MW00696191

# T APOSTATE

BY LLOYD EVANS

Dear Eric
Thanks for your
support!

Lloyd E

# THE RELUCTANT APOSTATE

## LEAVING JEHOVAH'S WITNESSES COMES AT A PRICE

BY LLOYD EVANS

JLE Publishing
2017

© 2017 Lloyd Evans

All rights reserved. This book or parts thereof may not be reproduced in any form, stored in any retrieval system, or transmitted in any form by any means—electronic, mechanical, photocopy, recording, or otherwise—without prior written permission of the publisher, except as provided by U.S. and/or international copyright law.

Published by JLE Services Ltd. t/a JLE Publishing

www.reluctantapostate.co

December 2016 printing

Unless otherwise indicated, Scripture quotations are from the modern-language *New World Translation of the Holy Scriptures,* 2013 edition, published by Watchtower Bible and Tract Society of New York, Inc.

Certain references to Watchtower publications are provided in shortened form. For further information, see "Abbreviations of Publication Titles" in *Watch Tower Publications Index.*

Photo Credits: ■ Pages 56, 99, 167, 348, 379, 391, 415, 420, 423, 427, 439, 449, 452, 455, 456, 460, 467, 469, 490, 493, 497, 553, 573: © Watch Tower Bible and Tract Society of Pennsylvania. ■ Pages 211, 214, 224, 235, 240, 276, 281, 297, 350, 377: Public domain (including expired copyright). ■ Pages 383, 400: © A. H. Macmillan. ■ Pages 398, 403: © R. V. Franz. ■ Pages 564, 576: © Royal Commission into Institutional Responses to Child Sexual Abuse. ■ Page 263: © M. J. Penton. ■ Page 41: Mapio.net. ■ Page 731: Wikipedia.org

All copyrighted material has been used per the "fair use" provisions of copyright law.

Trademarks: All trademarks are the property of their respective owners. The publisher is not associated with any product or vendor mentioned in this book.

Typeset in 10 pt/14 pt Merriweather Light
DTP services provided by Toon Media Publishing

Cover artwork: photography by Dijana Evans,
design by Lloyd Evans, Kyle Racki and Arthur Weber

*The Reluctant Apostate*

ISBN: 978-0-9956691-0-9

Made in Britain

Printed by

4edge LIMITED

7A Eldon Way
Eldon Way Industrial Estate
Hockley, Essex SS5 4AD
phone: +44 1702 200 242
fax: +44 1702 200 383
web: www.4edge.co.uk

*To Dijana,*
*Jessica*
*and Mum*

FOR WITNESSES

## TOPICS DISCUSSED IN "FOR WITNESSES" BOXES

# Contents

# Acknowledgements

*The Reluctant Apostate* was written sporadically over four years, during which time some of the events described took place. I thus had to *live* the story as well as write it. Over this period, many people have passed through my life and spurred me on in different ways, either through words of encouragement, or helpful guidance, or practical assistance. It is impossible to call to mind, by name, each and every individual who has contributed to my efforts. I can only write down a few names that come immediately to mind, and apologize in advance to the many whose names will inevitably be missing. I am grateful to *everyone* who has helped me in whatever small way—including a number who cannot be named because this would cause trouble for them due to the threat of shunning.

Among those I can gladly mention is Patrick Haeck, whose generosity was so incredible that it became part of the story! Dijana and I continue to be profoundly grateful both for his friendship, and that of his ever-growing "family," which includes Belinda, Delina, Oriana & Matthias, Amélie, "Oma," Bjorn & Priskilla, Tibni, Phebe, Jamin & Laurissa. The overwhelming love and kindness of the "crazy Belgians" came at a crucial time in our lives, and we look forward to many more years of joy and happiness with them.

I must pay special tribute to John A. Hoyle, who is a wonderful man—my good friend and trusted mentor. John is, in my view, an overlooked hero of the ex-Witness movement, and his behind-the-scenes contribution over the years toward making online resources available has been immense. I will always be thankful that he took a chance on a boisterous, controversial newcomer named "Cedars" back in 2011, and built a website that has gone on to improve so many lives. Our mutual friends Richard E. Kelly and his dear wife Helen have also been a reliable source of love, kindness and encouragement over the years, and Dijana and I are very thankful for their friendship.

Other fellow cult survivors and activists who have, at various times, supported and assisted me include Barbara Anderson, Steven Hassan, Paul Grundy, Randy Watters, David A. Reed, Eric Bottorff, Vincent Deporter, Julia Barrick, William J. Fitten, Ruben Looij, Chris Shelton, Amber Scorah, Sue Hall, Jeni Lundblom, Annette Getzschman, Frances Peters, Mike Rinder, Scott Terry, Brett Griffin-Young, Imtiaz Shams, Theramin Trees, Phil Dunne, Kathleen and Candace Conti, Robert Crompton, Javier Ortiz, Kyle Racki, Karenne Saylor, Elisa Kireeff, Ryan J. Morse, Claire Beecham, Joanna Foreman, Howie Rutledge Tran, Merice Ewart Marshall, Bill Hahn, Sean McGee, Ethan Hatcher, Pierre Burmester, Amelia Louise Ashton-Brooke, Ruben Ortiz, Gregorio Smith, Chip LaFleur, Debbie McDaniel, Robert and Marvina Benzekri, Johnny Kozák, Lisa L. Osborne, Esther Yvonne, Barbara Kohout, Victoria Summers, Catalin Bontea, Masoud Banisadr, Mariuca Rofick, Alex Strait, Janiene Adamse, Terry E. Walstrom, Benny & Pym Bonte, Néstor & Toni Kuilan, Angus & Jane Robertson, Susan Barber, Carrie Bee, "WifiBandit," Neil Gardner, Jerome Griff, Sheila Andersen, Don Brumfield, Jill Davis Long, Olli Schuster, Heather Bennett, Rowland Nelken, Misha Verollet, John and Mary Viney, Karen Morgan, "Toledo Squad," James Payten, Louise Goode, Stephanie Hammond, Patricia Russell, Daniel & Devon Genser, "Mr. Watchtower," Lydia Finch and Deborah Frances-White. I also value the solidarity shown by non-Witnesses like

Hemant Mehta, Regina Spiess and Trey Bundy, each of whom have summoned the compassion to highlight Watchtower abuse and injustice without requiring a Witness background in order to grasp the severity of the issues.

One of the joys of waking up from cult indoctrination is that of reforging lost friendships and family bonds. I want to give special mention to those who knew me as a Jehovah's Witness and have reached out with love and kindness since my awakening: my cousins Derek Phillips, Becky Phillips and Jenny Brooker, and my dear friends Mark Taylor, Carrie-Ann McClenahan and Jennifer Mason. There are others like these who have reconnected and have been supporting me from the sidelines, but I fear I would only make their lives more complicated by naming them.

Someone who is worthy of special mention is Arthur Weber. If you are impressed with the layout and aesthetics of the book you are holding in your hands (or swiping with your fingers, if you are reading on a Kindle device) you should know that this is due to his involvement. Arthur has repeatedly exceeded my expectations with his passion for the project, his patience and dedication, and his almost fanatical attention to detail. Arthur's extraordinary knowledge of Watchtower and its history, as well as his mastery of English grammar, punctuation and spelling (uncanny for a Romanian!) has also served to greatly smooth the process of getting this book over the finish line. The many weeks I have spent working closely with him have been an absolute pleasure. Any writers, including myself, looking to get future books published would be lucky to have his assistance.

Of course, it doesn't matter how good a book looks if it is not well written, and I will always be immensely grateful to my team of editors (each of whom I am also proud to call dear friends) for giving up so much of their time and energy toward (1) keeping my grammar and punctuation in check, (2) keeping my English *American* rather than British (for the benefit of the overwhelming majority of my readers), and (3) helping with mopping up any errors that slipped through: Rob & Blair Russell, Arthur Weber (again!), "Covert Fade," Mark & Kimberly O'Donnell and Graeme Hammond. "Covert Fade," Mark and Kimberly deserve extra credit for the dedication and tireless work they have poured into JWsurvey.org as fellow members of the website's editorial team. I am also thankful to Abigail Parker, Isaac Harris, Lee Elder, Peter Jeuck, Robert Crompton and Jim Penton for making their expertise available to me on certain matters as the need arose.

I further need to express my sincere appreciation to the following individuals, along with the many others who assisted with funding the publishing of this book via Indiegogo: Nel Welvaarts, Troy King, Louise Crack, Édith Châteauvert, Eddie Puric, Andrew and Myrna Vodopich, Patrice Gates, Nathan Hamlitsch, Tom Richardson, Ashley Latham, Janai Zecora Sparlock, Sarah Keirsey, Charles McCoy, Jarred Booth, Lisa Cook Osborne, Adam Heckathorn, Kirk Hemphill, Benny Bonte, Paul Watson, Jerome Griff, Mary Strauser, Dustin Condon, Andrew Kass, Greg Evans, Louczyshyn Roman, Pollie E. Hogue, Robert Andrésen, Neil Buckley, George Harris, Robert L. Chappel III, Daniel and Mie Månsson, Heidi L. Nordberg, the Zieman family, Martin Haugh, Sonia Mallet, Ryan & Story Johnson, Barbara Weed, Raffaela Hosbein, Mike Dennis, Mary Melinda Owens, Dumitru G., Janiel Baez, Malen Cross, Jonas Ropponen, Andrew Melton, Rob & Blair Russell, Rose Jorgensen, Gennadiy Kaliberda, Max Elfelt, Nathan Kincaid, Sue Hall, Michael Bryson, Sera-Marie Capaldi, the Şandor family (Raul, Cristina, Alex & Maya), Andrew Gregory Mercer, Louise Barbour, John Austin, Philip

Hickey, Benjamin Schaich, Robert L. Rogers, Mark Ellis, Jason M. Wynne, Ronald Feller, David C. J. Priest, Carrie L. Chaney, John Reeder, David Ferreira, Tyler A. Berg, Ramil & Cristy Espera, Michelle Bonin, Simon & Birnette, Roberto Secco, Pamela Dawn Land, Stephen Bowyer, Jackie Shaw, Jorian Micom, Shane E. Stapley, Scott Clarkson, Emily Thoresen, John A. Hoyle, Vincent and Michele Tylor, Valorie Kappmeyer, Tiina Torenius-Marttinen, Nicole Buesen, Cindy Crispin, "Birdy," James & Crystal Henson, Mike Beauman, Gabe & Angela Rellamas, Carmelo Rosado III, Kelly Perazzolo, Frank Jepsen, Craig A. Uherek, Brittany Gatchell, Travis G. Pryor, Philippe Malenfant, Rob Horan, Palo Roman, Przemek Ozgo, Mark Lacasse, Derek Edwards, the Nazaroff family, Kurtis Janda, Topher Spinnato, Nubia Adams, Jennifer Haugh, Natasha Freestone, Brett Griffin-Young, Christine Vail-Clarke, Donna L. Baynes, Jonathan Hosier, Karl Moloney, Christina Shirley Murrin, Michał Oborzyński, Peter Vagn Jensen, Alan Gunderson, Guillermo Iris Urena Jr., Geoff Dexter, Michael Tucker, Kate Harper, Linda S. Allen, Verushka Yearwood, Joan M. Miller and Jennifer Mason.

And finally, I need to profoundly thank my loving wife Dijana for surrendering her husband for four months between August and November of 2016 so that this book could finally be completed. Dijana also deserves credit for letting me divulge so many personal aspects of our lives by telling a story that she partially shares. It is by no means easy to give up so much private information that most people under similar circumstances would rather be forgotten, but Dijana shares my desire to make a difference in this world and I can't thank her enough for her unflinching love and support.

# Author's Note

I have made every effort to provide sources for quoted material. If the reference for a quote is not included in the text itself, it will normally be found in the "Notes" section. When it comes to past conversations forming part of my personal story, I do not claim to have recounted all of these verbatim. Rather, I have presented what was said with a desire to be fair and honest, and with the utmost accuracy that my fallible memory will allow.

# Foreword

TWO Jehovah's Witnesses recently knocked on my door. The smiling husband and wife team offered to give me some reading material from the Watch Tower Society and discuss their faith with me. I politely said no—I had errands to run—and closed the door. Almost immediately, I regretted it. I realized I had so many questions I wanted to ask them—questions I wouldn't have asked a couple of years ago because they just wouldn't have crossed my mind.

I became an atheist at age 14 because I stopped believing in God, but it wasn't until much later that I began to understand just how toxic religious institutions can be. When I think of the Catholic Church today, I can't separate it from the child sex abuse scandals. Evangelical Christians? I immediately think of a group that is antigay, antiwomen, antiscience, antidoubt, and anti-whatever-the-Democrats-are-doing. Scientologists went from being the odd group that counted Tom Cruise as a member to an institution that turns followers against their families while raking in millions of dollars in tax-free donations.

I didn't seek out this information. It turned up in my media diet: newspapers, books, television shows, and magazine articles. Even today, I'll see comedians holding little back in their criticism of religion, documentaries exposing the inner workings of these religions, and websites started by people who escaped various cults. The point is: I don't have to work very hard to hear people discussing these topics.

And yet, in all this time, I knew virtually nothing about Jehovah's Witnesses. My understanding of their beliefs, for the longest time, boiled down to "kind of Christian, but with a few quirks." I knew they didn't accept blood transfusions. That was probably the worst of it.

I could not have been more ignorant.

It was only in the past few years that I learned about apostasy trials, the practice of disfellowshipping, the criticism of higher education, the sexual abuse cover-ups, the homophobia, the way evolution is thought of as some sort of conspiracy, and the fear of anyone stepping outside the Watchtower-approved bubble. I had no idea Witnesses felt love was conditional. Forget the idea of blood being thicker than water. If you dare to disagree about Jehovah, that blood loses its viscosity in a heartbeat. Sons and daughters become dead to the very people who gave them life, and moms and dads are treated as invisible by those whom they cradled in their arms as babies. What a pernicious set of beliefs! And none of it was on my radar until I began reading Lloyd Evans' JWsurvey.org blog.

His articles, his accurate explanations of JW beliefs, and his ability to lay out the problems within the faith (because he experienced many of them personally) have opened my eyes to issues I never knew existed. Who knew those kind people knocking on my door were offering me little more than a Trojan horse? If you accept what they're giving you, your life will be worse off for it.

In my own work as an atheist activist, I've had the good fortune to speak with many people who escaped the religions of their youth. And every time I meet ex-Jehovah's Witnesses, I always ask them if they're familiar with Lloyd's work. "Of course we are!" they inevitably respond.

Lloyd is not only *the* go-to guide for people like me seeking to learn more about the inner workings of the Watch Tower Society, he has also become a safe haven for those who have left the faith—including those whose family members will no longer speak to them—because they are so relieved to discover they're not alone.

I have a lot of respect for anyone who walks away from the comfort of religion because they realize their once-cherished beliefs no longer hold up under examination. But, my goodness, think of the courage it takes to go public with your story so that others may one day join you on your journey. That's what Lloyd has done with his website and videos, and that's what he does in much greater detail in this book.

If you are currently a devout Witness, I hope you can better understand what one well-meaning "apostate" has experienced. His criticisms are fair and deserve your responses. If you are a Witness who has doubts, realize that your concerns are valid and there are many, many people who have asked the same questions running through your mind right now. This book will show you that leaving the faith, while difficult, is also the beginning of a wonderful next chapter of your life.

And if you're an atheist like me, let this book teach you about a faith that gets very little public scrutiny. Convincing people to start valuing evidence over dogma is meaningless if we can't also help them deal with the consequences of that decision. We need to understand what Jehovah's Witnesses go through to help them walk away.

I'm proud to call Lloyd a friend, and I'm incredibly inspired by his work. If he can leave the Witnesses, anyone can.

If any other Jehovah's Witnesses knock on my door, I'll invite them in and accept their reading material. But I'm also going to give them a copy of this book. Maybe they can learn something, too.

*—Hemant Mehta, editor of FriendlyAtheist.com*

# Introduction

THE world is a wonderful place. It bursts with variety and potential. Sure, life has its share of pain and suffering, but humanity overall trudges on undaunted, ever striving to better itself, ever pondering what lies beyond the horizon. The more we learn about our universe, the more we realize how special we are as thinking beings and what a privilege it is to be alive and capable of beginning to understand our place among the stars.

*The world is ours.* It is everything we are and will be. It compels us to move forward and progress.

If, however, you are one of Jehovah's Witnesses, the world is *not* wonderful at all. It is filled with evil and temptation; lost souls who, themselves pitifully estranged from their Creator, seek to hurt you or drag you off into depravity with them. If you are unfortunate enough to be one of the 99.9% of Earth's population who is not a Witness, then you are one of those cursed people—a "worldly" person. It is irrelevant whether you are religious or atheist, Christian or Buddhist. You could be a doctor or fireman, someone who works in a soup kitchen, or someone who helps old ladies across the street and rescues stray kittens. *It doesn't matter.* You are still worldly, in a "spiritually destitute condition," and therefore deemed a corrupting influence—unsuitable material for friendship or association.

But fear not, there is hope! Witnesses are, in their words, "untainted by the filth of Satan's world." Once you meet one of them, you will receive the opportunity to see the error of your ways and learn "the Truth" about God's plan for mankind. However, be warned: if you have the impudence to reject this generous offer, your name will be wiped from God's book of life. The purpose of your existence will be merely to await divine execution at Armageddon. You can only hope that your demise will be swift and not too excruciating. Birds will be summoned to dispense with your decaying remains. Conversely, all those who embraced the Truth when given the chance will be spared annihilation. Once the fiery wave of the apocalypse has passed, this chosen people will fashion the earth into a paradise where, as you might expect, everyone will be a Jehovah's Witness.

Despite their somewhat morbid and condescending outlook, Witnesses are mostly very pleasant people. They are individually capable of great love and kindness. If someone were to attack you or mug you in the street, the chances are they would *not* be a Witness. A Witness would be more likely to defend you against your assailant. As a rule, Witnesses do not drink excessively, nor do they smoke or take drugs. They are generally not violent or abusive. If you could picture the ideal citizen who is responsible and law-abiding, you could do far worse than call to mind a typical Jehovah's Witness.

The fundamental difference between an ordinary person and a Jehovah's Witness is that the life of a Witness is effectively micromanaged by a religious hierarchy based in America. "Jehovah's organization" is the term often employed by Witnesses to describe the Watch Tower Bible and Tract Society of Pennsylvania and its many affiliated legal entities, which I will collectively refer to as "Watchtower." Watchtower is controlled by a small group of men based in the state of New York who call themselves the "Governing Body."

This Governing Body claims to be used by God to direct what they will tell you is the earthly part of his organization. (God's organization has a heavenly part too, comprised of God, Jesus and the angels.) Sadly, not everything Watchtower asks Witnesses to do or believe is entirely loving or beneficial to them or others. I know this because I was one of Jehovah's Witnesses for 23 years before officially leaving on December 29, 2013.

This brings me to the title of this book. You might be wondering why I consider myself a *reluctant* apostate. Surely apostasy is something one does proudly, without regrets or inhibitions?

The truth is: when I first granted myself permission to start examining my beliefs objectively, I felt anything but proud of myself. Such was the fear and apprehension at viewing information critical of my long-held beliefs, I would not have been unduly surprised if a lightning bolt had ripped through the sky and zapped me to a crisp after my first few clicks on "apostate" websites.

Witnesses are trained to be gripped by horror and loathing at the mere mention of the A-word. It is hard to imagine a more fearsome bogeyman in a Witness's imagination than a bitter, mentally diseased, foaming-at-the-mouth apostate, hell-bent on ruining one's precious relationship with the Almighty (apart from Satan himself, of course). And even if you are able to somehow get past such deeply ingrained paranoia, there is the simple fact that nobody likes to be proven wrong. Nobody relishes the discovery that they have wasted years or decades of their finite time on this planet believing *and promoting belief in* something that is not true. This is especially so when the penalty for walking away from one's beliefs is total estrangement from believing family members. Few things can motivate someone against even considering leaving their faith like the constant threat of shunning by virtually everyone they have ever known or loved.

So yes, I was very reluctant. I wanted my investigations to reveal that I had been right all along—that the religion my parents had raised me in was indeed, by happy coincidence, the one and only "Truth." When my inquiries revealed the opposite, I had what most ex-Witnesses will refer to as an "awakening"—something by no means as pleasant or euphoric as it sounds, at least not to begin with. Not only do you get the jarring realization and intense frustration that you have wasted years supporting and promoting a harmful sect—you also have the pressing problem of how to extricate yourself, with as little damage as possible, from an existence defined by unquestioning allegiance to an organization. For some, this can feel like such a hopeless dilemma, with so many years invested and so many loved ones to disappoint, that they see no other choice than to simply pretend they believe for the rest of their lives in order to keep everyone happy. Others sink into depression or even contemplate suicide, since the prospect of living a lie or completely reconfiguring one's life and relationships can be simply too much to bear.

Thankfully, at least in my own case, reluctance soon gave way to relief, optimism and contentment. I was extremely fortunate to have married a patient, understanding, intelligent woman who also did not appreciate being taken for a fool, and whose love for me outweighed her dismay at my growing unbelief. I knew from the outset that even if everyone else in my life disowned me, my wife's love for me was there unconditionally so long as I wanted it. I had the time and space to figure things out and come to terms with my drastically altered reality knowing that not *everything* had to change if I did not want it to.

As I grew in wonder at discovering how thoroughly I had been deceived, I devoted more and more time and energy to helping others navigate their own way out of indoctrination. But this newfound calling had its own unique challenges. A bitter pill to swallow was the discovery that, wonderful though the world is, it is indeed broken. My decades of servitude to Watchtower were due, at least in part, to the failure of society in general to take religious fundamentalism and cult mind control seriously enough. In country after country, coercive organizations like Watchtower are even rewarded with tax exemption and charitable status despite their cruel, abusive ways. Compounding this frustration was the realization that the general public are largely ignorant of the true nature of my former faith, giving it enhanced prospects of misleading and enticing new generations of converts.

It was with these troubling considerations in mind that, in the winter of 2012, I embarked on writing this book. If telling my story and explaining the history and beliefs of Jehovah's Witnesses could help prevent people from ever facing the problems I experienced, or wasting the years I wasted, then it would be worth all the effort. I am therefore profoundly grateful to all non-Witnesses who take the time to read *The Reluctant Apostate* for the purpose of expanding their knowledge of this mostly overlooked and little-understood fringe faith.

I will try to be balanced and fair throughout these pages and present information without unduly insisting on how it should be interpreted. But I must ask you to keep in mind that it is impossible to do justice to this subject without discussing complex doctrinal matters that may seem incomprehensible to someone who has not undergone decades of tedious, systematic indoctrination as a Witness.

While reading these pages, you may feel at times as though you are on a roller coaster ride with information and events flying at you from all angles. I am mindful of this, and I realize that it is my responsibility as a writer to convey this material as smoothly and methodically as possible. Even so, I hope you can appreciate the scale of my challenge in doing so.

In particular, I would like you to be aware that we have a guest who is listening in on our discussion, quietly and unseen. Our guest is the Witness who picks up this book and dares to check whether it is being fair and accurate about his or her cherished faith. It would be remiss of me to write a book that essentially warns outsiders of the perils of being or becoming a Witness without also reaching out to those who are still trapped *inside* the faith, with little hope of ever discovering the joy of being mentally and emotionally free. After all, I was once that inquisitive, reluctant onlooker.

For this reason, you will notice that I will occasionally break off in my story to address our lurking guest directly using special boxes marked "For Witnesses." It is certainly a challenge to write a book of this nature with two vastly different audiences in mind, but it is a challenge I gladly accept.

Chapter One

# How to Make a Jehovah's Witness

*"Isn't it a remarkable coincidence that almost everyone has the same religion as their parents? And it always just happens to be the right religion."*
—Richard Dawkins

THE doorbell rings. You wonder who could possibly be visiting you at this time on a Saturday morning. Putting down your coffee, you shuffle to the door in your pajamas. The door opens to reveal two smartly dressed Jehovah's Witnesses perched on your doorstep. They greet you with broad smiles and splutter the briefest of small talk before offering you some Bible literature.

What happens next will depend on a variety of factors including how polite you are, your religious persuasion (or lack thereof), whether your visitors appear normal or slightly unhinged, and—most pressingly—the weather conditions. After all, if a freezing blast of cold winter air infiltrates the thin fabric of your pajamas, any enthusiasm to launch into a lengthy doorstep theological debate may soon dissipate.

In most cases, the above factors will generally conspire to elicit a response that Witnesses euphemistically refer to as a "conversation stopper." A conversation stopper is usually introduced with the words "I'm not interested" and climaxes with the door closing.

Now put yourself in the shoes of your crestfallen Witness visitors following such a defeat, and imagine being on the receiving end of this type of encounter repeatedly for over an hour—perhaps even two or three hours. Door after door closes with only the occasional person accepting whatever book, leaflet or magazines you are offering, often out of pity or in an attempt to get rid of you. Your predicament worsens if it is extremely cold or raining. You might find yourself checking your watch every few minutes to see how much longer you have before you can retreat to the car and go home, having done your duty for the day.

You now have a vague notion of what it is like to go preaching door-to-door as a Jehovah's Witness. From my own experience, a good number of Witnesses privately loathe the door-to-door preaching work, which they refer to as "the ministry," or "field service."

We humans are simply not programmed to enjoy repeated rejection; neither are many of us entirely comfortable with intruding on total strangers without an invitation. This is why door-to-door salesmen rarely look genuinely cheerful. Witnesses can only summon the courage to put themselves through this abnormal scenario week in, week out because (1) they feel obligated to do it, (2) they have come to view it as a social activity where they can spend time with fellow believers, or (3) they might just hit the jackpot and find someone at home who actually *wants* to talk to them. (Yes, this does sometimes happen—and when it does, it makes everything momentarily seem worthwhile.)

Let us go back to our initial encounter, with you answering the door, and imagine that a Witness somehow manages to overcome your conversation stopper. Suppose he raises a thought-provoking comment or question that confounds you. You might not know this, but Witnesses are trained to get past conversation stoppers wherever possible. For example, in the week of March 10, 2014, all Witnesses around the globe considered an article in their monthly newsletter under the heading "Improving Our Skills in the Ministry—Responding to Potential Conversation Stoppers."[1] The article offers the following advice:

> Imagine that you know that a natural disaster is imminent. People will die unless they flee to safety. You go to a neighbor's home to warn him, but he interrupts you, saying that he is busy. Surely, you would not quickly abandon your efforts to help him! Many in our territory turn us away, not realizing the life-saving value of our message. At the time of our visit, perhaps they are preoccupied. (Matt. 24:37-39) Or maybe they have been prejudiced by untrue rumors. (Matt. 11:18, 19) They might assume that we are no different from the religions that have produced bad fruitage. (2 Pet. 2:1, 2) If the householder initially is not interested, we should not be quick to give up.

Witnesses have perfected the art of not being "quick to give up" over many decades. From when I was a child until recently, Witnesses carried around with them a small brown book titled *Reasoning From the Scriptures.*[2]

---

[1] Until recently, the newsletter was called *Our Kingdom Ministry*. It is now known as the *Our Christian Life and Ministry—Meeting Workbook*.

[2] The *Reasoning* book was declared out-of-print in a memo to congregations in November 2015, but no official direction has yet been issued for Witnesses to abandon its use in the preaching work. I understand many still carry it in their book bags. Some Witnesses would probably argue that this book is "old light" and obsolete, but it is a book I am familiar with from my years as a Witness, and the information it contains is essentially the same as that found in more recent publications.

The *Reasoning* book (as it came to be known) had an entire section under the heading "How You Might Respond to Potential Conversation Stoppers." This section anticipated a plethora of householder rejections, and explained how they might be successfully bypassed by a proficient evangelist. For example, the book contains seven suggested rebuttals to "I'm not interested" from which one can choose. The first recommended response is 99 words long (if read in its entirety), and begins with the question: "Do you mean that you are not interested in the Bible, or is it religion in general that does not interest you?" Thus, even if a householder were to decline a conversation, they would get one anyway.

Let us assume such a strategy prevails, and you are somehow persuaded to forget all the reasons why you do not want to have a conversation about your personal beliefs at your front door. On a whim, and against your better judgment, you decide to indulge your uninvited guest in a conversation in which thoughts and opinions start to be exchanged.

As you might imagine, there is a world of difference between Witness beliefs and the beliefs of most ordinary, moderately well-informed people. To take one example, Witnesses believe that almost 4,400 years ago the entire earth, including (by implication) the peak of Mount Everest, was once immersed in the waters of Noah's flood.[3] To them, it is irrelevant that there is a total vacuum of geological and archaeological evidence to sustain this assertion—neither does it unduly disturb them that there are not enough water molecules

---

[3] If you want the exact year of this event, it is furnished in the 1963 Watchtower book *"All Scripture Is Inspired of God and Beneficial"*. 2370 B.C.E., according to page 294, was a year when umbrellas were advisable.

on the planet to accomplish this feat. In their minds, if Watchtower publications insist that the entire surface of the earth was deluged, this must be true. (*see box*)

**FOR WITNESSES**

## NOAH'S FLOOD

As uncomfortable as it may be, it would be worthwhile for you to spend a moment exploring the implications of the entire surface of the earth being inundated in Noah's day, as Watchtower strenuously asserts to have been the case.

If you were to melt all the ice caps, glaciers, and permanent snow on earth and put all this melted ice in one place, you would need a tank roughly 24 million cubic kilometers in size.* If you poured the contents of that tank into the sea, the sea levels would rise by roughly 70 meters. There would now be 1.386 billion cubic kilometers of water sloshing around in our oceans. The consequences of this would be devastating (the world would have to surrender all its coastal cities and low-lying land) but Mount Everest, which soars 8,848 meters above sea level, would be unfazed.

In order to transform Everest into the most shallow part of a global ocean, you would need to produce an extra 3 billion cubic kilometers of water from nothing, bringing the total volume of water on the planet up to at least 4.5 billion cubic kilometers. Such a stupendous mass of water is more than three times what you could hope to find on earth if you were to somehow squeeze every last droplet from our planet.

All this means that, if you really must cling to the belief that Noah's flood overwhelmed every piece of dry land, you

* These figures are based on information from The United States Geological Survey (http://water.usgs.gov/edu/earthhowmuch.html), The National Oceanic and Atmospheric Administration (http://sos.noaa.gov/Datasets/dataset.php?id=184) and RationalWiki.org (http://rationalwiki.org/wiki/Global_flood).

also need to insist that 4,400 years ago Jehovah saw fit to produce three times the planet's water from nowhere, and then spirit it away while simultaneously erasing any trace of this crushing mass of $H_2O$ from the archaeological or geological record for that period. You would also need to explain how kangaroos managed to make it back from the mountains of Turkey to Australia. Some explanation of how Noah, armed only with hammers and chisels, built a wooden ocean-going vessel larger than any that has been launched without sinking would also be helpful (research a ship called the *Wyoming*). And where do we even begin to untangle the logistical nightmare of cramming 6.5 million land-dwelling species into 40,000 cubic meters of ark?*

In short, there comes a point where the argument "Well, God just did it—okay?" must yield to the simple logic that if an all-wise, all-powerful entity wished to wipe out all living things apart from two of every kind of animal and one family of humans, he could have done it instantaneously without all the gory, implausible melodrama.

* *Insight on the Scriptures*, Vol. 1, is understandably vague on how many representative "kinds" boarded the ark to repopulate the planet. A number of only a few hundred is put forward that "could have produced the variety of species known today." Other creationists like Ken Ham are more generous, suggesting that 7,000 kinds accomplished this feat. Even if we take this larger figure, to suggest that 7,000 "kinds" ballooned into 6.5 million land-dwelling species in only 4,400 years requires an intensity and speed of natural selection that would baffle scientists. We would see, on average, approximately 1,500 new species evolving every year.

There is therefore a strong likelihood that, whatever you say to your Witness visitor, he will consider the majority of your opinions to be quaint and charming, but ultimately wrong. Once the conversation has ended and you have closed the door, he will retreat to a safe distance and make a careful handwritten note of your strange ideas so that he can return at a later date (usually within two weeks, or one week if he is extremely efficient) and tactfully explain precisely why you are so misguided and why Jehovah's Witnesses have all the answers for you.[4]

You might be thinking there is no way you would stomach more than one conversation with the Witnesses, but you would be underestimating their persistence and resourcefulness in extracting one from you. During this follow-up call (referred to by Witnesses as a "return visit"), let us suppose your visitor decided to apply the suggestions from his old copy of the *Reasoning* book in tackling any comments or questions you could conceivably throw his or her way.

For example, suppose you are feeling especially plucky and ask your new friend to explain what he would do if a doctor told him he would die without receiving a blood transfusion. This is a question that Witnesses are frequently asked and, once again, the *Reasoning* book had all its bases covered.

"If the situation is really that serious, can the doctor guarantee that the patient will not die if he is given blood?" asks the little brown book.[5] Rationality is swept aside and suddenly doctors are responsible for guaranteeing the outcome of any recommended treatment. "If possible," the book explains, "we try to put him in touch with a doctor who has the needed experience, or we engage the services of another doctor."

---

[4] Witnesses in many countries, including the United States, write notes about householders using a special slip of paper called an "S-8." In countries like the UK where data protection laws prohibit personal information being recorded on this kind of form, Witnesses use a simple notebook. The direction I was given was that, if passing on details of a particular householder to another Witness, I had to do this verbally.

[5] The same response appears almost verbatim on the final page of a 2016 worksheet titled "A Godly View of Life (Part 2)" downloadable from JW.org.

Bewildered by this response, you ponder for a moment and muster another question. Having remembered that Witnesses do not celebrate birthdays, you ask your visitor why this is so. He shows you two scriptures in the Bible, one in Genesis and one in the gospel of Matthew. On both of these occasions, some unfortunate individual is hung or beheaded at a birthday celebration. The relevant section in the *Reasoning* book thus concludes: "Jehovah's Witnesses take note that God's Word reports unfavorably about birthday celebrations and so shun these." Yes, the Bible's message is clear—celebrating birthdays is inadvisable and may lead to hanging or decapitation.

If you find yourself able to swallow this sort of argumentation, then there can be little doubt that you are destined to eventually become a Jehovah's Witness. Before you know it, you will be accepting a "free home Bible study" comprised of weekly hour-long discussions designed as a crash course on Witness doctrine. The Bible study will be oriented around a small 224-page book designed to inform you about what the Bible *really* teaches on a number of key subjects considered by the Witnesses to be of supreme importance. After reading each numbered paragraph, you will be asked a scripted question and your answer *must* correspond with the sentiments contained in the paragraph you have just read. Try to deviate in any way and you can expect to have the study discontinued before long. Reading your answers verbatim from the paragraph is frowned on, but still considered more desirable than voicing an honest opinion that differs from what has been prescribed for you by the book's writers.

What if you decide to be clever and, in your enthusiasm, you suggest to your Witness mentor that you might start using the internet to gather even more information on Witness beliefs so as to progress in your studies more quickly? This idea will be swiftly rejected. Jehovah's Witnesses do *not* want you consulting any independent sources of information on their beliefs—especially those available via the internet, which is riddled with information that debunks, disproves and discredits Witness theology. If you want to find out about the Witnesses, then you will need to study using only *their* literature or their approved website—JW.org.

If you somehow manage to stumble through all these stages without a flurry of red flags being raised, then the next logical step would be to start attending Witness meetings. There you will receive twice-weekly instruction on how to be an ideal Witness. You will find yourself surrounded by the friendly, smiling faces of "brothers and sisters" who will make you feel loved and appreciated. Your instructor will start taking you out in the door-to-door work, and if you keep this up and make all the right noises you will soon be awarded the status of "unbaptized publisher"—the final step before baptism.

Once you have grown more accustomed to your newfound faith and the adoration and encouragement of your devout new friends, you will likely respond favorably to the not-so-subtle nudges toward baptism, this being the final stop on your journey to becoming a Witness. To be accepted for baptism you will first need to successfully navigate three quiz sessions with an elder, who will go through a list of questions designed to ensure that you understand and agree with basic Witness dogma. Then, at the next Witness "regional convention" or "circuit assembly" you will be baptized in a pool by a man wearing a white T-shirt once you have answered a loud and affirmative "YES!" to two final questions, namely: "On the basis of the sacrifice of Jesus Christ, have you repented of your sins and dedicated yourself to Jehovah to do his will?" and "Do you understand that your dedication and baptism identify you as one of Jehovah's Witnesses in association with God's spirit-directed organization?"

Again, you are probably thinking there is no possible way you could stomach all of this *for any religion*, let alone one that declares itself "God's spirit-directed organization." You perhaps might even be leaning toward the conclusion that those who become Witnesses in this manner are just stupid or gullible, and therefore deserving of whatever negative consequences befall them. I understand why you might form this opinion, but I am afraid it really is not that simple.

Bear in mind that some people tend to lose their ability to think objectively and make rational decisions when they are depressed, lonely or otherwise emotionally vulnerable. Such individuals are the prime candidates to become Jehovah's Witnesses, because Witness beliefs and fellowship offer a strong sense of purpose and community. As cult expert Steven Hassan observes in his book *Freedom of Mind: Helping Loved Ones Leave Controlling People, Cults, and Beliefs*:

> The idea that people knowingly join destructive cults is patently wrong. Most cult recruits are recruited at a vulnerable moment, without understanding the forces that are being brought to bear on them.

Thus, though the mere thought of becoming a Witness may sound preposterous to you at this moment in your life, there is no telling what future personal calamities might render you susceptible to falling un-

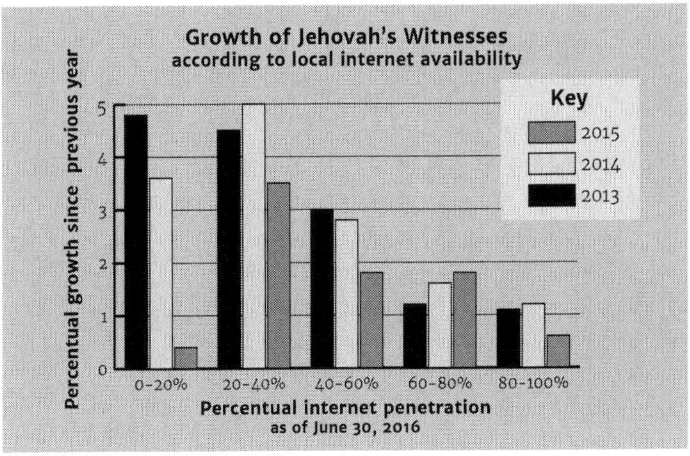


***To view the data used in making this chart, please see Appendix B.***

der the influence of a cult.[6] For anyone going through a divorce or bereavement, or suffering from depression or loneliness for any reason, the Witness package of instant friends and a structured, purposeful life can be hard to resist. It is such distressed, floundering souls who are normally able to make it all the way from doorstep to baptismal pool without hearing any alarm bells, as I have seen to be the case with my own family. That is why it is unfair to blame everyone who gets roped into a cult for their own sorry predicament. Things are often far more complicated than that.

Furthermore, it is worth noting that many Witnesses you meet will not have required conversion via the door-to-door work to begin with. Why? Because

[6] Like most cults, Jehovah's Witnesses strongly object to having their religion characterized as a cult. I personally find "cult" to be a problematic word, since it is a subjectively-applied pejorative that can cause people to become overly defensive. Suffice to say, my thoughts on cults, and the reasons why I believe the organization behind Jehovah's Witnesses can be considered a cult, will become clear in later chapters.

they have come "ready-made," having been born into their religion and raised in it by their parents. Such ones (like me) can hardly be painted as gullible or stupid for what amounts to little more than an accident of birth. I had absolutely no say in what I was taught to believe as fact from a very young age—and I am far from alone in that respect. There are many in my situation, often referred to as "born-ins," making up a sizable portion of Witnesses in most Western countries. If you were to walk into the average Kingdom Hall in Britain (my own country of birth) and ask the congregation to indicate, by a show of hands, who has become a Witness after being contacted in the door-to-door work, you are likely to be surprised at how few hands would be raised. This is because it is becoming almost impossible to make a Jehovah's Witness using the increasingly outdated doorstep method. Why is this?

The world has changed considerably in recent decades and the internet, in particular, has made it easier than ever for people to investigate and challenge dubious religious dogma. This is beginning to seriously impact on the Watchtower organization. For decades, it has reveled in the luxury of being able to dictate the beliefs of Witnesses without fear of contradiction. But now, the tide is turning. As the chart shown on the previous page demonstrates, the growth in Witness numbers is painfully slow in countries where the internet is widely available. The opposite trend is usually noticeable in lands with very little internet access.[7]

The internet's corrosive influence is being felt by the ordinary Witness on the street, for whom it is harder

---

[7] I am not suggesting that the internet is the sole reason for poor growth in developed countries (correlation does not equal causation), but it is certainly a contributing factor, as I will discuss at more length in a later chapter.

than ever to source new recruits. According to the latest available statistics (as of 2015), the average Witness baptism requires 7,429 hours of preaching work.[8] That is equivalent to over ten months of condensed 24-hour evangelism to produce each new convert—and the time needed is only increasing, as the graph below indicates.

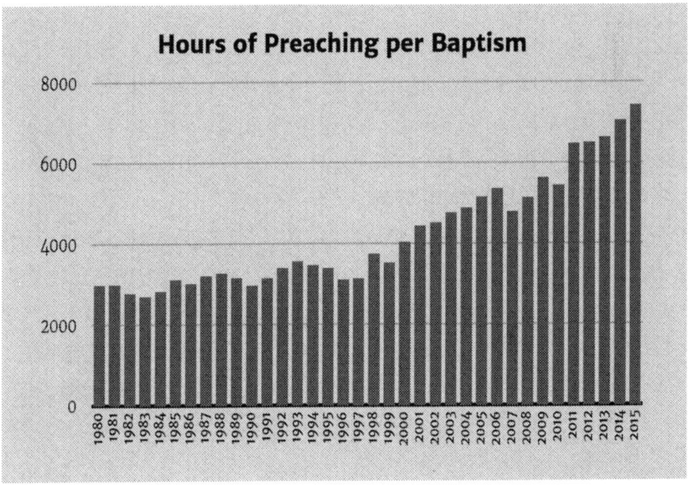


***Graph reproduced with permission from JWfacts.com.***

Put simply, the door-to-door work is already obsolete as a means of making new Jehovah's Witnesses. The only useful purpose it serves Watchtower is that of keeping Witnesses busy and giving them a means to show loyalty. If you want to turn someone into a Witness, your best bet is to indoctrinate him or her from childhood, as most Witness parents (many of whom were themselves raised in the faith) inevitably do with

[8] These numbers are based on statistics from the annual *Yearbook of Jehovah's Witnesses.* We can calculate the number of hours required per baptism by dividing the total number of preaching hours by the number of baptisms reported for the same year.

their children. My own mum and dad, with the very best of intentions, took the same approach with me.

I was a third-generation Jehovah's Witness. My family's connection with the religion stretches back as far as my father's parents—specifically his mother. "Nana," as my dear grandmother Isabel Evans liked to be called, was visited at her home in post-war Birkenhead (across the Mersey from Liverpool) in the aftermath of a period of family bereavement. It was around the time that both her parents had died (both following distressing periods of illness) that she began attending Witness meetings. I can well imagine how the resurrection hope offered by Watchtower must have been an appealing source of comfort and peace to her at a time of intense grief and despair.

Little could Nana have known that, by dedicating her life to the Witness cause, she was also effectively baptizing multiple generations of her descendants into the faith—beginning with my father and his siblings. This has continued down to this day with her great grandchildren, many of whom have been born into an organization that is almost unrecognizable from how it was when Nana first heard that knock at the door in 1953.[8]

Thirty-five miles east of Birkenhead you will find Eccles—a less-than-affluent corner of Manchester where my mother was raised. Unlike the other side of my

[8] This specific year is based on notes from a relative.

family, Mum's parents were not Witnesses and thus were without incentive to raise her as one.[9] But, like Nana, Mum also embraced her religion after being preached to amid times of tragedy and emotional upheaval.

*Mum in the '70s*

Mum, whose name was Lesley, was a kind and beautiful woman. She had what can only be described as a disastrous series of relationships as a young woman. Her first marriage ended in divorce after she discovered her husband was gay. (A relative once told me he wanted her as his "trophy wife.") And her second marriage ended in tragedy when her husband, Robin, a charming alcoholic whom she met at work, died in a house fire in 1974. (I was told he fell asleep in his armchair, cigarette in hand.)

---

[9] Mum's mother, Helen, was baptized as a Witness in later years, as were Mum's younger sister and brother, but I do not believe Grandma ever took the Witness faith particularly seriously. When taking my sister and I on our first overseas trip to Portugal in 1994, Grandma terrified us by having a brandy-fueled binge one night in our apartment, during which she heaped scorn on us for being Witnesses. She was also a heavy smoker, which is considered a disfellowshipping offense. Grandma only managed to evade judicial action by elders because there was never more than a single witness who could testify to her buying cigarettes at the shop, or answering the door of her flat, air freshener in hand, in a cloud of cigarette smoke (which were usually the circumstances in which I found her when visiting).

It was between these two ill-fated marriages that the Witnesses first contacted Mum, but with only limited success. (I will revisit the reasons for this later.) Finally, after being widowed, she found comfort and solace in the friendship and support extended by her Witness friends. Mum was baptized the year after Robin's death in 1975 (a year of considerable note to Jehovah's Witnesses, as I will explain in another chapter), and three years later she married my father, Jonathan, who had been raised by Nana as a Witness. By the time I was born, on September 10, 1979, there are no prizes for guessing what my religious affiliation would turn out to be.

I grew up in Wilmslow, a small Cheshire town 14 miles south of Manchester (when you fly into Manchester Airport, you are already only 10 minutes away by car). When I was a child, it was a quiet, leafy suburb where not much happened. Now it is a bustling upper-class haunt of WAGs[10] and businessmen, brimming with wine bars, coffee shops, supercar showrooms, and houses that ordinary people like me can seldom afford. It was Wilmslow where Robin and Mum had lived out their short, ill-fated marriage, so the first four years of my life were mostly spent in the same tall Victorian semi where the tragedy had unfolded. Later we moved to a smaller, detached house further from the center of town. This move coincided with my first attending primary school, which was a short walk from our new home.

My family attended the Wilmslow congregation of Jehovah's Witnesses at their local meeting place, or

---

[10] WAG is an acronym for "wives and girlfriends" of soccer players. Wilmslow, and nearby Alderley Edge, are very desirable when players for Premier League teams like Manchester United (the team I follow) and Manchester City are looking for homes.

***Wilmslow Kingdom Hall***

"Kingdom Hall," on the town's outskirts on the road to Knutsford.[11] From my earliest recollections, the Witness faith played a prominent role in my upbringing. Not only did we have three meetings to attend every week (two at the hall; one in the home of a Witness family)—we also had our private family study and regular participation in the door-to-door work. My younger sister and I had our friends at school, but the kids we spent the most time with were the children of other Witness parents.

We were immersed in the religion. As a small boy, I was keenly aware of my religious identity and how this made me different from other children. There was one incident in particular that served to drive home just how different I was.

---

[11] Wilmslow's Kingdom Hall is a beautiful building dating from the 19th century, and was formerly a church school. I was told the Wilmslow elders only managed to acquire it from the local church in the 1970s through a third party, because the church refused to sell to them directly. I understand the Kingdom Hall will soon be demolished to make way for a rebuild.

FOR WITNESSES

## CHRISTMAS

There is no denying that Christmas is of mostly pagan origin, as even the most cursory study of the history of its customs will reveal. However, even in this area of Witness belief there is good reason for you to ponder the celebration objectively—especially in deciding the extent to which you are prepared to dissuade others from observing it.

If you are reading this book as a married person, the chances are you are already observing at least one pagan custom on one of the hands with which you are holding the pages open. The humble wedding ring is widely recognized as having pagan origins extending as far back as Egyptian times.

The likelihood is that most married Witnesses who wear wedding rings do not wear them as a means of honoring pagan oaths. They wear them because, over the centuries, they have become a customary symbol of wedlock. As Watchtower publications will admit, "the wedding ring once had religious significance, but in most places today, it no longer does." The same article therefore acknowledges that "many true Christians accept the local custom of wearing a wedding ring to give evidence that a person is married."—*w92* 9/1 p. 30.

You might be interested to know that the exchanging of wedding rings is not the only tradition with religious origins to be shown tolerance by Watchtower. One *Awake!* magazine article titled "The Piñata—An Ancient Tradition" (*g03* 9/22 p. 22) concluded with the words: "A main concern is, not what the practice meant hundreds of years ago, but how it is viewed today in your area. Understandably, opinions may vary from one place to another. Hence, it is wise to avoid turning such matters into big issues. The Bible says: 'Let each one keep seeking, not his own advantage, but that of the other person.'—1 Corinthians 10:24."

It is regrettable that Watchtower cannot apply the same accommodating outlook to a custom that the overwhelming majority of people view, not as a pagan ritual, but as a celebration of family and an opportunity to show peace and goodwill to all men.

I must have been about seven years old when, one day, my teacher told all the children in my class to color in some posters to advertise the school's Christmas Fair. Christmas is just one in a long list of celebrations that Witnesses do not observe (*see box*). They consider it a pagan celebration that has nothing to do with Christ and is characterized by "ungodly conduct." New Year's celebrations are "marked by debauched behavior" and are thus to be similarly avoided. I was not sure what all the reasons were as a young lad, but I did feel strongly that coloring in a Christmas poster would be very wrong and something my parents would be very displeased about. I mustered up courage and calmly approached my teacher, informing her that I could not color in the poster because it was against my religion.

This news did not go down well.

"Lloyd doesn't want to help the school!" my teacher screeched in front of my classmates. If the public reproof were not bad enough, there was further humiliation to follow.

My teacher decided to punish me by sending me to stand alone in the middle of the school courtyard in the cold so that all the teachers and children could learn of my wickedness in disobeying her instructions. My school was (and still is) in a kind of rectangular doughnut shape with the courtyard in the middle. When standing in that central spot, one feels extremely conspicuous. I cannot remember for how long I stood there, or how cold it was (it must have been winter, by necessity) but I do not remember it being a remotely enjoyable experience.

When I told my parents of this, they were mortified—and came to the school demanding a meeting with my teacher. I was not present for their discussion, so I cannot tell you whether any apologies were forthcoming. I only remember the incident itself and how embarrassing and unfair it all felt at the time. As to whose fault the whole thing was, I am now able to view the matter a little more objectively. Yes, my teacher showed a lack of sensitivity and tolerance toward a pupil of a religious minority. And even if she felt her anger was justified, no child should be punished in that way—least of all for conscientious reasons. Nonetheless, this would never have happened in the first place if my parents had not been conditioned into training their child to refuse to do something as harmless as color in a school Christmas poster.

My punishment for taking a stand on a matter of faith was to have a profound effect on me. The experience made me feel even more different than I already was and served to reinforce the persecution complex and siege mentality that is instilled in all Witnesses from childhood. I now had proof that the world was out to get me.

But my parents had not finished locking horns with this particular teacher. One evening at the dinner table, not long after the Christmas poster incident, they asked me what I had learned at school that day. I told them I had learned about how fish once crawled out of the sea to become dinosaurs. I am sure this would not have precisely described what we had been taught, but it was certainly the way I had understood it.

Mum and Dad looked at each other aghast. I could tell they were extremely disturbed by what I had just said. They asked me to repeat myself. Their ears had not deceived them. To their horror, their young boy had been led astray with a lesson in the basic principles of evolution—a field of science that Witnesses reject entirely, believing that it "serves the purposes of Satan." (*see box*)

FOR WITNESSES

## EVOLUTION

Watchtower has long claimed that "the evolution theory is not only unscriptural but utterly without factual basis". (*w95* 5/15 p. 18) Despite this, you are probably aware that many who consider themselves Christians manage to accept it. This is not because they are stupid, or have allowed themselves to be misled by worldly thinking. Rather, it is because evolution is not just a theory—it is proven science.

Evolution is the reason hospital "superbugs" exist that are resistant to all antibiotics. Superbugs are the result of multiple inoculations killing off cells that offer no antibiotic resistance, allowing the surviving bacteria to replicate and thrive, ready for the next round of antibiotics to further sift the population. Finally, you are left with bacteria that can survive any antibiotic medication you can throw at them (causing a serious problem for doctors and pharmacists, I should add). This is evolution in action. You notice it more easily in bacteria because they live, replicate and die within minutes, hours or weeks rather than over many decades. (Bacteria can also share DNA between them, which also helps.) But just because it takes more time to observe changes in larger organisms over multiple generations, this does not mean humans and animals are somehow immune from similar transformative processes.

Part of the reason Watchtower refuses to accept evolution as proven fact stems from the creative days of Genesis. They argue that, since "God came to the completion of his work that he had made" at the end of the sixth creative day (or period), this must mean God has hit the pause button on the creative cycle. (Genesis 2:2) However, when we look at the physical world around us, we see that planet Earth is very much still a work in progress. The creative process never ended—it is continuing as you read these pages.

For example, even though Amos describes Jehovah as the "Former of the mountains," we now understand thanks to the scientific study of plate tectonics that mountains are in a constant state of being formed—albeit over many millions of years. (Amos 4:13) Where there is a mountain now, there may be an ocean millions of years in the future. The planet we live on is therefore clearly not a finished product, even though it may seem that way when you read certain scriptures. Hence, if the creation of the physical earth is ongoing, why should not the same be true of plants and animals? If you think about it, when a Christian dismisses evolution as "unscriptural," he might actually be inadvertently belittling a divinely-approved process from God's celestial toolkit.

Once again, my parents got in the car and headed to the school to have strong words with the teacher who, not content with persecuting young Lloyd over his beliefs, was now trying to fill his head with dangerous heretical nonsense about walking fish. When they returned, they told me they had left her with a copy of *Life—How Did It Get Here? By Evolution or by Creation?* The *Creation* book, as it is known by Witnesses, presents Watchtower's arguments against evolution—in large part through use of some appalling misquotes that have since been ruthlessly exposed.[12] In its concluding chapter it asserts: "The theory of evolution is contrary to reality, yes, effectively a 'lie.'"

If my parents had misgivings about my teacher's techniques, it could be suggested their own teaching

[12] Type "life how did it get here creation misquotes" into Google, and you will see what I mean. Richard Dawkins also devotes several pages to debunking various arguments from the *Creation* book in his well-known work *The God Delusion*.

methods were not above scrutiny. One evening, Dad decided to spice up our family study session by including an emergency drill for Armageddon. The telephone rang and he picked up the receiver to have what we later discovered was a feigned conversation with one of our congregation elders. (It was not too difficult to make the phone ring by itself.)

When Dad put the receiver back down, he had a panicked look on his face. He told us the great tribulation (or prelude to Armageddon) had begun. Our congregation was gathering at the Kingdom Hall so that we could all drive in convoy to Macclesfield Forest where we were to evade capture and persecution. The "nations of the UN beast" had finally turned on God's people and they were coming to get us.[13] I felt a rush of adrenalin, having suddenly found myself thrust into a real-life approximation of the final scenes from *The Sound of Music.*

To her credit, my younger sister was skeptical from the outset and did not believe this really was the end of the world. I, on the other hand, fell for it hook, line and sinker. After scrambling upstairs to my room I began stuffing a backpack with all manner of 'essential' equipment including binoculars, a compass, a flashlight, and a penknife. (I was heavily into Enid Blyton books at the time.) I was especially keen to include my Bible in this makeshift survival toolkit, along with a bright red book titled *Revelation—Its Grand Climax At Hand!*

The *Revelation* book was a Watchtower publication that had only just been released. At that time it was

---

[13] As I will explain in Chapter Eight, Jehovah's Witnesses believe the United Nations represents the scarlet-colored wild beast of Revelation. The UN is also sometimes referred to as the "image" of the beast.—*The Watchtower,* July 15, 2013, pp. 10, 11; *Revelation Climax* p. 195.

being enthusiastically studied and distributed by all Witnesses globally. Brimming with colorful and disturbing artwork, it explained how the Bible prophecies of Revelation (swarms of locusts, heavenly trumpet blasts, burning mountains crashing into the sea, etc.) mostly described symbolic events that took place in the early 20th century—specifically concerning the exploits of the early Witnesses (or "Bible Students" as they were then known).[14] A typical passage reads:

> The global congregation of Jehovah's Witnesses has shared in many conquests under the guidance of its conquering King. Outstandingly, he protected these Bible Students from annihilation in 1918, when they themselves were 'conquered' temporarily by Satan's political organization.

Despite such unabashed eccentricity, the *Revelation* book was greeted with excitement by Witnesses for two main reasons. Firstly, it reminded them that they were God's chosen people with a crucial role to play in the outworking of his purposes. Secondly, like most Watchtower publications, it made Armageddon *imminent.* With the majority of pre-apocalyptic prophecies having been neatly fulfilled by the early Witnesses in the first few decades of the 20th century, the arrival of God's day of wrath was a mere formality that could strike the planet at any moment.

I was too young to understand all the technicalities, but I thought the book might come in handy as a rough field guide to the apocalypse that now seemed

---

[14] The Bible Students, who still exist today, are followers of the teachings of Charles Taze Russell. After his death, they splintered into a number of sects including one that rebranded itself in 1931 as Jehovah's witnesses. The Witnesses are the most well-known and successful of these sects, in part, because they succeeded in keeping control of the Watch Tower Bible and Tract Society of Pennsylvania, which Russell founded.

to be unfolding before me. With my rucksack packed, I scurried downstairs expecting my family to be already waiting for me in the car with the engine running, ready to whisk me away to exile in Macclesfield Forest. You can only imagine how foolish and deflated I felt on realizing from the smirks on Mum and Dad's faces that it was all just a hoax. There was no great tribulation or Armageddon unfolding. The brothers were not waiting for us at the Kingdom Hall. It was only a drill.

It is difficult to look back on this episode without seeing the funny side. There is nothing wrong with parents having a bit of fun with their kids, and I do not think Dad meant any harm by this stunt. It was simply his way of making our family study a bit more enjoyable. However, there was also a serious lesson behind the ruse. Dad wanted us to view Armageddon as a *real event* that could strike at any moment. He wanted us to be mentally prepared for what, in his view, was certain to happen in the next few months or years. This was the overriding lesson that I took from this experience. From that point on, the end of the world was something that could befall me at *any* moment, whether I was ready or not.

It should go without saying that such religious indoctrination was hardly turning me into the most balanced, well-rounded kid to hang out with in the schoolyard. I found it impossible to make friends without feeling compelled to give them lengthy sermons about my beliefs. After all, did I not have some duty to warn them of what was to come?

I especially enjoyed regaling my bewildered pals with my knowledge of how Jehovah's Witnesses were persecuted during World War II—something I took great pride in. On other occasions, I recall singing aloud

Witness hymns (or "Kingdom songs"), much to the amusement of my schoolmates. This strange behavior, combined with my refusal to participate in a host of regular school activities (including school assemblies, because these involved singing church hymns) set me apart as different, making me a prime target for bullies—of which my school had more than its fair share.

One bully in particular would frequently chase me round the school field with his gang. The trouble was, I could not simply stand my ground with him, because my parents were constantly reminding me that, as a Witness, I was a strict pacifist. I was therefore never to resort to violence, even in self-defense. This meant that I had to avoid confrontation at all costs, which frequently involved running for long spells of the lunch break in a desperate attempt to escape the beating that was planned for me. It was explained to me that if I were chased to the end of a corridor, I was to clamber up the wall if possible to get away. Defending myself physically was simply not an option.

Suffice to say, the "Run, Forrest, run!" strategy rarely improved my situation, not least because I was not the most athletic of children. I was quite a tubby young boy, so a good deal of the bullying was because of my weight. (Mum's reassurances that I was not fat—I just had "big bones"—never quite seemed to convince other children.) But it was my reputation as a Bible-basher that really made me stand out from the crowd, and it was high on the list of reasons for bullies to make my life miserable in any way they could think of. Especially in the classroom, I remember some painful moments when kids would verbally ambush me with abuse and mockery about my religion and weekend door-knocking exploits the moment the teacher's back was turned.

Of course, my parents were concerned about all this, but in their minds there was little they could do. They were hardly going to stop raising me as a Witness, not when this was my only chance of making it through the impending apocalypse.

***A child of the '80s striking a pose***

Despite all the misery, my tormentors never succeeded in making me ashamed of being a Witness. Quite the opposite. The abuse I suffered emboldened me, and underscored what I was being taught by my parents and at the Kingdom Hall meetings: that God's true people had always been oppressed and always would be. After all, the Witnesses were persecuted to the point of death in the Nazi concentration camps.[15] Why should we have it any easier on the brink of Armageddon? If you are being persecuted, it is because you are preaching the "Truth" and making God happy. It matters not what anyone else says or thinks.

Throughout the nightmare of school life, I found small respite in my friendships with other Witness kids in the congregation. Around these friends, being a Witness did not make me different. It was actually *normal.* One boy I was very close to was Henry, who was only a year younger than I. Henry and his two sisters lived on the other side of town from me. He had a third sister in

---

[15] I will revisit this subject in Chapter Seven.

her teens, but she had left home after "disassociating" herself.[16] For that reason, her family never talked about her and neither did we. This is my earliest recollection of shunning someone, or pretending they do not exist, because they are no longer a Witness.[17]

Our two families grew quite close. As Henry and I entered our teens, we would all go on camping holidays to Wales together. As kids, we were both well behaved and tried our best to be model children at the Kingdom Hall. Mum would jokingly tell me to be more like Henry, and Henry's mother probably said the same thing to him about me. An unspoken rivalry developed between us as to who would get baptized first. Henry won this competition hands down, getting baptized when he was only nine. A year later, on December 15, 1990, I confirmed my own lifelong devotion to Watchtower at the Manchester Assembly Hall in Northenden. I was eleven.

I remember at the time my mum and dad did express some concern over how young I was, and even suggested that maybe I was only getting baptized to keep pace with Henry—but I was having none of it. Of course, I look back now and realize they were absolutely right, but I cannot help but feel that baptism was unavoidable for me as a Witness youth. It was not a matter of if, but when.

I will never forget how excited I felt when my big day arrived. Once I had made my vows, and the speaker had finished his dedication talk, I ran up the stairs at the assembly hall to get into the changing

---

16 Disassociating, disfellowshipping and shunning will be explained in more detail in later chapters.

17 Sadly, Henry would be shunned himself later in life after being disfellowshipped for being gay. His name has been changed for privacy reasons.

***Shortly after my baptism in 1990***

rooms at the back of the platform ahead of all the other baptismal candidates. I was determined to be first in line. Once I was back downstairs in my baptism uniform (white T-shirt and speedos) I realized I had forgotten my towel, so I hurried back up to get it. By the time I returned, I was frustrated to find myself near the back of the line.

The baptism seemed to be over very quickly. I remember seeing Mum in tears as I emerged with my wet hair and beaming face. I had made her so proud. She gave me a new Bible to commemorate the event. It was a leather-bound, maroon *New World Translation* with gold-edged pages, which I still have to this day (although the gold has faded with age and wear). On the inside cover, Mum wrote the words:

---

*To our dear son Lloyd*
*Baptized 15th December 1990*
*May Jehovah bless you and keep you.*
*May Jehovah make his face shine toward you*
*and may he favour you.*
*May Jehovah lift up his face toward you and*
*assign peace to you.*
*Numbers 6:24-26*
*With all our love from Mum & Dad*
*"Stay awake, stand firm, grow mighty"*

---

These words perfectly captured my outlook at this stage in my life. All I wanted to do was make my parents happy and proud—to make their faces "shine" toward me. I knew that the only way to be certain of this was to "stay awake, stand firm, and grow mighty" in God's one and only true religion. What is more, I believed every word of what I had been taught. There was not a shred of doubt in my mind that this was the "Truth"—at least not back then.

Armageddon was going to come at any moment and destroy all non-Witnesses (including the bullies at school) and my family would be spared by God to live together happily on an earth transformed into a paradise. In that respect, the baptismal vows I made to seal my lifelong commitment as a Witness were genuine. I just had no idea at the time that I was far too young, naive and misinformed to be making them. Neither could I have imagined that, within a few years, a book would be released by Watchtower that would cause me to start questioning everything.

CHAPTER TWO

# The Page-Folding Pioneer

*"The skeptic does not mean he who doubts, but he who investigates or researches, as opposed to he who asserts and thinks that he has found."*
—Miguel de Unamuno

*"Skepticism is the first step towards truth."*
—Denis Diderot

YOU might be under the impression that a Witness who calls at your home is doing so purely of his or her own volition and not under any coercion, or out of any sense of obligation. While it is true that Witnesses do not earn a salary for their evangelical work, it cannot honestly be said that they are under no pressure to engage in it.[1] You see, Witnesses keep a careful count of the exact number of hours they spend on people's doorsteps—indeed, *any* time that is spent in preaching. These "field service" hours are almost a form of currency among believers. The more hours a Witness writes down, the more spiritually-oriented he or she must be.

At the end of every month, it is the duty of all Witnesses to calculate the total number of hours they have spent preaching. They must then write this number down on a printed slip of paper called an S-4 *Field Service Report.* This is what it looks like:

---

[1] Some Witnesses designated as "special pioneers" earn a modest stipend to help cover their expenses. Such ones are expected to put in 130 hours of preaching per month.

**FIELD SERVICE REPORT**

**Name:** ..........................................................................

**Month:** ..........................................................................

| | |
|---|---|
| Placements (Printed and Electronic) | |
| Video Showings | |
| Hours | |
| Return Visits | |
| Number of *Different* Bible Studies Conducted | |

| |
|---|
| Comments: |

S-4-E 10/15

The S-4 slip is a kind of monthly spiritual bank statement. The more hours you are able to report, the more you are "storing up treasures in heaven." Your congregation secretary will compile the data from these slips on a special card charting your progress over the span of a year. These report cards are often consulted when deciding whether there are any spiritually weak ones who need a "shepherding visit"—a visit from elders that is generally used either to offer encouragement or warn against errant behavior.

Along with your field service hours, when filling in your S-4 you would also write down the exact number of "placements" you have left with people (these could be magazines, books, or digital files sent by email), the number of Watchtower videos you have shown, the number of times you have called back on someone who has expressed interest (i.e. "return visits"), and the number of individuals with whom you have conducted Bible studies over the month. If you knowingly fail to hand in a completed S-4 report slip for a month or more because you have not done any preaching, you would be considered by your local elders as being a spiritually weak "irregular" one. If things are really serious and you stop preaching for six months or more, you would be deemed "inactive."

You may consider the keeping of strict numerical records and monthly tallying of preaching statistics rather odd, but it serves a useful purpose. First, it allows Watchtower to gauge how well (or how badly) Witness evangelism is progressing, and how many Witnesses are engaged in what they believe is a vital work. Secondly, it serves as a constant monthly reminder to Witnesses of their personal commitment. More specifically, it gives Witnesses a guilt complex if they fail to put in the number of hours that other "publishers" in their region are reporting despite having to deal with similar, everyday challenges.[2] An act of worship thus becomes a form of competition.

As you can imagine, the number of hours an individual is able to accumulate varies considerably based on a number of factors. For example, elderly or infirm Witnesses are permitted to report as little as 15 minutes of preaching in a month and still be considered active Witnesses. Obviously, to benefit from this special provision you must be suitably old or unwell, and have clearance from your local body of elders.

For everyone else, the absolute minimum is one hour of preaching activity per month. But if you think reporting such a measly figure month after month would grant you a stress-free time as a bona fide Witness, think again. Any able-bodied person who submits such little time on their report would be considered spiritually weak by the elders and earmarked for a

---

[2] "Publisher" is a designation applied to all Witnesses who count time in the preaching work, whether baptized or not (i.e. "unbaptized publisher").

shepherding visit. Especially if you are a *man* in the congregation, and therefore deemed a suitable candidate to "reach out" for responsibilities, serious questions will be asked as to why you are not doing more in the preaching work.[3] For this reason, the unspoken rule is to at least hit the average number of hours that other Witnesses are reporting—a kind of "safety in numbers" approach. At a local level, this target might be 10 hours per publisher, per month. In poor countries where there is high unemployment, the average would usually be more. For 2015, the global monthly average was just over 20 hours per active Witness, which is no walk in the park for your typical working parent in the Western world.[4]

Of course, the accuracy with which you report your hours is left to you and your conscience. Within reason, unless you are regularly reporting abnormally high hours without attending any preaching arrangements, elders will usually not interrogate you or audit your report. For the most part, they will take you at your word. Still, most Witnesses who take their faith seriously will try to fill in their report as honestly as possible, even if the number of hours they report falls short of expectations.[5]

---

[3] Witnesses strictly adhere to the Bible's view (as expressed in the letters of Paul) that women should not be allowed to teach in the congregation. For this reason, only men are considered for roles and positions, as I will explain in Chapter Five.

[4] An average 7,987,279 monthly publishers reported a total of 1,933,473,727 hours for the service year running from September 1, 2014 to August 31, 2015.

[5] I have personally only ever heard of one case of a Witness deliberately faking his service report figures, but the practice seems to be widespread when comparing notes with other ex-JWs. With my own report, I always tried to be as honest

Clearly, it is in Watchtower's interests to continually heap pressure on Witnesses to be prolific in the number of hours they report and the number of Bible studies they conduct. Such pressure is wielded both in the organization's literature and from the platform. Specifically, every Witness is encouraged from a young age to enlist as a "regular pioneer." A 2013 *Watchtower* put it this way: "If you are not yet pioneering, ask, 'What adjustments can I make to begin doing so?'"

A regular pioneer can be thought of as an über-Witness who commits to spending at least 70 hours per month in the preaching work.[6] Like ordinary Witnesses, regular pioneers receive no payment for their efforts, despite devoting a considerable chunk of their time to promoting Watchtower's interests. In most cases, they will be expected to find part-time employment to support themselves financially.[7] If they have yet to fly the nest, their parents might choose to bankroll them. In exchange for their considerable sacrifice, regular pioneers (also known simply as "pioneers") receive the admiration and support of the congregation, including frequent mentions from the platform at the midweek meetings.

---

as possible, even if it resulted in trouble for not doing enough time (as was frequently the case)—although I tended to be rather generous in deciding how time could be counted.

[6] In contrast, "auxiliary pioneers" only need to report 50 hours per month (or as few as 30 hours during special campaigns). The option of auxiliary pioneering appeals to some Witnesses who are able to take time off from work to pioneer as the opportunity arises. If a Witness feels able to do 50 hours every month, he or she can apply to be a "*regular* auxiliary pioneer," but such ones generally do not enjoy the same prestige in the congregation as regular pioneers.

[7] You sometimes hear superhuman stories of regular pioneers holding down a full-time job while still managing to pioneer.

There are other perks but, for the most, part being a pioneer is all about recognition and a clear conscience.[8] If you manage to hit your target of 70 hours per month, you are setting an example to everyone else in the congregation, allowing you to sit comfortably in your seat while everyone else is being urged from the platform to do more. However, if you fail to fulfill your pledge of 840 hours for the year (i.e. 70 hours × 12 months), perhaps due to unforeseen health-related or financial constraints, you will soon find yourself under pressure to improve your game. If you persistently fail to respond to encouragement to this effect, you can expect to be unceremoniously stripped of your title. There are no prizes for *almost* succeeding.

You see, a regular pioneer makes a serious commitment, second only to the pledge of allegiance one makes at baptism. Good intentions count for very little if you fail to meet your hour quota. The fact that you are volunteering your time and forsaking a proper career and financial stability for little more than a title and a clean conscience counts for very little if you fall short for any reason.

Teenagers, in particular, find themselves under intense pressure to pioneer once they finish school. A typical example of the coercion they face can be seen in a 2002 promotional leaflet that pitched regular pioneering as a career opportunity not to be missed.

---

[8] Pioneers are described as being in "full time service" in the same way as those who work in Watchtower's branch facilities, or "Bethels." As such, they are allowed to stay at the local branches of Jehovah's Witnesses when they go on holiday. They also get to go to a six-day (formerly two-week) "Pioneer Service School" (or "pioneer school") after their first full "service year" stretching from September 1 to August 31 (and sometimes on special anniversaries of when they started pioneering), where they receive free food and accommodation throughout the course.

"What secular job could possibly be as exciting and satisfying?" it asked, adding: "The focus of a pioneer's life is, not his secular job, but his ministry—helping others to gain life!" It can be very difficult for a Witness teenager, especially one who is anxious to please his or her parents, to withstand such persuasion. After all, lives are supposedly in the balance.

Watchtower's recruitment drive targeting teenagers goes hand in hand with its stigmatization of higher education. Witness teenagers and their parents are conditioned at every turn to think of college and university as nothing more than worthless distractions threatening untold danger and risks. Those who pursue higher education, unless with the aim of better serving "Jehovah's organization" (with its "divine education" alternative) are considered foolish and misguided—especially since the end is claimed to be so very close.

One *Awake!* magazine cautioned: "If you are a young person, you also need to face the fact that you will never grow old in this present system of things." Why? Because "all the evidence in fulfillment of Bible prophecy indicates that this corrupt system is due to end in a few years." The article thus concluded:

> Therefore, as a young person, you will never fulfill any career that this system offers. If you are in high school and thinking about a college education, it means at least four, perhaps even six or eight more years to graduate into a specialized career. But where will this system of things be by that time? It will be well on the way toward its finish, if not actually gone!

I should perhaps mention that the above article was published in 1969. I will leave you to guess just how many people have both started and finished extremely productive careers in the nearly five decades since these words were printed without the end of the "present system of things" interfering with their retirement plans. You might assume the passage of time would prompt the organization to reconsider its approach and ease off in its assault on higher education, but you would, sadly, be mistaken.

A more recent edition of *The Watchtower* featured a list of scenarios in which a young Witness might be exposed to temptation. These grave dilemmas included being dared to smoke a cigarette, receiving an invitation to a party where there is alcohol and drugs, or being asked to share in watching a violent or risqué movie. Also ranked among this ominous list was the following sinister premise: "A well-intentioned teacher urges you to pursue higher education at a university." The article then asked: "If you are ever confronted with any of such situations, what will you do? Will you simply give in, or will you carefully consider what the 'end afterward' could be?" Higher education, regarded by the overwhelming majority of reasonably-minded people as the path to self-betterment, is thus relegated to an adolescent vice akin to smoking, doing drugs, or watching naughty films.

Watchtower's unbridled contempt for higher education stretches all the way up to the organization's upper echelons, with Governing Body members making it the subject of derision in their talks and videos. For example, Anthony Morris III appeared in a video in January 2015 with the following advice for young Witnesses:

> Young people, ask yourself: Why am I considering additional education? Is it because I'm pursuing a specific skill or trade to support my service to Jehovah? Or have I been pressured by the system into believing that higher education will somehow

make me a more respected person or lead me to a better life?

According to Morris, it is not Watchtower who is doing the pressuring, with the obvious ulterior motive of lining up fresh battalions of loyal workers to further its aims. Instead, it is Satan's system that is responsible for duping Witnesses into believing they can better themselves through learning.

Not done with traumatizing a new generation of teenagers into believing the world is out to deceive and exploit them, Morris had more wisdom to impart. After citing 1 Corinthians 15:33 as the "scriptural basis" for Watchtower's policy (a verse that cautions against "bad associations") Morris warned: "If we are in continued association with those who do not believe the same, it can erode our thinking and convictions." Thus, the true reason for the prohibition on higher education was revealed, albeit in such a way as to spin it to imply concern for the target audience: Watchtower is terrified of young people learning to evaluate their beliefs objectively through interaction with others in an environment where free thought is encouraged rather than stifled.[9]

Comparing the "bad association" a Witness at college or university might face with that of the workplace, Morris added: "It is one thing to work on a job with others, and quite another matter to immerse oneself in an institution of 'learning.'" (If you watch the video, you will see Morris raise his hands to gesticulate quotation marks for that last word, leaving his audience under no ambiguity as to the derision in which "institutions of learning" are to be held.)

---

[9] Some would argue that there is no "prohibition" because, so far, attending college or university has not been made a disfellowshipping offense. However, as you can plainly see from the provided quotes, it is strongly denounced.

As his rant continued, Morris decided to drive home the "danger" facing any who venture into university with the use of an anecdote:

> I have long said: the better the university, the greater the danger. The most intelligent and eloquent professors will be trying to reshape the thinking of your child, and their influence can be tremendous. One mom, I recall, asked me to try and help her son who was attending a prestigious-name university in Rhode Island. After visiting him, I later had to inform her that her son now believed in evolution. She refused to believe it until he finally told her himself. How sad.

Yes, a horrific tragedy awaits any Witness parent who allows their child to attend university: they might accept the science of evolution! (One can imagine Morris delivering the news to the mother in the same solemn way a doctor might convey news of a death or terminal illness.)

The end product of such overt fearmongering is generation after generation of Witnesses youths parachuting out of the education system immediately after finishing high school with little or no professional qualifications to support themselves or their future families—even though many of them are bright, intelligent, and brimming with potential to help make the world a better place.

You are probably wondering whether such demonizing of higher education and promotion of pioneering as a "career" had any influence on my decisions as a young person growing up as a Witness. Well, yes it did—despite my Witness parents being more open-minded about higher education than most.

In 1991, something unexpected happened: I started high school. Such a development would not surprise most parents, but mine were different. I distinctly remember Mum and Dad telling me they never expected me to need to go to high school in this "system of things." Apparently, they were expecting Armageddon to come first. With hindsight, the end of the world would probably have been less stressful than enduring what was in store for me as a Witness youth.

***A garden photoshoot in my uniform***

Less than a year had passed since my rather rushed baptism. I recall feeling happy and optimistic ahead of my first day. Mum had photographed me in my new uniform in our garden. I was anxious to see what high school life had to offer. I assumed it would be a vast improvement on my somewhat difficult primary school experience—but I was to be proven wrong.

As is the case with most schools, Wilmslow High had basically three types of students: the rich kids who were considered "cool" and popular, the crazy ones who did not give a damn and were only there to raise hell, and the nerds who were just trying to survive. I was firmly in the latter group.

By that time, I had shed much of my puppy fat and was heading toward the other end of the weight spectrum of being thin and gangly; so at least the calls of "fatty" became increasingly rare. Even so, I looked odd. I had an enormous nose (still do!) and a rather unstylish head of curly hair. These days it is cool for kids to constantly have their hoods up, which was how I wore mine at high school in the 1990s when the trend was the reverse: to keep your hood firmly down (even in the pouring rain)—or, better yet, have no hood at all. So, with my big floppy hood always up, combined with my big nose and bouncy hair, high school was never going to be kind to me. And it wasn't.

My choice of personal interests hardly helped. I was not all that keen on sports. In fact, I hated sports. I found football especially loathsome.[10] I had no interest in music and my knowledge of musical artists was limited to the likes of ABBA, Wham!, Alison Moyet, the Beatles and Mike Batt's awful *Wombles* albums (basically, Mum and Dad's combined record collection). This caused a major problem in one music lesson when we were asked to prepare a report on our favorite band or singer. I simply did not have one to talk about. I never really listened to music.

I went home and asked one of my uncles (whom I considered to be quite trendy) to recommend a band for my project.[11] He excitedly told me of an instrumental artist he was listening to at the time and played me a sample so that I could hear how awesome his music was. Convinced I had this project in the bag, I wrote an enthusiastic report on the musician for my presenta-

---

[10] This loathing of football (soccer), probably attributable to playground bullying in primary school, would reverse itself in my late teens. I would develop a taste for it just as my schoolmates were losing interest and becoming fascinated with girls.

[11] My uncle, Mum's younger brother, was baptized in 1995 (much to her delight), but he has since faded from the religion.

tion. The next day, I got more than a few raised eyebrows when, after watching my classmates rave about the likes of Nirvana, REM and Bon Jovi, I stood in front of everyone and declared my sudden appreciation for Mike Oldfield and his *Tubular Bells.*

Hopefully you are building a picture of how tortured my high school existence was. I am afraid it is a picture that gets worse. You see, my dad had grown up in the 1960s to be a huge fan of shows like *Thunderbirds* and *Star Trek.* These were making a bit of a comeback on British TV in the early 1990s and, as with his religion, he passed his tastes on to me. And so, while the other kids were all talking about the latest music icons or soccer stars, I could only get excited about uniformed puppets and the starship *Enterprise*—which is hardly the best strategy if your aim is to survive the high school experience.

Thankfully, I found a small group of friends who were almost as weird as me and seemed to humor my nerdish interests. But with my eccentric appearance and strange religious convictions, I was always facing an uphill battle in finding acceptance, even among them. My sister, who was a year behind me, simply could not bear the humiliation of being seen near me. I still have vivid recollections of Mum dropping us both off at the school gates in the morning and Hannah energetically moving herself as far away from me as possible. Looking back, I do not think I can blame her. It was every sibling for themselves.

Gradually, as my school years dragged on, things became progressively more difficult. As certain kids passed me in the corridors they would goad and heckle me incessantly, squealing my name in an irritating high-pitched way: "Lloooooyyyydd!" I started to develop something of a complex about it. To my surprise, things were not any easier for my much cooler sister. Despite being an attractive, likable and fairly unassuming girl, Hannah was also being relentlessly bullied. By 1995, things had come to a head for both of us. At my lowest ebb, I can remember crying into my pillow—pleading with Mum not to make me go to school the next day. I could tell she was heartbroken that both of her children were finding school so unbearable. Mum and Dad, on numerous occasions, tried speaking to the head teacher about bullying—but to no avail.

At their wits' end, our parents seriously discussed taking us both out of school to be taught at home, which is not an uncommon fallback strategy in Witness families. Home-schooling was hugely appealing to me, but I knew deep down that if I did not persevere with school for just one more year, I would regret it. I would miss out on my GCSEs and work would be much harder to find.[12] Hannah, on the other hand, still had two years to go, and the girls at school were being unspeakably cruel to her. She was under so much stress that she developed irritable bowel syndrome.

In the end, it was decided that I would try to somehow make it through one more year of high school, whereas Hannah would be pulled out. Looking back, I think we both made the right decisions. I left school with the full nine GCSEs. My grades were not astounding, but they never caused me any problems getting work. Hannah never got her GCSEs, but she attained some work-based qualifications in childcare that would

[12] GCSE stands for "General Certificate of Secondary Education." 5 GCSE passes at grade C or higher are roughly equivalent to a High School Diploma in the USA.

serve her well when applying for jobs as a nanny. I suppose only she could tell you whether her Witness background contributed in any way to her high school experience being so distressing and intolerable. Speaking for myself, my religious outlook made me view the majority of my classmates as inferior creatures who were all condemned to death if they failed to become Witnesses before the outbreak of Armageddon. As had been the case in primary school, this outlook prompted me to discuss my faith openly and frequently, making an already difficult situation much, much worse.

Having managed to make it through high school in one piece, the question now loomed: what to do next? By this stage I was acutely aware of the expectations for me to enter service as a pioneer. It was something I felt compelled to do rather than something I genuinely *wanted* to do. I admired and respected those who were pioneering in my congregation (all of whom were older than me) but I found it difficult to imagine spending almost every day knocking on doors alongside them. I especially feared having to spend whole days walking between doors in the pouring rain, which is typical weather for the North-West of England. I already found it hard enough to muster any enthusiasm to get up on Saturday mornings for just one hour of ministry with my parents, but back then the hour requirement for pioneers was 90 hours per month! This seemed simply impossible. The best solution, I concluded, was to kick everything into the long grass by postponing any decision on pioneering until things were a bit clearer.

As far as higher education was concerned, Mum and Dad were actually quite progressive and open-minded in comparison to most Witness parents. I think this was due, at least in part, to the fact that both of them had experienced quite austere childhoods. Neither of them came from a wealthy or privileged background. Both were raised to view financial security as something hard to attain and not to be taken for granted.

It was also around this period that Dad seemed to start getting fired from various jobs as a sales rep with increasing regularity. He had flunked school as a child due to his own problems with bullying, which he attributed to his dyslexia, and work as a salesman suited his skills and personality perfectly. Dad is a larger than life character; a talkative man with a good sense of humor and a gift for retaining information that most would consider useless. Even so, when it came to selling things, he did have his shortcomings. Mum once told me of an occasion when his boss sent him for an appraisal of his sales techniques. The conclusion? Apparently "he could talk anyone into buying something, but then talk them straight back out of it."

The occasions when Dad would come home and tell us he had been fired felt like a bomb going off in our family, leaving us all in shock. Mum took it especially hard, since she was the one running the household accounts and paying the bills. She felt the strain more than any of us.

When things got especially bad, Mum found work as a painter/decorator—a job she had a natural aptitude for due to her background as an art student. Her artistic streak and craftsmanship also enabled her to make some extra money from the occasional furniture restoration job. However, Mum suffered from severe migraines that were easily triggered by the fumes emanating from the paints and chemicals she used.

Never one to give up so easily, Mum managed to find a less hazardous job as a part-time nanny for a local wealthy family while still doing the odd decorating jobs here and there to make ends meet. I will always admire her resourcefulness and willingness to do her part in keeping food on the table. Mum was entirely selfless in putting the family's needs first. If Hannah and I needed clothes, she would not hesitate to go without buying any for herself to make sure we were presentable.

Even in our bleakest periods, I cannot bring myself to think of my family as poor. I have seen true poverty, so I could never frame my childhood experience in that context. Despite many setbacks, Mum and Dad did very well at keeping bread on the table and making our lives comfortable. We had all the usual gadgets and appliances. We lived in a nice house in a quiet neighborhood with a big garden. We had two cars in the driveway (our own car, and Dad's company car when he was in work). We managed a holiday each year even if it was only a camping trip to the Welsh coast.[13] Out of the dozen-or-so young families in our congregation, probably ours was among the better off financially. Nevertheless, money was certainly never taken for granted in our home, and I think the challenges faced by Mum and Dad gave them a more pragmatic approach to college education than most Witness parents.

This relative open-mindedness helped enormously in easing some of the pressure on me when it came to deciding what I would do on leaving school. Perplexed as to what my next step would be, the only thing I really knew for certain was that I could not be a pioneer—at least not yet. After much deliberation, my parents

---

[13] Looking back, credit must go to Dad for repeatedly surrendering himself to the camping experience when he never was the outdoors type at all.

and I finally resolved matters by deciding I would go to college for two years with a view to pioneering further down the line. With hindsight, this could have been a springboard to greater things. Had I chosen wisely, the two years could have ignited a hunger for learning in me that would only reveal itself in later years. Instead, I made some terrible decisions early on that rendered my time in college almost entirely pointless.

When speaking with my high school career advisor, I had told her of my interest in computers and drawing. She put the two together and suggested I should become a graphic designer. This was an excellent suggestion. If I had actually gone ahead and pursued this option (bear in mind: this was the mid-1990s, in the early days of the internet boom, when web development and computer graphics were still relatively in their infancy) I would potentially have had the basis for a long, successful career. Instead, I allowed an instructor at Macclesfield College to talk me into signing up for a more generic art and design course that included graphic design as one of the course elements. What little I ended up learning on that course about graphic design was not nearly comprehensive enough to get me into immediate paid work as a graphic designer once I finally had my qualification.[14] Everything I was taught was only intended as a stepping stone for other more advanced courses that one could take if aiming to become a professional artist.

I thus practically squandered two years mostly making pottery, painting abstract art, taking quirky

[14] I went for an interview for a part time graphic design job on finishing college. The interviewer quizzed me on my knowledge of fairly rudimentary graphic design techniques and I was unable to answer a single question, because none of it had been covered on my course.

photographs, and making batiks and lino prints. I was half-decent as an artist and, if I had used this course to advance to university, I could probably have forged some kind of career in the arts. My instructors seemed to think I had potential. However, it was never remotely in my mind to pursue such a route. I had more pressing matters in my head, such as the life-saving pioneer work I was supposed to be doing.

I was halfway through my college course by the time I realized it was not going to live up to my expectations. I then faced a similar dilemma to the one I had at high school—do I bail out now, or do I muddle through to get my qualifications? I decided on the latter. Even if the qualification was virtually meaningless, at least it was something to put on my resumé. Little could I have foreseen that my experience at college would have the overall effect of pulling me closer to my destiny as a pioneer rather than deflecting me from it.

College was not nearly as traumatic as high school—in many respects it was very enjoyable—but it was certainly challenging in ways I could not have expected. The best part was the social aspect. I was finally discovering what it meant to be popular. I discovered I had a sense of humor that my fellow students seemed to appreciate. They laughed at my jokes and, to my delight, accepted me for who I was without making a huge deal about my religion. I was starting to shed my obsession with science fiction and develop a taste for contemporary music and football. Even outside of college, I was broadening my social horizons—steadily gathering a more diverse group of Witness friends from beyond the confines of my congregation.

The challenges I faced were mostly hormonal. I was a hot-blooded teenager suddenly thrust into a situation where I was spending lots of time with so-called "worldly" girls in a college environment. To my astonishment, one or two actually *liked* me and were not shy about showing it. On one occasion, I found myself bundled into a storage closet with one of my admirers while everyone piled on the door to block our escape. It was dark inside, but there was just enough light for me to see her staring at me excitedly. I was embarrassed and immediately sensed I was in a very dangerous situation. Witnesses are not supposed to be alone with a member of the opposite sex unless it is their spouse. To the poor girl's surprise (and likely humiliation), I made my apologies before bursting every sinew to force the door open and break free. Making out with a girl was just not something I could bring myself to do, even if deep down I would have been fascinated to see what all the fuss was about.

Despite having a few friends on the course who were girls, for the most part I felt confident that I could stay out of trouble. Only one would emerge with the ability to test my loyalty as a Witness. Tracy, who was a year older than me, was a girl who I was genuinely enthralled by. She had captivating blue eyes and blonde hair, which she kept in a ponytail. She was kind, confident and witty. All the guys seemed to want her, and made little attempt to hide it.

Aside from a few flirty moments, if Tracy had any interest in me, she kept it well hidden. One such moment involved her asking me to pull up her bra strap, which had slipped down. She could not do it herself, because her hands were covered in ink from doing screen printing. Her friend was with us in the studio and seemed to find the situation hilarious. Do not ask me how, but I told her "no." I felt barred from indulging in any flirtatious behavior or revealing any kind of feelings. This was exactly the sort of situation I had been warned about throughout my childhood. Like Joseph, when Potiphar's wife attempted to seduce him in the story from Genesis, I had to stay chaste. Tracy was a "worldly girl" and I knew I had to view her as strictly off-limits.[15] We could only ever be friends—and even then, friends who did not socialize. Despite all this, I am sure Tracy knew I was smitten. I now look back in horror when I remember once trying to preach to her in an attempt to solve my dilemma. As you might guess, though she took the whole thing graciously, my efforts were unsuccessful.

Because Tracy and I both took the same bus into Macclesfield, we saw each other a lot. The closer we grew as friends, the more agonizing my situation became. One morning, when I was running late, I was so afraid of missing the bus that I hurtled across the road without paying any attention to the traffic. An armored security van slammed into me head-on, without having hardly any time to brake. To this day I cannot explain how it happened, but I got up off the road, climbed up the steps of the bus and collapsed in one of the seats. Within seconds, my vision started to turn pink. I could feel myself passing out. The driver was looking at me as though he was seeing a ghost. (He would later tell me: "When I saw you hit that van, I thought you were dead.

[15] Witnesses are not disfellowshipped for becoming "unevenly yoked" by marrying non-believers, but it is heavily stigmatized and repeatedly warned against. If you ignore the warnings, you will likely have to go through a period of "marking" (soft shunning) so that the congregation can show its disapproval for your ignoring the elders' council. (I will revisit the issue of marking in Chapter Five.) A male who marries a non-believer will almost certainly be denied any form of privilege or status, at least to begin with. Apart from all that, I was still considered too young to get into any kind of romantic relationship, because I was only about 17.

You went flying.") Tracy was immediately by my side, asking if I was okay. Gradually, her face became more blurry as I started to slip from consciousness. "Lloyd, stay awake! Stay awake!" she said. I am sure having her there was what kept me conscious all the way to the hospital, where the driver dropped us off. Tracy and her friend remained until Mum could be with me. When I called Mum on the phone and told her what happened, she immediately started crying. She had dropped me off just around the corner from the bus stop moments before the van hit, and driven home blissfully unaware of what was going on.

Incredibly, despite some heavy bruising and swelling on the side of my face that had merged with the asphalt, it turned out I was not badly injured and I recovered quickly.[16] Because of the incident, and Tracy's involvement, it felt easier to introduce her to Mum not long after, when Tracy was giving me a ride home in her car one afternoon. I can vividly remember Mum and Hannah running the rule over her in our kitchen. Mum was extremely good about everything. After meeting Tracy, I think she understood why I would not stop talking about her—even if I knew I was banned from pursuing anything. But before too long, my dilemma solved itself by ending in heartbreak. Tracy began a relationship with a guy in another class who I

---

[16] I remember a police officer coming into my bedroom to make it clear to me, as I lay convalescing with a face like the Phantom of the Opera, that I had broken the law by running out in the road like that. However, since I was the only one harmed, the matter would not be pursued. I also got a visit from the traumatized security van driver who thought he might have killed me. For many years, whenever reflecting on the incident, I would wonder whether my survival was an act of divine intervention. But I now realize I was just extremely fortunate. The laws of physics were in my favor that day.

would come to absolutely loathe, and that was the end of that.

I was distraught and began to turn my attention to my growing circle of Witness friends, on whom I felt I could rely to never let me down. In particular, one cute blonde pioneer from Stockport, Vicki, caught my interest. I allowed myself to be drawn into a small group of Witness guys who vied for her attention. Since her pioneer work meant she would nearly always be found in the ministry, I started joining up with some mutual friends to go on the preaching work in Manchester on Wednesdays in hopes of seeing her. Wednesdays happened to be the day when we had a free period in college, so long absences were generally forgiven by our instructors. To begin with, I would make the short journey North on the train, but Mum and Dad bought me a car soon after I passed my driving test, which I could then use to travel into the city and meet up with my new pioneer pals.

For once in my life, ministry was no longer a bore—it was actually fun! It was my way of forgetting the heartache of missing out on Tracy by pursuing a girl I was actually *allowed to date* if I could only convince her to return my interest. And I at least had a fighting chance of using my sense of humor (honed in the unforgiving proving grounds of college) to win over Vicki if we found ourselves as partners for a morning or afternoon in the door-to-door work. Things were finally falling into place.

By the time my art course ended in 1998, I was more or less sold on becoming a pioneer. I remember one of my instructors trying to talk me into staying on and doing the foundation course for university with the rest of my classmates, but I was having none of it.

Another two years of messing around with paint? What would that accomplish? I wanted to get out into the pioneer work, which was now both an obligation *and* a pleasure. I would worry about what to do with my rather pointless qualifications in art and design later. For now, my new life as a pioneer beckoned.

***Pioneering in 1998***

When September came, not only was I unveiled as Wilmslow's newest regular pioneer—I was also surprised to learn that my local elders had decided to appoint me as a ministerial servant, despite the fact that I had only just turned 19. Ministerial servants are effectively helpers to the elders. They are viewed as potential elders in training and can assist in certain aspects of running the congregation that do not involve disciplinary matters or shepherding visits.

My first assignment was to handle the congregation accounts, which seemed like a huge honor for a 19-year-old. Sure, it was a painstaking and tedious task involving lots of paperwork, and I probably only had the job because no one else wanted it, but that did not trouble me. So soon after leaving college, it felt as though I was being rewarded for staying focused on my life as a Witness. The future was looking bright and my life now had some direction. All I needed to do was honor my promise to report 90 hours of ministry every month and keep my congregation's accounts in perfect order and I was making my parents proud, and earning a good name with Jehovah, simultaneously. Of course, if these new responsibilities also made it easier to find a nice Witness girl, this would be no catastrophe!

Even though my parents were supporting me financially, I knew I still had to do my part. I got my first job while still in college, working the tills on Saturdays at a local store for £2.88 per hour. By the time I started pioneering I was working at a larger department store for £4 per hour—still doing mostly Saturday work.

As mentioned, the hour requirement for pioneers back then was 90 hours per month. I found this grueling but achievable, especially since I was only working weekends. Even so, I was relieved when the requirement was unexpectedly lowered to 70 hours in January 1999 (where it has remained ever since). This meant that I could work two or three days per week and still get my time in.

After quitting my job at the department store, I bobbed in and out of part-time and temp agency work, doing mostly administrative jobs such as filing, typing and data entry for local companies. It was low pay, but it seemed to suit me better than gardening or window cleaning, which was how most of my fellow pioneers were earning a living.[17] Most importantly, my part-time work was enabling me to pioneer and see more of my friends. I was especially thrilled at any fleeting opportunities to spend time with Vicki, even if it was

---

[17] I once attempted window cleaning for a few months, but decided it definitely wasn't for me after a few scary incidents in which my ladder parted company with the wall while I was on it.

becoming painfully obvious that she was not remotely interested in me.

Having my own car freed me to travel long distances and do preaching work with various Witness friends all over Manchester rather than confining myself to my own congregation territory in Wilmslow. This practice of frequently hopping to other territories is not exactly encouraged for Witness pioneers (elders would normally prefer them to focus their efforts in the congregation territory), but Wilmslow was a large congregation with a fairly easy-going body of elders, so nobody seemed to mind my absence. If anything, my parents appeared pleased that I was meeting new people within the "Truth" and spreading my wings.

At one meeting in 1999, an announcement was made requesting volunteers to help out in the Buxton congregation, where the local Witnesses had an immense rural territory spanning a sizable chunk of the Peak District National Park. I was only too pleased to go along and help out, and perhaps meet some new people in the process. I found myself working with a Buxton elder who mentioned he was looking for "exemplary" young brothers to join the Chairman's Office for the upcoming regional convention that summer.[18] Not long after meeting him, I got a phone call telling me I had been chosen to join the team for the "God's Prophetic Word" convention, to be held at the beginning of July.

Regional conventions are annual events, usually held at large-capacity sports venues or auditoriums. Thousands of Witnesses will typically assemble at these gatherings to listen to three days of talks, interviews and demonstrations designed to strengthen their

---

[18] Back then they were called "district conventions," but for ease of reading by current JWs, I will employ the latest lingo.

faith and keep them in a perpetually heightened sense of urgency regarding Armageddon. The Teaching Committee of the Governing Body organizes the program and prepares a series of talk scripts that are mostly read out almost verbatim by the speaker. The Chairman's Office of any given convention is entrusted with ensuring the event runs smoothly and that all items on the program are delivered precisely as the Governing Body has instructed.

The 1999 convention was among the first held at the Manchester Arena, which continues to host the event to this day, and my job was to escort speakers down to the platform to make sure they were not lost or delayed. This was hardly an intellectually draining task, but it was considered a huge privilege (as I was constantly reminded by the elder who was assigned as chairman). Apart from presenting an opportunity to mix with the who's who of Witness celebrities, including prominent elders, circuit overseers[19] and representatives from the branch office in London, the role carried the added perk of allowing me to spend the convention in a nice air-conditioned executive suite. From here, the talks could be listened to in relative comfort while the rank and file sweated and squirmed in their ordinary seats.

It felt very much like a huge leap forward in my promising rise through the Witness ranks. Not only was I a freshly-minted ministerial servant and regular pioneer—I was also now working in the Chairman's

---

[19] Circuit overseers are responsible for visiting designated "circuits" of congregations twice-annually to ensure all of them are worshipping in conformity with Watchtower guidelines. A "CO" reports directly to his nearest branch office (the Britain branch office is in London) and is responsible for appointing or deleting elders and ministerial servants.

Office at my local convention; rubbing shoulders with the top brass and making my parents very proud in the process.

But all of this is not the main reason why I remember the 1999 "God's Prophetic Word" regional convention more than any other. I now look back on this event as a turning point for other, more profound reasons. You see, a book was released at this event that was to have a monumental impact on the rest of my life, even if I could not fully grasp the significance at the time.

One of the highlights of my Witness upbringing was the release of new publications at the conventions. As someone who genuinely enjoyed reading from an early age, I could not wait for shiny new books and brochures to be revealed. I am sure I am not the only one who would inspect the convention program to speculate as to which talk would feature the "release" (usually it was the final talk of each day) and what the title of the new item would be.

Watchtower will normally send copies of a release to the convention in boxes that get hidden throughout the venue. These boxes are sent on the strict understanding that they will only be opened and the contents distributed once the speaker has revealed the new title (normally he will hold a copy aloft when doing so) and the talk has ended, which only adds to the suspense. In many cases, a publication will be released as a replacement of an existing publication on the same subject, especially if there have been a number of recent changes in Witness doctrine making such a reboot necessary. For me, the jackpot was a new release that addressed a Bible-related subject for the first time, or the first time in many years. *Pay Attention to Daniel's Prophecy!* was such a book.

The *Daniel* book, as it came to be known, was quite extraordinary. I devoured it voraciously the moment I got home, because it dealt with a book of the Bible that is rich in prophecy and was still regarded as mysterious by many Witnesses at the time. The prophecy of the "King of the North" in Daniel chapter 11 was a particular talking point, especially among older Witnesses who knew their Bibles. I wanted to get well acquainted with the book before the rest of the congregation studied it. I had been quite young and disengaged when the *Revelation* book was being studied and I always viewed it as being rather gaudy and eccentric. The *Daniel* book looked like it meant business and was released when I was old enough to begin to grasp the nuances of Bible prophecy in depth. This was just the sort of book I could get my teeth into and I felt mentally ready for it.

I powered through the first few chapters, marveling at the use of colorful illustrations and clear reasoning. The tables and references to archaeological records seemed to give the book a scholarly feel. The discussions on the Bible narrative of Daniel's exploits in Babylon were both riveting and inspiring.

Then I reached page 141, which discussed Daniel 7:25. In this verse, Daniel foresaw a wild beast (or world power) continually harassing the "holy ones" of the "supreme one." Page 142 declared these holy ones to be, in essence, the forerunners to Jehovah's Witnesses (or Bible Students) who were active around the time of 1914, which is the year in which Witnesses believe Christ became king in heaven and hurled Satan down to exile on earth.

The book went on to claim that the "time, times and half a time" (three and a half years) in which the holy ones were "given into the hand" of the beast referred to an exact period corresponding with World War I, during which the Bible Students preached despite being persecuted by the combined nations of Britain and America (represented by the beast). However, on page 143, the book insisted that this three-and-a-half-year period commenced in December 1914, more than four months after World War I began on July 28, 1914, and two months *after* Christ supposedly began his Kingdom rule on the 4th or 5th of October the same year.[20] Why the delay? It felt like the writers were trying to make dates in history fit with scripture.[21]

It was at this point that something very strange happened. I found myself consciously *disagreeing* with Watchtower's explanation of something. This probably sounds like an unremarkable, healthy thing to you, the reader. But to me, as a Witness raised in the faith who took it all extremely seriously, it felt very wrong indeed. I was overcome with guilt, as though I had committed a crime in my mind. The organization's publications were there to be read and accepted. They were not to be challenged or questioned.

---

[20] Page 97 of the *Daniel* book explains how the "seven times" of earth's domination by human rulership began with the destruction of Jerusalem in 607 B.C.E. and ended on October 4/5, 1914 (which is assumed to be when Christ began ruling as king). I will revisit the 607 B.C.E./1914 teaching in Chapter Six.

[21] The explanation offered by the writers: "By the end of 1914, they [the Witnesses] were expecting persecution." The sole evidence that forerunners of the Witnesses were "expecting persecution" when 1914 drew to a close is said to be the fact that the scripture they chose as the 1915 year text at the end of 1914 was Jesus' words at Matthew 20:22 (*King James Version*): "Are ye able to drink of My cup?" Even without the tenuous reasoning based on the year text, I felt that *expecting* persecution and actually *experiencing* it were two very different things.

These conflicted thoughts caused me to do something inexplicable. I folded the page with a diagonal crease so that the top edge of the page was now facing into the spine. I did this because it was the only way I could think of to discreetly mark the part of the book that I disagreed with as a form of silent protest without committing my heretical thoughts to writing. If I wrote anything down, or scribbled so much as a question mark, this could be found by someone else and I might be asked about it.

I assumed this would be the only occasion on which my page-folding protest would be needed, but I was in for a surprise. As I now flip through my old copy of the *Daniel* book, I see that the pages are folded on three more occasions, all in the final few chapters. Considering I had initially approached the book with such optimism, this was all very unexpected and utterly disappointing. For the first time, I began to look on the Governing Body, not as oracles of truth and wisdom guided by God's spirit, but as a group of men in Brooklyn who were just making it up as they went along—guessing at the meaning of scripture and shoehorning Bible prophecy to make it line up with events in the organization's history. Further evidence for these conclusions emerged when I summoned the bravery to reexamine the *Revelation* book with a critical eye and found it to be littered with similar contortions to the *Daniel* book.

But the *Daniel* book and Watchtower's dabbling with Bible prophecy was not my only area of concern. I was starting to notice other things that caused me to ponder. For example, I saw a poster at the convention listing the various events to be held at the arena that year. Our event was listed as the "Watchtower Convention." Why all this emphasis on "Watchtower" rather than

Jehovah's Witnesses? Why, for example, did an emblem of a watchtower appear at the end of each of our promotional videos and in some of our publications? Bear in mind that Witnesses are taught to view the use of symbols of any kind in worship (such as the cross) as idolatry, whether these draw inspiration from natural or man-made forms. It struck me that the prominent way in which the Watchtower name and logo were being used ignored this principle.

Against my better judgment, I found it hard to keep these disappointments to myself. I divulged some of my emerging doubts with two people—Mum and Nigel. Nigel was a guy in my congregation in his 40s whom I had befriended. He was a fairly new convert; full of enthusiasm for the preaching work. We worked together on the ministry regularly and would have long discussions about the "Truth" and my increasingly futile attempts to win over Vicki. I confided in him about my problems with the Watchtower symbol, as well as my disillusionment with certain parts of the *Daniel* book that made little or no sense to me.[22] At first he responded to these confessions with a mix of empathy and fascination, even suggesting at one point that I might be one of those few Witnesses who are spirit-anointed if I was so keenly motivated to dissect spiritual matters, in such depth.[23] I was having none of that. Anointed Christians were supposed

[22] Nigel's response to my issue with the Watchtower logo was to recommend that I write to the organization in New York regarding the matter, which I did. The letter I got back was dismissive of my concerns, saying that the use of the emblem was no more offensive to God than King Solomon's use of copper pomegranates in his decorations for the temple in Jerusalem. Unfortunately, I no longer have a copy of the letter.

[23] I will explain spirit-anointed Witnesses in more detail in Chapter Eight.

to have an unmistakable feeling that they are chosen by God to serve as kings and priests with Christ in heaven, and I had no such feeling—nor would I falsely claim to have one simply to give weight to my observations.

Over time, my conversations with Nigel became increasingly strained. I sensed that I was beginning to burden him with my reservations. Sure enough, there came a point where my congregation coordinator asked to speak with me.[24] A coordinator is responsible for coordinating the body of elders in each congregation, organizing meetings of elders and corresponding with the branch. One afternoon, when he and I were working together in the preaching work, he raised the issue of my doubts. It was clear Nigel had spoken to him.

My coordinator's name was Terry. He was an older man with big thick eyebrows, a warm personality and an unbridled enthusiasm for jazz and classical music. I would enjoy spending time with him in his car going on return visits and marvel at his uncanny ability to correctly name whatever piece of music was playing on Classic FM (a well known station for classical music) at any given moment. On this particular occasion, however, things were more serious. I was asked to explain to Terry the nature of my problems with the organization.

I briefly went through the basic gist of my issues with parts of the *Daniel* book and *Revelation* book. I told Terry that I felt as though some prophecies in the Bible had been poorly explained, giving the impression that scriptures had been forced to fit events in the or-

---

[24] The full title of a coordinator is the "coordinator of the body of elders." At the time of these events, a person with this role was known as the "presiding overseer." For simplicity, I will refer to the position according to the current terminology.

ganization's history. I told him that I had great respect for the Governing Body, but I failed to understand how they had arrived at some of their prophetic explanations.

Terry's response was unexpected. He said: "Tell me Lloyd, do you agree with our teaching regarding 1914?" I was baffled at this question, which seemed to ignore everything I had just said. When I answered that yes, I had no problem with the teaching of Christ's Kingdom starting in 1914, Terry more or less said: "Well that's all that matters!" We carried on as though nothing had happened. It seemed that any doubts I had about the Governing Body's prophetic interpretations were excusable so long as I embraced this central doctrine. I did not think for a moment that all Witnesses had such a flexible outlook, but Terry was my coordinator and at least I was "off the hook" as far as he was concerned.

I chose not to share my doubts with Mum, at least not to nearly the same extent as I had done with Nigel or Terry. Apart from anything else, I did not want to panic her by giving her the impression her son might be drifting into "apostasy"—a sin worthy of disfellowshipping and shunning. But I do recall one specific occasion when I told Mum of a problem I was having with the *Daniel* book shortly before we were due to consider that same section at our weekly book study group.

At the time, congregations of Jehovah's Witnesses were further subdivided into smaller, local study groups consisting of ten to twenty Witnesses who would meet in private homes during midweek to discuss an allocated Watchtower publication according to printed schedules from the organization. Soon after the *Daniel* book was released, all congregations of Jehovah's Witnesses studied the book from April 2000 through

January 2001. By the time 2001 rolled along, our book study group was being held in the home of a recently-widowed elderly Witness lady who lived a short walk from where we lived. Dad was responsible for taking the group and I was his assistant.[25]

Before we left to go to the study that evening, I remarked to Mum how strange it seemed that Daniel 12:12, 13—the *very last two verses* of the book of Daniel—had apparently found fulfillment in a 1926 *Watch Tower* article. It seemed inconceivable to me that God would inspire the ancient prophet Daniel to devote the final few words of his book to foretelling in cryptic language how a *Watch Tower* magazine writer would one day write something in an article that would make a few people happy.[26]

Mum double-checked with her book and confirmed that I had not misinterpreted what was written. She agreed that it was very odd. When the question came up for consideration during the book study, she boldly raised her hand and said before everyone: "I don't understand, Jonathan. Is this paragraph suggesting that the last prophecy in the book of Daniel was fulfilled by a *Watchtower article?*"

I remember Dad squirming in his chair and looking flustered. You are not supposed to publicly question somebody who is conducting a discussion of Watchtower materials. He will ask the questions and you will answer them according to the information in the para-

---

[25] As Dad's assistant, it was my responsibility to conduct the occasional book study in his absence—a job I did my best with whether I personally agreed with all of the sentiments in the publication under discussion or not.

[26] Prior to 1931, the magazine today known as *The Watchtower* was known as *The Watch Tower.* Even further back, from 1879 to 1909, it was known as *Zion's Watch Tower.*

graph. The fact that Dad's own wife was now quizzing him in front of his group was, I am sure, a source of great embarrassment. Dad gave an improvised answer to Mum's question that was vague and unconvincing, to the effect of "yes, that's how we understand it *at the moment.*"

This happened at the end of January 2001—and it gave me plenty to think about. It showed me that even my mother, whom I viewed as a real stalwart of the "Truth," was not afraid to openly question Watchtower publications if something did not make sense to her. Little did I know at the time that Mum was to be gone from my life only four months later. Her loss would turn my world upside down and cause me to rapidly reevaluate my growing disillusionment with the organization.

CHAPTER THREE

# God's Promise of Paradise

*"Those who promise us paradise on earth never produced anything but a hell."*
—Karl Popper

*"Religion looks forward to the destruction of the world. . . . Perhaps half aware that its unsupported arguments are not entirely persuasive, and perhaps uneasy about its own greedy accumulation of temporal power and wealth, religion has never ceased to proclaim the Apocalypse and the day of judgment."*
—Christopher Hitchens

FROM my earliest memories as a Witness child, two aspects of the beliefs I had inherited from my parents unsettled me. The first was the command to love Jehovah more than anyone else. Apart from it feeling odd to be commanded to love someone, I would think to myself: "Just how am I supposed to love Jehovah with my *whole* heart, my *whole* mind and my *whole* soul?" This Bible law found at Deuteronomy 6:5 and quoted repeatedly at Witness meetings troubled me, because I had never met God, and yet somehow I was expected to love him exclusively—more than I loved my parents, whom I loved immensely. I shared this quandary with Mum and Dad from time to time, but they could never unravel it for me in a way that made sense. I could understand loving God with some or even *most* of my heart—but *all of it?*

When not consumed by this conundrum, I allowed my mind to bask in less troubling thoughts of a future paradise. Witnesses believe that, once the great battle of Armageddon has been and gone, the whole planet will be landscaped into one delightful garden—a tranquil paradise to be enjoyed by all faithful Witnesses who have survived global annihilation. In this worldwide utopia, peace will prevail and food will be abundant. Sumptuous arrangements of fruit and vegetables will adorn every table. Nobody will go hungry.

The entire planet will be swathed in verdant forests, rolling fields and glassy lakes framed by snow-capped mountains (a bit like Switzerland but with a more tropical ambience). Deserts will vanish, to be replaced by fertile pastures—all of which will be apportioned fairly for Earth's new, filtered populace. Everyone will have a spacious self-built property on "just a little less than an acre" of land. Once fierce predators will revert to their original placid behavior from the Garden of Eden, embracing vegetarianism. Lions will forget that they are carnivores, and eat only grass. Sharks will use their razor sharp teeth to gorge on, one assumes, seaweed. Poisonous snakes will find an alternative use for their venom that does not involve incapacitating prey.

In this future Paradise, death will become a distant memory. Diseases will vanish, and humans will find it impossible to get into any life-threatening situations.[1] Mankind will discover the joy of living forever in a state of perfection, free from sin. Elderly Witnesses who survive Armageddon will become young again, and

---

[1] The March 24, 1926, issue of *The Golden Age* magazine (forerunner of *Awake!*) posited that inhabitants of the new world will be fitted with "individual negative gravity devices" that will keep them from injury as a result of gravity-related incidents, such as falling down elevator shafts.

their children who make it through will be allowed to grow to an agreeable state of youthful maturity before being locked into this age for all time. Basically, everyone will be 21—forever.[2]

Dead Witnesses will be resurrected into perfect human bodies to be welcomed back by their ecstatic families. Pre-Christian Bible characters will also be raised from the dead, as will those who died before Armageddon without knowing anything about Jehovah's Witnesses—especially those who were alive before it was possible to be affiliated with Watchtower (i.e. before the 1880s). (To make this less confusing: if you are not a Witness and you die before Armageddon strikes, you are in with a shot of being counted among the "unrighteous" of Acts 24:15 who can receive a resurrection. If Armageddon arrives with you and your children still having declined the opportunity to join the Witnesses, prepare to face God's wrath.)

The likes of Noah and Moses will spend their days regaling Armageddon survivors on what it was like to build the Ark, or how it felt to lead the Israelites through the Red Sea. Of course, any non-Witness resurrectees will need inducting into their new surroundings, and there will be no shortage of Witnesses with whom they can study. With nobody dying, new ones being born, and the righteous dead being raised, Earth's population will soon reach a pleasing fullness at which point God may "cause procreation to cease on

[2] It goes without saying that earth's new populace cannot keep having children with nobody dying, since the planet would eventually be over-populated. Older publications, such as a 1952 *Watchtower,* solved the problem by declaring that "childbearing ceases" when "the mandate to fill the earth is fulfilled." Current literature tends to avoid addressing the problem directly, while still featuring children in its depictions of paradise.

earth." The exact details of how all this will happen were always sketchy—a puzzle to be deciphered at some future point when "new scrolls" are opened.[3]

Though fanciful to say the least, Watchtower's vision of Paradise offered a blissful future on which to focus—especially to a young child with an imagination as vivid as mine. I would picture myself building sailing ships and tree-houses, riding elephants and befriending horses and monkeys. As a budding artist, I would frequently depict these fantasies on paper to the delight of my parents. They had raised me to think of Paradise as a future certainty, and my sketches and doodles were evidence that I was taking it all seriously.

The trouble was, Paradise came with strings attached—and this was the second area of my beliefs that troubled me from an early age. In order to take one's place in this utopia, one had to pass a test of loyalty to Jehovah, which really meant being loyal to his organization. If presented with a choice between loyalty to Watchtower and loyalty to one's family, family should always come off second best. This was the reason why Henry's family had ended all contact with Karen, his adopted sister. She had decided she no longer wanted to be a Witness, and the organization responded by directing her family to never speak to her again—a command to which they loyally held. Had they disobeyed, they would be showing more love for Karen than for Jehovah, and their place in Paradise would be compromised. The acre of land with their name on it might be revoked.

---

[3] The idea of "new scrolls," essentially an update to the Bible with information pertinent to Armageddon survivors, is based on Revelation 20:12—interpreted by a 2016 *Watchtower* as inferring that "scrolls will be opened to give us directions in new world living."

Of course, deviant Witness relatives are not the only ones who will be left behind when Armageddon strikes. "Worldly" non-Witnesses have every reason to panic. If you want to evade divine destruction, more will be required "than a superficial confession of faith or a last-minute effort to put things right with God." To be certain of making it through, you must become a Witness—and remain one. In fact, the only reason why Armageddon has not already come and gone is because God is mercifully holding the door open, "allowing for hundreds of thousands to be gathered" to the Witness fold before time is up and the slaughter commences.

Most Witnesses do not like to dwell on Armageddon's death toll, preferring instead to focus on the blissful and leafy end product of a cleansed paradise earth tailor-made to their needs. But it does not take much calculating to realize that with a planetary population of over 7 billion and only 8 million Witnesses (based on the latest available figures), the apocalypse that Witnesses salivate over would wipe out *billions* of people, including men, women and children. Their crime? Not wanting to be Jehovah's Witnesses. Were you to take a shovel to the foreseen utopia and start digging around, you would quickly discover that it has been sculpted over a mass grave of unimaginable proportions that would make the Holocaust pale in significance.

Most Witnesses flounder when cornered on their firm belief that such an unfathomable number of humans will be ruthlessly slain by the Almighty simply for not sharing their religious views irrespective of whether they are good people or not. However, those at the pinnacle of the organization, including Governing Body members, have occasionally been recorded enthusiastically elaborating on the massacre in talks at

Witness gatherings. For some reason, these ideas are never expressed in print in quite the same grisly detail as in the actual words of GB members when they are before an audience that they know will hang on their every word.

"The slain are gonna be from one end of the earth clear to the other end," warned GB member Anthony Morris III in one talk. "It's gonna be very numbing. Lotta dead people. Billions."[4]

During another of his talks, Morris drew from his military service as a medic during the Vietnam War to drill home the grim fate awaiting all non-Witnesses during the forthcoming apocalypse.[5] "I've seen what happens to humans when they're mangled," he revealed. "Until you've smelled human flesh burning from a helicopter crash, humans like a hot dog on a grill, blackened and splitting open—I know what's coming at Armageddon. Lotta dead people."[6] (One can

---

[4] I will revisit this Morris talk in Chapter Eight, because his comments on the need for Witness parents to coerce their children into baptism are especially disturbing. You can watch a video of the talk by searching "Anthony Morris Teenage Baptism" on YouTube.

[5] When reading Morris' life story in the May 15, 2015, *Watchtower*, it is not hard to form the impression that his Vietnam experience left him with PTSD. "In war, people do terrible things. I was no exception," he writes. "Jehovah looks at me through the blood of Jesus, and He has forgiven me for what I have done. Knowing that fact has enabled me to have a cleansed conscience and has motivated me to do all I can to help others come to know the truth about our merciful God, Jehovah!" How sad it would be if, driven by fantasies of divine slaughter, Morris is making millions of Witnesses pay the price for his inner turmoil.

[6] A video of Morris's "hot dog" remarks can be seen by searching "Anthony Morris Human Hot Dog" on YouTube. The recording is taken from a talk from the 2009-2010 special assembly day series.

only hope the audience did not have lunch too soon before listening to Morris' trip down memory lane.)

In another talk, fellow GB member Gerrit Lösch offered his own thoughts regarding the possible methods by which non-Witnesses will be reduced to smoldering hunks of meat during the day of God's wrath. Lösch read the rather gruesome portion of Scripture found at Zechariah 14:12, which describes how the flesh of God's enemies "will rot away while they stand on their feet, their eyes will rot away in their sockets, and their tongues will rot away in their mouths."

Lösch calmly proposed that this prophecy could well find a literal fulfillment during Armageddon. "Jehovah is perhaps gonna use radiation to cause this phenomena that people's flesh will rot away as they are standing on their feet," he mused. "It will be a destruction as mankind has never seen before."[7] So whereas Morris predicts that God will fire up his heavenly grill to dispense with unbelievers, Lösch's money is on some form of divine microwave being deployed. Different cooking methods, same end product.

Shortly after offering this chilling foregleam, Lösch boldly tackled the awkward problem of what Witnesses would do with all the billions of bodies left over in the wake of the apocalypse. "There will also be a lot of work to do," he warned. "Because we've mentioned that in Armageddon billions of people will die, and they

---

[7] You can watch a video of the recording of this talk by searching "Gerrit Lösch Armageddon" on YouTube. Not long after the video was widely available online in September 2012, Watchtower published a discussion of Zechariah 14 with a less morbid take on verse 12: "Whether literal or not, the scourge will silence terrifying threats. On that day, 'one's very eyes . . . and tongue will rot away' in that the attackers will be able to strike out only blindly and their defiant speech will be silenced."—*The Watchtower*, February 15, 2013, p. 20, par. 15.

have to be buried. The Bible indicates in the prophecy that there will be groups of people, of brothers and sisters, that will for a long time do nothing else than just bury the dead."

Despite Lösch's vision of "groups" of Witness grave diggers scouring the planet, the small matter of how the surplus of human cadavers will be spirited away from public view is never conclusively settled in Watchtower literature. A 2014 *Watchtower* article hints at a less labor-intensive means of accomplishing the task. "The carnage will be earth wide," advises the writer, before repeating the words of Jeremiah 25:33 (also quoted earlier by Morris) that "those slain by Jehovah in that day will be from one end of the earth clear to the other end of the earth." The following "parallel prophecy" from Revelation 19:17, 18 is then quoted:

> I saw also an angel standing in the sun, and he cried out with a loud voice and said to all the birds that fly in midheaven: "Come here, be gathered together to the great evening meal of God, so that you may eat the flesh of kings and the flesh of military commanders and the flesh of strong men and the flesh of horses and of those seated on them, and the flesh of all, of freemen as well as of slaves and of small ones and great."

In case the intended message is lost on the reader, a striking piece of artwork is shown depicting an angel hovering in front of the sun with a raven and various carrion birds flying in the foreground. The painting is captioned: "Birds will be called on to cleanse the earth."

Will birds do this job by themselves, or will they complement the work of the grave diggers? Or will there be a quadruple action of Morris' hot dog grill, Lösch's divine radiation, and a flurry of beaks and

***Image from "The Watchtower," February 15, 2014, p. 7***

feathers followed by the burial teams being summoned to get rid of whatever is left? The Governing Body would rather leave us guessing—or, to be more accurate, they would prefer us to refrain from dwelling for too long on the exact mechanics of the final solution. It would suit them better if we concentrate on the idyllic finale: the ends that justify the means.

Assuming you are a non-Witness, by this point you are probably balking in astonishment that a group of men who do not even know you are gleefully anticipating your future elimination and speculating as to the most expedient way for you to be blotted from history. If you happen to be reading this book in a developed country, at least be thankful that you have the opportunity to meet a Witness, learn the "Truth" and mend your ways before these dreadful things befall you and your dear ones. If you are reading this book in an Arab or communist country, then I hate to be the bearer of bad news but your outlook is considerably bleaker. This is because the odds of meeting a Witness in such lands and hearing their message of salvation are decidedly remote.

Every year in its *Yearbook*, Watchtower publishes a detailed country-by-country breakdown of figures related to its evangelism work. These figures tell you how many Witnesses are in each country, how many congregations they are organized into, how many Bible studies they are conducting, how many have been baptized, etc. (As you can probably guess, these statistics are mostly derived from the report slips referred to at the start of the previous chapter, which are diligently submitted by all Witnesses at the end of every month.)

A notable feature of the "Service Year Report of Jehovah's Witnesses Worldwide" can be found toward the end of the long list of countries and numbers. Positioned discreetly above the "Grand Total" is a row of figures attributed to "Other Lands." These *other lands* are countries where Witnesses are banned, or where the levels of persecution make it otherwise impossible for them to preach openly.[8] Such countries are nev-

[8] I personally do not believe the religiopolitical make-up of these countries is the sole factor making Witness evangelism problematic. Sometimes it is also a matter of culture. I recommend you read the story of Amber Scorah, who awakened from her religious indoctrination while preaching in one of these "other lands"—China. The difficulty Amber experienced conveying Witness beliefs in straightforward terms to the people she encountered played a key role in helping her reevaluate them for herself. You can read Amber's remarkable story by searching on Google for "Amber Scorah The Believer."

er named in the Yearbook, but it is relatively easy to identify them through a simple process of elimination. As of 2016 they include: Afghanistan, Algeria, Bahrain, Brunei, China, Djibouti, Egypt, Eritrea, Iran, Iraq, Jordan, Kuwait, Laos, Libya, Mauritania, Morocco, North Korea, Oman, Qatar, Saudi Arabia, Singapore, Somalia, Syria, Tajikistan, Tunisia, Turkmenistan, United Arab Emirates, Uzbekistan, Vietnam, Western Sahara and Yemen.[9]

The overall statistics related to Witness activity in these predominantly Muslim and communist countries are predictably disappointing. Rather than the *other lands* being evenly dispersed across the globe, we find them forming an almost unbroken chain stretching from West Africa to the Far East, accounting for just over 2 billion people, or 27% of the estimated global population. According to Watchtower's figures, however, these countries combined have only 38,833 Witnesses—or one Witness per 51,748 people (about the capacity of a large sports stadium). By way of comparison, the ratio for the United States is currently one in 261.[10]

Astonishingly, the ratio worsens for some Asian countries where governments *do* allow Witnesses to engage in their preaching work. If you live in Pakistan, the ratio is one in 185,039 people. If you are one of the 160 million living in Bangladesh, do not expect to be called on by a Witness any time soon. The ratio there is one in 631,355.

---

[9] As you can see, there are 31 countries on my list, but the *2016 Yearbook* says there are 30 of these "other lands." It is unclear why Watchtower says there are only 30 (it is possible that two "lands" have been grouped into one) but I can tell you that each of the 31 countries in my list do not feature in the most recent report.

[10] The data for this paragraph, including a map showing the other lands, is shown in Appendix C.

Three countries among the *other lands* are believed to have no Witnesses at all, namely North Korea, Somalia and Afghanistan.[11] Together, these account for roughly 68 million people. If you are unfortunate enough to live among those doomed souls, who are not receiving *any* warning of the impending day of God's wrath (or advice on what religion they must join to survive it), then I am sorry but you really are toast!

By now you have probably gathered that the Almighty is not scrambling to make sure Arabs and Asians are proportionally represented in his future utopia. Considering the monumental task that will shortly be facing Lösch's burial teams in that literally godforsaken part of the world, *not* surviving Armageddon may well be the least back-breaking option.

Despite the gaping disparity presented by the *other lands* figures, Watchtower literature remains defiantly upbeat about the success of the global preaching effort in relation to its expectations for the supposed nearness of Armageddon. According to Witnesses, one of the "signs" that we are in the last days can be found in Christ's words at Matthew 24:14, which says:

> And this good news of the Kingdom will be preached in all the inhabited earth for a witness to all the nations, and then the end will come.

Witnesses are satisfied that their "extensive preaching campaign going on worldwide is a direct fulfillment of Jesus' words," thus paving the way for Armageddon to strike at any moment. "Despite the opposition of Satan, his demons, and opposers among

---

[11] Though this is not widely publicized, these countries were named in a talk given by Watchtower representative James Rayford in January 2007. The relevant clip of the talk can be listened to by searching for the "30 Other Lands" video on my "John Cedars" YouTube channel.

mankind, Jehovah's people have enjoyed phenomenal success in carrying out their commission to make disciples," proclaims one *Watchtower*. "Today, they are preaching in 'all the inhabited earth,' from tropical jungles to frigid tundra, in mountains, in deserts, in cities, and in the most remote countryside." (Watchtower thus prefers not to think of "all the inhabited earth" in a literal sense, instead deeming a reasonable global smattering of Witnesses to be a job well done. Failure to reach more than a quarter of the world's populace can be overlooked so long as the geographical diversity of the preaching work is sufficiently impressive, encompassing tropical jungles and frigid tundra.)

Witnesses tend to buy into this sort of logic readily, especially when it comes to applauding an evangelical work in which they are all personally invested. After all, Witnesses may not be in every country, but they are in a hell of a lot of countries. Only the Catholic Church, with an estimated 12 million Catholics in China alone, can currently beat the Witnesses in terms of the global distribution of a Christian denomination. It was certainly a source of immense pride for me that, as a Witness, I could fly to almost anywhere in the world and find ready-made "friends" waiting for me—willing to show hospitality based on our shared allegiance.

No matter the language barrier, wherever you go on the planet Witnesses all believe exactly the same thing, and they all read exactly the same material translated into their native tongue. I could travel to a remote congregation in Bolivia and they would be studying precisely the same issue of *The Watchtower* at their weekend meeting as my hometown congregation in Wilmslow. Witnesses refer to such uniformity of worship as a "spiritual paradise." In other words, even though Armageddon has not yet purged the planet of

FOR WITNESSES

## EARTHLY PARADISE

Whether you were raised a Witness or became one after encountering Witnesses through the preaching work, in all likelihood you are looking forward to one day living in a blissful global paradise promised in the Bible. The trouble is, the Bible nowhere promises this.

The word translated as "paradise" in the Bible appears only four times in the *New World Translation.* These instances are in (1) Song of Solomon 4:13 ("Your shoots* are a paradise of pomegranates"), (2) Luke 23:43 ("And he said to him: 'Truly I tell you today, you will be with me in Paradise.'"), (3) 2 Corinthians 12:3,4 ("Yes, I know such a man—whether in the body or apart from the body, I do not know; God knows—who was caught away into paradise . . ."), and (4) Revelation 2:7 ("To the one who conquers I will grant to eat of the tree of life, which is in the paradise of God.").

Of these four quoted instances of the word translated as "paradise" in the Bible, the first is clearly used as a metaphor, and the second and fourth (in 2 Corinthians and Revelation) are applied by Watchtower as referring to heaven. Only the conversation between Christ and the criminal at Luke 23:43 is interpreted in the literature as referring to earth and not heaven. Watchtower explains that "Jesus will be with the criminal in that he will raise him from the dead and see that he is taken care of in the Paradise on earth." (*w13* 6/1 p. 14) Clearly, this is an arbitrary interpretation to make the verse fit with Watchtower teachings, since if "paradise" is either used metaphorically or applied to heavenly existence elsewhere in the Bible, the same can also be true here. In short, if Jehovah wants us to believe the vast majority of those who serve him will live on a cleansed paradise earth, he is extremely vague on the matter to say the least.

---

* The word "shoots" used to be rendered "skin" in earlier revisions of the *New World Translation.*

In reality, the Bible does not describe two hopes for humans who worship God—one earthly, and one heavenly. Instead, Watchtower's Paradise teaching is based on a combination of (1) the restoration texts in books of the Hebrew Scriptures predicting prosperous conditions for the restored Jewish people, (2) poetic verses in Psalms and Proverbs conveying the idea that good people will always prosper, and (3) the assumption that, if God created Adam and Eve in a paradise and asked them to "be fruitful and become many and fill the earth and subdue it," then surely that must still be his ultimate plan—it is simply on hold.

For most who profess Christianity, these are not good enough reasons to believe that the unnumbered "great crowd" of Revelation 7:9 applies to survivors of Armageddon who will inherit a future earthly utopia. When you read the verse, you will see it describes the great crowd as "standing before the throne and before the Lamb"—which is the clearest indication the writer could give that they are in heaven.

evildoers, Witnesses get a taste of the promised paradise whenever they all meet together, express the same beliefs, and show kindness to each other. This figurative interpretation of Paradise is certainly much more appealing and practical than the more literal and macabre alternative, but sadly you cannot have one without the other. You cannot have Watchtower's "spiritual paradise" in which everyone believes the same thing unless that same thing involves the imminent extermination of billions of non-Witnesses.

Despite the teaching of a future earthly paradise being based on extremely tenuous foundations (*see box*), it is a hope that forms the basic incentive for millions of Witnesses to radically set themselves apart from the world around them. It is what drives Witnesses to call at your door in all weather. It is what impels Witness parents to shun their wayward teenagers. It is what moves Witness parents to allow their children to die for want of a blood transfusion. They have been assured that by showing obedience now in everything Watchtower asks of them, whatever pain or hardship they may experience (including pain and hardship induced directly by the demands placed on them by their religion) will be compensated in God's cleansed earth.

In short, the hope of Paradise plays a huge role in motivating Witnesses to shake off any doubts or setbacks in pursuit of their faith. As a child, I would dwell on the Paradise a great deal, but these thoughts diminished considerably toward the end of my teenage years. Once doubts surrounding the *Daniel* book surfaced, any lingering convictions regarding Paradise began to evaporate.

But all of that was about to change.

The date was Friday, February 16, 2001. I found myself at a desk in the corner of the mailroom of a company that supplied hearing aids. This was one of my many low-paid temp agency jobs that were necessary at the time to make ends meet as a pioneer. My duty on this particular day was to seal envelopes ready for mailing out—hardly the most intellectually grueling task, but at least it was paid work.

The monotony was abruptly broken by someone rushing to my corner of the room with urgent news. My work was finished for the day. There was an emergency. Apparently my mother was in reception, and she desperately needed me to take her home.

I ran through to reception and, sure enough, there was Mum in the seating area. She was bent over in floods of tears. I sat down next to her and put my arm around her.

"What's wrong, Mum?"

Mum muttered something inaudible. Confused, I asked her to repeat herself. This she did, but it was hard to make out her words clearly due to her intense sobbing. Finally, a few words left Mum's lips that I could make out.

"It's in my liver."

I knew instantly what she meant. I pulled Mum up, took her outside to the car, got behind the wheel and began a 10-minute drive home that seemed to last an eternity.

Two years earlier, in January 1999, Mum had been diagnosed with cancer in her right breast. She had undergone chemotherapy, radiotherapy and, finally, a mastectomy before receiving the welcome news that her cancer was in remission.

From the moment cancer reared its ugly head in Mum's life, she did absolutely everything she could to fight it and live healthily. She would go swimming regularly, eat properly, take all her vitamins and nutrients, and cut out anything from her diet with even the slightest hint of a link to the disease. Every morning she would get up at 7 a.m. to take our dog Florence for a long walk around the neighborhood. She would go on hiking holidays in the Lake District. In short, I would say that throughout the year 2000 she was fitter and healthier than I was despite being in her early fifties. But none of this could prevent the cancer from returning.

In the days leading up to her arrival at my work, Mum had noticed a deterioration in her health. She was getting breathless easily, she could not swim as many lengths of the pool as normal, and she was losing small amounts of blood. This prompted an appointment at The Christie (then called "Christie's")[12]—the cancer hospital in Manchester that had treated her previously. This, in turn, led to an appointment for an ultrasound. Mum attended the scan on the Friday in question, assuming it was just a routine check. She was devastated when the radiologist detected the presence of cancer in her liver. Immediately, a bone and MRI scan were booked, and Mum left the hospital distraught. As she wrote in her diary, which forms the basis of much of what follows in these pages: "Don't know how but I drove to where Lloyd was working and got him to take me home."

Mum was still crying in the car, and I was desperately trying to process what was happening. Without any medical knowledge, my mind began scrambling for solutions as to how someone might get rid of cancer in their liver. If Mum had rid herself of breast cancer by having her breast removed could we not try a similar approach this time round?

"Mum, I don't understand. People have liver transplants. Surely you can have a liver transplant and get rid of it that way?"

Mum turned to me with a look that is etched on my memory. "Lloyd, people don't survive cancer in their liver."

---

[12] The Christie is a renowned and quite outstanding leading-edge cancer hospital. If you feel so inclined, please visit the web page at www.christie.nhs.uk, click on "The Christie Charity," and donate to its excellent work.

Those words hit me like a freight train. I have no idea how I continued driving but, from that point on, I knew my dear mother was dying.

When we got home, we did not get out of the car straight away. We lingered in the driveway crying, hugging, and trying to come to terms with what was happening. It was by no means easy for me to accept that Mum was not going to make it. I felt like my world was collapsing around me. But there was no choice in the matter—this was *going* to happen. And Mum seemed to appreciate being able to talk realistically with me rather than having to fight her way through any knee-jerk denial.

When we finally went in the house, it was time to start making phone calls. We called Dad. He told us he was on his way home. Mum also called Shirley, her best friend who lived across town. Shirley arrived in minutes. By the time Dad finally returned home, Mum and Shirley were locked in tearful conversation in the living room. I vividly recall Dad pacing in the dining room, waiting for a few moments alone with his wife. I felt sorry for him. I found myself wanting to help him process things.

"You know Mum's dying, don't you Dad?" I said.

"No she isn't," was his reply. He would not accept it.

As the three of us and Shirley wrestled with this bombshell, thoughts turned to my sister Hannah. As it happened, today was the final day of Hannah's "pioneer school," which was being conducted at a Kingdom Hall 20 minutes' drive away. Someone had to go and pick Hannah up, and it was decided that someone would be me. I quickly resolved that I would not be the one to break the news to her. For one thing, a guest would be joining us—a friend of the family, whom I would also be collecting along with Hannah. Cherry Midgley was a recently-widowed circuit overseer's wife—a bright and bubbly Scottish lady with a piercing laugh. She had tagged along during the final days of the school, and she would be staying with us for the weekend. I could not stomach the idea of spending a 20-minute car journey going through everything with Cherry while I was still reeling from the news myself.

And then there was Hannah, who could be extremely volatile with her emotions. If I had told her in the car while driving home, there is a strong likelihood we would never have completed our journey.

Hannah could sense something was wrong and kept badgering me, but my lips were sealed. The last thing we needed were more casualties, so I doggedly stayed quiet from the moment I entered the Kingdom Hall to fetch her and Cherry to the moment we pulled up in our driveway.

Hannah jumped out of the car and ran inside to see Mum, brimming with excitement and stories about her school. The ecstasy soon evaporated. She was in floods of tears the moment she heard the news. In the midst of all this sorrow was Cherry. For her it likely brought back memories of being widowed. In some ways it probably helped for us to have her there, because there was a reason to put on a brave face. As Mum later wrote in her diary: "After the shock and all the tears we shared some encouraging thoughts from pioneer school. Hannah has had a lovely time . . . I feel sad that I had to spoil her last day. We are all stunned."

In the weeks that followed, Mum had endless trips to The Christie for check-ups, scans, and chemotherapy courses. It was decided to try her on one of the most aggressive chemo treatments in a last ditch attempt to

***With Mum in 2001***

at least halt the cancer's progress. This took its toll on Mum. Apart from all the vomiting, her thick curly hair (which had fully regrown after previous treatments) soon fell out. She began taking morphine every night before she went to bed to help her sleep. At first Mum absolutely loathed the taste, but after a while it did not seem to bother her so much.

This was a surreal period for me. Ever since Mum first broke the news in the car on that fateful Friday, I had more or less grasped the severity of what was happening. The same could not be said of Dad and Hannah. If they were resigned to the fact that Mum's time with us was limited, they were not showing it. You certainly could not talk to them as though the situation were that grave. For them, Mum was going to pull through this, and we all just had to stay positive.

This meant that, of the three of us, I was really the only one Mum could speak to candidly with an eye on what was in store. We would have long conversations about all manner of things: both what lay ahead and what had happened in her past. One evening, she finally told me the full story about Robin, this mysterious man to whom I knew she had once been married. Up to that point, I had assumed Robin was her only previous husband, but for the first time Mum revealed her marriage prior to meeting Robin and the torment she experienced at the hands of Witness elders following her divorce.

Mum told me that back in the early '70s the organization would not acknowledge homosexual unfaithfulness by a spouse as adultery. Watchtower had decided at the time that it was only possible for an adulterous liaison to occur between a man and a woman. Therefore, even though Mum (then a stunning 22-year-old) was legally divorced from her first husband after he cheated on her with a male companion, the elders at the congregation where she was studying informed her she was not free to remarry with the organization's consent. They went so far as to warn would-be suitors away, telling them she was not available. Unsurprisingly, this absurd treatment drove Mum to cancel her study and distance herself from the Witnesses. This eventually led to her marrying Robin, her friend at work. Then, when Robin later died in the fire, it was the Witnesses who surrounded her and made her feel loved.

These revelations troubled me, particularly in light of my own recent conclusions about the organization, but now was not the time to turn my whole belief system on its head. Like many other pieces of damning evidence, this would need to be filed away in my mental pending tray for future processing.

Though emotionally draining, our conversations were invaluable to me and I cherish them to this day. In many ways, Mum was unknowingly preparing me for what was to come. After all, she told me the thought of dying did not scare her—she was only worried about what would happen to the three of us once she was gone. With this in mind, she would talk about her expectations for my future. Mum hoped I would one day meet someone special, being only too aware of the trouble I seemed to be having in this department. Mum also told me of her desire for me to go to MTS.

MTS, or Ministerial Training School, was an eight-week training course for single Witness men.[13] I had already expressed some interest in enrolling once I was old enough. It struck me as a more intellectual and less monastic alternative to going to work at London Bethel, Watchtower's headquarters in Britain. I could now see Mum was keen for me to attend the course. She even told me to film my graduation so that she could watch the tape with me some day in Paradise after her resurrection. This expectation of hers, and the conviction that inspired it, was embedded in my subconscious from that day forward. *I could not let Mum down.* Sure, MTS would be no walk in the park. It was an intense course, and not everyone who applied for it got accepted. But never mind that—if Mum wanted me to go that badly, I was going to go. I was not even sure whether Watchtower would allow the graduation to be filmed (it wouldn't), but I would worry about the details later. For now, being with Mum while I still had her was all that mattered.

As the weeks rolled by, the finite nature of my time with Mum began to be a source of frustration. It was like being in the final scenes of a movie that I did not

---

[13] Ministerial Training School was later renamed the "Bible School for Single Brothers," before being restructured and given its most recent name: the "School for Kingdom Evangelizers."

want to end without being able to hit the pause button. I would sometimes just stare at her, trying to somehow etch her face in my brain. I was terrified of forgetting her—forgetting *exactly* what she looked like. Sometimes it was all too much, and I would retreat to another room to play mindless computer games just to pass the time. I would then feel guilty for not spending every second with Mum that I had available, but looking back I suppose this was just my coping mechanism. After all, how do you deal with such a situation? What are you supposed to talk about when you know you are against the clock? To this day, it still troubles me that I might have better used those diminishing moments. I remind myself that nothing could have prepared me for what I was going through—what *all of us* were going through.

As Mum's chemo treatments continued to ravage her body, it became apparent that they were not making things better—only worse. Mum's face became gaunt, her lips parched, and her feet swollen. At the beginning of May, during one of Mum's many hospital visits, a young female doctor upset her by rather crassly asking whether she had looked around at any hospices. Things were clearly looking bleak.

We started to talk about whether Mum should come off her chemo altogether. At least that way we could just enjoy whatever time we had left. It was decided that this option would be explored with the doctors during the next weekly visit, which was scheduled for May 9.

I vividly remember the trip to The Christie with Mum and Dad that fateful day. Mum asked the doctor whether there was any sign that the chemo was working. He confirmed that there was not. In fact, there were now multiple tumors on her liver. Mum said that she would like to come off chemo and just enjoy whatever time was left. The doctor agreed to this without hesitation. Mum then asked how much time she could expect. "Three weeks to three months," was his reply.

These words floored me.

Up to that point, it felt like I was the only one in the family, other than Mum, who understood how serious this situation was. But when faced with hard numbers, the brutal reality of it came flooding in on me. I remember reeling for a few moments before getting myself out of the building as fast as I could and sobbing outside on the sidewalk, to the likely bewilderment of passers-by. I could not believe this was really happening—and so quickly.

As the shock subsided, thoughts turned to going on one final holiday together as a family while we still had some time. A holiday abroad was out of the question, so we decided to head for Cornwall—one of the most picturesque parts of the British Isles, and a place where we had spent holidays when Hannah and I were little. We packed our things and made the six-hour drive the following Saturday, May 12.

Almost as soon as we arrived in Cornwall, Mum's health seemed to deteriorate daily. She began to get confused easily, to the point where it was a challenge for her to convey even the simplest of thoughts or requests. On one occasion, instead of asking for a glass of water, she looked around, saw some socks, and asked for a glass of socks. We all looked at each other not knowing whether to laugh or cry.

There were pleasant moments of lucidity, and we made the most of these when they came. Usually when you go on holiday in Britain, even during the summer months, you are taking a gamble with the weather. But throughout our stay, the weather was mostly bright and sunny. Dad had done well in finding a gorgeous apartment perched on a hill overlooking the small fishing town of St Ives, a place so picturesque it is a magnet for landscape artists, and Mum was thrilled at being able to enjoy a nice view of the sea from the comfort of her sofa. We even managed the occasional trip down to the harbor front. On one of these occasions, Mum surprised us by abandoning her wheelchair and walking down on to the sand, assisted by Hannah and me. She was beside herself with joy at the simple pleasure of feeling the sand beneath her feet and the fresh sea air in her face.

As we neared the end of our first week, it became clear that Mum was fading more rapidly than we expected. She became ever more confused as the cancer spread throughout her body, besieging her brain. Before long it was obvious that we needed to get her to the local hospital, which was in Penzance. By that time, Mum's mind had faded so much that our last chance to say a proper goodbye had already passed.

We never got our "three weeks to three months" together. Mum passed away at around 6 p.m. on the 21st of May.

Dad, Hannah and I had spent the day by her bedside, hanging on her every breath, and noticing the time between the breaths getting steadily longer and longer. I cradled her forehead in my hand the same way she would do with me when I had been sick as a child. I hoped this would reassure her as it had me.

Eventually, once Mum had breathed her last, the doctor came in and pronounced her dead. Hannah went into hysterics, wailing uncontrollably. Shirley had made the journey down together with some other Witness friends, and they had been waiting patiently in one of the adjoining rooms. Once they heard Mum had passed away, they came in the room to try to console us. I will never forget the touch of Mum's skin once the life had left her body—cold and unresponsive.

We stayed in Cornwall a few more days to deal with the draining task of sorting out Mum's death certificate and arranging her funeral, for which her body needed to be transported back to Manchester ready for cremation. On our arrival home, friends and well-wishers would regularly stop by our house bringing gifts and trying to offer comfort in any way they could.

Wilmslow Kingdom Hall was inundated for Mum's funeral talk, which was given by our circuit overseer—another family friend.[14] As part of his talk, he read a letter I had written to Mum shortly before her death, which I had intended as my last goodbye. (I would give a great deal to be reunited with this letter, but it has since been lost from my possession.) In it, I thanked Mum for the moments we shared together.

In particular, my letter reminisced about a holiday to the Lake District the previous summer. During one glorious sunny day we went for a walk from our caravan to a nearby towering hill named Loughrigg Fell, which has a small lake at the bottom named Loughrigg Tarn. We were lost in conversation as we navigated the winding country lanes and fields. I had just been through my first break-up (a Witness girl from the Midlands I had met through friends), so I had plenty on my mind and needed Mum's counsel. In fact, I was

---

[14] If memory serves, the attendants said they stopped counting after 200. The Kingdom Hall was so full, people were standing in the parking lot.

**_In contemplative mood during the retreat to the Lake District (photo taken by Mum)_**

only there because Mum had urged me to come with her and Dad to help take my mind off things. Once we reached the hill, I clambered up it while Mum waited for me down by the lake.[15] Immediately after coming down I jumped in the lake to cool off, swimming for a while in the chilly waters as she strolled along the bank. As I explained in my letter, this experience felt like the closest to Paradise I had ever been—impossibly beautiful surroundings shared with someone I love.

Now Mum had left us, and the two years following her death remain to this day the worst in my life. Mum had been the backbone of our family; the crutch that we all leaned on. We needed her. As a parent, she compensated for Dad's emotional limitations. Whereas Dad was good at handling practical matters, Mum was the one Hannah and I would run to if we needed advice on anything, or a shoulder to cry on. Now she had vanished from our lives in little over three months.

Hannah, Dad and I each struggled in our own ways to come to terms with our loss—each wrestling with our own grief in the only way we knew how. Of the three of us, Hannah was most prone to projecting her grief on others, perhaps more than she would now be proud of.

Dad was the opposite. He could only recoil into himself, refusing to share his feelings with anyone. It would take a family shepherding visit from a circuit overseer for him to reveal his inner turmoil during a startling moment of frankness.

It came out that Dad was riddled with confusion as to whether Mum would want to marry him again in the resurrection. He did not know whether he would

---

[15] I would climb the hill again some time later with Dad and Hannah to help sprinkle Mum's ashes.

be allowed to even if she did. "Till death do us part" meant their marriage was now over, and Christ's words at Luke 20:34 indicated that the dead will not be able to remarry because they are "like the angels." This scripture makes perfect sense if you believe in a heavenly hope (as is the case with most Christians), but it is almost impossible to reconcile with the Witness teaching of an earthly resurrection into human form. Predictably, Watchtower publications respond to this scripture by giving it the widest possible berth and/or cloaking their answer in as much ambiguity as possible, even though it is a cause of great distress for the many Witnesses like my father who have lost spouses (*see box*).

**FOR WITNESSES**

## STATUS OF RESURRECTED SPOUSES

The hypothetical problem of whether Witnesses who die and are resurrected can stay married may not be a burning issue for all believers, but it can become a matter of great concern and anxiety once a Witness loses his or her mate. Widows and widowers might be justifiably worried as to whether they will be able to resume their relationships when reunited with their loved ones in paradise. So, what do Watchtower publications have to say on the matter?

A 1987 *Watchtower* article discussed, at length, Jesus' words at Luke 20:34. The writers explained that, according to the scripture, resurrected ones will not marry even when reunited with their spouses. "Human emotions today might make this a difficult conclusion to accept," the writer admitted, "but it is to be noted that nowhere does the Bible say that God's resurrecting the faithful means restoring their marital status."

The article went on to remind readers that "we have never lived as perfect humans." Therefore, it argued, "we cannot be sure how we will feel about past relationships if and when we gain perfect human life in a paradise." The trouble is: as humans we are defined by the relationships we develop with others. If human perfection could conceivably allow someone to deactivate their feelings for loved ones on a whim, then arguably human perfection is not worth having. What is the point of being perfect if it makes us indifferent to those whom we love?

After 1987, the organization understandably gave the issue a wide berth. "In Jehovah's due time, all will be revealed to our fullest satisfaction," declared *The Watchtower* in 2005.

Then, in 2014, the subject was raised again in a *Watchtower* article, but it was treated with more ambiguity. "Is there sound reason for hoping that resurrected ones will be able to marry?" asked the writer. "Put simply, the answer is that we cannot say." A number of possible arguments were then offered for interpreting Luke 20:34 in different ways, before the writer concluded: "But of this we can be sure: Obedient humans will be happy, for Jehovah will satisfy all their needs and desires in the best possible way." The reader is effectively told (as in the 2005 article): "Look, just don't worry about it. Everything will work out fine."

The real reason for the ambiguity and evasion is quite simple: Watchtower needs to keep people guessing, because otherwise Paradise is a strange place where a relationship that has lasted many years can suddenly count for very little. In reality, Luke 20:34 could not have been referring to an earthly resurrection because, as explained in the previous "For Witnesses" box, nowhere does the Bible describe a future earthly paradise. The Greek Scriptures exclusively describe Christians going to heaven when they die. But rather than admit this, Watchtower would prefer to keep widows and widowers locked in perpetual uncertainty as to what will become of their relationships.

Fortunately for me, I had no such issues with which to contend. When resurrected, Mum would still be Mum. Even so, I was left with a gaping hole in my life where she used to be and a religion that was telling me she was not *completely* dead—she was still alive in Jehovah's memory, and the only way to be sure of seeing her again was to busy myself in worship. This was precisely what I intended to do. Apart from anything else, I did not want to disappoint Mum when we were reunited in the resurrection and she asked to see my MTS graduation video. I, therefore, began applying for the school as soon as I could.[16] Applications were made on a yearly basis, and you would receive a form by attending one of the special MTS promotional meetings held at each circuit assembly.[17] The form asked a series of probing questions. One question in particular asked whether I was in full agreement with Watchtower publications. It pricked my conscience, but I responded in the affirmative. I was not going to let any nagging doubts from a few years ago get in the way of fulfilling one of Mum's dying wishes.

Though I was determined to get into MTS, it did present me with a dilemma. I was in my early 20s, still a virgin (obviously), and I yearned for companionship—especially now Mum's steadying influence was absent from my life. I had been in a brief six-month relationship the year before Mum died, but this had gone nowhere. Now I wanted more than anything to find someone who could help ease my feelings of loneliness

---

[16] The minimum age for applying for MTS at the time was 23. I began applying at 22 on the understanding that it may take some time for the form to be processed, by which point I may be eligible.

[17] A circuit assembly is a twice-yearly gathering of multiple congregations—not as large as a regional convention.

and despair. MTS, however, was only for *single* Witness males.[18] This meant that, not only did I need to choose a marriage partner from among only Witness girls (to avoid becoming "unevenly yoked" with an unbeliever), I also had to convince any such girl to wait until after I had graduated from MTS before officially starting a relationship.

This narrowed down the pool of potential partners significantly and led to me being extremely choosy as to whom I would or would not consider pursuing. "Yes, that girl might be attractive. Yes, she has a great sense of humor. But is she active enough in the 'Truth'? Could she be a pioneer partner for me in the future—a potential elder's wife?" Such questions plagued me. It seemed whenever I found someone I was genuinely attracted to, either she was not suitably "spiritual," or she simply was not interested in me. Whenever a girl came forward and made it clear, perhaps through friends, that she liked me, it was someone with whom I did not feel any chemistry. I wanted so desperately to feel that spark of excitement when someone you adore is in the room.

By this stage, internet chat rooms were in full swing and social networking was starting to take off. These offered some kind of solution to my unique predicament. I could interact with girls from all over the world from the privacy of my computer without commitment or physical contact, and ease some of my loneliness and sexual frustration with them. I got the thrill of chatting and flirting with normal girls without having to tie myself down to anything or hurt anyone's feelings. This sort of behavior, even if it is going on in

[18] The new "School for Kingdom Evangelizers" now also invites single women and married couples to attend.

cyberspace, is still a huge no-no as far as the organization is concerned, as countless *Watchtower* articles and letters to elders will attest. However, in my mind it was clearly not as bad as committing actual fornication with someone, and it was allowing me to remain single into my mid-20s when I was finding it increasingly difficult to find a girlfriend among Witnesses—especially given the limitations placed on me by MTS, which I simply *had* to attend to honor my mother's wishes. Hence, even though I knew what I was doing was technically wrong, it was easy to rationalize. Besides, if Watchtower could be so manifestly wrong over so many of its interpretations of Bible prophecy, what if it was also wrong about what young single people should or should not be doing in private on the internet?

Despite my actions making total sense to me, I would often be racked with guilt and feelings of worthlessness for resorting to measures that were clearly denounced as bad, even if they were not on a par with fornication. It weighed on my conscience.

Once Hannah had married and left home in 2003, my home life became much easier—at least for a while. Initially, Dad and I settled into what felt like a more relaxed atmosphere. But the tranquility was not to last. Before long, our personalities began to clash. I started to feel as though I was in a constant struggle to establish my independence. It seemed Dad felt the need to frequently remind me that he was the alpha male of the house with the authority to scrutinize my every word and action in Mum's absence. When we got into fights, Dad would threaten to call the elders to have them come and adjudicate. Things became intolerable.

With my home life deteriorating, I began to look beyond Wilmslow congregation for somewhere else to go—a new challenge. I needed to get out of Dad's shadow; to be no longer "Jonathan's son," but "Lloyd." At the time, Wilmslow had 18 elders, so there was little for me to do in the congregation as a young ministerial servant. I desperately wanted to find a place where I would be needed and evaluated on my own merits.

I asked my circuit overseer if he would assign me to a new congregation. I was thrilled when he wrote a letter confirming my assignment to neighboring Bramhall congregation, which then had only three elders and was in dire need of capable Witness men who could go in and help out with talks and leading the preaching work. My assignment began on September 1, 2004.

When I first started attending Bramhall meetings I was happy commuting the extra distance to the congregation's Kingdom Hall (the same hall from which I had collected my sister earlier in the chapter). But as my relationship with Dad worsened, it became obvious that I had to move out.

Renting even modest accommodation in the Wilmslow area was prohibitively expensive, but an opportunity presented itself when a one-bedroom apartment equidistant to Bramhall and Wilmslow became available. Greatly assisting my chances of getting it was the fact that it was owned by the mother of a friend from the Wilmslow congregation. I jumped at the chance to finally seize my independence, and found myself moving in before long. It felt strange and mildly scary to be on my own at last, but I knew it was for the best. Besides, hopefully it would not be too long before I could go to MTS, get married, and share my apartment and exciting new assignment with a wife.

Only weeks after moving into the flat a letter arrived from the Watch Tower Bible and Tract Society of Britain, dated January 10, 2005. The first two lines read, "Dear Brother Evans: Your application for enrollment in the Ministerial Training School has been accepted." I was beside myself with excitement. Everything was falling into place! Finally, my opportunity had arrived to go to MTS, thus fulfilling Mum's wishes.

But there was a catch. I had recently started a new job as a part-time secretary at a local real estate office. When I asked my boss for a two-month leave of absence to attend a Bible course, predictably she did not share my enthusiasm. My request was refused. I responded by handing in my notice. This, in turn, left me with another problem: I had just signed an agreement that tied me to paying full monthly rent on my flat, including for the two months that I would be away at MTS and without work.

Fortunately, there was a clause in the agreement that would free me if I could find someone else who would be willing to take over the flat rental—and I soon managed to find such a person. My landlady was thus good enough to release me from the agreement, leaving the monthly rent as no longer my concern.

And so, with no job and no place to live, I was finally free to pursue my pilgrimage to Ministerial Training School. There was little doubt in my mind that it would meet all my expectations and calm any lingering doubts about my beliefs.

Sadly, this optimism would prove to be misplaced.

CHAPTER FOUR

# Jehovah's Witnesses and Sex

*"Human sexuality had been regulated and shaped by men to serve men's needs."*
—Ana Castillo

*"I have no objection to anyone's sex life as long as they don't practice it in the street and frighten the horses."*
—Oscar Wilde

IN SEPTEMBER 2012, a very unusual video caused a stir on YouTube, clocking hundreds of thousands of views. It featured two men, both wearing suits, discussing masturbation in ASL (American Sign Language). In condemning the practice, the interpreters made erotic motions to indicate the stimulating of male and female genitalia. One of the men had a strange expression on his face during this portrayal—the sort of vacant look you might expect to see during orgasm.

The interpreters were Jehovah's Witnesses, and the maker of the video was the Watch Tower Bible and Tract Society of Pennsylvania. Someone had downloaded the footage from a page in the backwaters of Watchtower's official website (JW.org) and uploaded it to YouTube, whereupon it quickly went viral. Watchtower responded by issuing a flurry of DMCA takedown notices both for the first uploaded video and many of the mirrored videos that followed it, some of which had been set to music. Unfortunately for them, this action was not taken swiftly enough to prevent the material finding its way onto the popular TV network Comedy Central, where comedian Jeff Ross gleefully ripped into it on his show *The Burn.*

"I'm assuming most of you don't understand sign language, but check this out," said a smirking Ross. "The Jehovah Witnesses put this video out to tell deaf people not to masturbate." The studio audience chuckled as Ross played the clip.

"I don't know what he's saying, but I get the jizz of it." Ross quipped, adding, "Is there any way I can Jehovah's *un-witness* that?"

Though this unwanted exposure was no doubt acutely embarrassing for Watchtower (even more so for the interpreters themselves, one assumes), there was no escaping the fact that it was their production—an ASL presentation of the book *"Keep Yourselves in God's Love"* (published in 2008). The interpreters were conveying material from pages 218-219 under the heading "Gain the Victory Over Masturbation," a section that cautions Witnesses against the practice (*see box*). At the time of writing, the video can still be found on JW.org by searching through the sign language publications.[1] YouTube also continues to be awash with the video in various forms, with or without backing music.

For years, Watchtower has been relentless in its efforts to stigmatize masturbation, referring to it as "self-abuse" and, quite astonishingly, as a "stepping-stone to homosexuality." Unsurprisingly, such rhetoric

---

[1] The video is designated as "Chapter 22" in the list of ASL videos for *"Keep Yourselves in God's Love"* in the PUBLICATIONS > BOOKS & BROCHURES section on JW.org.

FOR WITNESSES

## MASTURBATION

Watchtower literature condemns masturbation as a "spiritually unhealthy habit." Pages 218-219 of the book *"Keep Yourselves in God's Love"* present ten scriptures in an attempt to support this argument. None of them refer directly to the act of masturbation. In fact, as one 2011 *Watchtower* admitted: "The Bible does not specifically mention masturbation—the deliberate self-stimulation that produces sexual arousal and orgasm."—*w11* 11/1 p. 7.

If the Bible does not specifically mention masturbation, then can it really be classified as a sin of any kind? Consider what was said in a 1950 *Watchtower* article on smoking: "It is true that the Bible does not specifically name tobacco-smoking as an evil to be avoided. If Christians should shun it, why does not the Bible definitely mention it? Because in the times when the Bible was written the smoking of tobacco was unknown."—*w50* 2/15 p. 59.

The same reasoning certainly cannot be applied to masturbation. People in ancient times had genitalia and knew how to derive pleasure from them. As one *Awake!* article admitted: "Masturbation was common in the Greek-speaking world during Bible times, and several Greek words were used to describe the practice. Interestingly, not one of these words is used in the Bible."—*g87* 9/8 p. 19.

Lest we forget, the Bible is not known for shying away when it comes to naming and shaming sexual practices that are to be viewed as abhorrent, including incest and bestiality. Intimate issues related to personal hygiene are also addressed without hesitation. The Hebrew Scriptures do not shirk from instructing Israelite women with a menstrual flow to quarantine themselves (Leviticus 15:19-30), or men who have a wet dream to "go outside the camp" to get themselves cleaned off. (Deuteronomy 23:10) So, why is the Bible silent on the act of masturbation if it is a condemned practice?

It seems Paul's words at Colossians 3:5 ("Deaden, therefore, your body members . . .") form the sole basis for Watchtower's long-standing prohibition on masturbation. The *New Living Translation* renders the same verse as follows: "So put to death the sinful, earthly things lurking within you. Have nothing to do with sexual sin, impurity, lust, and shameful desires. Don't be greedy for the good things of this life, for that is idolatry." Rather than prohibiting masturbation, this verse urges Christians to avoid falling into sinful temptation in line with Christ's words at Matthew 6:13, when he prayed, "Do not bring us into temptation, but deliver us from the wicked one." To read further into the verse than this general advice would surely be to "go beyond the things that are written."—1 Corinthians 4:6.

The simple truth is, masturbation is (and always has been) a perfectly normal practice and virtually everyone does it. In her book *The Great Sex for Life Toolkit*, Krisanna Jeffery lists several benefits to "self pleasuring," including a healthier prostate gland in men, increased ability to orgasm in women, and the creation of "positive neuro-transmitters known to boost the immune system and create positive moods." As she astutely observes: "No one has become pregnant or diseased by masturbation."

has led to overwhelming feelings of guilt on the part of countless Witness teenagers who have inevitably succumbed. "Feelings of guilt plagued me for many years," commented one Witness in a book intended as a guide for young people, "and it seriously affected my relationships with others and, above all, with Jehovah." (Note the circular reasoning indulged in by Watchtower: masturbation is proved to be wrong because of the guilt of the person doing it, because by masturbating he is ignoring the organization's warnings that masturbation is considered wrong.)

Watchtower's tough stance on masturbation can be considered a legacy of the '70s, when material on this and other sexual practices began to be printed with increasing regularity. As the sexual revolution reached its zenith in the late '60s, the Governing Body responded by passing down a raft of baffling sexual decrees with often far-reaching consequences. One particular *Watchtower* article, printed toward the end of 1969, fired the starting gun for nearly a decade of dabbling in the bedrooms of countless married Witnesses. It advised as follows:

> Some have contended, however, that absolutely anything done between husband and wife is permissible. However, that view is not supported in the Bible. In Romans 1:24-32, where it speaks of both men and women who participated in immoral sex practices, including lesbian and sodomite acts, the Bible mentions a "natural use of the female."

Despite branding oral and anal sex as "not approved by God," *even between married couples*, the article stopped short of prescribing precisely what disciplinary measures should be imposed on those falling short of this new prohibition. As the article stated, "beyond the above observations about conjugal acts we cannot go. With love, respect and unselfishness, marriage mates themselves must decide what they will do."

Watchtower's reluctance to enforce its "observations" would not last long. The book *Crisis of Conscience* by the late Ray Franz[2] offers a fascinating insider perspective on how things escalated. Franz was a member of the Governing Body during this turbulent period, but was later ousted from the organization in 1981 fol-

[2] Not to be confused with former Watchtower president Fred Franz, who was Ray's uncle.

lowing a purge of "apostates." I will discuss this period (and Ray in particular) in more detail in later chapters. For now, Franz's insight on the early Governing Body's handling of sexual relations between couples is invaluable to this discussion.

According to Franz's book, a letter was received at Brooklyn headquarters in 1972 regarding a Witness couple in California. Apparently, someone had entered their bedroom for reasons unknown and discovered "certain literature and photographs dealing with unusual sexual practices." This sparked an investigation and interrogation of the couple by local elders, who doubtless justified their intrusive actions using the aforementioned 1969 article. Having been alerted to the matter, the Watchtower president at that time, Nathan Knorr, convened the Governing Body to deliberate over the couple's fate. Up to that point, only Knorr had had the opportunity to give the matter any real thought, or consider what Bible verses might be applied. According to Franz, within "a couple of hours" the Governing Body decided that the husband and wife must be disfellowshipped.

It goes without saying that once you discipline one Witness couple for doing something, you must then apply the same standard to any who have followed a similar course. A *Watchtower* article was therefore printed in 1972 that made the new rules regarding oral and anal sex binding on all marriages. It warned that one or both spouses could be disfellowshipped for "gross unnatural conduct" if they were to "willfully show disrespect for Jehovah God's marital arrangements." The same article instructed that if a Witness wife were to receive requests for oral or anal sex from a non-believing husband, she should resist. It was made clear that "the situation is the same as if her husband demanded that she engage in some form of idolatry, in misuse of blood, dishonesty or other such wrong."

Another article published in a 1974 *Watchtower* went so far as to advise that "lewd practices on the part of a married person toward that one's own mate" were to be considered grounds for divorce. Up to that point, the only scriptural basis for divorce was adultery. However, references in the New Testament to *por·nei′a* (the Greek word from which "sexual immorality," or "fornication" according to older revisions of the *New World Translation*, is translated) were expanded to encompass "perversions within the marriage arrangement," meaning that adultery now effectively included oral sex between a married couple. As the article reasoned:

> That *por·nei′a* can rightly be considered as including perversions within the marriage arrangement is seen in that the man who forces his wife to have unnatural sex relations with him in effect "prostitutes" or "debauches" her. This makes him guilty of *por·nei′a*, for the related Greek verb *por·neu′o* means "to prostitute, debauch."
>
> Hence, circumstances could arise that would make lewd practices of a married person toward that one's marriage mate a Scriptural basis for divorce. For example, a wife may do what she reasonably can to prevent her husband from forcing upon her perversions such as are carried on in a brothel. Yet, due to his greater strength, he might overpower her and use her for perverted sex. So as not to be prostituted in this way at another time, a Christian wife may decide to get a divorce.

Such bizarre and unwarranted sexual legislature, backed up by harsh penalties including shunning and divorce, may seem far-fetched—but all of this had very real consequences. With so much at stake, married Witnesses came forward with confessions, and were interrogated as to what was going on between the sheets. As Franz related: "Women experienced painful embarrassment in such hearings as they responded to the elders' questions about the intimacies of their marital relations." It may seem too outrageous to believe that grown adults would submit to such a humiliating invasion of privacy, but as Franz explains (speaking from a Watchtower perspective): "To fail to come forward generally is viewed as indicative of an unrepentant attitude, and as weighing in favor of disfellowshipping." (In other words, better to come forward and hope for leniency than to be reported by someone else and have the concealment of your "sins" counted against you.)

In *Crisis of Conscience* Franz also provides examples of individuals who corresponded with Bethel during this insane period, whose lives were being seriously impacted by these strict new bedroom laws. One of the most heartrending is that of a Witness man who had become impotent by some twist of fate. Prior to the rules coming into effect he had been able to discover some sexual role in his relationship using an act that was now forbidden. This had allowed him to satisfy his wife and stop feeling like "half a man," but now this simple pleasure had been cruelly wrenched from him by the Governing Body's decree. Even though he confessed to not agreeing with the scriptural principles behind the ruling (or lack thereof) he told of how his wife was determined to obey them, so there was no sex at all anymore. He pleaded with the Governing Body to find some loophole that would allow him to continue as before because he was "crumbling" emotionally and feared for his marriage.

The poor man had every right to be concerned about his marriage. Franz quotes part of a memo (dated August 9, 1976) from a headquarters staff member who dealt with correspondence to the Governing Body. It offers a troubling glimpse into the havoc these new laws were wreaking:

> Many, many problems have resulted from the position taken, often where there is an unbelieving husband. Wives have refused to allow such husbands to stimulate them in this way or to stimulate the husbands in this way. As a result, marriages have broken up.

Around the same time as this mayhem was unfolding, laws were handed down regarding homosexuality and adultery. (I alluded to this development in the previous chapter, because it personally affected by mother following her divorce from her first husband.) A January 1972 *Watchtower* announced that adultery had not been committed if it did not involve sex between a man and a woman:

> While both homosexuality and bestiality are disgusting perversions, in the case of neither one is the marriage tie broken. It is broken only by acts that make an individual "one flesh" with a person of the opposite sex other than his or her legal marriage mate.

Thus, not only were homosexuality and sex with animals lumped together as equally "disgusting perversions"—but neither were deemed justifiable grounds for terminating a marriage (*see box*). Remarkably, gay sex and copulating with livestock were not the only ways in which a spouse could use his or her genitals out of wedlock and still be considered faithful to marital vows. Franz revealed that the Governing Body was asked to deliberate over the case of a Witness husband in South America who had confessed to having anal sex with another woman. The question was: would this man's wife be allowed to divorce him if his penis had

FOR WITNESSES

## HOMOSEXUALITY

Nobody would try to tell you for a moment that homosexuality is not strongly condemned in both the Hebrew and Greek Scriptures. Leviticus 20:13 calls for any man who "lies down with a male the same as one lies down with a woman" to be "put to death without fail," and the apostle Paul listed "men who submit to homosexual acts," and "men who practice homosexuality" among those who "will not inherit God's Kingdom." (1 Corinthians 6:9, 10) Even so, if you are a Jehovah's Witness, there are a number of things worth considering before approaching gay people and trying to persuade them not to be gay.

Firstly, despite the Bible's unequivocal condemnation of homosexuality, it should be noted that Jesus himself never went on record denouncing those who are attracted to the same sex, or demanding that they suppress their feelings. Instead, Jesus is presented as being a loving and tolerant man who treated with respect, mildness and compassion even those thought of as sinners by the religious leaders of his day.—Matthew 9:10-13.

It is also worth remembering that, despite repeated claims to the contrary in Watchtower literature, gay people do not choose to be attracted to the same gender—neither is their sexuality a "lifestyle" choice. Speak to any gay or lesbian person, and they will tell you they are simply not attracted to the opposite sex, and it has been that way for as long as they can remember. Insisting that they change their sexuality and embrace your heterosexual urges is just as unreasonable as if the roles were reversed, and they were to ask *you* to start being gay, lesbian or bisexual.

Thirdly and finally, gay people are not on some crusade to try to convert people to their sexuality, and their love for people of the same gender is not some contagious disease that you are at risk of catching if you show them tolerance. The only thing the LGBT community wants is for you to extend them the same kindness and dignity that you would expect for yourself. And when it comes to requests, there should be none more easy for a Christian to fulfill than that.—Matthew 7:12.

not entered the other woman's vagina? The Governing Body unanimously voted that no, she would not. The wife was instructed that she had to stick with her philandering husband or risk being disfellowshipped for adultery herself if she remarried without the organization's blessing.

Franz recounts that he experienced "emotional upset" as a result of having participated in the above unanimous vote despite being "genuinely disturbed" at the reasoning behind it. The incident prompted him to embark on a study of numerous Bible translations in an effort to determine the true meaning of *por·nei'a.* Franz's research was eventually presented in the form of a fourteen-page dossier of material for the rest of the Governing Body to consider.

To Franz's surprise, his colleagues not only read his dossier—they agreed with its conclusions. He was therefore assigned to prepare a *Watchtower* article (which would be published less than a year from the "one flesh" article) that effectively collapsed the organization's previous muddled understanding. After explaining at length what "new light" had revealed about *por·nei'a* as it related to the terms "fornication" and "adultery," the matter of divorce was discussed:

> What, then, is the significance of the Bible's use of these terms and what does it reveal as to the valid Biblical grounds for divorce? It shows that any married person who goes outside the marriage bond and engages in immoral sexual relations, whether with someone of the opposite sex or someone of the same sex, whether natural or unnatural and perverted, is guilty of committing por·nei'a or "fornication" in the Bible sense . . .
>
> Taking Jesus' words for what they mean, therefore, when a mate is guilty of such serious sexual immo-

> rality the innocent mate may Scripturally divorce such a one, if he or she so desires. One who obtains a divorce on such Scriptural grounds is also Scripturally free to remarry, not thereby being subject to a charge of adultery.

Franz's article on *por·nei'a* came slightly too late to rescue Mum from the meddling of her local elders as she attempted to move on from an unhappy marriage. Turning her back on an organization that appeared rule-obsessed and doctrinally conflicted, she wedded Robin on December 8, 1972, after Witness suitors had been hounded away. Though I now feel immense pride for Mum in taking this stand, I still find it baffling that the Governing Body has been able to wield so much power and influence over such intimate aspects of people's lives for so long.

The Governing Body's bizarre grace period for gay adultery was in place for less than a year, and yet this was just long enough to cause unnecessary anguish in my mother's life, sparking a chain of events that ultimately resulted in her meeting Dad and me being born. The fact that I am alive because of the Governing Body's interference in intimate affairs gives me no sense of endearment or gratitude toward them. Rather, I consider it a sobering personal reminder of just how disproportionate and far-reaching a religious organization's influence can be. It is also an irony of Watchtower history that a man who was later ousted from his position on the Governing Body over suspicions of apostasy appears to have been so instrumental in such sweeping changes to Witness doctrine on sexual morality—changes that are keenly observed by Witnesses to this day.

To summarize, not only has doctrinal tinkering by the Governing Body given generations of masturbating teenagers a guilt complex—it can also be blamed for breaking up countless good marriages and keeping many bad ones together. Admittedly (and commendably) the Governing Body's retreat from Witness marriage beds was almost complete by the mid-'80s.[3] (This was more likely a result of their being unable to keep up with the avalanche of confessions, allegations and controversies that their dabbling had provoked than anything else.) But by that time the damage had been done, and a culture of sexual paranoia and repression had been introduced that would linger for decades.

At the time of writing it is no longer possible for a married Witness to be automatically disfellowshipped for orally pleasuring his or her spouse—but this does not necessarily mean that Witness couples have license to do whatever they want under the sheets.[4] Problems can still arise "if it becomes known that a member of the congregation is practicing or openly advocating

---

[3] The March 15, 1983, *Watchtower* (pp. 30-31) commented: "How about sexual activity between married couples within the marriage bond? It is not for the elders to pry into the intimate lives of married Christians." Instead of elders policing the marriage bed, couples were urged to be mindful of "the Scriptural indications of God's thinking." They were instructed to "act in a way that will leave them with a clean conscience" and reminded that they would "do well to cultivate a hatred for everything that is unclean before Jehovah, including what are clearly perverted sexual practices."

[4] A vague statement appears in the August 2016 study edition of *The Watchtower* that appears to grant more latitude: "Although the Bible does not provide specific rules about the kinds and limits of love play that might be associated with natural sexual intimacy, it mentions displays of affection. (Song of Sol. 1:2; 2:6) Christian marriage partners should treat each other with tenderness." However, most Witnesses reading this would focus on the expression "natural sexual intimacy" as referring to sex acts that have not already been condemned as perverted.

perverted sex relations within the marriage bond," which would likely include loss of privileges in the congregation. This threat alone prevents many Witness couples from experimenting with oral sex, as I can personally attest. In this way, married Witnesses still keenly feel their religion's influence in their sex lives, even if what goes on in their bedrooms is no longer policed quite so rigorously.

April 6, 2005, finally arrived—my first day at Ministerial Training School as a student of the 29th class in Britain! I reported to Dudley Assembly Hall of Jehovah's Witnesses (an art deco style former cinema across the street from Dudley Zoo) to be swept along on an induction day filled with guided tours, handshakes and smiling faces. I knew instantly that this was where I belonged. This was my gateway to future opportunities.

In the three preceding months I had sacrificed my job and effectively made myself homeless in order to attend. My invitation letter had instructed me to read the entire New Testament in preparation for the course, which I had mostly succeeded in doing. I had also met with former MTS students and grilled them to find out how the course was conducted. From this information I had formulated an elaborate system of headed notepaper and special binders that would keep me organized and help me get the most from the experience. The end product would be a well-ordered repository of everything learned that I could easily use as a reference tool in the future. Additionally, I had the full complement of books and Watchtower materials that my invitation letter required me to bring, including a file of copies of

*Our Kingdom Ministry* dating all the way back to 1980. In short, I was prepared.

The only thing that niggled in the back of my mind on receiving my invitation was my private "issue" with masturbation. What if the course instructor started asking the class awkward questions on this matter, or unexpectedly began soliciting confessions? With such paranoid thoughts weighing me down, I decided to chasten myself by abstaining from the habit in the weeks leading up to the course. Then, if I could make it all the way through MTS in this "cleansed" state, hopefully the training provided would carry me the rest of the way. Receiving enlightenment that this truly is God's organization would be a huge incentive in observing this and other laws that so far made little or no sense to me. Besides, surely some (if not all) the other guys were doing it? Even if they were, my conscience tormented me.

The course itself proved to be extremely demanding and intense. I took along Dad's video camera and filmed sporadically over the eight weeks to document the course according to Mum's wishes. In the resulting movie, which I still have on DVD, you can see a marked difference between my giddy optimism on the first day and my more subdued and drained demeanor only a week later.[5] It was relentless. "It feels very much like we come home, we study, we go to bed and the next thing we know we're waking up and rushing in to the classes," I confess on camera.

---

[5] In case you are wondering, no I do not plan on making the full movie publicly available! My video editing skills were not as polished back then, so the film is rather long and tedious to watch for anyone but the students themselves. I also feel a responsibility to respect, to a reasonable extent, the privacy of my classmates.

***The 29th class in Britain assembles for its official photo—I am seated on the front row, just left of center in a light suit (our instructors are standing on the far left and right)***

At about 6 a.m. each morning I would get up, get ready, and leave my accommodation to report to the Assembly Hall for "morning worship" by 7:45. Morning worship is a ritual observed at the organization's Bethel facilities and (as in our case) on Watchtower-sponsored Bible courses. It involves reading the "daily text" (a Bible verse for the day that has been preselected by Watchtower) from a small book and considering the accompanying explanatory notes, which are usually based on a *Watchtower* article. The idea is that you read and discuss this material and then meditate on it throughout the day. Once morning worship was over, we could have our breakfast—prepared for us by a team of volunteer Witness caterers who also served a hot lunch (including dessert) every day of the course.

From 8:30 a.m. through to 4:40 p.m. we had four lessons punctuated by ten-minute breaks and nearly two hours for lunch. Despite the lengthy lunch period the Governing Body, in their infinite wisdom, had decided that there should be no midday break for the students. Instead, we were expected to put on work clothes, get organized into teams, and busy ourselves in a variety of menial chores designed to test our character. Our "work period" involved anything from painting fences to mopping floors. One particularly inexplicable task involved a mountain of chip bark that had been dumped in the corner of the parking lot of the facility. We were charged with shoveling it into bags and wheelbarrows, and redistributing it throughout the parking lot's borders so the bark covered the soil. We were clearly being made to do token work just for the sake of it, but we settled into our jobs and made as much fun of it as we could. As the course progressed, the "bark mountain" slowly diminished in size until finally it spelled the initials "M.T.S." for a photo opportunity.

***My classmates and I celebrate after vanquishing the bark mountain (I am in the middle of the group, jumping)***

The classes themselves mostly consisted of long sessions of listening to the instructor go through notes that had been prepared for him by the teaching committee of the Governing Body on a range of biblical/doctrinal/organizational issues. The vast majority of instruction was based on material taken from Watchtower literature and official correspondence. At various points in the discussion there would be question-and-answer sessions, or a student would be summoned to give a prearranged talk or comment dealing with a certain topic. If the student had somehow overlooked preparing for his piece (as happened to me on at least one occasion), then hard luck—he had to give it anyway! Student assignments would vary in duration, but were mostly between one and ten minutes. If you failed to conclude your talk or comment in the allotted time, the instructor would press his buzzer and you were expected to stop talking and return to your seat.

In the evening, there was homework. Lots of homework. The expectation was that you were to set aside an hour of preparation for each lesson the following day. There were four lessons, so this meant four hours of studying Watchtower publications every night before bed. You were then expected to commit additional time to preparing any forthcoming speaking assignments. I soon decided that I would spend slightly less time doing homework (30 to 45 minutes per lesson) so I could devote more time to my speaking assignments and, most importantly, go to sleep at a reasonable hour. This approach served me well. It meant that I was alert through most of the school, and my assignments generally seemed to go down well with both the class and the instructors. I was absolutely thrilled when I learned that I had been selected to give the "model" class demonstration of a "public talk"—a lecture that is given weekly in Witness congregations based on an outline from the Governing Body's teaching committee.[6] This was the longest possible speaking assignment that an MTS student could receive, and I was very proud to receive the privilege. It felt as though my efforts were paying off.

The two instructors assigned to our class had vastly different personalities. It almost seemed they had been deliberately paired to form some kind of "good cop, bad cop" combo. The good cop was a white Zimbabwean circuit overseer with a broad grin who was generous with his praise and encouragement, and seemed committed to making the course as pleasant as possible for everyone. The bad cop was a veteran circuit overseer and Gilead graduate who seemed to take everything extremely seriously, and did not hold back in his criticism if things were not precisely to his liking.[7]

---

[6] Public talks are now 30 minutes in length, but in 2005 they were 45 minutes.

[7] "Gilead" is the abbreviated name of the Watchtower Bible School of Gilead, which will be mentioned again in Chapter Eight. The school was launched in 1943 to train Witnesses to become missionaries. The MTS course was modeled on the Gilead course. It used to be that almost any married Witness couple could apply to attend, but since October 2011 invitations to

One classmate who felt the full force of Bad Cop's displeasure was an affable Irishman we nicknamed Dougal (he reminded us of a character from the *Father Ted* TV sitcom). Dougal had committed the mortal sin of starting a relationship with the daughter of the parents with whom he was staying. I had known about this for about 24 hours before it came to Bad Cop's attention, and only because I happened to be in Dougal's car party for getting to and from class. To the bewilderment of myself and other onlookers, Bad Cop approached Dougal's desk at the end of one lesson and counseled him about the scandal in front of everyone, reminding him that he was here to learn and not to get involved with girls.

This episode troubled me. Did Bad Cop really have to correct the lad in front of his friends? Why not take him for a quiet word in the instructor's office? Was his crime really so grave that it warranted public humiliation?

Another disturbing classroom incident, this time involving Good Cop, came during one lesson when we were asked to take our pens and cross out a sentence in one of our *Insight* volumes. *Insight on the Scriptures* is a two-volume set of Witness encyclopedias in which Bible-related names and topics are organized alphabetically. There was nothing overly profound in the fairly innocuous line we were asked to cross out.[8] Still,

---

Gilead have been limited to Witness couples already in certain forms of "full-time service."

[8] The forbidden line was: "So they must be understood to be standing in what was represented by the courtyard of the Gentiles, a special feature of the temple as rebuilt by Herod." It can be found on page 1081 of *Insight*, Vol. 2. The explanation for this deletion is to be found in the May 1, 2002, *Watchtower*, pages 30 and 31. The sentence no longer appears in the online version of the *Insight* volumes.

the very act of crossing out something in a Watchtower publication seemed like sacrilege to me, especially since this was a course where the application process involved pledging to agree with everything in the publications. If even the cherished *Insight* volumes were subject to alteration, then what sentences in other publications should we also be crossing out? And why were we so privileged? Why was there no direction for all Witnesses to make the same correction in their books?

I was left similarly deflated when it came to my hopes of reconciling long-held doubts over the organization's approach to Bible prophecy. The aging *Revelation* book (which by that time I considered an embarrassment) was repeatedly referred to during the course, and its fanciful take on Bible prophecy taught as sacrosanct. In one lesson we were issued a slip of paper with a timeline of the period between 1914 and 1922. It included various scriptures and references from Watchtower literature showing how certain dates had been arrived at. On close inspection it became obvious to me that the year 1919, which continues to carry enormous significance among Witnesses, had absolutely no correlation with any time periods mentioned in the Bible. It simply happened to be the year that early president Joseph Rutherford and some of his associates had been released from prison, having spent nine months incarcerated under charge of sedition. (More about this in Chapter Seven.) Because their exploits were deemed of great significance in the history of God's people, 1919 had been superimposed on Revelation's prophetic narrative. The three-and-a-half-year period prior to Rutherford's sentencing on June 21, 1918, just about stretched into the final days of 1914 (December 21) and was thus identified as the "42 months" of Revelation 11:2, 3.

**PERIODS OF TIME RECORDED IN REVELATION:**

| 1914 | 1915 | 1916 | 1917 | 1918 | 1919 | 1920 | 1921 | 1922 |
|---|---|---|---|---|---|---|---|---|
| 42 Months = DECEMBER – June | | | | 3½ Days | | 3½ Times = Spring – Autumn | | |
| REVELATION 11:2 – 3 | | | | Rev 11:9-11 | | REVELATION 12:14 | | |
| Ref: re: p164 Adjustment w 1/8/1994 | | | | re 168 | | re 184 | | |

***The timeline we were shown on our course***
***(the abbreviation "re" refers to pages of the "Revelation" book)***

Of further concern to me was the small matter of Rutherford's nine-month period of imprisonment not matching the period mentioned in the Bible at Revelation 11:9-11, which indicated a period of affliction for the "two prophets" (identified as being early Witnesses) lasting "three and a half days." Watchtower's explanation for this obvious discrepancy was that the three and a half days had been mentioned by the apostle John "to highlight that it would be only a short period compared with the actual three and a half years of activity that precede it." In other words, God made John write "three and a half days" rather than "nine months" because that would make things easier to understand.

But the instruction we were receiving, with its unflinching adherence to disjointed interpretations of Scripture, was not the only thing troubling me about MTS. As the course wore on, my vow regarding masturbation was becoming increasingly burdensome to the point where I was experiencing physical discomfort.[9]

As it turned out, the matter was discussed as part of our syllabus during the fifth week in a lesson titled "Sex and Marriage." Although none of us were chal-

---

[9] I would often wonder why men get pain in their testicles, or "blue balls," from not masturbating if masturbation is supposed to be wrong or unnatural.

lenged as to whether we had kept our hands in check, masturbation was predictably slammed as "self-abuse" based on arguments from a 1970s *Watchtower* article. This same article perpetuated the idea that masturbation "can, and frequently does, lead into homosexuality."[10] It also posited that masturbation is "abnormal and unnatural" using the following piece of logic:

> That masturbation is abnormal and unnatural is also indicated by the fact that abnormal, mentally deranged people are notorious masturbators.

This kind of silly argumentation, cobbled together before I was born by writers who were doubtless themselves victims of sexual repression, infuriated me. It was because of such nonsense that my balls were now aching and I could not get sex out of my mind, to the point where I would fantasize about the girls who were assigned to serve our lunches.

Our instructor rounded off his remarks by reminding us that masturbation could preclude a man from privileges of service. A Watchtower publication from 1973 was recommended for advice on ridding oneself of the habit. Here is a sample of its wisdom:

> Is one who practices masturbation 'deadening his body members as respects sexual appetite'? To the contrary, he is stimulating the sexual appetite. He develops a craving for activity that is not yet proper for him, so he satisfies the craving in an unclean way. (Ephesians 4:19) The Bible urges that one avoid the kind of thinking and conduct that leads to such problems, that he replace it with wholesome activity, and that he cultivate self-control. (Philippians 4:8; Galatians 5:22, 23) When earnest effort is put

---

[10] This bizarre claim also appears on page 39 of the 1976 book *Your Youth—Getting the Best out of It,* which was among my required reading as a Witness adolescent.

> forth to do this, such self-abuse can be avoided, with benefits mentally, emotionally and spiritually to the individual.

I had already tried to refrain from "self-abuse" by chastening myself for weeks of "wholesome activity" during which I was studying the Bible on an almost 24/7 basis. I had applied copious amounts of "self-control," refraining from touching myself for many weeks, and yet there had been absolutely no easing of my primal urges. This advice had been tested and clearly held no practical value.

After one particularly troublesome day, during which I found it almost impossible to concentrate, I finally succumbed to my frustrations and jerked off in the shower the following morning before class. The improvement in my overall mood was instant. I was now able to concentrate fully on the material being discussed. Moreover, I began to feel less guilt now that I could see plainly that the ban on masturbation was unsubstantiated in Scripture, especially since my instructors had failed to supply any logical justification when the matter was raised. This was just another of the many flaws in "God's organization" to store in my mental pending tray in hopes that it would all be ironed out by Jehovah in the fullness of time. Meanwhile, I just had to sit tight, play my part, and eventually everything would fall into place.

Of course, it never worked out that way, but this is how Witnesses with doubts are encouraged to think. It is called "waiting on Jehovah," and amounts to little more than consciously burying one's head in the sand.[11] A 2008 *Watchtower* explains it this way:

---

[11] *The Book of Mormon* musical contains a hilarious parody of this reasoning in the form of its song "Turn It Off."

> With hearts full of gratitude, we stay close to "the faithful and discreet slave whom his master appointed over his domestics, to give them their food at the proper time." Christ has appointed this slave "over all his belongings." (Matt. 24:45-47) Therefore, even if we as individuals do not fully understand a certain position taken by the slave class, that is no reason for us to reject it or return to Satan's world. Instead, loyalty will move us to act humbly and wait on Jehovah to clarify matters.

Admittedly, aside from my personal struggles and disappointments, on the whole I found MTS to be an uplifting experience. The 22 students represented eight different countries, and the varying backgrounds and personalities made for some lively banter and horseplay when the backs of our instructors were turned. Most of the guys were sincere, friendly and easy to get along with. A strong sense of camaraderie had developed as the course progressed over the eight weeks.

Once we entered the final week, thoughts turned to where we should all meet up for our class reunion in 2006, the following year. One student was from Malta, a suitably exotic place in my mind, so I pushed hard for us to go there. My second preference was for us to visit another student who lived in Rome.

Someone suggested we travel to visit Miroslav, a rather eccentric Croatian guy about my age who sat behind me in class and acted much older than he was. Miroslav's English was limited, but this did not stop him from being among the first to offer criticism of other students' speaking assignments. Despite his idiosyncrasies, he was capable of laughing at himself when teased.

I did not know much about Croatia (other than that it had hosted a brutal war when I was a teenager) but the

CERTIFICATE

MINISTERIAL
TRAINING SCHOOL

*Hereby be it known that*

**James Lloyd Evans**

*an ordained minister of the gospel, has shown himself qualified to engage in educational activity, promoting goodwill and working in behalf of permanent peace and the law of perfect order and righteousness, among all peoples. He is specifically recommended for service as a representative of the International Bible Students Association, and its associate corporation, Watch Tower Bible and Tract Society of Britain, to co-labour with them in preaching the good news of Jehovah God's Kingdom by Christ Jesus.—Matthew 24:14.*

*Issued at* Dudley, England

June 5, 2005
*Date*

***The certificate I received on my graduation***

idea of going there intrigued me. Somebody proposed that, instead of flying, we all drive there on a class road trip. Now this sounded interesting! I had long been fascinated by the idea of driving across Europe ever since my "cool" uncle had accomplished this feat when I was younger, and this seemed like the perfect excuse. Once the course was over, I would throw myself into making arrangements for our Croatian adventure.

By the time our graduation day was finally upon us on June 5, we were all sad that we needed to part ways. The assembly hall had been like a home to us for two months, so it was quite emotional to see our classroom being pulled apart the day before the ceremony to provide extra space for the hundreds of guests who would be flooding in. Each student had been issued a quota of tickets for friends and family to attend. I had invited Dad, Hannah and her husband, the couple I stayed with, and a few of my friends from back home.

The graduation featured a series of talks by a number of speakers, including our instructors and two representatives who had travelled up from London Bethel—Peter Ellis and Stephen Papps. I was interviewed about my personal hardships prior to attending the school. I was not the only student to have forsaken employment and housing for MTS, but the audience seemed very moved when I recounted the recent death of my mother. I recall saying that I had resolved to attend the course even if doing so would leave me "homeless and bankrupt." My interviewer commended me in his reply, saying that Mum would be very proud of me when she sees me again in the resurrection.

Once the ceremony was formally over, my classmates and I assembled at the front of the auditorium and serenaded the audience with a rendition of the rousing Witness song "Life Without End—At Last!" to thunderous applause. It felt like the perfect finale to my MTS experience, and I even managed to catch it on camera—just in case.

Readjusting to normal life on my return home was always going to be a challenge, but it was especially difficult for me since I had been emotionally invested for so long in attending the school. With my personal Everest conquered, what was left for me to do? All students received an assignment from Watchtower on graduating, and my assignment was to return to my previous congregation. Though there was an initial excitement when I was welcomed back in Bramhall, this would amount to little more than a brief honeymoon before I was forced to come to terms with my new predicament. I had to find work, and somewhere to live.

Thankfully, I had not burned all my bridges with my former employers. One of them (not a Witness) was glad to take me back into his company as a salesman. Also, an older couple in my congregation were kind enough to let me stay with them for a while until it was the right time to return to living with Dad again, who by now seemed to have mellowed considerably.

I threw myself back into service in the local congregation in whatever I was asked to do. People started talking about my potential as an elder, which was a position to which I aspired. The MTS course had included instructions on how to be a spiritual shepherd and handle various complicated judicial and organizational situations. I knew that only once I was an elder could I use this knowledge to the full. All the same, I felt it would be so much easier to fulfill these aspirations with a wife at my side. And now that MTS was over, there was no longer anything holding me back from starting a relationship if the right person came along.[12]

[12] For a number of years following the launch of MTS in the late '80s, graduates were not allowed to start relationships until a certain period had elapsed following their graduation. Our class was told that this requirement was dropped because it constituted celibacy, which Watchtower condemns in its literature when practiced by the Catholic Church.

In the months following MTS I continued my hunt for a girlfriend—a future capable wife of sound spiritual stock—but without much success. I arranged to spend a day in the preaching work with one quite pretty girl who I knew liked me, but whose feelings I struggled to reciprocate. I hoped that spending time with her would kindle some flame within me—but I got cold feet once I learned she had been telling her friends how excited she was about the arrangement. I ended up inviting another male friend of mine as a chaperone to put a dampener on things and take the pressure off the situation.

Another more embarrassing episode involved another girl with whom I arranged to spend the day preaching near her home in Wales—a good two-hour drive from where I lived. I do not know if it was her shapely figure or just the fact that I was sexually frustrated, but I recall spending most of the day going door-to-door with her, struggling to conceal an extremely unwelcome and ill-timed erection. The only way I could think of masking the protrusion was by keeping my hands in my pockets at all times, which must have looked very strange later on when we met up with a friend of hers to play soccer in the park. If she noticed my difficulties, she was kind enough not to let on. But it did not come as a shock when contact soon dwindled after that hellish day.

Frustrated by my failure to select from an extremely slim menu of potential partners, I once again turned to the internet to help ease my loneliness. One girl with whom I began to share some very intimate online exchanges was an American student who was studying in the Midlands. In one conversation I summoned the courage to share with her the fact that I was a Witness. She seemed to sympathize with my predicament and understand the relief our casual encounters were giving me. At first it felt blasphemous to be divulging my faith to her. I was giving her what Witnesses would call a "bad witness." Rather than converting her to the "Truth," she and I were using each other for cybersex. As with masturbation, I knew my actions were condemned by my faith—but so long as I steered clear of actual fornication I figured I was opting for the lesser of two evils, which surely counted for *something.*

This will not come as a surprise, but a 2001 *Watchtower* article had denounced such online encounters. Psychologist Dr. Al Cooper was quoted as declaring cybersex a "public health hazard."[13] In the same article, Dr. Cooper warned that those "whose sexuality may have been suppressed and limited all their lives" were especially prone to the practice. This described me perfectly, but the *Watchtower* article failed to acknowledge that, in the case of young Witnesses like me, much of this "sexual suppression" (or, more accurately, *repression*) originated from the organization itself—specifically through its tampering in the most private, emotionally-charged aspects of people's lives.

If all this repression were based on the Bible, that would at least be some justification—but even if Watchtower could find a biblical reason for banning premarital sex, it was another thing entirely to insist that I was only to choose a wife from among other Witnesses, and attach a guilt complex to masturba-

---

[13] Bernice Yeung wrote a comprehensive article on Dr. Cooper and his work on cybersexuality in the *SF Weekly* in 2004 (at the time of writing, the article can be read online at this URL: http://archives.sfweekly.com/sanfrancisco/sex-and-the-single-psychologist/Content?oid=2151348). According to Yeung, Dr. Cooper himself uses the internet for dating and claims to have met about 100 million women online.

tion if I failed in my efforts. At the very least it would have been helpful if I had reason to be convinced in my heart that Jehovah's Witnesses are unmistakably God's one true organization—but MTS, the much-anticipated spiritual zenith of my Witness experience, had failed utterly in helping to calm my doubts and confusion on that score.

Such internal conflicts led me to a point when I was able to excuse almost anything that could quell my raging libido apart from actual sex. After all, this was all for the greater good if it meant keeping my virginity until marriage and being in with a shout of seeing Mum again.

Occasionally, the American girl and I would discuss meeting up in person. One time she very nearly came to Manchester on the train to spend the weekend with me while Dad was out of the house, but I buckled at the last moment. I just could not bring myself to do it. She had told me she would not pressure me into anything I was not ready for—but it was me I was worried about, not her. I knew having a girl staying in my house who was willing to have sex with me would be just too much temptation to handle. I could easily see myself sliding beyond the threshold into sin and inevitable disfellowshipping. (I would have felt compelled to confess to elders.) We continued our chats online, but eventually our relationship waned. Though she clearly found it all very frustrating, I think she understood it was my religion that was pulling the strings.

All the while, I remained in touch with my MTS classmates, busily assisting in preparations for our first reunion in Croatia in May-June 2006. Nine of us would be making the journey to meet up with Miroslav. Though I could not help but fantasize a little about meeting a nice Croatian girl on the reunion, I was determined not to get my hopes up. In any case, I could not see myself marrying someone who spoke another language with all the communication issues this might entail. My focus was on having a real adventure with good friends and revisiting the camaraderie that had given so much enjoyment to my MTS experience.

Though we had initially planned to make the trip by road, all nine of us from the UK eventually opted to fly to Zagreb and travel from there to where Miroslav lived. I was the first to arrive in Sisak—a small industrial city about an hour south of the Croatian capital, straddling three rivers. On my arrival it felt as though the whole region was still locked in the early '90s. It was obvious that very little progress had been made since war had ravaged the country about 15 years earlier.

I was relieved to find Sisak congregation's coordinator, who spoke English, waiting for me at the bus station. Though I could not speak a word of Croatian, he invited me to give one of the talks at the meeting the next evening.

My talk seemed to go down well, even though it was greeted by an array of bemused looks from an audience who mostly could not understand a single word I was saying. I was also involved in an on-stage interview later that evening with some of my fellow classmates. (Now that I understand how few Croatians speak English—especially the older generation—I cannot help but wonder how the congregants managed to politely sit through a group of young guys babbling in an indecipherable language on their platform. Perhaps they enjoyed being reminded that their organization is international in its reach.)

At the end of the meeting, a pretty young girl with dark eyes and raven hair approached me. Her flawless features reminded me of the singer Katie Melua. In perfect English, she thanked me for my talk and said she had enjoyed it.

"By the way, I'm Deeyana," she said.

"Oh, like the princess!" I quipped. (If you have still not fathomed why I was having trouble getting a girl, this should be a clue.)

Laughing politely, Dijana (as her name is spelled) glided off to mingle elsewhere. She had made an impression.

The reunion turned out to be extremely enjoyable. A highlight of the trip was a visit to the Plitvice Lakes—a stunning UNESCO World Heritage site nestled in the Croatian mountains boasting a series of crystal clear lakes that cascade into each other via a labyrinth of waterfalls. Despite the relentless rain on the day of our visit (untypical for the time of year) everyone was in awe as we trudged along the wooden walkways and marveled at the beauty and splendor of our surroundings. In my mind, I was Adam in the Garden of Eden—and Dijana was my Eve.

I had discovered Dijana was a pioneer who was very highly spoken of by the local brothers, which ticked a major box on my list of requirements. I pursued her relentlessly with my camcorder, trying to get her attention. As you might expect, this paparazzi approach did little to endear me to her. To further complicate matters, it appeared I was not the only one smitten. A couple of the more handsome specimens from my class were moving in and trying their luck.

Finally, the time came for us to leave Croatia. As we awaited our return flight at Zagreb airport, I was stricken with sadness at having just been forced to say goodbye to Dijana. I felt I had blown my chances by acting the fool in an effort to get her attention.

It was not long before I heard Dijana's name raised in conversation among the other guys as our wait dragged on. One started making predictions as to who was in with the best shot of winning her over. It was suggested that, of three potential suitors, I was in third place. On hearing this, my mood instantly worsened. Sadness began to give way to irritation, annoyance—even jealousy. My friends seemed to expect me to join in with the banter, but I found it impossible to indulge them—not this time. This was not a game to me. Dijana was not some fairground prize. I had only just met her, but somehow she meant more to me than that. She had lit a flame inside me, and I feared I would never see her again.

CHAPTER FIVE

# Shepherd the Flock

*"The shepherd always tries to persuade the sheep that their interests and his own are the same."*
—Stendhal

*"Every seeming equality conceals a hierarchy."*
—Mason Cooley

IN 1985, something most peculiar happened in Bonham, Texas. A good number of the local congregation of Jehovah's Witnesses decided they no longer wished to be affiliated with the Watch Tower Society. This happened after letters containing theological questions were sent by the Bonham elders for Watchtower's attention, only to be answered with orders for them to stop being impertinent and get on with their assigned duties.

The situation came to a head in June when the organization sent a committee to Bonham to appoint a replacement body of elders who would be less troublesome. Once the new elders were chosen, the original elders were notified by letter that they had been disfellowshipped, and the locks were changed on Bonham's Kingdom Hall to prevent them from accessing the building.[1]

Before long, the controversy had escalated into a full-blown lawsuit for control of the Kingdom Hall.[2]

---

[1] The names of the ousted elders were: Wendel Baker, Trymer L. Berry, James E. Coleman, Ralph E. Deal, and Tony M. Jones.

The ousted elders had been named as trustees in the property's paperwork and were not going to walk away without a fight. Watchtower lost the suit, but only after its then vice president, Don Adams, made a remarkable statement in an affidavit revealing Watchtower's true nature:

> To implement their decisions, the Governing Body uses a hierarchical organization together with corporate entities, when appropriate, to accomplish its worldwide work of teaching and declaring the good news of God's established Kingdom.

This statement represented a U-turn from how Watchtower had hitherto described itself in its literature. The organization had nearly always used the word "hierarchy," or "hierarchical," in connection with "false religion," from which Witnesses were said to have escaped. A 1966 *Watchtower* declared Witnesses to "have freed themselves from the hierarchical, congregational and all other forms of church rule that are unscriptural," instead claiming that they were "governed by theocratic rule." In other words, it is not men who run Watchtower—it is God himself. But when push came to shove, and property ownership rights were in the balance, a high-ranking representative was willing to come clean about Watchtower's true nature as a religious hierarchy.

Eventually, Watchtower circumvented the whole issue by building their own Kingdom Hall in Bonham and establishing a new congregation for loyal Witnesses to attend. They also enacted a change to the arrangements for Kingdom Hall ownership as a means of insulating themselves against a repeat of the incident. Congrega-

---

[2] Facsimiles of local newspaper articles from the time can be found in Appendix D.

tions were asked to accept new instructions to the effect that trusteeship of a Kingdom Hall was dependent on being an elder or ministerial servant, and a congregation had the right to replace trustees if necessary.[3] This subtle change effectively handed complete control of all Kingdom Hall buildings to Watchtower, because if a body of elders did not use the building according to Watchtower's wishes they could no longer be elders and, therefore, their names could no longer be on the title.

This new arrangement would be tested some 25 years later when another body of elders in another part of the United States found itself in conflict with Watchtower—this time due to a disagreement over building renovations. It would now be the turn of the Menlo Park congregation in California to test Watchtower's mettle, and my friend and colleague John Hoyle (who lives in Oregon) would be on hand to cover the unfolding controversy in detail on his Ex-JW.com website via a series of articles that make for fascinating reading.

---

[3] This provision can be seen in a leaked Watchtower document titled *Information Regarding Ownership of Kingdom Halls*, dated September 1, 2005. "Where possible," it says, "elders or ministerial servants of the congregation should be appointed to act as trustees. In the event an elder or ministerial servant who has been appointed as a trustee no longer serves as an elder or ministerial servant, or is no longer a member of the congregation, he should be replaced where possible." The same document provides for trustees to be removed by the congregation if necessary: "The Declaration of Trust signed by trustees should include language recognizing the authority of the congregation to replace trustees and appoint substitute trustees." Another document, the *Congregation Property Ownership Checklist* (2009), insists that "corporation members or trustees do not have a say in congregation matters or in the disposition of congregation property beyond their roles as congregation members."

In mid-2011, the Menlo Park congregation had one of its twice-yearly visits by a circuit overseer named Paul Koehler. Koehler was an interesting character who seemed to relish his position and authority. According to Hoyle, he would regale audiences with stories of how he had once served in the military as a Navy SEAL, service that, it turned out, had strangely gone unrecorded by the U.S. Department of the Navy (as would be revealed when Witnesses irked by Koehler's platform boasts started digging).

During his visit, Koehler met with Jason Cobb and his fellow elders and suggested they agree to a refurbishment of the Kingdom Hall. When they respectfully declined the recommendation, Koehler responded by promptly arranging for all of them to be deleted as elders.

Understandably taken aback by this treatment, Cobb decided to file a number of suits against the Regional Building Committee, the local Watchtower circuit (and its overseer, Koehler) and the district (and its overseer).[4] He complained that his deletion was illegitimate and demanded it be reversed. Cobb had no licensed legal representation in bringing the case, and it was eventually dismissed.[5] In my opinion, in pursuing Watchtower legally over the matter, Cobb's naive assumption that it was Jehovah's organization, and that his deletion as an elder was the work of one or two rogue individuals rather than the inevitable consequence of defying a high-control cult, put him at a considerable disadvantage.[6]

---

4 There used to be an added tier of the Watchtower hierarchy between circuit overseer and branch office known as a "district overseer." This position no longer exists.

5 According to Hoyle, Watchtower somehow also managed to seize control of the congregation bank accounts, even though these were under Cobb's name as the primary signatory.

Calvin Rouse, a high-ranking attorney from Watchtower's legal department in Patterson, New York, represented the organization as defendants in the case.[7] After announcing himself as "general counsel for the National Organization of Jehovah's Witnesses out of Brooklyn, New York," Rouse explained why Cobb's demands were without legal merit:

> Ordinarily I wouldn't be here, but this is one of our 13,000 congregations in the United States. We are a hierarchical religion structured just like the Catholic Church. And when the order from the Pope comes down in the church defrocking a priest and kicking him out, he no longer has any say in any matter in the local parish priest—in the parish. The same situation as here. In his complaint he brings one claim. He claims that he wants to be reinstated as a director and an officer in the Menlo Park Congregation. This is contrary to our church rules and regulations and bylaws. We brought our organizational bylaws book, our rule book here, and we are prepared to present witnesses that this is a hierarchical organization.

The above statement, made in 2012, stands in stark contrast to a *Watchtower* magazine published just over 10 years earlier in 2001, which declared:

> In contrast with many religious groups in Christendom, Jehovah's Witnesses do not decide for themselves the form of spiritual government under which they operate. These sincere Christians endeavor to stick to Jehovah's standards. Overseers

---

[6] It also did not help that, according to Hoyle, Cobb "tended to be inflexible" with what he would share with the local media, who were initially interested in the case but whose interest soon waned in the face of his lack of cooperation.

[7] Copies of the court transcripts are available on Ex-JW.com under the article "Menlo Park Kingdom Hall: The State Lawsuit."

among them are not put into office by some congregational, hierarchical, or presbyterian form of church government.

The legal controversy involving Jason Cobb and the Menlo Park Kingdom Hall demonstrated the above words to be a total fabrication aimed at hoodwinking the reader into thinking Watchtower is something more elevated than it actually is—your run-of-the-mill religious hierarchy. As admitted by a legal representative of Watchtower in a court of law, Witness "overseers" (another term for elders) are quite clearly "put into office" by a "hierarchical church government," and they can just as easily be removed from said office by said hierarchy without any legal recourse—which is exactly what happened in both Menlo Park and Bonham.

Of course, most Witnesses are blissfully unaware of both legal altercations and thus continue under the impression that their religion is not a hierarchy but a "Theocracy." This is despite Watchtower recently being slightly more honest about its organizational structure in its literature. For example, an illustration published in a 2013 *Watchtower* depicts a clear hierarchy, with the Governing Body occupying the highest position in a line that has ordinary Witnesses on the bottom rung of the ladder.

Curiously absent from the picture opposite (or at least not clearly distinguishable) is Jesus Christ, who is claimed to be "the Head of the congregation." Instead, beneath a depiction of Jehovah on his heavenly chariot (based on a passage from the book of Ezekiel) you have the Governing Body seated around a boardroom table in plush leather chairs. Beneath them are the branch committees that care for countries or groups of countries (seated on slightly less comfortable chairs),

***Picture on page 29 of the April 15, 2013, "Watchtower"***

followed by traveling overseers like Koehler. Then you have the local bodies of elders and congregations before, finally, you reach the lowly "individual publishers" (the laity) at the bottom. Ascending vertically up the ladder from the bottom is by no means easy, no matter how skilled or intelligent you might be, or how genuine your motives are.

For example, not shown on the 2013 hierarchy illustration are ministerial servants, who occupy a position between normal publishers and elders. Only exemplary male publishers who "reach out" for privileges might find themselves elevated to this rank, which is based on Paul's writings at 1 Timothy 3:8-13. If you are not equipped with a penis, you need not apply.

If a congregation has a shortage of "qualified" brothers to cover menial tasks such as organizing the literature stocks or managing the sound system, only then will lowly women be granted the honor of caring for such "privileges." Interestingly, women (or "sisters") in the congregation are *not* barred from sharing in the "privilege" of vacuuming the carpet, polishing the woodwork or cleaning the toilets. But when it comes to the handling of sound equipment, the counting of donations, or the dispensing of books or magazines, these things are considered strictly male duties. (*see box*)

FOR WITNESSES

## SUBJECTION OF WOMEN

You will have been persuaded to believe that the way women are treated among Jehovah's Witnesses is perfectly normal. They are not to teach in the congregation by giving talks; if teaching a male Bible study without the presence of a male they are to wear a head covering, and even menial tasks such as operating sound equipment at meetings are considered above them.

A common scripture referred to in support of these rules is 1 Peter 3:1, in which husbands are told to assign honor to their wives "as to a weaker vessel, the feminine one." The argument made is that, by insulating women from doing the stressful work assumed by men, women are somehow elevated. Another equally misogynistic verse from the Greek Scriptures calls for women to stay quiet. "As in all the congregations of the holy ones, let the women keep silent in the congregations, for it is not permitted for them to speak," the apostle Paul writes. "Rather, let them be in subjection, as the Law also says. If they want to learn something, let them ask their husbands at home, for it is disgraceful for a woman to speak in the congregation." —1 Corinthians 14:33-35.

The truth is, women are not "weaker vessels" and there is no good reason for them to "keep silent." Women are every bit as capable as men of excelling in leadership roles, no matter how demanding, and share all the attributes needed for positions of oversight. The subjugation of women among Jehovah's Witnesses has nothing to do with any enlightened, scientifically-based wisdom. Rather, it is an embarrassing vestige of male Bible writers sharing vulgar, misogynistic views that reflect the primitive age in which they lived.

The extent to which Watchtower has embraced a demeaning view of women through many decades of its history is an embarrassment. For example, a 1967 *Awake!* article declared: "The female skull is lighter and its cranial capacity is about 10 percent smaller than that of a male, even as is the rest of the anatomy. The contour of the female skull is also more rounded and the facial bones are smoother. Apparently, with the lines of beauty goes less rugged strength." The writer of the same article (a male, one can only assume) concluded that "man is advantaged by a greater brain size."

Incredibly, current Governing Body member Samuel Herd repeated this line of reasoning in a talk that was recorded some years ago.* Among many other outrageously sexist remarks, he repeated the claim about cranial capacity from the 1967 *Awake!* before concluding: "So now this shows that she's just not equipped for the role of headship." In truth, though men on average do indeed have slightly larger cerebral, cerebellar and cerebral cortical lobar volumes, women tend to have a higher percentage of gray matter than men (gray matter contains all the synapses), so increased overall brain volume does not necessarily equate to increased intelligence.

Even so, it could be that, as a female Witness, you are more comfortable adhering to the Bible's insistence that it is simply not your place to hold certain roles in the congregation. Though you are, of course, entitled to this view,

---

* Clips of the talk recording are easily found by searching: "Sam Herd Women" on YouTube. It is believed to date to 1971, before Herd was a Governing Body member, when he was involved in traveling overseer work.

it is worth pondering the fact that women, like men, can supposedly be chosen by the holy spirit to rule with Jesus in heaven. That being the case, how is it that a woman can be given power over the earth itself as an immortal coruler and priest in Christ's heavenly government, but is not to assist with fairly menial, day-to-day matters in a congregation?

Further up the ladder from ministerial servants you will find elders, who are said to be chosen for their roles by holy spirit. As a 2010 *Watchtower* explains: "They are appointed after prayer and under the guidance of the holy spirit, so they too can be regarded as under Christ's direction, or guiding hand." In other words, when a man is being considered for appointment as an elder, the incumbent elders pray for holy spirit before discussing his credentials, thus guaranteeing that God will support whatever decision they reach. (The prayer before the discussion is therefore crucial. Without prayer, all you have is a bunch of guys deciding which of their male friends can join their exclusive club.)

Once the elders have decided which (if any) brothers in the congregation are fit for appointment, their recommendation is ratified by the circuit overseer, who has the authority to rubber-stamp appointments of servants and elders on behalf of the Governing Body.[8] The elder candidate is then discreetly approached and asked a series of questions before his appointment can be announced to the congregation, namely: "Is there anything from your past, even before baptism, or in

---

[8] This arrangement was introduced from September 1, 2014, onward. Prior to that, circuit overseers would pass recommendations for the appointments of elders and servants to the local branch office for approval.

your personal or family life that disqualifies you or would prevent you from accepting this appointment?" and "Is there any reason why your appointment should not be announced to the congregation?" Finally, only if the person has never served as an elder or ministerial servant before, should the following question be asked: "Have you ever been involved at any time in the past with child sexual molestation?"[9]

Of course, these are all fitting questions for someone about to take on a position of considerable trust and responsibility. There is just one problem: it is entirely down to the person's conscience as to whether he answers the questions honestly. In the case of the last question, most predatory child molesters are surely at least capable of giving a false answer when greater access to unsuspecting children beckons if only they can bring themselves to deny any previous abuse.

Thus, elders are basically "appointed by holy spirit" by means of a prayer and two or three questions. Once confirmed, the appointment is announced to the congregation and the new elder is issued with a copy of the "rule book" alluded to previously, which is titled *"Shepherd the Flock of God"—1 Peter 5:2.*[10] The *Shepherd* book is strictly for elders only, and is not to be read by any other Witnesses in the congregation. This was confirmed in a letter to elders accompanying the book's release, dated August 23, 2010:

> We would like to emphasize the importance of keeping these new textbooks secured and confidential, both before and after they are distributed.

---

9 The same questions are to be asked for those appointed as ministerial servants.

10 Published in 2010, the *Shepherd* book replaced the previous elders' rule book, *"Pay Attention to Yourselves and to All the Flock"* (published in 1991).

> The textbooks should not be left on tops of desks or in other places where they are easily accessible by family members or other individuals. The information is designed for use by the elders only, and other individuals should not have any opportunity to read the information.

Whether or not the information is "designed for use by the elders," it has long baffled me that Watchtower can justify insisting that procedural information that applies to *all* Witnesses is to be viewed only by an elite few, and not everyone. Not only are regular publishers prohibited from reading the *Shepherd* book, they are also prevented from reading material in regular correspondence sent from Watchtower to the local bodies of elders, otherwise known as "BOE letters" (BOE being an abbreviation of "body of elders"). The Bible certainly contains no precedent for rules to be circulated on a privileged "eyes only" basis, to be hidden from all but those responsible for enforcing them.

Of course, a degree of confidentiality is understandable wherever private information related to individuals is concerned. However, the *Shepherd* book and routine Watchtower correspondence for the attention of all bodies of elders are not of that nature. When you read the *Shepherd* book (as you can easily do by searching for a PDF of it online), you identify it almost immediately as a document setting forth a raft of rules governing a variety of scenarios applicable to ordinary Witnesses, as a cursory glance at the chapter titles indicates:

1. Shepherd the Flock of God
2. How Elders Work Together as a Body
3. Appointment and Deletion of Elders and Ministerial Servants
4. Assisting Those Who Are Weak

5. Determining Whether a Judicial Committee Should Be Formed
6. Preparing for the Judicial Hearing
7. Judicial Hearing Procedure
8. Appeal Hearing Procedure
9. Implications of Disassociation
10. Matters Related to Disfellowshipped and Disassociated Ones
11. Reinstatement Committee Procedure
12. Clarifications and Guidelines on Handling Certain Matters

BOE letters embellish (and occasionally replace) the guidance found in the *Shepherd* book when it becomes necessary to issue further instructions. While the majority of these letters make for extremely tedious reading to the uninitiated (i.e. how to manage literature stocks, what to do about letting Witnesses listen to the meeting over the telephone, etc.), the occasional BOE letter can be of clear relevance to ordinary members of the congregation—such as letters about the handling of child abuse, or how financial affairs are to be administered.

One such letter, dated March 29, 2014, announced sweeping changes to the means by which donations are to be collected from congregations.[11] The first page of the four-page document was to be read to the congregation, but concerning the remaining three-page postscript there was a sentence in bold print as follows:

> This postscript should not be read to the congregation, and this letter should not be posted on the information board.

---

[11] This letter was technically not a "BOE letter" because it was addressed "to all congregations." But as I explain, only the first page of the four-page later was to be read out to non-elders.

As you might expect, the postscript was the part of the letter of most interest to ordinary Witnesses. It detailed the means by which congregations would essentially be stealth-tithed through a new arrangement of regular, monthly donations to Watchtower—ostensibly to help pay for its pressing construction needs.

Under the new arrangement, previous loans being paid to the organization to reimburse a congregation's building or renovation expenses were to be cancelled, thus leaving congregations free to avail themselves of a new "opportunity" to send "at least the same amount" of money to Watchtower as their prior monthly donation toward a new centralized campaign of Kingdom Hall and Assembly Hall construction. Elders in more fiscally-autonomous congregations not previously indebted to Watchtower (who had not called on them for extensive building or renovation work) were instructed to establish a new monthly amount to be sent to the organization, calculated based on a survey of publishers using slips of paper:

> The elders in congregations without loans or those having standing resolutions to support Kingdom Hall construction worldwide should take a confidential survey of all publishers to determine the amount of the new resolution. This can be done by passing out slips of paper to be filled out anonymously by the publishers indicating how much they are able to contribute monthly toward local congregation expenses, including the resolution to support Kingdom Hall and Assembly Hall construction worldwide.

The postscript also requested that all congregations immediately donate their surplus funds, apart from money needed for minor repairs or operational costs, to Watchtower. In return for relinquishing the last vestiges of their autonomy, congregations would come under the umbrella of a new scheme whereby Watchtower would make itself accountable for the building and maintenance of all Kingdom Halls and Assembly Halls, while having full discretion when prioritizing the allocation of labor and funding.

Not contained in this or any other letter was an honest explanation of who *really* owns a Kingdom Hall in terms of deciding its use, and is thus responsible for its maintenance—namely, the Watch Tower Society. As the Menlo Park incident clearly illustrated, Watchtower has the final word on how Kingdom Halls are utilized and has no hesitation wielding this power when elders get too big for their boots. Moreover, if a Kingdom Hall ever needs to be sold for any reason, you can be sure the proceeds would not find their way back into the pockets of local Witnesses who over many years were persuaded to believe *they* were responsible for its construction, maintenance and upkeep.

A second letter from Watchtower on the matter followed, dated May 12, 2014. This time, because it was addressed only to elders, no part of it could be read out to ordinary Witnesses. The letter elaborated on the stipulation regarding surplus funds, ordering congregations to keep just $5,000 in their bank accounts, plus enough money to cover three months' worth of utility, supplies and servicing expenses, and hand over everything else to Watchtower. This demand marked the final death-knell for any notion of congregational autonomy. It meant that if Watchtower were to ever go bust for any reason (an eventuality I will explore in Chapter Eight), individual congregations can expect to be dragged down with it.

These far-reaching changes to the means by which donations are gathered by Watchtower were of direct relevance to ordinary Witnesses—especially those who donate portions of their hard-earned income to sustain the organization and their local congregations. But rather than involve Witnesses in matters that directly affect them, and be transparent regarding how changes are implemented, the service desk at Watchtower's headquarters (which is responsible for drafting and circulating these letters) apparently chose to keep the rank and file in the dark. All they want, it would seem, is their money and unquestioned allegiance. Regular publishers are pawns rather than partners.[12]

When it comes to Witness elders, all this secrecy serves a useful purpose—even if they do not consciously think of it in such a way. Privileged access to procedural, organizational guidelines and protocols imbues the role of elder with an aura of exclusivity. The "I know something you don't know" factor gives elders extra kudos, making them feel special and further elevating them in the minds of the rank and file.

As an elder you not only get to read materials that are forbidden for ordinary Witnesses—you also get to learn all the juicy stuff that goes on in your congregation behind the scenes. You know why Brother Smith has been reproved, or why Sister Jones and her husband are now giving each other the cold shoulder. You have insider knowledge on any scandals or misdemeanors, and people will freely approach you to confess their latest slip-ups. Of course, if you hear of anyone discussing your personal affairs or handling of matters, you have the option of denouncing and snuffing out any such talk as "gossip" and administering discipline as you see fit.

---

[12] As I will explain in Chapter Eight, the new donation arrangement just described was misrepresented by Governing Body member Stephen Lett in the May 2015 episode of JW Broadcasting.

When elders' meetings are convened, you get a say in far-reaching decisions affecting the way the congregation is run. You also get to arrange shepherding visits and use these as opportunities to impart "counsel" to wayward congregation members on anything that is not to your liking (if you are that way inclined).

Simply by virtue of the fact that you spend considerable time on the Kingdom Hall platform you are more visible as one "taking the lead" in the congregation. If you are a gifted speaker, you can expect invitations to travel to neighboring congregations to give talks. You might even be invited to deliver high-profile program items at assemblies or conventions in front of crowds numbering into the hundreds or thousands. The more you are seen on the platform, the more you will be showered with respect and reverence. If you have a family by your side in the congregation, they will be immensely proud of you for being such a marvelous role model and enhancing their own standing.

There is just one snag to all this: the role of elder leaves little room for individuality. An elder is essentially a line manager; an enforcer of Watchtower policies and rules that may not always make sense, but must be adhered to and defended vigorously and without a moment's hesitation. If you show any creativity beyond this narrow remit, you can expect your tenure as an elder to be brief and fraught with stress.

It is generally harder to "delete" an elder than it is to appoint one, simply because it involves no small amount of congregational upheaval and stress on all sides, with lengthy backroom meetings and endless finger pointing and bickering. Even so, you can and will find yourself facing serious difficulty as an elder if you do not toe the party line and do things the Watchtower way.

To my delight, a regular exchange of messages with Dijana via phone and internet in the weeks following the reunion soon spawned a relationship. I convinced her to come and live in the UK, initially as an au pair, so that we could be together. Apart from anything else, it was nice to have her in my life without paying for it in eye-watering three-digit phone bills!

After roughly six months of dating, I presented Dijana with a cheap silver ring (all I could afford at the time) bought in a hurry from an Ambleside jewelry store during an unplanned and scandalously-unchaperoned day out to the Lake District. We were in a rowing boat on a windswept Grasmere Lake when I took it out of my pocket. Dijana later joked that she felt more than a bit pressured, as it seemed like a choice between saying "yes" and returning to the safety of the shore, or lingering precariously in a small boat on a choppy lake as she deliberated her answer.

We wed in the registry office at Malinska, a picturesque town on the Croatian coast, on July 14, 2007. After officially tying the knot we had a Witness ceremony on the balcony of a local hotel. The view across the sun-drenched Adriatic from the top floor, where we later had our reception, was breathtaking. Our honeymoon was the drive back to the UK from Croatia across Europe, stopping off in Venice, the Swiss Alps, and Paris. It was an adventure neither of us will forget.

Our first home was a far cry from the luxury of our wedding and honeymoon. Neither of us had wealthy families on which to lean. We had both spent most of our youth pioneering, so we had little or no money for

***Dijana and I on our wedding day***

paying rent. The cheapest properties available were around £300 per month, and even this was a stretch for our virtually non-existent budget. By this point, we were already plunging the depths of credit card limits and cashing checks in order to get by as we struggled to find decent part-time work. Our financial constraints meant we were forced to settle for a basement flat in the center of Stockport on the outskirts of Manchester, which (as we later discovered) came with a complimentary late-night soundtrack of police sirens and drunken neighbors brawling.

By June 2008, we managed to flee our Stockport dungeon for more tranquil surroundings. Someone in our congregation had a non-Witness son who was working over in Dubai with his wife and kids, and he needed his four-bedroom house to be occupied for a token rent of £400 per month. By this time we both had jobs and were earning a little more money, so we were only too pleased to oblige.

We now had the use of a spacious house at the end of a cul-de-sac in a quiet suburb. A further cause for celebration came when, on April 28, 2008, I learned that I had finally been recommended to serve as an elder. As elated as I was to be appointed at the relatively young age of 28, it would soon become apparent that life as an elder was not what I had imagined. Within a few weeks I was already shedding any rose-tinted notions of elders being "spirit-appointed" spiritual men who work together in harmony, with only the interests of their flock at heart.

Principally to blame for this reality check was one elder I will call Geoffrey.[13] Geoffrey was the congregation's coordinator. He had been one of the first to welcome me when I walked through the door on my debut visit to Bramhall congregation, but this initial exchange should have served as an omen for what was to follow. Immediately after introducing himself, Geoffrey warned that the congregation had a problem involving various brothers gossiping about him. He told me that, if I heard any of this gossip, I was to report straight back to him with the names of those responsible.

---

[13] I will spare any undue embarrassment or difficulties by not using actual names in this account.

By the time I was appointed an elder, I had already figured out that, far from being spurious or mean-spirited, this "gossip" to which Geoffrey alluded was actually a strong undercurrent of justified hurt and unrest among individuals in the congregation as a consequence of his mean and overbearing nature.

***Reading a Bible verse from the platform at Bramhall Kingdom Hall***

Geoffrey's own sister had found herself on the wrong end of his autocratic streak soon after joining the congregation fresh from a marital breakdown. She was initially welcomed by her brother and his family, but things soon turned sour when she began dating a young man in the congregation before her divorce papers had come through. Geoffrey ordered her to end the relationship because, according to Watchtower rules, her unresolved marital status rendered her not "scripturally free" to remarry, or (more specifically) to date with the aim of marrying someone else. When she ignored his instructions, Geoffrey set about trying to coerce his fellow elders with the objective of having his sister "marked."[14]

I thus found myself, at one of my very first elder's meetings, locked in a convoluted discussion about marking and whether it should be applied toward Geoffrey's sister for her act of defiance in ignoring his counsel—even though her divorce papers had by this point come through. The poor girl ended up being marked anyway, together with her fiancé, despite my attempts to get Geoffrey and some of the other elders to see sense. I even found myself along with another elder being reprimanded in front of the body because we had been spotted helping out at a house-moving day at which Geoffrey's sister and her fiancé were also present.

Because the couple were popular and had many friends and family members in the congregation, the debacle seriously impacted on the peace and stability. Worse still, it would soon become apparent that Geoffrey's manufactured controversy—so clearly the product of a sibling dispute rather than a genuine attempt to extend spiritual help—was not a one-off incident. I began hearing of others who had found themselves on the wrong end of his bullying and intimidation. A young man with whom I was studying was reduced to such a nervous wreck that he broke out in terrible acne. The reason? Geoffrey had threatened him with

---

[14] As mentioned in one of the footnotes of Chapter Two, "marking" is a softer form of shunning. It is used to discipline Witnesses who behave rebelliously without committing what would be considered a "gross sin." Witnesses may still speak to someone who is marked, but they may not socialize with them. They can only have dealings with them at meetings or in the preaching work. Marking begins when the actions of the individual are spelled out and condemned in a special talk (in which the individual is not named), and ends when the elders take the lead in resuming social interaction with the individual.

having all his privileges removed if he did not stop seeing a girl in a neighboring congregation by a certain deadline. I also learned that Geoffrey was responsible for causing a sister to run out of the Kingdom Hall in a flood of tears during one meeting while her husband was on the platform. On making inquiries, it turned out this was connected to Geoffrey recently counseling the man for buying a Range Rover vehicle, which he had considered a materialistic "showy display."

The more it became apparent that Geoffrey had a problem with being overly-judgmental toward congregation members—whom we as elders were supposed to be supporting and encouraging—the more I felt duty-bound as a "shepherd" to try to do something about it. I assumed the best way to approach the matter was by adding an agenda item to my suggested points for discussion at a forthcoming quarterly elder's meeting. (Elders are usually asked to provide a written list of any issues affecting the congregation they feel need to be addressed at such meetings.) The idea would be to share some generic advice from Watchtower literature relevant to the matter without naming names or pointing any fingers.

Since Geoffrey was the coordinator, I had to hand him the printed sheet of paper with this and other recommendations, which I did before leaving the Kingdom Hall at the end of one meeting. What happened next is described in the following passage from a letter I would later be required to write to the London branch office giving my version of events (the only alteration to the original text is to insert "Geoffrey" in place of the coordinator's real name, and redact the name of another elder mentioned):

> I handed the document to Geoffrey after the meeting on Sunday 4th January. Geoffrey had arrived

> late after the meeting (as I recall, because he had been giving a talk elsewhere). I therefore handed my suggestions on a printout to Geoffrey before leaving to go to my car. Apparently once I had walked out Geoffrey read my comments and immediately approached another elder, [name removed], and asked him why I had put this particular subject on the agenda. [The other elder] referred Geoffrey to speak to me. Geoffrey then caught up with my wife as she was exiting the hall and told her to wait in the car park while he went to speak to me as I was waiting in my car.
>
> Geoffrey came into my car and asked why the subject had been put on the agenda. I told Geoffrey that I thought it might be good to have a general discussion on the principles concerning counsel as a reminder to make sure that the body was on the 'same page' when it came to that issue. Not content with my explanation Geoffrey pressed me for further details and asked me if there were specific instances that had led me to feel concern over this issue. At this stage I told Geoffrey that I would continue the conversation another time and promised to phone him to speak to him about it. Geoffrey seemed to assume that this was because I urgently needed to go somewhere but it was actually because I felt quite intimidated and wanted time to think about how to approach the subject, knowing full well that the areas of concern regarding counsel involved Geoffrey exclusively.

After this disturbing incident, and on taking the advice of the circuit overseer, I decided my only recourse was to reason with Geoffrey directly and try to plead with him to ease off with his eagerness to issue counsel. This turned out to be a monumental error of judgment.

I arranged to go to Geoffrey's home one evening, Bible in hand, to thrash things out. As I had anticipated, Geoffrey responded to my advice by being extremely intimidating and trying to put me in my place. "Be very careful, Lloyd," he warned, before listing all the reasons why I had disappointed him. By the end of our conversation, I could not get out of the door quickly enough.

This incident spilled over into months of bitter wrangling, as Geoffrey insisted I be deleted as an elder for being a disrupting influence to the congregation, and for being deceitful.[15] After numerous elders' meetings (some of which lasted long into the night) and letters to and from Bethel,[16] the whole affair ended with Geoffrey getting little more than a slapped wrist while continuing as the congregation's coordinator. I, meanwhile, was stripped of almost every congregational assignment apart from being an elder.[17]

---

[15] Especially after the parking lot incident I had been so fearful and uncertain of how Geoffrey would respond to my efforts to reason with him that I took along a concealed dictaphone as protection. I only revealed the existence of the dictaphone recording once Geoffrey began denying that he said certain things in our discussion. But the fact that I had secretly recorded a private conversation ended up being of more concern to my fellow elders (and the branch office) than the possibility that Geoffrey was being dishonest. Nobody ever listened to the recording.

[16] Bethel became involved only when the body of elders began to side with me, and Geoffrey sprung a surprise on us all by revealing that he had been feeding the service desk in London his version of events for many weeks. He told us Bethel would be dealing with our dispute directly from that point on. I had assumed this was a straightforward matter that the body was more than equipped to deal with themselves, but I had underestimated Geoffrey's knowledge of how to work the system.

[17] I was told I would no longer be the overseer of the weekly Theocratic Ministry School (a program I will mention again in Chapter Eight). Furthermore, Dijana and myself were stripped of our pioneer status. It was felt that neither of us had been sufficiently pulling our weight in terms of preaching hours, so I was asked to break the news to Dijana that her eight years

As painful as it was to see my sincere efforts to stand up to Geoffrey's bullying come to nothing, this experience would pale in significance compared with a far more harrowing ordeal in my personal life involving my disintegrating marriage.

It was a Friday morning. I ran downstairs to fetch the mail. When I came back into our bedroom, Dijana had my mobile phone in her hand and was staring at it aghast. The previous day, while she had been at work, I had been involved in cybersex with a girl I had met online. The girl had texted me back since then, and Dijana had just read the message.

My initial response was one of anger. In a flurry of tears and screaming I tried to wrench the phone from Dijana. Then, as reality slowly dawned, I realized she had every right to know that the man she had married and made so many sacrifices for was a messed up person with serious issues. Over my single years I had developed a fixation with chatting online with girls, and this behavior had tragically spilled over into my marriage.

The hours and days that followed were fraught with animosity, tears, and much soul-searching. I had spent the last three months trying to correct the conduct of a fellow elder in the congregation, and here I was with my own faults now in sharp focus.

The hypocrisy of it all stemmed from my ability to compartmentalize and excuse my darker side so that

---

of pioneering in two different countries were unceremoniously at an end. Though Geoffrey initially escaped the debacle seemingly unscathed, I later learned that he was eventually removed as coordinator in 2014 for reasons connected with his attitude.

it almost did not exist. I genuinely believed that the only thing that mattered was how many people were hurt by my actions. If Dijana did not know what I was doing online, then she could not be hurt. With the Friday morning discovery, the naivety of this thinking became glaringly obvious. There can be no secrets in a marriage. Everything will come out in the wash eventually.

As you would expect, Dijana was devastated. She assumed all of this somehow reflected on her as a wife. If I was engaging in online sexual encounters with other women, then in her mind, I must have no feelings for her whatsoever. I pleaded with her that this was not the case; that I loved her and wanted to be with her, but I was fighting powerful inner urges and needed help.

Initially I tried to talk Dijana into simply forgiving me so that we could move on without involving anyone else. I intuitively knew I had reached a crossroads. I explained to her that two paths lay ahead of us. One path involved soldiering on and trying to fix our marriage without involving others. The other path involved my seeking discipline through the congregation, losing all respect and standing in the organization, and being left with really nothing to be proud of or to fight for. I had a feeling of inevitability that I was on the cusp of a downward spiral from which, due to the mountain of doubts I was already suppressing, I would never recover. The only way out of this tailspin, in my mind, was for us to deal with these problems between us rather than involve the elders.

Dijana made it clear that she wanted the intervention of the elders, no matter the outcome. After all, this was not a one-off incident. Dijana had caught me in a similar situation only a few months after we were married, and previous attempts at sorting out my issues had clearly failed. There seemed no other option than to approach the elders this time. The trouble was, I had just come out of a long and bitter feud with Geoffrey, who I knew would relish the opportunity to exact vengeance. Dijana agreed that Geoffrey was the last person to involve in fixing our problems.

We therefore decided to move back to my home congregation in Wilmslow, where I would promptly stand down as an elder, confess my sins, and accept whatever discipline was to be handed out. Wilmslow would serve as a kind of spiritual maintenance pitstop on the way to what we both decided was our ultimate objective: a fresh start in Croatia.

We had been discussing this move for some time—but now that fixing our marriage was of utmost priority rather than pursuing any organizational opportunities, there was no longer anything holding us back. Also prominent in our thinking were Dijana's parents, whose health gave us cause for concern. Furthermore, living in the UK was becoming prohibitively expensive as the country, which by this point was entering the "credit crunch," slid into recession. We were spending over £170 per month just on property taxes before paying any rent or utility bills, and we had racked up a mountain of debt in overdrafts and credit card bills. In Croatia, we could live rent-free with Dijana's parents while slowly paying off our debts. We also had the option of finishing a semi-built apartment above their home if we wanted more privacy. We decided to go ahead with this plan, and moved out of the house we were renting. Dad agreed that we could move in with him for a couple of months before we made our final move abroad.

I drove to the home of the coordinator for Wilmslow congregation and delivered a letter through his door. It offered my resignation as an elder and went into quite some detail regarding my sexual misconduct. I had hoped the amount of detail would be sufficient for the elders to deliberate quickly over how to deal with me, but this would not prove to be the case.

In a series of disciplinary meetings before a "judicial committee" comprised of three elders I was asked to go into extremely intimate detail regarding the nature of my online encounters, what precisely these involved, with whom and how often.[18] These hearings were extremely emotional. I recall breaking down in tears on at least one occasion. At the time I did not feel the nature of questioning was overly invasive or inappropriate. I believed I was receiving needed discipline from God's organization, and I simply had to man up and see it through for the benefit of my marriage. Of course, I now cringe at the thought of sharing such personal matters with men who had no more right to this information than my local postman or storekeeper, but at the time I was convinced it was necessary.[19]

---

[18] One elder from Bramhall was drafted in to sit on the three-man committee. It would not surprise me if this was at Geoffrey's insistence. I now look back with some relief that, during my brief time as an elder, I was never called upon to deliberate at one of these tribunals.

[19] When preparing this chapter I came across the letters and emails I sent to Wilmslow and Bramhall elders over this period, which are still on my hard drive and now make for disturbing reading. The tone is self-abasing as I prostrate myself, scrambling to avoid disfellowshipping at a time when rescuing my marriage should have been my only concern. It is obvious that I was a completely different, more servile person than I am now, and acting under powerful forces I was then unable to comprehend.

Finally, a decision was reached that I would not be disfellowshipped. Instead, I would be "publicly reproved." This involved an announcement being read in both Bramhall and Wilmslow Kingdom Halls that I had been reproved for some unspecified sin. Normally such an announcement is deemed necessary only if the indiscretion is widely known, but for some reason (I believe due to my recent dispute with Geoffrey) it was decided that members of both congregations needed to know that I had done something seriously wrong. As well as no longer being an elder, "restrictions" would be imposed. I would be prohibited from offering comments during meeting items or giving talks for some months.

It felt as though my downfall was complete, but I was prepared to go through the disgrace and humiliation if this was the price for correcting my problems and starting a new life with Dijana. After everything that I had put her through, she would be my focus from this point forward.

Before long, it was time for us to relocate. We had decided to tow our belongings in a horse-box trailer that we bought on eBay—but we were unaware when collecting it that it dated to the '50s, and the wheels (one of which fell off shortly after we bought it) were so outdated it was impossible to replace them. We paid a Wilmslow elder who was also a mechanic to perform a makeshift repair and resolved to drive at 50 mph or slower all the way to Croatia. However, we only made it as far as Birmingham (85 miles) before beholding the terrifying spectacle of one of our trailer wheels rolling past our car as we snaked downhill across several lanes of the M6 freeway. After regaining control and pulling over, we called the tow truck and had it take the horse-box back to Manchester while we carried on in our old Ford Mondeo with less than half our belongings. The car had an overheating engine, so we had to stop every two hours to top off the water during the long drive across Europe. I am still not sure how we completed the journey.[20]

After a stressful two days on the road we were relieved to make it to Croatia on August 30, 2009. Dijana's parents were delighted to finally have us with them. They had been without their daughter for three years, and I could tell they had missed her. Their house, where we still live, is in a small one-road village 20 minutes' drive south of Sisak. From living in the suburbs of Manchester, we now found ourselves in a quiet rural community where people grow their own produce and keep livestock. Tractor engines chugging, roosters crowing, geese honking and dogs barking make up a large part of the typical ambience. When we first arrived, it felt like an idyllic place to take some time out and build a new life together without disturbance.

The local Sisak congregation was extremely welcoming. In the time it takes to find your seat at the Kingdom Hall you feel like you have shaken the hands of everyone in the town, such is the warmth and enthusiasm. At the time, the congregation had approximately 100 publishers and only a handful of elders. There was initial excitement when I arrived because, being an MTS graduate, it was assumed I could help ease the burden on the overstretched elder body. But I made it clear as soon as I arrived that this would not be possible, at least for some time. I told them I was under restrictions that had been placed on me back in the UK, concerning which they would shortly be informed.[21]

---

[20] The car would die completely a month after our arrival.

[21] Usually when a person moves between congregations a "letter of recommendation" needs to follow them from their

For the time being I would only be allowed to attend meetings and go in the preaching work. Not that this presented a huge problem for me, since I could barely speak Croatian anyway and would have found it daunting to prepare meaningful comments or talks.

It would take nine months for my restrictions to be lifted, but by the end of this period I had undergone an unexpected transformation. The cautionary advice given to me by a close friend back home was to prove extremely astute.

Christian had been the best man at my wedding. It was he who had collected me at the train station in Manchester when I first began my forays from college to meet up with the pioneers more than ten years earlier. We had been through a great deal together: navigating girl troubles, writing songs, playing in a wedding band and going on numerous vacations. He had even joined me on a trip to New York to tour Watchtower's Brooklyn, Patterson and Wallkill facilities in 2003. Christian was the only one of my close friends to make the drive down to Cornwall to be with me when Mum died. He was, without a doubt, my best friend. He was also one of the most sincere believers I knew, and he was visibly shaken when I told him of the reasons for my reproof. When Dijana and I then revealed our plans for Croatia, Christian was adamant that we should not make the move. He warned that I would essentially be disconnecting myself from the organization for a while due to the language barrier. Christian had served in foreign-language congregations in the UK, so he knew how challenging it was to

---

old congregation to tell the new elders whether they are in "good standing" or not. Quite often, the letter takes some time to arrive—especially if it needs to be translated by the branch office.

maintain interest at meetings when you can comprehend so little of what is said.

I shrugged off the advice, convinced that a fresh start in Croatia was precisely what Dijana and I needed. I felt that, despite what had happened, my faith could withstand anything that lay ahead. I could not conceive ever letting the language barrier get in the way of my relationship with Jehovah.

But it did not take long for Christian's concerns to be vindicated. Though I was attending meetings twice-weekly, this soon became a mere formality as I could barely understand a word of what was said. I found the whole routine of meetings, ministry and assemblies intensely boring and uninspiring. Devoid of any intellectual stimulation during these periods, I would often retreat into my thoughts. I began to ask myself: "What do I *really* believe?"

Long-suppressed doubts began to surface. Unplugged from the constant flow of indoctrination for the first time in my life, I soon made an alarming discovery: in my heart, I had stopped being a Witness a long time ago. It occurred to me that the lack of sincere commitment to my beliefs was at least partly to blame for the game of brinksmanship I had been playing with the rules on sex over the years. I had tried to offset the repression imposed on me since puberty by exploiting any loopholes that could keep my conscience and libido in some state of equilibrium. In my heart I had known it was not the "Truth" all along, so I had never given the moral codes the reverence I was supposed to. There was no impetus to observe rules I had suspected were manmade from the start.

It took only four months after our move for me to feel the need to address the reality that my faith was collapsing. After an emotional exchange with Dijana, I decided to retreat to another part of the house to write her a letter attempting to explain what was going on in my mind. I found it easier to articulate my feelings in writing rather than risk feeling pressured, in the heat of the moment, to say something I did not mean. The handwritten letter, dated January 1, 2010, was the only way I could bring myself to put into words the shocking realization I had come to. Here is the crucial part:

> You asked me moments ago what the "bottom line" is, and the bottom line is I'm scared to death. I've never been more anxious in my life. For the first time I am seriously considering disassociating myself as one of Jehovah's Witnesses. That sounds terrible and I can't believe I've just put it in writing, but that's how I feel.

I had reached a tipping point. Even though I was nowhere near fully awake from my indoctrination, the very fact that I could commit the idea of leaving to words on a page showed that it was only a matter of time.

Dijana was incredibly supportive given the circumstances. Though still a believer, she understood that my doubts were genuine. Her only concern was whether I might be using them as a pretext to leave her, but I was able to convince her this was not the case. I really was losing my faith, but it did not have to mean the end of our relationship.

With all this off my chest, over the months that followed I was content to go through the motions of pretending to be a Witness, at least heartened that I did not have to keep anything secret from my wife. By the early summer of 2010, I was back on the platform giving Bible readings for the Theocratic Ministry School component of the meeting. This was the most basic assignment a male Witness could receive at the time, but it was all my limited Croatian would allow. During my time as an elder, I would often be called on to not only act as "school overseer" (host for the school) introducing the students, but also to stand in for them occasionally by giving impromptu talk segments on various topics if students did not show up. Now, though, here I was fighting my way through the most basic Bible recitation in a strange language.

In October 2010, we had a visit from my dad. He and I were in the habit of speaking every week on the phone, but it was nice to finally have him with us in person for the first time since our move. Toward the end of his stay, he and I made the one-hour journey into Zagreb. Dijana had arranged for the two of us to receive a tour of the Croatian Bethel complex. Dad seemed to enjoy the whole thing immensely. The journey back home, however, would prove less pleasurable. During the drive, I blurted out: "Dad, I don't think this is God's organization."

Dad, who was driving, was visibly stunned.

"I don't know what to say Lloyd," he said. "I wish I could help you, but I don't think I would be the best person because it's too emotional for me."

And that was all that was said on the matter. The remainder of the journey passed mostly in silence.

Soon it was time for Dad to return home. He gave me a lingering hug before getting in his car and driving back to the UK. I felt a mixture of pride and shame: pride that I had verbalized to my father how I sincerely felt; shame that I had so clearly disappointed him.

As hard as I tried to be an active but secretly non-believing Witness, by May 2011 I had reached another crossroads. One Sunday morning I skipped the meeting and, while the house was empty, I wrote down a list of grievances with the organization: nine things I was dubious about, or no longer agreed with.[22] Seeing all my doubts together on paper in front of me somehow made them more real, and I felt regret at having suppressed them for so long. When Dijana returned home I showed her the list. She could not refute any of my criticisms. In fact, she agreed with many of them.

By now I was doing the bare minimum of one hour per month of ministry to keep myself from being noted as "irregular." This involved briefly accompanying Dijana or someone from the congregation in the preaching work without saying anything, because—quite apart from no longer believing—my limited Croatian was still completely insufficient for me to say anything thought-provoking.

I felt as though I was living somebody else's life, and I simply could not take it any longer. A few days after compiling my nine grievances I wrote another emotional letter to Dijana. The relevant parts are as follows:

> To get to the point, one of the things I've definitely decided is that I am definitely going to become an "inactive publisher." It's no longer a case of "if" but "when." It may even be as soon as the end of this month, because I don't think I can face anoth-

[22] The nine grievances were: (1) claims that an increase in numbers proves divine blessing, (2) the focus on Bible prophecy applying to early Witnesses, (3) the rules on masturbation, (4) the denial of evolution, (5) an inconsistent prophetic explanation in the *Daniel* book related to the "King of the North," (6) the stigmatizing of higher education, (7) the "new light" teaching, (8) claims that the Governing Body "represents" spirit-anointed Christians without contacting them, and (9) suspicions over the number of memorial partakers never dropping below 7,000 (as it turned out, this number would soon start rising).

> er hour of "fake" ministry, or another costly and completely pointless trip to some basketball court in Zagreb for a convention. . . .
>
> Another reason why I strongly believe I should become inactive sooner rather than wait any longer is because I want to leave while I still have a shred of respect for JWs. The more I go to meetings and assemblies, the more angry it makes me, and I'm afraid that if I carry on much longer it will make me very bitter and openly opposed to JWs, and I don't want that at all.

Dijana again sympathized with my situation. It could not have been easy for her to process the rapidly shifting parameters of our relationship, especially since she had once told me that the only reason she could think of for no longer loving me would be if I were to abandon the "Truth." But Dijana knew she was under no pressure to join me in dropping long-held beliefs. This was about me being true to myself and no longer living a lie. She therefore helped me with writing a letter to the Sisak elders communicating my decision to be "inactive"—to cease all activities as a Jehovah's Witness. The relevant part read as follows:

> I am writing to tell you about my intention to stop reporting as an active publisher from the end of this month. I will also no longer be attending meetings for the foreseeable future, and for these reasons I will obviously need to stand aside from my participation in the Theocratic Ministry School as well as my microphone responsibilities, although I would like to thank you for these privileges, which I have enjoyed.
>
> My decision was by no means taken lightly, but with a great deal of thought after a long and gradual process of soul-searching on my part ever since my reproving two years ago.

> My inability to rekindle my enthusiasm for service has been due to serious doubts about my beliefs and Jehovah's Witnesses as an organization, particularly the legitimacy of the Governing Body as God's earthly representatives. . . .
>
> Since I arrived in Croatia, I have been happy to attend meetings for the benefit of my family so as not to cause any embarrassment to them. However, I don't believe that this alone is sufficient reason for someone to continue joining themselves to a religion that they no longer believe. Everyone should "make the truth their own," and as I no longer feel in my heart that this is the truth, despite knowing more than many about the history and beliefs of Jehovah's Witnesses, I no longer think it appropriate that I should pretend to be one.
>
> My most compelling reason for becoming inactive is that I am becoming increasingly agitated at what I hear and observe within the organization, and I think it's important to leave now rather than allow any bitterness to develop, which could lead to apostasy (i.e. trying to turn people away from the organization). I would rather leave now while I still have some respect and positive thoughts about Jehovah's Witnesses in general.

I look back on that letter now with astonishment that my elders did not accept it as a letter of "disassociation," since I essentially told them I no longer believed and did not want to continue as a Witness in any meaningful sense. Most elders reading this would have taken it as a resignation and washed their hands of me there and then. Instead, two elders decided to pay me a visit as a last throw of the dice at convincing me to continue worshipping with the congregation.[23]

[23] I will explain what disassociation is, and how it differs from disfellowshipping, in a later chapter.

I made it clear to them that I harbored no animosity, that the brothers could stop by and visit any time they wanted, and that I would still be attending the Memorial each year. These assurances seemed to satisfy them somewhat.[24] I went on to tell them that, despite lacking resentment and ill-feeling, I had reached an impasse with my faith and it was improper for me to try to convince people of something I could not be sure of myself.

The meeting turned out to be very emotional. At one point all three of us were sobbing. More tears were shed when I later phoned Dad to inform him of my decision. I could sense in his voice that he was devastated. There are few worse feelings for most sons than the awareness of failing to live up to a father's expectations. It was soul-crushing for me to process this new reality. From being an elder and source of pride in Dad's eyes just a few months ago, I would now forever be a cause of shame and disappointment.

Despite the painful reverberations of my decision among dismayed Witness family and friends, becoming inactive proved to be an enormous relief. There was a strong sense of standing up for oneself and

---

[24] The Memorial is the annual commemoration of Christ's death, held by Jehovah's Witnesses after sundown on Nisan 14 of the Jewish calendar. An explanatory talk is given and the two "emblems" of the Last Supper (or Lord's Evening Meal), namely the wine and unleavened bread, are passed from person to person in respectful silence. Only someone who is convinced that they are going to heaven is permitted to "partake" of the emblems by eating the bread or drinking the wine. Attendance at the Memorial is normally higher than for normal meetings, because failure to attend is considered a lack of respect for the ransom and a sign of no longer believing. In 2015, 19,862,783 attended the Memorial—more than double the 8,220,105 peak Witnesses for the same year. Only 15,177 partook of the emblems. I will discuss Memorial partakers in more detail in Chapter Eight.

finally gaining some freedom. Almost instantly I had diminished reservations about seriously scrutinizing the beliefs with which I had been indoctrinated. Up to that point I had steadfastly observed Watchtower's guidance to do research using only the organization's publications. Books or websites that could be considered "apostate" in nature are considered strictly off limits for Witnesses, who are warned that their "safety lies in avoiding apostate propaganda as though it were poison, which in fact it is."

At some subconscious level I had always suspected the scorn hurled at apostate websites to be more about fostering paranoia in pursuit of Watchtower's interests than any genuine desire to protect Witnesses. Even so, crossing the threshold into viewing information that is considered contraband by Watchtower gave me a knot in the stomach—a tangible sense of danger and foreboding. I was rebelling against everything I knew, but there was little to hold me back now that I had made my stand known to both my family and the local congregation.

I had already laid some groundwork for my investigations with visits to Wikipedia over previous months. The idea had been to gain a neutral, third party perspective on my faith.[25] I had also been rattled when Wikipedia was derided in Watchtower's *2011 Yearbook*, which cited it as an example of "poorly documented Web entries written by unidentified or unqualified persons." This criticism incensed me, since exactly the same accusations could be leveled at those writing articles in *Watchtower* magazines—individuals who

---

[25] I have since learned that Wikipedia articles are edited by both current and former Witnesses, making the website a bit of a battleground between the two opposing camps.

never give any names and cite no credentials. And why the need for such an attack? In lambasting an objective website like Wikipedia, what was the organization so anxious to hide?

It turned out Wikipedia indeed had some interesting things to say about the Witnesses that aligned closely with my own misgivings. One entry in particular noted a significant oddity about the Governing Body, namely the fact that (at that time) they were claiming to act as representatives of the few thousand Witnesses who had a hope of going to heaven, despite putting forth no effort whatsoever to consult with such ones.[26] This simple observation made an impact on me, so much so that it had been included on my list of nine grievances. But here I was, now officially an inactive Witness, and ready to move up a gear. The time had come to finally take the plunge and see what a dreaded "apostate" website had to say.

I visited JWfacts.com.

Before delving too deeply into its pages, I skirted through the website in an effort to find out who was behind it in the hope of establishing his or her intentions. The site's owner, Paul Grundy, had posted a picture of himself with his young boy. I felt instantly reassured that Paul appeared to be a normal guy, a family man—not some crazy, sinister-looking fanatic. Once at ease with actually reading the pages, I noticed that Paul had a very non-confrontational tone toward Witnesses. He acknowledged that his visitors were entitled to continue in their beliefs despite reading his research if they so wished. He also had an open offer for anyone noticing anything nonfactual on his website to contact him so that he could correct it.

---

[26] I will touch on this in more detail in Chapter Eight.

As I took in more information, I found the revelations on JWfacts simply astounding. Rutherford wrote a letter to Hitler trying to reconcile with him? Watchtower was once an NGO member of the United Nations?[26] It quickly became obvious that my nine grievances were just the tip of the iceberg in comparison with the many scandals and false teachings strewn across Watchtower's history.

Among the sources cited by one of the articles was a book titled *Crisis of Conscience*, by Raymond Franz. I had heard of this book before. A former member of the Governing Body had turned apostate and written a book encouraging other Witnesses to do the same—or so I had been told. But was that the full story? I managed to find a website offering a PDF download of the book for five dollars. The revelations Franz's book presented, including events he had witnessed first-hand over his nine years at the very pinnacle of the organization, were mind-blowing. I felt much like the character Dorothy in *The Wizard of Oz* in the scene where the curtain is pulled back to reveal an old man flailing around with levers. My eyes were opened, and I could not unsee what I had seen even if I wanted to. Watchtower was now exposed for what it truly was: just one in a long line of religious scams masquerading as God's one true church.

At first I found it almost impossible to contain my astonishment at what I was learning. I made the mistake of emailing one or two Witness friends and family members to let them know about my inactivity and how this was based on a number of issues I was unable to resolve. Two friends immediately offered

---

[27] Both of these matters will be explored in detail in later chapters.

to fly to Croatia to try to talk some sense into me. I began a lengthy email exchange with one of them (an MTS classmate) in an attempt to explain what I was learning, but it soon became apparent that this was a fruitless and potentially dangerous course to pursue. If I said anything to identify myself as an "apostate" I could soon end up disfellowshipped and cut off from my family. I therefore decided it was pointless trying to defend my position. After making some excuses about being depressed, I abandoned any further attempts to share my discoveries with friends back home.

Meanwhile, it seemed my local elders in Sisak were beginning to regret letting me off the hook so leniently. Even though they had initially dealt with my decision gracefully, things turned sour after one elder joined the congregation from the branch office in Zagreb. In contrast to his amiable, not-so-trigger-happy counterparts, he was an *enforcer*—more clued-in regarding organizational procedure and intent on laying down the law. On learning of my sudden inactivity, he was apparently frustrated that his fellow elders had not given me more of a roasting regarding my motives. In his mind, it seemed, I had escaped too easily and there were questions that needed answering. Was there some hidden sin that required further discipline? Might this sin be the reason why I was distancing myself from the congregation?

Things came to a head when, at the end of one meeting (at which I was not present) the Enforcer pulled Dijana to one side and quizzed her in a backroom as to the reasons for my inactivity. It was explained that I must be involved in some wrongdoing requiring the intervention of the elders. The Enforcer then set about trying to extract information from Dijana by telling her (in Croatian): "I know Lloyd treats you like a rag for cleaning the floor." Dijana was taken aback by his tone. She certainly did not feel I was treating her in such a way, and was amazed that an elder who did not know me and had barely spoken more than a few words to me since his arrival could leap to such a scathing conclusion.

When I learned of this incident, I felt a sinking feeling. It seemed the net was closing. If the elders were breaking their own rules in their enthusiasm to incriminate me, then surely it was only a matter of time before I would be facing judicial action. My apprehension was only exacerbated by reading of how Ray Franz had been hounded from the organization in 1980-1981.[28]

It occurred to me that I urgently needed to brace Dad for the worst while there was still time. In a phone conversation I relayed what had happened at the Kingdom Hall, and told him it was possible I would soon be disfellowshipped. Dad's response to this news shocked me. He confirmed that, if that were to happen, even if on an unjust basis, he would shun me nonetheless.

"It would kill me to do it Lloyd, but I would do it all the same," he said.

Though I was devastated to learn that Dad was willing to put his loyalty to the Governing Body ahead of his relationship with his own son, I knew I could not be mad at him. He was reacting as any loyal Witness is expected to. If Watchtower tells you to do something, you do it—no matter how painful or inexplicable. As a subsequent *Watchtower* article would put it (describing the need for compliance as Armageddon approaches):

> All of us must be ready to obey any instructions we may receive, whether these appear sound from a strategic or human standpoint or not.

---

[28] This will be discussed in more detail in Chapter Eight.

As my predicament worsened, I received a phone call asking if it would be possible for the elders to meet with me. Dijana took the call, due to my limited Croatian. When she asked about the reason for the meeting, she was told it was merely to offer me "encouragement." Dijana thanked the elder, but told him this would not be needed. She was then informed of a second reason for the visit.

Not long before, the elder who was now calling had invited us for a meal at his home. During the evening, as part of the small talk the elder had asked various questions about our translation business, which was keeping us financially afloat following our move from the UK.[29] We had mentioned in passing that occasionally we would swap work with other Witness translators, and outsource projects to them on a freelance basis if we had too much to handle by ourselves. This innocuous nugget of information was now apparently deemed evidence of my conspiring to stay inside the organization purely so I could extract cheap labor from Witnesses who worked for me. Again, a damning verdict had been reached based on nothing but my elders' apparent haste to think the very worst of one of their "sheep."

The request for a meeting took on an even more serious tone when the elder let slip that he felt I was having difficulties that they needed to "sort out before the circuit overseer's visit." I was therefore a problem to be "sorted out" by a certain deadline. The impending visit of this Watchtower representative meant the clock was well and truly ticking.

---

[29] I am not particularly good at translating myself, since my Croatian is not fluent enough. However, because Dijana speaks both languages we can provide good quality translations, since Dijana can translate into native-standard Croatian, and I can proofread any translations from Croatian into fluent English.

As the phone call continued, I could tell Dijana was floundering under the pressure. She was at this point a believing Witness and still under the illusion that her elders had authority over her. I told her to end the call and tell the elder we would call him back with a decision. After discussing the situation together, we quickly agreed that there was absolutely no way the elders should be allowed to visit—especially considering the way they had handled the situation thus far. When Dijana called the elder back, she communicated a message from me that I felt they were conducting their affairs entirely contrary to the procedures outlined for them by the organization. If their version of offering "encouragement" entailed pulling my wife to one side at the Kingdom Hall and interrogating her about her husband, accusing him of treating her "like a rag for cleaning the floor" without him being present, then I would have to decline their offer. From that moment on, I would accept no elder visits until an apology was forthcoming.

As I fully expected, no apology came. Thus commenced a lengthy stand-off that would buy me some time and keep me beyond the reach of my elders, at least for a while. In the intervening window, I had the space to continue my research into the organization and figure out precisely how I had been deceived.

I took up the pseudonym "John Cedars" and joined a number of discussions on ex-JW forums, gathering information and then turning my findings into forum posts and blog articles.[30] I soon struck up a friendship

[30] I came up with this pseudonym so that I could post anonymously on an ex-JW forum. The thread on which I made my first ever post as an "apostate" was concerning a historic Bible Student convention at Cedar Point, Ohio, in 1922. I had shared some information with Paul Grundy about the DVD *Je-*

with a veteran ex-JW activist named John Hoyle, whom you will remember from earlier in this chapter. John was the webmaster for a number of JW-related websites. When I found myself involved in a controversy with other ex-JWs on a forum post, he came to my rescue out of the blue.

Still rather naive and bristling with ideas, I had proposed that a survey should be launched to find out how many current and former Witnesses disagreed with Watchtower teachings. I suspected this would require money, but I felt the end product would be well worth it—and I was more than willing to do the legwork and arrange everything. I worked out I would need $400 for a year's subscription to SurveyMonkey.com—a professional online survey provider—and began asking for this amount to get things moving. Predictably, this did not go down well with my fellow forum members. There was a fierce backlash, in which I was accused of trying to run a scam.

John contacted me privately and offered to help. He said he could build a website to host my survey. To my astonishment, he asked for nothing in return, and said it would not cost anything to set up.

It all seemed too good to be true, but I had nothing to lose. I accepted John's offer, and JWsurvey.org was launched in October 2011. Still going strong today with

---

*hovah's Witnesses—Faith in Action, Part 1: Out of Darkness* which presented a reenactment of the convention in such a way that the American flag, which can be seen on black-and-white photos of the event, was no longer in view. This, in my opinion, was an attempt to doctor the historical record of evidence that Jehovah's Witnesses (or Bible Students, as Watchtower followers were then called) were once just as nationalistic as any other group. After seeing people commenting on the subject, I chose the first name that sprang to mind, "Cedars," so that I could join the fray.

around 110,000 visits per month, the website now has a small editorial team covering JW-related news stories, and hosts a regular survey for canvassing opinions on JW beliefs and practices. In 2015, this survey attracted 6,083 participants, over a thousand of whom claimed to be active Witnesses.[31]

The first few years after my awakening were certainly a roller-coaster ride—a ride that continues in many ways. But before I take you further along in my story, perhaps it would be best to hit the rewind button to give you a deeper insight into the history of Jehovah's Witnesses. I firmly believe that only by understanding the origins of this little-understood movement can one fully appreciate how it has come to be so influential in the lives of millions of people, myself included.

---

[31] The results of these global surveys are published yearly on JWsurvey.org.

CHAPTER SIX

# The Pastor

*"Never make predictions, especially about the future."*
—Casey Stengel

*"Expectation is the root of all heartache."*
—William Shakespeare

1844 was a remarkable year. It was a year in which two fledgling American evangelical movements reached their respective formative crossroads. June 27 saw Joseph Smith Jr., founder of the Mormons, lying in a pool of blood after being shot in a jail in Carthage, Illinois. Smith's death plunged the early Mormon church into a leadership crisis, from which Brigham Young would emerge as successor.

Nearly four months later, early Adventism was to go through its own upheaval when the predicted date of Christ's second coming on October 22 yielded no such thing. The date would go down in history as the "Great Disappointment," since thousands of followers of William Miller bought into his prediction that this date would mark the Lord's return. Some frustrated believers, for whom "disappointment" seems a massive understatement, even sold all their belongings in expectation of a rapture that was not to be.

One man who had fallen under Miller's spell, although apparently not to the point of destitution, was George Storrs. Once a Methodist minister, Storrs had something of an epiphany in 1837 after picking up and reading a leaflet on a train journey.[1] Penned by a certain Henry Grew, the leaflet persuaded Storrs to believe in "conditionalism"—the concept that the soul does not automatically survive a person's death, and that you can only achieve immortality on condition that this is bestowed on you as a gift from God through Christ. This and other doctrinal deviations from what Storrs had previously believed moved him to resign from the Methodist church in 1840 and pursue his own investigations into the Bible, which led him to briefly align with Miller and his end-time predictions.

By 1842, Storrs had become a leading promoter of Miller's claim that Christ's return (or "advent") would occur some time between March 21, 1843, and March 21, 1844. When that period passed with no evidence of the Lord's return, Miller and his followers returned to the drawing board and came up with a revised date of April 18, 1844. When this date also failed, October 22, 1844, was settled on. Needless to say, only further anticlimax ensued.

After this string of failures, Storrs finally admitted he had allowed himself to become "drawn into Mr. Miller's theory for a time." He thus abandoned a movement that would go on to spawn a plethora of sects such as the Christadelphians, the Life and Advent Union, the Advent Christian Church, the Seventh-Day Adventists and—well into the 20th century—the Worldwide Church of God. All of these denominations were to enshrine the concept of conditionalism in their

[1] You will find this fateful train journey reenacted at around the 9-minute mark on the DVD *Jehovah's Witnesses—Faith in Action, Part 1: Out of Darkness.* The video is also available for viewing or downloading on JW.org.

teachings, arguably thanks to Storrs' fleeting but influential involvement.

It was during the countdown to the Great Disappointment that Storrs launched a newspaper titled *The Bible Examiner* in 1843. Through this journal and other publications, Storrs' unique brand of Christianity would decades later come to the attention of someone who was not even a twinkle in his parents' eyes when the first issue of *The Bible Examiner* rolled off the press—a Pennsylvania businessman by the name of Charles Taze Russell. Russell was born in 1852 in Pittsburgh to Joseph Lytel and Eliza Birney Russell, of Scottish-Irish descent. At age fourteen he began taking an active role in his father's clothing store. By the time Russell was in his late twenties, he and his father had expanded the business into a number of stores through which they amassed considerable wealth.

**Charles Taze Russell**

Despite taking an interest in religion as a boy, Russell had become disillusioned with Christianity by around the age of sixteen. He would later write: "Brought up a Presbyterian, indoctrinated from the Catechism, and being naturally of an enquiring mind, I fell a ready prey to the logic of infidelity, as soon as I began to think for myself."

But Russell's flirtation with atheism was to be fleeting. In 1869, he happened upon an Adventist meeting in Allegheny, Pennsylvania, where a preacher by the name of Jonas Wendell was giving a sermon. Though Wendell's sermon did little to persuade young Russell to become an Adventist, it did succeed in reinvigorating his interest in the Bible. As a result, Russell set up a small study group with his father and a few friends, and began scrutinizing some of the ideas being shared around at the time.

Though a number of Russell's contemporaries and predecessors contributed greatly to the formulation of his teachings, he only ever accredited the influence of three individuals by name in his writings—two of them appreciatively, the third not so. As he later wrote in 1906:

> I should and do gratefully mention assistance rendered by Brothers Geo[rge] Stetson and Geo[rge] Storrs, the latter the editor of *The Bible Examiner,* both now deceased. The study of the Word of God with these dear brethren led, step by step, into greener pastures and brighter hopes for the world.

M. James Penton is a former Witness, retired professor of history and religious studies, and noted Watchtower scholar. His book *Apocalypse Delayed: The Story of Jehovah's Witnesses* (now in its third edition) is the definitive reference work on the early history of Jehovah's Witnesses, and has a lot to say about Russell in particular—including those who influenced him. Penton remarks that "it is quite obvious that Storrs contributed much to the young [Russell's] thinking," adding:

> An examination of the *Bible Examiner* indicates clearly that Russell learned the doctrines of the ransom atonement of Christ and the restitution of mankind to a paradise earth directly from Storrs and his associates plus, of course, the doctrine of

> conditionalism. It is evident, too, that the practice of celebrating the Memorial of the Lord's Supper once a year on the supposed date of the Jewish Passover, 14 Nisan, as is done by Jehovah's Witnesses today, was learned by Russell from the editor of the *Bible Examiner.*

(So next time a Jehovah's Witness thrusts a Memorial invitation into your hands, remember you have George Storrs to thank.)

But these were not the only beliefs that Russell would assimilate during his early studies. He also developed a keen interest in Bible chronology, thanks in no small measure to the writings of one Dr. Nelson H. Barbour, who makes up the third, less celebrated member in the aforementioned trinity of Russell's acknowledged early mentors alongside Storrs and Stetson.[2]

Barbour, like Storrs, had been swept along by the Millerite movement in expectation of Christ's return in 1843-1844. He later wrote despairingly of the aftermath of the Great Disappointment:

> We held together until the autumn of 1844. Then, as if a raft floating in deep water should suddenly disappear from under its living burden, so our platform went from under us, and we made for shore in every direction; but our unity was gone, and, like drowning men, we caught at straws.

Left thoroughly despondent by his experiences with Miller, Barbour immersed himself in a colorful array of mostly nonclerical pursuits. He first made a living as a

---

[2] George Stetson was an Advent Christian minister and associate of Jonas Wendell, George Storrs, Charles Taze Russell and Henry Grew (who penned the leaflet found by Storrs on the train). Stetson lived with Watchtower's little-known first president, William Henry Conley (president of Zion's Watch Tower Tract Society from 1881 to 1884), for the final year of his life. His dying wish was that Russell deliver his funeral sermon.

***William Miller (1782–1849)***

***George Storrs (1796–1879)***

***George Stetson (1815–1879)***

***Nelson Barbour (1824–1905)***

"medical electrician"—someone who electrocuted people as a form of "therapy." Later he tried his hand as an inventor, and even prospected for gold in Australia.

It was during Barbour's 1859 return voyage from Australia that a shipboard conversation with a clergyman is said to have rejuvenated his interest in Bible prophecy. On returning home, Barbour immersed himself in study and quickly concluded that he had been wrong all along about Christ's second coming. It was actually scheduled for 1873—29 years later than

Miller had predicted. So convinced was Barbour of his calculations that he enthusiastically declared the good news in various publications, most notably his own newspaper—*Herald of the Morning.*

As 1873 drew to a close without incident, Barbour made a minor adjustment. "I am still enforcing the 1873 arguments with more faith and a greater zeal than ever," he wrote, "though I do not expect the Lord until the seventh month of 1874." When 1874 proved similarly uneventful, Barbour and his growing band of followers were not overly disheartened. They concluded that Christ *had* arrived in that year after all, but had simply chosen to do so invisibly. This conclusion was reached after someone rather conveniently pointed out that *pa·rou·si′a*, the Greek word used in the Bible to denote Christ's coming, can also mean "presence," thus putting a whole new spin on things. The fact that there was no visible evidence of Christ's arrival in 1874 did not necessarily mean he was not there. (Needless to say, if Miller had only come up with this idea in 1844, probably fewer people would have been quite so disappointed.)

Less than three years later, in January 1876, Charles Russell opened his mail to find a copy of Barbour's *Herald of the Morning.* As Russell later wrote, somewhat tongue-in-cheek:

> When I opened it I at once identified it with Adventism from the picture on its cover, and examined it with some curiosity to see what time they would next set for the burning of the world.

To his surprise, despite his well-founded reservations about Adventists being a group then obsessed with apocalyptic date-setting, Russell found himself nodding along with Barbour's ideas—especially the rather neat concept of Christ's presence being invisible.

This chimed with what he and his own associates were coming to understand about Christ's second coming: that its purpose would be "not to destroy, but to bless all the families of the earth, and that his coming would be thieflike, and not in flesh, but as a spirit-being, invisible to men."

Thus, the *pa·rou·si′a* concept, which was arguably invented out of necessity by Adventists who were desperate to resuscitate Barbour's failed 1874 prediction, came to be the catalyst for Russell's enthusiastic pursuit of a new line of inquiry: Bible prophecy and end-time chronology. These, in turn, were to become foundational elements of the Witness faith. Events of biblical magnitude no longer had to be observable in order to be proclaimed as underway. Lack of visual verification was of little concern. It was all simply a matter of faith (and knowing a thing or two about Greek).

Invigorated by Barbour's predictions, which were the missing piece in his doctrinal jigsaw, Russell arranged to meet the man in person. As he later wrote:

> I paid Mr. Barbour's expenses to come to see me at Philadelphia . . . to show me fully and Scripturally, if he could, that the prophecies indicated 1874 as the date at which the Lord's presence and 'the harvest' began. He came, and the evidence satisfied me.

Russell found in Barbour someone who was able to fill in the blanks in his own Bible research, giving everything a sense of tremendous urgency. End-time Bible prophecies did not merely foretell events in the distant future, but events that were either already in progress or due imminently. The two men, along with their colleagues, thus decided to join forces in spreading the word about their revelation. The world needed to know that Christ had been ruling in heaven since

1874, and was now gathering his "harvest" of true Christians unto him.

As eccentric and naive as their beliefs now appear, it is at least heartening to note the apparent sincerity with which Russell and Barbour embarked on their evangelical escapades. Russell in particular not only sold his business and invested his fortune in pursuit of spreading the message—he also pinned his name and reputation on the outlandish predictions of someone who had previously electrocuted people for a living, despite knowing his new partner's claims had only a brief window before being proven true or false. Such reckless, self-defeating actions do not speak of a calculated, cynical scam artist—more of a credulous fool who was rather too easily persuaded to open his checkbook.

Russell thus used his financial clout to bankroll Barbour's ailing newspaper *Herald of the Morning*, the masthead of which began to carry his name as one of the assistant editors. He also gave Barbour "money and instructions to prepare in concise book-form the good tidings so far as then understood, including the time features." The resulting volume, published in 1877, was given the arresting title *Three Worlds, and the Harvest of This World* in reference to Barbour's ideas that the history of mankind could be divided into three "worlds," or periods of time.

The aim of *Three Worlds* was to explain the math behind Barbour's rather convoluted eschatological beliefs, and in so doing declare the imminent fulfillment of Bible prophecy just a few months from its publication. According to its bold predictions, the "saints" (i.e. Barbour, Russell, and their growing band of associates) could expect to be caught up to heaven by Christ by no later than April 6, 1878. "Let me urge you," warned

Barbour, "a few months and 'The harvest will be past, the summer ended.'" Barbour and Russell were setting themselves up for yet another great disappointment.

Though Russell was enthused by the message of *Three Worlds* and sponsored its publication and distribution, his colleague George Storrs was understandably more guarded, having learned more from 1844 than Barbour evidently had. In the *Bible Examiner* of July 1877, Storrs wrote:

> The Chronology is the best I have ever seen; but it is impossible for me to assent to all the conclusions the writer has arrived at, as to the events; yet I feel no disposition to oppose his views by way of controversy. A few months will determine the accuracy of the ground he has taken as to the withdrawal of the saints from the earth.

Storrs' pragmatic "let's wait and see" approach apparently did not sit well with Russell, who expected unqualified support for *Three Worlds* from his mentor. Taking to the pages of *Herald of the Morning,* Russell expressed his dismay at Storrs' "criticism." Storrs, in turn, replied through the next issue of *The Bible Examiner* by elaborating on his reasons for skepticism.

"I object to the time setting in any limited period, because I believe it is a disregard of our Lord's teaching on the subject," Storrs explained. "The disappointments of the past, I think, should teach us it is an error to attempt to do more than to show the return of our Lord from heaven 'is near, even at the door.'"

Given that Storrs had already burned his fingers as a follower of William Miller, no one could really blame him for not falling over himself to embrace Barbour's predictions. But if Russell was irked by Storrs' unwillingness to deliver a ringing endorsement, he was in for an even greater letdown from Barbour himself. As you would expect, April 6, 1878, passed with Barbour and Russell, and everyone else for that matter, utterly failing to be raptured. Russell managed to brush this off with some doctrinal tinkering, insisting that those "dying in the Lord" from 1878 onward would receive an immediate heavenly reward rather than sleeping in their graves.

But Barbour could not dismiss his errors quite so readily. Clearly rattled by his latest failure, he went back to the drawing board and radically revised, not just his date-setting, but his entire approach to Christianity. Among the casualties of his doctrinal purge was "substitution"—the notion that Christ's death was required as a vicarious atonement for the sin of mankind. Barbour was unequivocal in divorcing himself from this teaching in an article of the August 1878 issue of *Herald of the Morning* that would be identified today as surprisingly atheist in tone.

"The doctrine of substitution," wrote Barbour, "that is, punishing the innocent in place of the guilty, is unscriptural, and obnoxious to all our ideas of justice, or of right and wrong."

Russell was dumbfounded by what he saw as the betrayal of a foundational tenet of Christianity by his editor and colleague. In the very next issue of *Herald*, he sounded his discontent:

> Unpleasant though it be, I feel it necessary to take exceptions to an article by my brother upon this subject, in the last number of this paper. I make the objection not from a spirit of controversy, but because I believe the doctrine of substitution assailed in that article to be one of the most important teachings of God's word.

Russell decided to part ways with Barbour and start up his own magazine: *Zion's Watch Tower and Herald of*

*Christ's Presence*, the first issue of which was published in July 1879. Shortly thereafter, in 1881, Zion's Watch Tower Tract Society was formed, with a man named William Henry Conley as president.[3] Finally, in 1884, the Society was legally incorporated as the Watch Tower Bible and Tract Society of Pennsylvania, with Charles Taze Russell as president. By this point, Russell had expanded the movement to a number of congregations (or "ecclesias") along the Eastern seaboard and as far west as Ohio, all of which were modeled on his home congregation in Allegheny, Pittsburgh. Each year these congregations would elect Russell as their "Pastor." Hence, despite never having any formal theological training, Charles Taze Russell became "Pastor Russell."

The early Bible Student movement, though being very much a product of Russell's enthusiasm, charisma and resourcefulness, still bore many hallmarks of the involvement of his early mentor, Barbour. The most notable example was the group's fixation with 1914, a date undoubtedly borrowed from Barbour by Russell. As any Witness will tell you, 1914 continues to be key to Watchtower eschatology to this day. (*see box*)

1914, so Witnesses are now taught, was the beginning of the "last days." It was the year that Christ re-

[3] Not much is known about Conley other than that he was a businessman and philanthropist with a penchant for helping religious causes. During his brief tenure as Watch Tower president, Conley helped finance a three-part series of books by George N. H. Peters. This evidently did not meet with Russell's approval, because the May 1883 issue of *Zion's Watch Tower* criticized Peters' books and dissuaded readers from studying them. Whether this incident was instrumental in Conley making way for Russell to assume the presidency in 1884 cannot be known for certain. It is, however, telling that the first president's death in July 1897 received no mention in *The Watch Tower,* nor did the magazine feature any posthumous references to Conley's involvement with the fledgling movement.

FOR WITNESSES

## 607 B.C.E. AND 1914

You might be surprised to learn that Jehovah's Witnesses are virtually the only ones who believe Jerusalem was destroyed by Nebuchadnezzar in 607 B.C.E. Historians and archaeologists are in agreement that this event can be reliably dated twenty years later, to 586/587 B.C.E.

The 607 B.C.E. teaching is a remnant of the writings of Charles Taze Russell, who became convinced that a period known as the "Gentile times" began in 606 B.C.E. and ended in 1914. 606 B.C.E. was eventually amended to 607 B.C.E. in the 1940s, once Watchtower writers realized there was no "zero year" between 1 B.C.E. and 1 C.E.*

The length of the Gentile times was supposed to be exactly 2,520 years. This 2,520 number was arrived at, not by Russell, but by John Aquila Brown in 1823. Brown's figure was then used by a string of 19th century writers to predict a steady stream of exotic dates for Christ's second coming. At least three writers other than Russell used the 2,520 number to suggest 1914 as the end of the Gentile times. One of these was Nelson Barbour, and it was Barbour's writings that inspired Russell.

The fact that the 2,520 number is a product of pure speculation and supposition can be determined through a simple reading of Nebuchadnezzar's dream in Daniel chapter 4. The dream is interpreted as being a premonition: a warning of a period of madness for the king during which his kingship would be preserved. There is no hint of any grander fulfillment in the verse itself. Instead, the writer of Daniel

---

* Interestingly, Russell was given the opportunity to check his calculations regarding the "zero" year as early as 1909. According to the book *What Pastor Russell Said*, he was asked: "If the 'Times of the Gentiles' began in October, 606 B. C., will they not end in October, 1915, instead of October, 1914?" Russell rather missed the point with his answer: "We think not . . . You should remember that in figuring chronology you count backward from A. D. for the 606, and forward from A. D. for the 1914."

simply declares: "All of this befell King Nebuchadnezzar." (Daniel 4:28) If Daniel chapter 4 has a more profound meaning beyond what is expressly mentioned by the writer, then the same can be said of countless Bible passages.

Watchtower not only uses the borrowed 2,520 calculation to arrive at 607 B.C.E. for Jerusalem's destruction—it also insists that a 70-year period of desolation was prophesied by Jeremiah to begin in 607 B.C.E., ending with the return of the Jews from exile, which they claim happened in 537 B.C.E. However, a careful reading of Jeremiah 25:11-12 reveals that the 70-year period applied, not to Jerusalem's desolation, but to the subjugation of Judah and surrounding nations to Babylonian rule. Furthermore, Jeremiah's 70-year period is said to end *not with the rebuilding of Jerusalem*, but with the king of Babylon being "called to account"—which would refer to 539 B.C.E., when Babylon was captured by Cyrus the Great.

Finally, the meticulous record-keeping of the ancient Babylonians makes it possible for modern historians to pinpoint when the reigns of different kings began and ended. The tens of thousands of cuneiform documents so far discovered by archaeologists form a seamless timeline for the Neo-Babylonian era, and the dates they give us include astronomical observations that can be verified by modern astronomers. One such document, VAT 4956, dates to the 37th year of Nebuchadnezzar and lists various positions of the moon and planets that can only correspond with 568/567 B.C.E. Since the Bible mentions, at 2 Kings 25:8, 9, that Nebuchadnezzar destroyed Jerusalem in the 19th year of his reign, this would date the destruction to 587/586 B.C.E.—not 20 years *earlier* in 607 B.C.E., a date chosen by Watchtower purely because it conforms to the cherished 2,520 number.

There is much more that could be said about the 607 B.C.E./1914 controversy. An excellent resource is the book *The Gentile Times Reconsidered* by Carl Olof Jonsson. Jonsson, who is the leading expert on the subject, has also written essays on Watchtower's more recent attempts to defend 607 B.C.E. that are freely available online as PDF downloads.

turned to rule invisibly in heaven, and promptly exiled Satan to earth. The outbreak of World War I in 1914 is pointed to as evidence that Satan was orchestrating earth's affairs from that time onward, having been confined to earth's stratosphere.

The ensuing period, between 1914 and 1919, is presently understood to be when Jesus turned his attention to inspecting the religions of the day. After fixing his gaze on the Bible Students, Jesus apparently waited for Russell's eventual death in 1916 before appointing, in 1919, the next generation of Watchtower leaders, beginning with Joseph Rutherford and his associates, to be his "faithful and discreet slave"—God's sole mouthpiece on the earth. According to Watchtower's present teachings, whoever happened to be among the organization's leadership from Rutherford's time onward can be thought of as part of this "slave."

Without 1914 you therefore have no last days, no Armageddon, no faithful and discreet slave and, frankly, no basis for any claims made by Jehovah's Witnesses about themselves or the times in which we live. But what few Witnesses realize is that the 1914 teaching balances rather precariously on a number that is little more than a cringeworthy vestige of 19th century dabbling in apocalyptic end-time date-setting. That number is 2,520.

As far back as 1823, a man named John Aquila Brown suggested that a passage in the book of Daniel mentioning "seven times" referred to a timespan of 2,520 years. The passage in question was Daniel chapter 4, in which King Nebuchadnezzar dreams of an immense tree that is cut down and abandoned for seven times. In the same chapter, Daniel explains that the dream was a premonition that Nebuchadnezzar would go mad for a period, during which his kingship would be put on hold. But Brown decided the verse had an alternative, or grander meaning. The period for which the tree in Nebuchadnezzar's dream was cut down was said to be a metaphor for a gap in world history between the last divinely-appointed king reigning in Judah (Zedekiah), and the return of Christ. This gap, in which Gentiles (non-Jews) would be allowed to rule for centuries without a divine mandate, came to be referred to as the "Gentile times."

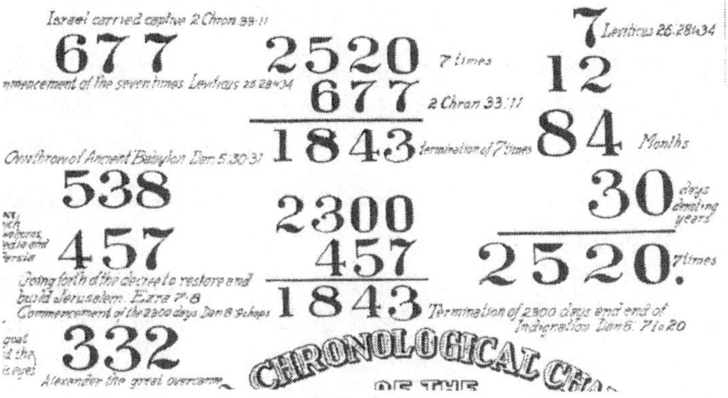

**A close-up of a chart used by William Miller's followers to show his calculations for 1843–1844 (note the use of Brown's 2,520 years)**

Once these "Gentile times," based as they were on a fairly innocuous and rather odd Bible verse, were assigned a specific length of time by Brown, a string of theories could proliferate as to which dates constituted the beginning and end. The most famous of these came to be William Miller's failed prediction concerning 1844. In that same year, coincidentally, an English clergyman named Edward Bishop Elliott published his *Horae Apocalypticae* ("Hours With the Apocalypse") in which he used the 2,520 number to instead generate 1914 as one of several potential dates for "the end." Elliot wrote:

> Of course, if calculated from Nebuchadnezzar's own accession and invasion of Judah, B.C. 606, the end is much later, being 1914.

Elliot would not be the last to use Brown's 2,520 years to hint at 1914 as being a date of apocalyptic significance. Barbour pursued the same line of inquiry, and succeeded in convincing Russell of his own version of the 2,520-year chronology, which had Christ returning invisibly in 1874 and bringing his day of wrath forty years later in 1914. Russell was so thoroughly sold on the matter that, as mentioned, he would continue to cling to the 1914 teaching long after his split from Barbour.

To explain these ideas in more detail, in the mid-1880s Russell began work on a new series of books that would unveil his rehashed chronology to the masses. The series was first titled *Millennial Dawn*—a reference to the dawn of Christ's thousand-year rule—but was later rebranded *Studies in the Scriptures* amid concerns *Millennial Dawn* sounded too much like a novel. In 1886 the first book in the series was published, titled *The Divine Plan of the Ages*, laying the groundwork for what was to follow: a labyrinth of convoluted teachings heralded as God's new revelation to mankind.[4] By 1910, Russell's complete six-volume set of *Studies in the Scriptures* was considered as "practically the Bible topically arranged," and studying these books was deemed more beneficial than reading the Bible on its own terms.[5]

---

[4] On its initial release in 1886, the book was titled *The Plan of the Ages*.

[5] The *Watch Tower* article in which this statement appears became the subject of a video released by the organization in 2016. In the video, Governing Body helper Kenneth Flodin claimed apostates had been deceitful by sharing a doctored version of the 1910 magazine article with someone who wrote

Despite the considerable hype, Russell's new books were hardly definitive, respected Bible commentaries and they brimmed with fanciful ideas.[6] Among the more eccentric of these was the notion that God had influenced the building of the Great Pyramid of Gizeh, and had subtly used the inner dimensions of his "stone witness" to foretell time spans of biblical significance including, as you might guess, the chronology pointing to 1914. But as with so many of his teachings, rather than birthing the theory entirely by himself, Russell turned to his contemporaries for inspiration.

John Taylor holds the distinction of being the first to unleash the boundless eccentricity of pyramidology with his 1859 book *The Great Pyramid: Why Was It Built? And Who Built It?* Charles Piazzi Smyth followed up in 1864 with his book *Our Inheritance in the Great Pyramid.* Smyth would later contribute further works on the subject after inspecting the pyramid in 1865 and taking precise measurements.

Borrowing heavily from the conclusions drawn by both Taylor and Smyth, in 1891 Russell published the third installment in his *Studies* series: *Thy King-*

---

in to Bethel. To see my video on this, including my rebuttal to Flodin's comments, search for "Apostates Deceitful Flodin" on YouTube.

[6] For example, in Volume VI of his *Studies* series (titled *The New Creation*), Russell propounded the view, based on Job 38:31, that the Pleiades star cluster is the location of the throne of God. He wrote: "Pleiades, in the north, has long been esteemed the center of the universe, the throne of Jehovah." This remarkable claim would be repeated in the writings of Russell's successor, Joseph Rutherford. In his 1928 book *Reconciliation* Rutherford wrote: "The constellation [*sic*] of the Pleiades is a small one compared with others which scientific instruments disclose to the wondering eyes of man. But the greatness in size of other stars or planets is small when compared with the Pleiades in importance, because the Pleiades is the place of the eternal throne of God."

*dom Come.* The final chapter, titled "The Testimony of God's Stone Witness and Prophet, the Great Pyramid in Egypt," began with a letter from Smyth praising Russell's conclusions. In this chapter, Russell insisted that various scriptures in the Bible pointed to the pyramid's significance and divine origins.[7] He claimed that the pyramid was built at the direction of the pre-exodus Bible character Melchizedek during a peaceful invasion[8] of Egypt around 2170 B.C.E.[9] Diagrams were produced showing various pyramid chambers and passageways, and Russell declared that the measurements of these (when inches were converted into years) denoted specific periods of time in human history. In summing up, Russell remarked:

> The ancient structure thus being repeatedly referred to in the Scriptures, we cannot doubt that, if questioned, this 'Witness' of the Lord in the land of Egypt will bear such testimony as will honor Jehovah, and fully correspond with his written Word.

---

7 E.g. Isaiah 19:19-20; Job 38:5-7 and Ephesians 2:20-21.

8 Russell explains on page 322 of *Thy Kingdom Come*, in a passage dripping with supposition and guesswork: "It is conjectured that Melchizedek, though not himself an Egyptian, used Egyptian labor for the construction of the Great Pyramid. And to some extent the traditions of Egypt support such a theory. They reveal the fact that Egypt had a peculiar invasion about this date by a people whom tradition merely denominates Hyksos (i.e. Shepherd Kings or Peaceful Kings). These invaders seem not to have attempted to disturb the general government of Egypt, and, after staying a time for some purpose not recognized by the tradition, they left Egypt as peacefully as they had come. These Hyksos or Peaceful Kings are supposed to include Melchizedek, and are assumed to have been the builders of the Great Pyramid—God's altar and 'Witness' in the land of Egypt."

9 Egyptologists understand the pyramid to have been completed around 2560 B.C.E. as a tomb for Pharaoh Khufu (of the fourth Egyptian dynasty) by Khufu's vizier Hemiunu.

Today, few Witnesses are familiar with Russell's pyramid obsession. Some have an awareness of the matter, perhaps thanks to old copies of *Studies in the Scriptures* volumes with charts depicting the Great Pyramid. The fact that Russell was buried near a large pyramid-shaped monument erected by his followers at the Rosemont United Cemetery in Pittsburgh is also a strong clue.[10]

Of the precious few Witnesses who are conscious of Watchtower's bizarre flirtation with pyramidology, fewer still are aware of the remarkable longevity of the teaching. In all of its 750 pages, the organization's official history book *Jehovah's Witnesses—Proclaimers of God's Kingdom* offers only this grudging acknowledgement:

> For some 35 years, Pastor Russell thought that the Great Pyramid of Gizeh was God's stone witness, corroborating Biblical time periods. (Isa. 19:19) But Jehovah's Witnesses have abandoned the idea that an Egyptian pyramid has anything to do with true worship.

A Witness reading this would be forgiven for assuming the pyramid teaching survived for 35 years before ending abruptly with Russell's death, but this is not so. From when it was first showcased in 1881, the teaching remained part of Watchtower doctrine for nearly half a century before finally being expunged in a 1928 two-part article by Russell's successor, Joseph Rutherford, who wrote:

---

[10] Some attribute Russell's fascination with pyramidology, as well as his use of certain symbols of Masonic origin, as evidence that he was a Freemason. In the absence of definitive proof to support this claim, and with the Freemasons denying that Russell was a member, I choose not to give it too much credence.

> We now wonder why we ever believed in or devoted any time to the study of the pyramid of Gizeh. Not only will we abandon such a study now, but we will ask God to forgive us for wasting the time that we put in on it and redeem the time by hurrying on to obey his commandments.

But rather than simply dismissing the Great Pyramid's divine significance and imploring God's forgiveness for being so silly, Rutherford went one step further. He claimed the whole thing was a conspiracy of Satan, who had orchestrated the pyramid's construction as a "subtle scheme" to "draw men away from Jehovah and his service." Hence, after 47 years, one preposterous idea (that God built the Great Pyramid of Gizeh) was merely supplanted by another (that Satan did). Rutherford's baffling claim has been given no further corrective treatment in subsequent publications, nor has it ever been retracted.

Another embarrassing and altogether more alarming feature of Russell's writings concerned his controversial views on race. Not only did Russell harbor strange fantasies about the "Ethiopian's skin," both believing and propounding the idea that, on reaching perfection, the skin of black people would be turned to its "original" white color—he also stooped to segregation and discrimination on grounds of ethnicity.

It should be stressed at this juncture that Jehovah's Witnesses today have an extremely healthy attitude toward race. Modern Watchtower literature insists that all races were created equal in God's image, and illustrations of future paradise almost uniformly depict people of different ethnicities and national garb coexisting peacefully. But few Witnesses are aware that their religion's acceptance of racial equality is more a product of societal progress, specifically the civil rights movement of the 1950s and 1960s, than something Watchtower literature has always championed.

One of the earliest examples of racist rhetoric in *Zion's Watch Tower* involved Russell expressing his wish that the magazine's distribution should be accomplished, at least in part, with skin color as a consideration.

Back in those early days, distribution of Russell's writings was almost entirely dependent on the work of Watchtower volunteers, later known as "colporteurs" (the forerunners of today's "pioneers"). Colporteurs were tasked with offering subscriptions to readers. You would expect Russell to have been grateful and welcoming of any and all who volunteered their time to circulate literature on Watchtower's behalf, but this was not quite the case. In the March 1, 1900, issue of *Zion's Watch Tower*, Russell's selection criteria for volunteers were expressly confined to members of "white Protestant churches."

Understandably, the black Bible Students at that time were none too pleased about being discriminated against and some wrote to the Society's headquarters to register their complaints. Russell responded by suggesting that "colored people have less education than whites—many of them quite insufficient to permit them to profit by such reading as we have to give forth," adding:

> Our conclusion therefore is based upon the supposition that reading matter distributed to a colored congregation would more than half of it be utterly wasted, and a very small percentage indeed likely to yield good results. We advise, therefore, that where the Watch Tower literature is introduced to colored people it be not by promiscuous circulation, but only to those who give evidence of some ear for the truth.

Russell's magazine thus freely acknowledged that its discriminatory advertisement for volunteers was based on a stereotype of black people as being uneducated, using this as a basis to claim that any literature distributed among them was "utterly wasted." It seems difficult to fathom how Russell, who privately admitted to being God's "faithful and wise servant," could harbor and promote such a deplorably backward and patronizing attitude toward his black followers.

Russell's bizarre views concerning black people were to continually resurface, most notably when touching on his outlandish ideas about "the Ethiopian's skin." In another 1900 *Zion's Watch Tower* article titled "Can Restitution Change the Ethiopian's Skin?" Russell recounted the story of a black preacher claiming to have developed white skin after praying for it. Reverend Draper, who apparently told others that "if he could only be white like his employer, he would be happy," started praying thirty years prior to the article's publication, and experienced a transformation. Once his skin was completely white, he returned to his former church and reportedly had a hard time convincing congregants of his identity.

Obviously we now understand this "miraculous" transformation to be the likely result of Vitiligo, a medical condition resulting in depigmentation of areas of skin. Vitiligo is by no means uncommon, but Russell was apparently so taken by the notion of black people becoming white that he would accept any related report as evidence that this might happen on a larger scale in the future. Accordingly, the February 15, 1904, *Zion's Watch Tower* reported a similar incident involving a nine-year-old boy named Julius Jackson under the heading "Can the Ethiopian Change His Skin?" Before relating the boy's story, the article opened with these introductory remarks:

> CAN THE ETHIOPIAN CHANGE HIS SKIN?
>
> We answer, No. But all will admit that what the Ethiopian cannot do for himself God could readily do for him. The difference between the races of men and the differences between their languages have long been arguments against the solidarity of the human family. The doctrine of restitution has also raised the question. How could all men be brought to perfection and which color of skin was the original? The answer is now provided. God can change the Ethopian's skin in his own due time.

It is difficult to fathom what drove Russell to preoccupy himself with the concept of blacks becoming whites. What was so wrong, from his perspective, about the skin color of black people? Why would the pigmentation of a person's skin make any difference to a God who, according to Acts 10:34, is "not partial?"

A 1902 *Zion's Watch Tower* article furnishes yet another telling insight into the Pastor's views on the matter. Under the heading "The Negro Not a Beast," the article represented an attempt at banishing the grossly offensive idea being circulated in a book of the period that black men and women were to be thought of as on a par with animals. Despite its commendable opposition to this outrageous suggestion, the magazine's rebuttal was tainted by more than a hint of the writer's own bigotry:

> We are not to forget that Africa is inhabited by various tribes or nations of Negroes—some more and some less degraded than the average.

How could a journal that fancied itself as a vehicle of divine wisdom consider the use of the word "degraded" appropriate in describing Africans? But, sadly, more would follow:

> While it is true that the white race exhibits some qualities of superiority over any other, we are to remember that there are wide differences in the same Caucasian (Semitic and Aryan) family; and also we should remember that some of the qualities which have given this branch of the human family its preeminence in the world are not such as can be pointed to as in all respects admirable.

Having asserted the "superiority" of Caucasians, the writer (a Caucasian, one assumes) continues:

> The secret of the greater intelligence and aptitude of the Caucasian undoubtedly in great measure is to be attributed to the commingling of blood amongst its various branches, and this was evidently forced in large measure by circumstances under divine control.

Hence, not only did white people enjoy a "greater intelligence and aptitude," but this was revealed to be the product of divine influence over their "commingling of blood." Thankfully, there was good news for non-Caucasians who aspired to their offspring becoming as "superior" as white people:

> It remains to be proven that the similar commingling of the various tribes of Chinese for several centuries would not equally brighten their intellects; and the same with the peoples of India and Africa.

It should be acknowledged at this juncture that Charles Taze Russell did not personally write each and every magazine article himself. *Zion's Watch Tower* had a number of regular contributors. However, Russell was the chief editor and, as such, would have checked each article personally before approving it for print. Even if he had not written a certain article himself, he would have signed off on it before publication in a magazine for which he was legally accountable. Therefore, we may consider any article published under Russell's editorship as representing his views. We can certainly say that Russell would have scrapped any article without the slightest hesitation if it conflicted with his own opinions.

It should also be noted that attitudes toward race and equality were nowhere near as enlightened in the early 20th century as they are now.[11] By quoting from Russell's publications on this matter I am not suggesting he was unique among his contemporaries in perpetuating racial bigotry. However, Russell's antiquated, distasteful, small-minded attitudes toward ethnic groups deemed inferior by his contemporaries must surely be weighed against his aspirations as a conduit of divine wisdom and his perceived role as a favored founding member of "Jehovah's organization."

Another alarming example of Russell's condescension against the "colored brethren" came in 1914 at a screening of *The Photo-Drama of Creation. The Photo-Drama* is often heralded by Watchtower as emblematic of the organization's forward-thinking and ability to embrace technology in furthering its message. At an eye-watering eight hours' duration, it remains one of the longest cinematic films ever produced. The length, combined with Russell's cringeworthy, scientifically-dubious[12] narration makes it something of an ordeal to the modern viewer. (I would be surprised if any

---

[11] I write this aware that there are currently heightened racial tensions in America, and fears over blacks being disproportionately targeted by police. Without question, we still have a long way to go as a species in fully understanding that we are all humans and there is really no such thing as "race." Nevertheless, the situation now is still far more tolerable than it was a century ago.

[12] Russell informed his audience that the seven creative days of Genesis totaled 49,000 years, with each "day" 7,000

***A poster advertising "The Photo-Drama of Creation"***

---

years in length. Modern geologists estimate our planet to be 4.5 *billion* years old. He also described the sun as a "fixed star," and suggested that Noah's flood was the result of a Saturn-like ring of water, hitherto held aloft by centrifugal forces, collapsing. Expanding on this "Vailian theory" he said: "There are scientists who claim that the Earth still has one ring about it, an electrical ring which, falling, will in a few years destroy fermentation, microbes and parasites, and greatly assist plant and animal life."

modern Witnesses have been able to sit through the whole thing, I certainly can't.) But, on its release, it was considered a cutting-edge must-see cinematic event. It was, after all, the first major screenplay to incorporate moving film, color slides and synchronized sound in the form of recorded speech. Production began in 1912, and by 1914 the rambling spectacle was ready. But Russell had his own ideas as to what his preferred audience would look like.

In January 1914, at a screening of *The Photo-Drama* at The Temple, West 63rd Street, New York, a number of black audience members were segregated from whites and forced to sit separately on the balcony of the auditorium. This caused understandable outrage. Several wrote angry letters to Watchtower, furious at suffering such indignity at the hands of their "brothers." A response was printed in the April 1, 1914, *Watch Tower* under the heading "The Color Line Found Necessary." It read, in part, as follows:

> We might have anticipated that many colored people would be deeply interested in this Drama. But it did not impress itself upon us until gradually their numbers increased to about twenty-five per cent of the whole audience. Of course, we were glad to see them, glad that they were interested in the Drama. We had the same feeling respecting them as others; but it was quickly discerned that it was not a case of feeling, but that, whereas the colored people of New York city are about five per cent of the population, in our audience they are about twenty-five per cent and the number increasing. What shall we do? As the attendance of the colored people would increase, proportionately the number of whites would decrease; for explain it how we will, a majority of whites prefer not to intermingle closely with other races.

> Recognizing that it meant either the success or the failure of the enterprise of the Drama as respects the whites, we have been compelled to assign the colored friends to the gallery, which, however, is just as good for seeing and hearing as any other part of The Temple. Some were offended at this arrangement.

I can barely imagine the humiliation of arriving at a screening of *The Photo-Drama* as a fan of Russell at the time, brimming with excitement and wonder, only to be herded like an animal into a separate part of the theater on account of the color of my skin. It would only add insult to injury if I were told that this was necessary so that my presence would not offend any of the white guests, because "explain it how you will, a majority of whites prefer not to intermingle with other races." I cannot imagine wishing to continue my association with the Bible Students after suffering such shameful treatment. I would wonder how this could possibly be Christ's church if "the success . . . of the enterprise of the Drama as respects the whites" was considered more important than treating people with dignity and upholding equality.

But apparently not all "colored brethren" were repulsed by this incident. At least according to the above-quoted magazine article, the organization's success-over-equality line of reasoning proved "entirely satisfactory to all of the fully consecrated" with only a few "tenacious and quarrelsome" individuals objecting. It seems that, as respects this incident, everything boiled down to humility. As the article itself concluded, in a clear reference to slavery:

> If nature favors the colored brethren and sisters in the exercise of humility it is that much to their advantage, if they are rightly exercised by it.

In further summation, the article revisited Russell's fascination with the "Ethiopian's skin" by claiming that, in due course, all mankind will experience "restitution to the perfection of mind and body, feature and color, to the grand original standard, which God declared 'very good.'" Quite why a Christian would need to have the color of his or her skin changed to a "grand original standard" is anyone's guess. But a strong hint of racism was not to be the only blight on Russell's copybook as Watchtower's esteemed founder. The steady and very public deterioration of his marriage arguably supplied the most controversy during his presidency.

The omens were not favorable from the outset of Russell's ill-fated marriage to Maria Frances Ackley on March 13, 1879. Only a year later, in 1880, Russell's widowed father Joseph would marry Maria's sister, Emma Ackley, making Russell's sister-in-law also his stepmother. If that were not sufficiently complicated, Russell and his wife vowed that their marriage would be a celibate one, without sex or cohabitation. Regardless of their puritanical justification for the arrangement, namely their expectations of imminent rapture and a literal interpretation of Matthew 19:12, this was no basis for a long, happy, healthy marriage, as they were both to discover at some cost.

Things began relatively cordially. Maria was allowed to play a leading role in the formation of the fledgling Bible Student movement. Not only did she get to be secretary-treasurer of the Watch Tower Society—she was also an editor and writer for the *Zion's Watch Tower* magazine. Maria even later claimed to have coauthored the first four volumes of *Studies in the*

*Scriptures*—a claim not to be taken lightly since she was, after all, better educated than her husband, having made it through high school and received training as a teacher. Maria was also apparently fiercely loyal to her husband, at least to begin with. In 1894, when a schism arose over Russell's increasingly authoritarian leanings, it was Maria who was deployed on a lecture tour of Bible Student congregations in defense of the Pastor. On her return, she went so far as to declare him the "faithful and wise servant" of Matthew 24:45-47. Maria also resisted overtures from opponents of Russell who, pointing to perceived ill-treatment of her, sought to recruit her in making a case against him as a bad husband.

Given Maria's determined commitment to her husband's work and willingness to defend him, she must have been devastated when, in 1895, Russell insisted on separation. In a sworn statement she would later recount:

> He proposed that on the ground of incompatibility that we agree to separate, and if I would do so he would give me that house in which we were living, and when I broke down at the suggestion, he said if I did not agree to it, that I would not get anything.

The situation continued to deteriorate until, in 1906, Maria filed suit for divorce from bed and board citing mental cruelty. It became apparent in her testimony that she was especially aggrieved by Russell's relationship with Rose Ball, a young woman who worked as a secretary at the Society's offices, and who had been taken in by the Russells' almost as a foster daughter.

Maria told the court she became suspicious after catching Russell alone with Rose in her bedroom on multiple occasions, and had confronted him on the

Charles and Maria Russell

matter. Her testimony was eventually ruled out, not because of concerns over accuracy or truthfulness (as Russell and his supporters would later imply) but because the events she described did not happen within the timeframe stipulated in Maria's bill of complaint. The crucial part of Maria's testimony, given to a packed courthouse on April 26, 1906, was later printed verbatim in the *Brooklyn Daily Eagle* based on court records:

> Q. I want you to tell us what your husband did in company with this woman Rose, in your presence and in your home.
>
> A. In the first place I considered it—(*objected to and witness was not permitted to finish.*)
>
> Q. Tell us what you saw and what he said was done.
>
> A. One evening he spent the evening downstairs and our library and bedroom were next to each other upstairs on the second floor, and I spent the evening downstairs reading, and I went upstairs about 10 o'clock to my room, and I supposed that: he was either in the library or had retired, and when I went up there I found that he was in neither place, and I stepped out in the hall, and I found that he was in his night robe, sitting beside Miss Ball's bed and she was in bed. On other occasions I found him going in there and I found she called him in and said she wasn't well and wanted him in, and I objected to this, and I said that it was highly improper, and I said: "We have people about the

house, and what kind of a name will be attached in this house if you do that sort of thing?" and he got angry.

Q. You state that you found him doing this at other times. How often after that?

A. I found him a number of times; I don't remember how often.

Q. In her room?

A. Yes, sir. And I found him in the servant girl's room as well, and I found him locked in the servant girl's room.

Q. Did he make any explanation why he was in the girl's room?

A. No. He did not; he just got angry.

Q. What did you say to him about this conduct and what did he say.

A. I said to him, "We have a great work on our hands," and I said, "In this work you and I have to walk very circumspectly before the world and if you are going to do things like this, what will happen? Suppose you are all right, don't you suppose people will talk about things like this?" and I said, "I am not satisfied with it," and he said he wasn't going to be ruled by me. But I felt distressed about that.

Q. What did Rose do at the Watch Tower?

A. She attended to the correspondence.

Q. Where was her desk with reference to the desk of Mr. Russell of the Watch Tower Society?

A. It wasn't near his; it was in the office.

Q. When would he go to the Watch Tower, in the morning?

A. I don't remember; he generally went down alone.

Q. Who would return with him?

A. She came with him in the evening and they came about 11 o'clock and the young men that were in the office—she was the only girl, and the young men would go home, and he wouldn't allow her to go home with them, and she must wait and always go with him.

*(Objected to.)* Q. I want the mere fact, did this girl Rose go home with your husband?

A. Yes, sir.

Q. What year was that?

A. In the fall of 1894. *(By Mr. Porter, attorney for the plaintiff.)*

Q. Did you state to your husband at this meeting any endearing terms?

A. Yes, sir.

Q. What were they?

A. I said "She tells me that one evening you came home—" I asked her when did these things occur. I said to him, "She says they occurred down at the office when she stayed down there with him in the evening after the rest had gone, and at home at any time when I wasn't around."

Q. Now, about the endearing terms?

A. She said one evening when she came home with him, just as she got inside the hall, it was late in the evening, about 11 o'clock, he put his arms around her and kissed her. This was in the vestibule before they entered the hall, and he called her his little wife, but she said "I am not your wife." and he said "I will call you daughter, and a daughter has nearly all the privileges of a wife."

Q. What other terms were used?

A. Then he said, "I am like a jellyfish. I float around here and there. I touch this one and that one, and if she responds I take her to me, and if not, I float on to others;" and she wrote that out so that I could remember it for sure when I would speak to him about it. And he confessed that he said those things.

Q. And the young men came home ahead of them?

A. Yes, sir.

Q. State to the court and jury what talk, if any, you had with this girl Rose, in regard to her relations with your husband, which you communicated to your husband?

*This question was objected to and it was changed to read as follows: Q. You are to tell what you stated to your husband that Rose had said and his reply to you.*

A. I told him that I had learned something that was very serious and I didn't tell him right away. I let a day elapse until I felt I had control of myself and could talk and then I told him that I had something very serious to tell him about this matter, and he said, "What is it?" and I said, "Rose has told me that you have been intimate with her, that you have been in the habit of hugging and kissing her and having her sit on your knee and fondling each other, and she tells me you bid her under no account to tell me, but she couldn't keep it any longer. She said if I was distressed about it she felt that she would have to come and make a confession to me, and she has done that. (*By the court.*)

Q. What did he say?

A. He tried to make light of it at first and I said, "Husband, you can't do that. I know the whole thing. She has told me straight and I know it to be true." Well, he said he was sorry; it was true, but he was sorry. He said he didn't mean any harm. I said, "I don't see how you could do an act like that without meaning harm."

Maria's testimony was explosive. Her husband was a Christian minister who urged his followers to "remember the higher interpretation of adultery and murder set forth in the New Testament: that whoever desires adultery, and is merely restrained from it by outward circumstances or fears, is really an adulterer in his heart." He went so far as to warn his followers that any "who find themselves in any degree of sympathy" with adultery "are deceived if they think themselves to be the Lord's people." And yet the Pastor seemed to insist on a level of familiarity with young women under his roof that belied his moral pronouncements. How could Russell have any basis for preaching morality to his followers with such a track record?

Russell's only option was to discredit Maria and deny her testimony with his own conflicting version of events, which he duly did in the July 15, 1906, *Zion's Watch Tower:*

> "Rose" was quite childish in appearance, wore short dresses, and looked to Mr. Russell to be about 13 years old. He did not know her age, but another who knew her guessed that she was only 10 years old. She may have been older than 13 in 1888.

Incredibly, it seems the Pastor believed raising the possibility of Rose being a minor when the incident happened made the whole scandal *less* outrageous. Russell further elaborated on his version of events by recounting how an emotional young Rose, distraught at her mistreatment by Mrs. Russell, had climbed on his knee and kissed him out of the blue:

> It was some months later that Mr. Russell in the Watch Tower office, hearing sobbing, turned to find "Rose" in tears. Inquiring the cause, "Rose," still weeping, came over and sat on his knee, and complained that Mrs. Russell had worked her too hard before she started for the office; and that she felt weary and friendless. He told her that all that was a mistake. He defended Mrs. Russell as not un-

> kind or unreasonable, and told "Rose" to do what she was able to do cheerfully, and then to explain her weariness and that he was sure nothing unreasonable would be asked. Then, suddenly, drying her tears, "Rose kissed Mr. Russell. Although surprised at all this Mr. R. did not resent it nor reprove it; but having reproved himself for not having been previously more fatherly. That very night he talked with his wife about "Rose" and pointed out that she was surely lonely since her brother's death, and that it would be a duty to look after her interests more carefully.
>
> Mrs. Russell agreed, and it was mutually arranged that "Rose" thereafter should be considered and treated as an adopted daughter.

Hence, according to Russell, his only crime in this whole affair was his failure to be sufficiently "fatherly" to a schoolgirl from whom his overbearing wife was extracting child labor.

No doubt many of the Pastor's doting followers, who sorely wanted him to be their spiritual mentor and role model, will have happily swallowed this half-baked attempt at self-exoneration. Russell's version was similarly endorsed by his lawyer, a certain Joseph Rutherford, who would later publish a 64-page booklet entirely devoted to putting out the many fires that were by then raging as to the Pastor's character (including a controversy surrounding "miracle wheat").[13] Regarding

---

[13] The booklet in question was Rutherford's *A Great Battle in the Ecclesiastical Heavens.* The "miracle wheat" controversy arose after a Virginian man named K. B. Stoner (not a Bible Student) discovered a productive strain of wheat and two Bible Students donated 30 bushels of it to the Society to be sold on as seed grain. The *Watch Tower* magazine made fantastic claims about the grain's properties and raised $1,800 selling it to subscribers. The *Brooklyn Daily Eagle* published a scathing exposé, replete with cartoon, ridiculing the whole thing as a commer-

Rose's age, the man who would come to style himself as the "Judge" wrote the following:

> But the most conclusive facts disclosed by the record showing [Mrs. Russell's] statement to be untrue are these: Miss Ball came to them in 1889, a child of ten, and was taken into the home of Mr. and Mrs. Russell. She was treated as a member of the family. She was an orphan. She kissed both Mr. and Mrs. Russell good night each evening when she retired. They treated her as their own child. (Court Record, pages 90, 91.) Mrs. Russell testified that the "jelly-fish" incident transpired in 1894, when the girl could not have been more than fifteen years of age. (Page 15, Record.)

But there was a problem with Rutherford's "conclusive facts": they were utter hogwash and easily proven as such. Rose Ball was not a minor, either in 1888/1889 when she came to live with the Russells, or in 1894 when the events recounted by Maria were said to have transpired. She was born in Buffalo, New York, on March 19, 1869, making her 19 years old in 1888, and a 25-year-old woman in 1894. Russell even listed Rose as a director of the Watch Tower Society in the April 25, 1894, *Extra Edition of Zion's Watch Tower.* She was hardly, therefore, an over-exuberant young schoolgirl in pigtails.

Instead of exonerating him, the Pastor's demonstrably-false reimagining of the jellyfish story only served to discredit him further, making Maria's version more plausible. After all, if Russell could lie so readily

---

cial racket. Russell sued for libel, and lost. Though the affair represented terrible judgment on Russell's part, both for mixing his ministry with commerce and for invoking "the power of God" in promoting what amounted to an agricultural fad, it was hardly the full-scale commercial scam many critics like to suggest.

about Rose's age at the time of the incident, he could lie about pretty much anything.

Incredibly, despite all this, Watchtower continues to stand by Russell and paint him as the victim of a scheming, vindictive wife bent on his humiliation. The 1993 *Proclaimers* book (page 646) raises four key arguments against the suggestion that Russell was "an immoral man and hence unfit to be a minister of God," namely: (1) Maria Russell answered "no" when asked by her lawyer if she was accusing her husband of adultery, (2) Maria failed to mention her accusations when questioned by an all-male tribunal in 1897, (3) a judge later told someone seeking a record of the testimony that the grounds for the case and subsequent verdict were "'indignities' and not adultery," and (4) Maria mourned the loss of Russell at his funeral and left some flowers accompanied by the message: "To My Beloved Husband."

None of the above arguments negate the specific claims made by Maria in her testimony. The second and fourth points speak of a conflicted wife who tried to make a success of her marriage even after the incident and continued to love her husband to the bitter end, despite his treatment of her. The first and third points are an attempt at conflating the "indignities" described in Maria's testimony with cold, hard evidence of adultery, which she never claimed to have (and most likely did not *want* to have). When you read the full transcript, you notice that Maria's denial of adultery comes immediately *before* she tells the jellyfish story, not after. This suggests Maria was disinclined to charge her husband with adultery (knowing there would be ramifications for doing so without evidence), but was still very certain in her mind that he had behaved in an undignified manner with more than one young woman, and could well have gone further than "fondling" with the opportunities he had engineered for himself.[14]

Maria's reluctance to brand her husband an adulterer showed great honesty and prudence on her part, but in no way did it let her husband off the hook regarding the specific events she recounted. Russell was, at least in the eyes of his wife, far from the image of chastity his sanctimonious writings implied. And the incredible lies he propagated in his attempts to absolve himself only strengthened her case.

In the wake of his humiliation at the divorce trial and the subsequent media storm,[15] Russell was sorely in need of drawing a line under the episode and reestablishing himself as a beacon of moral virtue. In March 1908, he asked all Watchtower representatives to pledge themselves to a vow he had devised, a significant component of which involved dealings with the opposite sex. The vow, which was printed in the June 15, 1908, *Zion's Watch Tower*, included the following:

> . . . and, so far as reasonably possible, I will avoid being in the same room with any of the opposite sex alone, unless the door to the room stand wide open.—wife, children, mother and sisters excepted.

---

[14] It is also quite conceivable that she did not want to think of her husband as an adulterer in the fullest sense. She lived, after all, at a time when being the wife of such a man carried more of a stigma than it does today.

[15] Shortly after the divorce trial, *The Washington Post* gleefully published a crude hack job lampooning Russell over the jellyfish story. Russell sued the paper and was awarded one dollar in damages. When he appealed the judgment, the paper offered a settlement, which included a full retraction and an invitation to print Russell's sermons. Another paper, the *Mission Friend* in Chicago, similarly overindulged and were sued. They also settled, with a full retraction.

The vow managed to itself become a subject of considerable controversy. Some Bible Students refused to accede to it, citing earlier writings of Russell that were firmly against the taking of vows. Nobody minded Russell taking a vow if his conscience compelled him to do so, but suggesting that every full or part-time "pilgrim" (traveling representative) and Bible House worker (Bethelite) should take it, and publishing the names of those who did as a further means of coercion, seemed a step too far.[16] This dispute, combined with doctrinal disagreements over the "New Covenant" and precisely who benefited from having Christ as mediator, eventually led to several hundred disgruntled Bible Students parting ways with their Pastor.[17]

Interestingly, Russell's vow finds a modern incarnation in the 32-page booklet *Dwelling Together in Unity*—a breathtakingly-pedantic set of house rules issued to all who sign up for Bethel service.[18] Under the section "Conduct, Dress and Grooming," we find the following injunction:

> It is required that you leave the door of your room wide open and be in full view of passersby if you are alone with one of the opposite sex who is not your marriage mate, parent, fleshly brother or

---

16 Russell later relented in publishing the names of those who took the vow, but still insisted on keeping records of vow-takers that critics claimed amounted to little more than a loyalty list.

17 Russell came to teach that the heaven-bound 144,000 did not have or need a mediator. He was adamant that only the rest of mankind had a mediator, which was Christ and his church together as one body. Others saw things differently.

18 I managed to obtain a 2004 copy of the *Dwelling Together in Unity* booklet from a former Bethelite. Thankfully, it must have slipped his mind to relinquish it when leaving Bethel, as all Bethelites are required to do.

sister, or other close relative. The same principle applies to offices.

The *Dwelling Together* booklet cites 1 Timothy 5:2 ("with all chasteness") as the basis for the "wide open door" policy, leaving newly-initiated Bethelites oblivious to the strong likelihood of it having more to do with the roving hands of their organization's founder.

As if the scandal and embarrassment of Russell's marital tribulations were not indignity enough, the Pastor also had to suffer the humiliation of surviving long enough to see his predictions for 1914 unequivocally disproved. But rather than admit defeat, he did what he had by now grown accustomed to doing: he moved the goalposts.

The following are all quotes about 1914 from Watchtower publications printed long before that date:

> "In this chapter we present the Bible evidence proving that the full end of the Times of the Gentiles, i. e., the full end of their lease of dominion, will be reached in A. D. 1914; and that that date will be the farthest limit of the rule of imperfect men."—*The Time Is at Hand*, 1889, p. 77[19]

---

[19] The same passage from *The Time Is at Hand* lists seven predictions for 1914 (or before 1914) that could be summarized thus: (1) the Kingdom of God would obtain "full universal control," being established "on the ruins of present institutions," (2) "Gentile governments" would be overthrown, (3) some time before 1914 the last member of the "royal priesthood" would be raptured, (4) Jerusalem would no longer be "trodden down of the Gentiles," (5) Israel's "blindness" would begin to be turned away, (6) the great tribulation would reach its climax in "a world-wide reign of anarchy," and (7) God's Kingdom would "smite and crush the Gentile image" mentioned in Daniel chapter 2. This list of predictions would subsequently be doctored in post-1914 editions of the volume, as later discussed.

"In view of this strong Bible evidence concerning the Times of the Gentiles, we consider it an established truth that the final end of the kingdoms of this world, and the full establishment of the Kingdom of God, will be accomplished at the end of A. D. 1914."—*The Time Is at Hand*, 1889, p. 99

". . . the 'battle of the great day of God Almighty' (Rev. 16:14), which will end in A. D. 1914 with the complete overthrow of earth's present rulership, is already commenced."—*The Time Is at Hand*, 1889, p. 101

"And the parallelism continues to the full end of the harvest of this dispensation—until the overthrow of the professedly Christian kingdoms, really 'kingdoms of this world,' and the full establishment of the Kingdom of God in the earth at A. D. 1914 . . ." —*Thy Kingdom Come*, 1891, p. 126

"And with the end of A. D. 1914, what God calls Babylon, and what men call Christendom, will have passed away, as already shown from prophecy." —*Thy Kingdom Come*, 1891, p. 153

". . . the deliverance [rapture] of the saints must take place some time before 1914 . . . Just how long before 1914 the last living members of the body of Christ will be glorified, we are not directly informed . . ."—*Thy Kingdom Come*, 1891, p. 228

"Call to mind that the Scriptures showed us that the full end of Gentile power in the world, and of the time of trouble which brings its overthrow, will be in the end of A. D. 1914, and that some time before that date the last members of the Church of Christ will have been 'changed,' glorified."—*Thy Kingdom Come*, 1891, p. 362

"The date of the close of that 'battle' is definitely marked in Scripture as October, 1914. It is already in progress, its beginning dating from October 1874." —*Zion's Watch Tower*, January 15, 1892

> "But bear in mind that the end of 1914 is not the date for the beginning, but for the end of the time of trouble."—*Zion's Watch Tower,* July 15, 1894

I hope you will notice that all of the above quotes were penned before the turn of the century. Only after 1900, as 1914 began to loom closer, did Russell's tone start to sound suitably cautious. "We have never claimed our calculations to be infallibly correct," he warned in the October 1, 1907, *Zion's Watch Tower.* "Our claim has always been that they are based on *faith.*" By 1912, Russell had conceded that "there surely is room for slight differences of opinion on this subject," reassuring his followers that nothing was set in stone. "We have merely pointed out what the Scriptures say, giving our views respecting their meaning and asking our readers to judge, each for himself, what they signify."

1914 was thus still a future date when Bible Students were already being urged not to take previous claims too seriously. If they put too much stock in their Pastor's predictions, the fault was theirs—not his. The problem with such a disingenuous strategy, which would be revisited by later generations of Watchtower leaders, was that these "calculations" were on record. In making his case for 1914 marking the end, the pre-1900 Russell had been emphatic and unflinching. Far from being offered on a take-it-or-leave-it basis, the 1914 teaching was presented as "established truth," "definitely marked in Scripture." In the July 15, 1894, issue of *Zion's Watch Tower,* Russell ventured as far as to say: "We see no reason for changing the figures—nor could we change them if we would. They are, we believe, God's dates, not ours." It is difficult to conceive of a more final, emphatic way of presenting a prediction as a copper-bottomed, absolute guarantee in the mind of a believer than to couch it in such terms.

In the decade or so leading up to 1914, Russell could not help but let his growing uncertainty temper his rhetoric as world events refused to square with his doomsday vision. As 1914 gave way to 1915, he must have known at some level that he was just as guilty of indulging in false prophecy as Miller and Barbour before him. Yet another disappointment was being visited on a new generation, only this time history was consciously being allowed to repeat itself.

True, there is no shame in an honest mistake. Russell undoubtedly allowed his enthusiasm to get the better of him. He took a gamble and assumed he would be right where others were wrong, and he lost. But Russell's approach of masking the extent of his certainty over the 1914 teaching only after its failure was apparent was thoroughly dishonest—and he did his best to ensure future converts would be kept in the dark.

Copies of his *Studies in the Scriptures* series published from 1915 onward were altered in parts where the passage of time had rendered the text obsolete. These changes were listed in the March 1, 1915, *Watch Tower* under the heading "Changes in 'Scripture Studies'":

> We call attention to a few slight changes which have been made in four pages of Vol. II. and six pages of Vol. III., "STUDIES IN THE SCRIPTURES." These are all trivial and do not alter the real sense and lesson, but conform to the facts as we have them today. The pages containing these corrections are as follows:
>
> Vol. II., page 77, line 1, "will be the farthest limit," reads "will see the disintegration."
>
> Vol. II., page 77, line 6, "will obtain full universal control," reads "will begin to assume control."
>
> Vol. II., page 77, lines 16, 17, "end of A.D. 1914," reads "end of the overthrow."

Vol. II., page 81, line 9, "can date only from A.D. 1914," reads "could not precede A.D. 1915."

Vol. II., page 170, line 16, "at that time they will all be overturned."

Vol. II., page 221, line 25, "full favor until A.D. 1914," reads "full favor until after 1915."

Vol. III., page 94, line 29, "in this end or harvest," reads "at the end of this harvest."

Vol. III., page 126, line 12, "at A.D. 1914," reads "after 1914."

Vol. III., page 133, line 21, "ere the harvest is fully ended."

Vol. III., page 228, line 11, "some time before 1914," reads "very soon after 1914."

Vol. III., page 228, line 15, "just how long before," reads "just how long after."

Vol. III., page 362, line 11, "some time before," reads "some time near."

Vol. III., page 364, line 14, "must not only witness," reads "may not only witness."

Without even referring to the original texts for which these amendments are intended (I have already listed some of them for you on the previous pages), hopefully it is clear from a cursory glance that what were shrugged off as "a few slight changes" were actually quite comprehensive and significant. Russell was whitewashing his false predictions—especially those related to what he said would happen in (or before) 1914. Rather than humbly hold his hands up and say: "I'm sorry, I got it wrong. The rapture and the end of worldly governments and religion didn't come about by 1914 as I predicted," the Pastor could only reach for the eraser.

Despite worsening health, Russell soldiered on into 1916, continuing to exude a sense of urgency. Yes, he was utterly wrong with the timing of his predictions, but the war raging in Europe offered a glimmer of hope that he could regain some credibility. In Russell's mind, the conflict itself was proof that apocalyptic events were afoot that would eventually climax in what he had been waiting for. The Pastor therefore busied himself with ministering to an increasingly international flock of believers, which by then boasted offices in Britain, Australia, Denmark, Sweden, Switzerland and South Africa. But he was to be spared the indignity of witnessing the Great War's failure to usher in Armageddon. On October 31, 1916, Russell breathed his last on a train in the Southwestern United States. The December 1, 1916, *Watch Tower* recounted events:

> Seven hours before his death, addressing his traveling companion, Brother Menta Sturgeon, he [Russell] said: "Make me a Roman toga." Using the bed sheets, Brother Sturgeon made a toga, which Brother Russell put on himself. He stood erect for a moment, and then lying down on the couch in his Pullman drawing room, closed his eyes, thus in symbolical language speaking of death. A great deal of the Bible is written in symbolical language, and it was quite appropriate that he should speak his last message in symbols. It is interesting here to know what a Roman toga symbolizes. Augustus' Poet Laureate, said, "It is by the toga that the royal nation is recognized." The word toga means a covering garment (white robe). It was the official robe of higher magistrates, priests and of persons discharging vows, and was worn on special occasions, such as celebrating a triumph . . . By wearing the toga Brother Russell in effect said, "I have fought the good fight; I have triumphed and shall be received as a member of the royal family of heaven."

Thus, wrapped in a toga, the founder of a religious movement that would come to influence millions worldwide departed the land of the living. When reading the account in full, the toga request seems more to do with practicality, or perhaps diminished lucidity, than any grand symbolic gesture. Russell was apparently in a great deal of pain and wanted to be comfortable. But it is revealing to note the readiness with which his followers ascribed profound spiritual meaning to a repurposed bed sheet—even borrowing prose from Roman poets in their eagerness to put a few final, grand words in the mouth of their deceased hero.

The episode reminds me of the scene in Monty Python's *Life of Brian* in which Brian is trying to escape a mob desperate to appoint him as their new Messiah. One of Brian's sandals detaches itself in the scramble to flee and is picked up by the pursuing fanatics. "He has given us a shoe!" shrieks Michael Palin. "The shoe is the sign," urges John Cleese. "Let us, like him, hold up one shoe, for this is his sign that all who follow him shall do likewise." Each holding one shoe aloft, the crazed rabble resume their chase. It is hard not to see similar depths of silliness and credulity in those who would interpret the wearing of bedlinen as a final message of triumph by a departing member of the "royal family of heaven."

Writers and historians have long agonized over whether the Pastor was good or bad, cynical or deluded. I honestly struggle to look on him favorably, and not just because such a large percentage of the unpleasantness in my life stems from the movement he birthed. Russell allowed himself to be swept along on a tide of late 19th century evangelical hysteria at a time when almost anyone with a bit of money and charisma—and preferably an unconventional take on the Bible—would probably have had little difficulty attracting an audience. Rather than shy away from the power his followers seemed determined to lavish on him, he developed a taste for it. That much is obvious when reviewing the 1917 book *What Pastor Russell Said*, a posthumous collection of answers to questions put to him at lectures and sermons. Doting followers would seek their Pastor's wisdom on everything from the extent to which letters could be sent and received, to managing household spending, to taking out insurance, to whether children could be sent to college and university.[20] Russell's devotees wanted him to instruct them on every aspect of living, and in many cases he was only too happy to oblige.

Throw into the equation the fact that Russell was a habitual megaphone for false predictions, a subscriber to crackpot pyramid theories, a casual racist, and a man who resorted to deception in an attempt to conceal his marital indiscretions, and we are left with an individual who is unrecognizable from the wise, unassuming, grandfatherly figure Watchtower would have us imagine.

At best, Russell was a gullible and eccentric entrepreneur with more money than sense who let fame and adulation go to his head. At worst, he was a crank, charlatan and narcissist whose role as founder of a religious movement with pretensions of equality, family

---

[20] Russell's answer was eerily similar to that of Watchtower today: "I advise all Christians not to send their children to colleges or universities; for if they do, they will risk a great deal through infidelity and unbelief, and they will be doing their children a positive injury."

values and moral purity is entirely at odds with his writings and conduct. In either case, by forming an organization with such apocalyptic, authoritarian underpinnings, Russell unknowingly created a monster that would go on to wreak havoc in the lives of millions. And it was a monster that would get its teeth under the tenure of his successor.

CHAPTER SEVEN

# The Judge

*"Whoever undertakes to set himself up as a judge of Truth and Knowledge is shipwrecked by the laughter of the gods."*
—Albert Einstein

*"Any fool can criticize, condemn and complain—and most fools do."*
—Benjamin Franklin

IN EARLY 1894, two women entered the Missouri office of a lawyer in his mid-20s. They were Bible Students, and they were keen to spread the news of God's plan for mankind as revealed to them by Pastor Russell. The lawyer was preoccupied with his work, but decided the most expedient way to end the intrusion was to buy three volumes of *Millennial Dawn* from them (later retitled *Studies in the Scriptures*). What happened next is recounted in the lawyer's subsequent letter to *The Watch Tower*, which was sent along with an order for more literature:

> I took the books home, and thought little of them, until a few weeks ago, when I had some spare time, I began reading the first volume, and it was so very interesting that I could not stop. The result is, my dear wife and myself have read these books with the keenest interest, and we consider it a God-send and a great blessing that we have had the opportunity of coming in contact with them. They are indeed a "helping hand" to the study of the Bible.

> The great truths revealed in the study of this series have simply reversed our earthly aspirations; and realizing to some extent, at least, the great opportunity for doing something for Christ, we intend to take advantage of this opportunity in distributing these books, first, among our nearest relatives and friends, and then among the poor who desire to read them and are unable to purchase; and for that reason we desire these extra copies. As soon as these are exhausted, we will order more, and try to do what we can in this way, be it ever so little.

The young lawyer had no way of knowing that these three books would change his life far more profoundly than he could possibly have imagined. Indeed, his enthrallment with Russell's writings would change not only *his* life, but the lives of generations to follow—for the lawyer's name was Joseph Franklin Rutherford. After joining himself to Watchtower's cause, Rutherford would rapidly rise through the organization's ranks to become the Pastor's successor. He would go on and author 21 books and a multitude of booklets and magazine articles. Quite apart from being a prolific writer, this lawyer would end up being the inventor of the name "Jehovah's witnesses."

Rutherford was born on November 8, 1869, in Versailles, Morgan County, Missouri. His Baptist parents, James Calvin and Lenora Strickland Rutherford, were farmers. When their teenage son showed an interest in pursuing a career in law, they insisted he pay the wages of a farm laborer as his replacement in addition to paying for his studies. Young Rutherford was able to meet their condition by securing a loan and selling encyclopedias from house to house.

On completing his education, Rutherford worked for a while as a court reporter. On May 5, 1892, aged 22, he passed his bar examinations to practice law in Missouri, working from the offices of a firm named Draffen & Wright as a trial lawyer. Rutherford would also serve four years as public prosecutor for Boonville, Missouri. On occasion he would be called upon to act as a stand-in judge for the Eighth Judicial Circuit Court of Missouri.[1] Despite these being only fleeting positions of no great significance or prestige, Rutherford would still leverage them to style himself as "Judge Rutherford" upon finally securing the reins of power at Watchtower—but all of that was still to come.

Despite the "God-send" and "great blessing" of purchasing three volumes of *Millennial Dawn* in 1894, Rutherford was apparently in no great hurry to drop everything and follow the Pastor. In 1896, he was more interested in campaigning for his hero, William Jennings Bryan, to become America's next president. (Rutherford would, for the rest of his life, sport Bryan's turned-up collar style—long after the trend had passed.) It would not be until 1906 that baptism would beckon, with Rutherford beginning work as a "pilgrim," or traveling Watchtower representative, soon thereafter.

With the Pastor facing mounting legal battles, most notably over his ugly split with Maria, what he

---

[1] In his 2003 book *The Four Presidents of the Watch Tower Society,* Watchtower historian Edmond Gruss relates how Rutherford would be dispatched by his landlord attorney to fill in for the traveling magistrate due to bad weather and/or illness. The occasions on which he was called upon to do this totaled "four or five days," and these days could be quite uneventful. "According to Hayden Covington," Gruss writes, "one day the only case scheduled resulted in a thirty-day jail sentence imposed on a hungry black man for stealing a watermelon to eat."

needed more than anything was a good lawyer—and Rutherford was happy to oblige, offering his services pro bono. To that end, in 1909 Rutherford joined the New York State Bar and developed a reputation among his fellow brethren as a zealous defender of their beloved Pastor. As mentioned in the previous chapter, in 1915 he went to the trouble of penning a 64-page booklet titled *A Great Battle in the Ecclesiastical Heavens* in which he showed a great talent for contorting the facts to get his point across—especially in his misrepresentation of the age of Rose Ball during the notorious jellyfish incident. (One has to wonder what Rutherford's chances of securing the presidency would have been if the Pastor had not had quite so many scandals and tribulations requiring his intervention.)

In addition to his legal work, Rutherford would also be called upon to deputize for the Pastor at debates and on trips abroad. By the time of Russell's death on October 31, 1916, Rutherford was sufficiently well-positioned in Watchtower's pecking order to be considered the Pastor's obvious successor—at least by those that mattered—and subsequent events would reveal him to be more than keen to assume that role.

But there was just one problem. Pastor Russell had left a will indicating that he did not want supreme power to rest with one individual as it had done under his own presidency. The will was published posthumously in the December 1, 1916, issue of *The Watch Tower*, and stipulated, in part, as follows:

> I direct that the entire editorial charge of ZION'S WATCH TOWER shall be in the hands of a committee of five brethren, whom I exhort to great carefulness and fidelity to the Truth. All articles appearing in the columns of ZION'S WATCH TOWER shall

> have the unqualified approval of at least three of the committee of five, and I urge that if any matter approved by three be known or supposed to be contrary to the views of one or both of the other members of the committee, such articles shall be held over for thought, prayer and discussion for three months before being published—that so far as possible the unity of the faith and the bonds of peace may be maintained in the Editorial management of the journal.

***Joseph Franklin Rutherford***

What Russell insisted on was a leadership arrangement much more familiar to Witnesses today—a governing "Editorial Committee of five" who would share in deliberating over material to be printed in *The Watch Tower*, thereby steering the theology of the organization. But incredibly, through a series of very clever political and legal maneuverings, Rutherford was able to effectively tear up the Pastor's will. The controversy he would generate in so doing would reverberate for decades, leading to a major split in the religion. By 1919, one seventh of Bible Students had parted ways with Watchtower, and thousands more would follow in the years ahead. It is in large part because of the 1917 leadership crisis that, to this day, Jehovah's Witnesses and the Bible Student movement are two distinct denominations.

When it comes to piecing together the chain of events you will get different stories depending on which sources you consult. There were two opposing factions—Rutherford and his supporters in the red corner, and in the blue corner a group of Watchtower directors and their supporters who deeply resented the direction in which the organization was being taken. Both factions wrote extensively about what transpired in their attempts to bring Russell's followers round to their point of view, and both felt fully vindicated in their actions.

To simplify things, I will use Watchtower's narrative as found in the *Proclaimers* book as the basis for the following few pages, and introduce other sources as appropriate to shed light on events. (I would have preferred to use the more recent *God's Kingdom Rules!* book, but it has absolutely nothing to say about this pivotal point in the organization's history. Indeed, the 240-page book only mentions Rutherford by name 21 times.) It should, however, come as little surprise if I tell you beforehand that the official Watchtower version of events is misleading to say the least.

For example, consider the following from page 66 of the *Proclaimers* book concerning a few at headquarters who are said to have "resented" Rutherford:

> The fact that the work was moving ahead and that he was making every effort to follow the arrangements that had been put in place by Russell did not seem to impress them.

As we have already seen, the "arrangements that had been put in place by Russell" involved stewardship of the *Watch Tower* magazine being shared by the members of an editorial committee, effectively reducing the role of the Society's president to little more than an administrative figurehead (similar to the role formerly occupied by Conley). But Rutherford's actions following Russell's death showed a clear disregard for his much-loved predecessor's instructions. As his presidency unfolded, it would become painfully apparent that he considered the Pastor's "arrangements" for the editorial committee as a hindrance to be brushed aside.

Rutherford was elected on January 6, 1917, two months after Russell's death. Despite not being an officer of the Society, and not even being on Russell's suggested shortlist for the "committee of five" (his name only featured along with five other potential substitutes on a B-list) he somehow managed to win over key players in the post-Russell interim management—most notably A. H. Macmillan, Russell's former assistant, and W. E. Van Amburgh, the Society's secretary-treasurer. Both of these men had considerable voting power for electing the next president, because they each held proxy votes on behalf of other members of the Society who could not attend the election in person, but who trusted their judgment. Hence, having ingratiated himself with these kingmakers, Rutherford had little difficulty securing the presidency. He was also careful to make sure his powers as president were increased by promptly having bylaws enacted that would effectively grant him full executive control of the Society. A brochure titled *Light After Darkness*, released by the Society directors who later tried to oppose him, described the nature of these bylaws:

> One of the by-laws, which was suggested at the shareholders' meeting, reads:
>
> "The President of the Society shall always be the Executive Officer and General Manager of the Corporation, having in charge the management of its affairs and work, both in America and in foreign countries."

> Another by-law, the one to which the Committee especially objected, authorized the President to appoint an Advisory Committee of three, of which the Secretary and Treasurer, Brother Van Amburgh, was to be a permanent member. These by-laws and such a Committee would naturally be thought by some to supplant the Directors in their advisory and executive capacity.

Rutherford had these bylaws read out and agreed to at the Society's annual shareholders' meeting at which he was elected president. However, according to the Society's charter, they could only become binding once passed by the board of directors. It was therefore in the hands of the board of directors to consent to measures that would effectively limit their control. Concerning this crucial moment, *Light After Darkness* adds:

> Like the dear sheep who were in attendance at the shareholders' meeting, unsuspicious and anxious to do anything to aid the new President, the Directors decided without protest to spread [the bylaws] upon the minutes of their meeting. It was this action that made the by-laws genuine and legal, an act which the Board hoped at the time would prove to be for the best interests of the work.

However well-meaning they may have been, by naively granting their new president so much latitude the directors were the architects of their own downfall. Rutherford now had the power to do whatever he wanted, and it did not take long for four of them (Robert H. Hirsh, Alfred I. Ritchie, Isaac F. Hoskins and James D. Wright) to grasp the enormity of their error. What happened next is described this way in the *Proclaimers* book:

> Opposition soon mounted. Four members of the board of directors of the Society went so far as to endeavor to wrest administrative control from Rutherford's hands.

Or, to put it more accurately, a *majority* of the board of directors (there were seven in total) endeavored to rectify their error by wresting administrative control *back* from Rutherford's hands, as Raymond Franz observed in *Crisis of Conscience:*

> Early in his presidency, four of the seven Directors (a majority) took issue with what they viewed as arbitrary action on the part of the president. He was not recognizing the Board of Directors and working with it as a body but was acting unilaterally, taking actions and then informing them later of what he had decided to do.

An early example of Rutherford's "arbitrary action" came with his handling of a controversy surrounding Watchtower representative Paul S. L. Johnson. Johnson had been dispatched to the organization's London offices by Rutherford shortly before his election as president, but during his trip he had apparently run amok, having been overcome by delusions of grandeur. He dismissed two of Watchtower's local officers and declared himself to be Russell's heir apparent and a key figure in the outworking of various Bible prophecies. (As crazy as this may sound, in the fullness of time, Rutherford could be considered guilty of doing more-or-less the same thing at the Society's headquarters.)

After some considerable drama involving seized funds, legal action, and an escape down a drainpipe,[2]

---

[2] Penton explains the debacle in *Apocalypse Delayed:* "Using the statement of powers granted him when he had been sent to Britain, [Johnson] tied up the International Bible Students' bank account and took over the London offices of the IBSA. He and another Bible Student named Housden seized all mails, opened the association's safe, and took all its on-hand funds. As a result, Rutherford, by then president, sent written cancellation of Johnson's appointment, and the latter's lawyer was forced to drop a suit to prohibit Rutherford loy-

Johnson was forced to return to America to be reprimanded by Rutherford, who reorganized the affairs of the London office and restored order. However, the four directors were unhappy with the president's arbitrary handling of matters. In particular, they believed Johnson had been deprived of a fair hearing. According to *Light After Darkness*, Rutherford cautioned them that "the management was in his hands and that it was none of their business," at which point they resolved among themselves to take action and withdraw the powers with which they had bestowed him:

> At a meeting of the Board of Directors in June . . . a resolution was presented to rescind the by-laws. This was the last meeting ever held by the Directors over which Brother Rutherford presided. When the resolution came up the President raised such a storm of opposition that the brethren yielded to his appeal to hold the resolution over until the next meeting, which was announced for July 20th. Although two or three requests were subsequently made for a meeting prior thereto, these were refused by the President until July 17.

Once again, it seems the directors had entirely underestimated Rutherford's determination and cunning. By letting him "hold the resolution over until the next week" they were granting him precious time to outmaneuver them and orchestrate their expulsion. In those crucial weeks between June 20 (the date of the "last meeting") and July 17 before the board was to be reconvened, Rutherford gained a legal opinion from a

---

alists from using £800 which had been temporarily tied up in the bank. Led by Rutherford loyalist Jesse Hemery, a group of Bible Students at the IBSA's London offices and residence eventually barricaded Johnson in his room. To escape, he was forced to leave by his window and climb down an outside drainpipe."

lawyer in Philadelphia to the effect that, since the four dissenting directors had not been appointed to office at the January shareholder's meeting, and were only appointees of Russell, they had no legal rights to control of the Society. The *Proclaimers* book picks up the story:

> It turned out that although the four opposing directors had been appointed by Brother Russell, these appointments had never been confirmed by vote of the corporation members at the annual meeting of the Society. Therefore, the four of them were not legal members of the board of directors at all! Rutherford had been aware of this but had not mentioned it at first. Why not? He had wanted to avoid giving the impression that he was going against Brother Russell's wishes. However, when it became evident that they would not discontinue their opposition, Rutherford acted within his authority and responsibility as president to replace them with four others whose appointments were to be confirmed at the next annual meeting, to be held in January 1918.

Again, the *Proclaimers* book is guilty of grossly misrepresenting events—this time by giving the impression Rutherford exercised restraint by not mentioning "at first" that he had the right to remove the directors. This myth of patience on the part of Rutherford perhaps stems at least partly from A. H. Macmillan, who decades later would write in a shamefully one-sided account that Rutherford "did everything that he could to help his opposers see their mistake, holding a number of meetings with them, trying to reason with them and trying to show them how contrary their course was to the Society's charter and the entire program Russell had followed since the organization was formed." In reality, no patience or restraint was extended, neither were any meaningful attempts at reconciliation made.

The *Proclaimers* narrative merely blurs the story so that the order and timing of events is obscured. Once Rutherford learned of the desire of the four directors to repeal his powers, he acted swiftly and decisively. That much is clear, at least from the account in *Light After Darkness:*

> On his homeward journey [from acquiring the legal opinion] he visited Pittsburgh and appointed brethren to take our places, whom no doubt he felt certain would never attempt to rescind his by-laws, as this was his only cause for complaint against us.
>
> At the noonday meal in the Bethel Dining Room on July 17, Brother Rutherford made the startling announcement to all gathered there that the Directors of the Society had never been legally elected, and that he had declared the offices of four of them vacant and appointed new ones in their places. All the old Directors were present and the Brethren he had appointed were also present.

Put simply, before the four-director majority could have a second chance at repealing Rutherford's new powers, he replaced them with four yes-men (A. H. Macmillan, W. E. Spill, J. A. Bohnet and George H. Fisher) who could be counted on to do his bidding. Less than a month had passed since the directors' botched attempt at stopping Rutherford and already he had succeeded in dispensing with their services. The "Judge" was now able to rule unopposed.

Watchtower continues to point to the legal opinion of a single lawyer as justification for Rutherford's "hard-fisted church politics" (to quote Penton). What the *Proclaimers* book declines to mention is that, following their abrupt demotion, the ex-directors sought several of their own legal opinions to the effect that they had been dismissed illegally:

> In this connection we might add that several lawyers have volunteered opinions upon the merits of this case. Some live in Pennsylvania, New York and New Jersey, and without a single exception all have agreed that, even aside from the moral wrong, Brother Rutherford's course is wholly unlawful.

Interestingly, Watchtower's 1959 precursor to the *Proclaimers* book, titled *Jehovah's Witnesses in the Divine Purpose,* attempted to mislead Witnesses on this detail. It claimed the directors approached a single attorney who "merely confirmed Brother Rutherford's position that they had never been members of the board of directors." But the directors went on record as having consulted *multiple* attorneys, at least one of whom they named so that Bible Students caught in the crossfire could verify his support of their position.[3]

In his book *Apocalypse Delayed,* Penton writes that "had Rutherford ever been taken to court for dismissing the four directors, he might very well have lost."[4] He adds that Rutherford's claim that the directors had not been legally elected "does not bear up under close scrutiny." Penton further suggests that, if Rutherford's logic were followed through consistently, then neither he nor the Society's other two officers (Pierson, the vice president, and Van Amburgh, the secretary-treasurer) had legal powers, since they were

---

3 On page 23 of *Light After Darkness* the directors write: "Upon the best legal advice we can obtain, and concurred in by Attorney Brother McGee, assistant to the Attorney General of Jersey, it appears that Brother Rutherford's interpretation of these technicalities is erroneous, and we are still the legal Directors of the Society."

4 Edmond Gruss concurs with this view, writing: "Legal consultants say his position was weak, and had the ousted directors pursued the matter legally, Rutherford would have lost."

not legally-elected directors when appointed at the January meeting.

But the four ousted directors were in no mood to drag their dispute with Rutherford through the courts, and once expelled from the board they had missed their chance to correct their mistake of granting Rutherford expanded powers. Having successfully consolidated control, the Judge instantly began wielding power more brazenly. On July 17, at the same time as declaring the directors' removal, Rutherford announced the release of a controversial new book titled *The Finished Mystery,* described as follows by the *Proclaimers* book:

> Brother Russell had been unable to produce [the seventh volume of *Studies in the Scriptures*] during his lifetime, though he had hoped to do so. Following his death, the Executive Committee of the Society arranged for two associates, Clayton J. Woodworth and George H. Fisher, to prepare this book, which was a commentary on Revelation, The Song of Solomon, and Ezekiel. In part, it was based on what Russell had written about these Bible books, and other comments and explanations were added.

An "Explanatory Note" in the opening pages of *The Finished Mystery* heralds it as the "posthumous work of Pastor Russell," although the fact that this is false advertising could not have gone unnoticed when the book was released in the Bethel dining room. As the *Proclaimers* book indicates, *The Finished Mystery* was not in any meaningful sense the work of Charles Taze Russell, but had instead been prepared by Clayton Woodworth and George Fisher. Concerning their authorship, in his book *Counting the Days to Armageddon* Robert Crompton notes:

> Indeed, it is obvious, even upon a fairly cursory reading of *The Finished Mystery,* that it was not in any straightforward sense the result of editing

> Russell's papers; rather it was in large measure the original work of Woodworth and Fisher at the behest of the new President.

Apart from the spurious claims regarding authorship, *The Finished Mystery* would prove controversial for a number of reasons—most pressingly, at least for the Bethel family at its unveiling, because it had been rushed through publication without the knowledge of the full board of directors and without the approval of the editorial committee. This editorial committee, you will recall, had been entrusted with formulating the Society's official teachings per Russell's will. But the will also charged them with publishing "no other periodicals" and "no other publications in any manner or degree"—and yet here was the Society's new president, having already disregarded the spirit of the Pastor's will by engineering executive powers for himself, releasing a new publication falsely styled the posthumous work of the Pastor against the Pastor's expressed instructions. Unsurprisingly, the *Proclaimers* book describes a dramatic reception for Rutherford's announcement:

> It was as if a bombshell had exploded! The four ousted directors seized upon the occasion and stirred up a five-hour controversy before the Bethel family over the administration of the Society's affairs. A number of the Bethel family sympathized with the opposers. The opposition continued for several weeks, with the disturbers threatening to "overthrow the existing tyranny," as they put it.

Rutherford and his supporters would have been well advised to listen to the "opposers" and shelve plans for *The Finished Mystery,* as later events would amply bear out. Instead, the Judge pressed ahead with publication, and by August 8 he had succeeded in evicting "the disgruntled ex-directors and their supporters" from headquarters.

At least according to one account concerning the eviction of Paul Johnson, this communist-style purge was carried out quite forcefully. On July 27, Johnson was ordered to leave Bethel. Following an altercation over a letter that Rutherford refused to let Johnson read out before the Bethel family, Rutherford "hastened to him and using physical force, which nearly pulled Brother Johnson off his feet, said in a fit of passion: 'You will leave this house before night; if you do not go, you will be put out.'" This, we are told, proved to be no idle threat. "Brother Johnson's personal effects were literally set outside the Bethel Home and brethren, as watchmen, were placed at various doors to prevent him from entering the house again."

But the dust had barely settled on the Judge's hard-won consolidation of power before the storm clouds of controversy would gather, thanks to his refusal to listen to reason regarding *The Finished Mystery.* Quite apart from the legal furor that would ensue from its publication, it should have been obvious from the outset that the volume was entirely unfit for distribution. There is no polite way of putting it: the book was (is) a slow-motion train wreck from start to finish, and its publication would go on to generate considerable unnecessary misery for the very individuals who championed its creation.

Firstly, there was the book's unbounded glorification of the Pastor, who was all but deified in its pages. "The amount of work that Pastor Russell performed is incredible, and it is doubtful whether it was ever equalled by any other human being," the writer insisted. The same page also marvels that the Pastor managed his unparalleled work despite poor health—

including "such distressing hemorrhoids that it was impossible for him to rest in the easiest chair."

Not only did *The Finished Mystery* confirm Russell as the "faithful and wise servant"—it also declared him to be the "seventh angel" mentioned in Revelation. (pp. 4-6, 53, 169) Though dead, Russell was described as supervising the harvest work, and Ezekiel 33:22 was invoked to claim he was speaking from beyond the grave through the pages of *The Finished Mystery.* (pp. 144, 256, 530) The "loud voice" of Revelation 14:18 was reimagined as a "disappointed cry" from Russell, because he did not have time to complete *The Finished Mystery* himself. (p. 227) Even Russell's marital problems were hailed as a fulfillment of Bible prophecy. It was explained that the book of Ezekiel had foretold that God would separate Russell from his wife and make her "dead" in his eyes. (pp. 483-484)

But the Pastor was not the only subject of the book's fantastic claims. The "behemoth" of Job chapter 40 was explained as being the stationary steam engine, and the "leviathan" of Job chapter 41 was revealed to be the steam locomotive. (pp. 84-85) Page 93 disclosed that the "valiant men" of Nahum 2:3 were the locomotive engineer and fireman. (The authors were apparently keen train enthusiasts.) The rider on the white horse in Revelation 6:2 was unmasked as the "Bishop of Rome," referred to as the "personal representative of Satan." (p. 106) The earth was revealed to be 48,000 years old. (p. 139) *The Finished Mystery* was described as "divinely provided" to humanity, and identified as the "incense burner" of Revelation 8:5. (p. 145) Michael and his angels from Revelation chapter 12 were determined as being the Pope and his bishops. (p. 188) England was condemned as having a "Satanic character." (p. 202) Revelation 14:20, it was claimed, predicted the precise traveling distance between where *The Finished Mystery* was written and where it was printed. (p. 230) Barbed wire, cash registers, typewriters and vacuum cleaners were among a list of inventions and discoveries resulting from increased enlightenment for the world since 1874 due to the glory of Christ, as foretold in Revelation 18:1. (p. 273) The "voice out of heaven" of Revelation 18:4 was explained as being the voice of the Watch Tower Society. (p. 276) Europeans were denounced as "the most cruel, bloodthirsty, quarrelsome, rapacious people on earth." (p. 307) And 1918 was pointed to as the year in which "God destroys the churches wholesale and the church members by the millions" while spirit-anointed Christians are raised to heaven, with 1931 later heralding the final establishment of Christ's kingdom on earth. (pp. 64, 485, 569)

***"The Finished Mystery," 1917 edition***

In short, the book reads like one long acid trip by someone who has spent an unhealthy amount of time immersed in the strange fantasies and endless predictions of Charles Taze Russell.[5] You would think the insanity I have enu-

[5] It can be argued that *The Finished Mystery* by itself debunks the prophetic claims of Jehovah's Witnesses, who teach that Christ was in the process of inspecting and cleansing their organization *while the book was being printed and distrib-*

merated above would by itself have been sufficient justification for Rutherford to consign *The Finished Mystery* to the shredder and erase it from history as expediently as possible—but that is not what happened.

To this day, despite repeatedly referring to the book as having played a significant role in Bible prophecy, Watchtower is generally far too embarrassed to quote directly from its pages—preferring instead to point to the storm of controversy it generated on its release as evidence of its importance.[6] But this storm was generated, not by any revolutionary theological wisdom Woodworth and Fisher had to dispense (they dispensed nothing of the sort—only page after page of unbridled, self-indulgent silliness), but because—at the height of war hysteria in America—*The Finished Mystery* denounced patriotism as "murder" and war as "an open and utter violation of Christianity." This, you might not be too surprised to learn, did not go down terribly well with the United States government, with Congress having only just passed the 1917 Espionage Act in the same month as the book's publication. Dr. Lon J. Strauss describes how events unfolded in his 2012 PhD thesis, titled *A Paranoid State: The American Public, Military Surveillance and the Espionage Act of 1917*:

---

*uted.* Only when you spend some time examining the contents of the book can you appreciate how preposterous it would be for a returning Jesus to give it his seal of approval.

[6] The *Revelation* book, despite acknowledging that *The Finished Mystery* "proved to be unsatisfactory as an explanation of Revelation," (p. 159) nevertheless points to it on page 208 as a means by which the two witnesses of Revelation 11 "struck the earth with every sort of plague." More recently, a 2016 *Watchtower* has applied Ezekiel's vision of a skeleton gaining flesh and coming to life as describing events leading up to 1919, with *The Finished Mystery* named as a tool that "strengthened God's people."

> The Committee on Public Information reported that IBSA members were promoting *The Finished Mystery*—supposedly the posthumously published writings of Pastor Russell—in the U.S. The Canadian government had recently banned the book as pro-German. . . . Dan W. Locke, a lawyer in Everett, Washington wrote to the Secretary of War, Newton D. Baker, informing him about a dire situation. He warned that members of the International Bible Students Association were engaged throughout the country preaching conscientious objection. Locke stated that he had attended a meeting of the IBSA and "listened as he (the preacher) spread his insidious doctrine, that Christ condemned murder" and therefore no true Christian could serve in the military. When Locke challenged the speaker regarding obligations of American citizens, the preacher answered that Christians were members of Christ's kingdom and therefore had no responsibilities to earthly nations. If this was not disloyal, then Locke demanded to know what was. Fearing that a national organization was influencing Americans toward pacifism, intelligence officers began investigating *The Finished Mystery* in late February [1918].

After examining the book, these intelligence officers—most of whom had been lawyers prior to the war—quickly concluded it was seditious material that contravened the Espionage Act of 1917. Of particular concern were pages 247 through 253, which were especially scathing in their condemnation of the "butchery" of war. Ironically, though, a considerable chunk of these pages had not been penned by Clayton Woodworth or George Fisher at all; neither by the Judge, nor the ghost of Charles Taze Russell, nor indeed anyone affiliated with Watchtower. The offending pages mostly comprised the words of a sermon by Reverend John Haynes Holmes of the "Church of the Messiah" in New York City—"an outspoken pacifist and opponent to the war"—whose speech was so scornful of America and its allies that portions of it had already been dropped on British troops on the Western Front as propaganda by the Germans. Hence, a considerable majority of the complaints against *The Finished Mystery* involved material that the writers had reproduced from what would be considered by Witnesses today as "Babylon the Great"—or a religious source outside Watchtower.

Once Rutherford learned that these pages were key to the government's pursuit of his organization, he attempted to have them removed in a last ditch attempt to forestall prosecution. Hence, a 1955 *Watchtower* admits to Bible Students "compromisingly cutting out pages 247-253 of *The Finished Mystery*, their seventh volume of *Studies in the Scriptures*, to please would-be censors."[7] As pressure intensified, Rutherford even began to backtrack on his antiwar stance, as Strauss relates:

> On May 5, Rutherford visited a Bible Students' meeting in Washington, D.C. A [*sic*] MID agent was in attendance, listening for disloyal remarks. Yet, the agent reported Rutherford "paid a glowing tribute to the President." Rutherford explained that the current war was foretold in the scriptures

---

[7] For many years it was believed that the woes experienced by the Bible Students in 1918 represented divine punishments as part of their emancipation from false religion. A 1992 *Watchtower* explained that "in 1918 Jehovah's servants came into a measure of bondage to Babylon the Great." (In other words, they were guilty of capitulating to pressure from false religion and therefore required discipline.) However, in the March 2016 *Watchtower* study edition "Questions From Readers" article, this teaching was reversed.

and that "those who engaged in it were following a Divine command; that those sacrificing their lives in behalf of their country would inherit eternal life as the result."

Strauss observes that this "glowing tribute" of President Woodrow Wilson and the war effort was "diametrically opposite" to the message Rutherford and his followers had hitherto been preaching. Indeed, less than three months earlier, on February 24, the Judge had delivered a speech with the theme "Millions Now Living May Never Die"[8] in which he had attacked the clergy for their endorsement of the war, claiming that "according to the Scriptures, the clergymen are the most reprehensible men on earth for the great war that is now afflicting mankind." It seems that, when needed, the Judge was capable of completely reversing his message to the point of saying things that he condemned others in the strongest possible terms for saying.

But despite his attempts at placating the authorities, senior government officials were hell-bent on seeing Rutherford and his associates behind bars. On May 7, 1918, they achieved their goal when warrants were issued for the arrest of the Judge and seven of his associates under charges of violating the 1917 Espionage Act.[9] Most historians will now look back on this and ensuing developments as among the more cringeworthy episodes in America's military history. They will generally admit that, quite apart from wartime hysteria, religious bias and interference from the clergy

[8] Rutherford would slightly modify this catchy slogan for the title of a future booklet.

[9] Interestingly, by being charged under the 1917 Espionage Act, Rutherford would join an extremely exclusive club that nearly a century later would also welcome Edward Snowden.

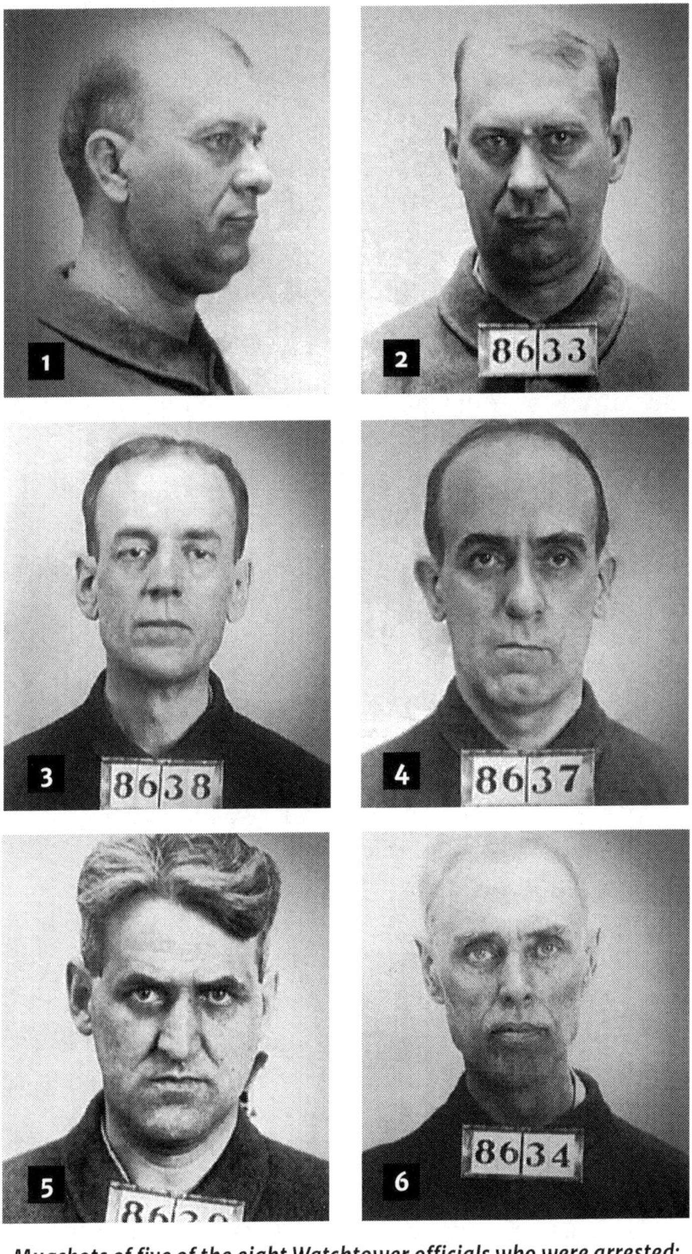


*Mugshots of five of the eight Watchtower officials who were arrested: Joseph F. Rutherford (1–2), Clayton J. Woodworth (3), George H. Fisher (4), Alexander H. Macmillan (5) and William E. Van Amburgh (6)*

played a not insignificant role in the grossly overblown chastisement of the Bible Students over a few ill-advised, mostly borrowed printed remarks. However, notwithstanding the cards being so heavily stacked against the eight who were arrested, there is evidence that considerable negligence on the part of Rutherford only served to exacerbate their predicament.

For example, the authorities were concerned about Watchtower undermining the war effort by indiscriminately handing out documents that could help young men avoid conscription on religious grounds. It came to light that Rutherford had put his signature to a number of blank affidavits—papers attesting to the IBSA (International Bible Students Association) being a legitimate religious organization—before going away on a trip, as Strauss explains:

> To make matters worse, Rutherford signed several blank affidavits. He left the registrant's name empty on the form, then left on a trip about mid-January 1918. This, coupled with the fact that Rutherford did not instruct his office personnel with who qualified for an affidavit, was disastrous. Even if Rutherford was simply being negligent, if those blank affidavits with his signature on them fell into the wrong hands, potentially, anyone's name could be filled in, consecrated member or not.

But this was not the only awkward truth to come to light during the trial. Under cross-examination, it turned out the Judge was not quite the ardent pacifist he had been previously leading people to believe:

> Rutherford, like other witnesses before him, stated that it was up to a man's individual conscience whether he would or would not take up arms for the government. "If you ask me individually I say my individual inclination is to go into war, because that

has been my ambition from youth to lead an army."

He would judge no man for his decision.

This startling piece of testimony speaks volumes about Rutherford's character. The 1917 presidency coup had already highlighted his burning "ambition" to "lead an army"—an ambition that drove him to act ruthlessly in sweeping aside the four directors, not to mention the last will and testament of the Pastor. Future events, and insights from those who worked closely with the Judge, would further attest to this combative, power-hungry streak.

As to Rutherford's somewhat conflicted stance on pacifism, Strauss relates that "when [prosecuting Judge] Oeland pressed him on whether a member could adhere to the draft and remain in good standing with IBSA, Rutherford said no." When further pressed on the matter, Rutherford gave a convoluted answer to the effect that Bible Students would not have a good standing with Watchtower if they went to war, but he had no problem with other Christians or members of other religions doing so. "For intelligence officers, who tirelessly worked on investigating the IBSA, Rutherford's statement was evasive," remarks Strauss.

A further controversy during the trial arose from the revelation that, despite going to considerable trouble to arrange the printing of *The Finished Mystery*, Rutherford had been less than thorough in proofreading the manuscript prior to publication, as Strauss further explains:

> At the trial, the prosecution inquired if Rutherford approved of the book, in its entirety. Rutherford read the manuscript he received from Woodworth and Fisher from February to April 1917 and at that time endorsed it. The version he saw did not include the lecture by John Hays [*sic*] Holmes. In fact, he

> did not read that portion until early March 1918. He assumed the version that would go to print was the manuscript he read and therefore never double-checked. Rutherford claimed he did not even reexamine the book after the Canadian government raised objections to it in early 1918.

Hence, several pages that were actually written by a non-Bible Student preacher—pages that formed the basis of much of the government's case against Watchtower—had not been properly checked by the new president. Even the banning of the book by the Canadian authorities was apparently not considered sufficient incentive for Rutherford to revisit those inflammatory pages or question the wisdom of giving some other preacher's anti-war tirade widespread distribution.

Again, it is worth stressing that Rutherford and his colleagues were by no means facing a fair trial. The political climate at the time meant the odds were firmly against them from the outset. To make matters worse, Judge Howe was "not the most unbiased person to preside over this case" according to Strauss, who also observed that "the judge seemed to be doing the prosecution's job" at times by, for example, refusing to allow Rutherford the opportunity to present his arguments in some instances. All the same, even without the obvious unfairness, Rutherford's ineptitude made it easy for a conviction to be achieved:

Even without the cards apparently stacked against him, Rutherford did not make a good impression at the trial. His actions smacked of negligence. First, he did not proofread a final version of The Finished Mystery before it was printed. In fact, there was little to no oversight of the publishers, who were also the authors. Second, with the difficulties in Canada, Rutherford should have taken steps to ensure something similar did not occur in the US. On the contrary, though, he appeared to desire a run-in with the government over his objection to war. On June 20, the jury found Rutherford and his seven associates guilty of violating the Espionage Act. The following day all but one were given twenty-year jail sentences. (The exception was an Italian Bible Student named Giovanni De Gecca who received a shorter, ten-year sentence.) Thus began the incarceration of eight senior Watchtower officials, including the Society's president, at Atlanta Penitentiary. By throwing Rutherford and his followers behind bars, with overblown accusations of "religious propaganda" that was "more harmful than a division of German soldiers" ringing in their ears, Judge Howe had given a despotic evangelical leader a gift beyond measure.

For years thereafter, Rutherford and his followers could claim, with some justification, that they were victims of unfair persecution. Before long, the Judge would even start pointing to his unjust treatment as the fulfillment of Bible prophecy—the affliction of God's people by Satan's wicked system from which he and his brothers had emerged triumphant. Not even the Pastor had been able to boast such a moving tale of martyrdom and and governmental oppression on his résumé! 1919, the year of the group's early release, would become etched in Witness dogma as the year Christ completed his inspection and cleansing of God's people—a process he had begun on his invisible arrival in 1914 when the "Gentile times" had ended.

But, for the time being, the Judge had more pressing matters to contend with, namely coming to terms with life as a lowly prisoner. Concerning this, his fellow inmate A. H. Macmillan offers the following anecdote:

At first we were put in the tailor shop making but-

> tonholes and sewing buttons on prisoners' clothes. They put Rutherford to making those little jackets the prisoners wear. There was no collar on them, just sleeves and pockets. Giovanni De Cecca, who is still a member of our headquarters staff, relates how Rutherford worked on one for a long time and even then he did not finish it. One of the guards, Giovanni said, was just a little fellow but he "trimmed the judge down," and Rutherford was a big man, six feet, four. But the guard was so unreasonable that some of the other prisoners, three or four Italians and some Jews, out of pity for him, took hold of the jacket and finished it in just a few minutes. For that consideration and kindness shown by these other prisoners who never had seen him before, Rutherford actually had tears in his eyes. Eventually Rutherford was transferred to the library, where he was much more at home with the work.

Witnesses today are familiar with the Judge as being a tall, intimidating figure—a powerful orator with a booming voice,[10] and yet, according to Macmillan, here he was reduced to tears because "three or four Italians and some Jews" had come to his rescue by relieving him of light manual labor. Unfortunately, the Judge would soon forget the "consideration and kindness" of his Jewish fellow inmates, as his words and actions in later years would indicate.

During his nine-month confinement, Rutherford feared the opponents he had successfully vanquished would return and sway the Society's members to re-

[10] Personally, I struggle to find either a booming voice or powerful oratory when listening to recordings of the Judge's speeches, which you can find on YouTube. To my ear, Rutherford had a mildly high-pitched voice, and at least by the '30s was accustomed to reading his speeches from a script rather than delivering them extemporaneously. Perhaps, as is so often the case, you had to be there.

pudiate his leadership, but these fears were to prove ill-founded. On January 2, 1919, the Judge received a telegram informing him he had been reelected as president at the Society's annual meeting—despite being behind bars and therefore unable to influence proceedings. This apparently convinced him that God had intervened and wanted him to continue as Watchtower's leader.

Finally, on March 25, 1919, Rutherford and his associates were released on bail. The judgment against them would soon be reversed and, over a year later, the government would announce that all charges had been dropped.

A free man once more, Rutherford wasted little time in furthering his work of reorganizing Watchtower to his tastes. On September 5, 1919, at a convention at Cedar Point, Ohio, Rutherford announced the launch of a new magazine titled *The Golden Age* (which, in later years, would be known by the name *Awake!*). Just as with *The Finished Mystery,* the launch of a new periodical was a flagrant violation of the Pastor's expressed wish that "no other periodicals" and "no other publications in any manner or degree" were to be published—but the window for protest had long passed. Within weeks, Bible Students were pressed into door-to-door distribution of this new magazine, described by the *Proclaimers* book as a "courageous journal." As quotes supplied in later pages will confirm, the "courage" of the *Golden Age* writers was necessitated more than anything else by their relentless discharge of incoherent, uneducated ramblings—including voluminous medical quackery, and even the occasional racist outburst.

With the Pastor's instructions regarding further

publications firmly discarded, there was nothing stopping the Judge from launching his own series of books, which Bible Students would be expected to enthusiastically "advertise, advertise, advertise" from 1922 onward.[11] He started in 1920 with the slender paperback booklet *Millions Now Living Will Never Die*—the title being a bolder version of the theme of his 1918 speech. Just as the Pastor before him had rested everything on the end of human rule coming in 1914, the *Millions* booklet would unveil the Judge's own signature false prediction—that 1925 would herald the return of various prominent Bible characters from the Old Testament who would help usher in God's Kingdom. Page 88 offered the following glimpse of the near future:

> What, then, should we expect to take place? . . . The chief thing to be restored is the human race to life; and since other Scriptures definitely fix the fact that there will be a resurrection of Abraham, Isaac, Jacob and other faithful ones of old, and that these will have the first favor, we may expect 1925 to witness the return of these faithful men of Israel from the condition of death, being resurrected and fully restored to perfect humanity and made the visible, legal representatives of the new order of things on earth.

So confident was Rutherford of his new teaching that it was referred to in his first hardbound book, released the following year, titled *The Harp of God.*

---

[11] On September 8, 1922, at a Bible Student convention at Cedar Point, Ohio, those in attendance were told to "Advertise, advertise, advertise the King and his Kingdom." Less than three years later in Rutherford's "Birth of a Nation" article (to be explained shortly), he would point to this event as the conclusion of the 1,260 days of Revelation chapter 12. To this day, Witnesses consider the 1922 Cedar Point convention as having prophetic significance.

"Abraham, Isaac, Jacob, and the other faithful prophets described by the apostle Paul in Hebrews 11" were to be "expected on earth within the next few years" and would "constitute the legal representatives of the Christ in the earth." A Watchtower book for children by William Van Amburgh, released in 1924 (only a year before the big event) and titled *The Way to Paradise*, expanded on the teaching even more imaginatively:

> We should, therefore, expect shortly after 1925 to see the awakening of Abel, Enoch, Noah, Abraham, Isaac, Jacob, Melchisedec, Job, Moses, Samuel, David, Isaiah, Jeremiah, Ezekiel, Daniel, John the Baptist, and others mentioned in the eleventh chapter of Hebrews.
>
> These will form a nucleus of the new kingdom on earth. One of the first things necessary will be to put Jerusalem in condition to be the capital of the world. . . .
>
> Old fashioned methods will not suffice. Already we see great changes coming in. The wireless and radio can carry messages half way around the world now; and by the time the princes are brought forth these inventions will be perfected to reach all the way round. . . .
>
> The princes can easily radio their instructions to any part of the world. Think of Prince Abraham having some general instructions to give, calling "Attention"; and all the people everywhere listening, and hearing every word he speaks, as easily as though he were addressing them from the platform of a public hall!
>
> Of course if any one desires to visit Jerusalem and personally interview the princes, or if the princes should desire to make a personal inspection of some public work, airplanes will soon be so perfected that it will be a matter of but a few hours

> ride to any part of the earth to or from Jerusalem. This will indeed be a new world, made glorious in every way.

Van Amburgh generously supplied the details of what Bible Students could expect to see in only a matter of months from his book's publication. An elite selection of Bible characters were to emerge from nowhere and seize control of earth's governance. From their world capital in Jerusalem, Abraham, Noah, Moses, King David and their corulers would fly out in airplanes to undertake "personal inspections" of their global domain, and issue instructions to their loyal subjects via radio.[12]

You would think Rutherford would have learned from the failure of his predecessor and exercised utmost caution with regard to offering extravagant predictions that could easily be debunked with the passage of a few years, but no such prudence was evident. If anything, the Judge was even more forthright in pushing 1925 as marking the end of human rule than the Pastor had been regarding 1914.

A 1922 *Watch Tower* insisted that the chronology pointing to 1925 "is not of man, but of God," further describing it as a "proven certainty." The very next issue declared expectations to be "of divine origin" and

---

[12] Rutherford had a strong fascination with the radio, which he considered as "God's provided means for communication between places of the earth" and a modern manifestation of the "lightning" referred to in Job 38:35. In 1924, he began broadcasting his sermons from Watchtower's own WBBR radio station. But, as his attacks on the clergy became increasingly strident, he was forced off the airwaves in the '30s. Livid at his treatment, the Judge predictably pointed to his censorship as further evidence of the oppression of God's people by Satan's system. He also issued his followers with phonographs so that his recorded messages could continue to be relayed.

"absolutely and unqualifiedly correct." A 1923 *Watch Tower* reminded Bible Students that "1925 is definitely settled by the Scriptures," and went so far as to argue that "the Christian now has much more upon which to base his faith then Noah had upon which to base his faith in a coming deluge." Then, only a year before the momentous date, *Watch Tower* readers were informed that "1925 is a date definitely and clearly marked in Scriptures, even more clearly than that of 1914."

When hopes for 1925 proved to be not quite as "absolutely and unqualifiedly correct" as had been suggested, the Judge executed a stunning U-turn, insisting he had never expressed his prediction with any certainty to begin with:

> Question: Have the ancient worthies returned?
>
> Answer: Certainly they have not returned. No one has seen them, and it would be foolish to make such an announcement. It was stated in the "Millions" book that we might reasonably expect them to return shortly after 1925, but this was merely an expressed opinion; besides it is still shortly after 1925.

Hence, what had so recently been a "proven certainty" was now "merely an expressed opinion." If Bible Students had been too excited by the prospect of Bible heroes soon returning and ruling over the earth, this was their own fault. Privately, though, the Judge knew he had been caught out just as the Pastor before him. Decades later, a footnote in a 1984 *Watchtower* would reveal that Rutherford gave Bethel workers the admission he should rightfully have offered to all his followers when he told them, regarding 1925: "I know I made an ass of myself."

Though 1925 did not mark the return of the Old Testament princes, it did mark a significant milestone in the Judge's presidency. It was the year Rutherford triumphed over the last remaining vestige of the Pastor's authority—the *Watch Tower* magazine's editorial committee. An article titled "Birth of the Nation" was published in the March 1, 1925, *Watch Tower* over the committee's objections. In it, the Judge dispensed with much of Russell's chronology, replacing it with his own fanciful prophetic interpretations. It was explained that Christ's kingdom had been established invisibly in heaven in 1914—not in 1874 as the Pastor had taught. With this in mind, Revelation chapter 12 was revealed to foretell the oppression suffered by the Bible Students following 1914—or, more precisely, the suffering of Rutherford and his associates in the first two years of his presidency. After all, if Satan had been hurled down to earth in 1914, would it not make perfect sense for him to take out his frustration on God's people?

Given the wholesale changes to their beloved Pastor's chronology, it is unsurprising that the editorial committee balked at Rutherford's ideas—but their opinions no longer mattered. The article would be printed anyway, redefining Watchtower teachings for decades to follow. Only two years later, in 1927, the organization would cease printing of *Studies in the Scriptures.* By 1931, the editorial committee had been dissolved entirely and the *1933 Year Book* would proclaim this development as evidence that "the Lord himself is running his organization."

With the Judge having finally purged the last remnants of Russell's influence, he set about slowly transforming Watchtower from a loose-knit "brethren" into a centralized "Theocracy."[13] But while Jehovah was os-

[13] Rutherford's idea of the "Theocracy" was explained in a 1940 issue of *Consolation:* "The Theocracy is at present admin-

tensibly the "Great Theocrat," it was the Judge who was to be relied on to interpret the divine will at all levels of the organization right down to congregation affairs—and even in deeply personal matters. Under Rutherford, the lives of followers of the organization began to be micromanaged to a degree never before seen. Perhaps nothing highlights this better than the Judge's bizarre resentment of beards—a resentment that is still felt by Witnesses to this day. In his book *30 Years a Watchtower Slave*, William Schnell gives his firsthand account of a remarkable incident at Watchtower's German office in Magdeburg in 1925:

> An amusing incident took place at the time of the Judge's visit. The Director of our German branch, as had many before him, had grown a large beard, patterned after Charles T. Russell's beard. The Judge did not want anything at all to remain which might remind him of Russell—not even the cultivation of a beard. So, sitting at the table for dinner one night within my earshot, the Director asked the Judge for one more large rotary press. The Judge said nothing for a while, merely ate. Then suddenly he looked up, his eyes pinned severely on the Director's huge beard and said, "I will buy you the press if you take that thing off," pointing to the beard. It surely shocked the Director's sensibilities, but he meekly heeded the warning and soon shamefacedly appeared minus his beard.[14]

In the decades following this incident, beards would become a major taboo among Witnesses. Illustrated publications released both during and following Rutherford's presidency would depict Bible characters

istered by the Watch Tower Bible and Tract Society, of which Judge Rutherford is the president and general manager."

[14] Schnell's story was verified in the *1974 Yearbook of Jehovah's Witnesses* on pages 97 and 98.

clean-shaven (yes, even Jesus!) and it would become generally understood that Witness males who insisted on sporting facial hair could expect diminished responsibilities.[15]

Obviously, the reasoning given for this comical stance could never be Bible-based, since nowhere in the Bible does it say anything close to "Thou shalt not grow a beard." (Quite the opposite, if you consult Leviticus 19:27.)[16] Instead, general advice is given to the effect that in certain cultures beards are "not the custom and are not considered acceptable for Christian ministers." "In fact," suggests a 2016 *Watchtower,* "having one may hinder a brother from bringing glory to God by his dress and grooming and his being irreprehensible."

Irrespective of the official justification, it seems more than likely that the incredible prohibition on beards that continues to impact the grooming habits of millions of male Witnesses deep into the 21st century stems from little more than petty resentment on Rutherford's part. It would appear that, at least in the Judge's troubled mind, anyone wearing a beard was signaling nostalgia for his predecessor—and that simply would

---

[15] The general rule is that a Witness male cannot give talks at Witness assemblies and conventions while having a beard, but the no-beard rule is enforced far more vigorously than that in practice. I know of one elder who finally succumbed to relentless pressure by shaving off his beard, which he had always been careful to keep neatly trimmed. The pressure came, not from his own body of elders per se, but from letters received from other congregations complaining that he should not have been dispatched to give a public talk at their Kingdom Hall while having facial hair.

[16] Because Watchtower now accepts that Bible characters wore beards, but frowns on Witness males wearing them, there is the strange phenomenon of fake beards being an awkward and ever-present feature of Watchtower-produced Bible dramatizations.

not be tolerated. Anything that could be linked with devotion to the Pastor or his teachings had to be purged.

Hence, within little over two decades of the Pastor's death, the Judge succeeded in fashioning a movement that was almost unrecognizable both organizationally and doctrinally from that which he inherited. Instead of Christ dying on a cross, it was decided he had died on an upright tree, or stake. Armageddon was not some period of anarchy and civil unrest preceding Christ's rule—it was a "universal war" during which "the very ground will revolt against the presence of the wicked horde . . . and it will heave up and shake itself against the enemy." The vindication of Jehovah's name through preaching, rather than character development or sanctification through works of Christian grace, became the primary goal incumbent on all true worshippers. Christmas was no longer a harmless celebration, but "of the Devil" and part of Satan's scheme to get the Christian church to "pander to all the pride and vanity and selfishness in the human family." Those who saluted the flag were deemed "covenant breakers" who are "guilty of death."[17] Even singing Christian songs at meetings would be abolished, for the reason that these

---

17 The refusal of Jehovah's Witnesses to salute the flag would result in Witness children in numerous states being expelled, and the controversy surrounding the issue would deteriorate into widespread mob violence against the Witnesses. However, the legal action pursued by Watchtower lawyers in defense of personal rights in this area would set valuable legal precedents. In his book *Fundamental Liberties of a Free People*, Milton R. Konvitz observes: "Fortunately for the development of civil liberties, the leaders of the sect followed an aggressive policy in the legal protection of the rights of Jehovah's Witnesses in the courts. We owe to their vigilance and constitutional militancy some of our most valuable legal precedents on the meaning and force of the First Amendment. It is to them that we owe credit for the decision of the Supreme Court that an expression of belief or sentiment may not be coerced."

"often express much that is out of harmony with the truth of and concerning God's kingdom."[18]

Given such sweeping changes, a total rebrand was only to be expected. Rather than thinking of themselves merely as Bible Students, from 1931, followers of Watchtower were to identify as "Jehovah's witnesses." Moreover, since they were advertisers of God's Kingdom, from 1935 even their places of worship were to get a new name: "Kingdom Halls." Congregation elders were gone, having been condemned as "parasites" who "think more highly of themselves than they ought to think, and are despicable in the eyes of the Lord," to be replaced by service directors charged with enforcing Watchtower policy.[19] Witnesses were to submit regular reports of their preaching activity to Watchtower for use in monitoring progress. "Zone servants," later known as circuit overseers, were to visit congregations to ensure they were keeping in line with the Judge's expectations.

These changes were significant and, with a few notable exceptions, many of them would become embedded in the fabric of Jehovah's Witness faith and culture for decades to follow. But beneath the veneer of piety and organizational "refinement" there was a darker, uglier side to Watchtower under Rutherford's presiden-

---

[18] The Judge's bizarre scrapping of singing would be reversed within two years of his death by his successors. The 1959 *Divine Purpose* book describes the release of the *Kingdom Service Song Book* at the 1944 assembly at Buffalo, New York, as follows: "This red-covered song book was received with genuine enthusiasm by the brothers, especially when it was announced that the book would be used at the weekly service meetings because, for some time prior to this, congregational singing had been dispensed with."

[19] This change would be revisited many years later, as we will see in the next chapter.

cy—a malevolence and bigotry that would occasionally surface in the literature and elsewhere. For example, as had been the case under the Pastor, Rutherford and his writers clearly had crude ideas about race that they were seemingly quite keen to extol—this time through the pages of *The Golden Age*. A 1919 issue spoke of the "desirability of sobering the southern negro" in a brief column on alcohol prohibition, and a 1928 issue observed that London schoolchildren enjoy "the heartiest laughs" when "watching a negro miner enjoying a square meal." Even Hispanics were rounded on in a 1927 issue of the magazine:

> Centuries before, anticipating the settlement of North America by a liberty-loving people, and the founding of a government favorable to enlightenment, Satan had sought to forestall it through the voyages of Columbus and the resulting effort to people it with Spaniards and other backward races under the influence of Rome. This undertaking failed.

These words were penned by a contributor named J. L. Bolling, who included them in a disturbing article that heaped scorn on Harriet Beacher Stowe for writing her famous novel *Uncle Tom's Cabin*—a work that proved to be instrumental in ending slavery in America. Bolling denounced the book as "the work of Satan" and heavily censured Stowe, who he accused of having "meddled in everything." Stowe, he argued, was "strongly influenced" by "demon manifestations" and "wicked spirits"

***Harriet Beacher Stowe: an unlikely target of Watchtower's condemnation***

through her husband, and wrote without sufficient knowledge of "the institution." Bolling also attacked Stowe for daring to claim inspiration from God as a female writer. "Not one single book of the Bible was written by a woman," he cautioned.[20]

But perhaps the most potent example of degenerate, racist ideology ever to shame the pages of a magazine that would, in later years, be renamed *Awake!* was printed in the 1929 issue (bold is mine):

> **It is generally believed that the curse which Noah pronounced upon Canaan was the origin of the black race.** Certain it is that when Noah said, "Cursed be Canaan, a servant of servants shall he be unto his brethren," he pictured the future of the Colored race. **They have been and are a race of servants,** but now in the dawn of the twentieth century, we are all coming to see this matter of service in its true light and to find that the only real joy in life is in serving others; not bossing them. **There is no servant in the world as good as a good Colored servant, and the joy that he gets from rendering faithful service is one of the purest joys there is in the world.**

Most likely the author of the above grotesque words was not the Judge but *The Golden Age* editor Clayton

[20] Bolling makes it difficult for us to nail him down as definitely for or against slavery. In one part of his rambling tirade, in which he describes America as God's "workshop and experimental laboratory of the time of the end," he writes that Satan had achieved a "triumph" when slavery was deemed constitutional. Bolling also concludes the article by describing Abraham Lincoln as "the great Emancipator." But he also suggests the Devil fomented "slavery agitation through the Abolition societies, churches, clergy, newspapers, etc." Indeed, the entire premise of his article seems to be the chastisement of Stowe for her perceived meddlesome role in the abolition of slavery rather than holding her to account for the bloodshed of the American Civil War.

Woodworth, or some other contributor. Regardless of who exactly penned these overtly racist sentiments that were sympathetic to slavery, they were published under Rutherford's presidency in a magazine that Witnesses today would be forced to accept as "spiritual food" from God's "faithful and discreet slave." Either this is so, and God is a racist who believes black people are intended as servants or, as is more likely, the foregoing is evidence that when small-minded men are put in positions of ecclesiastical authority, their primitive, backward views inevitably filter into their words. Further attestation of the latter would come to be furnished in Rutherford's incredible anti-Semitism in the build-up to World War II—another repugnant aspect of the Judge's character concerning which most Witnesses are entirely in the dark.

In his earlier writings, Rutherford appeared to have some sympathy for Jewish people. Works like *Comfort for the Jews* (1925), *Life* (1929), and the booklet *Restoration* (1927) reinforced his predecessor's Zionist notions that the Jews still had some role to play in God's purpose, and that the emergence of a Jewish state in Palestine had some significance in the establishment of divine rule over the planet. In *Life* he wrote:

> God promised to restore Palestine to the Jews. The rebuilding of Palestine is now beginning and is well under way. This is being done clearly in fulfillment of prophecy uttered as promises from Jehovah.

Despite perpetuating Russell's Zionism, which necessitated at least some level of respect for Jewish people, the Judge harbored a latent anti-Semitism that would yet find full expression. In a 1927 speech broadcast over the organization's WBBR radio station and subsequently printed in an issue of *The Golden Age*, Rutherford qualified which Jews he considered acceptable:

> Not every man who is a descendent of Abraham is a Jew, by any means. Be it known once and for all that those profiteering, conscienceless, selfish men who call themselves Jews, and who control the greater portion of the finances of the world, will never be the rulers in this new earth. God would not risk such selfish men with such an important position.

The Judge would further expand on who he felt made the grade as a Jew in his 1934 booklet *Favored People:*

> Before anyone can truly be a Jew within the meaning of the Scriptures he must have faith in God like that had by Abraham and he must be devoted to the service and praise of Jehovah God. If one is a descendant of Judah, and has the marks outwardly of a Jew, and yet does not believe and serve God and Jesus Christ, he is not really a Jew and is not entitled to be known by that name.

So, basically, only Jews who rejected their Jewish faith were "entitled" to be thought of as Jews. It seems Rutherford had time for them only if they embraced his beliefs and did not involve themselves in business or commerce. The moment a Jew tried to run a business or employ people, he morphed into one of "those profiteering, conscienceless, selfish men" plotting world domination.

It is remarkable that a man like Rutherford managed to write a book titled *Comfort for the Jews* while entertaining such primitive, vulgar views—but he had his ways of rationalizing things. For example, in *Life* he bemoaned the way "the New Testament has been made offensive to Jews, not because it is wrong, but because many so-called Christian preachers have used it as a club to chastise the Jews." (Apparently it was okay to dislike Jewish people so long as you were not blaming them for killing the Messiah.) But within only a few years of penning these words, Rutherford would himself pick up the "club" and start swinging it quite enthusiastically. At some point in 1932, just as anti-Semitism in Europe was being fanned by fascism into a blaze of hatred that would engulf the continent, a switch was flicked inside Rutherford's mind and he began firmly aligning himself with those same dark forces in a stunning U-turn from his previous Zionist position. *Life* was withdrawn from circulation, and in the second volume of his three-part *Vindication* series of books the Judge offered the following "wisdom":

> The Jews were evicted from Palestine and 'their house left unto them desolate' because they rejected Christ Jesus, the beloved and anointed King of Jehovah. To this day the Jews have not repented of this wrongful act committed by their forefathers. Many of them have been returned to the land of Palestine, but they have been induced to go there because of selfishness and for sentimental reasons. During the long period elapsing from the time of their expulsion to the present day the Jews have not "borne the shame of the heathen" for Jehovah's sake, nor for the name of Christ. . . . In 1917 the Balfour Declaration, sponsored by the heathen governments of Satan's organization, came forth, recognized the Jews, and bestowed upon them great favors. In this the seventh world power took the lead. Now Big Business and other wings of Satan's organization place the Jews alongside of and in the same category as the Gentiles. Heretofore even God's people have overlooked the fact that the affairs of God's kingdom with reference to the things of the earth are of far greater importance than the rehabilitation of that little strip of land on the eastern side of the Mediterranean sea. The Jews

> have received more attention at their hands than they have really deserved.

Hence, Rutherford decided that "heretofore" he (or "God's people" for whom he was self-appointed mouthpiece) had been wrong to give too much consideration to "that little strip of land" in the Eastern Mediterranean and that, perhaps, bashing the Jewish people for their "wrongful act" against Christ was not such a bad idea after all.[21] Earlier in the same book, the Judge also resumed his condemnation of the Jews over their perceived prominence in business:

> Among the powerful men who control the commerce of the sea are many Jews, so called, yet who are against God and against Christ and against the kingdom of God. All are representatives of the Devil, to be sure, and form a part of his organization, but the Lord is pointing them out as separate and integral parts of Satan's organization and gives his people a vision of them from different standpoints.

Two years later, in 1934, the Judge would intensify his scathing denunciation of the role of Jews in commerce:

> The people now on earth and which are called Jews are a commercial people. Among them are some of the richest and most avaricious men the world has ever known. Some of the chief men of Big Business are called Jews. Many of these people are very arrogant, self-important and extremely selfish.

---

[21] Rutherford's 1934 *Favored People* booklet would spell out the Jews' culpability for Christ's death even more clearly: "When the nation of the Jews repudiated their covenant with God and crucified Christ Jesus they were justly entitled to receive complete destruction. Jehovah God, however, declares he will have mercy on them. . . . When they rejected Christ Jesus God cast them away, and they have since been God's enemies because of their blindness."

With such unbridled contempt for Jewish people projected by Rutherford both before and after he parted ways with Zionism, you would think a certain contemporaneous German dictator would have had considerable sympathy for his ideas. And, as incredible as this may sound, the Judge would come to hope for the same.

On January 30, 1933, Adolf Hitler was appointed Chancellor by German president Paul von Hindenburg. Thereafter, a process of *Gleichschaltung* (or nazification) swept Germany as the country was prepared for totalitarian rule. It was during this period that, in April 1933, Prussian authorities stormed Watchtower's German offices in Magdeburg, seized its property, and outlawed the movement's religious activities. Fortunately for the organization, the U.S. State Department was able to intervene and the facilities were returned to its control by the end of the month. Even so, it was clear Jehovah's Witnesses in Germany were on borrowed time.

Watchtower publications portray the organization's response to this aggression as one of defiance against the Nazis. They point to Rutherford's "Declaration of Facts," a document penned by the Judge with the help of his German associates for distribution throughout Germany, as a fearless response to Hitler and his cronies. A 1955 *Watchtower* described the declaration as "a strong protest to Hitler and his government against their highhanded interferences with the witness work of the Society." In truth, the declaration was not a denunciation of the Nazis, but a last ditch attempt on Rutherford's part at establishing common ground with them. The declaration would be adopted at a Witness convention in Germany on June 25, 1933, and was reprinted in the *1934 Year Book.* It expressly praised the principles of the ruling party as being harmonious with those of the organization and God himself:

> Instead of being against the principles advocated by the government of Germany, we stand squarely for such principles, and point out that Jehovah God through Christ Jesus will bring about the full realization of these principles and will give to the people peace and prosperity and the greatest desire of every honest heart. . . . A careful examination of our books and literature will disclose the fact that the very high ideals held and promulgated by the present national government are set forth in and endorsed and strongly emphasized in our publications and show that Jehovah God will see to it that these high ideals in due time will be attained by all persons who love righteousness.

Yes, it seems the "very high ideals" of the Nazi-led German government were shared by Jehovah's Witnesses—ideals that would soon be realized by "Jehovah God through Jesus Christ." Though distasteful to say the least, this blatant groveling may seem like simple pragmatism on the part of Rutherford—an attempt at framing his followers as cooperative friends of Germany rather than enemies of it. But if this is so, the Judge had a very peculiar taste in friends.

In his attempts to ingratiate himself with the embryonic Third Reich, Rutherford made it perfectly clear that not *all* governments could expect such a warm embrace from his "Theocracy." Specifically, the very country that had intervened through diplomatic channels to secure the Magdeburg offices from Hitler's thugs, together with its future ally against the despot, received the Judge's scathing condemnation in the declaration:

> The greatest and the most oppressive empire on earth is the Anglo-American empire. By that is meant the British Empire, of which the United States of America forms a part.

Rutherford was convinced that the "Anglo-American empire," not Hitler's regime, was the real threat to world peace in the 1930s. And he would cling to his delusion that America and Britain were the true bad guys on an irreversible slide toward fascism until his final years. In his "Face the Facts" lecture at London's Royal Albert Hall on September 11, 1938 (apparently, when the Judge had something to say, it was a "fact"), he informed his audience that the USA, "once the bulwark of democracy, is all set to become a part of the totalitarian rule." In a style more reminiscent of the wide-eyed screeching conspiracy theorist Alex Jones than a font of Christian grace and wisdom, Rutherford grimly foretold:

> When the totalitarian Catholic combine gains control of the British Isles, which it is certain to do, then all liberties of the people will be at an end.

But all of that was to come. Back in 1933, the Judge had a would-be genocidal maniac to appease, and he knew he had common ground in their mutual loathing of Jews. Hot on the heels of his condemnation of the United States and Britain, Rutherford included the following in his declaration:

> It has been the commercial Jews of the British-American empire that have built up and carried on Big Business as a means of exploiting and oppressing the peoples of many nations. This fact particularly applies to the cities of London and New York, the stronghold of Big Business. This fact is so manifest in America that there is a proverb concerning the city of New York which says: "The Jews

> own it, the Irish Catholics rule it, and the Americans pay the bills."

Most people would read the above and immediately identify Rutherford's words as intensely bigoted and anti-Semitic. Jews are again painted as scheming, greedy, oppressive opportunists in hateful rhetoric that Josef Goebbels would have been proud of. But incredibly, rather than apologize for this outrageous material, Watchtower has since made moves to defend it.

A 1998 *Awake!* article defended both Rutherford's "Declaration of Facts" and other little-known details concerning the event at which it was unveiled. For example, most Witnesses are unaware that, according to at least one credible eyewitness account, when German Witnesses arrived for their 1933 convention to hear the declaration being read out they were greeted by the spectacle of swastikas hanging at the convention venue, and even opened their program with a hymn that had a melody identical to the German national anthem (or *Deutschlandlied*)—giving the event the look and feel of a Nazi party rally. The 1998 *Awake!* article downplays all this, as follows:

> For instance, critics claim that the Witnesses decorated the Wilmersdorfer Tennishallen with swastika flags. Photographs of the 1933 convention clearly show that they displayed no swastikas in the hall. Eyewitnesses confirm that there were no flags inside.
>
> It is possible, however, that there were flags on the building's exterior. A Nazi combat troop had used the hall on June 21, the Wednesday prior to the convention. Then just the day before the convention, crowds of young people along with units of the SS (*Schutzstaffel*, originally Hitler's Blackshirt bodyguards), SA, and others celebrated the summer

> solstice nearby. So Witnesses arriving at the Sunday convention might have been greeted with the sight of a building decked with swastika flags.
>
> Had there been swastika flags decorating the hall's exterior, corridors, or even its interior, the Witnesses would have left them alone. Even today, when Jehovah's Witnesses rent public facilities for meetings and conventions, they do not remove national symbols. But there is no evidence that the Witnesses themselves hung any flags or that they saluted them.
>
> Critics further state that the Witnesses opened the convention with the German national anthem. Actually, the convention began with "Zion's Glorious Hope," Song 64 in the Witnesses' religious songbook. The words of this song were set to music composed by Joseph Haydn in 1797. Song 64 had been in the Bible Students' songbook since at least 1905. In 1922 the German government adopted Haydn's melody with words by Hoffmann von Fallersleben as their national anthem. Nevertheless, the Bible Students in Germany still sang their Song 64 occasionally, as did Bible Students in other countries.
>
> The singing of a song about Zion could hardly be construed as an effort to placate the Nazis.

Regardless of how many years the melody for song 64 had been in use by Witnesses in Germany—or whether its lyrics were about Zion—a song that sounded like the German national anthem at a time when intense nationalism was sweeping the country was a curious choice for opening a convention at which a document prepared by Rutherford would pour vitriol on "the commercial Jews" and praise "the very high ideals held and promulgated by the present national government."

As to the swastika flags, the *Awake!* writer presents the first of a number of straw man arguments by suggesting that "critics" argue that the flags were placed there by the Witnesses themselves. Firstly, nobody has insisted that the swastikas were placed by Witnesses or, for that matter, that Witnesses were required to salute them. Secondly, the photographs shown in the article were taken from angles that do not establish whether there were swastikas in the hall's interior—but even if the swastikas were only on the outside of the building, it was still understandable that Witnesses at the time should have felt unnerved when arriving at an event where swastikas were on display. There was certainly nothing stopping the organizers from making alternative arrangements under the circumstances.

As for the "critic" on whose firsthand testimony the convention story is based, this was none other than Konrad Franke—a now-deceased branch overseer for Watchtower in Germany. In a recorded, two-part lecture he recounted his arrival at the 1933 convention to hear the Judge's declaration:

> When we entered, we found the hall bedecked with swastika flags! But not only that: when the meeting started, it was begun with a song that we had not sung for years, especially not in Germany, because of the melody. Though the lyrics were fine, the melody—well, the musicians who are here will recognize that the notes were [taken from] the melody of "Deutschland, Deutschland über alles"!
>
> Can you imagine how we felt? Many could not join in the singing. It was just as though their throats were throttled. What kind of leaders did we have who brought us [into] such dangers—and the danger of faltering under these circumstances—instead of helping and supporting us, so that we could take a fearless stand [against Nazism]. May all elders

> who are here among us learn something from these examples, and may they recognize their responsibilities in such matters in the near future.[22]

Hence, not only did the 1998 *Awake!* article misrepresent the claims made about the 1933 convention—it also misrepresented the honest concerns of a senior Watchtower official who attended the event as being those of an opponent of the organization.

Not content with merely obscuring controversial details surrounding the 1933 convention at which Rutherford's declaration was read out and adopted, the 1998 *Awake!* article also attempted to offer a defense of the Judge's shameful rhetoric about "the commercial Jews of the British-American empire":

> This statement clearly did not refer to the Jewish people in general, and it is regrettable if it has been misunderstood and has given cause for any offense. Some have claimed that Jehovah's Witnesses shared the hostility toward the Jews that was commonly taught in the German churches at the time. This is absolutely untrue. By their literature and conduct during the Nazi era, the Witnesses rejected anti-Semitic views and condemned the Nazi mistreatment of the Jews. Certainly, their kindness toward Jews who shared their lot in the concentration camps provides a resounding rebuttal to this false accusation.

Whether individual Jehovah's Witnesses were kind to Jews before, during or after the Second World War is beside the point. What matters is the approach taken by the leadership of the organization—an organization

---

[22] This is a translation of Konrad Franke's speech that is featured on page 25 of Penton's *Jehovah's Witnesses and the Third Reich*. Penton provides the original German transcript as a footnote.

claiming to operate under God's guidance as his sole channel with mankind. The language of the president in his "Declaration of Facts" is openly anti-Semitic, and no amount of denials by Watchtower or its apologists (of which there are many) can change this.

By condemning "the commercial Jews of the British-American empire that have built up and carried on Big Business" Rutherford was not condemning "Big Business" in general; neither could it be said that he was lambasting the greed of entrepreneurs irrespective of their religion or ethnicity. The Judge was singling out one ethnoreligious group of people and accusing them of being disproportionately involved in nefarious commercial activities. If Rutherford were purely against people being involved in "Big Business," regardless of race or religion, he could have easily said so. But he was addressing his declaration primarily to a Nazi leadership that he knew had an axe to grind with the Jews—and in that context he was revealing that he shared their hatred.

No matter how one chooses to spin it, Rutherford's vile "Declaration of Facts" and its swastika-strewn launch in Berlin hints strongly at a pro-Nazi undercurrent in the Watchtower leadership in the run-up to the Second World War. After its launch, the declaration would be distributed throughout Germany by the Witnesses, resulting in many of them being rounded up and arrested amid a fierce backlash by the authorities. A copy of the document would also be sent to the Führer himself, accompanied by a letter from Watchtower that would furnish further evidence of Nazi sympathies in the organization's hierarchy.

The infamous letter, copies of which can be easily found online, opened with the words "Sehr verehrter

Herr Reichskanzler!" or "Most Honored Mr. Chancellor!" The writer went on to explain that German Witnesses had met on June 25 to discuss the rising animosity against them. The persecution they faced was blamed on accusations "from clerical, especially Catholic quarters." It was insisted that the Watchtower leadership in Brooklyn "has been outstandingly friendly to Germany" in times past. As evidence of this, the sentencing of Rutherford and his associates "to 80 years imprisonment" was cited,[23] and it was pointed out that they had been incarcerated "because the president refused to use two magazines published by him in the United States for war propaganda against Germany." (This was not true. As already explained, Rutherford and his associates had been sentenced under the Espionage Act primarily for antiwar rhetoric printed in *The Finished Mystery.* As to the claim they refused to publish anti-German propaganda, an article in the June 1, 1918, *Watch Tower* had urged Bible Students to pray for an Allied victory over the German "autocracy.")[24] The letter went on to bemoan how Watchtower magazines had been "outlawed and suppressed in the United

---

[23] Each of the Watchtower officials, with the exception of Giovanni De Cecca, received four sentences of 20 years, to be served concurrently. (De Cecca's sentence was half of that of his colleagues.) Hence, citing 80 years as the length of the sentence when in practical terms it was 20 years was a clear exaggeration.

[24] The article in question proclaimed: "God was graciously pleased to cause this nation to be formed and to grow under the most favorable conditions in the world for the preservation of liberty, civil and religious." In its closing remarks, it urged: "Let there be praise and thanksgiving to God for the promised glorious outcome of the war, the breaking of the shackles of autocracy, the freeing of the captives (Isaiah 61:1) and making of the world safe for the common people—blessings all assured by the Word of God to the people of this country and of the whole world of mankind."

States during the war," which is surprising given that 38 consecutive issues of *The Watch Tower* were printed and distributed between April 6, 1917, when the United States entered the First World War, and November 11, 1918, when the war ended.

Apparently the German government did not fall for these outlandish deceptions, but these were by no means the only attempts to cajole Hitler in the letter. Just as with the "Declaration of Facts," the letter pointed to the Jews (along with Catholics, Rutherford's old foe) as being enemies of Germany from whom Watchtower wished to distance itself:

> In a similar manner, the administration of our Society not only refused to participate in the atrocity propaganda against Germany, but it took a position against it. This is emphasized by the attached declaration that refers to the fact that the circles that led [in promoting] atrocity propaganda in the United States (commercialistic Jews and Catholics) are also the most eager persecutors of our Society's work and its administration. These and other statements in our declaration are meant to serve as a rejection of the slanderous claim that the Bible Students are supported by Jews.

Apparently, Jews were among the "eager persecutors" of Watchtower along with Catholics, and thus the organization wished to stress that it received no financial support from them. In the declaration itself, Rutherford addressed this issue even more plainly by insisting:

> Up to this hour there never has been the slightest bit of money contributed to our work by Jews.

Having decisively distanced Watchtower from the "slanderous claim" that the organization benefited from Jewish financial backing, the letter to Hitler went on to reiterate admiration for his government's aspirations:

> At the convention, it was stated that there are no opposing views in the relationship between the German Bible Students and the National Government of the German Reich, but that, to the contrary, respecting the purely religious and apolitical goals and objectives of the Bible Students, it can be said that these are in complete harmony with the similar goals of the National Government of the German Reich.

Though the letter claimed Watchtower to be "apolitical," it went on to call for the "Anglo-American World Empire," and "especially England," to be "held responsible for the League of Nations and the unjustified treaties and burdens placed on Germany." Incredibly, the letter even promised that the Witnesses would be willing to observe the ban on their work, vowing that they would "continue to conform to the regulations of prohibition issued" in confidence that Hitler would finally see sense and "lift these measures." (I will revisit this concession later, which flatly contradicts the stance Jehovah's Witnesses are supposed to take when their preaching work is under ban.)

As should be obvious, the letter sent by Watchtower and its accompanying declaration is damning evidence that, far from mounting "a strong protest to Hitler and his government" in the aftermath of the Magdeburg branch closure, the organization stooped to incredible lows to placate the Nazis. But rather than concede that its approach was woefully mistaken, Watchtower deals with this period in its history in a way that is at best evasive and at worst downright dishonest. For example, the 1998 *Awake!* attempted to argue that "the Witnesses, along with millions of other Germans in early 1933, viewed the National Socialist Party as the legitimate ruling authority of the time." In other words, it was all just one big misunderstanding. Who could have known that the Nazi-led German Government hated the Jews and was not worth doing business with? If only that were the case.

The letter Watchtower sent to Hitler not only expressed admiration and willingness to conform to the "goals" of the German government, it also quoted directly from *Das Programm der NSDAP*—the Nazi Party Platform—in arguing that the Bible Students were in conformity with the fiercely anti-Semitic rhetoric found under Section 24. After suggesting that Hitler set up a commission to investigate the organization according to his own "just principles," the letter continued, as follows:

> By these principles we mean the statements in Section 24 of the Platform of the National Socialist German Workers Party:
>
> "We demand the freedom of all religious confessions in the state so long as they do not endanger its existence or conflict with the ethical and moral beliefs of the German race.
>
> "The Party, as such, represents the viewpoint of positive Christianity without associating itself with a specific confession. It opposes the Jewish-materialist spirit domestically and abroad and is convinced that a lasting recuperation of our people can only happen from the inside out . . ."
>
> We are firmly convinced that the National Government of Germany will find no reason to hinder our services or missionary activities if we are judged, first, without religious prejudice and, second, according to the Platform points quoted above.

So rather than beseeching the Nazis merely on the

understanding that they were the "legitimate ruling party" while being oblivious to their agenda, Watchtower's letter to Hitler quoted from and hence recognized a specific item from the Nazi Party Program targeting the Jews for discriminatory treatment. Watchtower was not ignorant to the fact that the Nazis were anti-Semitic—they appealed for leniency *on this basis* both by distancing themselves from financial involvement with Jews and by appealing on the basis of religious restrictions that unfairly targeted Jewish people.

By this point you may be wondering who authored this remarkable letter. Though ex-Witness sources tend to point to Rutherford as the author, it is unlikely that he wrote it himself (apart from anything else, the letter was written in German, not English).[25] Even so, as Penton argues, the Judge cannot be completely absolved of responsibility:

> This letter was probably written by the Watch Tower's German branch overseer, Paul Balzereit, or by someone directly under his supervision. Whether it was approved by Watchtower president J. F. Rutherford is impossible to say. However, it reflects what appears in the *Erklärung* [or "Declaration of Facts"] and was certainly in harmony with the general thrust of Rutherford's policies at the time.

Not only was the letter little more than a rewording of Rutherford's declaration, which it referenced frequently, but Watchtower itself admits that Balzereit (the likely author) was acting under the instructions of the Judge in this crucial period. The 1998 *Awake!* describes Rutherford as working "together with" Balzereit in pursuing his campaign to convince the Nazis that

---

25 Some may confuse the Watchtower letter of 1933 with a second, far less conciliatory letter sent to Hitler by Rutherford in 1934 that I will refer to shortly.

"Jehovah's Witnesses posed no threat to the German people and the State."

As part of these efforts, and as previously mentioned, Watchtower voluntarily agreed to cease all preaching activities—something that would be unthinkable for most Witnesses today who are taught to "obey God as ruler rather than men" (in observance of Acts 5:29) when it comes to preaching in countries where their work is restricted. In a letter sent from Watchtower's Magdeburg offices, dated August 28, 1933, *die deutschen Freunde* (the German friends) were instructed as follows:

> As authorized by the Watch Tower Bible & Tract Society, and especially as the proxy of the President, Judge Rutherford, I should like to ask you herewith to submit to all current governmental and police authorities' regulations [without] exception. Above all, I would like to entreat you not to disseminate banned publications and not to hold any meetings or lectures without permission issued by the police.

This was utter capitulation, which under the circumstances was the prudent course. If the German Witnesses had accepted the situation and adhered to practicing their faith privately without antagonizing their Nazi overlords, a strong argument could be made for their fate being far less bleak than it would turn out to be. Yes, they would have been unable to preach or hold meetings for over a decade—but at least they would not be deemed a threat to Nazi authority and, as such, could have expected more leniency. Instead, with his plan to win over the Nazis in tatters, Rutherford went on the offensive. The *Proclaimers* book briefly describes his change of strategy as follows:

> Early the following year [1934], a personal letter regarding the situation was written by J. F. Ruther-

> ford to Adolf Hitler and delivered to him by special messenger. Then the entire worldwide brotherhood went into action.

This personal letter was nothing short of a direct threat to Hitler that, if he did not lift the ban on Witnesses in Germany by an arbitrary date, the Judge would mobilize his worldwide following against the Reich. After advising the Führer that German officials "have been warned that those who oppose God and His kingdom shall be destroyed by the Lord at Armageddon," Rutherford commanded one of history's most notorious and ruthless dictators as follows:

> You may successfully resist any and all men, but you cannot successfully resist Jehovah God . . . Jehovah's witnesses have done everything within their power to show your government that they only want to freely worship Jehovah God and serve Him as He has commanded them, but their efforts have been ignored and their maltreatment continues by your officials. Once more in their behalf, as the president of the Society or organization under which they work, and in the name of Jehovah God and His anointed King, Christ Jesus, I demand that you give order to all officials and servants of your government that Jehovah's witnesses [who are of the EARNEST BIBLE STUDENTS and the WATCH TOWER BIBLE & TRACT SOCIETY] in Germany be permitted to peaceably assemble and without hindrance worship God and obey His commandments by teaching to the people the Bible truths concerning God's kingdom under Christ, for which kingdom all Christians have long hoped and prayed.
>
> If by the 24th day of March, 1934, there is no response to this earnest demand and nothing done by your government to grant the relief of the aforesaid Jehovah's witnesses in Germany, then

> God's people in other countries will begin the publication throughout the nations of the earth of the facts concerning Germany's wrongful treatment of Christian people there; and having delivered the testimony, we will submit our case and leave it to Jehovah God by and through Christ Jesus to administer the punishment of the guilty ones in His own good way. Permit me to remind you that Jehovah warns that no one shall oppress His anointed.

As you might expect, these self-indulgent, asinine, needlessly inflammatory words failed to achieve the desired outcome. If anything, the Judge's threats and eccentric posturing would only make matters worse for Witnesses in Germany.

Once the deadline had passed, Rutherford began using the pages of his "apolitical" literature to give Hitler and his regime the same scathing treatment the "Anglo-American Empire" was already receiving. Without regard for their precarious situation, Witnesses in Germany were called upon to assemble for preaching work in open defiance of the regime. They were instructed to send prepared Watchtower letters to German government officials—letters including statements to the effect that the authorities would "answer to Almighty God" for any violence or bloodshed against Rutherford's followers. Simultaneously, Witnesses in Britain and America sent a flurry of telegrams to Hitler, which read:

> Hitler Government, Berlin Germany. Your ill treatment of Jehovah's witnesses shocks all good people of earth and dishonors God's name. Refrain from further persecuting Jehovah's witnesses; otherwise God will destroy you and your national party.

On receiving these messages in October 1934, *Jehovah's Witnesses in the Divine Purpose* reports that Hitler "jumped to his feet and with clenched fists hysterically screamed: 'This brood will be exterminated in Germany.'" Though we have only one witness to this animated outburst, it has gone down in Witness folklore as proof that even the mightiest dictators cannot stand in the way of Jehovah. Hitler may have indeed been outlived by the "brood" he wished to exterminate, but the cruelty he unleashed on the Witnesses is not to be understated. By 1935, the Witness movement was officially outlawed in Germany, and those found guilty of promoting its message faced arrest and placement in "protective custody"—in other words: concentration camps. An estimated 10,000 were so imprisoned, and 1,200 would die in custody. (250 of these 1,200 are believed to have been executed, with the majority dying through maltreatment.) In summing up the role played by Rutherford in the persecution endured by Witnesses at the hands of the Nazis, Penton writes:

> It is true that the Witnesses would have suffered some severe persecution for maintaining their principles, and especially for refusing to *Heil Hitler* and to perform military service after Germany introduced universal male conscription in 1935. That said, had they not confronted the Nazis directly, they would have fared much better. But Rutherford seemed not to care about the safety of the Witnesses in Germany, any more than he cared about the safety of his brethren in the United States and other lands.

Indeed, while it was easy for Rutherford to issue threats and throw pronouncements of divine wrath at a genocidal dictator from the relative safety of his office on the other side of the Atlantic, it was Witnesses in Germany who suffered the backlash for this antagonism. The *Proclaimers* book reports that Witnesses in concentration camps were subjected to "the most cruel and sadistic treatment imaginable," which included being "cursed and kicked, then forced to do knee-bending, jumping, and crawling for hours on end, until they fainted or dropped from exhaustion, while guards laughed with glee." Others were "forced to stand naked or lightly clad in the courtyard in midwinter," or were "whipped until they were unconscious and their backs covered with blood."[26]

Even those who were spared the concentration camps faced considerable hardship. As Penton explains, "many ordinary German Witnesses lost their jobs, pensions, and social assistance cheques because they refused to *Heil Hitler* or to vote in the November 1933 Reichstag elections."

To summarize, though German Witnesses would have inevitably found themselves at odds with the Nazis due to their pacifism and refusal to venerate political leaders, this would surely have been less of an issue were they not also representing an organization that had positioned itself so aggressively against the regime, apparently as a vindictive response to having its flirtatious advances spurned. Watchtower and its president certainly did not prove worthy of the incredible courage and fortitude shown by those Witnesses

[26] The *1974 Yearbook* tells an especially sickening story of one Christmas Eve when the prisoners at Dachau, including "over a hundred Jehovah's witnesses," were assembled in a courtyard where the SS guards had erected a Christmas tree. The prisoners were told that the troops "wanted to celebrate Christmas with them this evening in their own particular way." A list of names was then read out "for almost an hour" of prisoners who had been recommended for punishment, and one by one these individuals were strapped to a block and beaten with steel whips by alternating SS men. All prisoners were expected to sing along during this grotesque spectacle as a band played *Silent Night*.

who never wavered in their principles even in the most testing circumstances imaginable.

The sad irony is that though most Witnesses are extremely well-acquainted with the suffering of their predecessors in the Nazi concentration camps, they are generally oblivious to the more unsavory elements of this episode in the organization's history. They have no clue that significant numbers of Witnesses relented when pressured to denounce their faith, with some prominent Watchtower officials even surrendering information to the Gestapo that would put their brothers at risk.[27] They know nothing of how, at least for a brief period, Witnesses were instructed to obey the Nazis by not preaching. They are unaware that Rutherford's "Declaration of Facts" expressed admiration for Nazi values and was adopted at a convention that, according to at least one credible eyewitness, had nationalistic overtones. And they are especially oblivious to any suggestion that there was a strong undercurrent of anti-Semitism running through the

---

[27] Penton cites official police records from the period revealing that, at least by 1938 (three years into the official ban) 516 Bible Students had been released from detention or incarceration having "obligated themselves, by written statement, not to become active any more on behalf of the illegal Bible Students Association nor to testify in future any more for the teachings of the same." Penton also includes in the Appendix section of his book *Jehovah's Witnesses and the Third Reich* copies of original Gestapo documents revealing that, under interrogation, senior Watchtower officials Erich Frost (who featured in the May 2016 JW Broadcasting episode), Fritz Winkler and Konrad Franke all gave information implicating their fellow believers. Of course, as Penton points out, these individuals could hardly be blamed for buckling under such extreme duress, but the available evidence casts doubt on repeated suggestions in Watchtower literature to the effect that Witnesses "did not compromise their faith" and "stood firm in the face of merciless assault."

Watchtower hierarchy that apparently emanated from the Judge himself.

It is worth underscoring at this point that Jehovah's Witnesses today are not an anti-Semitic organization, and do not espouse racism in any form. If anything, modern Watchtower materials champion racial equality, promoting the idea of a God who is "not partial" and who is keen to draw followers from "every nation" in the spirit of Acts 10:34. But as we have seen in both this chapter and the one before, it has not always been this way. There was a time when the leaders of "Jehovah's organization" were every bit as bigoted as others of their age—a fact that belies any claim that these men were handpicked by Christ, or otherwise conspicuous in their wisdom and enlightenment.

Racism is, in my opinion, symptomatic of a primitive, underdeveloped intellect, and yet it has muddied the pages of Watchtower literature from the days of the Pastor right through to the early presidency of Rutherford's successor, Nathan Knorr. It would be as late as 1952 that a *Watchtower* article would offer the following shameful observation—another strong hint that blacks are ideally suited to slavery:

> Really, our colored brothers have great cause for rejoicing. Their race is meek and teachable, and from it comes a high percentage of the theocratic increase.

Thankfully, by the mid-1950s Watchtower had largely shaken off such grotesque racist sentiments. While most Witnesses would be tempted to see this as evidence of continued organizational refinement under divine influence, a more likely explanation is that America's civil rights movement and changing attitudes in society in general had a reforming influence on Watchtower, to the extent that most Witnesses today would be shocked when confronted with the racism in the organization's early literature. It can therefore be argued that the track record of Jehovah's Witnesses on this issue is comparable with that of any other evangelical movement, and that external social influences—rather than the workings of the Holy Spirit—obliged Watchtower's hierarchy to make progress toward fully recognizing racial equality in its literature.

It is also worth noting that Watchtower's racism was not uniformly potent over its first few decades. While Russell's brand of racism seems to have been more a product of ignorance and misconceptions that were commonplace in his time, the racist material that emerged under Rutherford's presidency had an altogether more insidious, assertive tone. This is clearly seen both in the patronizing slurs against black people that disgraced the pages of *The Golden Age* and the stereotyping and scapegoating anti-Semitic sentiments from the Judge himself—vile rhetoric that would not have looked out of place in *Mein Kampf*—and yet when most Witnesses think of Rutherford, they think of someone who courageously stood up to Hitler rather than someone who sympathized with the Führer's dislike of Jews.

But Jews and "colored" people were not the only demographic that Rutherford looked down on. It is also painfully apparent from his writings that the Judge had an extremely unhealthy and condescending view of women. The omens were not good when the following was allowed to be printed in a 1930 *Golden Age* article:

> *QUESTION:* Will husband and wife live together after the resurrection is completed, if both are in harmony with God?
>
> **Answer:** The scriptures do not reveal what the relationship of men and women will be after the

> resurrection is completed. The most that we know is that there will be no children born during the last 100 years of the Millennium (Isa. 65:20), nor any born after that, because men and women do not have children after they reach the age of 100 years. Whether the identity of the sexes, as such, will be preserved, we do not know. There have been some well-authenticated instances in which women have been transformed into men, and it is possible that this transformation may become general and we shall all be brothers together.

Though Rutherford may not have penned the above personally, the fact that it could find its way into print under his presidency is very telling. Witnesses today would certainly be dumbfounded at the suggestion that a forerunner of the *Awake!* magazine once seriously suggested that women might need to have their gender changed in order to take their place in God's new world. (One assumes this transformation was to be imposed arbitrarily on all women by supernatural means, and that *The Golden Age* was not an early champion of gender reassignment surgery for the transgender community.)

A year on from this outpouring of eccentricity in *The Golden Age,* Rutherford would release the first volume of his *Vindication* book series—the same series mentioned earlier in which he began swinging his "club" against Jewish people. The first of these books, published in 1931, was chosen as the vehicle for a bizarre rant against women in which the Judge's sexism and misogyny was fully unleashed. In a section headed "Women to the Fore," the Judge bemoaned the "enfranchising" of women in "Christendom" (his word for the "Christian" nations, especially Britain and America). Rutherford even went so far as to link the empowerment of women with dabbling from Satan following the devil's recent ousting from heaven:

> It was in 1919 that the Federation of Churches of the United States issued a paper endorsing the League of Nations as the political expression of God's kingdom on earth. In that same year the Congress of the United States enfranchised women, and this act was ratified by such legislators in 1919 and early in 1920. Note that this was after the World War had ended and Satan had been cast out of heaven and had begun to prepare his forces for Armageddon. (Rev. 12:12; 16:13-16) The women of America in particular began to compete with the men as prophets of peace and to have a part in guiding and dictating the policies and political operations of Christendom. Since then they have wielded a great influence in the church organizations and in the councils of state. God foreknew this, to be sure, and caused his prophet Ezekiel to write concerning them: "Likewise, thou son of man, set thy face against the daughters of thy people, which prophesy out of their own heart; and prophesy thou against them."—13:17.

In Rutherford's mind, it was unthinkable for women to have any role of responsibility, either in religion or politics. To allow women any "influence" in these areas was to invite God's wrath, and the Judge saw it as his duty to warn against such depravity. Women, in his view, were to be put in their "proper place," and the failure of anyone else to notice this was not due to enlightened, progressive thinking—it was plain cowardice, as his *Vindication* rant went on to explain:

> In many of the church organizations women occupy the pulpit and preach and prophesy. The numerous women's clubs have become a part of the political and religious organizations of Christendom. These female prophets make a display of human foresight

> and prudence. They wield a powerful influence over the men. Politicians and political clergymen among men no longer dare to speak in plain terms of women's proper place in the church or in the home, for fear of losing political influence and support.

Rutherford felt somehow threatened by women having a "powerful influence over the men." When it came to *his* influence over the Bible Student community there was no problem, but women—in his backward view—were to stick to their "proper place." It was simply an abomination for their voices to be heard and given equal weight to those of their male counterparts.

But the Judge was by no means finished. As his remarkable tirade continued, he scorned acts of chivalry by men as being tantamount to worshipping women:

> The women make monkeys or dupes of men. The men have become effeminate, soft and easily influenced, and have lost their real manhood and sturdiness in the affairs of state and home. For instance, when men are sitting at a table and a woman approaches, all the men arise and pay her homage and thereby elevate her to a place above men. The men remove their hats upon entering an elevator, if a woman is present; and these things are said to be acts of respect and to show that a man is a gentleman. But it is subtle, and the real meaning is much different from that. It is a scheme of Satan to turn men away from God and from his announced rule of the proper position of man and woman. The Lord has declared that no effeminate man shall inherit the kingdom of heaven. (1 Cor. 6:9)[28] This proves that the scheme or habit of paying homage to women is not of God, but from

[28] Note Rutherford's conflation of "effeminate" men with gay men. How easily the Bible can be made to "declare" something on which it is silent.

> the great enemy of God. It is a veneer of being a proper thing, and therefore it is more subtle than otherwise.
>
> Every good man loves his wife, his mother and his sisters, and is kind and considerate to all women; but that does not mean that he should put women in a place contrary to the expressed will of God. . . . The modern practice of putting women to the fore in the affairs of religion and in the councils of state has much to do with destroying the sacredness of the home and with turning men away from God. Thus Satan has deceived and led the men and women in the wrong way, in order to turn them away from Jehovah God.

Hence, if you were affiliated with the organization in 1931 (the year Bible Students loyal to Watchtower became "Jehovah's witnesses") you were required to believe that the simple act of rising from the table when a woman approached, or removing one's hat when a woman entered the elevator, represented a subtle "scheme of Satan" aimed at contorting the "proper position of man and woman." Thankfully, Witnesses today are no longer bound by such nonsense. However, the shadow of Rutherford's misogyny still hangs over the organization when it comes to the way women are treated (as we saw in Chapter Five), with even the most trivial tasks at Kingdom Halls *apart from cleaning* off limits for Witness women.

Another Rutherfordian tradition still held to is that of not celebrating Mother's Day, and in *Vindication* the Judge did not mince his words in declaring it to be the devil's work:

> The father represents Jehovah, from whom comes every good thing, while the mother represents God's organization, used for his good purposes and to his glory. (Isa. 54: 5; 66: 8; Ps. 50: 20) Satan

> would turn the people away from this beautiful symbol, and therefore from God, and cause them to disregard the Word of the Lord. This he does in a very subtle way by organizing what in England and in America, the chief countries of Christendom, is called "Mother's Day". . . . The so-called "Mother's Day" was observed in America first in 1914, the very year that Satan's world ended and when he knew his time was short to get ready for the great battle of Armageddon. To induce the people to bestow special honor and worship upon mothers would be one step towards turning the people away from the worship of God; and this is one of his means of preparing for Armageddon. . . . On the face of it the arrangement of "Mother's Day" seems harmless and calculated to do good. But the people are in ignorance of Satan's subtle hand in the matter, and that he is back of the movement, to turn the people away from God. . . . The good mother is the one who serves and honors Jehovah and teaches her children to do likewise, and who renders her proper motherly duties in the home. Real men have great respect and great love for such mothers, but their worship is given to Jehovah God.

Incredibly, Rutherford believed that Mother's Day was an elaborate conspiracy by the devil to deflect "special honor and worship" away from God and toward women. The Judge was convinced that one of Satan's first orders of business on being ousted from heaven in 1914 was to influence world leaders to inaugurate the celebration of motherhood on a special day. This, apparently, was the devil's "subtle way" of getting ready for his showdown with God at Armageddon. (If only someone had told Satan he would have plenty of time to play with—over a century, in fact—so there was really no need to rush.)

Witnesses today would be forgiven for assuming they are long past such silliness, and that they have managed to come up with more sophisticated reasons for not honoring parents on a given day. Indeed, if you consult the *Reasoning* book you will be told paganism is to blame for Witnesses steering clear of giving their mothers a card and gift on the second Sunday of May. The reader is told that it is a "festival derived from the custom of mother worship in ancient Greece." But try finding the logic behind not celebrating Father's Day using current Watchtower materials, and explanations are harder to find.

You will be forced to hunt down an article in a 1956 *Awake!* magazine that opens with deeply unsatisfactory reasoning. We are advised that "nowhere in the Bible do we find that parents are to be worshiped, or that there should be a Father's Day and a Mother's Day kept in their honor." Firstly, nobody is suggesting that parents are to be worshipped on these occasions and, secondly, if you ban everything not mentioned in the Bible you will be forced to ban a great many things.

This begs the question: is there a more solid basis for Witnesses spurning those days? Well, it does not take long when reading the 1956 *Awake!* article for the true reason to become apparent. On the second page, a paragraph begins with the words: "On the face of it the arrangement of Mother's Day or Father's Day seems harmless and calculated to do good." The same paragraph ends with the suggestion: "Real men have great respect and great love for such mothers, but their worship they give to Jehovah God."

If these words sound strangely familiar, it is because you have only just read them in earlier paragraphs. Yes, entire sections of the 1956 *Awake!* article forbidding Mother's Day *and* Father's Day are copied almost verbatim from the Judge's words in *Vindication*, only with some of the more rambling rhetoric cut out and with "Father's Day" inserted alongside Mother's Day (apparently to avoid the inevitable confusion if one were to be allowed and one forbidden). Thus, if you happen to be a Witness, you now know the true reason why you must refrain from these celebrations. It is Rutherford and his 1931 jeremiad against the Satanic plot of respecting women that you must credit.

Having laid the groundwork for a prohibition on a harmless celebration that would linger in Witness tradition for decades to follow, Rutherford went on to quote from Revelation 2:20, in which the resurrected Jesus is claimed to say: "I have a few things against thee, because thou sufferest that woman Jezebel, which calleth herself a prophetess." (*King James Version*) In the Judge's mind, it was "fornication" for women to "teach and preach and prophesy in the churches." To further drive home his point about women not being granted opportunities for "seducing and misleading men," Paul's sentiments at 1 Timothy 2:12 were invoked, namely that women were not to teach, but were to "be in silence." Finally, to conclude his rant about the "creature worship" of women, the Judge offered the following olive branch:

> The purpose of here mentioning women is not to ridicule or to speak unkindly of them. There are good women wholly devoted to God and who are rendering good and faithful service unto him. Likewise there are men wholly devoted to God and serving him. But neither the man nor the woman is to be honored and worshiped for such.

As should hopefully be obvious by this point in the chapter, Rutherford's idea of "good and faithful service" basically involved willingness to distribute and promote his writings and recorded messages at every opportunity. Only the Judge was allowed to be "honored" in this way. The moment women in particular dared to voice an opinion on religious or political matters that was not merely parroting his views, they were forsaking their "proper place" and thinking too highly of themselves.

As shockingly sexist as the foregoing diatribe was, Rutherford saved his most vile denigration of women for the convention platform. One of the Judge's well-worn sayings when facing audiences was borrowed from an 1897 Rudyard Kipling poem titled *The Vampire*, the opening lines of which jeer at "the woman who did not care":

A fool there was and he made his prayer
(Even as you and I!)
To a rag and a bone and a hank of hair
(We called her the woman who did not care)
But the fool he called her his lady fair—
(Even as you and I!)

Clearly moved by Kipling's verbiage, the Judge decided to employ it when dispensing his advice on the virtues of staying single and avoiding romantic attachments to the opposite sex.[29] In his book *The Four*

---

[29] Rutherford clearly had a problem with people pursuing romantic love. His 1941 book *Children* tells the story of a model young couple name John and Eunice who decide to "defer" their marriage for "a few years . . . until lasting peace comes to the earth." ("When THE THEOCRACY is in full sway it will not be burdensome to have a family," reasons John.) And in a 1937 *Golden Age* article (that received a special "endorsement" in the March 1, 1937, *Watchtower*) Witnesses were urged to shun "the blight, the delusions and illusions of 'love' so called and 'courtship', which bring reproach upon the holy name of Jeho-

*Presidents of the Watch Tower Society,* Edmond Gruss relates how Rutherford "often said in his public talks that women were only 'a stack of bones and a hank of hair.'" Gruss tells of how his father heard the remark at a 1941 St. Louis convention—Rutherford's final convention appearance before his death, as it happens—and reported that "where he was seated, while a few of the women were offended, most sat numbly in their chairs with frozen smiles, nodding their heads in mesmerized agreement."

The Judge would have been well-advised to keep this obnoxious, second-hand expression out of print so that future Witnesses would have some pretext for dismissing the above story as "apostate" hearsay—but it seems he was either unable or unwilling to do so. A 1941 *Watchtower* features a comprehensive report by an "interested observer" at the same convention that brought the Judge's contemptible words reducing women to body parts into the organization's principal vehicle of "spiritual food" (words in quotation marks are Rutherford's, the rest is paraphrasing):

> Then the divine mandate shall be carried out, to fill the earth with a righteous, perfect offspring, and this by marriage and childbearing. "Some of these desecrators of His name claim that they only have the right to say who shall get married"; but they are presumptuous. In the kingdom the "great multitude" will look to the Lord to grade as to selecting each a mate for himself. "Why, then, should a man who has the prospect before him of being of the great multitude now tie himself up to a stack of bones and a hank of hair?" (Applause)

---

vah." Apparently Rutherford's life was devoid of love, and he insisted on the same being true of everyone else.

Despite his taste for degrading women in his writings and public speeches, there is reason to believe that—as is common with misogynists—the Judge was quite taken with them when they served a purpose. Less than ten years into his presidency, Rutherford was forced to fend off claims he had attended a performance of *Artists and Models* at New York's Winter Garden Theatre—a showgirl-strewn burlesque show starring well-known entertainer of the period, Al Jolson.

The timing of this alleged outing was especially shocking, at least to believers. In a letter sent by George Fisher (coauthor of *The Finished Mystery* and one of Rutherford's fellow inmates at Atlanta Penitentiary) to W. Nieman at Watchtower's offices in Magdeburg, dated April 27, 1926, the Judge was accused of going to see the show with two elders and a young woman the evening before Bible Students were to observe the Lord's Evening Meal, or Memorial. That Watchtower's president could have behaved so sacrilegiously was unthinkable to Fisher, who wanted Rutherford to face disciplinary action. As Penton relates:

> Fisher wanted to bring Rutherford, as an ex-officio elder of every Bible Student ecclesia, before the individual churches for discipline. Fisher claimed that he had the necessary Witnesses to do so. But in July of the same year Fisher died and the matter never got any further.

Taken on their own merits, Fisher's accusations are easily shrugged off as vindictive mudslinging by an embittered former associate—which is exactly how the organization framed them. A letter printed in a 1927 *Golden Age* duly condemned the "scurrilous" and "malicious" charges against the Judge, while leaving it largely to the readers' imagination as to what these charges actually were:

> The charge in George H. Fisher's letter is grossly false and libelous. He is dead, as you know. I have it from Judge Rutherford's own lips that he never saw Al Jolson in his life and does not know what he looks like. But he is too busy in the Lord's service to be drawn into a controversy such as this and I think that he is right in ignoring such malicious charges.

Interestingly, Rutherford's claim that he did not know what Al Jolson looked like was hardly an unequivocal denial of Fisher's complaint. In addition to this coyness, it is worth noting that, had the "grossly false and libelous" claims been completely ignored, *The Golden Age* should have been silent on the scandal. The issuing of a statement so clearly intended to quash specific rumors about something to do with Al Jolson suggests Bible Student tongues were wagging. And when this episode is added to other lines of inquiry, a picture emerges of a man who very likely enjoyed his "stacks of bones and hanks of hair" to a degree that renders laughable any claim that he played a leading role in purifying "Jehovah's organization."

Like the Pastor before him, Rutherford had a dysfunctional marriage (to put it mildly) that an ordinary Witness husband today would find himself heavily censured for if he attempted to replicate it. The Judge had been close to his "dear wife," if you remember, when he first encountered the Bible Student movement—but by the time of his death, his wife and son no longer had anything to do with him. Neither visited him on his deathbed, and both were absent at his funeral. Perhaps most alarming, at least for Jehovah's Witnesses taught to think of Rutherford as an early Watchtower leader headhunted by Christ, there are a number of lines of evidence hinting strongly at the Judge keeping at least one mistress.

In his book *Jehovah's Witnesses and the Third Reich,* Penton recounts the story of Mrs. Berta Peale, who was introduced to Rutherford by his stenographer, Bonnie Boyd.[30] After meeting the Judge in June 1938, Peale "abandoned her non-Jehovah's Witness husband of fifteen years and moved to the Brooklyn Bethel, where, at least outwardly, she became Rutherford's dietician and nurse." Her husband, Albert Peale—no doubt bewildered by the whole thing, to say the least—filed for divorce in November 1939, which was granted in March the following year.[31] After relating these details, Penton writes:

> Naturally, these facts raise serious questions. Why did Rutherford accept [Berta Peale] at Bethel when she had openly deserted her husband? Such behaviour was in clear violation of biblical teachings as understood by Jehovah's Witnesses. Why did the judge make her his nurse and dietician when he already had a male nurse and when she had no formal training as either a dietician or a nurse? And why, finally, did he take Mrs Peale, an attractive southern belle, with him wherever he went? That was something he did not do with his male nurse, Matthew Howlett.

Concerns over Rutherford's antics are by no means eased when considering the testimony of Hayden Cov-

---

[30] Bonnie Boyd was claimed to have received preferential treatment from Rutherford in a letter from Watchtower lawyer Olin Moyle, which I will deal with in the next few pages. While others had been forced to leave Bethel on getting married, Boyd, it was claimed, "was permitted to bring her husband into Bethel in spite of the printed rule providing that both marrying parties should have lived there for five years."

[31] Penton bases his account of Peale on information provided by Dr. Carl Thoronton, a grand-nephew of Berta Peale, as well as from transcripts from the Olin Moyle court case (*Moyle v. Franz et al.*) in which Peale's close association with Rutherford is referenced.

ington—a key Watchtower official who served under the Judge—who was interviewed by Dr. Jerry Bergman in 1974. (At the time of the interview, Bergman was still a Witness and Covington was disfellowshipped due to his alcoholism. The latter would be reinstated shortly before his death in 1978.) When Bergman asked Covington about the "philandering rumors" he angrily replied: "If your wife was paralyzed, what would you do?" "He seemed to acknowledge that Rutherford did have paramours, but defended him to the hilt," wrote Bergman.[32]

A further clue adding weight to claims that Rutherford was not quite the chaste spiritual leader that Watchtower would wish him to be is furnished in recorded testimony by Barbara Anderson, a former Bethelite.[32] In 1993, while still a Witness, Anderson was among a small party who visited Beth Sarim (Rutherford's former home in San Diego, which I will discuss in more detail in later pages). During this visit, according to Anderson, the then owner surprised the group with information about the property that they were not expecting.

> Then he pointed in the distance and he told us that when he bought Beth Sarim there were seven

---

[32] I will revisit the Bergman-Covington interview in the next chapter. Also noteworthy from the exchange was Covington's Rutherfordian male-chauvinist remarks about his wife. Bergman writes: "I also talked to [Covington's] wife during my visit. A very attractive, articulate woman, I was impressed with her . . . Some people you are really impressed with after only fifteen minutes. She was that kind of person. She had a good handle on both his, and the Society's, problems. I mentioned to Hayden that I was very impressed with her, and that I thought she was a good wife. He said something disparaging like: 'Well, she's a woman, she's supposed to take care of things,' clearly demeaning his wife. He felt she was a good wife because that is what a woman is supposed to do."

[33] Barbara Anderson is also a leading advocate against the mishandling of child sex abuse among Jehovah's Witnesses—a subject I will explore in more detail in Chapter Ten.

> small cabins located on the property where the Judge kept his women. And if we walked over to the area he said we could still see the foundation slabs of concrete where the cabins were. Well, we really laughed. Well, we were embarrassed—we didn't know what to say, so I changed the subject.

Naturally, the above account is a long way from representing ironclad evidence that Rutherford kept women in cabins on his property for sexual purposes. However, viewed in the context of what we know about the Judge—including (in the case of Covington) the testimony of one of his loyal lieutenants—it is at least *likely* that Rutherford was sexually active outside his marriage despite his elevated position in what he liked to call "the Theocracy."

The bare minimum we can say of Rutherford is that he could have done much more to shield himself from claims of extramarital impropriety. There would have been no scandal for him to answer to if he had continued cohabiting with his wife, or if he had not taken a beautiful woman away from her husband to be his constant companion under the pretext that she was his *unlicensed* dietician and nurse. If the Judge were still alive today, these facts alone would be enough to seriously compromise his authority as a Watchtower leader and possibly lead to judicial sanctions.[34] And yet,

---

[34] According to current directions to elders, Witnesses can be disfellowshipped for adultery based on circumstantial evidence. The *Shepherd* book advises (italics in the original): "In some cases adultery is not proved, but it is established by confession or by two or more witnesses that the mate stayed *all night* in the same house with a person of the opposite sex (or a known homosexual) *under improper circumstances*. The elders should carefully consider the situation. Were the individuals together *all night*? Were *improper* circumstances involved? For example, were the two persons alone? Is there evidence of a romantic relationship? What were the sleeping arrange-

according to the organization's current teachings, the Judge is still considered to have played a prominent role in the fulfillment of Bible prophecy concerning God's people.

Even setting aside Watchtower's wild eschatological claims about the Judge, the behavior of both him and his predecessor is frankly astonishing in the context of modern Witness teachings on marriage. As I will explain in more detail in Chapter Nine, the Governing Body insists on Witnesses upholding the sanctity of the marital bond to the point of forcing them to remain married to violent spouses. Separation without divorce is the only recourse for a battered Witness wife or husband in such cases. And yet neither Russell nor Rutherford can seriously be deemed to have fulfilled their duties in honoring the marriage arrangement. Given what we know about them now, neither would be considered exemplary or "above reproach" as husbands—which is a requirement for all who are considered for recommendation as Witness elders today.[35]

Watchtower's continued elevation of Rutherford in its theological narrative grows still more perplexing

---

ments?" (Disturbingly, the same willingness to consider circumstantial evidence is not extended when deliberating accusations of child sex abuse. Instead, eyewitnesses to the act must be presented before action can be taken in such cases, as I will explain in Chapter Ten.)

35 Regarding prospective elders who are separated, the *Shepherd* book asks: "Who is primarily to blame for the marital problems? What were the circumstances surrounding the separation or divorce? Who is responsible for the separation or pursued the divorce? Did both sign the decree indicating their agreement? How long ago did it occur? What is the brother doing to try to reconcile? . . . When separation and divorce are involved, there may be deficiencies on the part of both mates that make it necessary to limit special privileges because neither of them is exemplary."

when one considers aspects of the Judge's temperament and behavior that are more comprehensively documented than the admittedly scant information about his love life. For example, a letter penned by Watchtower lawyer Olin Moyle on July 21, 1939, caused a storm of controversy when it brought to the fore various unpleasant aspects of Bethel life under Rutherford's presidency that would shock Witnesses today.

Moyle had moved into Bethel in 1935, together with his wife, to head Watchtower's fledgling Legal Department. With the organization facing a barrage of legal battles in its fight for the religious freedom of its members, a capable lawyer who could take the heat off Rutherford and represent Watchtower in court alongside its lawyer-president was sorely needed—and Moyle wasted little time in distinguishing himself in this regard. He was instrumental in two Supreme Court victories that set precedents for First Amendment rights in America.[36] But, by 1939, Moyle had grown disillusioned with life at Bethel and was particularly disturbed by the way the president comported himself. He decided the best course of action would be to leave in protest, but with an offer to continue representing

---

[36] Moyle was involved in both the *Lovell v. City of Griffin* (1938) and the *Schneider v. State of New Jersey* (1939) Supreme Court cases—both decided in Watchtower's favor. After his departure, Hayden Covington took over as head of the legal department, and continued Moyle's impressive legacy of securing religious freedoms that would benefit Americans for generations to follow. It should be noted, however, that Watchtower is not keen to register pride in its contribution to society through groundbreaking legal victories, which it describes as a "side benefit" in its 2014 book *God's Kingdom Rules!*. The book points out that Witnesses "are not social reformers; nor are [they] interested in self-vindication. Above all, Jehovah's Witnesses have pursued their legal rights in the courts in an effort to establish and advance pure worship."

Watchtower from outside Bethel in lawsuits that were still pending, if so required.

Despite raising serious grievances about Rutherford's character and leadership style, the letter left by Moyle on the desk of the Bethel home lobby was bereft of bitterness or spite, as immediately striking in the opening words:

> Dear Brother Rutherford:
>
> This letter is to give you notice of our intention to leave Bethel on September 1st next. These reasons for leaving are stated herein and we ask that you give them careful and thoughtful consideration.
>
> Conditions at Bethel are a matter of concern to all of the Lord's people. Nowhere among imperfect men can there be perfect freedom from oppression, discrimination and unfair treatment, but at the Lord's headquarters on earth conditions should be such that injustice would be reduced to the minimum. That is not the case here at Bethel and a protest should be made against it. I am in a good position to make such protest because your treatment of me has been generally kind, considerate and fair. I can make this protest in the interests of the Bethel family and of the Kingdom work without any personal interest entering into the matter.

The letter went on to list Moyle's concerns about a number of aspects of life at headquarters, namely Rutherford's treatment of the Bethel family, perceived discrimination (especially the Judge's opulent living arrangements in comparison with ordinary Bethelites), the culture of alcohol use, and the proliferation of "filthy and vulgar" language.

Needless to say, the letter did not go down well with the Judge, who responded with a withering character assassination that he had printed in the October 15, 1939, *Watchtower.* Moyle's letter, it was insisted, was "filled with false, slanderous and libelous statements." Moyle was said to have identified himself "as one who speaks evil against the Lord's organization, and who is a murmurer and complainer, even as the Scriptures have foretold." Without being presented with a copy of the letter so that they could judge for themselves, Witness readers were informed that "every paragraph of that letter is false, filled with lies, and is a wicked slander and libel not only against the president but against the entire family." Moyle was accused of writing the letter "to justify himself and to 'cause division among the brethren,'" and his "slanderous paper" was said to be "against the interest of the Theocratic government" and "pleasing only to the Devil and his earthly agents."

Furthermore, since Moyle had been "entrusted with the confidential matters of the Society" as one of its legal representatives, and yet had "assault[ed] and malign[ed] those who trusted him," a predictable cliché was deployed: "Judas was entrusted by Christ Jesus with confidential matters, and Judas proved his unfaithfulness by furnishing to the enemy that which they could use and did use against the Lord." Having condemned Moyle as the ultimate traitor and "evil servant," the magazine concluded its rant with an instruction for Witnesses to either side with Moyle or "remain faithful to Jehovah and his government by Christ Jesus." "Choose whom you'll serve," was the final, rather menacing ultimatum put to bewildered readers.

Of course, Rutherford did not have to pursue the matter in such an aggressive, self-destructive manner. He could have either attempted to reconcile with Moyle (and, in so doing, showed himself to be humble and reasonable) or he could have ignored the letter and let it be slowly buried with the passage of time. Had Rutherford opted for the latter course, it is very likely that few people (if any) would know about Moyle or his letter today. Instead, the Judge issued a public statement in a well-distributed magazine accusing a clearly competent, practicing lawyer of "wicked slander and libel." The result was perhaps inevitable. Moyle sued Watchtower—successfully—and collected the then tidy sum of $15,000 in damages.[37] More significant than any financial considerations, Moyle's victory meant that the accusations he brought against Rutherford were given far more weight and credibility than if they had been left unanswered.

By now you might be wondering what claims Moyle's letter contained. Let us begin with his observations about bad language at Bethel:

> The Biblical injunctions against unclean, filthy speaking and jesting have never been abrogated. It is shocking and nauseating to hear vulgar speaking and smut at Bethel. It was stated by a sister that was one of the things you had to get used to at Bethel. The loudest laughter at the table comes when a filth or near filthy joke goes through, and your skirts are not clear.

Witnesses today observe strict rules on bad language and swearing.[38] A 2008 *Awake!* article aimed at young Witnesses insisted that profanity "shows disrespect for the Creator of speech." It therefore urged:

---

[37] Moyle was originally awarded $30,000 in damages, but this was reduced to $15,000 on appeal in 1944.

[38] In my personal experience, the extent to which swearing is tolerated among Witnesses can vary geographically. In the UK, any form of profanity in Kingdom Halls or in the preaching work is almost unheard of. However, I recall noticing slightly more latitude when visiting congregations in America.

> Think of how our Creator feels, then, when we misuse the gift of speech. Little wonder that God's Word states: "Let all malicious bitterness and anger and wrath and screaming and abusive speech be taken away from you along with all badness." —Ephesians 4:31.

And yet, according to Moyle, swearing and innuendo were commonplace at Bethel under Rutherford's presidency. It was something one had to "get used to," and something the Judge indulged in personally. But suggestions that Watchtower's president may have had a potty mouth and a dirty sense of humor were arguably the least of Moyle's accusations. His letter included scandalous reports of a pervasive drinking culture at the apex of Rutherford's "Theocracy":

> Under your tutelage there has grown up a glorification of alcohol and condemnation of total abstinence which is unseemly. Whether a servant of Jehovah drinks alcoholic liquor is none of my business, except in giving a helping hand to a brother who is stumbled thereby. Whether I am a total abstainer is nobody's business but my own. But not so at Bethel. There appears to be a definite policy of breaking in newcomers into the use of liquor, and resentment is shown against those who do not join them. The claim is made, "One can't be a real Bethelite without drinking beer." Shortly after we arrived it was arrogantly stated, "we can't do much with Moyle, but we'll make a man out of Peter." A New York brother intimated that I was out of harmony with the truth and with the Society because I didn't drink liquor. A New York sister stated that she had never used liquor or served it until some of the Bethel boys insisted upon it. A brother who used to drink liquor to excess became a total abstainer after getting the truth. He knew that a single drink of liquor would start him off to his former drinking

> habits, but in spite of that brethren from Bethel insisted upon his imbibing liquor and inferred that he was out of harmony with the organization through refusing. Total abstainers are looked upon with scorn as weaklings. You have publicly labeled total abstainers as prudes and therefore must assume your share of the responsibility for the Bacchus like attitude exhibited by members of the family.

To you, the reader, the idea of Rutherford being a keen drinker may not come as a huge surprise given some of his writings that we have already considered in this chapter. But to most Witnesses today, it would be unthinkable for such an instrumental figure in the history of "Jehovah's organization" to have been prone to booze.

Alcoholism is *not* tolerated among Witnesses.[39] And when it comes to elders and other senior officials "taking the lead" in the organization, they are expected to be "free from reproach" from this or any other vice. Though drinking is allowed for Witnesses *in moderation* (contrary to the Mormon practice of abstaining altogether) and attitudes toward alcohol tend to vary among Witnesses depending on the local customs, Watchtower takes a firm stand on drunkenness to the point of stipulating the following rule in its guidelines to Bethelites:

> Alcoholic beverages may be brought into the home, but they must be used in moderation in harmony

---

[39] "Drunkenness" is a disfellowshipping offense, and elders are asked to adjudicate based on how widely known the person's habit is. "A judicial committee is required when there is a practice of drunkenness or a single incident of drunkenness that brings notoriety," it says on pages 66 and 67 of the *Shepherd* book. In the event of someone getting drunk on a single occasion in their own home, and where "there was no notoriety," "it may suffice for the elder to give strong counsel."

> with local legal guidelines for drinking alcoholic beverages. Both heavy drinking and drunkenness are condemned by Jehovah and will not be tolerated. (Prov. 23:29-34; Eph. 5:17-19) Overindulgence will call into question an individual's Christian qualifications and may result in his being asked to leave Bethel. (Rom. 14:16-18) If it has not been your custom to use alcoholic beverages before coming to Bethel, there is no reason to start now just because you may see others using them.

Though you will occasionally hear stories of Bethelites drinking or getting drunk when their supervisors' backs are turned, generally the culture in modern Bethels is the polar opposite to the situation revealed by Moyle.[40] Whereas he described a tradition of "breaking in newcomers" and goading teetotalers, the current guidelines (at least as of 2004) make it clear that if a person was not previously in the habit of drinking any alcohol "there is no reason to start now."

Even more scandalous for current Witnesses would be the notion that it was under the "tutelage" of their former president that this drinking culture at headquarters thrived, with the Judge even labeling as "prudes" those who wished to abstain. As incompatible as such behavior may be with the pristine image of Rutherford that is fed to Witnesses today, the Judge made very little effort to hide the fact that he enjoyed alcohol—even during the years when doing so was forbidden in America.

Between January 1920 and December 1933, the laws on Prohibition made it illegal for alcohol to be manu-

---

[40] On one of my visits to London Bethel in the summer of 2001 (because I was pioneering I was allowed to stay in one of the apartments as a guest) I was invited to the Bethel family's barbecue in the gardens of Watchtower House. I will never forget everyone being rationed one bottle of beer—and no more!

factured, transported or sold in the United States. And yet, rather than meekly abiding by this law, in 1930 the Judge published a booklet titled *Prohibition and the League of Nations: Born of God or the Devil—Which?* Rutherford's 59-page illustrated rant about the importance of not banning alcohol lambasted the Anti-Saloon League (the leading organization behind lobbying for the Prohibition) as "the enemy of God," and accused it of "playing into the hands of Satan." As to the Prohibition law itself, the Judge declared:

> I am of the opinion that the American people were hoodwinked into adopting the Prohibition law because of the claim of the clergy and their allies and so-called "religious organizations" that God wanted them to do it. I am certain that the back of the whole scheme of Prohibition is the master mind of Satan and that his purpose is to use this Prohibition fiasco to turn the people away from Jehovah God.

While it is true that the "Prohibition fiasco" did more harm than good in the long run (hence the eventual repeal of the law), the fact that Rutherford could set aside his "apolitical" values to the extent of using Watchtower literature as a soapbox from which to publicly remonstrate over this particular issue is very telling. (And, again, such political dabbling would be alien to most Witnesses today.) We can justifiably ask: why would Rutherford go to such lengths to complain about Prohibition if it were not a deeply personal matter to him? By publishing his diatribe, the Judge left himself wide open to accusations of, as Shakespeare would put it, protesting "too much."

Admittedly, when it comes to deliberating over Rutherford's alleged alcoholism the majority of the evidence is inconclusive and/or anecdotal. Even so, the profusion of stories points strongly to there being more than just a conspiracy at the heart of the matter. Penton addresses the subject this way in *Apocalypse Delayed:*

> Although Jehovah's Witnesses have done everything possible to hide accounts of the judge's drinking habits, they are simply too notorious to be denied. Former workers at the Watch Tower's New York headquarters recount tales of his inebriation and drunken stupors. Others tell stories of how difficult it sometimes was to get him to the podium to give talks at conventions because of his drunkenness.

If your typical believing Witness were to be confronted with the foregoing, the immediate reaction would be something like: "That is just hearsay. Who is to say these rumors were not just fabricated by opposers?" While that is a defensible standpoint, it must also be remembered that we are dealing with a religious icon, the leader of a movement that espouses moral and spiritual purity, and it would be in Watchtower's interests to keep indiscretions of this or any other nature well buried. If Rutherford did have a drinking problem, how are we realistically to learn of it aside from through stories and rumors?

As it happens, however, rumors are not all we have to go on when investigating this issue. There is documented evidence from at least one credible source that the Judge went so far as to violate the laws against transporting alcohol by having whiskey secretly imported from Canada using Watchtower's Canadian facilities. We know about this because of a letter sent by another former Watchtower staff member who, before Moyle, came to be less than enamored with the president. His name was Walter Salter. As well as being a close friend and confidant of the Judge, Salter had also been the overseer for Watchtower's Canada branch. But after Salter began questioning Watchtower teachings in 1936, he soon found himself disfellowshipped. Not one to go out without a bang, Salter wrote a scathing letter to Rutherford following his exit, dated April 1, 1937. It included this astonishing admission:

***Walter Salter, as pictured in "The Messenger"—Watchtower's 1931 convention report***

> It was with this thought in mind that I, at your orders would purchase cases of whiskey at $60.00 a case, and cases of brandy and other liquors, to say nothing of untold cases of beer. A bottle or two of liquor would not do; it was for THE PRESIDENT and nothing was too good for THE PRESIDENT. He was heaven's favorite, why should not he have everything that would gratify his desires for comfort. True, I had a part therein for I partook of your hospitality, or shall I say the Society's hospitality for it was the Society's money but I partook, as above stated, being blinded with the idea the THE PRESIDENT was in charge and therefore responsible and not I. Today I see that the thought was absolutely wrong and that the squandering of the Society's money in that respect was a mis-appropriation of funds, and I should have taken no part therein whatsoever. I confess my wrong before the friends and before the Lord and ask their forgiveness and His.

Not only was Salter confessing to the misappropriation of Watchtower funds toward keeping the Judge lubricated—he was also confessing to his part in illegal activity. As previously mentioned, the transport of alcohol was outlawed during the Prohibition era. Witnesses today are told that they must respect the biblical injunction to "be in subjection to the superior authorities" in respectfully upholding the law, so long as it does not trespass on Bible commands, whether they personally agree with it or not. (Interestingly, Rutherford interpreted the "superior authorities," or "higher powers," of Romans 13:1 as referring to God and Christ, which no doubt helped ease his conscience somewhat. He was, after all, their sole mouthpiece.)[41] And yet, we have documented evidence from a credible source that if the law of the land came between the president of the Watch Tower Society and his whiskey, it could be disregarded.

But written evidence is not all there is when it comes to establishing Rutherford's love of the bottle. There are also strong visual clues pointing firmly in that direction. If you visit Barbara Anderson's WatchtowerDocuments.org website, you can read of the discoveries she made while working at Brooklyn headquarters in the late '80s and early '90s. Barbara tells of how, when doing research for the *Proclaimers* book, she found a box of photographs of Rutherford in the Bethel archives—including one image she describes as "one of the most disagreeable and revolting discoveries":

> Rutherford was clad in a dark-colored, one-piece, skin-tight, sleeveless swimsuit which covered him down to his thighs, a garment popular in the late

[41] On page 219 of his 1936 book *Riches,* Rutherford explained that the "higher powers" are "Jehovah God and Christ Jesus, that is, God and his royal house in heaven. The powers that rule the present wicked world and which are known as the 'temporal powers' are not ordained of God."

> 1920s and '30s. He had a huge belly, and appeared to be having fun romping on a large patio which overlooked the ocean. I seem to remember there were other people in a few photos lying on chaise lounges. The photo I'll never forget was a close-up of Rutherford's face; he was about a foot from the camera with his tongue stuck out as far as it could possibly go. He looked to me to be inebriated.

Unfortunately, until the photograph (or set of photographs) is released or somehow leaked, we have no means of beholding this cringeworthy spectacle for ourselves and thereby validating Barbara's story. Even so, there is other imagery of the Judge that adds credence to her account. For example, type "Joseph Rutherford drinking" into Google, and you will soon be directed to the picture below, which shows a seated Judge looking merry as drinks of some description are poured by what looks like his entourage.

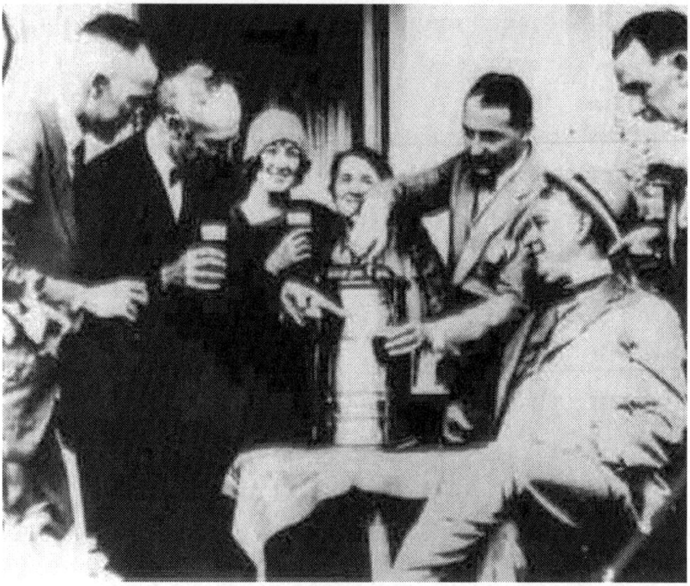

***Rutherford: apparently in the process of partaking***

Further visual hints that the Judge may have been partial to alcohol have been uploaded to YouTube in the form of rare 8 mm camera footage shot at Beth Sarim. The video was uploaded by Eric Bottorff, a fellow activist and former Bethelite, who came across it around 1990 after it was presented at the end of a Bethel "family night" (talent show) by a long-serving Bethelite named Michael Lubeck.[42]

The blurry, color, silent film shows the Judge frolicking in the grounds of his house and play-acting for the camera. At various points he is seen inspecting the gardens, cutting grass with a scythe, plowing soil with horses, surveying building work, and either picking fruit or playfully holding it in front of the camera. At two moments in the footage Rutherford jabs his tongue out in an almost reptilian manner—just as described by Anderson in the photo she discovered—and pulls odd facial expressions when doing so in behavior that is anything but presidential. Rutherford is also briefly shown inside the property but, instead of posing behind a desk or otherwise busying himself with his duties, he appears before the camera drinking something from an ornate glass.

Obviously, this video is not proof that Rutherford was a drunkard. For all we know, he could have been drinking orange juice from the glass, and was stone cold sober while cavorting in the gardens giving his tongue some air. But isn't it odd that the only film footage we have of the Judge not acting in some official capacity shows him behaving in this manner? Of all the things he could have shown himself to be doing when

---

[42] Eric runs the website JWstruggle.com, and his popular "JWStruggle" YouTube channel hosts the video in question, with his helpful commentary.

an 8 mm camera was pointed at him one day at Beth Sarim, acting like an imbecile should surely have been low on the list.

What would be the reaction if footage emerged of a current Governing Body member replicating Rutherford's behavior? Would Tony Morris be forgiven for prancing around sticking his tongue out like a lizard, and later being filmed drinking something? (Apologies if I have planted an unpleasant mental image.) Anyone can be caught off guard in this way, and there is nothing wrong with acting the fool when the mood takes you—we have all done it—but for someone claiming to be a conduit of divine wisdom to allow himself to be immortalized on camera in such an awkward state, especially given the documented complaints as to his drinking habits, reveals poor judgment at the very least.

As with the reports of Rutherford's philandering, it is quite possible we will never have conclusive evidence that the Judge had a drinking problem. There is no written confession to that effect, and such a document is unlikely to surface even if it exists. However, just as with the stories of Rutherford's extramarital escapades, there is much the Judge could have done to allay suspicions in this area. He could have put in place a robust, written drinking policy for all Bethelites, as is the case today. He didn't. He could have stayed silent on America's Prohibition laws, which really had nothing to do with Bible matters. He didn't. He could have made sure he was never filmed or photographed either drinking or in an apparently drunken state. He didn't. And he could have acted lawfully and responsibly by not having liquor illegally imported from Canada for his personal use (procured with dedicated funds, no less), but this—at least according to a confessed accomplice—is something he was unable to do. When the preponderance of evidence pointing to Rutherford's alcoholism is weighed against his failure to give anyone trying to clear his name the slightest morsel at which to grasp, it is reasonable to conclude that he was very likely a compulsive drinker and therefore, again, would have been discounted from any leadership position under current Watchtower rules.

We must, however, move on from the Judge's drinking habits and return to Moyle's letter, because it reveals more fascinating insights into Rutherford's character of which most Witnesses would, frankly, prefer to be ignorant. For example, when trying to imagine the ideal Christian role model, furthest from one's mind would be a tyrannical bully who publicly scolds and demeans any who fail to live up to his expectations. But according to Moyle, that is precisely the sort of man Watchtower's president was:

> Shortly after coming to Bethel we were shocked to witness the spectacle of our brethren receiving what is designated as a "trimming" from you. The first, if memory serves me correct, was a tongue lashing given to C. J. Woodworth. Woodworth in a personal letter to you stated something to the effect that it would be serving the devil to continue using our present day calendar. For that he was humiliated, called a jackass, and given a public lambasting. Others have been similarly treated. McCaughey, McCormick, Knorr, Prosser, Price, Van Sipma, Ness and others have been similarly scolded. They have been publicly called to account, condemned, and reprimanded without any previous notice. This summer some of the most unfair public reproaches have been given. J. Y. McCauley asked a question which carried with it a criticism of the

> present method of Watch Tower study. For that he was severely reprimanded. Your action constituted a violation of the principle for which we are fighting, towit, freedom of speech. It was the action of a boss and not that of a fellow servant. . . . Brother Worsley received a public denunciation from you because he prepared and handed to brethren a list of helpful Scripture citations on fundamental topics. How can we consistently condemn religionists for being intolerant when you exercise intolerance against those who work with you? Doesn't this prove that the only freedom permitted at Bethel is freedom to do and say that which you wish to be said and done? The Lord certainly never authorized you to exercise such high handed authority over your fellow servants.

This is not the image of Rutherford familiar to Witnesses from the organization's literature. A 1998 *Watchtower* printed the life story of a British pioneer and contemporary of the Judge, Gwendoline Matthews, who described him as a "kind, approachable man."[43] And in a 1994 issue of the magazine, Bethelite Robert Hatzfeld described him as "a kindly man" who "practiced what he preached." "He did not expect anything of others that he would not do himself," insisted Hatzfeld, adding that the Judge "was of the highest spiritual and moral character." It is hardly surprising that Watchtower is able to produce glowing testimonies from among believing Witnesses attesting to the character of a man who must by necessity be a paragon of

---

[43] When it was in the Judge's interests to project a light-hearted, humble side, it seems he was capable of doing so. In a 1941 interview with a reporter he is said to have jovially remarked: "To me, titles mean nothing. It doesn't matter whether I'm called Judge or jackass." I would have loved to witness the Judge's reaction to anyone taking him up on this invitation away from the media glare.

virtue according to their theology—an organizational figurehead who was supposedly among a select group entrusted by Christ with "the management of all his earthly belongings." In *Faith on the March*, A. H. Macmillan painted a similarly gushing (although slightly more realistic) portrait of his spiritual leader:

> Rutherford had always manifested a deep Christian love for his associates and was very kindhearted; but he was not naturally of the same gentle, quiet-mannered disposition as Russell. He was direct and outspoken and did not hide his feelings. His bluntness, even when spoken in kindness, was sometimes misunderstood.

Macmillan went on to write that, despite his "bluntness," it would become obvious that Jesus had chosen "the right man for the job" by selecting Rutherford in 1919. But given what we know about Rutherford—not just anecdotally but in documented evidence, *including his own printed words*—either Jesus is an appalling judge of character, or the pool of candidates from whom he made his selection that fateful year were even more prone to womanizing, racism, anti-Semitism, alcoholism, denigrating women, sympathizing with Nazis and bullying coworkers than the man who would go on to invent the name "Jehovah's witnesses."

The more one learns about Rutherford, the more incredible Watchtower's teaching regarding 1919 becomes—a teaching that can only be held to so long as ordinary Witnesses know as little about Rutherford's life and character as possible. (As mentioned earlier, the 2014 *God's Kingdom Rules!* book limits its discussion of Rutherford to the basic historical narrative, and keeps any commentary on his character and temperament to an absolute minimum.)

But I am afraid we are still not quite done with Moyle's "slanderous" letter, one of the most damning elements of which was the lawyer's scathing exposé of Rutherford's lavish living arrangements, and how these stood in stark contrast with those of ordinary Bethel workers:

> We publish to the world that all in the Lord's organization are treated alike, and receive the same as far as this world's goods are concerned. You know that is not the case. The facts cannot be denied. Take for instance the difference between the accommodations furnished to you, and your personal attendants, compared with those furnished to some of your brethren. You have many many homes, to wit, Bethel, Staten Island, California, etc. I am informed that even at the Kingdom Farm one house is kept for your sole use during the short periods you spend there. And what do the brethren at the farm receive? Small rooms, unheated thru the bitter cold winter weather. They live in their trunks like campers. That may be all right if necessary, but there are many houses on the farm standing idle or used for other purposes, which could be used to give some comfort to those who work so long and so hard.
>
> You work in a nice air conditioned room. You and your attendants spend a portion of the week in the quiet of country surroundings. The boys at the factory diligently work thru the hot summer months without such helps, or any effort made to give them. That is discrimination which should receive your thoughtful consideration.

In listing California as one of Rutherford's residences, Moyle was referring to a Spanish-style mansion built for the personal use of the Judge in San Diego. "Beth Sarim," as Rutherford named it, still stands to this day. In fact, my wife and I had the opportunity of seeing it for ourselves, thanks to the kindness and hospitality of some friends, while on a trip to the United States in May 2013. The present owners did not answer when I rang the doorbell, but noticeable on the wall of the property to the right of the front door was a bronze plaque identifying the site as a "historical landmark" for the city of San Diego.[44] I could not help but see irony in the fact that San Diego is more interested in drawing attention to the significance of Beth Sarim than its builders, the Watch Tower Society.

***Beth Sarim as it was when I visited in 2013***

The *Proclaimers* book's understandably terse acknowledgement of the property is limited to a small photo, three paragraphs and a footnote in a grey box on page 76. The footnote is the only part of the box that reveals the astonishing claims once made about the building. The writers admit that Beth Sarim was erected first and foremost as a private residence for

44 It is probably just as well that nobody was home, since I do not expect the current owners to be thrilled at the prospect of unannounced Witness and ex-Witness pilgrims descending on them, even if it could be argued that these come with the territory when you buy a piece of religious history.

Rutherford. They draw attention to the Judge's poor health, and insist that his winter-time work in San Diego (2,800 miles from Watchtower's Brooklyn headquarters) was "urged" by his doctor. The reader is left with the impression that the construction of a Californian mansion for the president's private use was a medical necessity.

Though Watchtower seems to be understandably ashamed of Beth Sarim, many former Witnesses are fascinated by the story behind it—and with good reason. The building is an awkward monument to the organization's failed predictions and a cautionary reminder that detachment from reality almost inevitably follows when religious leaders cloister themselves in ivory towers.

One of the most extensive discussions of Beth Sarim in official Watchtower publications can be found in an issue of an older Watchtower newsletter titled *The Messenger*—a convention report from 1931, some of which was devoted to answering a glut of derisory media attention about the property.[45] Under the heading "Beth-Sarim—Much Talked About House in San Diego," pages 6 and 8 defend Rutherford's need for the property in response to critical newspaper reports of the time:

> Judge Rutherford, president of the Watch Tower Society, is one of the hardest-worked men in the world. Anybody can be a Christian in peace-time, but Judge Rutherford was one of the war-time Christians; and, for daring so to be, went to Atlanta

[45] Quite apart from establishing the outlandish claims once made by the organization about Beth Sarim, the 1931 issue of *The Messenger* is well worth downloading by anyone who doubts the reverence that was lavished on Rutherford—a man who banned Mother's Day under the objection that it amounted to "creature worship." In the captions of two photos he is described as the "Generalissimo," and "Their Visible Leader."

> Penitentiary under four sentences of twenty years each. When he emerged he was in poor physical condition, and even now has the use of but one lung. Since his return from Atlanta, prudence and good common sense dictated that, working as hard as he constantly works, he should have the benefit of the most equable winter climate to be found.

One would think that if "prudence and good common sense" were applied to a situation in which a man is so gravely ill that normal work at his organization's headquarters is rendered impossible, the obvious solution would be for him to do less work, or step down from his duties altogether. Instead, living in a luxurious purpose-built residence on the opposite side of the continent from said headquarters was evidently considered the most practical solution.

In further explaining Rutherford's move to San Diego, Watchtower publications cite advice from his physician, Dr. Eckols. As the *Proclaimers* book succinctly puts it:

> In the 1920's, under a doctor's treatment, [Rutherford] went to San Diego, California, and the doctor urged him to spend as much time as possible there.

The reader is left with the impression that Rutherford was dispatched by his doctor from Brooklyn to the warmer climes of San Diego for the sake of his health. In truth, Dr. Eckols was based in San Diego, so his selection of that location was far from unbiased. And being told to spend "as much time as possible" in that part of the country does not explain the need for building a mansion there. After all, Rutherford had been using rented accommodation in the area for years before the decision was made to build Beth Sarim.

The funding behind Beth Sarim is one of the murkier aspects of this story. Watchtower literature repeatedly dismisses the suggestion that the property was built solely out of the organization's funds. "Beth Sarim was built with funds that were a direct contribution for that purpose," asserts the *Proclaimers* book. Watchtower's treasurer of the time, W. E. Van Amburgh, was more emphatic. "[N]o money has been drawn from the funds of the Watch Tower Bible & Tract Society, or any affiliated association . . . for the purpose of erecting, purchasing or acquiring the possession of any building or real estate in San Diego, California," he insisted.

Irrespective of who it was that paid the builders, we are left with a luxury residence erected using donated funds—a residence that, according to the deeds, was to be held in trust by the Watch Tower Society. After Rutherford died, it was Watchtower who pocketed the proceeds from its eventual sale in 1948. It was therefore as much a Watchtower-owned building as any other, and—as Moyle pointed out—it was allocated for the sole enjoyment of one man.

The timing of the Beth Sarim project is also a matter of some controversy. It was built in 1929, the year of the Wall Street crash that plunged America into the Great Depression. The construction costs were around $25,000—small change by today's standards, but a giddying sum of money back then. The architect, Richard S. Requa, drew inspiration from "some of the most beautiful residences" of the area. The building that emerged from his plans would be described by a neighbor as "one of the finest in Kensington Heights." It is understandable that Moyle could be so irked by the obvious extravagance—and he was not the only one.

In Salter's 1937 letter, he too balked at the obvious disparity between the opulence afforded Rutherford and the austerity endured by those who toiled to print and distribute his writings. Beth Sarim was listed among six "luxuries" at the president's disposal:

> 1. Not one but two 16-cylinder cars, one in California and one in New York. One would not suffice for THE PRESIDENT nor would a 6 cylinder car be big enough for THE PRESIDENT, but a 4 would do for a pioneer, or a bicycle or a hand-sleigh, or trudging along without any vehicle at all.
> 2. Your New York apartment, easily worth a rental of $10,000.00 a year. And its luxurious furnishings.
> 3. Your palatial residence on Staten Island, camouflaged as essential to the broadcasting station WBBR.
> 4. As though that residence were not sufficient, a further small place of seclusion in the woods of Staten Island where you can go and rest your weary body while the pioneers and others trudge from door to door.
> 5. Your further abode at San Diego, for which you yourself told me you were offered $75,000.00, but of course it could not be sold and the funds used to help the pioneers because it was deeded to David—what hypocrisy!
> 6. Commodious and expensive quarters in Magdeburg, Germany, for the convenience of THE PRESIDENT, to say nothing of the provision made for your comfort in London.

Salter's tone in his letter to Rutherford was regrettably scornful and sarcastic—especially in comparison to the mild, conciliatory spirit of Moyle's rebuke. Though this detracts somewhat from the information he presents, Salter's letter nonetheless offers documented evidence from a former Watchtower official that Rutherford leveraged his position as leader of an evangelical movement to live a life of needless extravagance. In that respect, there is little to differentiate the Judge from modern-day high-profile televangelists who shamelessly buy mansions and circle the globe in private jets while expecting, and in some cases demanding, that their devoted followers pick up the bill.

Take, as an example, those 16-cylinder Cadillacs—one of which was kept at Brooklyn, the other (a yellow coupé) in the garage at Beth Sarim. It was by no means imperative that the Judge should have owned *one* such vehicle, let alone two. "To place the value of this automobile in perspective, a new Ford in 1931 cost approximately 600 dollars," explains the 1987 book *Witnesses of Jehovah* by Leonard and Marjorie Chretien. "A 16-cylinder Cadillac cost between 5,400 and 9,200 dollars, depending on style."

As with Beth Sarim itself, it could be argued that these cars were not purchased by Watchtower but donated, perhaps by a well-to-do admirer of the Judge who wanted to see him ferried around in style. Even so, would it not behoove Rutherford to exercise some discretion? Was anything preventing him from repudiating "creature worship" by insisting on funds donated for his personal enjoyment being redirected to "the Lord's work" of printing and distributing God's life-saving message to mankind—especially given the sacrifices he expected others to make?

Despite apparently having no qualms in receiving the very best in life at the expense of his devotees, it seems Rutherford felt compelled to offer at least some excuse for having the sole benefit of Beth Sarim at a time of such austerity. He therefore insisted it be set aside for use by the princes, or "ancient worthies," who were running late from their expected appearance in 1925.[46] Apparently, Jerusalem had been ditched as the capital of Christ's government on earth. San Diego would now be the hub from which the likes of Abraham and Isaiah would issue instructions via radio. This extraordinary justification was elaborated in the *Messenger* article:

> Before Judge Rutherford would accept and use the home, he insisted upon writing the deed that it shall forever be held in trust by the Watch Tower Bible and Tract Society for the use of the Lord's work in the earth, with the expectation that in due time Abraham, Melchisedec, Joseph, Moses, Joshua, David, Isaiah or some others of the patriarchs or prophets of olden times will appear and will be glad to use this home which has been prepared for one or more of them in the western edge of the new world.

As laughable as this idea is, Rutherford was so taken with the notion of Bible "patriarchs or prophets of olden times" starting their comeback tour in San Diego that he drafted and signed arguably the most ridiculous title deed ever written, in which Bible characters were named as future owners of the property. Rutherford was so proud of the deed that he had it published in a 1930 issue of *The Golden Age.*

As you would expect, the bizarre claims of a prominent evangelist that he was living in a house that would soon belong to the likes of Moses, Samson and King David drew some attention from local journalists. A front-page article appeared in the *San Diego Sun* on January 9, 1931, under the headline: "David's House Waits for Owner." In it, Rutherford was asked what he

---

[46] Hence the name "Beth Sarim," or "House of Princes."

expected the princes to look like when they appeared, to which he replied:

> As perfect men. I interpret that to mean . . . that David, Gideon, Barak, Samson, Jepthae, Joseph and Samuel will be sent here to wrench the world from Satan's grasp, clothed in modern garb as we are, and able, with little effort to speak our tongue.

Yes, apparently the president of the Watch Tower Society was able to look a journalist in the eye and tell him straight-faced that Bible characters would soon appear on the streets of sunny San Diego, speaking perfect English and "wearing frock coats, high hats, canes and spats" (as the reporter put it). Presumably, the contemporary dress would have helped these Old Testament icons to be less conspicuous than if they had emerged in 1930s America wearing robes and sandals (or, in the case of Joseph, a coat of many colors). Their grasp of English "with little effort" would also have been convenient in compensating for the Judge's lack of fluency in Bible languages, not to mention considerably easing negotiations for laying claim to a piece of prime real estate.

The *Messenger* article goes even further in spelling out the detail with which this rendezvous had been planned for:

> The climate [in San Diego] is the same as that of Palestine. The place is planted with date and palm trees, such as would be familiar and pleasing sights to these men.

Indeed, how could a resurrected Bible character function effectively as one of Earth's new princes without being surrounded by vegetation that would remind him of home?

As incredibly silly and cringeworthy as Rutherford's ideas were, they were once part and parcel of Watchtower beliefs and cannot be denied, only concealed.[47] Whereas there was at least a mention of Beth Sarim in the *Proclaimers* book, there is no word of it in its successor, *God's Kingdom Rules!* If Witnesses want to learn about one of the most embarrassing teachings ever espoused by their religion, they must know where to look—and be prepared to do plenty of digging. Even then, a diehard Witness would often fall back on the argument: "Ah, but that was old light. We have moved on since then." But could not any religion say that about the skeletons in its closet? Is it not at least curious that an early leader of the movement, to whom prophetic significance continues to be attached, was capable of espousing such harebrained fantasies?

Of course, it is possible that the entire Beth Sarim project was little more than a publicity stunt, and that Rutherford's intentions were far more cynical than he led people to believe. We are unlikely to ever know for sure whether the Judge seriously expected to be called upon to allocate living quarters to the likes of Moses and King David. At least according to *The Messenger*, he was sincere:

> On the part of Judge Rutherford, the dedication of this home to God's work and for the use of these men was a simple act of faith.

And in Rutherford's 1939 book *Salvation*, he declared:

> The house has served as a testimony to many persons throughout the earth, and while the unbelievers have mocked concerning it and spoken contemptuously of it, yet it stands there as a testimony to Jehovah's name.

---

47 It would not be until a few years after Rutherford's death, in 1950, that Watchtower would scrap its teaching about the "ancient worthies" being resurrected *before* Armageddon.

Rutherford's funereal plans hinted even more strongly at sincerity on his part. He insisted on being buried at Beth Sarim "facing the rising sun, in an isolated part of the ground which would be administered by the princes, who should return from their graves." Little could the Judge have known that this bizarre request would lead to a protracted legal battle following his death from cancer on January 8, 1942. Watchtower lawyer Hayden Covington, and Rutherford's presidential successor, Nathan Knorr, were among those who fought to have the Judge laid to rest on the property in defiance of local residents, who were not overly keen on the idea of their neighborhood being turned into a cemetery or potential sacred monument.

To Watchtower's dismay, the residents won their battle. It was decided that the Judge would be denied his wish to be buried "facing the rising sun" at his beloved Beth Sarim. As a parting shot for their insolence, and with trademark Rutherfordian pomposity and melodrama, a 1942 issue of the *Consolation* magazine condemned the San Diego city officials for having "followed the course of Satan." "It was not the fate of the bones which they decided, but their own destiny," warned the writers. "Nor is their blood on anyone else's head, because they were told three times that to fight against God, or to tamper with His servant's bones even, would bring upon them the condemnation of the Lord."

And so, three and a half months after his death, under a cloud of controversy and acrimony entirely befitting his life and presidency, the Judge's remains were finally interred—even if, to this day, nobody can be entirely sure where.

Officially Rutherford was laid to rest in an unmarked grave on Staten Island, New York, with a notice posted to that effect in the *Time* magazine. (His funeral was attended by only four people, one of whom was A. H. Macmillan. Rutherford's surviving wife and son,[48] together with the next generation of Watchtower leaders, Nathan Knorr and Fred Franz, were reportedly conspicuous by their absence.)[49] Even so, rumors persist that the Judge's last wishes were honored in defiance of the court's ruling, with some claiming he was buried beneath the garage or driveway at Beth Sarim. According to Barbara Anderson, one of the property's subsequent owners (the same one alluded to previously who told her of Rutherford's "women") was convinced the Judge had become a permanent fixture:

> The owner and I began to talk about Rutherford. I asked, amongst other things, where was the hillside crypt that the Judge was supposed to be buried in before the San Diego County Commission said "no?" He pointed in the direction where, later on, we saw a small building, and then he asked if I knew where Rutherford was really buried. I said "Of course, yes, in Staten Island, New York!" He said, "No way!" He was very emphatic. He said: "You are standing on him!" I laughed. I looked down. I looked around. We all had quizzical looks on our faces, I'm sure. And he said, "I mean it! You're standing on the Judge. They didn't want him in New York, and so his followers buried him in this garage. The concrete was poured over him." I asked him how he knew, and he said Jehovah's Witnesses, old-

---

[48] Mary Rutherford continued as an active Witness up to her death in 1962 aged 93. Little is known about what became of the couple's son, Malcolm, other than his desire to have no part in his father's religion.

[49] In his 2003 book, Edmond Gruss writes that A. H. Macmillan divulged his attendance at the Staten Island funeral to Gruss' father. Macmillan was, apparently, "very disappointed in Knorr and Franz for not being present."

> er Jehovah's Witnesses who were connected closely with Rutherford and participated in the burial, told him after he had purchased the house.

With no physical evidence—not even a tombstone—to confirm precisely where Rutherford's remains are, his final whereabouts are likely to remain a mystery for some years to come, which is perhaps how it should be for such a colorful, bombastic, contentious character. Even on his death bed, the Judge wielded influence over the organization's destiny—somehow managing to plant the seeds of a power struggle that would only germinate decades after his demise. This fateful moment, in the days following the attack on Pearl Harbor, is touched on by Raymond Franz in *Crisis of Conscience*. Ray tells of how his uncle Fred was present along with two others:

> In late 1941, when Judge Rutherford lay on his deathbed at Beth Sarim in San Diego, California, he had called three men to his side: Nathan Knorr, Fred Franz and Hayden Covington. Rutherford told them that he wanted them to carry on after his death and that they should "stick together" as a team.

Even if the Judge really did only tell these three men to "stick together," it is clear that at least one of them left Beth Sarim with a far more profound interpretation of what had happened. As Ray Franz went on to explain, the same event would later be imbued with prophetic meaning in his uncle Fred's 1961 book *"Let Your Name Be Sanctified."* On pages 335 and 336, we find the following account:

> Rutherford was abed on the Pacific Coast when the United States of America was plunged into World War II Sunday, December 7, 1941. Two men of the anointed remnant (one since 1913 and one since

> 1922) and one of the "other sheep" (since 1934) were summoned from Brooklyn headquarters out to Rutherford's bedside at the home called "Beth-sarim," San Diego, California. On December 24, 1941, he gave these three his final instructions. For years he had been hoping to see the faithful prophets, including Elijah and Elisha, resurrected from the dead and installed as Kingdom "princes in all the earth" in God's new world.

Fred Franz proceeded to relate the story of how the Elijah passed on his powers as Jehovah's prophet to his understudy Elisha, hinting strongly that such a transference had also happened with the passing of Rutherford.[50]

> As viewed from our present time, it appears that there the Elijah work passed, to be succeeded by the Elisha work. . . . Elisha became heir to Elijah's official garment that had fallen from him. With it went its powers.

Hence, just as Elisha had received Elijah's official garment, or "mantle" (*King James Version*), when it drifted down from heaven in the events of 2 Kings chapter 2, so had the next generation of Watchtower leaders, Nathan Knorr, Fred Franz and Hayden Covington, received their commission as heirs of the Judge.[51]

---

[50] Fred Franz was fascinated with the concept of types and antitypes. He attributed almost everything in the Bible, especially in the Old Testament or "Hebrew Scriptures," as having its grander fulfillment, or "antitype," in the exploits of the modern "spirit-anointed" leaders of Jehovah's Witnesses and their "other sheep" companions. I will explain the distinction between the two in the next chapter.

[51] Also worthy of note in Fred Franz's fanciful interpretation of events surrounding Rutherford's death are some coy remarks concerning the lack of remains left behind by Elijah. On page 337 of the *Sanctified* book we read: "No mourning ceremonies were held for Elijah. Three days of search by fifty men

There would be no need for the unseemly leadership tussle that had tarnished the start of Rutherford's presidency. So long as Knorr, Franz and Covington could figure out some way of working together—something they had been forced to do anyway during the Judge's long periods of seclusion in San Diego—a stable, prosperous future for Watchtower was already mapped out. But despite being granted his power, none of these men could ever hope to live up to Rutherford's flamboyant legacy of drama and notoriety.

The Judge was quite simply one of a kind. A writer of Broadway musicals could certainly find worse subjects for a hit production than this scowling, charismatic, quintessential 20th century cult leader. The presidency of the Judge was a pantomime from beginning to end, and *Rutherford: The Musical* would have all the compelling plot elements needed for a show that would rival *The Book of Mormon* as a comedy tour de force: a leadership coup, a governmental investigation, a prison sentence that is later attributed to the fulfillment of Bible prophecy, failed apocalyptic predictions (including a claim that "millions now living will never die"), an estranged wife and son, a botched attempt at appeasing the Nazis, a female companion posing as a nurse and dietician, bootlegged whiskey, racism, reptile impersonations, a San Diego mansion built to entertain Bible characters who are always expected but never materialize, a passing of the "mantle" to the next generation of leaders—all rounded off with a controversial burial cloaked in animosity and intrigue.

But with the Judge dead, the age of charismatic, outspoken figurehead Watchtower presidents had

---

failed to find any dead body over which to mourn.—2 Kings 2:9-18."

drawn to a close. While Rutherford may have supplied no shortage of entertainment as one of the most fascinating characters in the organization's history, his presidency achieved little in terms of growing the movement.[52] What Watchtower desperately needed was a new leader who could be an effective administrator—someone prepared to sit back and let others thrash out the doctrinal details while quietly building Jehovah's Witnesses into a global brand. And, as it happens, this is precisely what Watchtower would get.

---

52 The Memorial attendance in 1917 was 21,274. By 1942, this figure had grown to 140,450. Though representing a 560% increase, Jehovah's Witnesses were still a relatively minor movement at the time of Rutherford's death after a quarter of a century of vigorous proselytizing. And the growth achieved by Rutherford would pale in significance compared to that of his successor.

Chapter Eight

# Rise of the Slave

*"They pretended, perhaps they even believed, that they had seized power unwillingly and for a limited time, and that just around the corner there lay a paradise where human beings would be free and equal. We are not like that. We know that no one ever seizes power with the intention of relinquishing it."*
—George Orwell

FEW Bible verses have had a more pronounced impact on the history of Jehovah's Witnesses than a fairly innocuous scripture found in Matthew chapter 24. During a conversation with his apostles on the Mount of Olives overlooking Jerusalem, Christ is described as giving a series of calamitous predictions for the conclusion of the system of things. War, famine and earthquakes are foreseen on an unprecedented scale. A "great tribulation" (or "great distress," or "greater anguish" depending on your preference of Bible translation) worse than anything hitherto observed is announced. Strange celestial phenomena are forecast, including the sun and moon being darkened and the stars falling from heaven. After these grim events are described, Christ asks his followers a question in verse 45:

> Who really is the faithful and discreet slave whom his master appointed over his domestics, to give them their food at the proper time?

Most Christians identify this verse as part of a parable intended to distinguish bona fide ministers from oppressive, overbearing pretenders. Others, though, insist Matthew 24:45 must have a special meaning. In their minds, Matthew 24 foretells, not just the end of the Jewish system of things with the destruction of Jerusalem by the Romans in 70 C.E., but the final apocalypse outlined in Revelation. That being the case, what if talk of a faithful slave is not just a parable, but a prophecy about a particular individual, or group of individuals, who would rise in the last days to exclusively dispense Bible truth? Almost since its inception, this is exactly the position Watchtower has taken. Hence, Russell considered himself, albeit in private, to be the "faithful and wise servant."

Soon after Russell's death, a 1917 tract titled *The Parable of the Penny* pointed to Rutherford as the successor to that role. But by 1927, it seems even the Judge could no longer stomach being the sole incumbent of such a lofty title. A *Watch Tower* article expanded the identity of the "Servant" to include, not only all Christians who professed a heavenly calling (referred to as the "anointed"), but Jesus himself:

> Seeing then that The Servant of Jehovah is The Christ, and that The Christ is composed of Jesus and the faithful members of his body, we find it proper to apply the term "Servant" to Jesus Christ alone or to Jesus Christ and the members of his body collectively as one; and sometimes it is applied only to the members of the body of Christ yet on earth.

This interpretation stuck—at least until "new light" politely nudged Christ out of the equation so that all anointed Witnesses who professed a heavenly calling (which in the days of Rutherford was pretty much all of them) were collectively referred to as the faithful "Servant" or (from the '50s onward) the

"Slave." Handing out "spiritual food" in the form of printed material drawing people to salvation was to be a responsibility shared among all associates of Watchtower who believed they were going to heaven.

There had to be some limit, however, on how big this Slave could be. Revelation chapter 7, it was insisted, restricted the total number of all anointed ones, including all approved Christians from history going back to just after Christ's death, to a relatively modest 144,000. Therefore, by mathematical necessity, the total number of anointed ones on earth in modern times had to be very small indeed. This was all very well if you happened to be a fledgling movement with only tens of thousands of followers, as was the situation on Russell's death in 1916. But what of a larger organization with perhaps hundreds of thousands, or even *millions* of followers—all of them heaven-bound?

Prior to 1935, if you were affiliated with Watchtower, you were basically going to heaven. There were rather complicated provisions for the better part of Earth's populace to colonize the cleansed planet post-Armageddon under Christ's heavenly rule but, for the most part, if you were a Watchtower follower you were principally interested in seeking out fellow future heavenly king-priest companions of Christ.

Then, in 1935, all of that changed. At a convention in Washington, D.C., Rutherford announced a new second tier of Christians—the "great crowd" (or "Jonadabs")—who could look forward to living forever on paradise earth while Rutherford and his associates ruled over them with Christ from heaven. Because 1935 became the year Witnesses expanded their search to looking for Christians with an "earthly hope" rather than just anointed ones, it came to be understood that

1935 marked the year when the bulk of the 144,000 had received their calling. The door to heaven was effectively closed. Hence, the number of Witnesses who claimed to be of the anointed began falling year-on-year before neatly constraining itself to manageable numbers of between 8,500 and 10,000 per year in the thirty years between 1978 and 2008.[1]

As tedious as this doctrinal detail may be, it is important to grasp if one is to understand the total transformation that Watchtower underwent in the seven decades between 1942 and 2012. Without giving away too many spoilers, we start off with a small but robust organization with a few scattered offices around the world, boasting only 115,240 members[2] but punching above its weight thanks to a young, tenacious new president who enjoyed the unquestioning allegiance of his subordinates. We end up with a powerful, global phenomenon with 8 million members, headed by a Governing Body claiming to wield power exclusively on behalf of Christ. It will be my job to explain over the following pages how this transformation unfolded.

In 1921, a student at the William Allen High School in Pennsylvania whose name we do not know got into a conversation about the Bible with another student

---

[1] These numbers are reported in the yearbooks of Jehovah's Witnesses each year as "Memorial partakers," since only Witnesses who believe they have been anointed to go to heaven may partake of the Memorial emblems at the yearly commemoration of Christ's death, i.e. eat the bread and drink the wine when these are passed around.

[2] The 115,240 membership figure is found in *Jehovah's Witnesses—The New World Society*, a 1955 Watchtower-approved book by Marley Cole.

whose name we *do* know: Nathan Homer Knorr.[3] The upshot of that encounter was that young Knorr, then 16, would become convinced that a small group known as the Bible Students—whose Pastor had died only a few years earlier—was the channel being used by God to communicate his plan to mankind. Moreover, within only 21 years of this fateful exchange, Knorr was to ascend to the pinnacle of the Watch Tower Society, eventually (albeit unknowingly) laying the groundwork for the present Governing Body arrangement.

***Nathan Knorr's 1923 high school yearbook photo***

Knorr was born in Bethlehem, Pennsylvania, on April 23, 1905. After graduating from high school at 18 in June 1923 he resigned his membership at the Reformed Church and was baptized a month later as one of the newest members of the Allentown Bible Student congregation. The same year he was invited to join the Bethel staff at Brooklyn headquarters.[4] From his hasty entry into Watchtower's inner sanctum straight from the baptismal pool, the speed of his rise through the organization's ranks would prove to be phenomenal.

---

3 The school was then known as Allentown High School. The main building from that period still stands today.

4 According to Edmond C. Gruss as recounted in his 2003 book *The Four Presidents of the Watch Tower Society,* Fred Franz told him in conversation that he conducted Knorr's baptism talk and Knorr used the opportunity to communicate his wish to serve in Bethel. If true, this would explain the rapidity of Knorr's recruitment.

Knorr began Bethel life as a worker in the shipping department, tasked with helping expedite the many books and brochures flowing from Rutherford's pen out into the wider world. After demonstrating "a flair for organization, and for getting things going," he was soon appointed to coordinate all printing activities at the Brooklyn printery. A 2014 *Watchtower* magazine contains an interesting anecdote from this period, as related by a long-serving Bethelite who knew Knorr personally:

> On one occasion, Brother Knorr spoke to me about the need for caring for what might be called small matters. To illustrate, he told me that when he was the factory overseer, Brother Rutherford would call him on the phone and say: "Brother Knorr, when you come over from the factory for dinner, bring me some pencil erasers. I need them at my desk." Brother Knorr said that the first thing he did was go to the supply room, get the erasers, and put them in his pocket. Then at noon he would take them to Brother Rutherford's office. It was such a little thing, but it was useful to Brother Rutherford. Then Brother Knorr told me: "I like to have sharpened pencils on my desk. So please have them there each morning." For many years, I made sure his pencils were sharpened.

Likely Knorr's willingness to leap at even the most menial requests from his superiors served him well in his steady rise through the Bethel ranks. According to Richard E. Kelly, another who served under Knorr at Bethel, older Bethelites who knew him from the Rutherford years would call him "Brownie" when talking about him between themselves—a reference to his brown-nosing, or readiness to curry favor.

As Knorr continued on his upward trajectory, he found himself under the tutelage of Robert J. Martin, then general manager of Watchtower's publishing of-

***An image of Rutherford flanked by Knorr (left) and Covington (right) from page 55 of the "God's Kingdom Rules!" book***

fice and plant. When Martin died in September 1932, Knorr was chosen as his replacement. The following year, he was already accompanying Rutherford in visiting the organization's branches in Europe. By 1934, Knorr had been elected as a director of the People's Pulpit Association (one of Watchtower's three main legal entities, which would soon become known as the Watchtower Bible and Tract Society of New York, Inc.), and within another year he was its vice president.

In 1940, Knorr also became director and vice president of Watchtower's parent corporation, the Watch Tower Bible and Tract Society of Pennsylvania (or the "Pennsylvania corporation" as it was known) so that, when Rutherford died, Knorr was the obvious candidate to replace him as president of both corporations, as well as Watchtower's legal arm in England—the International Bible Students Association. Nathan Homer Knorr was thus unanimously voted in as the organization's new leader in 1942.

A telling insight into just how powerful and revered the Watchtower president was in those days (and, by the same token, how foreign the idea of a "Governing Body" was) can be gleaned from an annual meeting "declaration" printed on pages 226 and 227 of the *1943 Yearbook* (the first to be published under Knorr's presidency). This remarkable document claims that Jehovah and Jesus are the "invisible Directors of the Watch Tower Bible and Tract Society," that Jehovah appoints the servants of his organization "as it pleases him," that Russell and Rutherford were both used by Jehovah "to oversee the affairs of the earthly part of Jehovah's organization under direction from the Lord," that the "Theocracy" operates "from the Top down, and not from the bottom up," and that "instructions come to the Lord's people on earth from the office of president of the Watch Tower Bible and Tract Society, filled by anointed men chosen of the Lord in his organization."

Point 6, in particular, makes it abundantly clear that Knorr was chosen to replace Rutherford by Jesus himself:

> We recognize before the Lord that Brother N. H. Knorr is His chosen servant to fill the office of president vacated by the passing on of Brother J. F. Rutherford to a higher office and field of service in Jehovah's organization; and that with this change in personnel in office the organization has not changed one bit, but that it has continued forward with greater speed and increase than ever before known in the history of God's earthly organization.

The declaration goes on to cite Bible verses in Isaiah promising increase and prosperity for God's people—verses that are said to find fulfillment under

Knorr's leadership. The glowing accolades then continue on into point 7:

> We declare to all our brethren throughout the earth that we are one hundred percent, wholeheartedly and joyfully behind the present president in every step that he takes in attempting to carry out the privileges and great responsibilities of his office, in an effort to serve Jehovah; and we rejoice in the privilege of continuing to march with him clear through the glorious portals of the New World to complete victory in this great fight for The Theocracy.

As it turns out, hopes that Knorr would steer the organization into an era of unprecedented increase proved to be not so wide of the mark. Knorr was, quite frankly, a brilliant administrator and an inspired choice as president—even if the inspiration did not necessarily come from heaven. Had Knorr not been plucked by Watchtower straight out of high school, he could well have gone on to enjoy considerable success in the corporate world. In measuring his influence on the organization, we can let the figures speak for themselves. When Knorr took office in 1942, he inherited an organization with 115,240 followers in 54 "lands."[5] Within 10 years, those numbers had quadrupled to 456,265 Witnesses in 127 lands. By his eventual death in 1977, Jehovah's Witnesses were a household name, boasting over 2 million members in 216 lands—a 1700% increase in the 35 years since Knorr first stepped into Rutherford's

5 The word "lands" is often used in relation to Watchtower statistics rather than "countries" or "nations." When somebody wrote a letter to Watchtower in 1997 to ask about this, they were told to "expect the land name list to differ from an atlas listing, reflecting rather the different lands and locations where the Kingdom work is being carried on without legally identifying them as separate countries with their own government."

shoes! By contrast, the organization grew 400% in the 37 years between 1977 and 2014—a feat Knorr managed in his first decade. It is hard to exaggerate the scope of Knorr's impact on Jehovah's Witnesses. The Pastor may have founded them. The Judge may have named them. But without Knorr's involvement, you would probably never have heard of them.

Unlike his predecessors, who were at least outwardly preoccupied with the impending earthly conquest of God's Kingdom, Knorr was a pragmatist.[6] This freed him to plan ahead to an extent that some found disconcerting given the urgency of Watchtower's doomsday tidings. As his wife related in her 2004 *Watchtower* life story:

> Nathan was very progressive, always planning ahead for future growth. Some considered this inappropriate, since the end of this system of things was considered to be very near. In fact, one who saw Nathan's plans asked him: "What is this, Brother Knorr? Don't you have any faith?" He replied: "Yes, I do, but if the end doesn't come as soon as we expect, we will be ready."

One area in which Knorr's forward-planning immediately found expression was his scrapping of the use of phonographs in doorstep evangelism. Under Rutherford, it was assumed that ordinary Witnesses

---

[6] When I spoke to Richard Kelly about his recollections from Bethel, he even suggested that Knorr and certain other senior officials did not strike him as being particularly sincere about the Witness faith: "While I do not know for sure, my guess is that Knorr was not a true believer. He was a cold business man, who knew what was going on. And I think his personal secretary, Don Adams, was in the same camp." Between 2000 and 2016, Adams was the president of Watchtower's parent "Pennsylvania corporation" (although, as will be explained, the role is now purely administrative in the Governing Body era).

lacked the skills to convey Watchtower's message effectively and could only do the "good news" justice by playing the Judge's recorded lectures at every opportunity.

**Nathan Homer Knorr**

Knorr saw things differently. He understood that ordinary Witnesses had the potential to serve as competent, persuasive preachers in their own right if only they could receive the proper training. In his mind, emancipating Witnesses from their lowly role as mere conduits of someone else's recorded words was not just the ideal way of escaping Rutherford's shadow—it was crucial to the organization's future growth.

Hence, in 1943, the Theocratic Ministry School was launched in every congregation aimed at churning out a steady stream of proficient evangelists and speakers. The same year, Knorr inaugurated the Watchtower Bible School of Gilead, which hinted more strongly at his ambitions for global expansion.[7] Gilead would furnish selected Witnesses with the required skills and knowl-

[7] Edmond C. Gruss, cited earlier, credits legal counsel Hayden Covington with coming up with the idea of the Theocratic Ministry School and Gilead due to his tiring of representing Witnesses in court whose lack of basic knowledge of their beliefs was embarrassing. This would no doubt have added momentum to the plans, but it should be noted that the schools were implemented under Knorr's direction and with the clear aim of making Witnesses proficient as speakers and evangelists, not merely with supplementing their doctrinal knowledge in the event of legal entanglements.

edge to promote the religion as missionaries around the world.

Under Knorr, the JW brand took on a truly global feel. Knorr began circling the globe to attend branch dedications and international conventions where his talks would be interpreted into various languages. The first book released under his presidency was titled *The New World*—a phrase that would become a mantra for Witnesses, especially since they were now promoting the idea of an earthly paradise to be inherited by millions rather than a few thousand tickets to heaven for a privileged few.

Hence, when Knorr decided it was time for Witnesses to have their own Bible, it had to be called the *New World Translation* (or *NWT*)—first released as a series of volumes between 1950 and 1960 (a few Bible books at a time) before finally being printed in one smart, green volume in 1961. (The *NWT* has since gone through several revisions, the latest being released in 2013. The most notable difference between the *NWT* and most other English translations is that it inserts the name "Jehovah" in certain places where God, or "LORD" is mentioned—even in the New Testament, where the earliest available Greek fragments indicate that "Lord" was used by the writers when referring to the Almighty.[8] The irony is that, although Witnesses pride

[8] Specifically, the *New World Translation* version of the New Testament inserts "Jehovah" wherever the original writers quoted from parts of the Old Testament that include the Tetragrammaton of the divine name. However, the very fact that the earliest New Testament fragments used "Lord" in these places proves Watchtower to be mistaken in insisting the early Christians departed from Jewish practice in restoring the name. Christians of other denominations will tell you there is much more wrong with the *New World Translation* than the way the New Testament text has been doctored to include "Jehovah."

themselves on promoting God's name, most scholars will tell you the closest approximation of the Tetragrammaton in English is "Yahweh." "Jehovah" is, as renowned scholar Bart Ehrman once put it, a "made-up English word"—a medieval Frankenstein's monster stitched together from Hebrew, English and European roots that gained ascendancy purely because it made it into the *King James Version,* which just so happened to be the preferred translation used by Russell.)

When it comes to gauging Knorr's character on a personal level, you will get different stories depending on which sources you consult. Anecdotes in Watchtower literature unsurprisingly portray him in a positive light, as a firm and driven but thoughtful, appreciative, fair man. Though Knorr undoubtedly had endearing qualities, he also had a ruthless, autocratic, occasionally mean-spirited streak reminiscent of the Judge. For example, in her 1978 memoir *Visions of Glory: A History and a Memory of Jehovah's Witnesses,* Barbara Grizzuti Harrison recounts Knorr's ugly (and alarmingly anti-Semitic) reprimanding of an elderly Bethelite who was caught selling a small supply of candy to fellow workers who could drop money into a box to cover the cost:

> Knorr heard about the little enterprise and read the old man out, at great length, in public. He tied his attack to the fact that the man was a Jew. The Jews, Knorr asserted, had always been willful, penny-grubbing ingrates. Jehovah had chosen them precisely to show that such unappetizing raw mate-

---

While there is some evidence of this translation being altered slightly to accommodate various Watchtower teachings, to my mind this is not such a pressing issue if you can accept that the Bible we have today can only ever be an imperfect copy of a copy, and according to most scholars its books show evidence of having been tampered with from their earliest origins.

> rial could be redeemed if they adhered to His laws. The candy seller was, Knorr said, demonstrating all the abysmal qualities that had led the Jews to kill Christ. And so on, for an hour, while I cringed.

Another former Bethelite, Néstor Kuilan, describes Knorr as someone who "would get sentimental and even make jokes," but could easily switch to being far more abrasive. "In Bethel he was feared, and he would scold the whole family when he was mad because somebody had broken the rules," Kuilan told me. "He'd mention the name of the person, his wrongdoing, and shame the person publicly."[9]

Accounts proliferate of cringeworthy dining room rants by Knorr about homosexual misdeeds by ousted members that went into detail bordering on the obsessive.[10] When I consulted one-time Bethelite Richard E. Kelly, he told of how Knorr seemed to almost enjoy recounting such explicit stories. Kelly also spoke of his perception of Knorr as a condescending and intimidating character. In his memoir *Growing Up in Mama's Club*, Kelly recalls the moment when a 1964 dining room exchange with Knorr brought his two-year stay at Bethel to a needlessly acrimonious end:

---

[9] Néstor Kuilan and his wife Toni were both friends of Raymond Franz, and feature in *Crisis of Conscience*. I will later mention their eventual ejection from Bethel in the 1980 purge, the story of which you can read in more detail in a 2013 JWsurvey.org article by Joanna Foreman titled "Nestor Kuilan—Surviving the Fall from Watchtower's Trapdoor."

[10] Edmond C. Gruss, cited earlier, claims in his 2003 book (p. 214) to have interviewed several Bethelites who testified to one notorious occasion in 1970 when Knorr regaled the Bethel family about a case of pedophilia in extremely graphic terms. One of these interviewees told of how he rushed to the bathroom when the recitation was finally over because he "felt like vomiting." Another said she noticed Knorr's eyes take on a "glazed look" as he went into the more intimate details, causing her to want to scream out: "Stop it! Stop it! That's enough."

***(Left) Néstor & Toni Kuilan; (right) Richard & Helen Kelly***

When he started pulling away from the table, I moved quickly toward him and asked if I could schedule time to talk. Up close, he stood tall, a big-boned man with an imposing aura—a white George Foreman, who did not smile. He gave me a stern look, crossed his arms, and rudely stated that now was as good a time as any. I noticed that several people stopped to look, no doubt curious why I was speaking to Knorr.

Without a hint of nervousness, I announced, "I want you to know that I will be leaving Bethel in two weeks, and I'd like to tell you why."

He never looked happy, but now he ratcheted up his already harsh demeanor. He glared and tauntingly inquired, "So, why are you leaving?"

He was interrogating me and it suddenly unnerved me! But I stayed calm. "Because I want to get married and . . ."

He held up his big right hand; his signal for me to stop and to listen. "So after you're married for a few years, do you think that you will leave your wife as well? Perhaps you will tire of her like you have of Bethel service. I wonder if you know anything about keeping commitments."

Kelly (who, I am pleased to report, is still happily married after fifty years and counting) was not the only one who found Knorr difficult to deal with. Hayden Covington, whom I introduced in the previous chapter, had precious few kind things to say about him when visited by Jerry Bergman in 1974, as Bergman would later relate:

> He kept calling N. H. Knorr, the president then, a "cobra." When I asked him why he said, "Do you know what a cobra does? They'll slither behind you, and they'll strike viciously." It became apparent that he detested Knorr.

In the same interview, Covington reportedly singled out one particular event as justification for his dislike of Knorr. In 1939, under Rutherford's presidency, a convention was held at Madison Square Garden that was famously interrupted when a fight broke out with Catholics who had gatecrashed the event for the purpose of raising mischief. Covington is said to have resented the fact that Knorr "snuck out like a coward" when he should have joined the fray and helped to "beat the shit out of those bastards."[11] (Covington was known for his strong language.)

Perhaps the most insightful appraisal of Knorr's character can be gleaned from *Crisis of Conscience*, in which Raymond Franz suggested that Knorr's over-

---

[11] In stark contrast to his animosity toward Knorr, Covington seems to have been very fond of Rutherford, most likely (as also observed by Bergman) because they were of similar combative temperament. For example, Rutherford shared the view that the Madison Square Garden protestors were to be forcibly repelled. He wrote in his 1940 book *Religion:* ". . . the ushers acted strictly within their rights and in the performance of their duty and certainly have the approval of the Lord in so doing. The ushers were not using carnal weapons in order to preach the gospel, but they were using force to compel the enemy to desist in efforts to prevent the preaching of the gospel."

bearing behavior was simply an almost-inevitable product of his supreme authority in the organization. Franz even admitted that, when Knorr was relaxed and not wearing his presidential persona, his company was quite enjoyable:

> When he was not in his president's "uniform" or role, I genuinely enjoyed my association with him. However, his official position, as is so often the case, did not generally let that side of him be seen and (again, doubtless due to his feeling that the role he carried out was according to God's will) he inclined to react very quickly and forcefully to any apparent infringement upon his presidential authority. People learned not to do this.

Franz went on to suggest that, had Knorr been on the Governing Body during the events of 1980-1981 (which I will come to shortly), he would not have "gone along" with the cruelty meted out toward him and others. Perhaps Franz was being a little too generous in his assessment of Knorr. Humiliating, abusive behavior by someone in a position of authority cannot be excused merely because he or she is pleasant to people when not wearing their leader hat. All the same, Franz's perspective is useful coming from one of the few people who worked alongside Knorr as almost an equal, thus allowing him to observe more facets of his personality than others would have.

For all his faults, one thing that can be said of Knorr is that he understood his limitations. Like all good administrators, he was gifted at identifying talent and delegating duties accordingly. Rather than present himself as a font of great spiritual wisdom, he drew on the skills of Fred Franz (the uncle of Raymond Franz) as his chief architect of Watchtower doctrine and policy. "Freddie," as some would call him,[12] came up with the teachings and, so long as Knorr found them agreeable, he would put the wheels in motion to make sure every Witness treated them as absolute "truth." For example, in 1952, during an altercation over a doctrinal matter with his editorial staff, Knorr reportedly told them: "Brothers, you can argue all you want about it, but when it gets off the sixth floor *it is the truth.*" (Watchtower's printing presses were on the sixth floor, so Knorr was saying that once doctrine finds its way into print, it is not to be questioned.)

Another fascinating insight into the doctrinal mechanics under Knorr's presidency came in the 1954 Walsh case—a Scottish lawsuit brought by Watchtower with the aim of establishing Jehovah's Witnesses as a formal religion in the UK and granting all Witnesses the right to be considered "ministers" under UK law (for the purpose of avoiding conscription).[13] Freddie flew out for the trial, along with fellow Watchtower heavy-weights Hayden Covington and Grant Suiter, and was quizzed on the organization's inner workings. Here is a fascinating piece of his testimony:

> Q. In matters spiritual has each member of the Board of Directors an equally valid voice?
>
> A. The president is the mouth-piece. He pronounces the speeches that show advancement of the under-

[12] For the purpose of more easily distinguishing between Raymond and Fred Franz, I will hereinafter be referring to Fred Franz as "Freddie."

[13] Judge Strachan would grant that Jehovah's Witnesses should be recognized as a religion, but not that all Witnesses be considered ministers. Watchtower appealed the case at both Scotland's High Court of Justiciary and the House of Lords, but both upheld the ruling. The case is mentioned in the June 1, 1955, *Watchtower* (pages 329-332), and the *1973 Yearbook* (pages 133-135).

***The Society's board of directors in the 1950s (from left: Lyman Swingle, Thomas J. Sullivan, Grant Suiter, Hugo Reimer, Nathan H. Knorr, Fred W. Franz and Milton G. Henschel)***

> standing of the scriptures. Then he may appoint other members of the headquarters temporarily to give other speeches that set forth any part of the Bible upon which further light has been thrown.
>
> Q. Tell me, are these advances, as you put it, voted upon by the Directors?
>
> A. No.
>
> Q. How do they become pronouncements?
>
> A. They go through the Editorial Committee and I give my O.K. after Scriptural examination. Then I pass them onto President Knorr, and President Knorr has the final O.K.
>
> Q. Does it not go before the Board of Directors at all?
>
> A. No.

For the most part, Knorr's partnership with Freddie worked brilliantly (with one or two notable exceptions, which I will come to later). But as the 1950s gave way to the 1960s, Watchtower found itself under mounting pressure to make itself more democratic—at least in appearance. Watchtower scholar M. James Penton describes "restlessness within the larger Witness community" over this period, and "unhappiness about the nature of the Witness organizational structure among Jehovah's Witnesses throughout the world."

Whether changing social attitudes were to blame for this undercurrent of resentment is hard to say, but you can hardly blame Witnesses for noticing that their religion was effectively being run according to the whims of some guy in an office. Of course, this was the way it had always been, but the elephant in the room likely became more noticeable as the Witnesses found themselves ballooning in size and vying for credibility. Things would start to come to a head in 1965 when Knorr assembled a committee tasked with compiling a new Bible encyclopedia that would later be published under the title *Aid to Bible Understanding.*[14] One of these committee members was former missionary and future *Crisis of Conscience* author Raymond Franz.

With their mandate to delve into the Scriptures and use even commentaries by "worldly" scholars to better understand the Bible's position on a number of topics, it was not long before Ray Franz and his colleagues realized that Watchtower's organizational structure deviated noticeably from what had been divinely prescribed. When preparing the material for the section headed "Older Man," Franz discovered that the organizational practice of having only one "congregation servant" or "congregation overseer" to preside over a congregation was entirely at odds with the New Testament model of a group of elders sharing this responsibility. Ironically, all congregations formerly had elders under Russell, but Rutherford had scrapped the arrangement in 1932, since he considered "elective elders" a threat to his

[14] *Aid to Bible Understanding* would subsequently be replaced by the two-volume *Insight on the Scriptures,* which was provisionally discontinued in print form in a memo to congregations dated November 2015.

authority.[15] But Franz was not afraid to suggest that, if the Bible precedent was for Christian congregations to have elders, maybe this should be reflected among Jehovah's modern-day people.

At first Franz's ideas were met with resistance, but after his uncle eventually gave the green light it became Watchtower policy that Witness congregations would henceforth have bodies of elders rather than just one person in charge. These changes would pave the way for similar reforms at the apex of the hierarchical pyramid. After all, if congregations could have a body of older men, why not the religion itself?

The exact chain of events that led to the formation of the first Governing Body is regrettably rather sketchy. Raymond Franz was one of the inaugural members in 1971, but even his account of the events of that year in *Crisis of Conscience* leaves much to the imagination. We do not know, for example, on what date the first official Governing Body meeting took place, in what manner the attendees were selected or under what circumstances it was convened (we will likely never know).[16] What we do know is that the term "governing body" (all lowercase) had already slipped into the Witness vocabulary from the 1940s onward, and was used to

---

[15] Rutherford repeatedly wrote of his disdain for "elective elders" in his books, describing them as corrupt and lazy troublemakers. It is worth noting that elders are still elected today, but by existing elders together with the circuit overseer rather than the congregation as a whole.

[16] Monday, September 6, 1971 is put forward in the December 15, 1971 *Watchtower* as the date of a Governing Body meeting when a rotating chairmanship was first decided on. This, you would think, would be a pressing agenda item for an inaugural Governing Body meeting, but the reader is left guessing.

describe the Watch Tower Society's board of directors.[17] The board of directors would meet with the president sporadically, always at his behest, and sometimes with months going by between meetings. The directors' approval on scriptural matters was not generally sought. They were simply there to receive instructions, give advice, or attend to corporate matters. Freddie confirmed the lack of doctrinal control as a matter of public record in the Walsh case, as we saw earlier. And Lyman Swingle (a member of the pre-GB board of directors), when asked to try to influence Knorr at a pre-1971 meeting of the writing staff, is said to have remarked: "Why me? What can I do? I'm only a director."

But on October 1, 1971, a change was announced. Freddie gave a talk that would go on to be described as the "tail wagging the dog talk" at the organization's annual meeting at an assembly hall in Buckingham, Pennsylvania.[18] The talk, which is more or less transcribed across eight pages in the December 15, 1971, *Watchtower*, informed Witnesses that matters related to the "strictly spiritual field" were thenceforth to be decided on by a Governing Body of rotating chairmanship in imitation of the first century apostles. The dog analogy was employed to drive home the point that the "Society," or Watchtower's parent corporation founded by Russell, was a legal entity that should be *at the disposal* of this new Governing Body—not the other way round. It was revealed that seven members of the board of directors had become eleven Governing Body mem-

---

[17] The *1970 Yearbook*, on page 65, says: "So really the governing body of Jehovah's witnesses is the board of directors of the Watch Tower Bible and Tract Society of Pennsylvania, all of whom are dedicated to Jehovah God and anointed by his holy spirit."

[18] I will abbreviate this to "dog tail talk" hereinafter.

bers.[19] From that point on, a Governing Body meeting in regular, weekly sessions—not the Society or its president—would be calling the shots.—*See box.*

At least, that was the theory.

Though the Slave finally had its mandate to rule, its control over Jehovah's Witnesses was still far from a done deal. Knorr may have indulged his trusted sidekick Freddie by letting him tinker with the process for deciding on the "strictly spiritual field," but he clearly had not grasped the full ramifications of this concession, as future events would affirm.

The Governing Body began meeting every Wednesday (as they still do). Agenda items were decided by Knorr and included rubber-stamping the assignment of Watchtower's traveling representatives (whom GB members had mostly never met). Sometimes the group would deliberate over doctrinal matters, such as what offenses should merit disfellowshipping. An example of the 'wisdom' that emanated from these discussions has already been related in Chapter Four, in which I told of how, for a brief spell in 1972, homosexuality was deemed to not constitute adultery, because it could not yield offspring (a collective brain fart that, as it turned out, shaped my mother's life dramatically).

Though some Governing Body members were cautious in introducing far-reaching injunctions that would impact on the private lives of countless followers worldwide, others were more dispassionate. At one such meeting when laws over sexual morality were being debated, future Society president Milton Henschel is said to have remarked: "If we let the brothers do this, there is no telling how far they will go."

---

19 The number would reach as high as 18 in 1977—a record that has never been surpassed.

FOR WITNESSES

### GOVERNING BODY

You might not have realized this, but the words "Governing Body" appear nowhere in the Bible. Because of this, Watchtower uses the account in Acts chapters 15 and 16, with its description of the "apostles and older men," as its scriptural basis for the Governing Body arrangement.

Watchtower argues that the apostles expanded their number by adding the "older men" in what is assumed then became a permanent ruling council. Interestingly, the term "apostles and older men" only appears six times in the Bible, and all of these occurrences are in Acts chapters 15 and 16 in connection with the handling of one issue, namely a controversy among Christians as to whether circumcision was still to be practiced.

To insist that this arrangement was permanent (even though it is mentioned nowhere else in the Greek Scriptures), and that the apostles and older men worked together on all decisions from the circumcision issue onward, is to assert something that simply is not described in the Bible. However, this is precisely what the Society repeatedly does in its literature in relation to the supposed existence of a first century equivalent to the Governing Body who directed all aspects of the preaching work.

Furthermore, as will later be explained in this chapter, there is evidence that not all affairs among the early Christians were administered from Jerusalem. For example, Paul and Barnabas are recorded as embarking on their first missionary tour after receiving instructions to that effect from the Antioch congregation.

But, despite these meetings, Knorr still held the reins of power in every meaningful sense. As Raymond Franz put it, the "administrative authority and responsibility rested exclusively with the corporation president." And for Franz and others, who had joined the Governing Body under the illusion (given by Freddie's "dog tail talk") that the Society and its president were under the authority of the Governing Body, not vice versa, this gradually became more of a sticking point.

According to Franz, he found himself in the unenviable position of being foremost in asking the awkward questions as to why the arrangement outlined in his uncle's talk (and, indeed, a *Watchtower* article that had left the "sixth floor") was not being implemented in practice. Knorr, it seems, took this extremely personally. On one occasion he is said to have gone into great detail about his workload (he certainly had every reason to take great pride in his accomplishments, at least statistically) and suggested he bring it all "down here and turn it over to Ray Franz and let him handle it." After Franz tried in vain to reassure Knorr that his suggestions were not a personal attack, the matter was buried for the time being.[20]

The issue would reemerge in 1975 when the Governing Body began receiving reports of an undercurrent of discontent among the headquarters Bethel family. The divide between management and ordinary workers was growing more noticeable, and the ensuing discussions on organizational structure spilled over into the obvious discrepancy between the arrangement outlined in the "dog tail talk," and the status quo (i.e. the Governing Body being little more than an advisory board to the president). As a result of these exchanges,

---

[20] Ray Franz does not give us a timescale for when this altercation took place. He only suggests that it was after the October 1971 "dog tail talk," and hints it was also after the publication of the December 1971 *Watchtower*—so likely late 1971 or early 1972.

***The Governing Body in 1975—visible are Fred Franz and Nathan Knorr (front row, second and third from left) and Ray Franz (back row, third from left)***

the Governing Body appointed a "Committee of Five" to investigate matters and report their recommendations.[21] But to suggest that this committee went about its work without the support of the president would be an understatement.

Watchtower's *Proclaimers* book (pages 108 and 109) implies that Knorr helped usher in the Governing Body arrangement, giving the impression that it arose out of necessity following the emergence of an inoperable brain tumor that "caused him to bump into things." It is hinted that Knorr could no longer fulfill his duties and thus ceded power to the Governing Body as his preferred successor.

Though Knorr certainly did help pave the way for the Governing Body arrangement, it seems he did so unwittingly, i.e. by giving Freddie a little too much leeway. At least according to the version of events related

[21] According to Raymond Franz, this committee was comprised of himself, Leo K. Greenlees, Albert D. Schroeder, Dan Sydlik, and John C. Booth.

by Raymond Franz, once the full reality of his error had sunk in, Knorr vehemently fought the arrangement right to the bitter end—only capitulating when he was left with no other choice.[22] Franz insisted that if Knorr's illness played any role in his relinquishing of power, this was not obvious from his words or actions. He further argued that the president's illness began to feature in Governing Body discussions only after the power struggle was over.

Knorr was so opposed to the Governing Body's ascendancy, said Franz, that he used opportunities when speaking before the Bethel family at morning worship to discredit the "investigation" being carried out by the committee of five and question the motives behind the process. He would remark: "Where is their proof that things aren't working well, that a change is needed?" while bemoaning the fact that "a few complainers" were trying to "overwhelm the joy of the majority." Franz even related how, on one such occasion, Knorr insisted that the proposed changes would only be made over his dead body (which, as Franz pointed out, nearly proved to be the case).[23]

But if Knorr felt threatened by the dramatic changes afoot, he was not the only one. Freddie was his

---

[22] It must be acknowledged that Franz does relate two instances in which Knorr tabled motions at Governing Body meetings in support of the new arrangement, but there is reason to believe neither of these were sincerely proffered. One described the new arrangement in melodramatic language (i.e. calling for the Governing Body's "takeover" of the Society's responsibilities), and the other more reasonably-worded motion (which Freddie later suggested was only made "under duress") he would himself later vote against.

[23] Words in quotations are from *Crisis of Conscience*, and according to Franz were noted down by him at the time, but also heard by thousands of Bethelites tied in by audio and video link.

Frederick William Franz

vice president and trusted lieutenant, and believed strongly that both he and Knorr had inherited a special "mantle" of power from Rutherford, as explained in the previous chapter. He had made a solemn vow to the Judge to support Knorr to the bitter end, and he intended to keep it.[24] Freddie thus embarked on a personal crusade of trying to undermine the concept of a Governing Body (a concept that he had previously championed) and even of the notion of committees (because it was a committee that was putting forward recommendations for the changes). On September 7, 1975, a matter of months before the new arrangement would go into full effect, Freddie used his talk at the Gilead graduation ceremony to mount a spirited, *biblically-based* argument against the whole concept of a Governing Body.[25]

Freddie argued, correctly, that Paul and Barnabas received their instructions from the Antioch congregation—*not* from the apostles in Jerusalem—and that instructions to the early Christians must therefore

---

[24] One could also point to the fact that Freddie was the obvious successor to Knorr as president on his demise, so diminished power for Knorr would inevitably translate to diminished power for Freddie.

[25] A detailed account by Raymond Franz of his uncle's talk, including transcripts, features on pages 90 to 98 of *Crisis of Conscience* and is well worth a read if you happen to be a Witness.

have originated directly from Jesus rather than from any human council or body. What Freddie said on that platform, before an assembled throng of bewildered Gilead graduates and their families, was essentially a Bible-based refutation of everything Watchtower stood for (and, indeed, continues to stand for). He reversed almost everything that had come from his own mouth in the "dog tail talk." According to Freddie's new reasoning, any congregation or group could do whatever they wanted provided they believed they had God's backing. There was, based on his logic, no need for an organization claiming God's influence in administering the affairs of Christians. A leadership comprising one or two individuals (such as he and Knorr) did not have to answer to anyone but Christ.

Ray Franz was in attendance at the event and his recollection of feeling "disturbed" by what he was hearing we can now reasonably equate with raging cognitive dissonance:

> I would be less than honest if I did not admit that I left the auditorium that day feeling not only deeply disturbed but also somewhat ill. It seemed that God's Word was something that could be made to fit one argument when circumstances made it advisable, and an opposite argument when circumstances were different. This disturbed me more than any other aspect of the matter.[26]

The irony here is that, despite giving what was arguably the single-most "apostate" talk that a senior Watchtower official will *ever* give in public, Freddie escaped censure. His nephew would not be so lucky, and would receive far greater punishment for far less damning "heresy," as I will go on to relate.

---

[26] Of course, many would argue that the same can be said of organized religion in general.

Finally, as 1975 drew to a close, the bitter wrangling reached its climax. The time had come for the committee of five's recommendations for the Governing Body to assume control of Watchtower to be voted on. Franz relates how, at a meeting on December 3, 1975, a show of hands was called for:

> All but two raised their hands in favor of the motion to implement the recommendations. The two who did not raise their hands were the president and the vice president.

It took until the next day, after further discord, for Knorr and Freddie to finally relent. And this, according to Franz, was only after Governing Body member Lloyd Barry, "his voice strained and shaking with emotion," had pleaded with Knorr to vote the changes through, because it was inevitable they would be passed anyway. When Knorr's hand finally went up, Freddie's followed. Thus, the keys of power were reluctantly passed from a presidency to a ruling council for the first time in Watchtower's history, despite this being recommended more than half a century earlier in the will left by Russell.

The changes were implemented from January 1, 1976. Knorr would succumb to his tumor 15 months later on June 8, 1977. The Slave finally had a meaningful grip on power—a grip that would only tighten with the passage of time.

By the late 1970s an increasingly disillusioned Raymond Franz felt that the perception of most Witnesses as to what went on at the summit of "Jehovah's organization" did not square with reality. As he would later confess:

> I now began to realize how large a measure of what I had based my entire adult life course on was . . . a myth—persistent, persuasive and unrealistic.

***Raymond Victor Franz***

Some of Franz's reservations were on doctrinal matters (he questioned the organization's emphasis on 1914, and felt that all Christians were spirit-anointed, or heaven-bound); others were more to do with the unloving spirit he observed among his peers.[27] He wrote of sharing some of his doubts among his closest friends, but insisted he was suitably discreet in so doing. "Up until 1980, aside from my wife I do not believe there were more than four or five persons on earth who knew to any real extent the concerns I had," he wrote. "And none of these knew all the reasons that caused these concerns." At least from Franz's perspective, he was not leading some uprising against Watchtower. He was merely sharing concerns with a handful of close friends and supporting the organization to the extent his conscience could permit.

Franz had already received some clue that the Governing Body's attitude was shifting in a troubling new direction now that members had settled into

---

[27] Ironically, according to Franz, even Knorr expressed doubts about 1914 not long before his death. On page 217 of *Crisis of Conscience*, Knorr is quoted as saying in a 1975 Governing Body session: "There are some things I know—I know that Jehovah is God, that Christ Jesus is his Son, that he gave his life as a ransom for us, that there is a resurrection. Other things I'm not so certain about. 1914—I don't know. We have talked about 1914 for a long time. We may be right and I hope we are."

their new, more powerful roles. He had, for example, been questioned in a meeting as to why he had failed to place his initials next to a number of *Watchtower* articles (the exact number was given) prior to their publication to indicate his approval. Franz had somehow escaped censure after saying that he could not conscientiously agree with the articles, but that he had not tried to block their publication. He had also offered to relinquish his place on the new Writing Committee if this made things easier. This offer was declined, but Franz could sense this was only the beginning. Something far more sinister and pervasive was brewing.

By late 1979, Ray Franz and his wife, Cynthia, had decided to take a leave of absence from Watchtower headquarters, citing health reasons. They departed Brooklyn to spend time with friends in Gadsden, Alabama, in March 1980. The Franz's planned to stay in a mobile home on the land of a Witness business-owner, Peter Gregerson, doing manual labor in lieu of rent. (The couple only had "about $600 in a savings account and a seven-year-old car" to show for decades of voluntary service to Watchtower.) The idea was to explore the possibility of finding somewhere to live and work if they were to take the plunge and leave Bethel permanently.

Then, only a month into his leave of absence, Franz began hearing disturbing reports emanating from Brooklyn. He received a phone call from his friend, Ed Dunlap, who was a respected member of the writing staff. Dunlap had been paid a visit by two Governing Body members, Lloyd Barry and Jack Barr, who interrogated him in his office as to his personal beliefs. The areas of concern all surrounded matters unique to Watchtower dogma, such as 1914 and the "anointed." No information was given as to who or what had prompted the inquiries. Dunlap was expected to answer questions, not ask them.

The great purge of 1980 was under way. A combustible atmosphere of suspicion and paranoia had been ignited by a simple phone call into Bethel. A Witness in New York named Joe Gould had called and been put through to Harley Miller, a member of the five-man Service Department committee. Gould reported that a fellow employee, named Humberto Godínez, had related having a conversation with a Bethelite who had expressed a number of ideas that did not conform to Watchtower teachings. When the name of this individual was asked for, it was produced: Cris Sánchez. As the discussion progressed, more names were supplied: Ed Dunlap, René Vázquez and Ray Franz.

Godínez and his wife were invited to come to Bethel to be interviewed by Miller about what they had related. During this interview, Miller asked Godínez if he could telephone Vázquez (who had a long record of loyal service to Watchtower) to see if he would say anything incriminating when "tactfully" probed on certain doctrinal matters. Godínez did, and the goal was achieved. Then followed another two-hour, recorded interview of Godínez and his wife by the Governing Body's Chairman's Committee. The accusations given on that occasion, and the recorded testimony gleaned, were used to launch a full-scale investigation into alleged apostasy, with teams set up to pursue different individuals under suspicion (which was what had prompted Barry and Barr to quiz Dunlap in his office). While Franz was still on leave in Alabama, his close associates were being systematically rounded up Stalin-style and asked to either implicate him as an apostate, name others, or admit to apostasy themselves—with disfellowshipping threatened as punishment for failure to cooperate.

The frenzied witch hunt came to a head in the week of April 21st to 26th. Among those who found themselves purged—deemed guilty by association—were Néstor and Toni Kuilan (whom I mentioned earlier). In a 2013 interview published on JWsurvey.org, Néstor related the cold manner in which he and his wife were disfellowshipped:

> The elder in the suit moved around the room and used a terroristic Gestapo tactic, sitting on top of the table with his leg on a chair, while I looked up at him. At the last meeting they told me if my attitude continued, I would end up in the street outside Bethel with posters and signs against the Watchtower; I would become a member of the Evil Slave. At that moment I became angry and I said, "I am an elder here like you, and you should respect me, so don't talk to me like that." The meeting ended; they disfellowshipped me that night by sending a note to our room.

In the midst of these remarkable events, Franz had a telephone conversation with then chairman of the Governing Body, Albert Schroeder, in which he directly asked what was going on. According to Franz, Schroeder shrugged off the question with a number of evasive remarks that had little or no bearing on the dramatic events unfolding. No mention was made of the fact that Franz and others had been implicated in charges of apostasy, or that a full investigation of such matters was in progress. In a subsequent, more open conversation, Franz agreed to return to New York Bethel on May 19, where two days later he met with the full Governing Body. He agreed to having the session recorded on the sole proviso that a recording be made available to him. His copy of the tape would never materialize.[28]

After giving his answers to a number of questions, Franz was asked to leave so the Governing Body could deliberate his fate. He would later be told that a number of members sought his disfellowshipping, but they could not achieve a majority in voting for that motion. Eventually, it was decided that Franz should resign, to which he agreed. He and his wife were offered a place on the "Infirm Special Pioneers" list, which would grant them a monthly stipend in exchange for a token amount of hours in the preaching work. They declined the offer, preferring not to obligate themselves to the organization in any way—even if the commitment to pioneer hours was only implied.

Despite Franz's resignation, it would not be long after their return to Alabama that he and his wife would find they were still very much on Watchtower's radar. A new circuit overseer began visiting the East Gadsden congregation and soon took a special interest in Franz's friend, boss and landlord, Peter Gregerson. Apparently rumors had started circulating that Gregerson's views did not fully correspond with Watchtower's in some relatively trivial area. Gregerson was visited at his home by the new overseer and one of the local elders. The resulting conversation seemed to end amicably. However, when the matter was later pursued and a further meeting requested, Gregerson decided to

---

[28] Franz documents the back-and-forth with headquarters about the tape that was promised to him. At first he was told a copy would be sent; then he was told it would not be because his "status" had changed from when the agreement was reached. Finally, Franz insisted that, if the recording was not sent to him, all copies should be destroyed. Watchtower sent Franz a letter saying this had been done, but obviously he only had their word on that.

preempt being subjected to any apostate witch hunt by disassociating on March 18, 1981.

Given the circumstances, this was the most prudent course for Gregerson. You see, there was a difference back then between a "disassociated" person and a "disfellowshipped" person. A disfellowshipped person is someone who has been expelled from the congregation for some perceived wrong; who must subsequently be shunned. A disassociated person could, at least at that time, still have contact with Witness friends and relatives despite no longer being a congregation member.

Apart from having a large family that would have been seriously impacted if he were shunned, it was important to Gregerson to not have relationships with his many Witness employees needlessly complicated by being disfellowshipped. But if Gregerson thought he had narrowly escaped his own inquisition thanks to a convenient loophole, he was mistaken. Only six months later a *Watchtower* article would be published that would recomplicate matters. I will revisit this significant magazine in further detail in Chapter Eleven, but it had the effect of changing the rules so that a disassociated person was to be shunned *in just the same way* as one who is disfellowshipped. The loophole had been closed.

Nobody can say for sure whether the September 15, 1981 rule-changing magazine was written purely to engineer a scenario whereby Ray Franz could be disfellowshipped, but the events that followed its publication and the rapidity with which they unfolded certainly leave that impression. Franz was reportedly told by others at the time: "They did everything but put your name and Peter Gregerson's in the magazine."

To sum up a rather unsettling account that Franz relates in great detail in his book, he was disfellowshipped not for apostasy or speaking against Watchtower, but for having one meal with his disassociated friend.

Two witnesses were produced at Franz's judicial hearing: one testified to his sharing a meal with Gregerson *before* the new *Watchtower* was published (and whose testimony was therefore irrelevant), and another saw him eating with Gregerson *after* its release. The latter Witness was a lady who admitted to herself eating with Gregerson on one occasion after the *Watchtower* was published, but she said she "knew it was not right and would never do it again."[29] Thus, based purely on the testimony of one witness—a witness who had confessed to the same "sin" but had been allowed to pardon herself—Franz's 43 years as a Witness came to an end on December 31, 1981. And Watchtower's fingerprints were everywhere.[30]

Of course, it did not have to be this way. The wisest course for the Governing Body would have been to leave Franz alone and let him enjoy his final years in peace.[31] He clearly considered himself a loyal Witness and ally of the organization regardless of the way he

---

[29] Gregerson would later tell Franz that the same woman had eaten with him on more than one occasion.

[30] There are a several reasons for concluding that the disfellowshipping of Franz was likely orchestrated from headquarters. Firstly, Franz was disfellowshipped for doing something trivial that had only just been made an offense, with apparently no effort to extend mercy or offer any leeway. Also, the magazine seemed to regulate the exact situation Franz found himself in from March 1981 onward as someone in close contact with a recently-disassociated person. Finally, according to Franz, the elders who led proceedings against Franz indicated themselves that their hurried actions had the approval of Watchtower's service department.

[31] Ray Franz died on June 2, 2010, shortly after falling and suffering a brain hemorrhage, aged 88. His widow, Cynthia, died of a heart attack on December 29, 2013, aged 78.

was treated and his private reservations in some areas. If the Slave truly considered him an enemy, they would have been well advised to heed the wisdom of the old proverb: "Keep your friends close, and your enemies closer." But the Governing Body could not resist chasing him and having him disfellowshipped by means of new rules on disfellowshipping and disassociation that would impact Witnesses for generations to follow.

Watchtower's heavy-handedness toward Franz would ultimately prove self-defeating, opening a Pandora's box in the form of his books *Crisis of Conscience* and *In Search of Christian Freedom.* Both of these books uncovered unsavory details of Watchtower's history and eviscerated its dogma, and continue to be a thorn in the organization's side to this day. The events of 1980-1981 also set a dangerous precedent for the Governing Body moving forward. No GB member would be allowed to think for himself, question the status quo, or bring radically new ideas to the table. From the 1980s onward, anyone aspiring to the highest echelon of Watchtower's hierarchy would have to be an organization man—a yes man. A GB member who thought progressively, who was keen to introduce more mercy and even-handedness when applying scripture, who sought to steer the religion into more mainstream waters, could expect a similar fate to Franz.

Hence, when the first new GB member following the resignation of Franz was appointed some 14 years later in 1994, it was someone who has since proven himself a stalwart defender of even the most gruesome aspects of Watchtower theology.

Gerrit Lösch, as already recounted in Chapter Three, has been recorded regaling audiences with his grim vision (based on a passage in Zechariah) of Armageddon victims being exterminated by some form of radiation and Witness burial teams scouring the planet to conceal surplus human cadavers left over from Jehovah's day of wrath. On another occasion, Lösch was taped comparing the ambition of young people to go through university with a mental disorder:

> So most of the college students go for that reason, to have a higher living standard. Some go for the fame, but most go for the money. Sometimes the children wouldn't even go but the parents push them to go. They want to be able to say "my son is a doctor." So is this really the thing to pursue this side of Armageddon? Now some have good motives. If they do, we will not judge them. It's a personal decision. Some pioneer throughout college and they have good motives. But we have lost really too many to the world already, and so it is a kind of danger.
>
> This reminds me of an experience that was mentioned in our literature about a young man that had a compulsory [*sic*] behavior. He was always forced like to wash his hands many many many times a day. He just couldn't stop doing that. He hated himself so much for it that finally he decided to kill himself. He bought himself a gun and he pulled the trigger. And the bullet went through his head, but he survived. And some went to college and survived.
>
> Now this young man survived and the bullet had hit this part of the brain that was responsible for his compulsive behavior. After he recovered he was normal. So the question is: yes he survived coll... in that case we can apply it to college. He survived that operation, the bullet operation. But would we recommend that to others? That's a different matter.

If you are the sort of person who can equate the desire of young people to better themselves and enhance their career prospects with the plight of OCD sufferers, you are perfect material for joining a group of men charged with promoting and perpetuating teachings that elevate an organization's prosperity over the needs and welfare of individuals. Appointments to the Governing Body since Lösch have similarly served only to supplement the radical leanings of the organization and, in some cases, accelerate its slide into extremism. Samuel Herd, Stephen Lett, David Splane and the late Guy Pierce were all appointed in 1999; Anthony Morris III and Geoffrey Jackson joined in 2005, and Mark Sanderson joined more recently in 2012. All have proved themselves as organization men—at the very least supporting and promoting the status quo, and in some cases going out of their way to voice opinions that serve to stretch organizational policy to new levels of absurdity. Progressive, liberal and open-minded these men certainly are not—or if they are, we await a crumb of evidence.

Three excellent specimens to highlight the fundamentalist leanings of the Slave's newest incarnation can be found in Anthony Morris III, David Splane and the relative newcomer—Mark Sanderson.

Morris arguably leads the way in the current crop of GB members when it comes to courting controversy and defying of common sense. It does not take long when listening to one of his talks to form the impression that Morris is acutely impressed with his own importance and wisdom. A perfect example of this came at the 2014 annual meeting when, while commenting on the need to support "Christ's brothers," he recounted this anecdote:

> I remember telling a friend of mine once where I wasn't treated too well in this particular branch

> territory, and I said to my friend: "Well, it's not me they need to worry about, it's my big brother. That's who they'd better worry about." Yeah, we've gotta pray for those men over there.

The story elicited laughter from the audience, but the message was nonetheless serious and intentional. In the mind of Morris, anyone who fails to show him the reverence he feels he deserves has Jesus himself to answer to.

A still more stunning display of Morris' eccentricity came at a United States branch visit,[32] also in 2014, when he unleashed a now infamous tirade against the vice of wearing tight clothing that is hilarious and disturbing in equal measure:

> Now, I have to mention this, something I've observed, I see it in the airports but, worldly women? This is what they do. And it's all jerry-rigged but sometimes even some of our sisters now—and I suppose they're probably really lovers of God and such, but you're not thinking of this verse—and what it is is this spanx. This skin-tight stuff they wear.
>
> Now, are any sisters wearing it in the ministry? No! I can't say I've ever seen that. But when they exercise they leave home and they're jogging in this stuff? Look at the verse. Is that appropriate? To wear skin-tight spanx, or whatever they call it? It's not modest, and it's certainly not sound of mind. It's really not appropriate.

---

[32] A branch visit is a periodic visit to a Watchtower branch office by a Governing Body member (or representative) to give attention to the way it operates in much the same way as a circuit overseer would visit a congregation. Quite why this is needed in the United States, where branch committee members share facilities with the Governing Body, is beyond me.

> There's nothing else to say about it. Now you wanna be in your home or your room and wear that stuff? That's your business. But don't go out in public like that, and say you worship the true God. "I'm just trying to stay in shape!" Uh uh, inappropriate.
>
> And the other one that needs addressing is for these younger fellas, 'cause the older ones aren't doing much of it, thankfully—it's the metrosexual look. We've addressed that in the past. We've said things about it. But what's happened now, it's really caught on more. Metrosexual—that's the tight suit jacket and the tight pants, better known as "tight pants." And they are tight, I mean tight, all the way down to the ankles. And that is not modest brothers. No. It's not appropriate. It's not sound of mind.

Morris went on to praise a circuit overseer who refused to go in the door-to-door work with a tight pants-wearing Witness before bringing his eyebrow-raising rant to a climax.

> And frankly, I have asked sister after sister, you know: "What do you think of this? Do you find that appealing, attractive? You know, I'm just curious, 'cause I'm not a woman." And you know what? I've not met one yet that thought they look good.
>
> But like I've been telling others, and this is a fact, the homosexuals that are designing these clothes, they like you in tight pants. That's who likes it. Not spiritual people.

At one point during the recording of Morris' diatribe the audience can be heard giving way to laughter, specifically at the part where he first singles out tight pants as immodest attire for young Witness men. But Morris was not joking—he was deadly serious. In his mind, tight pants are part of an elaborate conspiracy by homosexual fashion designers who are willing to stop

***An image from the January 2017 study edition of "The Watchtower" cautioning that wearing tight pants shows a "lack of modesty"***

at nothing for the momentary thrill of feasting their gaze on the male form.[33]

The tightness of male clothing is clearly something to which Morris has devoted a considerable amount of thought, as evidenced by a similar talk he delivered during a branch visit to Rome earlier the same year. His Italian audience had responded with similar hysterics, and nobody could blame those in attendance at either event for being unprepared for the spectacle of one of God's earthly representatives arbitrarily introducing a new rule that the Almighty judges you according to the tightness of your trousers.[34]

---

[33] For this particular claim, Morris received the dubious distinction of being named as one of 2014's craziest "right-wing nut-jobs" by Trudy Ring at the *Advocate* magazine.

[34] Perhaps unsurprisingly, Morris' tight pants rule eventually found its way into official Watchtower law. According to Chapter 10 of the leaked *Circuit Overseer Guidelines* (dated October 2015): "If the body of elders agrees that a brother or sister is blatantly and deliberately ignoring repeated counsel, and his or her dress and grooming is disturbing to the congregation, the elders may determine that the person no longer qualifies to share in the ministry. In such rare cases, no announcement would be made to the congregation." In other words, a Witness can be banned from preaching if his pants are too tight. (A PDF of the leaked *Guidelines* can be found relatively easily online.)

Though the tight pants debacle received modest online media exposure, Morris' far more chilling remarks about child baptism have passed mostly under the radar. The following words are from a recorded Tony Morris talk of unknown date and location:[35]

> What will be the disastrous result for those not serving Jehovah? The slain are gonna be from one end of the earth clear to the other end. And that's why I told you earlier, it's gonna be very numbing. Lotta dead people. And we don't take any delight in that, and neither does Jehovah, but he's been warning 'em, just like he did before the Flood. Lotta dead people. Billions.
>
> So in view of such warnings the Watchtower said about family heads and single parents that you do well to ask yourselves about your children who are old enough to reason. Not the little babies here. "Will your children"—I'm just paraphrasing a little differently *The Watchtower*—"will they survive this climactic event?"
>
> Well, they will if they're spiritually alive and strong. When they're old enough to reason, they cannot get through [Armageddon] on your coattail. We've never said that. If they're old enough to understand the need for dedication and baptism, and like some used to say: "Well, I don't think I'm old enough."
>
> I tell parents—'cause we raised sons, we know how it works—I say: "Well okay"—and one just got a little upset and, he was determined—"I'll tell you what, you tell him: okay when you turn 16. . ."—I dunno about your state, but. . .—". . . er, no driver's license!"

---

[35] Though the date and location of these particular comments are unknown, Morris was filmed making similar expressions about withholding a driver's license from unbaptized youths in a talk at the 2015 regional convention.

> "Oh no, I'm ready! I am ready! I know I can handle a car when I'm 16!"
>
> "But you can't dedicate your life and get baptized, huh?"
>
> Now we never force it, but don't, don't swallow that business. If they're old enough to understand the need to get into the city of refuge, exercise faith in Christ Jesus, they'd better do it! They're not getting in on your coattail when the end comes. Nope.

Such open fearmongering rarely makes it into print in Watchtower literature, because the Governing Body tends to shy away from incriminating itself in writing. But when Morris is given a microphone and a Witness audience willing to massage his ego with guaranteed respect and applause, outrageous words have been known to spill from his lips. In this case, parents are effectively told that their children will join the "billions" slaughtered at Armageddon (which, incidentally, clears any ambiguity over whether Jehovah will kill non-Witness children) unless they have their heads plunged beneath the surface of a pool by a man in a white T-shirt. And if children decline the opportunity to chain themselves to a religion for life at the first time of asking, parents are licensed to resort to blackmail in pursuit of this objective. As is frequently the case with cults like Watchtower, *the ends justify the means.*

This habit of coaxing parents to force their children into baptism was also indulged by David Splane during a branch visit to Malmö, Sweden, in 2013:

> Now sometimes young ones feel that, oh, they really, they don't want to follow the truth too much. They don't feel like getting up and going out on field service on Saturday mornings, or maybe not to attend the meetings. And the parents say: "Well, you know, I don't like to force my children to do

> something they don't want to do. I want it to come from their heart." But is that really wise?

Splane went on to admit that certain aspects of Witness life, such as meetings and preaching work, are done out of compulsion rather than enjoyment, before continuing:

> Now, when parents say that they don't ever want their children to do anything they don't want to do, they really don't mean it. Now, suppose that your son Christopher got a job this summer working at McDonald's. Now, the first day of work, you go into his room and wake him up: "Christopher, time to get up!" Christopher opens one eye and says: "Oh ma, let me sleep!"
>
> What you gonna do? Do you phone the manager of McDonald's and say: "Now, in our home we don't believe in forcing our children to do anything they don't want to do! Now, Christopher doesn't feel like going to work today, but don't worry, his father and I are going to try to touch his heart. And I'm sure that between now and the end of the month he'll feel like showing up, at least sometimes." I don't think you'd do that. You'd say: "Come on, get up! You're going to learn that there are things we have to do in life whether we feel like it or not!" And you would commend yourself. You'd say: "This is being a good parent." If you would do that for a Big Mac, why wouldn't you do that when your child's everlasting life is involved?"

Hopefully it does not need pointing out that taking a summer job at McDonald's is not the same as committing your life to a cult. (At least McDonald's pays the minimum wage.) Even so, Splane's example is revealing. He accepts that embracing the Witness faith is something all mankind must do "whether [they] feel like it or not." This underscores the fact that baptism for Witness youths is not a *choice* in any meaningful sense, unless a cashier during a bank robbery who opens the register at gunpoint can be considered as doing so of his own free will. Baptism is presented as a matter of *life and death*. Therefore, as with Morris and his bartering over the driver's license, Witness parents are expected to force the issue with their children, even if they are still not old enough to attend high school.

This brings us to Sanderson. In a talk given in Germany in May 2015, he singled out two couples whose faces he recognized in the audience before saying:

> You know, all five of us, we have something in common. We were all baptized between the ages of nine and eleven. It's the best decision I ever made. Let me ask you four here, was it the best decision you ever made? All four are nodding "yes!"

Sanderson went on to read a number of quotes from Watchtower publications to the effect that children should be steered toward baptism by their parents regardless of any misgivings (such as the justified fear that they might be disfellowshipped) before saying:

> If you're in God's righteous new world and you look around and you see that your children are there with you, that you taught them, you trained them to be servants of God, that will be the greatest joy that you will ever have. And it will never go away, because they will live forever with you. Please, brothers, take this reminder seriously.

It is hard to decide which is more distasteful: Sanderson's suggestion that Witness children should be baptized as young as nine simply because he feels it was the "best decision" he ever made (again, it can hardly be called a "decision"), or his telling parents how good they will feel in paradise having coerced their kids into baptism given the fact that (like all

*Mark Sanderson, pictured at a Gilead graduation ceremony in 2013*

present GB members apart from Morris) he is not a father and unlikely to become one any time soon.[36]

Of course, baptizing children cattle-dip-style with the threat of being disowned by their parents if they ever reverse their pledge makes perfect sense if you are an unscrupulous fundamentalist movement bent on self-preservation, but it is certainly not ethically or logically defensible. Children are usually prohibited by law from gaining employment, voting, buying or leasing property or entering into contracts—and for good reason. A childhood should be devoted to letting the child gradually establish his or her personal identity. Children are slowly gathering the tools and knowledge they will need to start making decisions on complex issues later in life, and thus cannot be held accountable in the same way as adults. I am not remotely the same person I was between the ages of nine and eleven, and neither—I would assume—are you, the reader (if you are an adult). How can it be considered proper for children of Witness parents as young as *nine years old* to make a commitment that will shackle them to a religious entity for the rest of their lives? How does allowing children to make such a pledge differ in any meaningful sense

[36] Sanderson is single at the time of writing, and if he were to marry he would be barred from having children as a Bethelite. I personally know of married Bethelites who have been sent home for having children.

from the Catholic tradition of baptizing infants—long condemned in Watchtower publications as an "unscriptural practice?"

The enthusiasm of the current crop of GB members to endorse child baptism openly in situations such as branch visits where they could easily deliver a more generic, uplifting Christian message, highlights the unyielding, party-line attitude that got them into their positions in the first place. They were chosen precisely because of their willingness to not only tolerate and maintain objectionable teachings inherited from their forebears, but to proudly advocate them. This requires a special kind of mindset—a deeply-entrenched arrogance potent enough to sustain delusions of grandeur on a scale few of us mere mortals can fathom. It should therefore have come as no surprise when, on October 6, 2012, the Governing Body informed those present for the Society's 128th annual meeting at the Jersey City Assembly Hall (or Stanley Theater) that they, the Governing Body, should thenceforth be considered as Christ's "faithful and discreet slave." In retrospect, the omens for this final move to consolidate ecclesiastical power had already been lining up for some time.

It started in 2007, when a *Watchtower* article had the effect of reopening the door to heaven by scrapping the long-held teaching that the heavenly calling ended in 1935. "We cannot set a specific date for when the calling of Christians to the heavenly hope ends," it was admitted. Some Witnesses evidently saw this as a green light to start claiming heavenly prospects. From 2007, the number of professed anointed Witnesses steadily increased. The Governing Body responded to the surge in 2011 by trying to undermine the aura of reverence associated with the anointed. A *Watchtower* article warned that "a number of factors—including past religious beliefs or even mental or emotional imbalance—might cause some to assume mistakenly that they have the heavenly calling."[37] Undeterred by the 2011 article, the ranks of the anointed continued to swell year-on-year. From between 8,500 and 10,000 Memorial partakers per year between 1978 and 2008 (as mentioned before), the number stands at 15,177 as of 2015. It would not be surprising if these developments, and the dilution of prestige associated with being of the anointed, played some role in the Governing Body's decision to effectively demote them.

A more pressing motive for the Slave to seize sole authority was the confusion and inconsistency surrounding the organization's prior teaching on Matthew 24:45. The problem with suggesting that an elite class of anointed Witnesses are, all of them, the "faithful and discreet slave" who give Christ's followers "their food at the proper time" was obvious to anyone who devoted sufficient thought to the matter. The "spiritual food" coming out of Watchtower was certainly not coming from 8,000-or-so individuals dotted around the globe. It was coming from a handful of men in New York and the various committees and departments over which they presided, the staff of which were overwhelmingly not of the heavenly calling. Prior to 2012, the Governing Body accounted for this glaring inconsistency by insisting they were to be thought of as "representative" of all anointed ones. Whenever they released a book, magazine or brochure, the words therein could be construed as coming from *all* anointed ones.

---

[37] Of course, when deciding on whether professed anointed Witnesses are crazy or not, the Governing Body members, all of whom must be anointed, are to be held above suspicion.

But this clearly did not address the problem. Did the Governing Body consult, even *periodically,* with the thousands of anointed ones to agree on what wisdom and guidance should be presented in their publications? One 2009 *Watchtower* article addressed the matter quite unabashedly:

> Are all these anointed ones throughout the earth part of a global network that is somehow involved in revealing new spiritual truths? No. Although as a composite body the slave class is responsible for feeding the spiritual household, not all individuals of the slave class have the same responsibilities or work assignments. (*Read 1 Corinthians 12:14–18.*) As noted earlier, in the first century, all were involved in the vital preaching work. But only a very limited number were used to write the books of the Bible and oversee the Christian congregation.

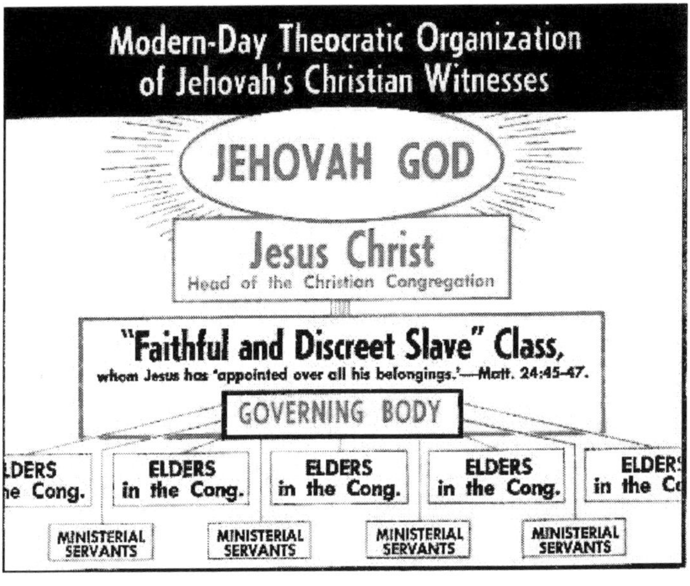


***An image from the December 15, 1971, "Watchtower" (note that the Governing Body was part of but slightly below the "'Faithful and Discreet Slave' Class")***

Everything, therefore, boiled down to trust. The anointed were collectively involved in "revealing new spiritual truths," but Witnesses just had to trust that Jesus had made the right call by head-hunting fewer than a dozen of these individuals (all of whom just so happened to have long track-records of Watchtower service) to speak on behalf of thousands of them. This, prior to October 6, 2012, was what you were required to believe as a Jehovah's Witness. But then it came time for the rise of the Slave to reach its climax.

At the 128th annual meeting, the Governing Body decided that that it was finally time to cut out the middle man. A flash of new light had revealed that they were exclusively the faithful and discreet slave, and the steadily increasing numbers of professed-anointed ones no longer enjoyed even a symbolic role in feeding God's people. A written explanation in a subsequent *Watchtower* was carefully worded to account for the fact that, despite apparently being selected by Christ as "the Slave" in 1919, the Governing Body had actually only existed since the 1970s:

> Who, then, is the faithful and discreet slave? In keeping with Jesus' pattern of feeding many through the hands of a few, that slave is made up of a small group of anointed brothers who are directly involved in preparing and dispensing spiritual food during Christ's presence. Throughout the last days, the anointed brothers who make up the faithful slave have served together at headquarters. In recent decades, that slave has been closely identified with the Governing Body of Jehovah's Witnesses. Note, however, that the word "slave" in Jesus' illustration is singular, indicating that this is a composite slave. The decisions of the Governing Body are thus made collectively.

Thus, Witnesses were now required to believe that in 1914 an invisible Jesus Christ swooped down to earth to carry out an inspection that eventuated in "a small band of loyal Bible Students," namely Joseph Rutherford and his underlings, being appointed five years later in 1919 as his channel for conveying divine wisdom to mankind. Not explained was how the Slave would continue after Rutherford's death, or the mechanism by which almost anyone who happened to find themselves in a position of sufficient authority at a New York-based religious movement automatically inherited the mantle of power first bestowed after World War I. It is left to one's imagination that Jesus would automatically confer the same power on new generations of Watchtower leaders out of the necessity imposed by these men dying off over many decades of the "short period of time"[38] between his 1914 heavenly enthronement and the vanquishing of God's enemies at Armageddon.

Not a moment's thought seems to have been given to the fact that by conveying power on an unbroken line of privileged individuals rather than a homogeneous cloud of Christians over many decades, Watchtower has embraced its own version of the Catholic tradition of "apostolic succession." (Apostolic succession is the teaching that the office of the Pope has received uninterrupted divine authority going all the way back to the apostle Peter. As it happens, Watchtower devotes an entire section to dismissing it as "not a Bible teaching" in its *Reasoning* book.)

Apparently missing the irony of this particular facet of the "new light," in his 2014 biographical *Watchtower* article "Losing a Father—Finding a Fa-

---

[38] See Revelation 12:12.

ther," Gerrit Lösch mentioned doubts over apostolic succession as being key to his rejecting his Catholic roots when first contacted by the Witnesses:

> No wonder that for many Catholics the teaching of apostolic succession is the most important teaching, since the correctness or incorrectness of other Catholic teachings hinges on it!

Precisely the same can be said of Watchtower's slave teaching. Without it, the Witness theology evaporates; the Governing Body becomes just another group of men doing their best to interpret scripture. But throw in claims of divine authority conveyed by Christ himself at some point in the murky past, with this mantle of power being passed in an unbroken line from one generation of Watchtower leaders to the next (as necessitated purely by the tendency of humans to die), and everything changes. Watchtower morphs from being just one of many religious movements into being "Jehovah's organization," and anyone who speaks against Watchtower's leaders is guilty of speaking against the Almighty himself.

Luckily for Watchtower, they can rely on the average Jehovah's Witness not giving all of this too much thought. If you desperately want to believe that you have invested years or decades in the one true faith, you will grab at the flimsiest of reasons to suspend belief. But for other more contemplative, inquiring Witnesses, the rise of the Governing Body to even greater power and prominence will not have proven so endearing. Previously, they had a credible claim to humility as a group of men who claimed to be spokespersons of a much more expansive "class" of future heavenly kings and priests. But in 2012, they arbitrarily seized all power for themselves from under the noses of those whom they once claimed to serve as "representatives."

***The Governing Body as shown in the July 15, 2013, "Watchtower" Clockwise from top left: David Splane, Anthony Morris III, Mark Sanderson, Geoffrey Jackson, M. Stephen Lett, Guy Pierce (deceased), Gerrit Lösch, Samuel Herd***

The narcissism of these maneuvers was only amplified by the manner in which the news was delivered. Normally when "new light" is dispensed by the organization, it comes in the form of a *Watchtower* article explaining some new understanding of scripture. The advantage of this method of relaying information is that millions of Witnesses globally receive their "spiritual food" at the same time, since the same article is translated into virtually all languages and considered at the same meeting on the same week (usually even on the same day) globally. But for this landmark unveiling of a significant new teaching, the Governing Body chose to disclose their epiphany to a select audience numbering only 15,514—namely those in attendance at the Stanley Theater together with Bethelites from various facilities tied in by video link. It would be over a month before the announcement would be confirmed on JW.org, by which point the news had spread like wildfire on the internet on Witness and ex-Witness forums. Even when the confirmation was presented on JW.org, it took a further month (December 2012) for the news report to be available in languages other than English. This meant that, depending on your language or nationality, as a Jehovah's Witness you could expect to wait weeks or even months for official confirmation in your native language of a teaching that redefined your religious beliefs.[39] That the Governing Body could opt for such a clumsy approach for sharing their momentous announcement would suggest that the pomp and ceremony of a grand unveiling at an auspicious event took precedence over the need to share the news evenly and efficiently among their global following. Rather than discharging its duties in a way that is faithful and discreet, the Slave seems more prone to posturing and fanfare.

But the 2012 "new light" was not the first or last indication that the faithful and discreet Slave might be, in reality, anything but. Throughout Watchtower's modern history since Knorr succeeded Rutherford as president, there have been notable lapses in judgment that, for the most part, have been carefully concealed from ordinary Witnesses. In the pages that follow, I will relate a few of the more outstanding examples.

## Mexico and Malawi

Jehovah's Witnesses pride themselves on maintaining strict political neutrality in the spirit of Christ's words to Pilate that his Kingdom is "no part of this world." This has resulted in young Witness men over many decades enduring long periods of imprisonment

---

[39] It would be April 2013, six months after the annual meeting, that the July 2013 *Watchtower* study article would be released explaining the "new light" on the new "faithful slave" teaching in detail. I was able to get my hands on a leaked copy in late March, meaning that JWsurvey.org readers had a summary of the article two weeks before ordinary Witnesses.

in countries where conscription is in force. For example, in South Korea, Witnesses are willing to spend up to 18 months in prison in order to avoid military service, even though the country already allows for non-combative service.[40] According to Watchtower's logic, a Witness who submits to the one month of combat training required for South Korean conscripts (presumably scrambling around in mud and learning how to clean, assemble and fire a weapon) is violating Isaiah 2:4, which demands that Christians should not so much as "learn war anymore." (Of course, the verse insists nothing of the sort but, as with many areas of its doctrine, Watchtower would rather go to extremes in enforcing its teachings than be seen to concede ground to "Satan's world" in any way.)

Though Watchtower's strong doctrinal aversion to compromising political neutrality has generally been consistently maintained, there have been notable exceptions. One example is the organization's covert flirtation with the United Nations in the 1990s, which I will come to later. Another is the period in the '60s, '70s and '80s when Watchtower allowed two entire-

[40] As of July 2016 there were 495 imprisoned JW conscientious objectors in South Korea, each serving 18-month sentences. A PDF download from JW.org disclosing this information also indicates that over the last 60 years more than 18,800 have been likewise detained, representing an accumulated confinement of more than 36,000 years. Of course, not helping the situation is the refusal of the South Korean government to recognize the rights of its citizens to conscientious objection on grounds of thought, conscience and religion. Fortunately, though, at the time of writing, there is hope of this changing. According to an August 17, 2016, piece by Kim Se-jeong in *The Korea Times*, district courts have acquitted nine Jehovah's Witnesses of violations of the Military Law thus far in 2016 alone. One district court even noted: "It is unjust to punish people who object to military service by criminal law without even making an effort to provide alternatives."

ly contradictory standards to apply to two countries, namely Mexico and Malawi. In the latter country, Watchtower's policies resulted in Witnesses suffering horrendous persecution, including destruction of property, beatings, rape and murder.

Much of what we know about this matter is gleaned from *Crisis of Conscience* in a chapter titled "Double Standards." Thankfully, when compiling his material on the subject, Raymond Franz understood the importance of presenting documented evidence to prove what amounts to gross negligence, recklessness and hypocrisy on Watchtower's part. Photocopies of key branch correspondence in support of his claims are therefore furnished in his book.[41] What follows is therefore based on Franz's evidence, at least as regards the situation in Mexico. The persecution in Malawi (and the reasoning behind it) is attested by Watchtower's own publications.

In Mexico, Witnesses had written to Watchtower requesting guidance on how to deal with difficulties presented by their refusal to undergo one year's military service. Only by fulfilling such service could a young man obtain a *cartilla* card (a certificate declaring one year's service complete), which enabled him to obtain a passport, driver's license, and so forth. Without their cartillas, Mexican Witnesses were considerably restricted in how much they could provide for themselves, or engage in work for Watchtower.

Watchtower's solution to the problem was spelled out in a letter sent from Brooklyn to the Mexican branch dated June 2, 1960. It effectively allowed Witnesses to obtain their cartillas through bribery on

---

[41] Paul Grundy has also reproduced the relevant documents on JWfacts.com on the page titled "Malawi, Mexico, Oath of Allegiance."

condition that officials were "willing to accept such an arrangement," and provided "the money paid does not go to the military establishment, but is appropriated by the individual who undertakes the arrangement."

Apparently baffled by the latitude granted them by Watchtower, the Mexican branch wrote to Watchtower again in a letter dated August 27, 1969, this time making it clear that bribery was not the only concern with the organization's proposed solution. If a Mexican Witness carried a cartilla card, this meant that he was automatically placed in the country's standing military reserves. Identifying oneself as part of a country's military through obtaining a certain document was hardly conducive with Watchtower's stance on "Christian neutrality."

Amazingly, Watchtower wrote back to the Mexican branch a week later and told them this still did not present a problem. "The letter that you quoted of February 4, 1960 (123) covers the whole matter," they insisted. "There is nothing more to be said." Mexican Witnesses were thus allowed to continue bribing officials into giving them a document that identified them as reserve soldiers so long as this allowed greater leeway with regard to employment and travel.

While this was happening, Jehovah's Witnesses in Malawi were being targeted for abominable treatment by the authorities over a similar issue. A first wave of violent attacks against Witnesses broke out in 1964, instigated by the ruling Malawi Congress Party, who were angered by the Witnesses' refusal to buy party membership cards. Then, in 1967, a more concerted campaign of aggression was mounted against the Witness community. Thousands were beaten by police and citizens. The violence escalated to the point where at least

50 Witnesses were murdered in 1972. Tens of thousands of Witnesses were forced to flee to neighboring Zambia, only to be mistreated in that country also.[42]

The following quote from a 1976 *Awake!* magazine makes it clear that the unbounded savagery inflicted on the Witnesses resulted from their refusal to buy a political card:

> It is because Jehovah's Witnesses refuse to buy the Malawi Congress Party card. This card declares the holder to be a member of the ruling political party of Malawi. But for Jehovah's Witnesses to buy a political card and thus join a political party would be an open denial of what they believe and stand for.

What the above quote does not mention is that Malawi was a single-party state. Hence, buying a card was not a matter of showing preference for one political party over another. There were no other parties available to reject. It was simply a matter of conforming to an arbitrary requirement imposed by the ruling government by indicating one's support thereof. Buying the card was no more a breach of "Christian neutrality" than paying for a passport identifying oneself as a citizen of a given country.

The following 1968 *Watchtower* quote paints a gruesome picture of just how much Witnesses suffered as a result of the ridiculous stand their leaders in Brooklyn had compelled them to take:

---

[42] According to Penton's *Apocalypse Delayed*, 21,000 Malawian Witnesses fled to Zambia in 1972 "where many died from malnutrition, lack of water, and ill treatment much to the shame of the Zambian authorities and the United Nations." He reports that "in November and December 1972 up to nine Witnesses a day were dying—many of them small children—and by 18 December, nearly 350 refugees had perished at that camp."

> At Lilongwe in central Malawi, 170 homes of these Christians were burned down in three nights. In the Fort Johnston district, slightly to the south, 34 homes and 18 food storage places were burned down toward the end of October. At Mbalame on October 27 the Christians of two congregations all had their homes burned down while they, including the women, were stripped of their clothes and brutally beaten.

And the following material from the *1999 Yearbook* goes into even more horrendous detail regarding the suffering:

> For some of our dear sisters, the persecution was especially harrowing. Many were the reports of rape, mutilation, and beating of Christian women. The sadistic attackers spared nobody. The elderly, the young, and even some pregnant sisters were put through such cruel ordeals. Some suffered miscarriages as a result. . . . The vicious attacks claimed many lives. In Cape Maclear, at the southern end of Lake Malawi, bundles of grass were tied around Zelphat Mbaiko. Petrol was poured on the grass and set alight. He was literally burned to death! Sisters also suffered terribly. Following their refusal to buy party cards, many were repeatedly raped by party officials. In Lilongwe, Sister Magola, along with many others, tried to flee the trouble. However, she was pregnant and could not run very fast. A mob, acting like a pack of wild dogs, caught up with her and beat her to death. At the campus of Bunda College of Agriculture, just outside of Lilongwe, six brothers and one sister were murdered and their bodies were horribly mutilated.

Hence, while Witnesses in one country were allowed to compromise their political neutrality by obtaining *through bribery* a card that falsely identified them as part of their country's militia, Witnesses in another country were prohibited from *legally* obtaining a document recognizing their allegiance to the ruling party *in a single-party state*, even though this prohibition led to them suffering the most brutal treatment imaginable.

Clearly, the liability of the Malawian regime is not to be understated. Witnesses in Malawi should never have been placed in a position by their own government where obedience to the unreasonable commands of their religious leaders carried such grotesque penalties. Without question the thugs who abused, raped and murdered peaceful worshippers should be held accountable, as should the leaders and politicians that sponsored and orchestrated their atrocities. Even so, the whole affair entirely contradicts any notion that Watchtower leaders from Knorr through to the first Governing Body members were "faithful and discreet" in weighing the far-reaching effects of their policies. In applying their foolish, inconsistent reasoning they delivered thousands of Witnesses to be brutalized by evil, barbaric monsters rather than allow them the same concession Mexican Witnesses, under far less grave circumstances, had already been granted. One cannot help but wonder whether events in Malawi would have turned out the same if those making the decisions on what it meant to be "no part of the world" had been among those personally affected.[43]

---

[43] As it turns out, there are examples of Watchtower leaders being more yielding when it comes to their own political neutrality (apart from the UN membership, to be discussed later). On the JWfacts.com page mentioned in a previous footnote, evidence is shown that both Rutherford and Knorr signed the United States "Oath of Allegiance" as Society presidents, which involves swearing to "support and defend the Constitution of the United States against all enemies, foreign and domestic."

## 1975

As we saw in the previous two chapters, a strong fascination with end-time chronology and apocalyptic date-setting has permeated Watchtower theology from the days of the Pastor. This preoccupation with forecasting the end of the world has produced some embarrassing results—most notably the dramatic predictions for 1914 and 1925. As the 1960s arrived, it was time for Freddie to try his hand at pulling a date from thin air, and the date he produced was 1975. (The fall of that year, to be precise.)

1975 made its debut in the 1966 book *Life Everlasting in Freedom of the Sons of God,* a red hardcover book with gold lettering on the cover and spine. The first chapter laid the groundwork for the new prediction by explaining the system of jubilee years that, according to the Bible, had been given to Israel by God at Sinai. This, it was explained, was a prophetic foregleam pointing to 1975.

Put simply, Israelites were to observe a system of Sabbath rests whereby every seventh year from the conquest of the promised land their fields were to lie fallow, giving the land chance to "rest" or recuperate. After seven of these seven-year cycles (7 × 7 = 49) there would be a 50th year, or jubilee year, to be marked with the sounding of a special horn. In this festival year, not only were all fields to continue to lie fallow,[44] but all debts were to be forgiven and all Israelites sold into

---

[44] If you were an Israelite farmer, you were expected to grow enough crops in the 48th year to see you through both the 49th "Sabbath" year, and the 50th "jubilee" year, until you could get back to growing crops on the 51st year when the cycle began afresh. God would miraculously make sure everyone had enough to last over the two-year period, provided all were obedient.

slavery in lieu of debt could be released.[45] Freddie reasoned that this divinely-prescribed arrangement was a "shadow" for a greater jubilee year involving freedom for all mankind through Christ's ransom. Since, according to Watchtower chronology, Adam had been created in the year 4026 B.C.E., this meant that 1975 would mark six thousand years from man's creation. According to Freddie, God viewed "a thousand years as one day"[46]—so it was extremely likely that the final thousand years of God's 7,000-year rest day (the seventh "creative day") would correspond with the 1,000-year reign of Christ foretold in Revelation. 1975 would hence mark the final thousand year period within God's 7,000-year "rest" day, ushering in a period of freedom for mankind. This would, in turn, require the intervention of God's divine wrath at Armageddon as a means of getting rid of. . . well, everyone who was not a Jehovah's Witness.[47]

Once introduced, 1975 was put forward with varying degrees of certainty. Occasionally, Freddie would hedge his bets by employing more vague language, saying things like: "Don't any of you be specific in saying anything that is going to happen between now and 1975."

---

45 The notion of humans being owned by other humans was thus an intrinsic part of this whole 'sacred' arrangement.

46 This leap in logic was achieved using scriptures like Psalm 90:4 and 2 Peter 3:8, both of which speak of God viewing one thousand years as one day. A similar trick was pulled by Russell when he promoted the 2,520 year period (borrowed from others) that produced 1914. The application of the 2,520 years depended on "year for a day" reasoning based on Numbers 14:34 and Ezekiel 4:6. The Bible, it seems, can be used to create any number of dates or spans of years depending on which multiplier verses one invokes.

47 See Appendix E for details of why the convoluted reasoning behind 1975 did not make sense even by Watchtower's standards.

But from the point of view of a believing Witness, the expectations for 1975 were clear and unambiguous. Consider the following text from the very chapter in the *Life Everlasting* book where the date was first unveiled, and try to imagine being a believing Witness in 1966 (with absolute trust in Watchtower as a channel for divine wisdom) when reading it (bold is mine):

> The Jubilee year of God's ancient law was a "shadow of the good things to come." The substantial reality that it foreshadowed must yet **without fail** be introduced for the good of all the groaning human creation. The blessed time for its introduction is **fast approaching. Shortly, within our own generation,** the symbolical trumpet **will** be sounded by divine power, proclaiming "liberty in the land to all its inhabitants." (Leviticus 25:8-10)

As someone who has been a Witness, I can tell you language such as the above would have pressed all the required buttons to elicit the impression: "They're telling us to be cautious, but really they *know* Armageddon is coming in 1975!" Similar rhetoric, further fanning the flames of frenzied expectation among Witnesses, would soon follow in Watchtower publications and from convention platforms. Consider the following words from a 1966 *Awake!* magazine:

> Does God's rest day parallel the time man has been on earth since his creation? Apparently so. In what year, then, would the first 6,000 years of man's existence and also the first 6,000 years of God's rest day come to an end? The year 1975. It means that within a relatively few years we will witness the fulfilment of the remaining prophecies that have to do with the "time of the end."

The following year, a district overseer named Charles Sunutko would speak the following words at a convention in Wisconsin (giving immortality to the phrase "Stay alive 'til '75"):

> Well now, as Jehovah's Witnesses, as runners, even though some of us have become a little weary, it almost seems as though Jehovah has provided meat in due season. Because he's held up before all of us a new goal. A new year. Something to reach out for and it just seems it has given all of us so much more energy and power in this final burst of speed to the finish line. And that's the year 1975. Well, we don't have to guess what the year 1975 means if we read *The Watchtower.* And don't wait till 1975. The door is going to be shut before then. As one brother put it: "Stay alive to Seventy-Five."

Then, in 1968, the following words were printed in the *Kingdom Ministry* (Watchtower's newsletter):

> Just think, brothers, there are only about ninety months left before 6,000 years of man's existence on earth is completed. Do you remember what we learned at the assemblies last summer? The majority of people living today will probably be alive when Armageddon breaks out, and there are no resurrection hopes for those that are destroyed then.

The same year, one *Watchtower* magazine incredibly urged Witnesses *against* being cautious as to keeping in mind a date for the end:

> This is not the time to be toying with the words of Jesus that "concerning that day and hour nobody knows, neither the angels of the heavens nor the Son, but only the Father." (Matt. 24:36) To the contrary, it is a time when one should be keenly aware that the end of this system of things is rapidly coming to its violent end.

These and other similar expressions dotted throughout various talks, books and magazines had the effect of convincing many Witnesses that the end really

***A lapel badge card for a Witness assembly in the early 1970s***

was coming in 1975, and that action was required. For example, a 1974 *Kingdom Ministry* article praised Witnesses who had responded to the prediction by selling their homes and property, and devoting themselves more fully to pioneer ministry:

> Reports are heard of brothers selling their homes and property and planning to finish out the rest of their days in this old system in the pioneer service. Certainly this is a fine way to spend the short time remaining before the wicked world's end.

Even more strident was an appeal made to Jehovah's Witnesses at a 1974 convention in the Netherlands by a Dutch branch overseer, who urged his audience to take up pioneer service as a matter of great urgency:

> Sell your house, sell everything you own and say, "Oh boy, how long can I carry on with my private means. That long?" Get rid of things! Pioneer! Plan to shower people with magazines during these last few months of this dying system of things!

M. James Penton, who was himself a Witness over this period, affirmed the zeal with which many believers responded to the 1975 teaching:

> Thousands of Witness young people became pioneers as did many new converts. Businessmen sold prospering businesses. Professional men gave up their jobs. Families sold their homes and moved to serve 'where the need [for evangelists] was greater.' Young couples delayed their marriages or at least refrained from having children if they did marry. Old couples sometimes withdrew all their pension funds at once. Many, both young and old, male and female, delayed having surgery or proper medical attention.

In short, it was Miller's 1844 "Great Disappointment" all over again.

Needless to say, the uneventful passing of 1975 left countless justifiably upset and frustrated people—people who deserved a heartfelt apology from a Watchtower leadership that had so clearly misled them, and with such far-reaching consequences. But rather than immediately recognize their error and apologize accordingly, an article appeared in a 1976 *Watchtower* that effectively chastised Witnesses for giving too much credence to what their spiritual leaders had told them:

> But it is not advisable for us to set our sights on a certain date, neglecting everyday things we would ordinarily care for as Christians, such as things that we and our families really need. We may be forgetting that, when the "day" comes, it will not change the principle that Christians must at all times take care of all their responsibilities. If anyone has been disappointed through not following this line of thought, he should now concentrate on adjusting his viewpoint, seeing that it was not the word of God that failed or deceived him and brought disappointment, but that his own understanding was based on wrong premises.

It would take more than four years *after* the obvious failure of 1975 before anything approaching a formal admission of guilt would be printed. And when it finally came, it was in the following few words from a 1980 *Watchtower* article:[48]

> With the appearance of the book *Life Everlasting in Freedom of the Sons of God*, and its comments as to how appropriate it would be for the millennial reign of Christ to parallel the seventh millennium of man's existence, considerable expectation was aroused regarding the year 1975. There were statements made then, and thereafter, stressing that this was only a possibility. Unfortunately, however, along with such cautionary information, there were other statements published that implied that such realization of hopes by that year was more of a probability than a mere possibility. It is to be regretted that these latter statements apparently overshadowed the cautionary ones and contributed to a buildup of the expectation already initiated.

The supreme irony of the 1975 prediction is that in the 1966 *Life Everlasting* book, in the pages *immediately preceding* those where the prediction first appeared, the following remarks were made in an apparent attempt to disparage "materialistic scientists" and exalt Watchtower as a beacon of truth and wisdom:

> Today materialistic scientists are continually interesting themselves in the laws of the universe

---

[48] According to Ray Franz in *Crisis of Conscience*, it was he who penned this 1980 article at the request of the Governing Body. Remarkably, one of his final acts on behalf of Watchtower prior to his expulsion was an attempt at mopping up the mess generated by his uncle. Franz suggested that the apology would have been more abject if he had not written it knowing it would need to pass a two-thirds majority at a Governing Body meeting before being printed.

> and probing deeper and deeper in order to discover them and understand them so as to get benefit from their discoveries. How much more should we interest ourselves in the Creator himself and in his laws for our human creation and earnestly seek to know and understand them. This is even more enlightening than the discovery of the universal laws and it works to our greater benefit. It frees us from bondage to superstition, idolatry, immoral practices, extreme fear of mortal men, devils, false religious doctrines and systems, and false hopes. Continued subjection to God's beneficial laws keeps us free from such hurtful, enslaving things.

Did not the insistence that Israel's jubilee years held some greater symbolic meaning applicable to our day prove to constitute a "false religious doctrine?" Did not the spurious prediction extracted from this teaching lead to "false hopes" surrounding the year 1975 on an epic scale? How could the writer here suggest that his religion's "enlightenment" was more beneficial than science—enlightenment that, only a few paragraphs later, would splurge out one of the most infamous apocalyptic predictions of the modern age?

The 1975 debacle not only annihilates any suggestion that Watchtower leaders throughout the organization's history have formed an unbroken chain of "faithful and discreet" custodians of divine wisdom. It also highlights the foolishness of elevating one's opinions to the point where even science, with its tried and tested methods and long record of improving the quality of human life, is deemed inferior. Give me scientists and their endless thirst for knowledge any day, the fruits of which are enjoyed even by the ignorant and indoctrinated (and often perversely used by such to attack the very source from whence they originated).

No scientist that I know of could be accused of forcing people to believe unfounded dogma based on fear and conjecture. And when scientists do make mistakes, they usually have the decency and fortitude to apologize, their humility aided by the fact that they do not normally purport to be earthly envoys of a supreme, infallible entity.

### United Nations NGO Membership

If you were to ask a devout Jehovah's Witness to name an organization that stands out as despicable and blasphemous in the sight of God, and will likely play a key role in the countdown to Armageddon, you would be hard-pressed to find one that does not reply "the United Nations." For decades, Witnesses have been taught to think of the UN as a diabolical abomination; a "disgusting thing that causes desolation" as affirmed in a recent *Watchtower* magazine:

> In the larger fulfillment [of Matthew 24:15, 16], the "standing" will occur when the United Nations (the modern-day "disgusting thing") attacks Christendom (which is holy in the eyes of nominal Christians) and the rest of Babylon the Great. The same attack is described at Revelation 17:16-18. That event will be the beginning of the great tribulation.

Why is an organization that was established in pursuit of world peace to be considered "disgusting?" Going all the way back to its predecessor, the League of Nations, Watchtower has interpreted its very existence as an affront to Christ's Kingdom rule. In their minds, only the Kingdom can usher humanity into lasting peace and unity. Anything else is not just a pretender, or a bit of healthy competition—it is outright blasphemy. As a 1989 *Watchtower* magazine put it:

> Ascribing to human organizations things that God's Kingdom alone will accomplish is blasphemous. Thus, the Bible foretells that after a short existence, the United Nations will go "off into destruction." Only God's perfect heavenly government can bring lasting peace to mankind.

The UN is also deemed worthy of destruction because it has been identified by Watchtower literature, including the *Revelation* book, as the "scarlet-colored wild beast" of Revelation—a machination of the devil intended to destroy the "harlot" of false religion (all religions that are not Jehovah's Witnesses) in the run-up to the apocalypse.

> Yes, the nations will use the scarlet-colored wild beast, the United Nations, in destroying Babylon the Great. They do not act on their own initiative, for Jehovah puts it into their hearts "even to carry out their one thought by giving their kingdom to the wild beast." When the time comes, the nations will evidently see the need to strengthen the United Nations. They will give it teeth, as it were, lending it whatever authority and power they possess so that it can turn upon false religion and fight successfully against her "until the words of God will have been accomplished." Thus, the ancient harlot will come to her complete end. And good riddance to her!

Given their intense acrimony toward the UN, you would expect the last thing Watchtower leaders would want to do is voluntarily approach it to apply for membership as an NGO (non-governmental organization). But, for reasons nobody really knows, this is precisely what they did in 1991. Watchtower was accepted as a member the following year, in 1992.

Watchtower's membership was with the UN's Department of Public Information, which requires members to agree to endorse the UN's charter and promote the UN as a force for good. Hence, incredibly, a slew of articles appeared in the *Watchtower* and *Awake!* magazines from 1992 onward that began to describe the UN in terms that were completely at odds with the utter condemnation of the 1988 *Revelation* book, released just a few years earlier. My personal favorite is this 1995 quote from the same *Watchtower* article that later told Witnesses to respect the UN and view it "as they do other governmental bodies of the world":

> For 50 years the United Nations organization has made notable efforts to bring about world peace and security. Arguably, it may have prevented a third world war, and the wholesale destruction of human life through the use of nuclear bombs has not been repeated. The United Nations has provided millions of children with food and medicine. It has contributed to improved health standards in many countries, providing, among other things, safer drinking water and immunization against dangerous diseases. Millions of refugees have received humanitarian assistance.

Despite this new, altogether more conciliatory tone, ordinary Witnesses were completely oblivious to the NGO membership. There was, after all, no reason for anyone to suspect anything. But, on October 8, 2001, the cat was let out of the bag when Stephen Bates, a reporter for the *Guardian* newspaper, uncovered the scandal under the headline "Jehovah's Witnesses Link to UN Queried":

> The United Nations is being asked to investigate why it has granted associate status to the Jehovah's Witnesses, the fundamentalist US-based Christian sect, which regards it as the scarlet beast predicted in the Book of Revelation. Disaffected members of the 6m-strong group, which has 130,000 followers

> in the UK, have accused the Witnesses' elderly governing body of hypocrisy in secretly accepting links with an organisation that they continue to denounce in apocalyptic terms. The UN itself admitted yesterday that it was surprised that the sect, whose formal name is the Watchtower Bible and Tract Society of New York, had been accepted on its list of non-governmental organisations for the last 10 years.

Witnesses and ex-Witnesses alike were left stunned by this revelation. UN headquarters was soon inundated with letters requesting confirmation. In response, the UN released open letters on official letterhead signed by Paul Hoeffel (chief of the NGO section of the Department of Public Information). These letters decisively proved that Watchtower applied for association in 1991, was accepted in 1992, and requested disassociation that became effective as of October 9, 2001—the day following Bates' article.[49] They also confirmed that criteria for Watchtower's association included "support and respect of the principles of the Charter of the United Nations and commitment and means to conduct effective information programs with its constituents and to a broader audience about UN activities."

The Slave was thus exposed as a hypocrite on two counts. Firstly, Watchtower sets extremely high standards for rank-and-file Witnesses when it comes to staying neutral with regard to Satan's world (to this day you can be forcibly disassociated and shunned for joining a "nonneutral organization," or refusing to quit employment that makes you "a clear accomplice in nonneutral activities"), and yet they had been caught red-handed entangling themselves in the world's political system. Secondly, how were Witnesses supposed

---

[49] Scans of these letters are reproduced in Appendix F.

to take the Slave's prophetic interpretations seriously if they had been effectively caught in bed with the same organization they had denounced as being the "scarlet-colored wild beast" of Revelation, the "disgusting thing" of Daniel and Matthew, and an insult to God's sovereignty?

Watchtower may have withdrawn from the UN within 24 hours of being busted, but the damage was done. The Slave had been exposed for its duplicity in courting the very entity it claimed to loathe. To this day, Watchtower has not published any explanation for the scandal in its literature.[50] As with other ugly aspects of Watchtower history, the Slave seems content to cover things over in the hope that not too many will stumble on evidence of their lengthy UN affiliation. And for the most part, this strategy continues to work brilliantly.

### The Generation Teaching

You may recall that I mentioned the *Reasoning* book back in Chapter One. First published in 1985, it was a constant companion of Witnesses—a mainstay of their book bags all the way through to its recent discontinuation. If you were to open that book at page 200, you would find part of a list of 10 beliefs of Witnesses that

---

[50] The closest Watchtower ever came to offering an explanation to Witnesses was in a leaked letter to branches about the scandal, dated November 1, 2001. More information on this and the various excuses offered by Watchtower apologists can be found in my 36-minute YouTube documentary *Watchtower and the United Nations—An Unexpected Affair*. There is also a thorough discussion about the scandal, including key documents, on the relevant page of JWfacts.com. Another excellent resource is Tami Dickerson's 2011 booklet *Jehovah's Witnesses and the United Nations: How the Watchtower Society Fooled Millions.*

"set them apart as different from other religions." Point 8 on this list, which was to be used in helping convert people to the Witness faith until as recently as 2013, reads as follows (bold is mine):

> (8) Last days: They believe that we are living now, since 1914, in the last days of this wicked system of things; **that some who saw the events of 1914 will also see the complete destruction of the present wicked world;** that lovers of righteousness will survive into a cleansed earth.

Hence, in the not-so-distant past, a key teaching of Witnesses was that "some who saw the events of 1914" would be alive when Armageddon arrives. This assertion was based on a verse in Matthew 24:34, in which Jesus tells his disciples that "this generation will by no means pass away until all these things happen." It is understood that, when saying "these things," Jesus was referring to the signs of the last days (that he had just outlined)—meaning that the "generation" he mentioned would survive these events through to the conquest of God's Kingdom over world governments. Naturally, Watchtower leaders assumed this generation involved *them;* specifically anointed, Witnesses who were around when Jesus began ruling in heaven in 1914.[51]

So intrinsic was this teaching to Watchtower that for many years it adorned the masthead of the *Awake!* magazine. Under the heading "Why *Awake!* Is Published" appeared a paragraph that concluded with the following words:

---

[51] Obviously there were no "Jehovah's Witnesses" prior to 1931 when this name was adopted, but Watchtower includes under the umbrella of "the anointed" all who were associated with Watchtower from the years when followers identified as Bible Students.

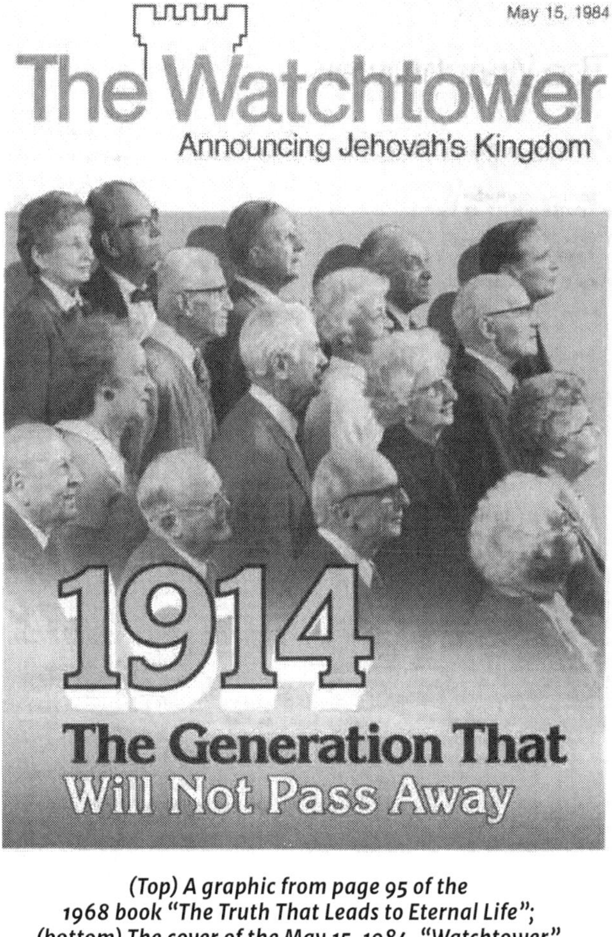


*(Top) A graphic from page 95 of the 1968 book "The Truth That Leads to Eternal Life"; (bottom) The cover of the May 15, 1984, "Watchtower" (all featured Witnesses were born before 1914, and all have since died)*

> Most important, this magazine builds confidence in the Creator's promise of a peaceful and secure new world before the generation that saw the events of 1914 pass away.

Curiously, the wording of this masthead was changed for the November 8, 1995, issue to read as follows:

> Most important, this magazine builds confidence in the Creator's promise of a peaceful and secure new world that is about to replace the present wicked, lawless system of things.

Somehow, between the issue of October 22, 1995, and the issue of November 8, 1995, the "Creator's promise" had changed. The word "generation" apparently now had slightly less to do with people who had actually witnessed the events of 1914. Why was this?

You will need to ask Watchtower for a definitive answer on what prompted the change, and you will most likely be told that in those two weeks the "light got brighter" on their understanding of Scripture. A more realistic explanation for the change would be that, as with the 1975 fiasco, the passage of time had rendered a Watchtower prediction obsolete. By 1995, it was becoming increasingly unlikely that somebody old enough to register world events in 1914 would live long enough to survive through to Armageddon. Watchtower had maintained this teaching in its literature since 1951,[52] but as the 20th century drew to a close and almost ev-

---

[52] We probably have Freddie to thank for the 1951 teaching. Prior to 1951, less emphasis was placed on who the "generation" might be, likely because 1914 was still relatively recent (as a year tying the modern age with Bible times) and there was not really any pressing need to explain the passage of time since that year. A useful webpage showing the history of the generation teaching and its various incarnations going back to Russell can be found on JWfacts.com.

eryone at headquarters baptized before 1914 was dead (including Freddie, who passed away on December 22, 1992, having been baptized in 1913), something had to give.

So, what was the new understanding? A rather vague 1995 *Watchtower* article informed Witnesses that the word "generation" as used by Jesus in Matthew was a "contemporary people of a certain historical period, with their identifying characteristics." It held that the group referred to were "the peoples of earth who see the sign of Christ's presence but fail to mend their ways." What was being described was an ongoing generation of people who saw the sign of Christ's presence, and who could do so at any point from 1914 onward for some indeterminate period. This certainly bought Watchtower a bit more time for Armageddon to come, but there was just one problem: it did not make the slightest bit of sense. The verse specifically uses the word "generation," which is not a word one normally employs when referring to everyone living from a certain point in history onward.

Later, in 2008, a subtle change was introduced. Instead of applying to the bad guys (i.e. incorrigible worldly people) the verse now applied to "the modern-day John class"—all anointed Witnesses over the same time period from 1914 "until the last of the faithful anointed ones dies and is resurrected." This understanding suffered from the same problem as its predecessor, namely a reliance on Witnesses accepting that a "generation" can be thought of as a group of people sharing a certain set of attributes living beyond a certain year.

Unsurprisingly, this revised "understanding" would prove short-lived. Within only two years the holy spirit

***David Splane gives Witnesses an "easy way to keep the generation straight"***

had gotten its act together and in 2010 finally delivered the *actual* meaning of the word "generation"—the meaning still held to today.[53] The "generation" of Matthew 24:34 again involved 1914, but this time another piece of mental gymnastics had come to the rescue. The generation that witnessed the events of 1914 had overlapped with another generation that worked alongside them for a period, creating one long, continuous, *overlapping generation.*

If you are scratching your head at this point, be assured you are not the only one. In fact, many Witnesses were left puzzled—so puzzled that Governing Body member David Splane would appear in a video in September 2015 in an attempt to explain the whole thing. A board was even produced, complete with pointy stick, as an "easy way to keep the generation straight" (to quote Splane). It showed the life course of Freddie as being illustrative of the new generation

---

[53] I have no doubt the "understanding" of the generation of Matthew 24:34 will change many more times in the history of Jehovah's Witnesses, but I am limited by the time in which I write and will just have to try to keep up in future editions.

understanding. Because Freddie had been baptized in November 1913, he could be thought of as being part of the original generation who witnessed the events of 1914. Any anointed Witnesses who were "contemporaries" of Freddie and his anointed associates before they died (1992 is cited "for the sake of argument," this being the year of Freddie's death) could be considered as forming the second component of the overlapping generation. Hence, you could not be part of the overlapping generation unless you were (1) an anointed Witness, and (2) your time as an anointed Witness overlapped at some point with the "generation" of which Freddie was a member.

Of course, all of this is pure nonsense. You cannot edit the English dictionary just to rescue a belief that is central to your particular faith. A generation is a generation, and by redefining the word the Governing Body are essentially ordering their followers to willfully bypass their logical thinking skills by asserting the incomprehensible as indisputable truth. If you can arbitrarily insist that a generation can be composed of two groups, why not have three, four, five—on into infinity? The word "generation" quickly loses all meaning.

As with other instances in Watchtower history when the Bible was forced to conform to fanciful eschatological claims, the ever-fluctuating generation teaching furnishes a fine example of religious "truth" that changes only as it is proven wrong by the passage of time.

### ***Become Jehovah's Friend* Cartoons**

Watchtower has long understood the benefits to be reaped from equipping Witnesses to indoctrinate their children as the next generation of loyal followers (note the *correct* use of the word!). For the most part, colorful publications like *My Book of Bible Stories* (1978) and *Learn From the Great Teacher* (2003) have served this purpose, but in 2012 a new resource for sculpting young minds was added to Watchtower's arsenal. A DVD was released at that year's convention titled *Become Jehovah's Friend—Listen, Obey and Be Blessed.* It introduced two CGI-animated cartoon children, Caleb and Sophia, whose fictional escapades would serve to teach both Witness parents and their offspring how to satisfy the Slave's expectations.

With opening remarks by Anthony Morris III (presumably picked because he was the only GB member with children), the DVD featured two episodes (or "lessons") with the promise of more to follow on JW.org. "Lesson 2" proved to be especially troubling. It showed a young Caleb being chastised by his mother for returning home with a plastic action figure, identified as "Sparlock the warrior wizard."[54]

"Caleb, who likes magic? Jehovah, or Satan?" asks Caleb's scowling mother at the dinner table, before invoking images of Adam and Eve condemned to misery and old age for failing to resist the devil's wiles. In order to no longer sadden Jehovah by playing with a plastic figurine that displeases him, Caleb is eventually forced to put his Sparlock toy—a gift from a friend—in the dumpster. The coercive nature of the video, so clearly designed to encourage parents to employ fear, threats and manipulation in enforcing the Slave's whims, was genuinely unsettling for ex-JWs to behold. A slew of scathing videos lambasting the cartoon were

54 Sparlock is a fictional creation of Watchtower, but he was quickly embraced by the ex-Jehovah's Witness community as emblematic of their struggle.

***A grisly depiction of Armageddon from the 2003 children's book "Learn From the Great Teacher"***

uploaded to YouTube by ex-Witnesses and non-Witnesses alike, but apart from issuing a few DMCA take-downs for copyright infringement, Watchtower seemed mostly unfazed by the backlash. They were clearly stepping up a gear in their quest for control of young ones, and a few outraged YouTubers were not going to stop them.

*Caleb and Sophia risk eternal destruction by failing to pay attention at the meeting*

In more recent years, Caleb and Sophia have been deployed to teach children that the Genesis account constitutes a literal retelling of the creation of earth and all living things (Lesson 9), that God will execute any who fail to pay attention at Kingdom Hall meetings (Lesson 15), that children should contribute their ice cream money to Watchtower (Lesson 19) and that Witness children should seek out schoolmates whose parents are gay or lesbian to let them know of the paradise that awaits those who repudiate the homosexual "lifestyle" (Lesson 22).

## Typhoon Haiyan Disaster

On November 8, 2013, Typhoon Haiyan ravaged the Philippines, leaving in its wake 6,300 dead, 28,000 injured, and more than $2 billion worth of damage. In addition to showcasing nature at its most deadly, Haiyan would also furnish a potent example of the Slave exploiting death, misery and suffering for propaganda purposes.

Within a week of the disaster, the Governing Body was mobilizing a camera crew to follow Mark Sanderson as he flew out to meet with local Witnesses amidst the clean-up effort.[55] "With the Philippines Typhoon Haiyan story it was very important to turn it around quickly," Bethel worker Todd Freund would later relate, "because it's a current news event and all the people, the brothers and sisters there that were suffering, we hoped it would be very encouraging for them to get this story quickly."[56]

The resulting video, titled *Philippines Typhoon—Faith Conquers Adversity,* was released in March 2014. It opened with reassuring noises that Watchtower was fully in control prior to Haiyan's arrival. "Before the storm hit, the Philippines branch office began coordinating the evacuation and relief efforts," the narrator explained. A circuit overseer was then interviewed, recounting how he was given advance notice by the local news service, whereupon he began texting elders of the congregations under his charge, urging them to evacuate to a "separate place." "We knew it was going to do tremendous damage," admitted Hubertus Hoefnagels of the Philippines branch office.

Anyone watching the video would be forgiven for assuming Watchtower was on top of the disaster from the get-go—and there is every reason why they should

---

[55] Sanderson was presumably chosen for the assignment because he is a former member of the Philippines branch committee.

[56] These comments appear in the November 2015 JW Broadcasting episode, hosted by Mark Sanderson. An entire segment is devoted to the making of the *Philippines Typhoon* video. The fact that footage recorded in the aftermath of the disaster (frequently referred to as a "story") was carefully spun for maximum emotional impact is barely concealed, and in some ways even celebrated.

have been. The International Federation of Red Cross and Red Crescent Societies was predicting a "dangerous" typhoon heading straight for Leyte and Samar (the two worst-affected provinces) as early as two days before Haiyan hit.

Regular warnings were sounded over television and social media. Even though some refused to treat these with the appropriate urgency, more than 750,000 across the central Philippines were successfully evacuated. These warnings also specifically cautioned citizens of a significant storm surge. Clare Nullis, spokeswoman for the UN's World Meteorological Organization, told *Reuters* that "certainly on Thursday and Friday, PAGASA, which is the Philippines' meteorological service, they were sending out regular warnings of a seven-meter (22 ft) storm surge. That was going out on an hourly basis."

So, with regular, specific warnings that a catastrophic typhoon was incoming, dragging a powerful storm surge that would almost certainly devastate low-lying coastal areas, you would think the Philippines branch would have canceled Thursday-evening meetings and urged all Witnesses to flee to higher ground. Unfortunately, as the video continues it becomes clear that, for whatever reason, this is not what happened.

Viewers are taken to one Kingdom Hall in Guiuan which, as it happens, is where the typhoon first made landfall at 4:40 a.m. on Friday. Incredibly, we are told that on the Thursday night, as the typhoon approached, the Guiuan congregation was *holding a meeting.* As conditions worsened following the meeting, local Witnesses huddled together inside their battered place of worship. At one point the roof flew off. Incredibly, despite such grave negligence, there was no loss of life—but the same could not be said elsewhere as Haiyan worked its way westward deeper into the Philippines, striking the coastal city of Tacloban. In one Kingdom Hall alone, we learn that 22 lost their lives by taking shelter in the structure rather than heeding the warnings to evacuate. One thirteen-year-old girl named Sheryl Gariando is revealed to have survived the catastrophe by climbing a tree, but she lost her whole family (with the exception of her younger brother) when the surge ripped through her Kingdom Hall.[57]

All of this raises a number of questions. Why were the Witness survivors featured in the video not among the 750,000 evacuated? Why were the Guiuan elders holding a meeting hours before the typhoon struck? Why were Witnesses in this region, including the 22 who perished at the Tacloban Kingdom Hall, not safely relocated to higher ground? Either Watchtower never ordered these congregations to evacuate, or they did but their warnings went ignored. If warnings were ignored, why was this not alluded to in the video if only for the purpose of clarifying that Watchtower had no culpability for the loss of life?

Concerns were not eased when the video showed a devastated Kingdom Hall in Tanuan that was lifted from its foundations and carried 15 meters by the rag-

---

[57] Sheryl's plight is made even more tragic by the fact that she is apparently unaware that her unimaginable loss has been exploited by the very organization that likely failed to prevent it. "The elders told me it was ok to cry, because it would get what was in my heart out into the open," she says in the video. "Going to meetings really helped. The brothers read scriptures that reminded me of the resurrection." In the November 2015 JW Broadcasting episode, it was disclosed that Sheryl had been moved to a Witness family close to the branch office, and had joined the auxiliary pioneer service.

***Top: The devastated Kingdom Hall in Tacloban;***
***Bottom: A JW family reveals their hoard of Watchtower literature***

ing waters. Here, again, Witnesses described taking shelter in their Kingdom Hall rather than fleeing for safety. "We stayed here until the typhoon arrived," says one elder named Levi. His mother, who cannot swim, relates how she was dragged out of the Kingdom Hall by the storm surge, only surviving by grabbing hold of a piece of wood. "I was strengthened by contemplating the meaning of the year text," Levi enthuses. "It says, 'Jehovah your God is with you.'"

We are then told that all 44 who sheltered in the structure survived. The message from this part of the video seems to be: "A Kingdom Hall is a place of refuge in times of disaster, much like Noah's ark. Flee to it, and dwell on spiritual things, and you will be delivered." Not only is such a message extremely insensitive in the context of the huge loss of life at Tacloban, where this strategy failed with catastrophic results—it is also grossly negligent to promote such a dangerous, superstitious recourse to a worldwide audience of Jehovah's Witnesses, some of whom may find themselves caught up in a similar disaster in the future.

In another part of the video, a family from the Central Tacloban congregation is interviewed in their home where, mercifully, they survived the typhoon (unlike many of their brothers and sisters over at the Kingdom Hall). The father, Richard, describes his vain attempts at keeping the roof from flying off. Then his daughter excitedly opens the refrigerator to show the Watchtower camera crew the contents. A section is revealed to be crammed full of Watchtower literature (including, quite prominently, the previously-mentioned *Become Jehovah's Friend* DVD). The message here seems to be: "In times of disaster, rescuing Watchtower literature takes priority over stock-piling basic provisions."

In the closing minutes of the video, the narrator discloses that 33 Witnesses were confirmed dead in the disaster, with 10 more missing, presumed dead.[58] This is

---

[58] Apart from the exploitative aspect of Watchtower's Haiyan coverage, families of the 43 Witnesses whose lives were claimed would be further insulted in the January 2016 JW Broadcasting episode. In this video, Travis Brooks, a design and construction worker for Watchtower, credits Jehovah with delivering sand needed for a Kingdom Hall extension project on Yap by means of a typhoon (likely Typhoon Maysak, which itself claimed four lives and injured ten). As I point out in an article for JWsurvey.org titled "Does Jehovah Control the Weather?" Witnesses are essentially asked to believe that God allowed one typhoon to kill 43 Witnesses, but used another to deliver building materials to Watchtower's advantage.

an enormous loss of life for one religious community in a natural disaster, which begs the question: how do the Witness deaths compare with the country in general?

The *2014 Yearbook* gives the rather precise figure of 97,701,745 as the population of the Philippines for the 2012/2013 service year, before the disaster occurred. As stated, Haiyan claimed the lives of 6,300—giving us a mortality rate of 0.0063% for the country as a whole. By comparison, Watchtower claims to have had 185,000 Witnesses in the Philippines at the time of the disaster. When we include the 10 presumed dead with the confirmed figures, this gives us a mortality rate of 0.024% among Witnesses for Typhoon Haiyan—nearly *four times* the national figure. Statistically speaking, being a Jehovah's Witness put you at a significant disadvantage as the typhoon approached, to say the least. How does the Governing Body account for this, given the fact that they released a video revealing that several congregations were ignoring official advice (to evacuate) by heading to their Kingdom Halls in those crucial remaining hours, with at least one group of elders conducting a meeting?

I firmly believe the Governing Body owes an explanation for what happened in the Philippines when Typhoon Haiyan struck. Even if it should transpire that they are, for reasons yet to be explained, entirely free from blame for the disproportionate number of Witnesses killed (news I would honestly welcome), their cheap attempt at exploiting the disaster for promotional, manipulative purposes was distasteful in the extreme. It seems that, when it comes to convincing Witnesses of the urgent need to put complete trust in them, there are few lines of decency the Slave will not cross. And it would not be long before they would further utilize video and internet technology to fashion the perfect vehicle for broadcasting their authority on an unprecedented scale.

### JW Broadcasting

At the annual meeting on October 4, 2014, the Slave announced a new provision for dispensing "spiritual food." Beginning the same month, available only on a new "JW Broadcasting" website (URL: tv.jw.org), there would be a monthly hour-long program hosted by Governing Body members on a rotating basis. Sure enough, a steady stream of highly-potent propaganda videos followed, including slick dramatizations and stirring experiences set to music.[59] The material shown continues to be clearly crafted with the aim of bypassing logic and reason, and appealing directly to the emotion of the intended audience by tugging at the heart strings.

These monthly episodes emphasize the need for reliance on Jehovah's organization in all aspects of life. Young ones are reminded of the need to avoid higher education. Witnesses are urged to sacrifice well-paying jobs in order to "simplify" their lives to serve Jehovah. Witness parents are instructed to indoctrinate their children at the earliest opportunity. Those who have put their lives on the line for Watchtower at various points in the organization's history are commended for doing so. And, beginning in April 2016, a regular feature of science denial was launched in which people with scientific backgrounds who happen to be Witnesses step forward to contradict the overwhelming scientific consensus regarding evolution (usually revealing their ignorance on the subject in so doing).

---

[59] I have produced a series of rebuttals to these videos on my "John Cedars" YouTube channel.

Apart from the obnoxious propaganda element, the obvious problem with the JW Broadcasting format is that it is self-defeating for the Slave. By increasing their visibility to the point where they are appearing in the living rooms of Witnesses on an almost monthly basis,[60] the Governing Body has removed the aura of mystery that once served a useful role in nurturing the respect and reverence of ordinary Witnesses.

It used to be that a Witness could confidently say: "I have no idea who the Governing Body members are, or what they look like—*that's* how humble they are!" I can still remember when the organization's *Proclaimers* history book was released in 1993 and for the first time I got to see, on page 116, smiling mug-shots of each of the GB members—then numbering 12 (as of January 1992). They appeared approachable and grandfatherly, and as a young Witness it felt special to get a rare glimpse of my spiritual leaders, all on one page. Prior to the *Proclaimers* book, unless you worked at Bethel, or were extremely fastidious with tracking organizational developments, it was difficult to know who these men were. I even recall touring the Brooklyn Bethel in 2003 and being introduced to a GB member who was passing our party in the corridor (my memory is vague, but I think it was Lösch). If our tour guide had not pointed him out to us and introduced him as a GB member, I would honestly not have had a clue who he was.

---

[60] Beginning with the December 2015 broadcast, it was decided that Governing Body members would alternate hosting duties with Governing Body "helpers"—or assistants of the various Governing Body committees. Hence, Governing Body members only now appear as hosts on a two-monthly basis. It would not surprise me if Governing Body members withdraw from hosting duties entirely in the fullness of time.

Fast forward a little over a decade, and the identities and likenesses of these men are almost inescapable. Any semblance of modesty or reclusiveness has vanished. JW Broadcasting has served to give Witnesses a glimpse behind the curtain that many would probably prefer to be without. Rather than coming across as astute, intellectual, eloquent and wise, the performances of the GB members reveal them to be cheesy, condescending, insincere, jewelry-brandishing televangelists who address their audience as though they are children.[61] And despite decades of Theocratic Ministry School training, they do not even appear to be especially competent as speakers.

It would have been much smarter for the Governing Body to stay behind the curtain and keep Witnesses guessing, but such is their obvious need for reverence and adoration it would seem they cannot help but pursue the limelight—even at the risk of cheapening their image. In that respect, no JW Broadcasting episode has served to drag the Slave down to earth quite like the May 2015 episode in which, for the first time, Witnesses were treated to the spectacle of "Jehovah's organization" begging for donations.

### Increased Begging for Funds

Watchtower used to have a long, proud history of not being too pushy when it came to requesting contributions. For all his faults, one thing we can credit Charles Taze Russell with is his pragmatism in ac-

[61] It should be noted that there has been a reduction in the amount of jewelry being brandished by Governing Body members in more recent JW Broadcasting episodes compared to the first few appearances, when expensive-looking watches and pinky rings were on show.

knowledging that if his movement truly enjoyed divine backing, the necessary funds would be supplied. Hence, Russell is frequently quoted in Watchtower publications as saying:

> "Zion's Watch Tower" has, we believe, JEHOVAH for its backer, and while this is the case it will never beg nor petition men for support. When He who says: "All the gold and silver of the mountains are mine," fails to provide necessary funds, we will understand it to be time to suspend the publication.

This pledge to "never beg nor petition" was underscored in Russell's comments at a meeting in 1913, as recorded on page 128 of the 1917 book *What Pastor Russell Said* (a compilation of his answers to various questions put to him by Bible Students):

> Years ago, dear friends, I had my experience when a Congregationalist. There was a fair and voting contest on and I remember very well that I solicited from one person, and he very promptly handed me two dollars and seemed pleased to give it. After receiving the two dollars I felt ashamed. I said, You begged. My answer was, You begged for the church. But you would be ashamed to beg for yourself. Yes I would, but this was for the Lord. But if you would be ashamed to beg for yourself should you not be more ashamed to beg for the Lord? Is the Lord poor? I said, No, and I will never beg or solicit again, nor have I from that time to now.
>
> The question is, How can we spend so much money when we solicit none? People voluntarily push it on us. That is no joke. People really say, "Brother Russell, I am deeply interested in these things and would like to put a little money in. Can I have a chance?" We say, Brother, there is all of the chance in the world.

***Stephen Lett in the May 2015 JW Broadcasting episode***

In recent years especially, Russell's noble, unobtrusive approach to gleaning donations has been all but swept aside by his modern-day successors. At no time in its history until now has Watchtower done this quite so blatantly as on the May 2015 JW Broadcasting episode, when Stephen Lett admitted to a shortfall between expected income from donations and the cost of the organization's planned projects:

> The Governing Body very much feels the urgency of accomplishing as much as we possibly can in behalf of Kingdom interests, knowing that the great day of Jehovah is near. So in an effort to inform you of the support that is needed for this great work, I have the following information to share.
>
> We have looked forward to this next fiscal year and projected the expenditures for all of the theocratic initiatives we are scheduling. In doing the math, we found that the amount of money flowing out will be much greater than the amount of money that we have coming in at this time. Well why is that? Does this represent a lack of appreciation for spiritual things? No, absolutely not!

Lett went on to list the many provisions Witnesses could be thankful for, such as printed publications, new Bibles, the JW.org website, and JW Broadcasting. He suggested that, though there was no lack of appreciation from ordinary Witnesses, the shortfall in funds could be due to a misconception among many that the organization was flush with money due to its recent decision to cancel congregation "loan repayments," not to mention the recent sale of Watchtower's lucrative Brooklyn properties, which have served as the organization's headquarters since 1909. (The properties were sold off one-by-one after a decision to move the organization's headquarters to Warwick, upstate New York, as announced at the 2011 annual meeting. At that event, the late Guy Pierce revealed that the Governing Body were "not yet certain of Jehovah's will regarding Warwick," but were proceeding with the plan regardless.)

So, what of Lett's claims as regards misconceptions among Witnesses? Both, I'm afraid, were misleading to say the least.

As explained in Chapter Five, the "canceling" of loan repayments and instituting of regular monthly donations *irrespective of whether congregations were previously indebted or not* was not an act of generosity by Watchtower. Rather, it amounted to stealth tithing—coercing Witnesses into supporting regular monthly congregation payments to the organization, and forcing congregations to send over any surplus funds as a one-off payment.

Furthermore, Lett continued the policy of keeping Witnesses completely in the dark over the total proceeds from the sale of the Brooklyn properties, which are likely to exceed $1.3 billion once the last few are

***Top: Brooklyn factory/residence buildings, sold by Watchtower for a combined $375 million in 2013 Middle: The iconic Brooklyn headquarters building at 25–30 Columbia Heights, sold in 2016 for $340 million Bottom: The new headquarters at Warwick***

sold.[62] Lett played down the windfall, claiming that the sale of one unnamed "significant" Brooklyn property would offset only a few weeks of normal operating expenses. But such a claim is meaningless without knowing the numbers involved, and rings even more hollow when it is remembered that Watchtower pocketed $375 million from one transaction alone (information that can only be gleaned from non-JW real estate websites).[63] Then there is the fact that the replacement Warwick complex has been budgeted at only a tiny fraction of Watchtower's Brooklyn proceeds.[64] Put simply, far from being a drop in the ocean, the income from the Brooklyn sell-offs was considerable and resulted from the milking of an enormous cash cow that has been steadily inflating over many decades thanks to voluntary funds, volunteer labor, and tax exemptions. And it is a cash cow that has been milked, as I will explain later, out of necessity.

Having made his case for Witnesses to empty their piggy-banks, Lett concluded:

---

[62] A September 22, 2016, article in *The Real Deal* reported: "At one point, the Witnesses held 4.5 million square feet over 30 buildings. They're down to nine buildings, having made about $1.25 billion on staggered sales since 2004, according to the CO [*Commercial Observer*]."

[63] The properties sold in this transaction, familiar to Witnesses from their publications, include the five factory buildings: 117 Adams Street, 175 Pearl Street, 55 Prospect Street, 81 Prospect Street and 77 Sands Street. The tallest of the buildings, 90 Sands Street, is a 30-story residential building completed in 1990 to house up to 1,000 Bethel workers and visitors.

[64] Four separate neutral sources, namely *The Brooklyn Paper, The Observer, The Real Deal* and the *New York Post* all cite an estimated figure of $11.5 million for the building costs of the Warwick headquarters—an unbelievably low sum, but the only one we have in the absence of any transparency from Watchtower.

> The Governing Body wanted to make you aware of the financial needs in the world field. And we are confident that with this knowledge, your appreciative hearts will move you to do what you can to support the work at hand.

Despite the unprecedented spectacle of a GB member going cap-in-hand in the May 2015 episode, it seems the response was underwhelming. Nine months later, Lett appeared again and commended his audience for increasing their donations by "more than 15%" over the two months following his plea. You have to wonder whether it was worth it for the Governing Body to ditch Russell's tradition of never begging or petitioning for the sake of such a meager return, further eroding their credibility to more astute observers in so doing.

It should go without saying that if you are planning something that you cannot afford to do, the thing to do is reduce the scale of your plans accordingly. If Jehovah wants to bless his chosen Slave, he will make funds available. If he doesn't—he won't. To plan for something you cannot afford and rely on the generosity of others to bail you out is hardly "discreet"—but this is the reality of Watchtower in the modern age. If they want to do something, and lack the necessary funds, it is down to the rank and file to stump up the cash.

Having touched on Watchtower's mounting desperation for funds, I will devote the final pages of our three-chapter whistle-stop tour of the organization's history to a glimpse of what the future might hold for the Slave.

It is hard for even the most cynical critic of Watchtower to envision it ever going bankrupt. After all, as organizations go, it is big. Very, very big. And with a devoted following of 8 million worshippers globally, you would expect its balance sheet to always be healthy.

Watchtower certainly manages to spend money as though there is no shortage. Take, for example, the amount it allocates to its special pioneers, missionaries and traveling overseers in their assignments—the only figure related to Watchtower finances that the Slave makes public. The figure given for 2015 (the latest to hand) was a hefty $236 million. This compares with $224 million in 2014, and $200 million in 2013.

But what do these figures mean when we do not know how much is going in and how much is going out? An organization can make a billion dollars a year, but if it is spending $1.1 billion dollars yearly the situation will soon become untenable. Any organization that is able to take out loans to help meet operating costs is capable of going bankrupt if it fails to keep up with repayments, and Watchtower is no exception. Furthermore, quite apart from Lett's embarrassing begging for donations in the May 2015 JW Broadcasting episode, there are telling clues that all is not well with Watchtower if you know where to look.

Firstly, there is the printing situation. When Watchtower reached its printing zenith in 2005, it was churning out just over 3 billion magazine pages per month. Then, gradually, it began reducing its commitments. Two 32-page *Watchtowers* and two 32-page *Awakes* per month became two 32-page *Watchtowers* and one 32-page *Awake!* in 2006. By 2013, there was one 32-page "study edition" *Watchtower*, one 16-page "public edition" *Watchtower*, and one 16-page *Awake!*, bringing total printing down to just shy of 1.9 billion pages per month. More recently, as of 2016, printing has dipped further

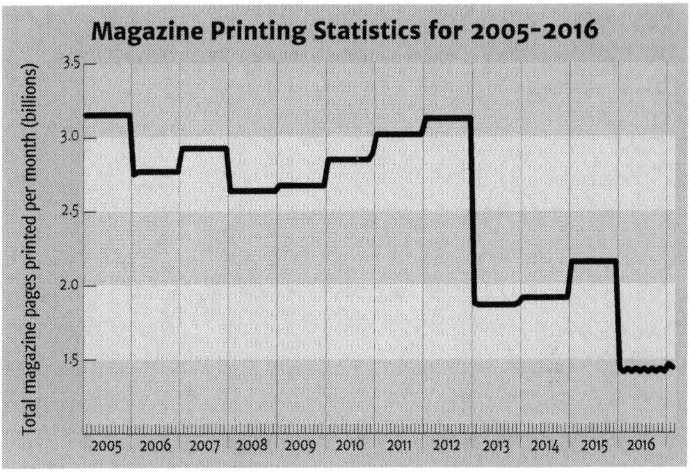


to 1.4 billion pages (one public 16-page *Watchtower* and *Awake!* issue every two months, plus the 32-page monthly *Watchtower* study edition). Despite ever-increasing circulation, we are still left with an astonishing drop in monthly magazine printing of 54.91% between 2005 and 2016.[65] Add to that the slew of books that were declared out-of-print in a memo dated November 2015, from golden oldies such as the *Revelation* book, the *Reasoning* book and the *Creation* book (all mentioned in previous chapters) to publications that were only released in recent years, i.e. *Live With Jehovah's Day in Mind* (2006), *"Come Be My Follower"* (2007), and *God's Word for Us Through Jeremiah* (2010),[66] and you get the distinct impression Watchtower is trying to distance itself from

---

65 The basis for these calculations is shown in Appendix G.

66 The discontinuation of these publications was announced in the November 2015 "Announcement to All Congregations" posted on all Kingdom Hall information boards. While some publications were completely discontinued, some (including *"Come Be My Follower,"* the *Daniel* book and the *Insight on the Scriptures* volumes) were discontinued with the option of being reissued at a later date.

printing as much as possible.[67] This makes no sense if you happen to believe that printed "spiritual food" is needed more urgently now, with Armageddon looming, than it was in 2005—and all the sense in the world when you factor in how costly printing is.

Then you have branch numbers. Not so long ago, Watchtower boasted 118 branches (for 2009), but by 2012 that figure had plummeted to 96. As of 2015, 89 branches were reported (a slight drop from 90 the year before). In the gung-ho, jet-setting days of Knorr, the organization prided itself on global expansion through colonizing new countries with branch offices, claiming this as evidence of God's blessing. But today's Slave has been quietly orchestrating the organization's retreat since 2010. As you might expect, Watchtower has downplayed the significance of this obvious downsizing. This is how the "merger" of a number of Central American branch offices with the Mexico branch was explained in a 2012 *Watchtower:*

> Because of this merger, the Bethel family in Mexico has become more multicultural and international. The influx of fellow believers from different lands has resulted in an interchange of encouragement. It is as if God took a huge eraser and eliminated national borders.

The reader is thus given the impression that the creation of a more multicultural Bethel family in Mexico and the elimination of national borders were the chief motivations for closing six branches, namely in Guatemala, Honduras, El Salvador,[68] Nicaragua, Costa

---

[67] No printed publications were released at all at the 2016 "Remain Loyal to Jehovah!" regional convention, the first time in living memory this has been the case.

[68] The *1990 Yearbook* describes the 1988 dedication ceremony of the El Salvador branch on page 26: "'Hail the Theocracy,

Rica and Panama. A more pragmatic reason is surely the realization of considerable savings by removing the expense of running facilities in all those countries.

Similar consolidation has been observed elsewhere. Iceland, Norway and Sweden are administered by Denmark's Scandinavian branch. Latvia, Estonia and Lithuania come under the Finland branch. New Zealand answers to Australia. Ireland answers to Britain. Austria, Switzerland and Luxembourg answer to the Central European branch located in Germany. As with the reductions in printing, the streamlining of Watchtower's global footprint makes sound business sense, but it is almost certainly borne of necessity due to the organization's diminished financial clout. If money were no object, Watchtower would undoubtedly prefer a full presence in all countries where there are Witnesses in significant numbers to be organized and administered.

A third compelling indication that Watchtower has money worries can be seen in its slashing of personnel. A letter read out to Bethel families worldwide on Wednesday, September 23, 2015, warned that, in addition to certain building projects being mothballed or canceled altogether, the number of Bethelites and special pioneers globally would be reduced. The following month, Samuel Herd read an announcement at the 2015 annual meeting that attempted to rationalize the cutbacks:[69]

---

ever increasing! Wondrous expansion is now taking place.' On Saturday, November 12, 1988, 22,091 voices joined together to sing those stirring words in celebration of the dedication of the new branch office and Bethel Home in the Central American country of El Salvador."

[69] The 2015 Herd announcement can currently be watched on YouTube.

> Every family head realizes that where the household income is limited, he must carefully budget available funds so that his wife and children will have the necessities of life. Well at Philippians chapter 1 verse 10 we are told to "make sure of the more important things." In harmony with this wise advice, we desire to give priority to those activities that contribute the most to the spiritual welfare of God's people and the advancement of the global preaching work.

It is hard to comprehend how reducing the number of special pioneers, who are able to dedicate 130 hours per month to preaching thanks to a monthly stipend from Watchtower, will contribute to the "advancement of the global preaching work." This point was raised by an individual claiming to be a jilted special pioneer from Germany. His open letter to the organization found its way onto a German ex-JW forum before finally reaching the ex-JW Reddit page. Here follows a partial translation:

> In the belief that the end is near and that the organization is [led] by Jehovah's spirit, I started pioneering in my youth. I [turned down getting] a good education in the hope that the organization needs me. Jehovah is the best employer, as I was told. And now you decided that my special pioneer service will end [on the first of] January 2016. I ask myself what changed that you do not need my service anymore after nearly 30 years? I am astonished that you advise me to serve as an normal pioneer in the future. If the end is near, why is my service as [a special pioneer] not necessary anymore? Is it the money? Am I too expensive for the organization?

Though one can sympathize that the services of someone who has sacrificed so much for the organization may have been so unceremoniously dispensed with, it seems fairly obvious that he (assuming he is credible) and other full-time Watchtower personnel *did* prove too expensive to maintain. Herd's announcement may have tried to frame the cuts as advantageous to the preaching work, but there can be no doubt that the need to "use available funds effectively" (as he would later say it in the same speech) was the primary imperative. As with the cuts in printing and branch numbers, these are not changes that a Watchtower flush with funds would eagerly make. What we are seeing is an organization forced to begrudgingly recalibrate its size to proportions that are more sustainable in relation to the money it can expect to receive in donations—a stream of revenue that is increasingly under threat.

To put it bluntly, Watchtower now finds itself at the wrong point in history. It was built to flourish and prosper in the 20th century, when anyone who was sufficiently persuasive and had access to a printing press could be guaranteed some kind of following. Now, though, the organization can no longer be the gatekeeper of information as it once was. It finds itself in the uncharted waters of the information age, in which spurious claims made by anyone can be thoroughly debunked in just a few clicks. The internet is proving lethal to a movement that was forged in the fires of ignorance, fear and credulity. The Slave may be able to convince their indoctrinated followers not to access websites and videos that dismantle their teachings, but they plainly cannot demand the same from the wider public from whom they *must* draw fresh converts in order to keep their heads above water.

Because the internet is so corrosive to its message, Watchtower is forced to rely on attracting new followers from developing countries with precious little online access. As already revealed in Chapter One, this is indeed where the most growth can be seen. But there are two notable problems with this strategy. Firstly, internet access in the developing world may be poor now, but realistically it can only improve. Google has already shown some commitment to making the internet freely available in the Third World. (Apart from humanitarian considerations, there are obvious financial incentives to Google expanding its reach in this way.) Secondly (and more pressingly), recruiting new followers from impoverished countries may keep Watchtower's membership numbers relatively buoyant, but the same cannot be said for its bank balance. Witnesses in such lands, where many are forced to live on less than a dollar a day, cannot be relied upon as a reliable source of revenue no matter how much the organization hounds them for donations. Growth in such countries thus creates a dangerous imbalance, because Watchtower is forced to allocate funds donated from wealthier countries in order to service Third World growth (by printing literature, building facilities, etc.)—but it is the wealthier countries where growth is slowing, thanks in large part to the internet. Put simply, Watchtower is spending funds from an ever-diminishing First World money pot on trying to find new followers in Third World lands where people are too poor to donate. This is clearly an unsustainable model, and I believe it lies at the heart of the organization's financial woes.

Compounding the problem is the mounting backlash over child abuse mishandling, which I will explore in more detail in Chapter Ten. Not only does Watchtower's reputation of covering up abuse severely handicap its ability to find fresh converts—there is also the drain on its resources from defending itself legally. And with each new case filed against Watchtower, more victims are emboldened to come forward. (If you happen to be a survivor of child abuse as a Jehovah's Witness, and Watchtower was liable in some way for your abuse, you would be well advised to sue the organization while there is still something to sue.)

Watchtower's strategy for addressing its increasingly toxic brand has been mostly to bury its head in the sand, pretend that everything is going swimmingly, and issue blanket denials when confronted by the press. The launch of JW.org in 2012 was an obvious attempt at bringing the internet to heel—but it was too little, too late. Statistics released by the organization show that its online propaganda tool is mostly preaching to the converted.[70]

Any organization facing the kind of PR nightmare besetting Watchtower would work feverishly to fix problems, implement reforms and issue apologies where necessary. If dwindling resources are an issue, an astute leadership would radically scale down operations to the bare minimum so that, rather than just keeping their heads above water, funds could start being set aside for a rainy day. But Watchtower does not consider itself to be just *any* organization. It is Jehovah's one true organization on earth; his sole channel with mankind. Watchtower must be seen to be not just *getting by*, but *thriving* under divine blessing. Any opposition to its teachings and practices must,

---

[70] The *2015 Yearbook* boasted that JW.org received 850,000,000+ total visits in the first two years from August 27, 2012, to August 31, 2014. This figure sounds impressive until you factor in the number of Jehovah's Witnesses—8 million. Assuming every active Witness visits their own official website at least once per week, you arrive at only a slightly lower figure of 832,000,000 visits over the two years (8,000,000 × 52 × 2).

by default, be the result of Satanic persecution. Ultimately, if the Slave can just hold on long enough, the winds of the apocalypse will be unleashed and it will find itself fully vindicated—its enemies vanquished. Such unbridled delusion at the helm is why I believe the eventual collapse of Watchtower is not a matter of if, but when.

Not only is Watchtower an obsolete dinosaur, an analog entity in a digital age—its undereducated, delusional leadership is devoid of the ingenuity and pragmatism needed to help it prosper long-term. The Slave is not nimble, shrewd or intelligent. It is the misshapen product of a kind of reverse evolution that has been moulding Watchtower's leadership since Knorr first started penning names for his Governing Body version 1.0 some day back in 1971. From that point forward, unquestioning, docile organization men have been whisked up the Watchtower ladder, while forward-thinking, progressive, intelligent visionaries like Raymond Franz have been deemed threats to the status quo and duly jettisoned or sidelined. The end product, after decades of picking the runts over the true leaders, is a Slave entirely unequipped for the 21st century; a Governing Body that can only ever plan for the short-term and is clueless when it comes to navigating the choppy waters of the information age.

Watchtower's only hope is to hunker down and make itself more like Scientology—a robust, highly-centralized cult sequestered in a smattering of compounds whose bark is much louder than its bite (thanks to the occasional Super Bowl ad). Witnesses who want to follow the Slave must do so from their own homes and keep the checks coming in. No more large-scale printing. No more Kingdom Halls or Assembly Halls—just the occasional glitzy gatherings for PR purposes and continued proselytizing on street corners to keep up appearances. Sure, the numbers will steadily fall as Witnesses begin to realize their religion is a mere shadow of its halcyon days—but if Scientology can bring itself to exaggerate its membership, so can Watchtower.[71] All that matters is that the leadership is comfortable and have a modest following who can sustain them for the next hundred years of waiting for the apocalypse.

Whether the Slave can bring itself to swallow humble pie and shrink Watchtower to quite this extent remains to be seen, but the present scale of the Governing Body's delusion suggests to me that they would sooner run the organization into the ground and claim bankruptcy as some attack by Satan's system and omen of the great tribulation than reduce it to a scale that, in their eyes, would represent capitulation and an open admission that they no longer enjoy Jehovah's backing.

Whatever happens to Watchtower, whether it collapses or somehow manages to soldier on in some form, one thing we can be certain of is that there will always be Jehovah's Witnesses. Religions, you see, are tenacious, virtually-indestructible things. They can exist long after their leaders have died—with

---

[71] A Scientology church spokeswoman, Beth Akiyama, is said to have estimated "10 million members affiliated with more than 5,000 groups and organizations in 156 countries" for a 2005 article in the *Pittsburgh Post-Gazette,* titled "Scientology Comes to Town." But according to a 2016 article by Scientology reporter Tony Ortega, the church is thought to have peaked at 100,000 members "around the year 1990," and as of 2013 was estimated to have a membership of "between 10 and 20 thousand." Ortega's article is titled "SCIENTOLOGY'S SPACE MAN: As of 2013, active Scientologists fewer than 20,000 worldwide."

or without organizations to service them. This fact is well demonstrated by the fact that Bible Students continue to exist to this day, more than a century after the predictions of their leader, Charles Taze Russell, failed spectacularly. (Miroslav, the Croatian MTS classmate who briefly featured in Chapter Four, and was instrumental in Dijana and I meeting, has since left the Witnesses to become a Bible Student. He has made several attempts to recruit me to join him in following the Pastor.)

If even the Pastor can keep a modest following a hundred years or more after his death, you can be certain there will always be a Slave of some kind and sufficient numbers who would do *anything* to prove their loyalty to it.

CHAPTER NINE

# Blood and Tears

*"This much have I learned: A man's life weighs more than glory, and a price paid in blood is a heavy reckoning."*
—Lloyd Alexander

IN 2016, Jehovah's Witnesses assembled at various locations around the world for their "Remain Loyal to Jehovah!" regional conventions. As can be easily surmised from the theme, the focus of the three-day event was to remind Witnesses of the importance of heeding the direction of the Governing Body in all aspects of life. "God's loyal love is more precious than life itself," the audience was advised in one talk.

To drill home this message of absolute loyalty, a number of videos were presented depicting Witnesses faced with various scenarios that would test their resolve to obey their leaders.[1] A final video, with a rousing musical score, featured as part of Sunday's concluding talk. It showed all characters from the previous videos basking in paradisaic conditions as a reward for their allegiance.

One of the characters revealed to have successfully made it into Paradise was a Russian man named Ser-

---

[1] I made these videos the subject of a special nine-part series on my YouTube channel, titled *Worst Convention Ever.*

gei. Sergei's fictional life story was the subject of seven videos shown on Friday afternoon. In the first video, Sergei is introduced as a young boy with a passion for playing the violin. When Sergei tells his father that he has been given an opportunity to join a program for young, gifted musicians, the response is emphatic. Sergei is barred from pursuing his talent professionally, because putting God's Kingdom first should take priority.

"You will be surrounded by people who don't love Jehovah," warns his father. "Can you handle that?"

"I don't know. But I really love it. And I'm not good at anything else! But I'm good at this!" pleads young Sergei, violin in hand. "Can I just try for a little bit?"

"I think it will make [things] only harder for you," his father replies, as Sergei finally concedes defeat. Apparently, all Witness parents are expected to similarly deprive their children of the chance to learn how to play instruments to a professional standard—or, for that matter, learn any skill that makes them stand out from the crowd and receive acclaim.

At various points in the series, Sergei is depicted enduring persecution under communism (Witnesses were banned in the Soviet era and continue to be censored and harassed in modern Russia) and resisting flattery from a JW friend who ends up vanishing from the congregation after reading an apostate leaflet.[2] The final video reveals Sergei to be a very sick man, with his grown daughter, Irina, visiting him in the hospital. Irina hands him an old photo taken when he

---

[2] The "vanishing" is quite literal. The apostate is shown fading from his seat at the Kingdom Hall with a vacant, miserable expression on his face.

was a child. A young Sergei can be seen clutching a violin beside his father.[3]

"I didn't know you played the violin," she says.

"I lost interest in it, I guess," says Sergei. (The audience by now understands that he "lost interest" after having his ambitions extinguished by his father.)

A doctor enters the room flanked by a colleague. After some terse small talk, he gets down to business.

"We have received your test results. I wish I had better news."

"Okay, go ahead," says Sergei.

"We have to operate."

"Alright, but remember—no blood!" insists Sergei, waving his finger.

"I will do my best, but your best option is a blood transfusion. Without it, your chances are much lower. Do you understand what I'm trying to say?"

"Yeah, I understand. And thank you, doctor, for doing your best and leaving this choice to me. My stand is the same."

"Very well. We will schedule the surgery for the end of this week. And, er, we have to run a few more tests this afternoon, but I will give you a few minutes first."

"Thank you," mutters Sergei as the doctors exit the room. He and his daughter are left to process what is happening.

---

[3] The daughter's name is revealed to be Irina in the series of videos, which begins with her handing Sergei the photo—thus prompting his trip down memory lane, which forms the basis for the "flashback" videos to follow. The same scene in which Irina hands Sergei the photo is repeated in the final video, allowing us to see his response.

"I love you, Papa," says Irina, hugging him. "I know you'll make it through. Mama always said you were strong."

"I love you, too, sweetheart," replies Sergei. "And, should something happen, keep your hope anchored on that wonderful day—the day when your mom and I will be reunited with you in the new world. Promise me?"

Irina hesitates as a doctor returns to the room, apparently to collect her father. Sergei wipes a tear from her cheek. Before leaving, she speaks the words he wants to hear: "I promise. I'll see you outside."

Now alone, Sergei removes his glasses and, with steely determination, utters the following passage from Romans 8:38-39:

> For I am convinced that neither death nor life nor angels nor governments nor things now here nor things to come nor powers nor height nor depth nor any other creation will be able to separate us from God's love that is in Christ Jesus our Lord.

"For I am convinced," repeats Sergei as the camera fades, leaving the viewer guessing as to whether he will be forced to pay the ultimate price for refusing blood.

Of course, the above never happened. It is a fictional drama intended as propaganda. But it is also a scenario that is played out in countless hospitals all over the world whenever blood is the only option for saving the life of a Witness. And the Governing Body wants Jehovah's Witnesses to know exactly how they should respond when the chips are down: loyalty to Jehovah (or more accurately: "Jehovah's organization") comes first; preservation of life comes second.

The depiction of Sergei's apparent martyrdom was introduced with a symposium talk titled "Be Loyal as Jesus Was—When Facing Death." The speakers assigned to deliver this talk were required by the Governing Body's Teaching Committee to say words similar to the following:

> Many people would preserve their own life at all costs
>
> Jehovah's people view life as a gift from God and will not be disloyal to him in an attempt to preserve life (Ps 36:9)
>
> Death cannot separate us from God's love for us [Read Romans 8:38, 39] However, the choices we make when facing death could distance us from Jehovah when we need him most

Thus "preserving life" can be an act of disloyalty if the wrong means are employed. To resort to illicit measures in furthering one's existence would be to *distance a Witness from his or her Creator*, causing him or her to lose out on being resurrected in the future Paradise. As one 1970 *Watchtower* put it: "How foolish it would be to gamble away the prospect of life eternal for the very uncertain promise of a cure by blood transfusion!" And the current Bible study tool of Jehovah's Witnesses, the book *What Does the Bible Really Teach?*, offers the following explanation on pages 130–131:

> Would a Christian break God's law just to stay alive a little longer in this system of things? Jesus said: "Whoever wants to save his life will lose it, but whoever loses his life for my sake will find it." (Matthew 16:25) We do not want to die. But if we tried to save our present life by breaking God's law, we would be in danger of losing everlasting life.

To underscore this threat of forgoing everlasting life, Governing Body member Anthony Morris III, on at least two occasions, used his concluding remarks at the 2016 regional convention to revisit a heartbreaking experience from an old *Awake!* article.[4] The story was that of a teenager named Joshua Walker who died refusing blood in 1994, aged just 15.

Joshua was diagnosed with acute myeloid leukemia and treated at a hospital in Canada. Under Canadian law, so long as two doctors could attest to him being a *mature minor*, he could legally decline life-saving treatment. Two doctors at the hospital (the doctor treating him and the department head) concluded he met the criteria, having spoken with him personally and noted that he was "very adamant" about his stance. The fact that the Walkers' family doctor also deemed him a mature minor meant that Joshua had three doctors supporting his position—so, more than enough. Despite this, the hospital chose to pursue a court decision in order to cover itself legally. This resulted in a judge ruling that Joshua did not have the right to refuse treatment, which meant that doctors could transfuse him despite his protests.

Joshua's lawyers, at least one of whom was a Witness, took the case to the Court of Appeal.[5] A panel of

---

[4] Conventions are held on different dates for different locations. Not all conventions feature Governing Body members as speakers, but occasionally they will appear at such events—especially when it is an international convention. Morris made the comments that follow on at least two occasions. The relevant remarks can be seen on Part 7 of my "Worst Convention Ever" YouTube series, as well as on another YouTube video that can be found by searching "No Blood Governing Body Member."

[5] The *Awake!* article does not specify whether Watchtower was directly involved in Joshua's legal representation. However, the only one of Joshua's lawyers named in the article, Daniel Pole, is (or was) certainly a Witness. According to an article dated August 1, 2012 on the *Legal Feeds* blog, Pole was once censured by a judge for failing to disclose to a former client who left part of his estate to Watchtower that, as a Witness elder, he had a conflict of interest. (URL: http://www.canadian

five judges overruled the lower court judge, sealing Joshua's fate. The article that appears in *Awake!* makes for painful reading for anyone yet to be convinced that life should be surrendered if this is required by unfounded religious dogma. The writer praises the legal victory and acclaims Joshua's role in paving the way for others to refuse medical treatment.

When quoting from the article at the convention, Morris appeared moved by Joshua's story. "Well, this is quite touching," he said. "Having raised two sons, it can get emotional." His voice then trembled slightly as he read the following part of the account:[6]

> One night when Josh was in the hospital, he said: "Mom, a lot of times when you go to the bathroom or go to get Dad, the doctors come in and say: 'Josh, you need a blood transfusion. Without it you will die. We want to help you.' 'Then please respect my wishes about blood,' I would reply. I told one doctor who tried to get me to take blood: 'You may think I'm crazy, but I have all my thinking abilities. I just want to live by Jehovah's law on blood. He knows what is best for us. The best thing for me is to respect the sanctity of life, and if I die I will live again.'"

Joshua almost certainly was not crazy, but the expectations imposed on him by his religion unquestionably were—and his parents, though themselves deluded, were at least partly responsible for his death.

---

lawyermag.com/legalfeeds/1439/judge-criticizes-lawyer-for-failing-to-disclose-connection-to-church.html)

[6] I have no reason to doubt that Morris' emotional reaction was genuine, at least on some level. One of the most disturbing elements of cult indoctrination is that it can allow the mind to become so partitioned that someone like Morris can be anguished by reading about a tragedy while refusing to take action to stop the same fate befalling others. The sincerity of such delusion in no way dilutes the evil it can produce.

"We don't want Josh to die," Joshua's father Jerry reportedly told *The Evening Times Globe* (whose coverage was sufficiently pro-Watchtower to be cited in *Awake!*). "We're doing everything medically to keep him alive." (We can safely assume he meant "everything medically" *apart from allowing blood.*)

"We're not here to watch him die," Jerry continued. "We're here to get that boy better, so he can walk out and go back to his trains, go back to the Kingdom Hall, to his meetings and his service, and maybe go back to some basketball." But there would be no meetings, service (door-to-door preaching) or basketball for Joshua. Once the last attempts to save him through legal avenues had been successfully neutralized, Joshua could only wait to die in his hospital bed—convinced to the very end that his outlook was far less bleak than it actually was.

***A photo of Joshua Walker from the January 22, 1995 "Awake!" magazine***

"Jeffrey, you stop crying," Joshua is recorded as telling his brother. "I'm a winner either way. Don't worry about me." The *Awake!* article explains that Joshua was indeed victorious because "if he recovered from his illness, he was a winner; if he didn't and he died and was resurrected into the Paradise earth, then he was undoubtedly a winner!"

"I'm in Jehovah's hands," Joshua reportedly told his mother, Sandra, on another occasion. "I want all of you to stay in the truth so you can welcome me back in the resurrection. I can tell you this, Mom, with all certainty: I know Jehovah is definitely going to bring me back in the resurrection. He has read my heart, and I truly love him."

As the end neared for Joshua, his mother resigned herself to her loss. "Josh, as much as I hate to let go, it would only be selfish on our part to want you to stay," she told her son. (Apparently, wanting your children to outlive you is selfish.)

"Mom, I know, and really I am kind of tired of fighting," he replied.

Almost as alarming as the clear delusion of both Joshua and his parents is the extent to which the media lavished them with praise for their stand, at least if the quotes reproduced in *Awake!* are to be taken at face value. In an article titled "A 'Minor' Victory" (note the sickly play on words), the *Telegraph-Journal* reported:

> The New Brunswick Court of Appeal's decision that 15-year-old Joshua Walker has the right to consent to or refuse medical treatment is a victory not just for Jehovah's Witnesses, but for us all. . . . Sometimes the decisions an individual makes may seem too hard for society to bear, especially hard if the life or death of a young person is at stake. But even harder to bear would be a society that routinely violates the bodies and souls of its citizens. Joshua Walker has done his part to keep us safe from that.

Nobody would argue that "a society that routinely violates the bodies and souls of its citizens" would be an intolerable proposition, but the journalist responsible for this piece misses the point entirely by spinning the court's decision to allow Joshua to martyr himself as a repudiation of totalitarianism. Joshua was not victorious against totalitarianism—he was a *victim* of it.

Joshua had been coerced by a religious hierarchy into believing he would forfeit eternal life with his family if he allowed his doctors to perform a routine medical procedure. It was the duty of his country's judiciary to shield him, a minor, from a cult that prizes its own dogma and authority over the lives of its followers. Instead, pro-Watchtower lawyers were allowed to work their magic and convince the judges at the Court of Appeal that allowing a child to be manipulated by his religious leaders into killing himself was a "victory" for democracy.

To add insult to injury, twenty years later, the story of Joshua would be leveraged for propaganda value on a convention platform by a senior representative of the same organization that effectively killed him. After reading the *Awake!* article, Anthony Morris III would laud Joshua's martyrdom as "a good example of faith in the face of incredible stress and persecution." (It would appear that by doing everything they could to save Joshua's life, his doctors were persecuting him.) "And when he's resurrected you'll hear more from him, because Jehovah loves that little fella," added Morris to applause from the convention audience. In their hijacked minds, Joshua *must* be making his comeback in the near future, because one seventh of Jehovah's "faithful and discreet slave" has just said so.

Incredibly, the Joshua story is not the only time the Governing Body has celebrated the death of a child of Witness parents due to their blood prohibition. A 1994 issue of *Awake!*—carrying the title "Youths Who Put God First"—was dedicated to recounting multiple, similar stories. The article summary on the inside cover romanticized the issue in this way:

> In former times thousands of youths died for putting God first. They are still doing it, only today the drama is played out in hospitals and courtrooms, with blood transfusions the issue.

Three smiling children feature on the front cover. The next thirteen pages then tell, story by story, of how they were never allowed to make it to adulthood.[7]

***The front and inside cover of the May 22, 1994 "Awake!" magazine***

Adrian from Newfoundland died on September 13, 1993, aged 15, having refused treatment with blood for a stomach tumor. ("I could just not live with myself if I am given blood," he told his doctors.) Lenae from California died nine days later on September 22, 1993, aged

[7] The May 22, 1994 *Awake!* magazine is commonly understood to feature 26 martyred Witness children, because 26 faces are shown on the front cover. However, of the 26 faces, only the three in the foreground appear to be actual victims of refusing blood whose stories are told in the magazine. The rest are apparently generic pictures of children selected by the art department.

12, having similarly refused treatment for leukemia. ("I don't want any blood or blood products," she insisted. "I would rather accept death, if necessary, than to break my promise to Jehovah God to do his will.") Lisa from Toronto, also a leukemia sufferer, died at home in the arms of her parents on an unknown date after refusing blood. (Lisa had threatened to "fight and kick the IV pole down and rip out the IV no matter how much it would hurt, and poke holes in the blood" if transfused against her will.)

The stories of two other children, Crystal Moore and Ernestine Gregory, are related in an attempt to balance out the otherwise morbid narrative. Ernestine, a 17-year-old leukemia patient, is described as forcibly receiving blood "in spite of her vigorous protests" after doctors were granted a court order overruling her and her parents. She later prevailed in having the order overturned, blocking any further transfusions. The story concludes as follows:

> Ernestine had no further transfusions, and she did not die from her leukemia. Ernestine stood firm and put God first, like the other young people mentioned previously. Each one received "power beyond what is normal."—2 Corinthians 4:7.

Crystal, meanwhile, is said to have declined blood for her "inflammatory bowel disease" after being told by doctors that she would otherwise die in 24 hours. As it turned out, no blood was needed. Crystal is described as being later discharged from hospital and making a full recovery. Despite writing of three other Witness children who were not so fortunate, the *Awake!* writer has no qualms in using Crystal's apparent mistaken prognosis to drive home his point:

> When doctors wanting court orders to give blood declare blatantly that if the judge doesn't comply

immediately, the patient will die, let them remember the case of Crystal Moore.

Rather than weakening the case for court intervention, these stories demonstrate the clear duty of both judges and legislators to protect children from being made to pay the ultimate price for their indoctrination as Jehovah's Witnesses. While it can be argued that adult Witnesses have the right to decline treatment, the same cannot be true of minors who do so out of compliance with beliefs planted in their minds by their parents—no matter how convinced they may appear.

Children are hardwired to trust their parents and believe what they are told—especially in matters of life and death. It is this basic, primal trust that makes child indoctrination so successful as the driving force behind religion. But whereas most religious dogma passed from parent to child is only harmful insofar as it is not true (or cannot be substantiated by evidence), Jehovah's Witness beliefs have the potential to end a child's life.

Thankfully, legislators and judiciaries are becoming wise to this lethal situation and stories are emerging of the state successfully intervening to save Witness children from their parents. For example, in 2013, a 10-month-old baby girl in New Zealand, diagnosed with neuroblastoma, was taken under court guardianship after her Witness parents attempted to deny her life-saving treatment with blood products. Justice Helen Winkelmann, in placing the child under High Court guardianship to allow treatment, recognized the dilemma of the parents. "Their ongoing support and care for [the baby] is crucial," she said. "And the making of these orders, I hope, resolves the difficult position they presently find themselves in."

In commenting on Winkelmann's ruling, Peter Le Cren, a health lawyer and former medicolegal counsel, indicated that such cases are relatively common in New Zealand, arising on approximately a yearly basis.[8] Le Cren even suggested that Witness parents are usually relieved when the matter is taken out of their hands. "It gives the clinicians and the family involved a lot more comfort having the sanction of the court," he explained. "These families are in a very difficult situation. They feel hugely torn." Similar stories continue to surface in other countries and give one hope that being born to Witness parents does not need to be a death sentence for all such children who end up in need of blood.[9] Even so, *some* Witness children are bound to slip through the net, and clearly they are at substantially higher risk than children whose parents do *not* believe receiving someone else's blood will harm your prospects in the afterlife.

By now you may be wondering why Jehovah's Witnesses feel so strongly about blood transfusions that they are prepared to let their own children die by not receiving them. The short answer is: Witnesses view blood as sacred—as representing the very soul or life of a creature. They consider the only legitimate use of blood to be sacrificial, i.e. the pouring out of the blood of Jesus in redeeming mankind. They understand any other use of blood, especially taking it into the body in any form (including one's own stored blood), as strictly prohibited under the law given to Moses as recorded at

---

[8] Ian McEwan makes the quandary faced by a judge intervening in such a case the basis for his 2014 novel *The Children Act*.

[9] We have tried to document some of these stories on JWsurvey.org, which can be found by clicking on the "Blood transfusions" menu link.

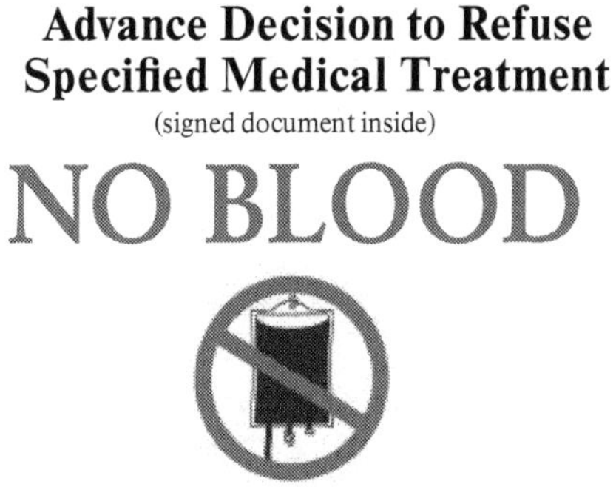


***A "no blood" warning on a "Durable Power of Attorney," or "blood card," carried by Witnesses (the document is normally carried in the purse or wallet, and is designed to be folded in such a way that if medical staff check the person's belongings, this is the first part they will see)***

Leviticus chapter 17.[10] This law, they believe, was transferred across from Judaism into Christianity at Acts 15:29 when the apostles and elders told the early Christians to "keep abstaining from things sacrificed to idols, from blood, from what is strangled."

Clearly, the Bible writers could not possibly have envisioned the medical use of blood to save lives when penning this command. It would not be until the early 19th century that the first successful blood transfusions would be performed on humans. Even so, Watchtower

---

[10] The prohibition against donating one's own blood in anticipation of future use was clearly spelled out in a 2000 *Watchtower* article: "Occasionally, a doctor will urge a patient to deposit his own blood weeks before surgery (preoperative autologous blood donation, or PAD) so that if the need arises, he could transfuse the patient with his own stored blood. However, such collecting, storing, and transfusing of blood directly contradicts what is said in Leviticus and Deuteronomy. Blood is not to be stored; it is to be poured out—returned to God, as it were." Interestingly, the use of stored blood for medical purposes is given the green light when it comes to blood derivatives (fractions and vaccines), which Witnesses are allowed.

has become extremely adept at convincing Jehovah's Witnesses that abstinence from eating blood also means abstinence from receiving it intravenously. (*see box*)

FOR WITNESSES

## BLOOD TRANSFUSIONS

More than likely you are familiar with the importance of correctly understanding the principle behind a divine law. By appreciating the intent of a law, it is much easier to discern how it is to be applied. With this in mind, it would be worthwhile revisiting the words found at Acts 15:29—especially the counsel that Christians are to "keep abstaining from things sacrificed to idols, from blood, from what is strangled, and from sexual immorality."* What were the reasons for this guidance? And to what extent were Christians intended to observe it?

In 1 Corinthians chapter 8, Paul wrote that he had nothing against those who eat food sacrificed to idols because, as he put it, "we know that an idol is nothing in the world and that there is no God but one." Nevertheless, he urged his readers to refrain from eating such food so as to avoid stumbling others. "But keep watching that your right to choose does not somehow become a stumbling block to those who are weak," he cautioned in verse 9.

It was for this same reason that the prohibition on eating blood, a vestige from the Mosaic law code that had already been nailed to the torture stake, was to be nonethe-

* In case you are wondering why "sexual immorality" was included in this list, this is because the apostles and elders were quoting from a passage in Leviticus 17:1 to 18:27—a part of the Law of Moses that was read aloud at the synagogues every Sabbath. This list of four requirements also appears in the exact same order in Acts 21:25, and formed the mandatory rules for both Israelites and foreigners living in ancient Israel. In other words, the writers were reciting a list of laws that were familiar to the reader, having been drummed into the Jewish people by rote. They were not necessarily of equal moral importance.

less observed by Christians. (Colossians 2:13, 14) There was nothing inherently wrong with eating blood—it was simply a courtesy to Christians who had converted from Judaism and who might be easily offended on seeing other Christians eating something they considered sacred. As Charles Taze Russell explained in a 1909 *Watch Tower* article on the matter, "it was advisable that the Gentile Christians abstain from the use of their liberty in this direction, out of deference to the weaker brethren, Jews and Gentiles, who could not so deeply philosophize and whose consciences might be injured."

Despite the context of the verse helping us to understand its true intent regarding stumbling, Watchtower continues to lean primarily on Acts 15:29 as the basis for its blood transfusion prohibition—a prohibition that was only introduced in 1945—a quarter of a century after Jesus supposedly chose the organization in 1919. (You have to wonder: if abstaining from blood transfusions is so urgent and has divine backing, why did it take 25 years for the "faithful slave" to figure this out?)

It is also worth pondering whether the writer of Acts really intended for Christians living centuries in the future to lay down their lives by refusing medical treatment with blood. For one thing, blood transfusions were unheard of in the first century, so it is impossible that the writers could have had such an extreme application in mind.

Watchtower attempts to sidestep this argument by saying that if something is prohibited for humans, it should not matter how it is taken into the body. "Suppose a doctor were to tell you to abstain from alcoholic beverages," argues the *Bible Teach* book on page 131. "Would that simply mean that you should not drink alcohol but that you could have it injected into your veins? Of course not! Likewise, abstaining from blood means not taking it into our bodies at all."

This is fallacious reasoning, rooted in a poor analogy. Both blood and alcohol are broken down by the digestive system when ingested, but they behave completely differently when entering the circulatory system. Injecting alcohol straight into your blood could cause serious harm (because the body has not had time to break it down), whereas once blood enters your body it circulates and functions as blood. Also, doctors would have no hesitation in using alcohol to clean the wound on an alcoholic patient if necessary.

Finally, before resolving to lay down your life in observance of Watchtower's blood teaching, you would do well do to research the rabbinic principle of *pikuach nephesh*, which was frequently appealed to by Jesus when trying to reason with the Jewish religious leaders. Jesus argued that the preservation of life takes priority over fastidious observance of rules that are intended to enhance life, not terminate it. "If you have one sheep and that sheep falls into a pit on the Sabbath, is there a man among you who will not grab hold of it and lift it out?" Jesus is said to have asked. "How much more valuable is a man than a sheep!"

Now that you have some grasp of the basic reason for Watchtower's blood prohibition, you may be wondering how it originated and what penalties are imposed on a Witness who breaks the rules.

The first material condemning blood transfusions surfaced in the 1940s during the early presidency of Knorr. Incredibly, in a 1940 issue of *Consolation* (a forerunner to *Awake!*) printed under the tenure of Knorr's predecessor, a brief story was featured, titled "The Mending of a Heart," describing a blood transfusion without a hint of condemnation:

> In New York city a housewife in moving a boarder's things accidentally shot herself through the heart with his revolver. She was rushed to a hospital, her left breast was cut around, four ribs were cut away, the heart was lifted out, three stitches were taken,

> one of the attending physicians in the great emergency gave a quart of his blood for transfusion, and today the woman lives and smiles gaily over what happened to her in the busiest 23 minutes of her life.

One would be forgiven for assuming blood transfusions were practically *advisable* for Witnesses based on the above, but by 1945 the tone of the organization's literature had completely changed. A 1945 *Watchtower* article insisted that "it behooves all worshipers of Jehovah who seek eternal life in his new world of righteousness to respect the sanctity of blood" by not taking blood "directly into the human body." By 1961, accepting blood transfusions carried the punishment of disfellowshipping. A Witness who donated or accepted blood, or promoted doing so, was to be considered "deliberately opposed to God's requirements." "As a rebellious opposer and unfaithful example to fellow members of the Christian congregation he must be cut off therefrom by disfellowshiping," the article decreed.[11]

As things currently stand, a Witness who accepts a blood transfusion will be considered as having disassociated from the faith (in other words: signaled that they no longer consider themselves to be a Witness) if they do not express regret for their decision. This is spelled out clearly in the following instructions from pages 111–112 of the *Shepherd* book (bold in the original):

> **Willingly and unrepentantly taking blood.** If someone willingly takes blood, perhaps because of being under extreme pressure, the committee should obtain the facts and determine the individual's attitude. If he is repentant, the committee

[11] Do not ask me why, but in the early 1980s Watchtower added an extra "p" to the word "disfellowshipping." I guess "new light" comes in a variety of forms.

> should provide spiritual assistance in the spirit of Galatians 6:1 and Jude 22, 23. Since he is spiritually weak, he would not qualify for special privileges for a period of time, and it may be necessary to remove certain basic privileges. Depending on the circumstances, the committee may also need to arrange for an announcement to the congregation: **"The elders have handled a matter having to do with [name of person]. You will be glad to know that spiritual shepherds are endeavoring to render assistance."** On the other hand, if the elders on the committee determine that he is unrepentant, they should announce his disassociation.

Identical instructions for one who "willfully and unrepentantly takes a blood transfusion" and "thereby chooses to reject the Scriptural sanctity of blood" are found in an even more secretive Watchtower document titled *Correspondence Guidelines.* These guidelines are issued to key staff at Bethels around the world—especially staff who are responsible for answering letters from elders or rank and file Witnesses. They contain cookie-cutter responses to a long list of scenarios in which Watchtower doctrine might apply. (A 2011 version of the guidelines was leaked by an insider in October 2015.) Interestingly, the document advises that there should be no penalties for a doctor or nurse who administers blood to a patient under the instructions of a superior:

> A Christian who is a nurse or a doctor respects the Scriptures and therefore would not recommend or order a blood transfusion for a patient. If he or she as an employee is not responsible for deciding the matter and is directed by a superior to administer a transfusion to a non-Witness, whether to obey is a matter for personal, conscientious decision.—*w99* 4/15 28-30; *w75* 4/1 215-16.

However, according to the same document, a Witness farmer who allows a blood transfusion for one of his livestock should expect a slapped wrist at the very least:

> It is not proper for a Christian to administer a blood transfusion to an animal owned by him or to authorize another to do so.—*w64* 2/15 127-8.

Hence, the prohibition on blood even extends into the animal kingdom, despite the fact that animals are not supposed to be party to the arrangements by which Christ is said to have redeemed mankind. You will have to ask Watchtower for the reasoning behind this and to what extent the rules apply. Would a Witness zookeeper be forced to find alternative employment if asked to feed unbled meat to the lions? Would a Witness biologist be liable for disassociation if he unrepentantly breeds mosquitoes or leaches for release into the wild? The hypothetical scenarios are almost endless.

As incredible as it may seem that Watchtower has devoted so much thought to the various nuances of its blood policy, this should come as no surprise to those familiar with the organization's history. Watchtower's preoccupation with medicine and trying to regulate what forms of it are considered unacceptable for Christians stretches even further back than the end of the Second World War.

During Rutherford's presidency, numerous articles spewing all manner of medical quackery appeared in the organization's literature—most notably in *The Golden Age* (later renamed *Consolation* before finally becoming *Awake!*). All human ailments, it was declared, "have their start in the intestines." Pacifiers for babies were declared "one of the chief causes of diseased and enlarged tonsils and adenoid growths." Air baths, in which one was to "bob up and down for a while" after stripping naked, were claimed to be "good for preventing colds." X-rays were to be avoided, because "they are destructive and sure to harm the grandchildren of those exposed to them." Aluminum cookware was deemed "a curse to humanity," and it was recommended that its manufacture and use "should be forbidden by law." Kerosene (also known as lamp oil), when "applied to cuts" was said to allow them to "heal sooner." Suicide, it was advised, was preferable to having your tonsils removed. ("It's cheaper and less painful," suggested a 1926 *Golden Age*.) The germ theory of disease was dismissed in a 1924 *Golden Age*, which announced that "it has never been proven that a single disease is due to germs." And in 1929, the writers of the same magazine even felt moved to offer advice on sleeping. "Sleep on the right side or flat on your back," the reader was urged, "with the head toward the north so as to get benefit of the earth's magnetic currents."

We cannot be certain as to who was individually responsible for each of these eruptions of absurdity, which apparently burst forth from heaven into the Slave's printed "spiritual food."[12] We can, however, acknowledge that Rutherford allowed it to proliferate, thus paving the way for the organization's fixation with health and medicine to spill over into official dogma.

For example, vaccination (which according to a 1921 *Golden Age* "never prevented anything and never will, and is the most barbarous practice") was banned for Witnesses right up to 1952, when a *Watchtower* admitted

---

12 Clayton Woodworth was editor of *The Golden Age* and almost certainly wrote the majority of its spurious medical content. Woodworth, who also coauthored *The Finished Mystery*, died in 1951 and is widely regarded as having played a key role in the origins of the blood teaching.

the matter was "for the individual that has to face it to decide for himself." And from 1967 through 1980, Witnesses were blocked from receiving organ transplants, deemed by the organization to be tantamount to cannibalism. (Witnesses were also warned of the possibility of "personality transplant" from donor organs. "The recipient in some cases has seemed to adopt certain personality factors of the person from whom the organ came," cautioned a 1975 *Watchtower*.)[13]

The obvious problem facing any religious group that prohibits certain medical treatments is that once it starts down such a road there is no turning back. The leaders may later see reason and want to reverse their prohibition, but they cannot do so without automatically acknowledging liability for all the lives lost while it was in place.

It is all very well telling Witnesses that they are now permitted to receive vaccinations or organ transplants, but what about all the children who died due to not being vaccinated before 1952? Or what recourse is there for all those who died refusing organ transplants between 1967 and 1980? How are these victims, or their families, to be compensated for Watchtower's blunder in trying to determine *and dictate* God's will in this area? The Governing Body faces a similar problem with the organization's blood prohibition: they cannot

[13] Incredibly, the risk of personality transplant was cited among the reasons to abstain from blood in a September 15, 1961 *Watchtower* article. The article quotes a Dr. Américo Valério (a "Brazilian doctor and surgeon for over forty years") as saying: "Moral insanity, sexual perversions, repression, inferiority complexes, petty crimes—these often follow in the wake of a blood transfusion." The article then bemoans the fact that "organizations whose blood supply is considered reliable obtain blood for transfusion from criminals who are known to have such characteristics."

abandon it without acknowledging that it has needlessly and recklessly killed generations of Witnesses. The only thing they can do is try to phase it out, so that gradually, without anyone noticing, blood becomes increasingly acceptable. We saw the first move in this direction at the dawn of the 21st century.

In a 2000 *Watchtower*, a distinction was made between what are widely considered the primary components of blood (red cells, white cells, platelets and plasma) and "fractions" derived from these. After listing the components, the article stated:

> Jehovah's Witnesses hold that accepting whole blood or any of those four primary components violates God's law. Significantly, keeping to this Bible-based position has protected them from many risks, including such diseases as hepatitis and AIDS that can be contracted from blood.
>
> However, since blood can be processed beyond those primary components, questions arise about fractions derived from the primary blood components. How are such fractions used, and what should a Christian consider when deciding on them?

The article went on to give examples of how "doctors might prescribe injections of gamma globulin, extracted from the blood plasma" or how platelets could be processed "to extract a wound-healing factor."[14] The writer then asked:

---

[14] We can be grateful that, in allowing gamma globulin injections, Watchtower so readily ignores its strong stance against the harvesting of blood. As Ray Franz notes in *In Search of Christian Freedom:* "To produce sufficient gamma globulin for one injection by syringe (a vaccination persons, including Jehovah's Witnesses, traveling to certain southern countries may take as protection against cholera) close to 3 liters of blood are needed as the source of supply. This is still more blood than is generally employed for a common blood transfusion. And again, the gamma globulin is drawn from blood that

> Should Christians accept these fractions in medical treatment? We cannot say. The Bible does not give details, so a Christian must make his own conscientious decision before God.

Hence, suddenly Witnesses had some degree of choice. As with vaccinations and organ transplants, "new light" had come to the rescue—at least partially. It turned out the apostles and older men in Acts 15:29 had more in mind when talking about "abstaining from blood" than their terse statement originally implied. This was brilliantly highlighted by Paul Grundy with his revised version of the same verse on JWfacts.com:

> . . . keep abstaining from things sacrificed to idols and from blood, [that is; whole blood and four fractionated components, namely red cells, white cells, platelets and plasma. However, one may freely partake of other components or the aforementioned components provided they have been further fractionated, unless your conscience should disallow these too.] and from things strangled . . .

As welcome as it was (and still is) that Witnesses living in the 21st century and in urgent need of blood products have slightly improved survival odds than their counterparts across the millennial divide, there is still no escaping the minefield of contradictions thrown up by the rule change. In his book *In Search of Christian Freedom*, Ray Franz reproduced correspondence from an associate that brutally exposed the absurdity of the fractions provision:

> The blood, it is claimed, belongs to God. But that is conveniently forgotten when the use of blood

---

is stored, not 'poured out.'" According to a 2005 medical paper titled *Clinical Uses of Intravenous Immunoglobulin:* "Intravenous immunoglobulin (IVIG) [another name for gamma globulin] is a blood product prepared from the serum of between 1,000 and 15,000 donors per batch."

> "fractions" is pronounced tolerable! But it would hardly do to accept for any secular use what exclusively belongs to God, because that would be the same as using stolen property! A stolen car is a stolen car and it would not make the theft more tolerable if the car is separated into "primary components," say the motor, coach and the transmission, and then separated further into "fractions" such as carburetor, pistons, hood, doors and drive shaft. Only if the car is not stolen would one have the right to take it apart and use or sell it as small parts. And if the car is not stolen, all parts, both big and small, can properly be separated and used at will. So if blood "fractions" can be tolerated, certainly the "major components" and even whole blood can!

The argument is compelling. If you are going to insist that blood belongs to God and the only acceptable use for it is in divinely-mandated sacrifice (aside from which it should be poured out on the ground) you must accept that it should not be used in medicine *at all* if you are going to be consistent. Something that is stolen does not become *unstolen* simply by dismantling it into its various smaller components.

A further problem with the fractions provision is the way Watchtower has arbitrarily applied religious significance to the major components of blood. If you put a vial of blood into a laboratory centrifuge and spin it for a while, you will find that the red blood cells naturally drift toward the bottom, the clear plasma lurches toward the top, and the white cells and platelets form a "buffy coat" sitting between the two. That is how blood is fractionated into its component parts. But what would the Bible writers have known about laboratory centrifuges? Why is the Creator's view of blood components established according to how they respond to centrifugal forces? Why is physics the final arbiter in determining the religious significance of the material making up your body?

Though red blood cells, white blood cells, plasma and platelets indeed perform vital functions, it turns out there are parts of these major components without which they would be rendered almost useless. For example, the hemoglobin in red blood cells accounts for over 15% of the volume of your blood. It is the protein responsible for circulating oxygen throughout your body. It is the reason your blood is red! If you were to somehow remove the membrane, or wrapper, from a red blood cell, you would mostly be left with this oozing, red protein. If you are looking for a substance that is most responsible for the basic function of blood (i.e. the oxygenation of your body cells and removal of carbon dioxide) you would be hard-pressed to find a better candidate than hemoglobin. 97% of the oxygen carried through your veins and arteries is riding on hemoglobin molecules (the remaining 3% gets dissolved in the plasma). And yet, according to Watchtower, though having red blood cells transfused would be breaking God's law, if you could somehow remove the wrapper and use the hemoglobin inside —this would be fine.

Of course, injecting raw hemoglobin will not do you much good (it can actually do quite a lot of harm) which is why scientists are scrambling to develop "artificial blood" that can exploit the properties of hemoglobin safely while having a much longer shelf life than natural blood.[15] At present, HBOCs (hemoglo-

---

[15] Early candidates for viable artificial blood products included PolyHeme, Hemospan and Hemopure, but of these all but Hemospan seem to have fallen by the wayside. A 2010 article in *The Independent* indicated research into this and other

bin-based oxygen carriers) are still in development, but once widely available they *will be allowed* for Witnesses according to Watchtower's current rules on fractions. Below is a section of a worksheet that appeared in a 2006 *Our Kingdom Ministry* newsletter. As you can see, Witnesses are allowed to check to say they are prepared to receive hemoglobin if this is available:

| | |
|---|---|
| **HEMOGLOBIN—33% OF RED CELLS**<br>A protein that transports oxygen throughout the body and carbon dioxide to the lungs. Products being developed from human or animal hemoglobin could be used to treat patients with acute anemia or massive blood loss. | __ I accept hemoglobin<br>or<br>__ I refuse hemoglobin |

The significance of this is not to be understated. If you are reading this book years or decades in the future, it is possible you are already living at a time when the death of Jehovah's Witnesses due to refusal of blood transfusions is almost unheard of, because hemoglobin-based artificial blood is, by your time, in common use. Of course, Watchtower would undoubtedly laud this as proof that its pioneering stance on bloodless medicine finally reaped dividends, motivating the medical community to get its act together to find a solution to the benefit of Witnesses and non-Witnesses alike.

---

hemoglobin-based alternatives such as HBOC-201 is yielding results: "In one trial involving 688 patients undergoing elective orthopaedic surgery, the men and women received either one unit of real blood or two units of blood substitute HBOC-201, a haemoglobin-based product from Biopure. Made from a bovine source, the substitute can be kept at room temperature for up to three years and does not need to be matched with blood type." Another potentially promising treatment involves "genetically modifying haemoglobin to make it less toxic, and then wrapping it in a special long-life plastic cocoon. In such an environment, the protein could work its magic on oxygen supply and carbon-dioxide removal without the risk of toxic effects."

They are unlikely to admit that such an eventuality would be more due to (1) the need for science to create a universal blood substitute to suit all blood types that can be stored almost indefinitely without going off, and (2) the Governing Body partially relenting in 2000 and splitting hairs to the extent that red blood cells are prohibited but the hemoglobin inside is not.[16]

Especially is it doubtful that the Governing Body would acknowledge its role in the deaths of scores of Witnesses who were simply not born in time for science to save them. There would be untold numbers who would owe their continued existence to a combination of scientific progress and their leaders plumbing the depths of pedantry in differentiating theologically between a red blood cell and the stuff that makes it work. The lunacy of Watchtower's position on hemoglobin was perfectly summed up by the same contributor quoted above from Ray Franz's second book:

> With or without the peel an orange is still an orange. If a method to remove the segments of an orange and arrange the segments in groups of four without peel is invented, the product will still be orange, and nobody would call it anything else. In the same way slimmed red cells, freed and prepared hemoglobin, will remain blood. Therefore, to say that taking in red blood cells is a sin while accepting the freed vital hemoglobin is not is downright Pharisaic hypocrisy.

---

[16] It is possible that artificial blood products that do not use hemoglobin (such as perfluorocarbons, or "PFCs") could overtake their hemoglobin-based counterparts. Even if Witnesses end up getting access to artificial blood that is not directly based on blood derivatives, Witnesses would still have science to thank for rescuing them from the predicament imposed on them by their leaders.

When someone loses a lot of blood, usually the two most important things they need are blood volume, and oxygen. Without sufficient blood volume, the body enters hypovolemic shock (also called hemorrhagic shock), which happens when the heart is not receiving enough blood volume to keep pumping it. With the onset of severe hypovolemia, organs fail and the body starts shutting down. Though volume expanders (aqueous solutions of mineral salts or other water-soluble molecules) can help delay this, what the body most desperately needs when blood loss reaches a critical stage is oxygen. Hemoglobin is the essential ingredient in your blood that makes it possible for your body to "breathe." Without it, in every practical sense your body is drowning; suffocating. Hemoglobin, carried along by red blood cells, must be circulating in suitable quantities in order for vital oxygen to be delivered and harmful carbon dioxide expelled.

But, according to Watchtower, the Bible has something to say about all this. The writers of Leviticus and Acts would have had strong views on the extent to which doctors of the future were to keep the body's vital processes from collapsing. Apparently, these men from the ancient Middle East, if consulted, would have been fine with pure hemoglobin being administered, but would have considered the same substance an abomination in its packaged, natural form.

Witnesses are needlessly dying every day this nonsensical rule remains in force—a rule that amounts to insisting that someone (or something)[17] else's hemoglobin can only enter the bloodstream and start ferrying oxygen if its natural casing (the thing that

---

[17] As you may have noticed in an earlier footnote, hemoglobin for use in HBOCs can be derived from bovine blood.

stops it from behaving like a poison) is exchanged for an artificial one.

Of course, as vital as it is for your blood to ferry around oxygen, that is by no means the only role it fulfills. White blood cells (or leukocytes), for example, are your body's defense force. Unlike red blood cells, leukocytes do not come in a uniform structure. We only refer to them collectively as "white blood cells" because the "buffy coat" (between the red blood cells and the plasma) that emerges when spinning blood centrifugally is whitish. Some of this whitish stuff is platelets—fragments of cells that mass together to form a clot if you get cut or scraped. The rest is leukocytes.

Leukocytes are a sophisticated army comprising divisions of neutrophils, eosinophils, basophils, lymphocytes and monocytes. Each of these divisions have their own specialized role in protecting the body. Neutrophils, for example, are the most abundant of all the leukocytes (60-70%). They are like foot soldiers: heroically throwing themselves at bacterial or fungal infections for the greater good of the body's defense. (If you see pus on a wound, you are looking at the battlefield remains of countless neutrophils who have valiantly died defending their host body.)

You might assume that leukocytes have been banned by Watchtower as a major component of blood because they make up a substantial volume of it but, in fact, this is not the case. In healthy adults, leukocytes account for a mere 1% of the blood volume. Compare that with hemoglobin at 15%, and you will likely be just as puzzled as me that, despite serving a similarly vital role, leukocytes are somehow not deemed "kosher" by the Slave. Your confusion may only increase if I tell you that leukocytes are transfused naturally between a mother and her baby during pregnancy. Apparently, however, this is the *only time in your life* when unrepentantly receiving someone else's neutrophils, eosinophils, basophils, lymphocytes and monocytes does not carry the penalty of extermination at Armageddon.[18]

Perhaps the worst thing about the fractions provision is that, despite being an improvement on the total blood ban in place previously, it is still *too little, too late.* It may seem reasonable to leave it up to the consciences of Witnesses as to whether they will accept fractions or not, but for every Witness who accepts fractions there will be many others who will refuse on principle if there is any ambiguity.

I remember vividly how I reacted as a Witness when the fractions provision was introduced. My attitude was: "But where do these blood products come from? If they come from blood, then blood has to be donated. Am I seriously supposed to take blood from someone without being willing to donate any myself?" I could not fathom how it could be right to accept something that was only available from "Satan's world" as a result of worldly people feeling compelled to donate it altruistically. If all non-JWs were to suddenly vanish with only Witnesses left behind, from where would these fractions be derived? These questions perplexed me. Since the fractions policy was presented on an "it's

---

[18] Even more incredibly, some red blood cells are exchanged between mother and fetus, leading to problems if the mother is Rh negative and her baby is Rh positive. In "Rh Sensitization"—a quite common immune system response—antibodies in the mother become sensitized to her baby's red cells so that they are effectively programmed to attack Rh positive cells in future pregnancies. Hence, a Witness who argues that blood transfusions are unnatural must explain why Jehovah designed mother and child to exchange both white and red blood cells during pregnancy.

up to you" basis (which it was), I preferred to err on the side of caution—especially with my eternal life at stake. And I cannot have been the only one. Thankfully, I woke up before ever having my conviction put to the test, but the same cannot be said of the countless others who have been called on to take a stand.

The true body count resulting from the blood ban will perhaps always remain a mystery. (Despite being proud of its stance, Watchtower is not quite proud enough to report the number of Witnesses who die observing it.) But, every now and then, we find clues hinting at the scale of the carnage. For example, a paper was published in 2011 titled *Clinical Benefits and Cost-effectiveness of Allogeneic Red-blood-cell Transfusion in Severe Symptomatic Anaemia.* The paper gave a chilling insight into the rates of Witness mortality due to blood refusal. Results were shown from a study of four major public hospitals in New Zealand from 1998 to 2007. It found that out of 103 Witness patients who suffered severe anemia (lack of hemoglobin in the blood), 21 died. All 103 refused blood, but were agreeable to alternative treatments. When 103 non-Witness patients in similar circumstances were randomly picked, it was found that only two of these died. Hence, over the same period, the mortality rate of Witnesses who refused blood was *ten times* that of non-Witnesses who did not.

Attempts have been made to use figures such as these to extrapolate what the yearly death toll might be worldwide—but with so many variables to consider, gleaning data that can be used in any meaningful way is problematic at best. Even so, the New Zealand study paints a horrifying picture of just how many Witness lives are being lost due to the blood prohibition with or without the fractions provision.

In the absence of firm data, the most direct means of grasping the colossal waste of life arising from the blood teaching is through anecdotes, which essentially come in three forms: stories printed in Watchtower literature, occasional media reports, and experiences from those who have been personally impacted but are not (or are no longer) sympathetic to Watchtower teachings. As we have already seen, Watchtower anecdotes tend to spin the issue in such a way as to portray Witnesses as brave champions of conscientious freedom who are both pleasing God and contributing to society through their sacrifice. Media reports are usually more objective in giving us the raw facts minus the emotional or religious element, and generally offer minimal explanatory material on the blood prohibition itself (usually a Watchtower spokesperson is allowed to tell the public that blood transfusions are unbiblical).

Arguably least heard are those free from the organization's influence who have either themselves stared death in the face or were very close to someone who did. I will now relate two such stories: one from a survivor of the blood ban, and one from the sister of someone who was not so fortunate.

Phil Dunne is a now-awakened ex-Witness from Florida who kindly agreed to an interview during his vacation in Croatia.[19] Having been raised in the faith after his mother converted, Phil was baptized at 17 and got married only three years later.

Shortly after the couple moved to California, Phil came to the realization that something was seriously wrong with his health. He discovered he had a tumor blocking the head of his pancreas, leaving him jaun-

[19] You should be able to find the video on my "John Cedars" YouTube channel under the title *A Conversation With Phil Dunne.*

***Phil Dunne***

diced and in a lot of pain. Doctors struggled to find a precise diagnosis. Then one night while Phil was watching TV he was overcome with pain and nausea. He ran to the bathroom to throw up, only to end up passed out on the floor in a seizure.

After Phil was rushed to hospital, doctors discovered a tumor had torn a hole in his stomach. It became clear he had Non-Hodgkin's lymphoma—a cancer of the blood. Treatment would involve intense chemotherapy—but there was a more pressing problem. The tumor in Phil's stomach was causing internal bleeding, and he was told he would die within a "couple of days" without a blood transfusion.

Phil resigned himself to his fate and began getting his affairs in order, even writing out an informal will for his family. His doctors pleaded with him to reconsider and suggested he receive blood secretly in such a way that his Witness friends and family would never know.

"I could've easily gotten around it," Phil told me. "If you've never been in that situation you don't know, but doctors will come in privately and they will tell you that they can give you blood without anybody ever knowing. They even can have bags that are not labeled, that are not see-through. They told me that you could even have somebody in the room and they wouldn't know that you were getting a blood transfusion." But even though Phil was not 100% convinced of the soundness of the blood prohibition, he could not bring himself to accept this offer. Not only did he trust that the Governing Body *must* know best—he also could not imagine living with himself after defying the Slave's guidance in order to prolong his life.

"I was terrified of dying, but at the same time, I felt that I couldn't live with the guilt of having had a blood transfusion," he explained. "Having to keep it secret from my family, it would probably just tear me apart." Phil dreaded the scenario of being continually showered with praise for keeping his resolve and being pointed to as a role model of unflinching faith and integrity when deep down he would feel like a fraud.

Despite making his decision, Phil felt conflicted. "Even though I wasn't sure at the time whether or not I really believed that I was gonna wake up in Paradise if I'd died, I really was on the fence about it," he admitted. "I just knew that I couldn't go on living my life with that kind of guilt if I'd taken the blood transfusion."

Having made his mind up to die for his religion, that should really have been the end of the road for Phil. But suddenly and unexpectedly, the situation changed. His doctors had come up with a plan.

"They said it probably wouldn't work," he related, "but they were gonna do ten straight days of targeted intense radiation directed straight at that tumor that was giving me internal bleeding, and they were hoping that they could shrink it enough to be able to cauterize the hole to stop the internal bleeding—and then they can put me through chemotherapy."

To everyone's surprise, this bold strategy worked. After three weeks, Phil was discharged from the hospital and, shortly thereafter, began a course of chemotherapy that would eventually force his cancer into remission.

Phil had cheated death, but his elation was tempered by a growing sense of unease. What if things had gone slightly differently? What if there had been no miracle cure? How was he to reconcile the fact that his religious beliefs had very nearly killed him? Phil felt himself sliding into an existential crisis.

"The main feeling I had was: 'Do I really believe this?' If I had grown up in India would I believe that I was a Hindu? If I grew up in the Middle East somewhere would I have believed Islamic teachings?" Phil could feel his faith starting to unravel. "I wanted it to be real, so I studied harder than I ever have studied before. I got into the blood issue . . . a lot of things with the blood issue really disturbed me as far as certain hypocritical aspects of it—like we're not allowed to take whole white blood cells, but mothers' breast milk has trillions of white blood cells in it, so are we not allowed to breast feed our children? There were so many things that didn't make sense."

Phil needed answers. Rather than take his faith at face value, he decided to revisit the writings that had formed the basis of his Witness upbringing. "I decided to, for the first time ever, go through those books with a critical eye." Phil's discoveries led him to the realization that his convictions were built on an intricate web of lies, unfounded dogma and spurious claims. It dawned on him that he had had a narrow escape and very nearly died for nothing.

Finally faced with reality, Phil now had a challenging road ahead of him. His devout wife had no interest whatsoever in entertaining his discoveries or the smallest likelihood that her devotion to Watchtower was misguided. The couple finally conceded that their marriage was over and knew a separation was inevitable. Worse still, as Phil's absence from meetings became noticeable, his Witness friends began to withdraw. "Besides a handful of people that I won't mention because I don't want them to get in trouble with their respective congregations, everyone has pretty much cut me out of their lives," he admitted.

Even so, Phil has no regrets about embracing reality. If anything, his narrow brush with death at the hands of one group's perverse teachings has helped him value life as never before. He especially longs for the chance to thank his doctors for keeping him alive despite him very nearly frustrating their efforts. "I wish that I could personally apologize to all of them, because that just must have been so hard for them to watch someone die when they know they could save them."

When speaking to Phil, I could not help but notice how healthy he appeared. It was hard to reconcile this vibrant, driven individual with his description of a stricken, anemic patient on the brink of death. But thanks to pioneering work by skilled professionals—students of higher education from "Satan's world"—here he was relating his story to me years later in the Zagreb sunshine. One has to wonder how many like Phil were not so fortunate, instead joining the legions of forgotten martyrs who will never be able to breathe a sigh of relief at *only just* escaping self-inflicted oblivion.

One such silenced victim is Donald, a Jehovah's Witness ministerial servant who died refusing blood on February 2, 1986. Donald was not raised a Witness, but was attracted to the religion in his late teens, getting baptized at 20. His younger sister, Karenne, was never a baptized Witness, but remains profoundly affected by what happened to her brother during his years under Watchtower's influence. She shared his story in an article titled "The Friday Column: The Blood Issue and Leukemia: One Man's Story." (Karenne's article was uploaded to JWsurvey.org on February 12, 2016, which would have been her brother's 58th birthday.)

Donald knew something was wrong when he started experiencing discomfort while on a trip to Arizona in the autumn of 1985. A local doctor diagnosed him with pleurisy and advised him to return home to Florida. When he did this and sought further medical advice, he learned his illness was infinitely more serious. He had Acute Myelogenous Leukemia, or AML. Karenne explains the diagnosis in more detail:

> Bloodwork and a bone marrow biopsy revealed that Donald had tons of immature white blood cells (leukocytes) that were interfering with his bone marrow's ability to produce normal red blood cells. His red blood cells were misshapen (not round) and were not able to do their job of transporting oxygen. His bone marrow was full of these immature white blood cells and misshapen red blood cells.

The normal treatment for AML is blood transfusions and bone marrow transplants. Donald refused both. Although bone marrow had been de-prohibited by Watchtower in 1980 (when the ban on organ transplants was lifted), this did not help Donald. An AML patient would have to receive multiple pints of blood in preparation for receiving bone marrow to ensure that his or her body is sufficiently strengthened. Thus, having resolved to die for his beliefs, Donald was told he had one to six weeks to live.

Karenne returned home from a visit to her town's library one late afternoon and was told by her father to call her sister-in-law, Carole. When she made the call, Carole told her to fly out to Florida as soon as possible. "She explained the situation to me and said that the doctor told her that my brother might die within one week," Karenne says.

Karenne and her family wasted no time in flying out to Florida, although they were scarcely able to process what was happening. On seeing her brother, Karenne noticed a huge difference from the glowing, buoyant man she remembered. "He was wrapped in a sheet; his lips were completely white and he was breathing like a rabbit—rapid and shallow breaths."

Immediately noticeable was the presence of elders at Donald's bedside. In fact, it was an elder's wife who first greeted the family on arrival and conducted them to a waiting area. (This was before Watchtower arrangements for close supervision of Witnesses faced with the blood dilemma became more coordinated and widespread. Today, hospitalized Witnesses in this predicament can expect frequent visits by specialist groups of elders known as "Hospital Liaison Committees.")[20] Karenne and her family grew increasingly annoyed by elders being virtually camped out by Donald's bedside, seemingly in a shift pattern. The elders were

---

[20] The *Proclaimers* book describes the purpose of Hospital Liaison Committees as follows: "To support Jehovah's Witnesses in [their] determination to prevent their being given blood transfusions, to clear away misunderstandings on the part of doctors and hospitals, and to establish a more cooperative spirit between medical institutions and Witness patients." In reality, HLÇs are Watchtower enforcement units; groups of elders tasked with making sure the ban on blood is upheld in hospitals, where Witnesses are otherwise out of sight of the congregation and more likely to relent when faced with the real prospect of having to die for their beliefs. It goes without saying that if refusing blood is truly a personal decision made by Witnesses without being under any coercion or duress, HLCs should be entirely redundant. Hospitals would be well-advised to restrict access to Witness patients by HLC representatives, or anyone visiting in a religious/ministerial capacity.

heard reading scriptures to him, reminding him to keep his "eyes on the prize." Their apparent agenda was to nullify any potential attempts by Donald's "worldly" family to urge him to accept treatment.

Eventually, the unease spilled over into a frank request by Karenne for them to leave. "I asked them to go home," relates Karenne. "I told them that my time with Donald was limited and I wanted them to give us time to be a family." To Karenne's relief, the elders respected her wishes and left—but they had already robbed her of precious time. "I was only able to be in Florida for one week, so by the time the elders finally went home, I only had two full days to spend with Donald."

***Donald wrapped in bedsheets as his condition worsened***

In what little time she had left, Karenne held a vigil by her brother's bedside. She would lie awake on the floor beside his bed through the night, holding his hand as the TV flickered in front of them. Karenne writes of how one night she drifted into sleep, and her hand slipped from his. Donald immediately yelled "Karenne!" at the top of his voice, despite only being able to whisper and speak softly hitherto. "Donald explained to me that the reason he wanted me to hold his hand all night was because he wanted someone to be awake in case he died," Karenne explains. "He didn't want to die in the middle of the night, all alone, while everyone slept."

Soon Karenne's time was up. It was time for her to leave, along with her mother and brother. For a while, the family had communication with Donald through letters that he punched out on a typewriter (his failing vision made handwriting difficult), but this final flurry of contact would soon be cut short.

Donald died sitting on his bed, leaning against Carole. He had told her, "I'm going to die today," to which she had replied, "Don't say that. You will be fine. We're going to get through this." Donald then said he could no longer see. A silence of about ten minutes followed before his last words were uttered: "I'll see you when I wake up."

Donald had joined the Witnesses with hopes of living forever. When Karenne had asked him how he felt about dying, he brimmed with confidence. "Don't feel bad for me," he told his sister. "I have the easy part. All I have to do is go to sleep. Then I get to wake up in the new system." But there was nothing "easy" about Donald's death, or its aftermath. Karenne told me his loss had a devastating impact on his wife and children. (Carole has since died of cancer, so the two children—both of whom are not Witnesses—are without parents.) Thoughts of paradise may have offered Donald some comfort, but they were little more than an illusion sold to him by an organization desperate to win his loyalty.

To add insult to injury, some of Donald's precious final moments were spent hunched over his typewriter completing a talk assignment for his local congregation's Theocratic Ministry School that would be delivered posthumously. The title? "Why it is better NOT to have a blood transfusion." Even after his death, Donald would be enlisted to assert the Slave's right to interfere in medical decisions.

Both Donald and Phil were showered with praise for not relenting by their respective congregations. When stories like theirs emerge, whether they end in triumph or tragedy, they are typically heralded as proof that Witnesses are blessed when they take the ultimate stand. I recall a similar story in Bramhall congregation of a young Witness who beat incredible odds as a leukemia patient and survived refusing blood despite staring death in the face. (Of course, the tireless efforts and expertise of the medical personnel is nearly always marginalized, with "power beyond what is normal" from God pointed to as the main source of the miracle.) Nobody stops to think that maybe, just maybe, the blood ban might be mistaken—a sinister product of leaders who have grown accustomed to attaching far too much importance to their narrow-minded, convoluted interpretations of Scripture. Perhaps the worst irony of Watchtower history is that, for all the constant talk of persecution at the hands of Satan's system, no despot, government or agency has been as prolific at killing Jehovah's Witnesses as Watchtower itself.[21]

---

[21] Adolf Hitler, who allegedly vowed to "exterminate this brood in Germany" in reference to Jehovah's Witnesses, would be responsible for the death of an estimated 1,200 of them—a tiny fraction of the number that must have died refusing blood in the decades that followed World War II.

The prohibition on storing and transfusing blood and major blood components well highlights the callousness and dogmatism infesting the heart of the organization and corrupting the thinking of its leaders. As far as the Governing Body is concerned, preserving the *sanctity* of life is more important than preserving *life itself.*

But sadly, blood transfusions are not the only area in which the Slave leans on such perverse reasoning with catastrophic consequences on the lives of Witnesses. We see similarly twisted logic in other areas, such as Watchtower's horrendous approach to domestic violence.

According to the organization's understanding of scripture, the only way for a Witness to obtain a divorce is if his or her partner commits adultery. This rule is based on words attributed to Jesus at Matthew 19:9:

> I say to you that whoever divorces his wife, except on the grounds of sexual immorality, and marries another commits adultery.

Hence, to leave a marriage except on the grounds of adultery is itself deemed adultery. Common sense would dictate that if a Witness's life were threatened by a violent husband or wife, the urgent need for him or her to preserve their physical well-being by abandoning such a relationship would override any concerns over fidelity—but this is not how Watchtower sees things. The only way out for a Witness in such a situation is "separation," meaning that—though living apart—the abuse victim must remain married and cannot marry anyone else until evidence for unfaithfulness by either party is presented. Abused Witness spouses are thus potentially made to pay for their poor choice of marriage partner for the rest of their lives.

This madness all stems from Watchtower's insistence that the preservation of the marital bond is of more pressing concern than the need to preserve the life or well-being of abused wives or husbands. Such perverse reasoning, in turn, forms the basis for truly horrendous advice for abused spouses finding its way into print—a perfect example of which appeared in a 2012 *Watchtower:*

> Selma recalls a lesson she learned from the Witness who studied with her. "On one particular day," says Selma, "I didn't want to have a Bible study. The night before, Steve had hit me as I had tried to prove a point, and I was feeling sad and sorry for myself. After I told the sister what had happened and how I felt, she asked me to read 1 Corinthians 13:4-7. As I did, I began to reason, 'Steve never does any of these loving things for me.' But the sister made me think differently by asking, 'How many of those acts of love do you show toward your husband?' My answer was, 'None, for he is so difficult to live with.' The sister softly said, 'Selma, who is trying to be a Christian here? You or Steve?' Realizing that I needed to adjust my thinking, I prayed to Jehovah to help me be more loving toward Steve. Slowly, things started to change." After 17 years, Steve accepted the truth.

Whether this story is true or fabricated, the message is clear: a man hitting his wife is not a huge deal, and an abusive husband may even relent in his violence if his wife is willing to adjust her behavior and set a good example. The onus, at least in this case, is on the victim to improve her situation.

I wish I could tell you the above material is a one-off, but it is only the most recent in a string of

Watchtower quotes in which abused wives are reminded that their non-believing violent husbands can be transformed by the Witness faith—often by being "won without a word" (quoting 1 Peter 3:1, 2) by the respectful, subservient attitude of their victim.[22] You would think it obvious that any wife (or husband) on the receiving end of violence would be well advised to flee to safety, notify the police, and give serious consideration to ending the relationship—but again, the sanctity of marriage comes first in the minds of the Governing Body. Divorce is simply not an option. Even if a legal divorce is obtained by appealing to the courts outside the congregation, this is not considered a basis for remarrying for an abused Witness husband or wife. In the eyes of the Slave, they are bound to their abuser until evidence of adultery is uncovered.

The worst case scenario of this insane policy was played out in a tragic story featured in a documentary film, available on YouTube at the time of writing, titled *Deadly Devotion—Witness to Murder.* (Though the pounding, suspenseful music is a little distracting and over-the-top for my tastes, the quality of interviewees and commitment to explaining events is generally excellent.)[23] It tells the harrowing story of Kim Anderson,

---

[22] In addition to the February 15, 2012, *Watchtower* (p. 29), quoted above, examples of similar advice can be found in the following references: *w69* 12/15 p. 740; *g70* 12/8 p. 10; *g74* 1/8 p. 11; *w76* 5/15 pp. 292-293; *w82* 7/15 p. 7; *w86* 8/1 p. 21; *w90* 8/15 p. 21; *yb90* p. 64; *yb93* pp. 179-180; *w94* 4/15 pp. 27-29; *yb94* p. 145; *w96* 5/1 pp. 22-23; *g97* 4/22 p. 31; *w99* 1/1 p. 3; *yb99* p. 60; *w04* 8/15 p. 10; *w07* 4/15 p. 6.

[23] The documentary contains a handful of discrepancies in the reenactments, such as referring to an expected "rapture" in 1975 and portraying elders in an uncharacteristically aggressive manner for dramatic effect. Jim Kostelniuk, who participated, addressed these issues in an article for Watchtower-Watch.com (another of John Hoyle's websites) saying: "But to

who together with her two children, was murdered by her husband, Jim Anderson, on August 29, 1985.

Kim, from Burnaby in North-West Canada, had originally been married to a Witness named Jim Kostelniuk.[24] But when Armageddon failed to arrive in 1975 according to Watchtower's predictions, Jim became vocal in his disillusionment with the faith. Kim's elders put pressure on Kim to distance herself from Jim and, before long, the marriage was over. Kim obtained a divorce, taking the two children Juri and Lindsay with her. She would marry again—this time to a Texan named Jeff Anderson whom she had met at an organized retreat for Witnesses in Maui. However, within only weeks of their marriage in August 1981, Jeff revealed himself to be a violently abusive husband—and Kim even suspected him of sexually abusing her daughter, Lindsay. When Kim fled the couple's apartment in Texas, taking her children with her back to Canada, she found her elders less than supportive. She was told her claims regarding molestation could not be substantiated. The elders instructed Kim to remain with her husband and try to make the marriage work.

Jeff was thus invited to come and reunite with his wife in Canada where, predictably, his abuse soon resumed. Fears mounted over his interest in Lindsay. After further appeals for the elders to intervene were

---

me, these are minor changes that occurred because of audience-relevance, limitations on time and composition—things that don't detract from the message: that the Watchtower Society and their elders screw around with people's minds, and messes up their families."

[24] In addition to appearing in the documentary, Jim Kostelniuk has also authored a book about the tragedy titled *Wolves Among Sheep—The True Story of Murder in a Jehovah's Witness Community.*

rebuffed, Kim had Jeff leave the house—only to find him immediately take up residence across the street in a basement apartment. Jeff began stalking the mother and her two children. Then, on the fateful morning, he entered the property with a shotgun after Kim neglected to lock the door. Police were alerted because Kim had been on the phone to her mother when Jeff emerged with the weapon. The property was quickly surrounded and hostage negotiations commenced, but law enforcement was unsuccessful in preventing Jeff from gunning down Kim in front of her two children before turning the weapon on them. Lindsay, who was eight, died in the arms of her brother Juri, who was ten.

His murderous rampage complete, the killer surrendered himself to police and received three life sentences—one for each of his victims. Though Jeff Parsons was undoubtedly a sociopath who allowed his inability to handle rejection to turn him into a mindless killer, the role played by Kim's elders in this tragedy is not to be downplayed. Not only were they instrumental in dismantling her first marriage to the "apostate" father of her children—they also put pressure on her to persevere with the clearly abusive relationship that arose from their meddling with devastating consequences. And in handling matters in this way, they were operating entirely within the guidelines regarding marriage that remain incumbent on Witnesses to this day.

It is admittedly rare, for reasons I will explain shortly, to hear of such stories in which elders turn a blind eye to spousal violence—but they *are* out there if you go looking for them. I received my own powerful, firsthand testimony in the summer of 2015, when I traveled to interview ex-Witness Janiene Adamse in the Netherlands.[25] Janiene was raised a Witness and married a fellow believer at a very young age. She was 17—he was 20. "I was happy for one week of the marriage," she told me. "And then it started."

Janiene related how she was mentally and physically abused over four and a half years by her Witness husband. When she pleaded with the elders of her congregation in Antwerp, Belgium to do something, they somehow spun the situation so that it was her fault. She was urged to be a better wife, to be more submissive. Incredibly, she found no more empathy when she went to the police with her plight.

Eventually, her husband was disfellowshipped and started working in the sex industry. Janiene learned that he was having an affair with a female colleague and discovered his car had been outside the woman's house overnight. When she went to the elders, expecting them to confirm this as a cut-and-dried case of adultery so that she could get her divorce, they told her nothing could be done because there were no witnesses. (Her friend, who had tipped her off that the car was outside the house, was not counted as a Witness because she was "worldly.")

Janiene had already resolved to leave her husband if there was any infidelity, but he had threatened to track her down and kill her if she did so. Despite this threat, Janiene fled to a shelter for abused women—but finding the conditions there intolerable, she moved back to the home of her Witness parents in the Netherlands. After about six months, her mother approached her and asked when she would be moving back in with her husband. Shocked that her mother would want her to place

---

[25] You can watch the interview on my YouTube channel by searching: "Janiene Adamse domestic abuse."

herself in harm's way again, Janiene moved out of her parents' home and found her own apartment.

*Janiene and Jean-Pierre*

Soon thereafter, Janiene met Jean-Pierre, her present husband. By this point, she was legally divorced but not considered by her elders to be "scripturally" free to remarry. Once they discovered the romance, she was disfellowshipped for adultery. Janiene broke down in tears when she told me of her words on returning home to Jean-Pierre after the judicial committee: "You will never know how much I love you, because I've just given up my life for you."

These words were no exaggeration as far as Janiene was concerned. Still a believer, she was effectively being punished with estrangement from all her friends and family simply for moving on from an abusive relationship. "I felt very lonely because all the people that I'd grown up with, everybody that I knew, all my friends were in the Kingdom Hall—and all of a sudden you have nobody at all," Janiene explained. She told me it took her "years to recover" from the low self-esteem her husband had implanted in her mind. Janiene even attempted suicide. When I asked her what had prompted her to want to take her life, she replied without hesitation that it was due to her firm belief that she would be killed at Armageddon for failure to live up to the expectations placed on her by what she believed to be God's one and only true people. With such a grim prospect hanging over her, Janiene felt her life was meaningless.[26]

It took twenty years for Janiene, despite being disfellowshipped and shunned by her religion, to shake off the fear of Armageddon. During this period, she even tried to get reinstated—but without success. It was a chance encounter through work with an ex-Witness named Patrick Haeck (who features in a later chapter) that finally pulled her out of her indoctrination. Patrick encouraged her to read *Crisis of Conscience,* which she did in only two days. Finally, after being trapped in a no man's land of guilt and fear for two decades—an alien to "Satan's world" and an outcast from her own faith—Janiene was able to shake herself free from Watchtower's influence and fully enjoy life.

It is impossible to say how many more Janienes are out there who have either suffered in the past, or are suffering right at this moment as a result of Watchtower's shameful domestic violence policy—a policy that gives victims only two choices: more abuse (to the point of death, at least in the case of Kim Anderson), or celibacy. Worse still, the nature of the problem makes it extremely difficult for victims to step forward. Once you are married to someone, you are committed to spending your entire life with them for better or worse. In the case of a believing Witness wife with an abusive husband, unless there is some drastic change in circumstances, she will very likely take the secrets of her ordeal to her grave. If she were to speak out, or try to move on with her life in any meaningful sense, she would risk losing everything—especially if there are believing children

---

[26] There is plentiful anecdotal evidence of shunning—or the threat of shunning—resulting in suicide, or attempted suicide. Unfortunately, without statistical evidence, it is impossible to verify how many lives have been senselessly ended in this way.

who would be prepared to shun her as an adulteress. All of this makes it almost impossible to quantify the scale of the damage being wrought on abused spouses by Watchtower's twisted teachings on marriage.

Another area of abuse among Jehovah's Witnesses concerning which we can only scratch the surface is that of child molestation. Here too, Watchtower has policies in place that serve to amplify suffering and extend virtual immunity to perpetrators. A significant difference, however, is that child abuse victims are not normally bound to their abusers for life, giving them greater freedom to take action in later years once they understand the devastating effects of the brutality that was wrought on them. As a result, Watchtower is currently besieged with legal action by victims of pedophilia who are stepping forward and pursuing justice. These brave souls have experienced unimaginable barbarity and absolutely refuse to allow more children to suffer as they did.

CHAPTER TEN

# Suffer the Little Children

*"The only thing necessary for the triumph of evil is for good men to do nothing."*
—Edmund Burke

ON JULY 14, 2002, I found myself seated in a Kingdom Hall in Dolgellau, a small market town nestled in the majestic valleys of North Wales. It was Sunday morning. I was on a weekend break with some friends, and the meeting was drawing to a close. At the time, I was still a heavily-indoctrinated Witness. Mum had died just over a year earlier, and I firmly believed being reunited with her was contingent on how tightly I could cling to the organization's bosom.

Just before the meeting ended, an elder stepped onto the platform and read a letter from the London branch office. This was most unorthodox. The reading of letters was usually reserved for midweek meetings as part of the weekly announcements. The Sunday meeting was more of a showcase event with a "public talk" designed to attract newcomers. What could possibly be important enough to warrant a special message from Watchtower to all congregations on a Sunday morning?

As the letter was read, it became clear that it was about child abuse. The rather defensive tone made it clear that we were being prepared for a negative media onslaught about the organization's child abuse policies. It read, in part:

> In recent weeks, the press in this country has focused attention on the way accusations of child abuse are handled by various religious organizations. Such reports may cause some sincere individuals to ask about the procedures followed by Jehovah's Witnesses. Therefore, we believe that it will be beneficial to review with you our Bible-based position, so that you will "know how you ought to give an answer" to any who may inquire.—Colossians 4:6.
>
> Simply stated, we abhor the sexual abuse of children and will not protect any perpetrator of such repugnant acts from the consequences of his gross sin. (Romans 12:9) We expect the elders to investigate every allegation of child abuse. Even one abused child is one too many. However, in evaluating the evidence, they must bear in mind the Bible's clear direction: "No single witness should rise up against a man respecting any error or any sin. . . . At the mouth of two witnesses or at the mouth of three witnesses the matter should stand good." (Deuteronomy 19:15)

Up to that point, I had not heard the slightest whisper of my religion having any problems with child molesters. To my knowledge, there had been no abuse in my congregation or further afield. If any stories of that nature did exist, then I had been successfully kept in the dark. And if the unthinkable happened and a pedophile were to infiltrate, the measures outlined in the letter seemed quite reasonable. Why would the elders not investigate such allegations? Was it not their job to protect the congregation? As to the stuff about "two witnesses," if I were to be accused of molesting someone's child I would not think it unreasonable to expect my accuser to be able to corroborate his or her claims.

Later that day, I parted with my friends and drove home to Wilmslow, where I was still living at the time with Dad and Hannah. The letter had also been read at their meeting, and it was generally understood that it was intended to preempt a *Panorama* documentary that would be aired by the BBC that evening. Since the letter did not expressly prohibit us from watching the documentary, or even imply that we were to avoid it, none of us minded seeing what all the fuss was about. After all, it felt prudent to arm ourselves, in case, while engaged in our preaching work, we were confronted by members of the public who did not have the complete picture.

The documentary, titled *Suffer the Little Children*, turned out to be a stomach-churning experience. The BBC's tenacious and persistent investigative reporter, Betsan Powys, spoke to victims of child abuse from different parts of Britain and the United States. A story soon emerged of horrendous abuse ignored by elders, of victims told to remain silent, of police having their investigations disrupted, of Witnesses siding with the perpetrator rather than the victim, and of an organization that simply refused to grasp its responsibility to protect children.

Even though I found the program disturbing, I still felt an overwhelming urge to show loyalty. As the end credits rolled, Hannah was visibly outraged. She began asking why the organization had allowed this abuse to happen. I pleaded with her: "No, you don't understand. All these people who molested children have since been dealt with. These are just a few bad individuals. They've all been disfellowshipped, or the elders who didn't do their jobs properly have stood down."

I desperately wanted to think of Watchtower as Jehovah's clean, pure organization. I refused to accept that it could be so negligent on such a grave issue. But nine years later, when I finally awakened from my indoctrination, I realized there really was a serious problem. Betsan Powys was not just some mischief-maker stirring up trouble as an agent of "Satan's media." She was on to something.

In my relatively short time as an activist, I have often been asked by outsiders about child abuse—including journalists researching the organization. Non-Witnesses seem genuinely perplexed as to how such a polite, well-mannered, morally fastidious religious community as Jehovah's Witnesses could have an obvious problem with child abuse in their ranks. (And when I say it is *obvious*, I refer not only to the steady stream of media attention and legal cases, but also the fact that Governing Body member Geoffrey Jackson, while before a Royal Commission in Australia, acknowledged that the organization was "not immune" from child sexual abuse. I will revisit the Royal Commission and Jackson's testimony later.)

The reasons why Jehovah's Witnesses have a problem in this area are complex and can be challenging to comprehend—especially by those unfamiliar with the beliefs and culture of the organization. In my opinion, there are five main factors behind the phenomenon, which I will do my best to explain.

### The Two-Witness Rule

Elders are instructed in their *Shepherd* books that anyone who accuses another of wrongdoing must be able to present another (or second) witness. This rule applies even in cases of child abuse where, for understandable reasons, there is rarely a bystander watching the abuse take place. Accordingly, Chapter Five of the *Shepherd* book contains the following guidance on pages 72-73 (bold is mine):

> If the accuser or the accused is unwilling to meet with the elders or if the accused continues to deny the accusation of a single witness and the wrongdoing is not established, **the elders will leave matters in Jehovah's hands.** (Deut. 19:15-17; 1 Tim. 5:19, 24, 25; *w95* 11/1 pp. 28-29) The investigating elders should compose a record, sign it, put it in a sealed envelope, and place it in the congregation's confidential file. Additional evidence may later come to light to establish matters.

Therefore, elders can only take an accusation of child abuse seriously if the molester admits to his actions or someone else other than the victim saw him do it. But it should not take a genius to appreciate that not all pedophiles are anxious to admit to their crimes, and they are extremely unlikely to prey on children in front of spectators who can later act as witnesses.

The only exception to the two-witness rule is a loophole referred to by some as the two-*victim* rule, whereby if another victim of the same abuser comes forward, his or her evidence can be counted as the second witness. The obvious problem with this provision is that it leaves a child molester free to abuse a second child before facing justice. It also relegates the harrowing, life-altering experience of either the first or second victim to little more than part of an evidence-gathering process. It would be the same as saying of an accused murderer: "We'll be able to convict him of murder if we let him loose and he murders someone else!"

## Culture of Confidentiality

Organizations that pride themselves on being progressive tend to value the respect and credibility that comes with openness and transparency, and letting the public know how responsible they can be when problems arise—but Watchtower is not like that. Watchtower has long been obsessed with confidentiality and secrecy. In a letter dated July 1, 1989, the following guidance was given to elders (bold is mine):

> Elders share the obligation to shepherd the flock. However, they must be careful not to divulge information about personal matters to unauthorized persons. There is "a time to keep quiet," when "your words should prove to be few." (Ecclesiastes 3:7; 5:2) Proverbs 10:19 warns: "In the abundance of words there does not fail to be transgression, but the one keeping his lips in check is acting discreetly." **Problems are created when elders unwisely reveal matters that should be kept confidential.** Elders must give special heed to the counsel: "Do not reveal the confidential talk of another." (Proverbs 25:9) Often the peace, unity, and spiritual well-being of the congregation are at stake. **Improper use of the tongue by an elder can result in serious legal problems for the individual, the congregation, and even the Society.**

In a more recent letter to elders, dated November 6, 2014, the organization went as far as to insist that if elders are judicially investigating a wrongdoing that is also a crime, they should keep it a secret:

> In some cases, the elders will form a judicial committee to handle alleged wrongdoing that may also constitute a violation of criminal law (e.g., murder, rape, child abuse, fraud, theft, assault). Generally, the elders should not delay the judicial committee process, but strict confidentiality must be main-

> tained to avoid unnecessary entanglement with secular authorities who may be conducting a criminal investigation of the matter. For example, even the fact that a judicial committee has been formed should not be disclosed to persons not entitled to know.

To maintain its secrecy, Watchtower is adamant that it will only report accusations of child abuse to the authorities if the local laws in the country or state specifically require elders to do this.

You might be thinking: "Well that's perfectly reasonable. So long as no laws are broken, what's the harm in not reporting someone else's crime?" But such reasoning overlooks both the gravity of child abuse as a crime, and the moral imperative of reporting it.

Just imagine going on vacation, only to return to find that your home has been broken into. To your horror, you find that some irreplaceable family heirlooms have been pilfered. Because you were away when the thieves struck, you would have no clue as to their identity. Then you remember that your neighbor has a video surveillance system, so you call on him and ask to review his footage for clues. To your astonishment, your neighbor says "no." The footage belongs to him; it is his private property and he is not legally required by the local laws to show it to anyone. He refuses to help you get your things back or help to bring justice to those who broke into your home.

That is essentially the attitude Watchtower is displaying every time it refuses to report the crime of child molestation to law enforcement. But rather than a person's home and belongings being violated, we are talking about a child being robbed of its mental and emotional well-being, leaving it permanently damaged. A person may not be legally obliged to do something, but they are still morally obliged to do the *right* thing.

### Perceived Separation From the World

A third factor is the firm belief that Jehovah's Witnesses should keep themselves as separate as possible from the world in general. This isolationist attitude is manifested repeatedly in Watchtower publications, which hardly foster a healthy attitude toward the world outside the organization. As the May 15, 2014, *Watchtower* put it:

> Satan's system of things will soon come to its end, but God's organization will survive the last days.

Or, if you prefer, the January 1, 1990, *Watchtower:*

> It may not be too long, but we must endure! In Satan's system, we have to put up a hard fight for the faith, as the world's immorality, corruption, and hatreds surround us on all sides.

The siege mentality among Witnesses can and does translate into an assumption that all problems between them should be sorted out internally, with the help of the elders. After all, why would you involve the police or courts of law when these are all elements of Satan's doomed system, that "will soon come to an end"? This aversion to taking legal action against fellow believers was perfectly summed up in the March 15, 1996, *Watchtower* on page 15 (bold is mine):

> Loyalty to Jehovah God will also keep us from doing anything that would bring reproach upon his name and Kingdom. For example, **two Christians once got into such difficulty with each other that they improperly resorted to a worldly law court. The judge asked, 'Are both of you Jehovah's Witnesses?' Evidently he could not understand what they were doing in court. What a reproach that**

> **was!** Loyalty to Jehovah God would have caused those brothers to heed the counsel of the apostle Paul: "Really, then, it means altogether a defeat for you that you are having lawsuits with one another. Why do you not rather let yourselves be wronged? Why do you not rather let yourselves be defrauded?" (1 Corinthians 6:7) **Certainly, the course of loyalty to Jehovah God is to suffer personal loss rather than bring reproach upon Jehovah and his organization.**

Thus, at least in the mind of a Witness, suffering personal injury will often be of lesser concern compared to the unthinkable prospect of bringing Jehovah's organization into reproach.

## Misconceptions Surrounding Forgiveness

Like many Christian denominations, Jehovah's Witnesses teach that any sin can be forgiven, no matter how serious.[1] But how far should this go when it comes to pedophilia? Should someone who molests children be forgiven to the extent that he is appointed to a position of trust within a congregation? Should it be possible for a pedophile to serve as an elder? As recently as October 2012, Watchtower sent a letter[2] to all bodies of elders that replied in the affirmative:

> It cannot be said in every case that one who has sexually abused a child could never qualify for privileges of service in the congregation.

That same letter informed elders that notoriety was a key factor in deciding whether a pedophile could serve as

---

[1] Witnesses are taught that "blaspheming against the spirit" is not forgivable, but it is left to God, not humans, to determine whether this offense has been committed.

[2] The October 1, 2012, letter has since been replaced by a newer letter dated August 1, 2016, which I will discuss later in this chapter.

an elder or not. If nobody in the congregation knew about the person's history, the pedophile could be deemed "irreprehensible," or "free from accusation," and therefore fit for appointment. But such reasoning overlooks the very nature of child abuse, namely that it is carried out in secret, behind closed doors, away from the public gaze. A congregation cannot be aware of a child molester if there are policies in place specifically designed to keep them in the dark. And the fact that a congregation is unaware of a pedophile's crimes does not make him a more desirable candidate as a congregation leader!

Moreover, in allowing pedophiles the potential to serve as elders by way of extending forgiveness, Watchtower seriously overlooks the very nature of pedophilia. It is not something that simply comes and goes, or can be banished by prayer, confessions, and religious counseling. Small progress is being made in rehabilitation techniques, but it is being made by skilled professionals with years of experience in working with offenders—and even they will admit that some pedophiles simply cannot be rehabilitated.

Forgiveness of pedophiles on religious grounds is therefore an entirely misguided concept, especially when used to justify letting child molesters assume positions of trust. If a person is capable of raping a child, they are clearly not a suitable candidate to run for political office, work as a teacher or family doctor, or become any kind of responsible church leader.

### Onus on Sinfulness of Child Abuse

Finally, there is a problem that overshadows each of these four factors. I am referring to the perception among Witnesses that child abuse is first and foremost a *sin*, and only a crime by coincidence.

For example, on the first point just mentioned, if the Governing Body were to treat child abuse as a crime in the same way as murder is a crime, they would not insist on having two witnesses, or two victims of the same perpetrator. They would tell elders to make sure all victims go to the police straight away, and let justice take its course. On the second point, if the Governing Body fully acknowledged the criminality of child abuse, the preservation of confidentiality and shielding of the organization's reputation would be a non-issue compared to the urgent need to protect vulnerable ones in the congregations. As to the third point—separation from the world—if Witness parents were able to truly grasp that child abuse is a crime, they would not think twice about pursuing justice against a perpetrator regardless of whether he or she happened to share the same religious views. And regarding the fourth point—forgiveness—it should be obvious that a man who rapes a child is no less undesirable for a position of trust in a congregation as someone convicted for crimes such as murder or fraud.

Hence, most of the problems surrounding child abuse could be easily rectified if the Governing Body were to embrace the mantra:

LET THE BIBLE JUDGE SIN, LET THE LAW JUDGE CRIME

But because, in their minds, the sinfulness of child abuse outweighs all other considerations, this can and does lead to child molesters being sheltered from justice. (Interestingly, as a side note, despite there being rules in the Jewish law code against a variety of intimate acts—including prohibitions related to menstruation, wet dreams and incest—nowhere in the Old or New Testament does it expressly state that it is wrong for an adult to have sex with a child. Arguably, the strong revulsion of most people to pedophilia has more to do with our innate sense of right and wrong than the commands of any sacred text.)

Having considered the reasons why child abuse flourishes among Jehovah's Witnesses, we can now approach the question: How long have we known about it? Institutional child sex abuse has not been a matter of public concern for as long as you might expect. In the United States, it was not until 1986 that Congress passed the first laws aimed at giving victims of child sex abuse the right to make a civil claim, thus holding organizations accountable for abuse perpetrated by individuals.

Ten years later, in 1996, Megan's Law was enacted. This gave American citizens the right to know the details of sex offenders throughout the country. A similar provision known as the Child Sex Offender Disclosure Scheme, or "Sarah's Law," was rolled out in parts of the UK as recently as 2011.

With legislation came increased prosecution and detection of cases. By the dawn of the 21st century, old stigmas and taboos had been sufficiently swept aside for the media to take a more active role in raising awareness, and the Catholic Church was among the first institutions to be investigated. The 2015 Oscar-winning movie *Spotlight* documents the superb efforts and professionalism of investigative journalists at *The Boston Globe* who exposed widespread child abuse by local Catholic priests in 2001 and 2002. It is a must-see movie—with outstanding performances by Michael Keaton, Mark Ruffalo, Rachel McAdams and Liev Schreiber—and I can strongly recommend it if you have not already had the pleasure.

It was also in 2002 that two hard-hitting documentaries were released focusing attention on the covering up of child abuse by Jehovah's Witnesses. One was an NBC *Dateline* program titled *Witness for the Prosecution.* The other was the previously-mentioned *Panorama* program.[3]

Before it aired, Witnesses throughout Britain had been assured that, in the organization's eyes, "even one abused child is one too many"—but the facts presented by Betsan Powys revealed that this was hardly the case in practice. If anything, the number of pedophiles being effectively concealed by the organization's strict regime of secrecy appeared to be much higher than expected. When former elder Bill Bowen was interviewed, he told Powys that, based on contact from informants within the organization, the number of unreported pedophiles on Watchtower's database for the USA, Canada and Europe was a staggering 23,720—a figure that, though uncorroborated, seemed too precise to be a total fabrication.

The program later showed Powys, armed with this information, confronting a now-deceased member of the Governing Body, Theodore Jaracz, who was less than cooperative. Accosting him as he exited the stage at a convention in Oklahoma, Powys asked a disconcertingly smug Jaracz about his justifications for keeping any number of pedophiles on a secret database that is inaccessible to the authorities. Jaracz could only babble about the need for privacy, and boast of how Jehovah's Witnesses do as Paul urges in 1 Corinthians 4:6 by not going "beyond the things that are written"—thus implying that Watchtower's

---

3 At the time of writing, it is possible to watch the *Panorama* program on YouTube.

policies, including the keeping of the database, have biblical warrant. Powys' important questions were effectively left unanswered.

Despite refusing to grant any interviews to *Panorama*, the organization did send a fax to the BBC on May 9, 2002, two months before the film aired. In it they admitted to the existence of the database, but disputed the numbers cited by Bowen:

> You have been told that here in the United States we have compiled a list of 23,720 names of child abusers. That is false. First of all, the total number of names in our records is considerably lower than that. In addition, it is not meaningful to focus on the number of names we have in our records. This is because our figures include the names of many persons who have only been accused of child abuse whereas the charges have not been substantiated.

Though, to this day, nobody knows how many alleged child molesters are recorded within the organization's database, the fact that the database exists and is currently sitting safely on Watchtower hard drives is beyond doubt. I will later cite further proof of its existence, and offer a recent insight into just how many names it may conceal. For now, we can say with confidence that the problem of child abuse among Jehovah's Witnesses has been well documented for some considerable time. Certainly since 2001-2002, around the time widespread abuse was first uncovered in the Catholic Church, former Witnesses such as Bill Bowen and Barbara Anderson have been assisting the media and speaking out about it openly.

Barbara Anderson, whom I introduced in Chapter Seven, is particularly well-positioned to comment on the issue having worked at Watchtower headquarters in the writing department. Her superb website, WatchtowerDocuments.org, explains how she first came to learn of the child abuse problem as a Bethelite back in 1992. What she discovered led to her leaving the organization in 1998, and starting her activism work shortly thereafter.

Prior to the 1990s, we do not know of anyone—inside or outside Watchtower—who knew there was a significant problem with child sexual abuse, let alone how bad it was. Only with fairly recent improvements in legislation and growing media scrutiny could the full scope of the problem begin to be understood—and in many ways, we are still just scratching the surface in our understanding. For every documented case brought to light, it is reasonable to assume there are many more shrouded in secrecy. However, to give you a thumbnail sketch of the problem, I will relate the stories of seven victims whose cases have propelled the mishandling of child abuse by Watchtower into the spotlight. Three of these victims are from the United States: Candace Conti, José Lopez and Debbie McDaniel. A further two are from the United Kingdom: Karen Morgan, from South Wales, and a victim we will refer to as "Amelia." And, for privacy reasons, our last two victims are known only as "BCB" and "BCG"—both from Australia.

In June 2012, Candace Conti was awarded $28 million in damages by a jury in California for the abuse she suffered at the hands of a Witness named Jonathan Kendrick between 1995 and 1996 when she was 9-10 years old. Watchtower was found responsible because, prior to Conti's abuse, Kendrick's elders knew that he had molested his stepdaughter, but did nothing to prevent him from moving on to other children. All they did was remove him as a ministerial servant. They even allowed Kendrick to pair off with Conti in the preaching work.

***Candace Conti***

After the verdict was announced, a lengthy appeal process ensued in which Watchtower tried to get the decision reversed. At least partially, they succeeded. The appeals court determined that Watchtower's leadership had no legal duty to warn parents in Conti's congregation that a confessed child molester had access to their children. The court removed the punitive part of the verdict, but still insisted Conti receive $2.8 million in compensation. It was decided that, whether there was a legal duty to protect children or not, Conti's elders had still knowingly paired a nine-year-old girl with a pedophile in the preaching work, which was considered a "church-sponsored activity." Not long after the appeal verdict was announced, the case was settled.

Despite ending in something of an anticlimax, the Candace Conti case will go down in history as ground-breaking. It was, after all, the first time a jury had ruled against Watchtower in a child sex abuse case. And by going public with her story, Conti inspired a flood of other victims to step forward and pursue justice. One such victim was José Lopez.

Lopez had been one of eight children abused by a Witness named Gonzalo Campos between 1982 and 1995 in the San Diego area. Elders knew Campos was a child molester as early as 1982, but took no action. Instead, even while Campos was accumulating more victims, they rewarded him with congregation privileges—first by making him a ministerial servant in 1988, then by appointing him as an elder in 1993. It was not until 1995 that Campos was finally disfellowshipped, but by 2000 he had succeeded in getting reinstated. In 2009, Campos' victims learned that he was regularly attending meetings, and began pursuing legal action. Soon after, in 2010, Campos fled to Mexico, where he has remained ever since.

Though Campos managed to evade the justice system, the organization that had for so long shielded his crimes was less fortunate. In February 2013, one of the victims, José Lopez, filed suit against Watchtower for his abuse after his fellow victims had each received substantial settlements from the organization. Lopez won the case in October 2014, and Superior Court Judge Joan Lewis awarded damages totaling $13.5 million. Of special note in this case is the fact that Watchtower lost, at least in part, because it refused to cooperate with the requests of the court, leaving Judge Lewis no choice but to rule against the organization by default.

So, what requests did Watchtower refuse?

This brings us back to the database. Lopez's legal team, led by Irwin Zalkin, successfully argued that the database was a key piece of evidence in demonstrating the organization's failure to report child molesters. It was duly subpoenaed. However, a Watchtower official named Richard Ashe testified under oath that it would be impossible to produce it due to its vast size, and the fact that it was tangled up in all manner of other documents:

> Honestly, Mr. Zalkin, the efforts that we've made up to this point is just trying to figure out how on earth we could ever do that in our filing system. You're talking about 14,000 congregations and over 3 million documents that have been scanned and that would have to be searched. . . . It would take years to do that.

Unconvinced by Ashe, Zalkin consulted a software expert who testified that Watchtower's database, which it had been revealed was run on Microsoft SharePoint software, could be produced within two months or even *two days* if search terms were used. At this point, Watchtower's lawyers bluntly refused to surrender the information, effectively opting to instead pick up the $13.5 million tab for having their defense thrown out by default. (In April 2016, Watchtower succeeded in getting the Lopez ruling reversed by an appeals court, but on condition that they produce their records—effectively resetting the case, with the organization getting one more chance to comply. As of early November 2016, when this book was in final edits, the database had still not been produced.)

But refusing a court order to produce its database was not the only act of defiance for which Watchtower was punished in the Lopez case. The organization also refused a subpoena for the appearance of its most senior Governing Body member, Gerrit Lösch. This was cited by Judge Lewis as another reason for her ruling.

As it happens, the April 2016 appeal judgment overturning Judge Lewis' ruling agreed with Watchtower that Lösch should not have been forced to give deposition because Zalkin and his team had failed to establish that he was key to the case as the most senior Governing Body member. Even so, whether Lösch's appearance should have been compulsory

***Gerrit Lösch, as pictured in the July 15, 2014 "Watchtower"***

or not, Zalkin's request was not unreasonable and presented Lösch with an excellent opportunity to defend "Jehovah's organization"—something he should have been only too willing to do under the circumstances. But rather than acquiesce, Lösch was so anxious to avoid appearing on the stand that he filed a statement on February 5, 2014, in which he emphatically argued against having *any* involvement with Watchtower's child abuse policy (bold is mine):

> I am not, and never have been, a corporate officer, director, managing agent, member, or employee of Watchtower. I do not direct, and have never directed, the day-to-day operations of Watchtower. **I do not answer to Watchtower.** I do not have, and never have had, any authority as an individual to make or determine corporate policy for Watchtower or any department of Watchtower. **Watchtower does not have, and never has had, any authority over me.**[4]

I shudder to think what would happen to an ordinary Witness if he or she were to try saying words similar to that at a congregation meeting!

After the initial verdict, Lopez's lawyer Zalkin was interviewed by a team of former Witness activists, including myself, as part of a podcast episode. During our interview, I will never forget Zalkin relating a chilling

[4] You can read Lösch's full statement in Appendix G.

exchange he claims to have had with one of Watchtower's lawyers during the case:

> Our goal is not to destroy the Jehovah's Witnesses. They may think that's what we're after—we are really after trying to get them to change what are really just antiquated and dangerous policies. And when we resolved our first few cases with them, one of the things I asked their lawyers, and Mario Moreno in particular, was "what can we do to change this, so that this doesn't keep happening?" And he looked at me and said, "we're never changing this."

If this account is accurate, it would seem to indicate that the Governing Body is in no mood to learn its lessons despite multiple courtroom defeats, millions of dollars in settlements in the United States alone, and a barrage of negative media exposure.

A good example of the hard-hitting media scrutiny Watchtower has been forced to contend with can be found in the coverage of Debbie McDaniel's experience, which featured in several reports by journalist Trey Bundy on the *Reveal* website in 2015. (In addition to Bundy's articles, Debbie's remarkable story is recounted in her book *Out With Consequences*, available on Amazon. The account that follows is based on Debbie's recollections from the book.)

Debbie's story is noteworthy for a number of reasons, not least of which is her family's pedigree in Witness circles. Her father, an elder in McAlester, Oklahoma, has a 1982 *Watchtower* article devoted to his account of walking away from a promising career as a NASA engineer on the Gemini and Apollo programs soon after embracing the Witness faith.[5]

---

[5] The story of Wendell Marley appears in the May 1, 1982, *Watchtower*, and is titled "In Search of Success."

Wendell Marley was clearly a clever man. His daughter Debbie was born in 1969, the same year he watched from the control room at Houston as Neil Armstrong took his first steps on the lunar surface after being safely delivered there by a spacecraft Marley had helped design and build. But for all his early promise and undoubted engineering brilliance, it turns out Marley was not quite so adept at fatherhood—even after the epiphany that led to him becoming a Witness and moving his family to Oklahoma to pursue a life of devotion to Watchtower.

When Debbie was seven years old, she woke from sleeping at a friend's house to find an erect penis being forced into her mouth by the son of some Witness friends her parents were visiting. On learning of this, Debbie's father is said to have responded by taking her home and beating her until she could scarcely breathe before shunning her for weeks.

A year later, when Debbie was eight years old, the presiding elder (coordinator) in the family's new Kingdom Hall in McAlester began to take an interest in her. His name was Ronald (or "Ronnie") Lawrence. It began with Lawrence placing her hand on his erection while the two were alone in his car one morning during preaching work (behavior that, by this stage, young Debbie was beginning to consider normal) and advanced to him violating her with his fingers and even a wooden spoon at his home while his wife watched TV, oblivious. Debbie would plead with her parents not to be taken to Ronnie's house, but to no avail. It was considered a privilege for him to take such a keen interest in the "spiritual development" of the children in the congregation.

Lawrence continued to abuse Debbie until she was 13, by which point she had been reduced to a wreck—

suffering from depression, hair loss and eating disorders. In the years that followed, Debbie increasingly rebelled against her Witness upbringing until finally leaving home at 18. Lawrence soon began staking out her apartment detective-style, apparently eager to discover whether she was having sex with her new worldly friends. It was not long before Debbie was faced with the bitter irony of being ejected from her religion, including all contact with her family, by the same man who had violated her as a child—all in the name of keeping Jehovah's congregation "clean" from someone who had had premarital sex.

So distraught was Debbie at the shunning that resulted from her disfellowshipping that she soon began begging Lawrence for reinstatement. After many months of attending meetings while being shunned by an entire congregation, Debbie's reinstatement was finally announced. Her father, however, insisted she apologize to him personally before he would start speaking to her again.

Before long, it became apparent that Debbie was by no means the only one to have been molested by Lawrence as a child. A group of his victims approached her and asked if she had also been abused. "It's time to come forward," they told her.

"What followed was chaos—months and months of it," Debbie writes in her book. She and other victims were "required to face [Lawrence] with their accusations." Finally, after a needlessly excruciating judicial process in which his victims were asked to relive their ordeals, Lawrence was himself disfellowshipped. When Debbie asked the elders whether the police should be involved, she was told Lawrence's abuse did not merit their intervention. "On more than a couple of occasions, I inquired about notifying the authorities of the molestations," Debbie recalls. "The elders assured me that they had been notified and law enforcement had declined to take an interest. For years to come, I fully accepted their explanation."

It was not until after 2012, with Lawrence having been twice reinstated, that these assurances were discovered to be terrible lies. By this point, Debbie had again been disfellowshipped—this time for embracing the fact that she was lesbian and starting a new life with her now-wife, Crystal. After reaching breaking point amid a torrent of abuse and manipulation over her attempts to gain joint custody of her daughter from her Witness ex-husband, Debbie burst into her local police station one morning yelling: "I'm not leaving here until someone helps me with the harassment from Jehovah's Witnesses!"

***Debbie McDaniel***

The police listened patiently as Debbie began to tell her full story, including her abuse as a child. As a result of this moment of desperation, authorities were finally alerted to Lawrence's crimes. The district attorney mounted a case against both McAlester congregation and Watchtower for the systematic cover-up of Lawrence's abuse of multiple victims over many years. Journalists descended on McAlester, and news cameras filmed Lawrence walking out of police custody and into a car after a Witness paid his $50,000 bond. Three other Lawrence victims, themselves no longer in the faith, came forward as plaintiffs. However, because many of the victims were still Witnesses, the four of them stood alone. When the day came for the case to be deliberated in court, the victims were astonished to find local Witnesses turning out overwhelmingly in support of Lawrence—including Debbie's parents, who sat on the side of the man who had molested their daughter.

It was hoped that, though the statute of limitations had lapsed (the offenses dated back to the '80s), a provision could be leveraged that would allow the case to be pursued. However, the judge failed to agree with the district attorney's interpretation of the law, and threw the case out. At least until lawmakers revisit the statute of limitations in Oklahoma, it appears Watchtower has succeeded in keeping a loathsome individual they know to be a predatory pedophile cocooned from justice.

Another abuse victim who is no stranger to the appalling tendency of Witnesses to spring to the defense of "forgiven" pedophiles is Karen Morgan. Karen was around 12 years old and growing up in Barry, South Wales, when she began to suffer abuse from her uncle, Mark Sewell, who was then a ministerial servant. Sewell started kissing her on the lips and progressed to engineering situations for them to be alone so he could kiss her with his tongue. Sewell would also get Karen to lie on top of him, and would caress her back while in his underwear. Halfway through his abuse of Karen, Sewell was appointed as an elder.

When Karen finally told her parents, they took her to confront Sewell—but Sewell denied the allegations and accused Karen of lying. More meetings with elders followed, but far from being productive they only

*Karen Morgan*

made things worse, as Karen was repeatedly made to confront her abuser. Finally, a seven-man committee of elders was appointed by the London branch office, and Sewell was stripped of his position as an elder and disfellowshipped. However, he was disfellowshipped, not for his abuse of Karen, but for having a belligerent and unforgiving attitude. Karen was told that because two witnesses could not be produced, there was nothing the organization could do.

Years later, after more of Sewell's victims came forward, he was arrested by police and put on trial. By that time, he had been reinstated as a Witness. Jehovah's Witnesses gave no help or cooperation to police and prosecutors throughout their investigations. During the trial, it came to light that evidence against Sewell dating back 20 years had been shredded by the organization. Furthermore, out of eight or nine elders who were involved in judicial hearings against Sewell following the abuse, only one agreed to give evidence in court (and he attempted to retract his statement).

The trial culminated in a guilty verdict for Sewell, who was imprisoned for 14 years on eight sex charges, including rape. When interviewed by the BBC in the wake of the verdict, Karen told of how the bungling intervention of the elders only served to exacerbate the emotional damage of her ordeal.[6]

---

[6] Karen's BBC interview, along with news footage of various other cases mentioned, features in my 90-minute 2016

I caught up with Karen in August 2015 and asked her about the case. She told me that though elders "came looking" for her to disfellowship her for having a perfectly normal relationship with her boyfriend after moving on from the Witnesses, they were much less eager to cleanse their congregation of a convicted pedophile. In fact, so concerned were they about Sewell's spiritual welfare that they were giving him regular shepherding visits behind bars, where he was active in trying to convert fellow inmates.

Karen's father, John Viney, also gave a helpful insight into why, as a Jehovah's Witness parent, he was slow to pursue justice for his daughter after she first approached him:

> The process of being a Jehovah's Witness has a profound effect on you, and it has an effect on you as a father. And to a degree I think, and I'd have to be honest now, and say that my children and my family didn't always come first because of either congregation responsibilities or trying to be loyal to what I believed. On some occasions, I think I was not as robust at protecting my children as I could've been.

Another UK Jehovah's Witness victim of child abuse who has received extensive media attention has been referred to by the press as "Amelia." Between 1989 and 1994, when Amelia was between the ages of four and nine, she was abused by a ministerial servant named Peter Stewart. Shortly after the abuse began, Stewart was discovered molesting another child. But Stewart's elders allowed him to keep his privileges as a ministerial servant, thus granting him free license

---

documentary film *Jehovah's Witnesses and Child Abuse—Is There a Problem?* This chapter is based on my script for that video, which should be easily found on YouTube.

to continue abusing Amelia. The attacks took place in Amelia's home, in Stewart's home, in a shed, in cars, at the Kingdom Hall, during the Tuesday night book study group, during preaching work (Stewart would lead the group and assign himself to work with Amelia), and even at conventions. Stewart tormented Amelia, telling her she was sinning, that she had committed fornication, and that she would be killed at Armageddon.

In 1995, Stewart was convicted of assaulting another child and sent to prison for five years. On his release, Amelia was terrified his abuse might resume, so she contacted both her elders and the police. The police took matters very seriously, and 72-year-old Stewart was arrested and charged—although he died in 2001 before the case came to trial. The elders, however, had little sympathy. They told Amelia that, because there had not been two victims to her abuse, there was nothing they could do.

At the urging of her husband, Amelia eventually took legal action against Watchtower. Her lawyers consulted with Candace Conti's lawyers back in America in bringing the case. In June 2015, the High Court ruled in Amelia's favor, awarding her £275,000 in compensation—making her the first person to win a civil suit against Watchtower in the UK.[7] Watchtower contested the ruling, but their efforts at appealing proved unfruitful. In July 2016, in addition to the damages due to Amelia, Watchtower was ordered to pay £1 million in legal fees—money that will have come straight out of dedicated funds for preaching the "good news."[8]

---

[7] Watchtower was also forced to pay Amelia's £455,000 legal costs, bringing the full amount to £730,000.

[8] The £1 million figure was reported in the *Leicester Mercury*, but I understand the precise amount of legal fees was to be determined by Amelia's lawyers.

Despite the victory, nothing can ever fix the damage inflicted on Amelia—not just by her abuser, but by those who shielded him from justice. She has already attempted suicide, and is on record as telling her lawyers, AO Advocates, that she does not expect to live beyond the age of 30. When I was researching for his chapter, Amelia told me: "I thought that my only options at that time were to kill myself or run away to escape him. I begged my elders to make him attend meetings at a different Kingdom Hall—this was while he was attempting to get reinstated—but they said they couldn't do this."

When the case was finally brought to a conclusion in Amelia's favor, her lawyers went on record saying: "Following the original trial and judgment, we have always maintained that this is the time for apologies not appeals, and we now hope that after years of litigation our client can finally move on with her life and put this court case behind her." Amelia is hopeful that her experience of pursuing justice will embolden other victims to come forward. "Having them up on the stand and hopefully feeling some measure of what they made me feel when I was 14 while they were 'investigating the abuse' was a deeply healing process," she explained to me. "I wouldn't call it revenge, as it was too positive an emotion for that, but the whole process was cathartic and healing."

Like the Conti and Lopez cases in the United States, Amelia's hard-fought victory against Watchtower is extremely significant. It not only resulted in justice being served, but also dealt Watchtower a bloody nose financially, thus providing a powerful incentive for reform. Policies that, for so long, have caused immeasurable harm to countless children are now finally hurting Watchtower on the balance sheet.

A further crushing blow to the organization came with Australia's Royal Commission into Institutional Responses to Child Sexual Abuse, which considered Jehovah's Witnesses as case study 29 in the summer of 2015. It is hard to overstate the significance of the Commission in dragging Watchtower's dreadful policies firmly under the spotlight, or the elation felt by ex-JW activists like myself at the sheer spectacle of such a draconian, overbearing religious entity for once being on the receiving end of intense judgment and scrutiny. Finally, the authorities of a modern democracy were seen to be giving the organization's negligence the close attention it warranted. The live feeds of Watchtower officials being questioned before the Commission soon found their way onto YouTube, and made for compelling, almost addictive viewing.

Angus Stewart, SC, a slender South African Oxford graduate and brilliant lawyer, proved to be the Commission's inspired choice as counsel for the case study. From the outset, he demonstrated an uncanny ability to absorb mountains of tedious details about Watchtower doctrine and policy, and become fully conversant in its various nuances (no easy thing for someone not raised as a Witness). Stewart wielded this remarkable ability with devastating effect when grilling the various elders and Watchtower representatives who had the unenviable task of being forced to defend the organization under his relentless, probing cross-examination.

Much of the proceedings revolved around the abhorrent treatment of two women who were identified only as "BCB" and "BCG," both of whom gave testimony. Their ordeals perfectly highlighted the appalling inadequacy of Watchtower's child abuse policies when put into practice, and how inconsistent elders can be when trusted to enforce them.

***Angus Stewart***

BCB was raised on a farm in Western Australia. She began attending meetings from the age of 10, and was baptized at 18. From when she was 15, BCB was groomed and sexually abused by an elder named Bill Neill, who was the father of one of her friends. Neill was one of only two elders in her congregation—the other was Max Horley. Years later, when BCB and her husband went to speak to Horley about the abuse, a meeting was arranged with the circuit overseer and Neill, who—astonishingly—was brought into BCB's home by the elders for this all-male tribunal. Neill was defiant and defensive, and accused BCB of walking around his home wearing revealing clothing—a typical blame-the-victim routine.

Horley told the Commission that even though he had no reason to doubt BCB's allegations, he was powerless to pursue judicial action against Neill because there was no second witness to the abuse. Incredibly, he had also instructed BCB not to mention her abuse to anyone out of respect for Neill's family. Horley and the circuit overseer believed BCB enough to insist Neill step down as an elder for "uncleanness," but not enough to take judicial action against him or report the matter to authorities. Even after being removed as an elder, Neill still held an active role in the congregation, and BCB was required to see him several times a week—including at meetings at his home. In a letter to Watchtower, Horley and the circuit overseer said that they would like Neill to serve as an elder again "once this has died down."

Exasperated by her treatment, BCB had, by 2014, decided to take her accusations to the Royal Commission. Learning of this, an elder telephoned her husband and asked whether she really wanted to "drag Jehovah's name through the mud." The same elder, Joe Bello, admitted before the Commission that such a statement completely contradicted the organization's own guidelines to never dissuade victims from going to the authorities. In giving evidence, BCB explained the crushing effects of her experience:

> The abuse definitely changed who I was. It destroyed my confidence and my self-esteem. Even though the sexual abuse stopped when I was 19, I have continued to feel like Bill's victim well into my adult life. I've had a lot of therapy to address what Bill did to me, but I still have trouble feeling a sense of closure about what happened. I still feel that Bill was never made to face any consequences for what he did to me. I felt like Bill's position as an elder contributed to his power over me.

Similarly traumatized by her ordeal was BCG, from Queensland. When BCG was 13 years old, her father was appointed a ministerial servant. When she was 17, her father sexually abused her multiple times over a two-week period while the rest of the family were away on vacation. Shortly after the incident, BCG approached two elders in her congregation who happened to be friends with her father. She told the Commission that both refused to speak to her until she confronted her father, or unless he was present at the meeting.

It was eight months before a meeting was finally arranged between BCG and her elders at the insistence of her boyfriend. By that point, BCG's father was already being investigated by the elders for an extramarital relationship. It would become clear that marital infidelity was of more pressing concern to the elders than a man's sexual assault of his teenage daughter.

BCG was interviewed several times—again by an all-male tribunal. In one of those meetings, BCG's father was brought before her, causing her to feel terrified. She related how he threatened her verbally and physically, and blamed her for seducing him. Around this time, BCG learned that her father had abused not only her, but her older sister and two younger sisters. She told the Commission that when she informed the elders of these new allegations, the two elders refused to accept the testimony of her sisters even though these should have been considered under the two victim rule. According to BCG, she was told by the elders that the evidence of her sisters could not be considered because they were too young to know what they were talking about, and were not witnesses to the same event.

Under examination by Stewart, all three elders denied remembering anything about these extra allegations concerning the abuse of BCG's sisters. They also admitted to believing BCG to be a genuine abuse victim, but said they were powerless to take action because they lacked sufficient evidence.

But things began to unravel when one of the elders, Dino Ali, was shown notes that he had taken at the time of the investigation. These handwritten notes proved that the elders were aware of the allegations of abuse by BCG's sisters, one of whom was as young as two or three when she was first molested. The notes also revealed that BCG's father had confessed to assaulting her, meaning that the elders had all the grounds they needed to disfellowship him—not just under the two-*victim* rule, but also under the two-*witness* rule. Amazingly, they neglected to do this. Instead, BCG's elders disfellowshipped the father—someone they believed to be a pedophile—purely on the grounds of lying and "loose conduct" in an extramarital affair. Worse still, the elders' notes revealed that BCG was ordered never to mention her abuse to anyone—not even her soon-to-be fiancé. As with BCB, the dreadful treatment of BCG by her elders left lasting scars, as she recounted in her testimony:

> At trial, my father denied all charges against him. It took six years and three trials before he was finally convicted for the indecent assault of me. The elders who presided over the committee meetings and the appeal committee meetings gave evidence at the committal and at a voir dire during the first trial but the trial resulted in a hung jury. The second trial was declared a mistrial. My father was convicted at the third trial at the end of 2004. He was sentenced to three years imprisonment.
>
> The trials were easy compared to what I had been through with the elders during the committee meetings. I would go through it 20 more times if I had to. At least the court has rules when questioning survivor witnesses. The Jehovah's Witnesses can do and insinuate whatever they want, and there are no protections for the victims at all.
>
> I've had no contact with any of the elders involved in the committee meetings or from the Mareeba congregation or from the Watchtower since my father was convicted.

> During my teens, I was at times depressed and suicidal and this became worse after my father's sexual abuse of me while my mother was away at Expo 88. I also attempted suicide several months after the committee meetings in 1989 as a result of my experience of the committee meetings with the elders, and I couldn't bear the judgment of those around me, the public vilification and ostracism, I wanted to dig a hole and die.
>
> The only time I felt my upset feelings were heard, was when I went to the police. Nobody else, up until that point, had acknowledged that what my father did to me was wrong and he should be made to answer for it. I have at times lived a life in fear of being ostracized, shunned and vilified by those around me. I have always lived in fear of my father. I have lived in fear of Jehovah. I thought I had done all the right things, had put my trust in Jehovah, but nobody protected me. They only made it worse.

Again, an abuse victim was silenced. Again, evidence was ignored. Again, the police were left out altogether. And again, incompetent men failed miserably in implementing the organization's already-flawed guidelines. But all of this was only the tip of the iceberg. Before the Commission began delving into the cases of BCB and BCG, Stewart explained how the government inquiry had summonsed Watchtower Australia to produce its records related to child abuse. This brings us back, once more, to the elusive database.

When the Commission received the 5,000 documents representing the records for the Australia branch alone, what it found was astonishing. A total of 1,006 case files emerged relating to allegations of child sexual abuse made against Jehovah's Witnesses in Australia going as far back as 1950, with each file representing a different alleged perpetrator. This nauseating discovery brought long-held fears over Watchtower's database into sharp focus. Rumor and speculation collided abruptly with reality. Watchtower's Australian arm had been keeping secret records on 1,006 alleged pedophiles between 1950 and 2014—and bear in mind these records would only have been generated *due to judicial action being taken.* Hence, these 1,006 individuals would have had their guilt established by elders, and would have all been either disfellowshipped or reproved over the 65-year period. But as Stewart continued his opening address to the Commission, the full horror unfolded:

> Evidence will be put before the Royal Commission that of the 1,006 alleged perpetrators of child sexual abuse identified by the Jehovah's Witness Church since 1950, not one was reported by the Church to secular authorities. This suggests that it is the practice of the Jehovah's Witness Church to retain information regarding child sexual abuse offenses but not to report allegations of child sexual abuse to the police or other relevant authorities.

So 1,006 pedophiles—all of them either reproved or disfellowshipped for child sex abuse between 1950 and 2014—and not a single one reported to the police! Stewart would later reveal that these case files related to at least 1,800 victims, all of whom will have had their abuse effectively covered up by the organization.

After having some time to absorb the magnitude of this disclosure, I decided to try extrapolating what the numbers might be if Jehovah's Witnesses in countries like the United States, Canada and Britain were to have the same pedophile rates as Australia. I checked the publisher numbers from the last 65 years of Watchtower yearbooks, and used this data to produce an estimated number of victims and perpetrators. Based on my calculations, with the same rates as Australia, between 1950 and 2014 the Britain branch would have had details of 2,324 perpetrators and 4,159 victims. The Canada branch would have had 1,965 perpetrators and 3,515 victims. And the United States branch would have had 17,084 perpetrators and 30,568 victims. The combined estimated totals for Australia, Canada, Britain and the United States: 22,379 perpetrators and 40,041 victims.[9]

Again, I would go to pains to point out that these are just *extrapolations*, and there is no way of being certain of any numbers until Watchtower releases the records in its database for all countries as it was forced to do in Australia.[10] Even so, if my extrapolation turns out to be indicative of the true picture, we are talking about tens of thousands of pedophiles who have never faced justice. Bowen's number—23,720—was not quite so unbelievable after all.

Given the scale of Watchtower's pedophile problem over 65 years in Australia alone, it would not be unreasonable to expect a degree of humility and introspection from the Governing Body. An apology to decades' worth of victims, backed up with offers of compensation and remedial action, would certainly be welcome even if belated.[11] At the very least, it would be reassuring to

---

9 The data from which these calculations are derived may be found in Appendix H.

10 At the time of writing there is a case brought by another of Gonzalo Campos' victims, Osbaldo Padron (also represented by Irwin Zalkin) in which the judge is again insisting that Watchtower release its records—even introducing a $4,000-per-day fine until these materialize. True to form, Watchtower is so far refusing to comply. Whether Watchtower finally relinquishes the database in this case or as a result of some other legal intervention, it is hard to believe it can keep such damning evidence shrouded in secrecy forever.

11 For example, consider the following statement on a Catholic website under the heading "How does the Church help

think that measures are being put in place now so that future generations of children are protected. But at the time of writing, Watchtower seems happy to continue to weather the storm of negative media, costly settlements and legal defeats rather than introduce urgently-needed reforms. Neither is there any cause for optimism when reviewing the rhetoric and actions of those Governing Body members who have been called upon to answer for the organization on this matter. Their behavior can be summed up in two words: defiance and denial.

As of 2016, the Governing Body is made up of seven members—four of whom have had some involvement in the issue: Gerrit Lösch, Stephen Lett, Anthony Morris III and Geoffrey Jackson. I have already mentioned Gerrit Lösch's no-show in the Lopez case. Those of a Christian persuasion might call to mind the words of Christ to his disciples at Luke 21:12:

> But before all these things happen, people will lay their hands on you and persecute you, handing you over to the synagogues and prisons. You will be brought before kings and governors for the sake of my name.

By insisting that Lösch give evidence on a matter of such importance, nobody was persecuting him or treating him harshly. Instead, he had an opportunity

---

victims?": "The Archdiocese of Baltimore has long been committed to the treatment and healing of those who have been harmed through abuse. We apologize and offer counseling assistance and pastoral services. The Archdiocese also recognizes the importance of offering support to family members. We do this for as long as it is helpful, and regardless of the age of the incident. We provide this support regardless of lawsuits and statutes of limitations. We have paid $2.8 million in victim counseling, and more than $7.6 million in direct payments to victims/survivors. The Archdiocese continues to spend hundreds of thousands of dollars annually to assist victims and protect children."

to set the record straight regarding Watchtower's child abuse policies, and defend the reputation of "Jehovah's organization" before a court of law. He refused, despite risking considerable ramifications for his failure to appear, and stooped to utter dishonesty regarding his relationship with Watchtower in doing so.

Less timid about publicly airing his thoughts on the organization's track record on child abuse was Stephen Lett. In a video sermon aired on JW Broadcasting, he said (bold is mine):

> Another way we can contribute to the oneness: rejecting false stories that are designed to separate us from Jehovah's organization. As an example, **think about the apostate-driven lies and dishonesties that Jehovah's organization is permissive toward pedophiles. I mean, that is ridiculous, isn't it?** If anybody takes action against someone who would threaten our young ones and takes action to protect our young ones, it's Jehovah's organization. We reject outright such lies.

Hopefully by this point it is painfully obvious that Watchtower's mishandling of child abuse is anything but "apostate-driven lies and dishonesties." Lett's denial is itself an outrageous lie given all the court cases and settlements he must be aware of as a Governing Body member. His reaction amounts to little more than burying his head in the sand, and demanding his followers do the same. (The straw man in Lett's comments should also be noted, namely the false claim that apostates accuse the organization of being "permissive toward pedophiles." Activists like myself do not for one moment suggest that Watchtower literature *condones* pedophilia. Rather, policies such as the two-witness rule have the effect, whether intended or not, of *shielding pedophiles from justice*—a distinction Lett was happy to blur for the sake of rousing the disgust of his audience against their unseen and muted apostate foe.)

Equally adept at employing insinuation and falsehood in denying the organization's culpability in this area is Anthony Morris III, who also addressed child abuse during his appearance in the July 2015 JW Broadcasting episode. Morris began by reassuring Witnesses on the matter of reporting to police:

> Our policy as an organization is that one professing to be a victim or his parents should never be discouraged from reporting the incident to the appropriate authorities.

This represents an obfuscation; a clever play on words. Watchtower elders are now instructed not to *dissuade* parents from reporting the abuse of their children to the police if that is what they want to do, but there is an enormous difference between not dissuading someone from reporting and *encouraging* them to do so—especially in the context of an organization that preaches confidentiality, promotes distrust of the outside world, elevates and exaggerates the power and remit of elders, and advocates not taking one's "brother" to court.

***On a JW Broadcasting episode, Anthony Morris III holds aloft an "Awake!" magazine from 1982***

Morris went on to boast of how Watchtower has actually been proactive in addressing child molestation:

> As the awareness of child abuse became more and more known, we published a landmark *Awake!* magazine over 30 years ago. It was the issue of June 22, 1982. There are five article titles that nailed the subject in a very straightforward manner. The first article was entitled: "The New Morality." And then, "Chickens and Hawks" was the second article. It warned about homosexual men who prey on and advocate the right to use boys for sex. Shame on them!

Hence, rather than admit to serious organizational problems with the mishandling of child sexual abuse (for which there is no end of supporting evidence), Morris essentially pinned the blame on homosexuals. He also claimed that, far from being naive, the organization was actually way ahead of the game! As proof he brandished a 1982 *Awake!* magazine, not one single page of which advocates reporting to authorities in all cases where child abuse is suspected. (As it turns out, this is a notable flaw across *all* published Watchtower material on this subject.) In summing up, Morris went as far as to express pride for the organization's track record in this area:

> While we cannot control everything that an individual might say, it is clear that over the decades protecting children from abuse is a top priority for this organization. We are proud of our reputation in this regard, and we look forward to the time in God's new world where no one, young or old, will ever again be a victim of abuse.

These comments, in my view, typify the Governing Body's willful ignorance of the urgent need to take meaningful action to protect children. It is not just that these men are *proud* of their appalling reputation in this area—they also fail to recognize their own duties and responsibilities *in the here and now,* instead choosing to shift the problem of ending child abuse upward. In their view, the new world order over which they will soon preside as kings and priests in heaven with Christ will render the earth a child abuse-free zone. This is precisely the attitude expressed decades ago in the 1982 *Awake!* magazine lauded by Morris:

> In God's due time all who embrace his kingdom under Christ will become able to keep this law of love perfectly. Then will come fulfillment of Proverbs 2:21, 22: "The upright are the ones who will reside in the earth, and the blameless are the ones that will be left over in it. As regards the wicked, they will be cut off from the very earth; and as for the treacherous, they will be torn away from it."
>
> This is the only way, the final way, to end child abuse.

Our final example of Governing Body arrogance and denial comes in the ample form of Geoffrey Jackson. Earlier I mentioned that Jackson, in his appearance before the Royal Commission, admitted that Jehovah's Witnesses do have some kind of problem with child abuse—even if it is a problem Jackson considers the organization to be on top of:

> I accept that child abuse is a problem right throughout the community and it's something that we've had to deal with as well . . . There have been changes in policies over the last 20 or 30 years, where we've tried to address some of those problem areas, and by the fact that they have changed the policy would indicate that the original policies weren't perfect.

It seems very likely that when Stewart asked the questions that prompted those remarks, he did so

***Geoffrey Jackson testifies by video link before the Australian Royal Commission***

knowing that Stephen Lett had recently dismissed all claims about child abuse as "apostate-driven lies and dishonesties." Indeed, later in the proceedings, Stewart went on to specifically ask Jackson whether claims of child sex abuse among Jehovah's Witnesses amount to "apostate lies":

> Stewart: Would you disagree, then, with anyone who said that the efforts to highlight and deal with child sexual abuse in the Jehovah's Witness church are engaging in apostate lies?
>
> Jackson: I guess that's a broad question, because sometimes those who make these accusations make many other accusations as well. But let me assure you, the person making the accusation is not the main thing. The main thing is: is there some basis to the accusation. And if there is some way that we could improve, the Governing Body is always interested in seeing how we can refine our policies. You see, Mr. Stewart, could I just emphasize, as a religion, two very strong things we feel. One is, we try to keep a high moral standard. Secondly, there is love among the organization. So we want to treat victims in a loving way.

Rather than agree or disagree with the sentiments of his colleague, Jackson could only offer a vague and evasive answer about there being love in the organization. Even worse, when Stewart later showed Jackson from the Bible that the Governing Body could actually bypass the two-witness rule altogether if they so wished, Jackson refused to play ball. Stewart drew Jackson's attention to a passage at Deuteronomy 22:23-27, in which a scenario involving rape is discussed:

> If a virgin is engaged to a man, and another man happens to meet her in the city and lies down with her, you should bring them both out to the gate of that city and stone them to death, the girl because she did not scream in the city and the man because he humiliated the wife of his fellow man. So you must remove what is evil from your midst.
>
> If, however, the man happened to meet the engaged girl in the field and the man overpowered her and lay down with her, the man who lay down with her is to die by himself, and you must do nothing to the girl. The girl has not committed a sin deserving of death. This case is the same as when a man attacks his fellow man and murders him. For he happened to meet her in the field, and the engaged girl screamed, but there was no one to rescue her.

What Stewart was offering was a "get out of jail free" card. The Governing Body, if they wanted, could allow accused pedophiles to face justice *without* two witnesses and still claim a scriptural basis for such a policy. After all, a man raping a virgin in a field without witnesses must be just as culpable, for the sake of argument, as an adult raping a child without anyone watching. Stewart therefore landed his punch brilliantly by asking Jackson:

> Is it not the case that had Jesus been asked about a case of sexual abuse, he may have referred back

> to this part of Deuteronomy and said that it's not required to have two witnesses?

Jackson could only reply:

> I certainly would like to ask Jesus that, and I can't at the moment, I hope to in the future. But that's a hypothetical question which, if we had an answer, then we could support what you said.

Weeks after appearing before the Commission, Jackson sent written testimony entirely dismissing the scriptural loophole Stewart had presented. In his letter, Jackson wrote:

> It is important to note that the two contrasting situations in verses 23 to 27 of Deuteronomy chapter 22 do not deal with proving whether the man is guilty in either situation. His guilt is assumed in both instances. In saying that he:
>
> "happened to meet her in the city and lay down with her"
>
> or he:
>
> "happened to meet the engaged girl in the field and the man overpowered her and lay down with her"
>
> in both instances, the man had already been proved guilty and worthy of death, this being determined by proper procedure earlier in the judges' inquiry. But the question at this point before the judges (having established that improper sexual relations had occurred between the man and the woman) was whether the engaged woman had been guilty of immorality or was a victim of rape. This is a different issue, although related, to establishing the man's guilt.

Jackson was effectively arguing that the two witness rule overrides the provision for adjudicating cases of rape in Deuteronomy. In his opinion, the rapist in Deuteronomy 22 would have already had his guilt established without the woman's testimony. Essentially, Jackson trusts that the rapist would have given a full confession to elders of raping the woman in the field, despite facing the penalty of death by stoning for coming clean. Not only does this argument make no logical sense, it is also interesting to note that—in the space of just *three weeks*—Jackson had gone from hoping to ask Jesus a question about a certain verse in Deuteronomy to suddenly having all the answers about that same verse. "New light" had been dispatched in record time, and it had given the Governing Body a free pass to continue applying the two-witness rule even in cases of child rape.

Stewart summed up his understandable frustration over all this in his written findings to the Commission:

> It is submitted that Mr. Jackson was evasive and unhelpful in assisting the Royal Commission to understand whether there is scope for interpretation of the two-witness rule such that would allow for action to be taken in circumstances where there is only one direct witness to an incident of child sexual abuse.
>
> It is further submitted that the current position is that where the victim is the only witness to an incident of child sexual abuse and the abuser does not confess, the Jehovah's Witness organization will not take action until such time as a second child is abused in similar circumstances by the same accused person. It is submitted that this position is untenable and is completely at odds with the organization's expression of abhorrence of child sexual abuse.

Hence, despite the best efforts of the Australian Royal Commission, Geoffrey Jackson's testimony did not move them any closer to addressing the main problems with the Governing Body's flawed policy.[12] Even when presented with a golden opportunity to bypass the archaic two-witness requirement when deliberating over reports of child rape, the Governing Body rigidly stuck to its guns—meaning that countless Witness children will continue to be placed in harm's way.

Another noteworthy part of Jackson's testimony came in the following exchange with Stewart when he declared that he would actually *like* to see the reporting laws changed so that Watchtower would have no choice but to comply:

> Stewart: Perhaps you can address that question specifically, which is this: is there a scriptural basis to that policy or practice, being not to report child sexual abuse allegations to the authorities unless required by law to do so?
>
> Jackson: Thank you for the opportunity to explain this. I think very clearly Mr. Toole pointed out that if the Australian government, in all the states, was to make mandatory reporting, it would make it so much easier for us . . . So if the government does happen to make mandatory reporting, that will make this dilemma so much easier for us, because we all want the same goal, that children will be cared for properly.

The approach to policy-making described here by Jackson is extraordinary. We have already learned that

---

[12] Thankfully, it seems the Commission's scrutiny of the organization is not yet over. In November 2016, when this book was in final edits, its official website made the following announcement: "The Royal Commission into Institutional Responses to Child Sexual Abuse will hold a public hearing commencing in February 2017 into the current policies and procedures of each religious institution named below in relation to child protection and child-safe standards, including responding to allegations of child sexual abuse." Jehovah's Witnesses were included on the list.

Watchtower's modus operandi is to report accusations of child abuse only if it is commanded to do so by law. But Jackson is here suggesting that he would prefer the Australian government to *force* Watchtower to do the right thing by making reporting compulsory throughout the country. If the Governing Body is so anxious for this outcome, why not be proactive and report all accusations regardless of the local reporting laws?

Any Jehovah's Witness reading this would do well to ponder the fact that out of four Governing Body members who have either addressed or been called upon to address child abuse in the organization: one has breached a subpoena and refused to defend the policy in court, even denying his involvement with Watchtower altogether; one has described allegations of covering up child abuse as "apostate-driven lies and dishonesties;" one has similarly denied problems with child abuse, claiming the organization has a brilliant reputation and blaming the whole thing on gay people, and one has admitted there is a problem but refuses to do anything about it even after being presented with a scriptural basis for dropping the two-witness rule—even suggesting that the only thing preventing the organization from doing the right thing is that they are not always commanded to do so by the state.

In one's wildest imaginings it is difficult to conceive a more irresponsible, ham-fisted, negligent attitude toward the safety of children—but this, unfortunately, is the reality of how the revered leaders of a religion numbering eight million choose to confront rampant child sex abuse in their ranks. As nice as it would be to believe that these men understand the problem—and how best to fix it so that millions of

Witnesses children will be protected henceforth—the evidence points strongly to this not being the case. So long as the Governing Body clings to its obsession with the two-witness rule, children will be at risk from being molested and having their abuse concealed.

All the Governing Body needs to do to fix the problem is send a letter to all bodies of elders saying quite simply:

> *"Dear brothers, you are advised with immediate effect to contact the police or local authorities, regardless of the local reporting laws, if you hear of any accusations of child molestation within your congregation. Judicial handling of such matters may be pursued with the guidance of the branch, but your main priority should be to notify the authorities, assist them in pursuing their investigations, and follow their recommendations to protect the children in the congregation. Child molesters are not to engage in preaching activity on behalf of the congregation, or serve in any positions of trust."*

Unfortunately this letter does not exist, and is not likely to exist either—at least not for the foreseeable future. After all, if Watchtower is happy to lose millions in legal costs and expose itself to a steady flow of negative media rather than protect children, why should they budge on the issue any time soon?

Though it is impossible to peer into the minds of the Governing Body members and fully grasp their perspective and logic, it seems very likely that they are deluded enough to consider this whole matter a case of satanic persecution and a test of loyalty to Jehovah. Even if the organization were to go bankrupt over its mishandling of child abuse, I believe this—in the minds of Lösch, Lett, Morris and Jackson—would only be proof that Armageddon is imminent, and that Satan has launched his attack on Jehovah's people.

Yes, that is the level of delusion I believe we are dealing with.

I would hope that you, dear reader, are unreservedly appalled and disgusted at the full scale of neglect and incompetence surrounding Jehovah's Witnesses and child sex abuse after considering what has been so far explained in this chapter. Even so, if you have never been a Witness, you might be tempted to reason: "Yes, this is all very terrible, and I do feel bad for this situation, but this is an internal problem for a fringe religious movement. The fact that they refuse to address the problem of pedophilia may affect eight million Jehovah's Witnesses, but it doesn't affect me and my family."

Well, it is not quite that simple.

Rick Simons, the lawyer for Candace Conti, drew a rather obvious conclusion when being interviewed for *ABC News:*

> If ever there was a group that needs the sun to shine on them it's this one, because when your doorbell rings on Saturday morning, and your kid answers the door, you don't want that guy to be a child molester.

This chilling vision of a Witness pedophile calling at people's homes may sound too horrendous to contemplate, but it was played out on camera in a video posted to YouTube in August 2016 by an ex-JW going by the name of "Roman Vargas." (The video has since been removed from YouTube, but the incident was later reported on by a local news team.) On seeing the video I was able to reach out to Roman and get more background behind the encounter.

Roman lives in Colorado Springs, and had recently befriended a fellow ex-JW living locally who warned him of a convicted pedophile, Waymon Ivery, also living in his area. Appalled by this discovery, Roman consulted the sex offender's registry. Sure enough, he found that Ivery was living within a mile of his home. He was listed with a conviction for first-degree sexual assault on a child dating to December 1992. Horrified by the prospect of Ivery proselytizing in his neighborhood, Roman memorized Ivery's face so that he would recognize him if his worst fears were ever realized.

Then, one morning, Roman heard his dogs barking. He went to the window and saw a group of Witnesses standing by a car opposite his home. One of them was Ivery. Grabbing his phone to film the incident, Roman went outside and yelled: "Waymon!" When Ivery responded, Roman approached and established again that he was indeed Waymon Ivery.

The highly-charged conversation that ensued makes for shocking viewing. Ivery is seen retreating into his friend's vehicle as Roman asks him why he is out calling on people's homes despite being a convicted child rapist. Ivery can only respond with denials, telling Roman he has it "all wrong."[13] Another Witness inside the car is seen covering his ears, clearly traumatized by the confrontation, before the engine starts and the car pulls away.

As disturbing as the video is to watch, it represents the first irrefutable evidence that congregation elders *do* allow known pedophiles to engage in door-to-door

---

[13] Ivery has since admitted his crime and commented on his denials when confronted by Roman in an interview with Carlos Vergara for *News 5 Investigates*, which is available on YouTube at the time of writing.

preaching, despite the clear threat to children in the community.

Anyone who has been a Witness will tell you that there are countless instances when a door will be answered by a child. Of these cases, very occasionally the child will say that nobody is home. The ramifications for this situation if a pedophile is the one visiting do not bear thinking about. Even if someone like Ivery is accompanied by others, there are still clear opportunities for someone like him to exploit. For example, there is nothing stopping him from returning to a certain address by himself at another time.

It is simply unacceptable for Witness elders to hold door-to-door preaching as so sacrosanct for Witnesses as a form of worship that they should be required to engage in it even when they are convicted child molesters. Firstly, there are a number of forms of preaching that do not involve someone calling on the homes of children (i.e. cart witnessing, phone witnessing, or letter writing). Secondly, a Watchtower ban on pedophiles engaging in preaching would not be without precedent. If elders are already authorized to ban Witnesses from preaching just because their "dress and grooming is disturbing to the congregation," why can they not wield the same prohibition on convicted pedophiles?[14] What is of more pressing priority: chastising someone for wearing tight-fitting clothing, or protecting children from sexual predators?

Watchtower's negligence toward the safety of children in the community was further underscored by the testimony of Kevin Bowditch, one of the elders

---

[14] Further details of this bizarre rule, which can be found in the *Circuit Overseer Guidelines* document, are provided in footnote 34 in Chapter Eight.

questioned before the Royal Commission about the case involving BCG. Bowditch was specifically asked about risks posed to the public by child molesters who are cast out of Witness congregations:

> Stewart: And when a person is disfellowshipped, they then can still attend meetings, and so on, but under some restriction; is that right?
>
> Bowditch: Under a lot of restrictions.
>
> Stewart: And members of the congregation cannot associate with them socially?
>
> Bowditch: Socially or spiritually.
>
> Stewart: But the person is still, otherwise, in the world and can associate with people outside of the church?
>
> Bowditch: Yes.
>
> Stewart: And you don't take into consideration, do you, how people outside of the church might be kept safe from such a person whom you are not satisfied will not reoffend?
>
> Bowditch: If they were outside the church and they were a close friend, I would tell them.
>
> Stewart: How would you know if they were a close friend and outside of the church?
>
> Bowditch: If they are a close friend of mine.
>
> Stewart: A close friend of yours?
>
> Bowditch: Yes, if I was—if I had associated with them.
>
> Stewart: What about people who are not close friends of yours, others outside of the church—you don't take any steps, do you, to protect them from this potential reoffending?
>
> Bowditch: [blank stare]
>
> Stewart: You don't, do you? You are concerned with the congregation principally, aren't you?

Bowditch: Yes, we are concerned with the congregation. We are shepherds of the congregation.

Stewart: And you are not a shepherd to those who are not in the congregation?

Bowditch: No.

Stewart: And as an organization, in your experience, you don't seek to protect or take care of children who are outside of the congregation?

Bowditch: That's a broad statement.

Stewart: Well, I can limit it.

Bowditch: Yes, limit it, please.

Stewart: In your decision on whether or not to disfellowship someone, you don't take consideration of children outside of the congregation?

Bowditch: We do take consideration of them, but what ability have we got to protect every child in Australia?

Stewart: Well, what you can do is you can report to the child protection authorities.

Bowditch: And that is done in some cases.

Stewart: But generally it's not done, is it?

Bowditch: No.

Stewart: It's not done unless there is a legal requirement for it to be done, is it?

Bowditch: That is true.

This awkward exchange, combined with the Ivery incident, demonstrates Watchtower's appalling lack of awareness regarding its responsibility to the wider community. The expectation that Witnesses should be able to preach door-to-door even if they have a history of child molestation represents a clear threat even to children whose families have nothing to do with the Witness faith. And even if a pedophile is cast out of the religion and therefore can no longer preach, he still poses a threat. If he is disfellowshipped without being reported, he is effectively being unleashed into the community without being on the radar of the authorities—free to offend again. This problem really does affect *everyone*, but there is precious little to suggest the Governing Body will grasp the urgent need to take action any time soon.

The most recent instructions issued by Watchtower available at the time of writing come in the form of a letter to elders dated August 1, 2016. This six-page document, which replaces the October 1, 2012, instructions issued in the wake of the Conti verdict, was sent out almost exactly 12 months after Watchtower's policies were savaged by the Australian Royal Commission.[15] But despite being apparently written in a way that is more wary of external scrutiny, astonishingly little has changed. The two-witness rule remains in force even if, unlike in the 2012 letter, it is nowhere expressly mentioned.[16] Elders must continue to defer to the branch office and receive instructions from the legal and service departments in all matters, including whether to report to authorities or not. The writers seem under the impression that known predatory Witness pedophiles can be persuaded by elders "never to be alone with a

---

[15] I would very much like to be able to produce this and other letters for the reader's inspection as part of the Appendix. However, I have received legal threats in the past from Watchtower for reproducing its "copyrighted" letters to elders, and I would prefer to shield this book from legal action wherever possible. Suffice to say, the August 1, 2016 letter should be easily found online by those determined enough to seek it out.

[16] Paragraph 13 of the letter urges elders to "carefully follow Scriptural procedures and the Bible-based direction" when investigating child abuse allegations, especially according to the guidance in Chapter Five of the *Shepherd* book—the same chapter that tells elders to "leave matters in Jehovah's hands" if a second witness is not forthcoming.

minor, not to cultivate friendships with minors, not to display affection for minors, and so forth," simply by being cautioned to that effect. And, despite receiving advice to the contrary at the Royal Commission,[17] Watchtower still seems under the illusion that announcing the reproof of someone known to them as a pedophile for an unspecified offense will "serve as a protection" to parents and children:

> If wrongdoing is established and the wrongdoer is not repentant, he should be disfellowshipped. (*ks10* chap. 7 par. 26) On the other hand, if the wrongdoer is repentant and is reproved, the reproof should be announced to the congregation. (*ks10* chap. 7 pars. 20-21) This announcement will serve as a protection for the congregation.

In two ways this letter even *regresses* the child abuse policy from its already sorry state. Rather than bodies of elders having autonomy to warn other bodies of elders if a known predator is moving from one congregation to another, the letter insists that the branch must first be consulted—thus adding a needless tier of bureaucracy to what should be a straightforward matter of elders in congregation A warning elders in congregation B that a child molester is likely to start

---

[17] On page 86 (points F50 to F52) of his submissions to the Commission, Stewart writes: "Since it is the policy or practice of the Jehovah's Witness organisation not to report allegations of child sexual abuse to the police (other than if required by law to do so), if a known abuser is found to be repentant and for that reason merely reproved rather than disfellowshipped he remains in the congregation and a risk to children in the congregation. The system of not announcing the reasons for reproval means that members of the congregation are not warned about the risk that such a wrongdoer poses to children in the congregation. The sanction of reproval therefore does nothing to protect children in the congregation and in the broader community."

visiting their Kingdom Hall. The relevant paragraphs in the *Shepherd* book granting such autonomy are even to be crossed out (which raises the question of just how seriously the *Shepherd* book can be taken if entire paragraphs can be so swiftly rendered obsolete). And, incredibly, the "Do Not Call" list—designed to prevent Witnesses from bothering those who have expressly requested them not to visit—is henceforth expected to double-up as a child safeguarding tool. If elders learn that a disfellowshipped pedophile has moved into their territory, or if the authorities notify them of a pedophile at a certain address, paragraphs 22 and 23 urge that "the elders should list that address on the appropriate congregation territory card as a 'Do Not Call.'" Anyone who has any experience of door-to-door preaching as a Witness will appreciate that Witnesses frequently call on do-not-calls by mistake, perhaps after becoming engrossed in conversation with their partner. If a Witness inadvertently stumbles on a do-not-call, they assume the worst that is likely to happen is that they will find themselves on the wrong end of a severe tongue-lashing. But if a Witness working with a minor, or two young teenagers working together, mistakenly stumble on a pedophile's address, the worst case scenario does not bear contemplating.

Despite these disturbing new instructions, the letter offers a glimmer of hope that, at least in one area, the Governing Body is finally beginning to understand the gravity of what they are dealing with:

> One who has engaged in child sexual abuse does not qualify to receive any privileges in the congregation for many years, if ever. This includes seemingly minor privileges. Elders should keep in mind what is stated in the January 1, 1997, *Watchtower* article "Let Us Abhor What Is Wicked," page 29,

> paragraph 2: "Child sexual abuse reveals an unnatural fleshly weakness. Experience has shown that such an adult may well molest other children. True, not every child molester repeats the sin, but many do. And the congregation cannot read hearts to tell who is and who is not liable to molest children again. (Jeremiah 17:9) Hence, Paul's counsel to Timothy applies with special force in the case of baptized adults who have molested children: 'Never lay your hands hastily upon any man; neither be a sharer in the sins of others.' (1 Timothy 5:22)." Therefore, if the body of elders believes that one who has engaged in child sexual abuse decades ago may now qualify for minor privileges, such as carrying or adjusting microphones, operating audio/video equipment, or assisting with accounts, literature, magazines, or territories, they should assign two elders to call the Service Department. The assigned elders should call the Service Department before any congregation privileges are extended.

Though not quite sufficiently robust, the above guidance is a welcome reversal of the 2012 letter, mentioned earlier, in which elders were informed: "It cannot be said in every case that one who has sexually abused a child could never qualify for privileges of service in the congregation." True, the door remains slightly ajar for a pedophile Witness who harbors ambitions of performing fairly menial Kingdom Hall duties (such as dispensing literature or operating the sound system) "decades" after his abuse. However, of more pressing concern is the blocking of pedophiles from ever becoming elders and ministerial servants, which are positions of respect and trust. Most elders reading this part of the letter would understand it to mean that the risks of "laying their hands hastily" are far too high when a known pedophile is being considered for such appointments.[18] Let us therefore hope that, henceforth, there will be no new Gonzalo Campos-like cases of pedophiles being elevated into such positions, and that future guidance to elders firmly and unequivocally precludes this from happening. (Of course, how congregations are to deal with pedophile elders and servants who have *already* managed to climb back up the ladder while they still could is, of course, another matter entirely—a matter on which the 2016 letter is silent.)

As with most aspects of Watchtower policy and teachings, writing about the organization's child abuse policies can be a frustrating exercise. One is essentially trying to aim at a moving target. Cases won in court can be appealed. Significant new cases can surface, shedding light on certain matters previously not known or considered. Governing Body members can die off and be replaced by new members with more (or less) progressive ideas. New Governing Body instructions to elders can replace older publications and letters. If you are reading this more than ten years in the future, assuming Watchtower has not bankrupted itself by then, doubtless there will have been several changes in policy in the intervening years.

It is my sincere hope that, sooner or later, Jehovah's Witnesses will become a religion with procedures that make it impossible for pedophiles to exploit the trust of parents and children, or rely on organizational bureaucracy to effectively conceal their crimes. I will be among the first to rejoice when the day comes that

---

[18] Based on 1 Timothy 5:22, the principle of not "laying hands hastily" requires elders not to be quick to appoint men to privileges of service who might not qualify.

the Governing Body finally *truly* grasps that "even one abused child is one too many," and that child molestation is to be treated as a crime first, and a sin second. But as things stand, we are still painfully far off from that day dawning, and the true horror of it all is that Watchtower's problems are self-inflicted. It never had to be this way.

My fear is that it will take many more years of courtroom defeats and negative media exposure for the organization's hierarchy to adequately address the problem by ditching the two-witness rule, allowing reporting of *all* allegations, and guaranteeing that no pedophile Witness is (or ever will be) in a position of trust, or able to visit the homes of children in the community. And even when this eureka moment finally arrives, the Governing Body will still be left with the onerous task of paying compensation to the multitude of victims accumulated over the decades before the problem was addressed—which alone would surely bankrupt whatever is left of "Jehovah's organization." Thus, whichever way you look at the mishandling of child abuse by Watchtower, the damage has already been done and *nothing* can ever put it right, as should be immediately obvious when talking to anyone whose life has been irreversibly scarred by the Slave's stubborn refusal to protect children from the very worst of humanity.

Regrettably, however, negligence surrounding child abuse is not the only means by which the Jehovah's Witness hierarchy has ruined lives. The trauma of shunning has also been wielded to devastating effect by successive Watchtower leaders as a tool for keeping multiple generations of Witnesses mentally imprisoned, as I can personally attest.

CHAPTER ELEVEN

# 8 Million Hostages

*"You only have power over people so long as you don't take everything away from them. But when you've robbed a man of everything, he's no longer in your power—he's free again."*
—Aleksandr Solzhenitsyn

IN HIS brilliant book *The End of Faith*, Sam Harris touches on the desperate plight of the North Korean people, who currently languish under the fear and tyranny of a dynasty of maniacal despots of which Kim Jong-un is the present incumbent. Though published in 2005, when the world political landscape was somewhat different, Harris' insightful words thoroughly resonate:

> We should, I think, look upon modern despotisms as hostage crises. Kim Jong Il has thirty million. Saddam Hussein had twenty-five million. The clerics in Iran have seventy million more. It does not matter that many hostages have been so brainwashed that they will fight their would-be liberators to the death. They are held prisoner twice over—by tyranny and by their own ignorance. The developed world must, somehow, come to their rescue.

Hopefully you are sufficiently persuaded by the preceding material in this volume to understand why I believe the above words tick so many boxes when it comes to Jehovah's Witnesses. I am not suggesting for one moment that the likes of Mark Sanderson, Geoffrey Jackson and Tony Morris on their most despotic days can match the North Korean leadership in all its gratuitous savagery. There is clearly a distinction to be drawn between a bunch of deluded men who coerce people to follow them, to the detriment of their health or family if necessary, and a merciless dictator capable of executing one of his generals with an antiaircraft gun for falling asleep at an inopportune moment (as Kim Jong-un reportedly once did).

No, the similarity lies, not in the violence and savagery, but in the fact that, like North Koreans, Jehovah's Witnesses are *hostages*—all eight million of them.[1] As Harris points out: strip away the barbed wire and sentry towers from North Korea's borders and, though a mass defection would almost inevitably ensue, any army of would-be liberators would still have their work cut out fighting to emancipate a significant portion of the population from their leader and his notebook-carrying cronies. Why? Because North Koreans are brainwashed morning, noon and night to *adore* Kim Jong-un. They genuinely believe they are reliant on him for their prosperity. They are kept prisoner, not by barbed wire, guns and sentry towers, but by their own reconditioned minds.

The same is true of Jehovah's Witnesses. Substitute the barbed wire for Watchtower's shunning policy, which serves as a powerful deterrent against defection, and you have the same scenario. Even if you could somehow reverse the shunning rules and make it so that Witnesses are allowed to leave while still

---

[1] The latest available *Yearbook* figures indicate between 7,987,279 (average) and 8,220,105 (peak) active Witness publishers for 2015, although this number will no doubt fluctuate in the future.

maintaining a normal relationship with their believing loved ones, a considerable majority would willingly remain shackled to their dear leaders and vehemently oppose any efforts to wrest power from the Governing Body. Why? Because they are held captive in their own minds through *brainwashing*—a systematic development of emotional bias and dependency using fear and the meticulous control of information—exactly the same means by which Kim Jong-un, despite being such an overwhelmingly undesirable choice as leader, continues to have an entire country as his personal plaything.

Of course, I understand "brainwashing" is a strong word to use—a word that many would consider alarmist or sensationalist—but it accurately describes the process cult victims go through: the conditioning of one's mind so that authentic impulses and desires are supplanted or overruled by those of a person, group or government. It is an accurate word that, in my view, is not used nearly enough in explaining the otherwise confounding beliefs and behavior of people under oppressive regimes and wacky cults, from North Korea to Scientology, from ISIS to the Westboro Baptist Church.[2] Even in the ex-cult community, there seems to be understandable aversion to embracing the B-word for fear of losing credibility. Cult experts like Steven Hassan (a former Moonie) with his illuminating BITE model tend to favor less abrasive terms such as "mind control," "exploitative persuasion" and the legal term "undue influence."[3] Even more politically-correct,

---

[2] I will discuss the use of the word "cult" more extensively in the next chapter.

[3] BITE is an acronym for Behavior control, Information control, Thought control and Emotional control. Hassan's BITE model is helpful in highlighting how cults use these elements

media-friendly alternatives might be "grooming" or "radicalization"—although the more one steers toward political correctness, the more one's words become shrouded in ambiguity. (What really is "radicalization"? Who gets to decide what is "radical," and what isn't?) All of these terms describe more or less the same process and can be used almost interchangeably, depending on the disposition of the audience. But, since this is my book, I get to choose the word I consider to be the closest fit.

Brainwashing is very much real and flourishing in the heart of civilization deep in this 21st century, and I am afraid it is the only way for us to make sense of the fact that eight million people currently identify as Jehovah's Witnesses despite being at least vaguely familiar with much of what you have read in the preceding chapters. Sadly, however, most people fortunate enough to be on the outside of cults, political regimes and other coercive brainwashing movements tend to balk at the suggestion that the human mind is reducible to a computer that can be programmed by others given the right circumstances. They reason that, if someone gets involved in a cult, it must have been—at least at some level—a conscious decision. But by embarking on this line of reasoning, one is essentially indulging in victim-blaming. Nobody *wants* to be used and lied to.

For example, take a look at some guidance dispensed by Graham Norton, a talented and funny comedian and talk show host who occasionally doubles as an advice columnist for *The Telegraph.* When approached by a man with a wife of 24 years who, since joining the

---

to influence their followers. For more information, I would recommend Hassan's *Combating Cult Mind Control—25th Anniversary Edition* which, in the interests of full disclosure, features a more concise version of my story on pages 175-177.

Witnesses, was a "completely different person" with views that caused "daily conflict" in their relationship, Norton's advice was thus:

> This is very hard. From where you are standing, the Jehovah's Witnesses have stolen your wife; but the truth is she gave herself away. It is hard to accept but the woman you married was clearly not happy—or at very least was not getting everything she needed from you and her children.

I can only sympathize with the poor fellow on the receiving end of Norton's "wisdom," who has been left feeling that he was not making his wife happy or giving her what she needed in their relationship. Even the children were apparently guilty in this respect. What Norton does not seem to understand is that nobody "gives themselves away" to a destructive cult, just as nobody knowingly signs up to a timeshare scam, or enthusiastically downloads a Trojan onto their computer, or runs out to buy a second-hand car anxious to acquire one that is actually two cars welded together. All of these rackets involve significant elements of deception and subterfuge to bait people into doing something they would not dream of doing with full knowledge, and in that respect cults like Jehovah's Witnesses are no different.

I am not suggesting for a moment that the Witness who calls at your door on a Saturday morning is fully cognizant that he is peddling nonsense and deliberately aims to pull the wool over your eyes. Rather, the Witness faith has evolved over more than a century into a self-perpetuating scam, so that even those in the higher echelons of the organization are deluded enough to be unaware that they are tricking people. For example, despite adorning the bookshelves of millions of Witnesses, at the time of writing, the previously-mentioned *Revelation* book is nowhere to be found in the extensive list of publications available to read or download on JW.org.[4] A Witness might shrug this off as either an oversight, or the necessary removal of "old light," or a well-meaning attempt on the Slave's part to shield the uninitiated from material that might be too profound or confusing. Whatever the conscious justification for withholding the *Revelation* book, the omission still amounts to deception—a lack of transparency.

The *Revelation* book is toxic to the aims of JW.org, and the Governing Body knows it. It presents a litany of absurdities that only begin to make sense once you have already been bombarded with extensive indoctrination to the point of embracing various foundational claims, i.e. that Jesus had a tussle with Satan in heaven in 1914 and threw him down to our biosphere, where he has been confined ever since. If you were to ask someone oblivious to Witness doctrine if they would consider signing up based solely on this proposition and other similar "gems" from the publication, the best response you could hope for would be a polite "thanks, but no thanks." Thus, by keeping this and other damning material at arm's length, Watchtower is deceiving the general public in precisely the same way a timeshare scammer or disreputable used car salesman would—by controlling the flow of information and baiting people with only the most attractive, universally appealing (and mostly fabricated) selling points. Once the critical thinking faculties of the prospective cult member have been pummeled into submission with promises

---

[4] It would not surprise me if a new book on prophecy is released in the near future, since so many Watchtower books dealing with prophecy are now obsolete due to the organization's ever-changing teachings.

of loved ones being resurrected and an eternity in a panda-strewn paradise, *then* you can introduce all the crazy stuff to your heart's content.

Deception, whether knowing or unknowing, is the reason why anyone becomes a Witness, whether they are indoctrinated from childhood or converted as adults. Deception, and not any failure on the part of her husband or children, was what drove the wife of the man who wrote to Graham Norton to distance herself from her family. Deception is the basic fuel that courses through the brainwashing engine, empowering all manner of nefarious, opportunistic enterprises, whether these are religious, political, commercial or therapy-based. As threatening and deeply unsatisfying as this thought may be, deception, when fully harnessed, can turn a human being into little more than a robot—capable of almost anything. It can override a parent's love for its child, or a child's love for its parent. It can even drive someone to kill themselves, or kill their loved ones, or kill total strangers.

Perhaps as a vestige of our religious heritage most of us are averse to the idea that we humans can, under certain conditions, be reduced to mindless automatons capable of doing unmentionable things at someone else's bidding. We like to think we are smarter than this as a species. We perhaps aspire to a more privileged position in the cosmos in which the basic integrity of the self, the essence of who we are, is sacred ground that can never be trespassed. But I am afraid that underestimating the weaknesses of our species and complacency on the issue will not stem the steady tide of damage being wrought on society by groups and individuals only too willing to exploit our collective ignorance and indecision.

To fix a problem, one must first acknowledge it—but even in the case of the clear threat posed to civilization by Islamist brainwashing, at the time of writing I am not convinced we are even close to that stage.[5] Cults are flourishing amid our hesitancy as a species to confront, question and criticize anything calling itself a religion. Jehovah's Witnesses in particular will continue to be held hostage by leaders every bit as deluded as their followers so long as the harm being unleashed, much of which has been catalogued in previous chapters, goes unchecked. It would be some consolation if governments, despite refusing to proactively tackle harmful cults, were at least not *rewarding* their cruelty with tax exemptions and even (I shudder to even write this) *charitable status*—but we are still a long way from reaching even this modest milestone.

One of the most depressing realizations awaiting those who wake up from cults is how indifferent the world is to the threat these movements pose, despite the immense power they wield in making people do things against their better judgment. You realize *it really is* a broken world after all—a world that, though slowly edging forward, continues to be infested with ignorance and apathy in all tiers of society. I can liken the intense frustration to successfully escaping from a concentration camp deep in a forest and stumbling into the local village in search of aid and solace, only to discover the villagers *knew* of the existence of the camp all along but were completely unfazed by it. ("Oh, you're saying they treated you badly and kept you there *against your will?* We thought it was a holiday camp and

---

[5] If you are looking for a book that superbly dissects the threat posed by Islamism, and the various nuances of Islamist conviction, I would recommend *Islam and the Future of Tolerance: A Dialogue* by Sam Harris and Maajid Nawaz.

everyone stayed there through choice! Are you *absolutely sure* it is not a holiday camp? It certainly looks like one!") In other words, popular apathy and/or refusal to take brainwashing seriously only adds insult to injury for the cult survivor, reminding him or her why these cults have been allowed to prosper and flourish in the first place for so many years and in so many forms.

At least in the UK, religions are allowed to get away with pretty much anything so long as nobody gets shot, kidnapped or blown up. It simply "isn't cricket" to ask questions of anything calling itself a religion so long as the harm it causes is of a more abstract kind: mental or emotional rather than physical or violent. A "hear no evil, see no evil" cycle of perpetual passivity holds sway whereby the government will take no action against mentally or emotionally abusive 'religions' if there is insufficient interest from the media, and the media will not take an interest unless there is a whiff of sex, or celebrities, or people getting shot, kidnapped or blown up. Families getting torn apart by religiously-mandated shunning simply does not sell newspapers, so it may as well not be happening.

It can be a rude awakening to see one's basic human rights dismissed so casually by those who have the power to insist they are respected. Still more sobering is the realization that, at least in its portrayal of society's leaders as fickle, superficial and well-meaning but ultimately ineffectual, the Slave's condemnation of "Satan's system" is not completely wide of the mark.

At this point you might be thinking: "Whoa, did you just say *human rights*? What do human rights have to do with all this?" When I say this is a human rights issue, I am not being melodramatic. I am referring specifically to Article 18 of the United Nations' Universal

Declaration of Human Rights, which reads as follows (bold is mine):

> Everyone has the right to freedom of thought, conscience and religion; **this right includes freedom to change his religion or belief,** and freedom, either alone or in community with others and in public or private, to manifest his religion or belief in teaching, practice, worship and observance.

In a twisted irony, the above article is often invoked by Witness lawyers when defending the religious freedoms of Witnesses, whether fighting for their rights to go about their preaching work unhindered or to abstain from military service as conscientious objectors (as in South Korea).[6] Watchtower sees no hypocrisy in appealing to the rights afforded it by "Satan's system" while simultaneously trampling on the very same rights of countless former believers like myself through mandatory shunning—an abominable practice that directly violates one's freedom of thought, conscience and religion by making it impossible to leave one's faith without devastating consequences.

Shunning is wielded by Watchtower as a punitive instrument that visits pain and misery on people long after they have fled the boundaries of its control and

---

[6] The corresponding Article 9 of the European Convention on Human Rights has also been used by Watchtower lawyers in defending the rights of Witnesses. In 2014, Watchtower managed to convince Nils Muižnieks, Council of Europe Commissioner for Human Rights, to appear in one of its propaganda videos to discuss Article 9 in relation to the organization's struggle in various countries regarding conscientious objection. I responded by uploading a video rebuttal to my YouTube channel in which I questioned Mr. Muižnieks' judgment in appearing in a video for an organization that was depriving me of my human rights, and called on him to take action. I posted the video to Mr. Muižnieks' Facebook page to make sure he saw it. I still await a response.

influence. The practice of disfellowshipping (or in my case "disassociation," which carries the same penalty) is an open act of emotional blackmail designed to make the estranged one return to the fold if only to regain contact with family members, who are coerced in Watchtower materials to treat former members as though they do not exist. As an example, here is some guidance from a 2012 *Watchtower* blatantly urging that disfellowshipped ones should be incentivised to return (bold is mine):

> **Consider just one example of the good that can come when a family loyally upholds Jehovah's decree not to associate with disfellowshipped relatives.** A young man had been disfellowshipped for over ten years, during which time his father, mother, and four brothers "quit mixing in company" with him. At times, he tried to involve himself in their activities, but to their credit, each member of the family was steadfast in not having any contact with him. After he was reinstated, he said that he always missed the association with his family, especially at night when he was alone. But, he admitted, had the family associated with him even a little, that small dose would have satisfied him. **However, because he did not receive even the slightest communication from any of his family, the burning desire to be with them became one motivating factor in his restoring his relationship with Jehovah. Think of that if you are ever tempted to violate God's command not to associate with your disfellowshipped relatives.**

Such overt coercion and guilt-tripping has a tangible effect on family relationships, as you will see if you read on to the events surrounding my own exit in the winter of 2013—events no person living in a 21st century civilized democracy should be forced to contend with. Suffice to say, my wife and I—on an almost daily basis—continue to feel the punishment radiating from a cult we have long since escaped both physically and mentally.

It has been known for the emotional trauma of shunning, or even just the threat of it, to induce people to suicide.[7] As research by the likes of Dr. Kip Williams of Purdue University is showing, the effects of ostracism can be deep-rooted and long-lasting.[8] We humans are social creatures who thrive on communal acceptance and engagement with others. When you find yourself inexplicably or unjustly severed from social interaction, even from interaction with someone you have barely met (perhaps because they suddenly start ignoring you, or walk away from you mid-conversation without explanation), the frustration bordering on aggression can be palpable. This increases exponentially into untold misery and despair depending on how close you are to the person shunning you, and the duration over which you are shunned.

Many would argue that the Universal Declaration of Human Rights applies to governments and public bodies, and is not something to which religions can be held accountable. However, it should be obvious that we clearly have a problem whenever a government or public body incentivizes or subsidizes a religion that is guilty of human rights abuses by extending tax

---

[7] Evidence of Watchtower-mandated shunning leading to deaths from suicide is so far limited to anecdotes. Hopefully, somebody somewhere with the skills or resources might eventually be compelled to make the death toll among those being shunned due to cults an area of serious academic study.

[8] A fascinating insight into Professor Williams' pioneering work on ostracism can be gleaned from his BBC radio interview, which is presently searchable on YouTube using the keywords "Kip Williams ostracism shunning effects ostracised."

breaks and, as already mentioned, even charitable status. In England and Wales, the Charity Commission is responsible for regulating charities and making sure they conform to basic standards, including the "public benefit" requirement. According to legislation passed in the Charities Acts of 2006 and 2011, an organization that fails to contribute services that benefit the wider public, and not just its own members, cannot qualify as a charity. But this requirement is only helpful so long as it is enforced. In the case of Watchtower, in paperwork submitted to the Charity Commission it is basically allowed to self-certify itself as benefiting "persons residing in the United Kingdom and elsewhere, both Jehovah's Witnesses and the wider public" merely on the basis that it hands out free literature and its meetings are free to attend.

It should go without saying that, irrespective of whether an organization's literature and meetings are "free," if these disseminate information that is demonstrably spurious and aimed predominantly at coercing people to follow a group of leaders, this does not benefit the "wider public." Neither are the public benefited if, on joining such a group, their families are dismantled as a punitive measure just because somebody has been excommunicated. But the Charity Commission, under the constraints currently imposed on it by UK law, is forced to take everything at face value.[9] It is essentially forced

[9] At the time of writing, the Charity Commission has a statutory inquiry under way against various UK entities of Jehovah's Witnesses that are registered as charities, including the Watch Tower Bible and Tract Society of Britain (Charity no. 1077961). The inquiry is looking into concerns about child safeguarding, shunning, and domestic violence. I am pleased to be included among those who have registered official complaints against Watchtower with the Commission, and I appreciate the Commission's persistence in pursuing its investiga-

to recognize the charitable status of an organization whose printing presses disgorge material instructing its members to *not even email* relatives who are guilty of leaving the "charity," using paper and ink procured with at least a helping hand from tax exemptions and Gift Aid windfalls. Similar latitude is afforded Watchtower in other countries such as the movement's heartland, the United States, where the IRS seems all too easily persuaded to grant tax breaks to almost anything calling itself a religion, including organizations like Watchtower and Scientology[10]—regardless of the devastation visited by these cults on thousands of people on a daily basis.

Charitable status and human rights aside, a further infuriating element of Watchtower's shunning policy is that it is ultimately self-defeating. As previously mentioned, though shunning is claimed to be an act of love designed to keep "Jehovah's organization" clean, in reality the threat of estrangement is used as a fence to keep Witnesses hostage. But hostage-taking

---

tion in the face of vigorous legal challenges from Watchtower in an attempt to block it (Watchtower has appealed all the way to the Supreme Court). That said, current UK law significantly limits the Commission in the extent to which it can regulate charities. At present, I understand the Commission cannot withdraw an organization's charitable status—it can only "deregister" it, which has no impact on that organization's religious/tax exempt status. Until the Charity Commission is legally equipped to revoke the charitable status of groups that are obviously not charities, it seems to me their influence on cults like Watchtower will always be critically undermined. In short, the system itself is flawed, sabotaged by a legacy of deference to religion, and I know of survivors from other abusive religious groups (also registered as charities) who are similarly frustrated by the obvious unfairness of the status quo.

[10] Scientology's tax-free status is arguably due to its successful campaigns of harassment and intimidation of IRS personnel more than anything else. The same excuse cannot be made of Watchtower.

only yields diminishing returns for any organization—particularly one whose objective is to attract new members. If Watchtower wishes to jettison its growing reputation as a cult, it would be a good idea for it to stop acting like one. Yes, there would be an exodus if the Governing Body were to reverse its shunning policy and instruct Witnesses to maintain or establish contact with disfellowshipped family members. Thousands, or even millions, would jump at the opportunity to drop the pretense and seize their freedom. But at least the Governing Body would have the satisfaction of knowing that the millions who remain are truly loyal to them. And former members like me would have less incentive to make YouTube videos and write books and blog articles exposing in detail Watchtower's flaws if contact with our indoctrinated loved ones were restored.

Getting rid of shunning would not only be a masterstroke for the Governing Body from a PR standpoint—taking the wind from the sails of its critics, and rendering the internet a more Watchtower-friendly place—it would also have a knock-on positive influence on all the other major problems, such as the policies on child abuse, domestic violence, blood transfusions and higher education, because for the first time Witnesses would be able to vote with their feet. If a Witness objected to any of the abusive teachings and practices elaborated in previous chapters, he or she could walk away without fear of reprisals. Such liberation of individual members would, in turn, have a modernizing influence on Watchtower as a whole. Rather than making far-reaching decisions with total impunity, the Governing Body members would be wary of ill-advised policies impacting on them personally. Continued prohibition of life-saving medical treatments, or failure to bring child abuse standards in line with legal requirements, would start to show in the attendance figures and, most pressingly, on the balance sheet. In short, dropping shunning would disincentivize critics like me to give Watchtower a hard time, while incentivizing the Governing Body to make life better for Witnesses.

If all this talk of dropping shunning sounds like fanciful conjecture, it is worth remembering that, rather than representing a total U-turn, such a move would be more of a reversion (or "flip-flop") to the way things were in Watchtower's more amiable past. Few Witnesses realize that, not only is their shunning policy without biblical justification (*see box*)—it is also

---

**FOR WITNESSES**

## DISFELLOWSHIPPING

Though frequently portrayed as an act of love designed to induce an erring one to return to the fold, the truth is that nowhere in the Bible will you find justification for the practice of disfellowshipping as enforced by Watchtower. To the contrary, Christ urged his followers to cherish the family bond, as we can discern from his parable of the prodigal son.

The account in Luke 15:11–32 tells of how a young man squanders his inheritance with prostitutes only to be embraced by his father on his return. Though Watchtower publications tend to gloss over the part where the father runs to embrace his son "while he was still a long way off," this detail indicates that the father's love for his son was more important to him than whether he was repentant or not. And, considered hypothetically, Witness elders today would have had a strong case for disfellowshipping the prodigal son on his return. Why? Because he only returned *after* exhausting his food and money, and not before. This could be deemed as "worldly sadness"—a stronger regret for the adverse consequences of wrongdoing than for the sin itself.

A common biblical justification offered by Watchtower for its shunning policy is 1 Corinthians 5:11, in which Paul writes: "But now I am writing you to stop keeping company with anyone called a brother who is sexually immoral or a greedy person or an idolater or a reviler or a drunkard or an extortioner, not even eating with such a man."

Two things are noteworthy about this scripture. Firstly, it is clear that when referring to "anyone called a brother" Paul was referring to brothers in the congregation to whom one might be tempted to extend hospitality, i.e. by sharing a meal. To insist that Paul was referring to anyone *including family members* is to superimpose on the text what is not there. Even Watchtower recognizes that there must be some flexibility when applying this verse to family, which is why disfellowshipped parents can still be spoken to by their young children, or disfellowshipped husbands or wives can still be spoken to by their spouses. The trouble is, Watchtower does not go far enough in applying mercy by acknowledging that *all* family bonds should be preserved and respected when wrongdoing is committed. And wherever there is ambiguity as to how such principles are to be applied, Jesus made it clear that mercy should be the primary consideration.—Matthew 9:13.

The second noticeable aspect of Paul's words is that nowhere do they mention *not even talking* to a disfellowshipped person, which is how they are interpreted by Watchtower. It should be possible to talk to someone and have normal, healthy interaction with them without "keeping company" (associating) or sharing meals with them. In fact, when viewed objectively, the punitive measures described in 1 Corinthians chapter 5 correspond perfectly with the measures Watchtower uses for its "marking" policy, as found at 2 Thessalonians 3:14 where Paul wrote: "But if anyone is not obedient to our word through this letter, keep this one marked and stop associating with him, so that he may become ashamed." Despite these two sets of instructions apparently referring to the *same* situation of admonishing a wrongdoer, Watchtower applies both verses completely differently, using 2 Thessalonians as grounds for a far more lenient measure than full-blown shunning: "marking." When there is a case of marking, Witnesses are dissuaded from associating with anyone whose actions correspond with those of the marked person (as described in a talk), but they can still acknowledge his existence by speaking to him.

In summary, Watchtower's practice of disfellowshipping finds no basis in Scripture. It is one thing to keep a congregation free from hypocrisy by insisting that willful sinners are not to be considered as members. It is another thing entirely to insist that disfellowshipping should apply even inside the family circle and to the extent that a disfellowshipped relative may not even be communicated with.

relatively recent. To demonstrate, take a look at how a 1947 edition of the *Awake!* magazine discussed the Catholic practice of "excommunication," which Watchtower acknowledges to be equivalent to disfellowshipping[11] (bold is mine):

> The authority for excommunication, they [the Roman Catholic Hierarchy] claim, is based on the teachings of Christ and the apostles, as found in the following scriptures: Matthew 18:15-19; 1 Corinthians 5:3-5; 16:22; Galatians 1:8,9; 1 Timothy 1:20; Titus 3:10. **But the Hierarchy's excommunication, as a punishment and "medicinal" remedy (*Catholic Encyclopedia*), finds no support in these scriptures. In fact, it is altogether foreign to Bible teachings.**—Hebrews 10:26-31.

[11] A 1996 *Watchtower* equated excommunication with disfellowshipping as follows: "If the religions of Christendom were conscientiously to apply the Christian principle of disfellowshipping, or excommunication, for all the lawless acts committed by those claiming to be its members, what would happen?"

> Where, then, did this practice originate? The *Encyclopædia Britannica* says that **papal excommunication is not without pagan influence,** "and its variations cannot be adequately explained unless account be taken of several non-Christian analogues of excommunication." The superstitious Greeks believed that when an excommunicated person died the Devil entered the body, and therefore, "in order to prevent it, the relatives of the diseased cut his body in pieces and boil them in wine." Even the Druids had a method of expelling those who lost faith in their religious superstitions. It was therefore after Catholicism adopted its pagan practices, A.D. 325, that this new chapter in religious excommunication was written.
>
> Thereafter, as the pretensions of the Hierarchy increased, **the weapon of excommunication became the instrument by which the clergy attained a combination of ecclesiastical power and secular tyranny that finds no parallel in history.**

The above quote is so foreign to current Watchtower dogma that I can well imagine some Witness readers assuming it to be a forgery, so I have taken the liberty of including original scans of the article in Appendix J. Suffice to say, denouncing excommunication as a "punishment" and a "weapon" that is "altogether foreign to Bible teachings" and "not without pagan influence" is a universe away from the support for disfellowshipping found in current Watchtower literature. And, amazingly, it would take only a few years from the printing of this anti-excommunication article for Watchtower to embrace disfellowshipping as a punishment for wrongdoing, which it did in 1952.

Before 1947, most notably under the presidencies of Russell and Rutherford, judicial matters were dealt with in a much less cloak-and-dagger way, with those charged with wrongdoing being tried before the entire congregation. The accuser would state the charges, the accused would offer his defense, and there would be a show of hands to determine the guilt and/or outcome. As awkward as these proceedings would have likely been depending on the nature of the offense, at least controversies could be "discussed and argued out," with the accused getting to face his or her accuser and defend themselves publicly. The public nature of the process would also have made accusers think twice before bringing false or exaggerated charges, and no doubt incentivized thrashing out problems and disputes in private before things had chance to escalate. Contrast this state of affairs with the present solution for dealing with judicial issues: a kangaroo court of three men playing judge, jury and executioner; a back-room confession-based interrogation with no obligation to reveal from whom the charges originate, and I know which arrangement would have been my preference.

Also, not insignificantly, the maximum punishment prescribed in those early years was far less draconian—at least according to this description in a 1919 *Watch Tower* (bold is mine):

> According to this Scripture ["Vengeance is mine; I will repay."—Romans 12:19-21] the very most that the church could do would be that, after having vainly endeavored to get the brother to repent and reform, it should **withdraw special brotherly fellowship from him** [the wrongdoer] until such time as he would express willingness thereafter to do right. Then he should be received again into full fellowship.
>
> **In the meantime the brother may merely be treated in the kindly, courteous way in which it would**

**be proper for us to treat any publican or Gentile, withholding the special rights or privileges or greetings or voting opportunities that belong to the church as a class separate from the world.**

Without doubt the above represented a far more civilized arrangement, in which the convicted wrongdoer was no longer considered part of the congregation, but was still to be treated in a "kindly, courteous way." Family ties were respected and, as stated, rather than matters being dealt with behind closed doors, they were settled publicly.

Things changed slightly in 1944 under Knorr's presidency when, instead of holding public hearings, it was decided that judicial matters were to be "quietly laid before the representative members of the congregation or company, the ones that are charged with the responsibility for the spiritual welfare of the brethren and for the direction of their service to the Lord." Though this change moved things a step closer to the judicial committee arrangement of today, with handpicked representatives deliberating over evidence of wrongdoing, there were still no clear-cut demands for those found guilty to be ostracized. Rather, the wrongdoer was to be stripped of "assignments of service" and was not to be "followed or imitated by others of the congregation, but should be helped to see the error of his way." Shunning was still not on the agenda. "Count him not as an enemy, but admonish him as a brother" was the Bible-based mantra, based on 2 Thessalonians 3:14, 15.[12]

---

[12] As discussed in the "For Witnesses" box on disfellowshipping, Paul's words in 2 Thessalonians chapter 3 and 1 Corinthians chapter 5 apparently refer to an identical situation in which wrongdoers are to be admonished. But Watchtower presently draws a distinction between the two, insisting

But the prospects for those deemed to be sinners would worsen significantly with the arrangement introduced by a *Watchtower* magazine in 1952, just five years after the *Awake!* article on excommunication (bold is mine):

> What is the congregation going to do now with such an individual? We must keep in mind that this person has been disfellowshiped and is not a member of our company. **We want to avoid him, we want nothing to do with him.**
>
> Now meetings that are open to the public he can attend as long as he behaves himself and acts orderly. If that individual comes into a public meeting, say, a public lecture in a public auditorium, or Kingdom Hall, or city park, or a *Watchtower* study or a service meeting, it is public, the doors are open, and he may be admitted. If he comes into that meeting and sits down, as long as he is orderly, minds his business, **we have nothing to say to him. Those who are acquainted with the situation in the congregation should never say "Hello" or "Good-by" [*sic*] to him. He is not welcome in our midst, we avoid him.** If this one should be sitting in the *Watchtower* study and raise his hand, the chairman should never recognize him or allow him to make a comment. **He is not one of us. He is not a recognized member in God's congregation. Those who are informed and know the individual certainly should avoid him, have nothing to say to him.**

Hence, for the first time, Witnesses were instructed to *not even speak* to a disfellowshipped individual.

---

that 1 Corinthians 5 refers to *disfellowshipping* for serious sin whereas 2 Thessalonians 3 refers to the lesser punishment of *marking* (a kind of "shunning-lite" for minor indiscretions). There is no evidence for such a distinction in the Bible itself.

If such a person sought to regain his position in the congregation, perhaps through mortal fear of being destroyed in an impending fiery apocalypse, he first had to endure the humiliation of sitting silently in meetings over many months in hopes of eventually being reinstated—all the while surrounded by people who were expected to pretend he did not exist.

Worse still, the new disfellowshipping arrangement was to apply *even within families* so as to frustrate "Satan's influence" (bold is mine):

> Satan's influence through the disfellowshiped member of the family will be to cause the other member or members of the family who are in the truth to join the disfellowshiped member in his course or in his position toward God's organization. To do this would be disastrous, and so **the faithful family member must recognize and conform to the disfellowship order.** How would or could this be done while living under the same roof or in personal, physical contact daily with the disfellowshiped? In this way: By refusing to have religious relationship with the disfellowshiped.

A small olive branch had been extended. If a disfellowshipped family member was living *under the same roof* he could have contact so long as this did not include religious dialogue (i.e. criticism of the organization). But beyond the shelter of the family "roof," this loophole no longer applied. Disfellowshipped relatives living outside the "immediate family circle" were to be confined to "only the contacts absolutely necessary in matters pertaining to family interests"—or as this later came to be known in Witness jargon: *necessary contact.* If somebody died, or an important family-related matter arose requiring urgent attention, a disfellowshipped family member could be spoken to. Apart from that, all the small-talk and day-to-day banter that is an essential component of any meaningful human relationship was to be snuffed out.

As abominably draconian as this arrangement was, it was *still* not as bad as the hellish arrangement that exists today—the arrangement under which eight million Witnesses are held hostage. Why? Because in the '50s, '60s and '70s you could still vote with your feet if you wanted no part of this nonsense by "disassociating" yourself as one of Jehovah's Witnesses. Concerning "disassociated" ones, a 1970 *Watchtower* had this to say (bold is mine):

> Say, for purposes of illustration, that an individual **persistently neglects to attend meetings.** He comes to the point where he is **completely disassociated from the congregation,** not having any concern at all for Jehovah's arrangements for His people to meet together. **The congregation does not take any action against him;** they have recognized his wrong course and have tried to help him; but **he has on his own drifted away and disassociated himself.**

This loophole, where one could "completely disassociate" from the congregation without facing congregation judicial action, offered a way out for anyone who woke up to the lunacy of the cult. Back then, you could walk away from Watchtower while still keeping hold of precious family ties and not expect to be treated like a criminal when Witnesses encountered you in the street.

But this was not to last, as we saw in Chapter Eight. In 1981, the door finally slammed shut in dramatic fashion with the publication of the *Watchtower* article that was used as the pretext for Raymond Franz to be ejected from the organization. According to the revised rules, disfellowshipping and disassociation would *both* merit shunning by believing family and other Witnesses:

> Persons who make themselves "not of our sort" by deliberately rejecting the faith and beliefs of Jehovah's Witnesses should appropriately be viewed and treated as are those who have been disfellowshiped for wrongdoing.

I was only three years old when these events took place; enjoying my childhood somewhere in leafy Northern England under the quaint assumption that the parental love I was then enjoying was permanent and unconditional. But 31 years later, the above-quoted words from the dreaded September 15, 1981, *Watchtower* article were to catch up with me with dramatic, life-changing consequences.

The phone rang one Friday evening in late December 2013. Before lifting the receiver I knew who it was, and what he wanted. My mother-in-law had been approached at the Kingdom Hall by our congregation coordinator the evening before. He had told her I should expect a phone call, and she could tell from his sullen demeanor that it would not be to discuss the weather. The elders wanted to arrange a judicial committee, and I would be the one on trial.

To explain how I knew this was what they wanted, perhaps I should rewind events a little.

Two months earlier, I had enjoyed my final holiday with Dad after persuading him to fly out to Croatia to see us. Though we had casually discussed the prospect of his visit for some time during our regular phone conversations, it was with particular urgency that I pressed him to go ahead and book the plane tickets for late October. Dijana was pregnant, and by now fully awakened from her indoctrination. We had both determined that we could never countenance our child being raised as a Witness. We knew that if we stayed as Witnesses, even if in name only (by being "inactive"), Witness relatives would seize any opportunity to indoctrinate our child with the excuse that they were only doing what we should be doing. We knew the only way to guarantee our child's freedom was to make a clean break by formally disassociating ourselves. Before we did this, I wanted one last holiday with Dad—a final throw of the dice at pleading with him face-to-face not to shun us once the inevitable happened.

Rather than leap on him the moment he stepped off the plane, we resolved to spend some relaxing days with him for the start of his visit. This was, after all, supposed to be a holiday.

We spent a couple of days in the beautiful hill country of Northern Croatia along the border with Slovenia. The house where we were staying had its own vineyard that produced exquisite dry white wine (like champagne but without the fizz). Dijana and I bought a bottle to save for when the baby would be born. The autumn colors were vibrant and the scenery majestic as the three of us gleefully explored the winding roads in my Ford Cougar.

Once we were home and settled, I nervously took Dad to one side late one evening. I had briefly prepared what I wanted to say and even had some laminated scans of newspaper articles to show him. All the same, I knew this would not be easy. The "Truth" meant the world to him. It was his whole life. It was the lens through which he interpreted everything—from his troubled childhood right through to the loss of his wife. Looking back, I realize I was naive to even attempt an "intervention" on someone so heavily indoctrinated but, if only for my unborn child's sake, I felt I had to at least try.

I broke the news that Dijana and I would be disassociating. We had irreconcilable grievances with the organization and, given all that was at stake, it was important that he should at least listen to what a few of these were. Dad sat on the edge of the bed with me as I showed him the laminated articles. One was of the 2001 *Guardian* piece in which Watchtower had been exposed by Stephen Bates for being an NGO member of the United Nations. For reasons explained back in Chapter Eight, this scandal had floored me when I first learned of it on JWfacts.com. There was simply no escaping the fact that the Governing Body had allied themselves with the very political entity they claimed to loathe for *nine years*, all the while disfellowshipping anyone who failed to observe their strict rules on Christian neutrality. Furthermore, a key requirement for their membership was that they were to endorse the UN's charter and promote its various programs. How could they be so hypocritical?

Dad was shell-shocked, having clearly been hitherto oblivious to the scandal. He burbled some attempt at a rebuttal—something along the lines of: "But what does the UN Charter *actually say?*" I told him he could read up on the UN Charter whenever he wanted, but by supporting the UN Charter, Watchtower was supporting the UN—the very organization it had denounced as satanic in its literature. Moreover, the association was only hurriedly terminated *after* Watchtower was rumbled by a reporter. If the NGO status was somehow justified, why had Watchtower ended it so hastily? And why had the Governing Body not come clean about the whole affair to Witnesses in the literature? Why were they so secretive if there was nothing to hide?

Dad was silent.

Continuing with the theme of Watchtower being surreptitious and deceitful, I showed Dad a 2011 newspaper article from *The Independent*—one I was especially familiar with because I had been instrumental in its publication.[13] The article discussed the fall-out (or "war of words") following the publication of a hate-strewn study edition of *The Watchtower* a few months earlier, which included the following quote (bold is mine):

> Suppose that a doctor told you to avoid contact with someone who is infected with a contagious, deadly disease. You would know what the doctor means, and you would strictly heed his warning. **Well, apostates are "mentally diseased," and they seek to infect others with their disloyal teachings.** (1 Tim. 6:3, 4) Jehovah, the Great Physician, tells us to avoid contact with them. We know what he means, but are we determined to heed his warning in all respects?

"Apostates" like myself, whose only "crime" was that of defying Watchtower, had every right to feel incensed at being labeled "mentally diseased"—a slur that is offensive both to former Witnesses and those who genuinely suffer from mental illness.[14] As it turned

---

[13] The *Independent* article, by Jerome Taylor, has been reproduced in Appendix K.

[14] As you can see from the quote, Watchtower writers lifted the term "mentally diseased" from 1 Timothy 6:3, 4 in the 1984 edition of the *New World Translation*. Other more respected Bible translations render the original Greek in much milder language in the same verse, and indeed Watchtower's 2013 revision to the New World Translation quietly replaced "mentally diseased" with "obsessed," which carries a completely

out, a number of fellow ex-Witnesses whom I had met on an online forum shared my sense of outrage. One of these, who happened to live in the UK, decided to report the matter to her local police, since religious hate speech is taken extremely seriously by the UK authorities. This lady soon had a visit from police officers who reviewed the material and took it to be examined by their superiors. When I emailed PDF versions of the offending magazine to a handful of journalists to alert them to our modest success, Jerome Taylor from *The Independent* responded and expressed an interest in writing about the controversy. I ended up being cited as a "current member" (which technically, I was) in the following quote from Jerome's resulting "war of words" piece:

> A copy of the magazine, distributed by Jehovah's Witnesses around the world, was given to *The Independent* by a current member of the church who has become unhappy with official teaching but is afraid to leave for fear of losing his family.
>
> "Many like me remain associated with the Witnesses out of fear of being uncovered as an 'apostate' and ousted, not just from the organisation, but from their own friends and families," said the man, who would only give the name John. "I find I am now branded as 'mentally diseased'—giving any who discover my true beliefs free licence to treat me with disdain."

---

different and far less offensive connotation. But rather than issue any retraction or apology for using the spurious "mentally diseased" quote in the July 15, 2011, *Watchtower* in reference to apostates, Watchtower seems happy to let that slur stick in the minds of Witnesses, even including it in material for speakers as part of a symposium in the 2013 "God's Word Is Truth" convention series (search "2013 Human Apostates" on YouTube), which was delivered in the same year as the release of the less offensive Bible revision.

I showed Dad my laminated copy of the "War of Words" article, explaining that I was the "John" referred to. I also showed him Watchtower's official response to Jerome Taylor:

> Rick Fenton, a spokesperson for the Watchtower Society, insisted last night that ostracisation was "a personal matter for each individual to decide for himself". "Any one of Jehovah's Witnesses is free to express their feelings and to ask questions," he said. "If a person changes their mind about Bible-based teachings they once held dear, we recognise their right to leave."

Dad did not need me to tell him who Rick Fenton was. Rick had once been a member of Wilmslow congregation, where Dad was still serving as an elder. His mother had joined the Witnesses at some point in the late '80s and early '90s. Rick and I had been on backpacking trips together and he was one of the pioneers I most looked up to when I first left school and was considering pioneering. (I can still remember my embarrassment when Mum mildly scolded him one evening when he came to pick me up after school to take me on "return visits" in his red MG convertible after I had mentioned to her what a fast driver he was.)

In 1996, Rick had decided to leave pioneering to go and work as a Bethelite at Watchtower's London headquarters, where I visited him occasionally. After starting off in the Bethel garage fixing cars and trucks, Rick had risen through the ranks to serve Watchtower as one of its publicity officers. Only recently, Dad, Dijana and I had joined him and his wife for lunch at his mother's house on one of our trips back to the UK. But now, my old friend and I found ourselves pitched against each other as adversaries—at opposite ends of a significant debate in a national newspaper article in which Rick, to my horror and dismay, had chosen to tell a barefaced lie.[15] Jehovah's Witnesses are not "free to express their feelings and to ask questions" in any meaningful sense, and by visiting punishment on former members by means of its brutal shunning policy the Governing Body certainly does not "recognize their right to leave."

As I pointed out to Dad, if shunning of former Witnesses was fair and proper, why be ashamed of it? Why had Rick found it necessary to offer such a brazen fabrication to the media? Why had he gone on record with a national newspaper saying that shunning was a "personal matter for each individual to decide for himself," when shunning is characterized in Watchtower literature as a "command" from Jehovah and a matter of loyalty for all Witnesses?

By this point, Dad's cognitive dissonance seemed to be at boiling point. He had reached his threshold.

"I'm sorry, Lloyd, thank you for showing me all this but I'm afraid it's a lot to take in and I'm feeling rather nauseous and tired. I think I'd better go to bed if that's okay with you," he said.

"Of course, Dad."

I remembered only too well how overwhelming the waking-up experience had been for me, and how jaw-dropping it was to see clear examples of Watchtower subterfuge and deception when I first began my research. Though I slightly suspected Dad of running away at the first hurdle when I desperately wanted him

---

[15] This would not be the last time Rick would misrepresent the Witnesses in his official capacity as Watchtower spokesperson. For another example, please search for my YouTube video titled *Dear Rick Fenton, Please Stop Lying*!

to challenge me on this, I knew I had to let him process things at his own pace.

In the small room where Dad was staying there was a wood-burning stove facing his bed—clean, unused and not yet connected to the chimney. Just before he finally called in for the night I positioned my copy of *Crisis of Conscience* prominently inside the stove so he could see it. On the first few pages I put a sticky note on which I scribbled the words: "Thanks for looking behind the curtain! Love you Dad."

Dad never picked up the book, and never read the note.

The next day, Dad was extremely evasive. We had other relatives staying and he spent most of his time chatting and joking with them. I was devastated by his lack of willingness to engage with me at such a crucial juncture and with such grave consequences looming, but I decided to give him the benefit of the doubt. I hoped he would come round if given enough time and space.

Finally, Dad asked to speak with me. We went upstairs to the same room that had been the setting for our conversation the evening before. What Dad said once the door closed was devastating. He coolly confirmed that he *would* be shunning me, Dijana and our child once we disassociated ourselves. This was not open to discussion. There was no point trying to show him any more information. His mind was made up.

I immediately collapsed in tears, overwhelmed with emotion.

"You're a hypocrite!" I yelled. "How can you go round calling on people telling them to examine *their* beliefs and reject them in favor of yours when you refuse to have your own beliefs examined?"

Dad replied to the effect that he saw no contradiction.

My anger and exasperation intensified as I continued to recoil from the bombshell that Dad would be surrendering me without a fight. Though I was not yet a father, I could at least imagine the love I would have for my child and the fervor with which I would battle the *slightest* threat to our relationship. Dad was not putting up any fight at all—he was running away the moment his beliefs were challenged. Was he not supposed to be an elder—a spiritual shepherd? Surely if he absolutely *knew* he had the "Truth" he should be sitting me down and allowing me, indeed *begging me,* to give him my absolute worst—fully confident that he had all the answers? Surely if he really loved me he would do everything possible to win me back and help me see the light? Instead, two newspaper articles were all it took to put him in full flight, abandoning his son, daughter-in-law, and future grandchild. How could he be so coldhearted, so robotic?

Finally moved by how distraught I was, Dad approached me to give me a hug. I recoiled.

"Don't you dare pretend to love me!" I shouted. It would take more than a cuddle to make up for the fact that he was abandoning his son.

Dad exited the room, leaving me scrambling to come to terms with what had just happened. On his way downstairs, he passed Dijana and calmly told her: "You'd better go to see Lloyd, I think he's a bit upset."

For the rest of Dad's stay, the matter was not discussed any further. The hour-long drive to the airport passed in total silence. There was one final hug when I dropped him at the terminal before getting straight back in the car and driving home. I knew if I tried pleading with him in our final few moments together I would only make things worse.

Almost as soon as I came home I set to work on a new JWsurvey.org blog article titled "The Story of Cedars—A Prisoner No More." From when I had first started my activism in 2011, I had yearned to show my face and tell my story. Now that I had prepared Dad for my exit and witnessed his shocking response, there was no longer anything holding me back. If anything, the brutality of Dad's rejection served as a catalyst, hastening my exit. I had been shaken into the realization that a stand must be taken against this despicable cult.

The article, finally posted on November 6, 2013, was a tell-all account of my life to date. I made sure I was completely honest about all my reasons for leaving, including the problems of a sexual nature that had turned out to be instrumental in my exit. Even though many of these details were really only the business of Dijana and myself, and nobody else, I wanted to be completely transparent. I knew my article would eventually be picked apart by my old friends and family, perhaps including my dad and sister. I wanted nobody to be able to point the finger and say: "Look, he's setting himself up as some kind of guru, and ignoring all the skeletons in his closet! Typical hypocritical apostate!"

The article was well received, attracting thousands of visits within the first 24 hours of going online. I found myself inundated with messages of support and solidarity from other ex-Witnesses, many of whom could relate to my story and found parallels with their own experiences. I fully expected my blog article to finally come to the attention of the local elders in Sisak. In fact, I *wanted* them to see it. I could not wait to get out of this hideous organization and drop the pretense—and I would not have long to wait. It was barely two months after my article went up before I was notified by my mother-in-law of the impending phone call from my congregation coordinator, whom I will refer to as Marko.[16]

Marko is a likable guy who rose through the ranks rapidly following his baptism. When I first met him in 2006, on my first visit to Croatia, his baptism had been only a couple of years earlier—and now he was my congregation's coordinator. Marko would probably have still been handling the microphones if he were a Witness in Britain or the United States, but you would need to try extremely hard, or be incredibly inept, not to rocket through the ranks in a country as thinly-populated with Witnesses as Croatia. Though somewhat lacking in charisma and experience, Marko exudes kindness and positivity—always wearing a big smile on his face. When he telephoned, however, I sensed he was not smiling.

"We know about your website," Marko said in his broken English.

"I see," I replied.

"Could you come to meet with us at the Kingdom Hall on Sunday night, six o'clock?"

"Yes," I said. "But on one condition."

I told Marko that I refused to allow the two elders who had hounded my wife and I to have any part in the meeting. (One, you will recall, had dragged Dijana into the back room at the Kingdom Hall to interrogate her without me being present. The other had speculated

[16] This was not the same coordinator who met me at the bus station in Chapter Four. There had been a change in personnel since then.

that I was running an exploitative business scam based on the passing mention that I occasionally gave work to freelance translators who were Witnesses.) These men would have no part in the final act of my 23 years as a Witness, and if I saw them I would turn around and walk straight out. Marko agreed to my condition. He also agreed that, because I am English with a weak command of Croatian, the meeting would be held in English to the extent possible. It was for this reason, he said, that an elder from Watchtower's branch office in Zagreb would be attending.

When Sunday evening finally came, I felt reasonably in control. I knew this was essentially a formality. Some of my ex-JW friends were suggesting I take along a lawyer, but I could not imagine why this would be necessary. After all, both parties wanted the same thing—a parting of the ways between me and Watchtower. Others suggested I record the meeting and upload the recording to YouTube as others had done. My wife and I discussed this possibility and both reached the same conclusion. It would be unkind to Marko and the other elders to push them into the limelight on my YouTube channel without their permission. I would also almost certainly be asked whether I was carrying any recording equipment. I wanted to go into the meeting confident, with my head held high and nothing to hide. I was also not comfortable lying on tape as to whether I was recording or not. Not recording the meeting and simply writing about it on my blog later seemed the best option.

In the hours leading up to my judicial committee hearing, there was a flurry of messages of support and solidarity from others who had been through the same ordeal. Emails, Facebook messages and tweets came flooding in, from which I drew strength. One particularly heartwarming tweet came from Misha Verollet, an Austrian writer and follower of my blog who would later become an activist colleague.[17] It simply read: "All the best for your trial. Don't forget: you've already won. Greetings from Vienna."

Misha was right. I *had* already won. These guys had no power over me. They were simply bewildered spectators in my ongoing struggle with a cruel authoritarian cult that threatened my family. In fact, were it not for my desire to protect my family, I would not have gone to the trouble of indulging them in the first place. It was possible for me to simply let them disassociate me *in absentia*—but I had my reasons for attending. I needed to let Watchtower know what would happen if my local elders made things worse for me than they needed to.

Moments before I was due to get in the car, I received an email from Dad. I had emailed him two days earlier to let him know of my judicial committee, inviting him to call me if it was not too distressing for him to do so. He replied as follows:

> You're right, it is too much, heart-breaking I think for us both. The happiest and most rewarding times of my life as well as the darkest convince me of my beliefs. I am so sad that that has not been your experience. The hardest thing for a parent is to let go when you feel they are making a bad choice. It's yours to take and I must respect that.
>
> We both must stand the consequences of our determination. You soon will become a parent yourself you will do your best I am sure to give her what you believe to be the best, that's all your mum and I wanted for you.

---

[17] Misha would go on to author the German-language book *Goodbye Jehova!* under the pen name Misha Anouk.

> I will never give up my hope for you despite your making it clear that if you are put outside you will never return.
>
> I do not know how I will bear it if you reject the way I have chosen to walk, but despite how you feel about my sincerity I cannot put into words the love I feel for you, Dijana, and my prospective grandchild.
>
> Love Dad

Despite the finality of Dad's rejection when we were in person, his email still came as a hammer blow. My mind was already grappling with my impending face-off with the elders, and I now had Dad's email to ponder. Why did he assume I doubted his sincerity? It seemed my angry outbursts when we were together might have prompted that remark. In my reply, I knew I needed to put his mind at ease on that score. I did not (and still do not) question my father's sincerity at all. I know he is brainwashed to be sincere about what he believes, and to be convinced that his actions are right and proper. The only thing troubling me—and which will continue to haunt me even in the unlikely scenario that he awakens some day—was his willingness to jettison me from his life without putting up a fight. I will always struggle to reconcile his evasive actions with those of a concerned, devoted father.

In his email, Dad had also highlighted a fundamental difference between us. For him, the times of happiness and sadness in life were the driving force behind his beliefs. For me, periods of good and bad fortune and emotional responses to the same are meaningless when it comes to evaluating the validity of religious propositions. There is no room for sentimentality in this regard, especially when family ties are in the balance.

What is of overriding importance to me is *what is true, and what isn't.*

Sadly, Dad could not, and still cannot, see things that way. He cannot see that, in placing unquestioning trust in a group of religious leaders just because it makes him feel good, he does not differ in any meaningful sense from the billions of followers of other creeds across the globe. It was this contradiction that I had tried to show him in our last face-to-face encounter, even if calling him a hypocrite was undoubtedly not the best way I could have chosen to do this.

Though rattled by Dad's last-minute message, I tried to put it to the back of my mind. If anything, this email was further proof that I was doing the right thing. No son should ever have to face such rejection from his father. My daughter would certainly never see me abandon my relationship with her for any reason, let alone divergent personal beliefs. A line would need to be drawn in my family between a generation stupefied and entranced by false promises of paradise, and the generation who said "enough is enough!"

And this line would be drawn tonight.

I parked around the corner from the Kingdom Hall on the banks of the Kupa River, which flows through Sisak. After filming a quick video in my car to document the event for YouTube, I walked the short distance through the rain to the Kingdom Hall.

The gates to the building were open. The lights were on, and there were two cars in the parking lot. I stepped inside and was greeted by Marko. On entering the auditorium, two more elders greeted me in perfect English, neither of whom I recognized. One, named

Davor, was from the Croatian branch office. He must have been in his 40s, and was schoolteacher-like in appearance. The other elder from Zagreb (about my age, or perhaps younger?) was named Dejan. He seemed jolly and likable. Marko joked that this was not the same Dejan I had specified, so he assumed it was okay to invite him. I said this was fine by me.

***Sisak Kingdom Hall—scene of my final minutes as a Jehovah's Witness***

We sat down facing each other over a small table that seemed to serve mostly as Davor's desk. It quickly became obvious that Davor would be chairing the meeting. He asked if it would be okay to conduct at least part of it in Croatian. I said this might be a problem, since my Croatian is extremely poor, so if the meeting was to benefit me I would appreciate if they could use English as much as possible, but I would not mind if I heard the occasional Croatian. They were fine with this.

They asked if it was okay for them to open in prayer, to which I said "yes." All bowed their heads and Marko said a prayer in Croatian, none of which I could follow—not that I was really trying. I had too much on my mind. I went along with the prayer and said a loud "amen" at the end in hopes that this might help put them at ease.

I was told that this was a judicial committee, formed on the basis that I was accused of apostasy. Did I understand this?

"Yes."

For the sake of my own privacy, this meeting would not be recorded, and it would be appreciated if I did not record the meeting. I found this reasoning strange, since I had no objections over privacy and would have welcomed any opportunity to have the conversation recorded, but this was clearly the Watchtower way of saying: "We don't want you to record this meeting."

I assured them I was not recording it, and stressed that it was important to me that they understood this. They seemed relieved.

Davor explained that the purpose of the meeting was twofold. They wished to "offer help" to me spiritually but, as he went on to insist later, doctrine was not to be discussed. I could not help but find this amusing. How could they help me spiritually without discussing doctrine if the whole reason I was before them was due to my doctrinal objections? This encapsulated how futile the whole thing was.

Davor then made a throwaway remark to the effect that I was free to leave any religion if I so wished. I had to interject.

"Respectfully, no! I am *not* free to leave this religion. I will not have any of you tell me that. If I were not being faced with repercussions for leaving, *then* you could say that I am free to leave. But I have had an email only this evening from my father telling me that he will shun me once I have left. My family is being used by Watchtower as a weapon against me. So you can say whatever you like, but I will not have it said that I am free to leave this religion. *Is that absolutely clear?*"

There was an awkward silence, a begrudging acknowledgment, and the meeting resumed.

The second purpose of the meeting, it was explained, was to protect the congregation. Two scriptures in the book of Galatians were read, namely Galatians 6:1 ("Brothers, even if a man takes a false step before he is aware of it, you who have spiritual qualifications try to readjust such a man in a spirit of mildness") and Galatians 5:9 ("A little leaven ferments the whole batch of dough").

I had to chuckle at that last scripture. Did they realize they were insulting me by referring to me as leaven that might corrupt others? Apparently not. I was to take it on the chin that I was no better than a lump of yeast in their eyes. And again, how were they hoping to "readjust" me with a "spirit of mildness" while refusing to discuss my issues with the organization?

With the scriptural pretext to the meeting out of the way, conversation swiftly turned to my apostasy. Davor explained that they had discovered my website. A stapled printout of one of my articles was produced and placed on Davor's table, facing him. I was asked if these were my words. I strained from my position to see which article it was, since the text was facing away from me. Davor noticed that I was having difficulty, and swiveled the printout so I could read it. I then saw that it was my "coming out" article written only a few weeks earlier—"The Story of Cedars—A Prisoner

No More." I could see that some sentences had been marked in pink highlighter.

"Did you write these words, and do you stand by them?"

"Absolutely," I responded, without hesitation. "I would also add that there is a promise on my website that if there is anything wrong, or incorrect, or misleading on its pages I will change or remove it if it is brought to my attention. I have never had a serious email asking me to make changes in reference to this promise—only the occasional angry email from a Witness who stumbles on my site and complains about some point or other because they do not know as much about the organization as I do."

Again, my words received begrudging acknowledgment. Davor continued.

"Do you still consider yourself as one of Jehovah's Witnesses?"

"No, I do not."

Davor then brought up that I had mentioned in my article about my wife and I preparing letters of disassociation. I was asked if I had brought these letters with me. I said that yes, I had.

"In that case, the matter is settled," said Davor. "You are no longer one of Jehovah's Witnesses. Do you have anything to add?" I replied that yes, I did have a few things to say. First, I would appreciate being told how they came to learn about the website. Davor looked at Marko, and Marko said that it was a sister in Croatia who had found the website and emailed him about it. Apparently, this sister was not in our congregation. I was slightly disappointed. I had hoped for a more romantic story involving frenzied phone calls between Brooklyn and Zagreb, but it seemed it was a simple case of a local snitch.[18] Apparently, the circumstances surrounding this woman's discovery of my website, and precisely what she had been doing on it, were of no pressing concern. She had reported to her superiors like a good, loyal Witness. The ends, as always, had justified the means.

I then explained that my reason for attending the meeting had to do with my family. My Croatian in-laws, who share the same house and attend Sisak congregation, have an interdependent relationship with my wife and I. I had already tried sharing information about Watchtower history with them, and (like my father) they were adamant that they would not entertain any negative talk about the organization. With these boundaries established, we had all agreed that not discussing religious matters was the easiest and least distressing solution for all concerned.

I was also mindful of the impact it would have on Dijana's parents if I were to pursue other members of the congregation, or Witnesses elsewhere in Croatia, with the aim of waking them up from their indoctrination. This too would distress my in-laws and place a strain on a relationship on which we were mutually reliant. I explained to Davor that my wife and I could live with the status quo, and that I was happy for my activism work to be limited to English-speaking countries—without encompassing the country I was living in—if this was the price I had to pay for caring for my family.

If, however, my in-laws were to be coerced into not speaking to us, this would complicate matters. I would

[18] I was later told by someone still inside the organization and in contact with my former elders in the UK that there was more behind my judicial committee than this, but I suppose this will have to remain a mystery for now.

no longer have anything holding me back from turning my attention to Croatia, with its modest 5,000-or-so publishers. Newspapers would be contacted. Television and radio appearances would be arranged. Websites would be set up. Leaflets would be distributed, and respectful presentations outside conventions could be expected. The choice was therefore theirs. They could leave me alone and allow my in-laws to deal with the situation in their own way without coercion, or they could make things harder for Dijana and I—thus removing any incentive for me to not create havoc for Watchtower in Croatia.

The elders looked at each other.

"We can only tell your parents-in-law, if they approach us, what it instructs them to do in the Bible," said Davor. The others nodded.

I could feel myself losing my calm. They were ignoring my threat.

"So you're saying that you will tell my parents-in-law to shun us, even though this will create problems both for them and you?"

"We can only tell them what it says in the Bible. The Bible is our only authority." Again, the others nodded. A look of confidence spread across Davor's face as my frustration mounted.

Fortunately, as the situation deteriorated, I managed to gather my thoughts and find a route past his reasoning. This was one of two occasions during the meeting when my feelings got the better of me and I struggled before somehow managing to regain composure.

"Ah, if you're saying that you will tell them to do what it says in the Bible that is fine by me," I said, "because nowhere in the Bible does it say family members should shun each other. In fact, it says the opposite."

They stared at me in silence.

"In the parable of the prodigal son, which I'm sure you're all familiar with, the son only returns to his father for—I forget the exact phrase—insincere reasons. He did not show true repentance according to the organization's rules by abandoning his course of conduct." (I struggled to remember the organizational phrase "worldly sadness," which is the term used for when someone only returns to the congregation out of sadness due to the adverse consequences of their sin rather than a sincere determination to cease wrongdoing, but the official jargon escaped me in the moment.) "The son goes away and has sex with prostitutes. He lives a life of sin and debauchery. And what is the only reason that he decides to return to his father?" I paused, inviting Davor or one of the other elders to answer. There was only silence.

"We know the answer to your question," Davor said coolly.

"Great, if you know the answer to my question, then what is it?" I asked.

"We don't need to answer your question," he replied nonchalantly.

"What do you mean you don't need to answer my question? It's a simple answer. What is it?"

"None of us need to answer your scriptural question. We know what it is. We don't need to answer any scriptural questions," Davor asserted. His eyes seemed vacant. The friendly schoolteacher was gone—replaced by a cold Watchtower interface.

"That's very interesting. Very interesting indeed," I said. "I have asked you a simple scriptural question, in much the same way as Jesus would have asked the Pharisees a scriptural question, and you have refused to answer it. That tells me a lot."

I lingered for just a moment to allow that point to sink in.

"The reason why the prodigal son returned to his father is. . ." I paused, placing my hands on my stomach, "because he was hungry! He only came back to his father because he was hungry, not because of any real repentance. And how did his father respond?" I gestured with my arms, spreading them as if to receive the son in a warm embrace.

My point was made. In the prodigal son parable, the family bond surpasses everything—including perceived wrongdoing. The elders looked at each other and offered no reply.

"There is just something I'm not sure about," Dejan interjected. The other two looked at him. Dejan had been mostly silent throughout, simply observing the proceedings. I was beginning to warm to him, and was intrigued as to what he would say.

"You seem like a really nice man," he said. "What I don't understand is why would a nice man like you threaten us? It doesn't make sense to me. It's like. . ." Dejan struggled to find the proper word to complete his question in English. A brief discussion ensued in Croatian as the other two tried to help him. I waited for them to quieten down before answering.

"That's a very good question Dejan. All I would say is this: you can take a lot of things from a man. You can take his house. You can take his money. You can take his car. You can take his pet. All of these things a man can cope with losing. But if you take a man's family away from him, you will find he is capable of doing a lot of things. And threats of building a website are the least of the things you need to worry about. You have to understand that, from my perspective, Watchtower is the aggressor here. I am the one being threatened, and I am only warning you all of what will happen if you remove my reasons for not doing anything."

Dejan seemed bewildered. Perhaps he was feigning disapproval in front of the others, or maybe what I said had been lost in translation. All the same, when I look back I doubt I could have expressed myself better. Watchtower were the bullies in this scenario—not me. I had to get that point across, if nothing else.

"Right," said Davor, "well I think that brings things to a conclusion. I just need to see the letters of disassociation."

"Of course," I said, reaching for my folder and handing over a piece of paper containing handwritten, signed statements from both my wife and I. The finish line was in sight.

Davor placed the paper in front of him and began reading it aloud, beginning with my wife's message in Croatian. My wife had written it rather hurriedly as I was making my way out the door. She had offered to read it to me, but I told her she could tell me what it said when I got back. I was therefore in the dark as to what she had written.

Davor finished reading the letter and muttered something in Croatian to the other two, who nodded. He then read my letter aloud, which simply stated:

> To whom it may concern,
>
> From henceforth, let it be known that I, James Lloyd Evans, am no longer one of Jehovah's Witnesses—nor do I have or seek any affiliation with the Watch Tower Bible and Tract Society.
>
> Yours sincerely, [signed]

I confess, I enjoyed hearing them read this! But there was bad news in store.

"We can accept your letter," said Davor. "It's very clear and unequivocal. However, we cannot accept your wife's letter. She doesn't quite make it clear enough that she no longer wants to be a Witness."

I was in disbelief. All manner of thoughts began flying through my head. Up to this point, the meeting had gone almost entirely according to plan. Now, it seemed, Dijana had not been clear enough in her letter? I could not imagine how that could be.

"Why, what does she say?" I asked.

"It says that she no longer *feels* like she is a Witness. It isn't clear enough," said Davor.

This actually made sense. My wife is the ultimate peacemaker and hates upsetting or offending people. It did not surprise me that, in her efforts to be diplomatic, she had failed to be quite as forceful in her statement as this judicial committee, intent on salvaging her from my apostate talons, required.

"No problem," I said. "I don't have credit on my phone but I see you have a phone there. Do you mind if I use it to call my wife and have her speak to you? I'm sure we can sort this out."

"No, that won't be necessary," said Davor.

"Please, it won't take a moment."

"No," said Davor, "that wouldn't be appropriate."

"Listen, one way or another this ends tonight," I said, my frustration mounting. "Do you want me to go and drive her here through the pouring rain so she can tell you how she feels herself?"

"No, it would be too stressful for her," said Davor, "we will arrange a separate meeting just for her."

"Look, there's absolutely no way my wife will meet with you," I said. "Marko can tell you what she was like when he called me the other day to arrange this meeting. She refused to even come to the phone to translate for him. She just cannot handle anything like that."

Marko nodded in agreement.

"You must understand," said Davor, "we are meeting to discuss you, not your wife. We will need to arrange to meet with her separately so that we can find out how she feels and offer spiritual help."

I could feel my anger swelling. My protective instincts began to kick in.

"Are you seriously telling me that you can't accept her letter even though she says she no longer feels like a Jehovah's Witness?" I said.

Davor nodded.

"So let me get this straight. You're saying that even if my wife had written exactly the same words that I had written, you wouldn't have accepted it because this meeting is about me and not her?"

"Yes, that's correct."

"So why did you even read her letter if this meeting is only about me?" I asked.

"She wrote us a letter, and we wanted to see what she said!" Davor replied smugly.

"I feel as though you've tricked me. Right at the beginning you asked if we *both* had letters. You made it sound as though you were ready to receive statements of disassociation from both of us."

"Lloyd, you know how this works," said Davor. "You've been an elder. You know we need to follow procedures handed to us, and the procedures clearly state that we need to meet with your wife separately."

At that moment, as had happened over the shunning issue, the fog in my mind suddenly lifted. From somewhere I regained my "elder head" and was able to find another way around the problem.

"Okay, this is very simple," I said. "All my wife needs to do is write the same letter that I have written and make sure Marko gets it, and then you will have to accept it as her letter of disassociation."

Davor's smug demeanor vanished. He had been busted.

"Er, we would not want to encourage you or your wife to do that," he spluttered.

"No problem," I said, calmness restored. "That's precisely what we'll do. I'll tell my wife she needs to send Marko a letter as soon as possible. Not that I want you thinking I'm telling her what to do—this is her decision."

And with that, the meeting was over. There was no final prayer. All four of us rose from our seats.

"Can we shake hands?" I asked Davor. He said I could. I shook the hands of all three enthusiastically, lingering a moment with Dejan as he stifled an unexpected sneeze. I then thanked all three and headed for the exit. Marko watched to see me leave before returning to be with the others as I walked out the door.

I walked back to the car with a smile on my face. Yes, it had been a painful and arduous process—not made easier by my father's eleventh-hour message—but a line had been drawn. A stand had been taken. The next generation now had a fighting chance of mental freedom.

After 23 years of cult servitude I was no longer a Jehovah's Witness—*and it felt great!*

CHAPTER TWELVE

# A Prisoner No More

*"Beware the irrational, however seductive. Shun the 'transcendent' and all who invite you to subordinate or annihilate yourself. . . . Never be a spectator of unfairness or stupidity. Seek out argument and disputation for their own sake; the grave will supply plenty of time for silence."*
—Christopher Hitchens

WHAT is a cult? The word can be applied in different ways depending on who you speak to. It is also problematic when used to describe a well-known, successful organization with millions of members. Most journalists, writers and scholars will shy away from using any form of pejorative for a popular religious movement lest they are accused of bigotry. Ultimately, any judgment on whether something is or is not a cult can only be subjective. For example, you can declare someone a criminal if a conviction by a court of law makes this an objective fact, but who or what has the final word on whether a given movement can be labeled a cult?

Watchtower, according to its website, rejects the word because Jehovah's Witnesses "have not invented a new religion" but "pattern [their] worship after that of the first-century Christians." In other words, if Jehovah's Witnesses are a cult, then so were the early followers of Jesus. (Good luck trying to find a branch of Christianity that *doesn't* claim to model itself on the

New Testament!) Watchtower also asserts that Witnesses "do not look to any human as their leader"—a claim that is dubious at best given what we have considered in previous chapters.

Some see the word "cult" as applying only to religions—specifically *small* religions. Sam Harris, whom I quoted at the beginning of the previous chapter, once recorded a special podcast episode in which he turned his attention to the cult phenomenon. When focusing on one of the extreme examples of cults—Marshall Applewhite's doomed Heaven's Gate movement, for which 39 followers committed suicide—Harris remarked:

> One can view cults as a kind of lens through which to view the phenomenon of the true believer. Of course, every religion is a kind of cult which just has more subscribers. That's how we differentiate cults from religions. If you have millions of subscribers, you are a religion. If you have thousands—or, in this case [of Heaven's Gate], 40—then you are a cult.

Harris thus deftly exposed the flawed logic at the heart of how the word "cult" is deployed. He correctly observed that "every religion is a kind of cult which just has more subscribers," while conceding (in a tongue-in-cheek way) that religions tend to evade being identified as cults once they attract a sufficiently impressive following. This focus on numbers is echoed in the *Oxford Dictionary's* definition of "cult" (bold is mine):

> Definition of cult in English:
>
> noun:
>
> A system of religious veneration and devotion directed towards a particular figure or object: the cult of St Olaf
>
> 1.1 **A relatively small group of people having religious beliefs or practices regarded by others**

**as strange or as imposing excessive control over members:** a network of Satan-worshipping cults

1.2 A misplaced or excessive admiration for a particular thing: the cult of the pursuit of money as an end in itself

A glaring problem with the above "relatively small" criterion is that it rewards successful cults by upgrading them to religions once they have exceeded a certain membership threshold. But a favorable consensus from a sufficient number of people does not turn bad ideas into good ones. If popular wisdom imposes any kind of numerical limit on how big (or small) a cult can be, this only aids cults by gifting them a convenient get-out-of-jail card. It is akin to saying: "Dupe enough people, and you're off the hook!"

To put all this in context, let us imagine that, in 1997, Marshall Applewhite somehow succeeded in convincing the entire population of the State of California—then numbering some 32 million individuals—to join his Heaven's Gate group and commit mass suicide by asphyxiation as a means of reaching an imaginary spacecraft trailing the Hale-Bopp comet. Can you imagine, in reporting the unimaginable carnage of 32 million corpses strewn across California, the world's media dropping the word "cult" in favor of "religion?" Or, if at Jonestown, in 1978. Jim Jones had somehow managed to massacre, not just 900, but several million converts to his People's Temple using poisoned Kool-Aid, would history remember him as a religious figure rather than a cult leader?

The sooner we rid ourselves of this tiresome cliché that only small groups get to be called cults, the better. Large cults like Watchtower are taking full advantage of our confusion and reticence in this regard; flourishing unchecked while smaller, easier targets in the cult spectrum—such as Scientology and the Westboro Baptist

Church, both of which harm fewer people due to their small size—take most of the media punches. I can well understand how, if you are a journalist and you want to offend the least number of readers with a gripping cult exposé for your TV documentary or newspaper article, picking on the cult with the least followers is the prudent course—but this is hardly a fair or intellectually defensible approach. High numbers should not make a cult *less* worthy of criticism—quite the opposite.

Neither should it be assumed that all cults must be religious in nature, as Steven Hassan points out in *Combating Cult Mind Control* (bold is mine):

> It is also important to recognize that there are different kinds of cults and they often operate quite differently. Different cults appeal to the many different human impulses: such as desire to belong; to improve oneself and others; to understand the meaning and purpose of life. **Religious cults** are the most well known. They often have a charismatic leader and operate with religious dogma. **Political cults,** often in the news, are organized around a simplistic political theory, sometimes with a religious cloak. **Psychotherapy/educational cults,** which have enjoyed great popularity, purport to give the participant "insight" and "enlightenment." **Commercial cults** play on people's desires to make money. They typically promise riches but actually enslave people, and compel them to turn money over to the group. None of these destructive cults deliver what they promise and glittering dreams eventually turn out to be paths to psychological enslavement.[1]

In August 2014, I attended a special "undue influence" workshop in London hosted by Hassan, at which

[1] Hassan's book also lists human traffickers as a form of cult due to the coercive techniques used by the ringleaders of such groups.

I was introduced to Masoud Banisadr.[2] Masoud spent 20 years as a member of the Islamic-Marxist political organization Mojahedin e Khalq (or MeK), which was once formally classed as a terrorist group by the United States. During his lengthy indoctrination, he was successfully coerced into divorcing his wife (the love of his life) and estranging himself from his children. Though there were undoubtedly Islamic elements to the MeK ideology, it was first and foremost a political cult with explicit political aims—to sweep the leader, Massoud Rajavi, to power in Iran. Masoud is now free of his indoctrination and an effective advocate for raising awareness of the threat posed by political cults, but he knows that he has his work cut out in fighting the common misconception that cults must only be religious.[3]

The proliferation of such a wide spectrum of cults, the diversity and ingenuity of which shows signs of only increasing rather than diminishing, makes it all the more urgent that we remind ourselves of what cults are *at their very essence*. We must abandon this fanciful notion that a neat line can be drawn along some imagined boundary to demarcate where a religion ends and a cult begins (or vice versa). The exact positioning of any such line would always be subjective and malleable according to the religious or cultural preferences of whoever assumes the role of adjudicating.

For example, would the average person raised to revere the Torah be quick to condemn as cultish the

---

[2] Masoud's story is told in his book *Masoud: Memoirs of an Iranian Rebel*, available on Amazon.

[3] Other representatives of what one might call "alternative" cults at the undue influence workshop included victims of psychotherapy cults, who spoke of how they had been exploited sexually by their leaders into believing that sleeping with them was the only means by which they could be cured of their psychological maladies.

practice of ultra-Orthodox rabbis circumcising infant boys by sucking their penises? (This particular barbarism continues to needlessly claim lives through herpes infections well into the 21st century.[4]) Would the average person raised to respect the Qur'ān and ḥadīths reject as cultish threats of violence against those who draw cartoons of Muḥammad? Would the average person raised in a fundamentalist Christian family fall over themselves to denounce homophobia as a narrow-minded, cultish abhorrence?

We need to agree on a definition of "cult" that transcends subjectivity. I would therefore submit that *a cult is any movement, large or small, religious or nonreligious, that inflicts harm on followers and/or non-followers as a result of deception.* By this simple definition, I believe it logically follows that, as Harris suggested, *all* religions are cults. I can well understand why this claim would be fervently contested by many of my dear friends and colleagues who join me in the fight against cult influence who are themselves religious, but I have yet to encounter a more satisfactory, straightforward means of objectively establishing what cults are.

Many would argue that religious teachings are not automatically harmful simply because they are based on faith rather than fact, but what benefit does a child derive from being programmed with a revised understanding of the cosmos that is without factual basis? Life is too short to believe things that are not true, no matter how much inner bliss or satisfaction such beliefs may offer, or how consoling we may find them. The simple determining factor based on which

[4] A *Daily Mail* article dated April 5, 2013, reported that 13 infants in the New York City area were infected with a deadly form of herpes through the practice since 2000. Two of these babies died and a further two suffered brain damage.

any claim, religious or otherwise, should be appraised as worthy of a moment's consideration should be: *"Is it true, or isn't it?"* How enriched or reassured one feels by dwelling on propositions that are without factual basis is, quite frankly, irrelevant—or, at the very least, no more relevant than the euphoria experienced by people of myriad other faiths and cultures who are conditioned to embrace conflicting propositions. All of this was brilliantly expressed by Harris in one of his speeches that was based on an analogy in his book *The End of Faith:*

> Imagine if your neighbor claimed to believe that there was a diamond buried in his backyard that's the size of a refrigerator. And you ask him, "Why?" You see him out on his lawn digging every Sunday with his family. Imagine how you would feel about his mental faculties if he said: "Well this belief gives my life a tremendous amount of meaning—my family and I really enjoy digging for this on Sundays and it has a remarkable bonding effect on us." Or what if he said: "I wouldn't want to live in a universe where there wasn't a diamond buried in my backyard." It's pretty clear that these responses are inadequate—deeply inadequate—and yet change the subject to the existence of God, who can hear your prayers, who's looking out for you, despite all of the other devastation we see in the world going on each day God is protecting you and your family—you change the subject to that proposition and all bets are off. In fact you could not possibly get elected to office in [the United States] unless you endorsed that kind of thinking.[5]

Variations on the faith model are the basic product of all religions, who without exception rely on their

[5] This speech is searchable on YouTube via the keywords: "Sam Harris Diamond Backyard."

followers embracing as true claims that cannot be substantiated—claims that would sound preposterous if religious devotion were not appealed to as validation. I would add my voice to many others before me who have argued that belief in things that can only be imagined and never seen—which is what faith ultimately is—cannot be considered a virtue in any meaningful sense. (As Hebrews 11:1 puts it with admirable candor: "Faith is the assured expectation of what is hoped for, the evident demonstration of realities that are not seen.")

To believe something without requiring evidence is to impede oneself intellectually, which has to be considered detrimental if one's goal is to make the most of one's fleeting journey through life by operating—to the extent possible—under the premise that knowing things that are true is more desirable than knowing things that are not. Hence, if you can accept my earlier, fairly reasonable proposition that a cult can be defined as any harmful movement that employs deception, and if you find yourself a member of a religious movement that teaches things that are not true (or cannot be objectively substantiated as being true), I would regretfully suggest that you are indulging in a variation of a cult.

Naturally, I can sympathize with any resentment you may feel toward me for characterizing your cherished belief system with a pejorative that carries such a loathsome stigma. But, as humanity continues on its overall upward trajectory toward a fuller understanding of our universe, ever distancing itself from the crude legacies of its less-informed forebears, I can confidently reassure you that I am only approximating how future generations living centuries hence will come to evaluate the object of your devotion.

"But you're being ridiculous!" you might answer. "I can come and go from my church/synagogue/mosque whenever I please without any form of shunning. My leaders embrace my individuality. They do not expect money or unquestioned loyalty from me. I am free to live my life the way I please. And you say I'm in a cult?"

I am very pleased to hear it. If all those things are true, you would certainly be in a much *softer* cult than Jehovah's Witnesses, leaving you exposed to far less harm. But by agreeing with Harris and others who say that all religions are cults, I am not remotely suggesting that all religions or cults are equally bad. I am merely acknowledging that believing or extolling as dogma things that are not true, or are at the very least unverifiable, is harmful. It impedes us. In no way can committing ourselves to spurious claims about the nature of our existence be advantageous to the human experience.

This is especially so when it comes to children, who deserve the very best start in life. Every child is owed an upbringing rich in discovery and wonder; free from undue reverence to the beliefs and traditions of ancestors whose window of opportunity to enjoy sentient existence has long since closed. But rather than help children make the most of their capacity to absorb knowledge, religions exploit it. To underscore this point, I can hardly do better than repeat this painfully accurate observation by Richard Dawkins, part of which I used to introduce the first chapter:

> Isn't it a remarkable coincidence that almost everyone has the same religion as their parents? And it always just happens to be the right religion. Religions run in families. If we'd been brought up in ancient Greece we would all be worshipping Zeus and Apollo. If we had been born Vikings we would

be worshipping Wotan and Thor. How does this come about? Through childhood indoctrination.

Though there will always be exceptions to the rule (not *every* ancient Greek will have worshipped Zeus and Apollo), hopefully my own story sufficiently attests to the almost inevitable replication of religious convictions between parents and their children, and the paramount role played by child indoctrination in perpetuating religious belief. Child indoctrination is the lifeblood of all religions past and present, no matter where you look on our planet. If your parents believed something, there is a strong chance you will believe it too. Hence, religious belief merits no more reverence and admiration than nationalism, since both one's religious beliefs and one's nationality are largely accidents of birth, and any claims of superiority arising from them ("My religion is the truth!" or "My country is the greatest!") can only ever be subjective.[6]

Ultimately, the major selling point of nearly all religious faith is the refutation of human mortality. Few people relish the thought of dying, so it is unsurprising that a belief system will be appealing if it offers the assurance that death is not *really* the end—only the beginning. Many faiths, including Jehovah's Witnesses, go even further by recommending the notion that you can, indeed *must*, forgo pleasure and fulfillment in this life in favor of cashing in your chips in the next—the "store up treasures in heaven" philosophy.

---

[6] It could be argued that atheism might also be an accident of birth if both a child's parents are atheist, but it is a mistake to conflate atheism with religion. As Penn Jillette remarked: "Atheism is a religion like not collecting stamps is a hobby." Atheism is not a religious belief—it is a lack of religious belief. A child raised to atheist parents is therefore given a blank canvass—an opportunity to evaluate religious claims on their merits rather than under the assumption they must be true.

(Watchtower's vile blood teaching is one of the more distressing examples of this destructive ideology, but by no means the only one.) Since the dead are unable to return and warn us of what a dreadful folly such thinking is, we are reliant on our own reasoning faculties to grasp what an extremely rare gift life is—a gift we have been incredibly fortunate to receive as the culmination of a fantastically improbable series of events stretching back across millennia, involving no small amount of death and suffering. To take this gift for granted by wasting time and energy on unverifiable propositions is undesirable at best. All religions are therefore culpable if only for trying to distract us with a fake product—a placebo. They may not all be ruining people's lives per se, but they do all cause harm if only by disseminating unhelpful, unsubstantiated assertions as fact.

That said, clearly there are religious groups that are more worthy of being highlighted as cults than others due to the severity and scale of damage they are wreaking on humanity.[7] Without prioritizing or making *some* distinction as to which groups should be especially targeted it would be impossible to mount any meaningful resistance to the worst offenders. But I believe we must move on from a tiresome "This religion is a cult, this religion is not a cult, because I say

[7] Anticult organizations like infoSekta in Switzerland do fantastic work in this regard by raising awareness of the movements we should be especially worried about and trying to combat the harm they are causing. Let me give one example of infoSekta's work. In January 2015 they invited me to speak at an event at the Zürich University of Teacher Education. The event was organized for the purpose of informing teachers and psychologists who have Jehovah's Witness students or patients as to the best ways of dealing with the often-times far-reaching psychological issues unique to this religion.

so!" mentality. If we do not drop this futile attempt at pigeon-holing, future generations will step in and do it for us. What really matters is not whether a religion is a cult or not, but what specific harm it is causing and how many people are affected.

Naturally, not all religions cause the same amount of harm and the harm they cause does not affect equal numbers of people. There are *soft cults* that are guilty of little more than promoting spurious teachings, and *extreme cults* whose teachings result in terrible suffering on an enormous scale. When it comes to battling epidemics, doctors and scientists rightly prioritize and allocate resources according to how virulent the disease is and how quickly it can spread—in other words, how many people are at risk. It would be unthinkable for millions of dollars to be spent on combatting an infection that only gives a negligible number of people a brief headache, but an epidemic that severely impacts on the quality of life—or is even fatal in some cases—would rightly have all available resources thrown at it. Governments should, I believe, start applying the same approach to tackling harmful cults.

If a group has teachings that are damaging, or even potentially deadly, it should be censured accordingly. And the urgency with which sanctions are enforced should be proportionate to how many people are impacted. In the case of Jehovah's Witnesses, you have a religion boasting millions of members that is covering up child abuse, promoting the dismantling of families on religious grounds, and advocating death as preferable to receiving a blood transfusion. As argued in the previous chapter, *at the very least* Watchtower should not be rewarded with tax exemptions or charitable status with such a track record. Extending such benefits is not only a grave insult to those who have been victimized—it also blemishes a country's record on human rights.

I would never go as far as urging the banning of Jehovah's Witnesses—the course that has been pursued in Russia—because I believe strongly in freedom of speech and freedom of religion. It is the personal right of everyone to believe and practice a religion even if it is detrimental to his or her well-being. But if a religion is coercing people to die from refusing medicine, measures should be put in place to reduce the chances of this happening.[8] (Fatalities of this kind should be rendered impossible in the case of legal minors.) If a religion is found covering up or in any way facilitating child abuse, it should be criminally prosecuted and fined, and those personally responsible for creating harmful policies should be similarly punished. School-children should also be warned as early as possible of the threat posed by brainwashing, its basic mechanics and what to look out for. Critical thinking should be a mandatory component of school curriculums. In short, there are any number of ways for a government

---

[8] For example, as I write these final pages, the Canadian media is reporting the distressing death of 26-year-old Éloïse Dupuis, who died refusing blood following complications when delivering a baby boy. The Health Minister for Quebec, Gaétan Barrette, went on record saying: "She was informed, she signed documents many times. She knew, and she made it clear, that if something was to happen, because of her religion she didn't want any transfusion." In making this statement, Barrette entirely overlooked the role played by undue influence in Éloïse's death. Her non-Witness relatives report that Éloïse was surrounded by Witness elders, the "hospital liaison committee," in her final hours, which would have made it almost impossible for doctors to persuade her to accept life-saving treatment with blood. Such manipulative tactics to enforce what is supposed to be a "personal decision" should be outlawed. Religious representatives should not be allowed near patients under such circumstances.

to protect its citizens from harmful cults without trespassing human rights, but at this stage in history the civilized world has fallen woefully behind in this regard and is essentially giving anything calling itself a "religion" a free pass. The victims of religion may not always be conspicuous, but they *are* out there—and their suffering deserves recognition and the application of justice.

By now you are likely wondering how someone like yours truly, who was once a fiercely evangelical Jehovah's Witness "Bible-basher," can now be so outspoken against religion in general.

When I first exited my Witness indoctrination, I did put forth some effort to salvage my identity as a Christian. For example, my prayers before meals at restaurants would cause Dijana considerable embarrassment before I finally quit the habit. (The ritual of praying before meals is one of the first things to go for many who awaken from religion, but I always liked the idea of showing gratitude, even if I was not fully convinced that anyone was listening.) When reading the words of Raymond Franz—who extolled "Christian freedom"—I assumed I could at least take the Bible at face value, even if I could safely jettison the Watchtower dogma with which I had been saddled through my upbringing. But it was only a matter of time before I started extending the parameters of my critical thinking from my Witness heritage to Christianity in general.

I soon found that the Bible held no greater claim to divine origin than any other holy book or sacred text. I came to accept that some of the grim passages (1) advocating genocide, (2) legislating for slavery,

(3) proposing the punishment of people for the crimes of their ancestors, (4) suggesting that a baby girl makes her mother more "impure" than a baby boy, (5) describing (in some places gleefully) the murder of children, (6) decreeing the mutilation of infant genitals, (7) urging the stoning to death of someone for collecting wood on the wrong day, and (8) prescribing the death penalty for those who are gay, offended rather than refined my innate sense of morality.[9] I found myself reasoning that—apart from those dreadful passages—if God really exists, he would be worthy of neither admiration nor worship if he has given me free will only to begrudge my use of it in questioning him. A Creator who punishes my honest reservations as to his existence and moral judgments is not worthy of my respect or worship. A God who rewards only those who accept his existence based on bad evidence is toying with his creation in a very distasteful way. If free will is a gift with strings attached, then it is no gift at all.

We can go even further, if you like, and suggest that if the God of the Bible really exists, the universe is an extremely messed-up place. The actor Stephen Fry made this point superbly in the following exchange during a televised interview (searchable on YouTube), which left his interviewer, Gay Byrne of Ireland's RTÉ One channel, visibly stunned:

---

[9] (1) Numbers 31:13-18 (verse 18 also hints strongly at female virgins being spared slaughter for use as sex slaves if you compare different translations), (2) Leviticus 25:44-45 and 1 Peter 2:18, (3) Exodus 20:4-6, (4) Leviticus 12:1-5, (5) Exodus 11:5 (the "firstborn" would have had to include firstborn infants), 2 Samuel 12:13-18, 2 Kings 2:23-24 and Psalm 137:8-9, (6) Leviticus 12:3, (7) Numbers 15:32-36, (8) Leviticus 20:13. (A video discussing some of these verses can be found on my YouTube channel and is titled *My Top 10 Most Immoral Bible Verses*.)

Gay Byrne: Suppose it's all true and you walk up to the pearly gates and you are confronted by God. What would Stephen Fry say to him, her, or it?

Stephen Fry: I will basically (it's known as theodicy I think) I'll say, "Bone cancer in children? What's that about? How dare you! How dare you create a world where there is such misery that is not our fault! It's not right. It is utterly, utterly evil. Why should I respect a capricious, mean-minded, stupid god who creates a world that is so full of injustice and pain." That's what I'd say.

Byrne: And you think you're going to get in?

Fry: Oh, but I wouldn't want to. I wouldn't want to get in on his terms. They're wrong. Now, if I died and it was Pluto, Hades and if it were the twelve Greek gods, then I'd have more truck with it because the Greeks didn't pretend not to be human in their appetites, and in their capriciousness and their unreasonableness; they didn't present themselves as being all-seeing, all-wise, all-kind, all-munificent; because the god who created this universe (if it was created by God) is, quite clearly, a maniac—utter maniac, totally selfish. We have to spend our life on our knees thanking him? What kind of god would do that? Yes, the world is very splendid, but it also has in it insects whose whole life-cycle is to burrow into the eyes of children and make them blind. They eat outwards from the eyes. "Why did you do that? Why? Why did you do that to us? You could easily have made a creation where that didn't exist. It is simply not acceptable." So, you know, atheism is not just about not believing there's a god—but, on the assumption there is one, what kind of god is it? It's perfectly apparent that he is monstrous, utterly monstrous, and deserves no respect whatsoever. The moment you banish him your life becomes simpler, purer, cleaner—more worth living in my opinion.

Fry thus brilliantly and succinctly reveals why the bridge between atheism and anti-theism is so easily crossed. Once you stop assuming that God exists and shed your fear of displeasing him, you are free to deliberate hypothetically over his character. Even if you put God's Old Testament tantrums to one side and focus purely on the issue of human suffering, God's character will be found wanting according to the most rudimentary standards of morality.

Sam Harris has also expounded the anti-theist argument very well using the horrendous statistic of the number of children who die every year before they reach the age of five: *nine million.* After quoting this figure in a speech, he broke it down further to "24,000 children a day, a thousand an hour, 17 or so a minute," adding that "some few children, very likely, will have died in terror and agony" with their parents' frenzied prayers for God's intervention going unanswered. What was Harris' conclusion?

> Any God who would allow children by the millions to suffer and die in this way, and their parents to grieve in this way, either can do nothing to help them, or doesn't care to. He is therefore either impotent or evil.[10]

If you were to present a Witness with this objection to God's toleration of suffering, most would be ready with an answer. (Or they *should* be, because the question of suffering is arguably the issue with which Witnesses are most frequently confronted.) They argue that if God were to intervene in human affairs to end suffering, he would trespass against the divine laws he established to vindicate his sovereignty, according

[10] The speech is easily found on YouTube with the keywords "Sam Harris Christian Morality."

to which humans have been granted sufficient time to prove themselves inept at ruling independently without his help. But who exactly is God trying to impress with such a convoluted arrangement? Surely an all-wise, all-powerful Creator could conceive a more elegant means of ridding the earth of suffering than to tolerate it for millennia—indeed to be the *direct cause* of it in some cases by creating certain insects, bacteria and viruses that visit suffering on humans by design?

Once you allow yourself to accept that humans are not the focal point of the cosmos, that the universe cares not whether humans flourish or flounder, that it has been around for 13.8 billion years before our species emerged and will soldier on for billions of years after we have joined the 99 percent of all lifeforms on earth that are now extinct, all these riddles disappear. You realize that death and suffering are as inevitable for humans as for all other creatures.

Not that coming to terms with one's mortality is by any means easy. In my own case, I have had to accept not just that death really means death for me personally, but that promises made about seeing Mum again were nothing more than an illusion—an elaborate fantasy sold to me with the aim of securing my allegiance. As distressing as it can be to let go of these cherished promises, I have personally found life to be much richer and more enjoyable by doing so. Time on this planet is now a rare and precious opportunity to be savored rather than squandered. And when problems arise, I know I must accept the responsibility of solving them myself rather than expecting God to swoop down and fix things for me. Freedom from religion has helped me to take my mortality seriously, to understand my place in the cosmos and kinship with all other living things, and to embrace a sense of duty toward improving the prospects for humanity where possible—if only for the benefit of posterity.

But dealing with death is not the only challenge facing ex-Witnesses. Usually they must also deal with the collapse of their entire sense of community when social bonds are severed through shunning. When in "good standing," without any punitive sanctions against them, Witnesses find it almost effortless to integrate themselves in their local congregation and forge lasting relationships. They enjoy a strong sense of purpose in serving a perceived greater good, and are conditioned to believe that friendship among fellow believers is compulsory. Failure to "widen out," or forge social bonds with people based on shared faith, is seen as indicative of spiritual weakness.[11]

But when a Witness suddenly finds themselves cast adrift in "Satan's world" with no guaranteed friends on whom to depend, it can be extremely distressing. Bereft of their sense of belonging, ex-Witnesses often scramble to build new connections and forge some form of replacement community while still not fully understanding who they are in terms of their authentic identity. They can often wrongly assume that everyone who has the same Watchtower stamp in their cult passport will instantly be compatible as a friend due to the shared experience, which makes the disappointment even more crushing when they learn the hard way that simply being an ex-Witness does not make someone a pleasant person. If someone is nasty, vindictive or antisocial as a Witness, the likelihood is they will continue to be those things as an ex-Witness.

---

[11] The November 15, 2009, *Watchtower* urges Witnesses to heed 2 Corinthians 6:11-13 by expanding their social network, saying: "If we 'widen out,' our circle of friends will grow, intensifying the love that unites us in true worship."

Even ex-Witnesses who succeed in building new friendships have their work cut out in fully coming to terms with what has been done to them mentally and emotionally. The experience of being in a cult leaves deep, lasting scars. I will never forget Jon Atack, an expert on Scientology, making the following poignant observation at the press conference for the 2014 undue influence workshop in London:[12]

> It can take people many years to recover. In fact, two experts, Conway and Siegelman, said of Scientology it has the most debilitating set of rituals of any cult in America, and that they anticipated recovery time unaided to be twelve and a half years. I would say they were wrong. It's not twelve and a half years. In the most part, people who have been involved in something this invasive do not recover without help. They go to their graves with this stuff still restricting them and preventing them from helping society.

These words resonated powerfully because, despite by that time being completely awakened from my loyalty to Watchtower, I knew my cultic identity was still a strong part of my psyche. It continues to punish me occasionally with sudden flushes of doubt, guilt and fear—feelings that can only be vanquished with heavy doses of logic and reason, including reminders of exactly *why* Watchtower teachings are false and harmful. Sometimes it feels as though there are two Lloyds inhabiting my mind: my cultic identity, or "JW Lloyd," and my emancipated, authentic self. As unwelcome as JW Lloyd is, and as much as I would like to forever purge him from my psyche, I admit that I often draw

[12] The video in which these comments are made can be found on YouTube by typing in "undue influence press conference."

on him for inspiration when I am writing articles, preparing videos, or even writing this book. It is JW Lloyd on whom I can rely whenever the brutally honest, assertive prose of authentic Lloyd must be softened in order to make my material more palatable and helpful for those I am trying to reach. And it is JW Lloyd who is summoned whenever I need to decode some new Watchtower article with its convoluted "new light" explanations of Scripture.

I have noticed that JW Lloyd is getting weaker and less conspicuous as the years pass by since my exit, to the point where I will often, instead, turn to my wife (who is a year behind me in her awakening) for help in reaching through to believing Witnesses. But I suspect JW Lloyd will always be cowering, Gollum-like, somewhere in the far recesses of my mind—a scar on my subconscious that will never fully heal.

The permanence of the damage caused by brainwashing, and its ability to haunt someone for years after they have either been ejected from a cult or awakened from its influence, must not be underestimated. It is not just Witnesses who need to wake up from their brainwashing-induced stupor, it is a good deal of ex-Witnesses too—perhaps the majority. This is why I try to remind those newly freed from Watchtower's influence not to rest on their laurels. It is imperative that they build up their cultic immune system by buttressing their psyche with as much information as possible. The golden rule for chasing away the ghosts of cult indoctrination is and always will be "the three R's": *Research, Research, Research!*

It is one thing to be free of the *ritualistic* aspects of being a Jehovah's Witness (perhaps by ceasing to go to meetings and assemblies, or in the preaching work, or to the Memorial), but it is another thing entirely to rid oneself of the residual effects of years of layered, highly potent cognitive and behavioral conditioning. Total, permanent detox from sustained cult brainwashing to which one has been exposed for any significant period is a condition that, in my opinion, can never be fully attained. You can claim to have attained it, perhaps by ignoring everything to do with Jehovah's Witnesses and living your life completely free of any reminders of your former faith, but—if my own experience is anything to go by—I would respectfully suggest that you would be living in denial.

For a number of years I have been an extremely vocal activist against Watchtower. I have become sufficiently well versed in the false teachings, historical scandals, and harmful practices as to create a number of resources—including blog articles, videos, and this book—all detailing my findings and setting out my case against the organization. I am absolutely convinced that the religion of Jehovah's Witnesses is not just untrue, but deeply detrimental to humanity to the extent that, in some cases, it is deleterious to the well-being of children and even a threat to human life. And yet, I refuse to deny that JW Lloyd is *still* a part of me. It is still possible, despite what I know, to have those gnawing feelings of doubt and guilt. I can therefore only imagine how tortured are those ex-Witnesses who convince themselves they do not need to do *any* research because they "just know" deep down it is not true. We cannot afford to underestimate how multi-faceted and complex the human subconscious is. It is one thing for someone to *know* something is not true—it is another thing entirely for this realization to filter down to the subconscious catacombs where many of our deepest fears and insecurities prowl.

Occasionally, I will still be taunted by other ex-JW activists to the effect that nothing I say or do in my articles or videos will wake up believing Jehovah's Witnesses. They reason that anybody who ventures online to read one of my articles or watch one of my videos is already awake and thus gleans only validation rather than enlightenment from material criticizing Watchtower. But I have learned enough from my own experience to understand that cult brainwashing is far more complex than that. When awakening from unwavering belief in one's indoctrination, there is rarely a sudden flash of revelation that it is all complete nonsense. A believing Witness does not go to bed one night and wake up the next morning cured of his or her dependency on "Jehovah's organization." The process is far more gradual and staggered.

A Witness's mind might sway to and fro with progressions and regressions. He or she might resolve to abandon a key element of their indoctrination ("Armageddon isn't coming, it's all just scaremongering. . .") only to embrace it again later through deep-seated fear, or a rousing talk or touching experience. This to-ing and fro-ing might continue, perhaps over many years, until the Witness finally wrenches free of enough of these tendrils of belief for the whole house of cards to collapse in a "eureka" moment—leaving them completely awake, but still with work ahead. The assistance of activists who have been through this process already and know how to successfully navigate the labyrinth of emotions is critical to achieving a recovery that, while hardly ever complete in an absolute sense, can at least be considered successful.

In one of my videos (in which I answer critics who suggest I should "move on" from my activism), I use the illustration of two sides of a river spanned by a bridge. One side is populated by the millions on our planet who are convinced that Watchtower is God's organization, whether they are Witnesses in "good standing" or former Witnesses who have been disfellowshipped for some perceived wrongdoing and are still riddled with fear and self-loathing. The other side is populated by current[13] and former Witnesses who have sufficiently purged themselves of reverence for Watchtower and the Governing Body. Both groups are aware of the bridge between the two states of mind, even if they both have very different perceptions of it. Indoctrinated Witnesses can, when they are ready, use the bridge to cross over to the other side and into mental freedom. Mentally free Witnesses are no more desirous of crossing over to the indoctrinated side than they would be to have themselves thrown in jail, but some of them will stand in the middle of the bridge to help those on the other side escape. Those who do this are the *activists*—anyone who uses their time and energy to try to help Witnesses wake up.

The deeper the indoctrination of the Witness, the more fearful and suspicious they will be of the bridge, and what lies beyond. Witnesses who are completely under Watchtower's spell have allowed themselves to be convinced that their side of the river is the only safe place to be, and that grave danger lurks along the riverbank—especially at the bridge. Devout Witnesses therefore throng together at the furthest extremity of their domain away from the river. But, every now and then, a Witness cannot help but stray toward the bridge—perhaps out of curiosity in a fleeting mo-

[13] Some Witnesses wake up from their indoctrination but, for various reasons—usually connected with family and the wish to avoid shunning—decide to stay inside the organization.

ment of doubt. Some become so overwhelmed by their doubts that they furtively position themselves almost on the bridge, teetering on the threshold, fascinated by what awaits them if they were to cross over. If they can muster the courage to venture as far as the middle of the bridge, a hand will be extended by one of the ex-Witness activists on the other side to help them the final few steps to freedom. The hand could be that of an evangelical Christian activist, who immediately bombards the Witness with alarmist claims that they will not be saved unless they give themselves over to Christ and are born again. While this sort of approach will inevitably appeal to a tiny percentage of Witnesses, for most it will frighten them all the way back to where their fiercely-loyal fellow believers are huddled together—and they will think twice before approaching the bridge again.

If a doubting Witness is more fortunate, the hand that reaches out to grab theirs could be that of Paul Grundy, whose excellent, thoroughly-researched, religiously-neutral JWfacts.com resource is written to appeal to almost any religious or nonreligious persuasion.[14] Another helping hand providing a firm wrench into reality is that of Raymond Franz. Though Franz died in 2010, he is still on the bridge and helping untold numbers of traumatized victims of the Watchtower cult, myself included, cross over to the other side with his kind, nonconfrontational style of writing. Franz's writings were undoubtedly motivated, at least in part, by his strong Christian convictions. Even so, he predominantly appealed to logic and reason in his books, leaving the reader to reach his or her own conclusions

---

[14] Paul is not religious, but is careful to keep a neutral tone on his website regarding belief and unbelief, which I have tried my best to replicate on JWsurvey.

based on the available evidence. *Crisis of Conscience*, in particular, provides an invaluable stepping stone from mental enslavement to Watchtower to either a less dogmatic, black-and-white, us-versus-them flavor of Christianity or—as turned out to be the case with me—no religious belief at all.

That Franz could reach out through his activism so persuasively without insisting that his own beliefs be embraced by everyone is, I believe, a wonderful model to follow for all activists, whatever their convictions. Faith may be an indulgence that humanity is slowly learning it is better off without, but some people seem to need it in their lives. Believers and unbelievers alike can be of considerable value in the battle to extricate Jehovah's Witnesses from their indoctrination, and when it comes to finding a productive outlet for the pain and anger of cultic abuse there is no nobler a use for such energy than helping future generations avoid the same fate. Few aspects of my activism give me more gleeful satisfaction than the thought of children who haven't even been born yet avoiding a Witness upbringing because of something I have said or written that helped persuade their parents or grandparents. I firmly believe the most pressing duty of any ex-cult activist is to save the next generation from fear and ignorance, and to make it easier, not harder, for harmful cults in whatever incarnation to face the scrutiny, contempt and criticism they deserve. By doing this, we can achieve the worthy goal of leaving the universe a slightly more agreeable place than we found it, which is as good as any reason for living that I can think of.

As I drove home from the hospital at around midnight on May 7, 2014, my feelings suddenly overwhelmed me. I gripped the steering wheel hard and allowed myself an unrestrained roar of delight. I had just witnessed the birth of my daughter, Jessica Liberty Evans. I felt as though nothing in the world could possibly make me happier—not even winning the lottery several times over![15]

This joyous event was all the more welcome for the months of turmoil that had preceded it. In the aftermath of our disassociation, the tension and animosity from my JW in-laws became so unbearable that Dijana and I felt the need to abandon living downstairs in their part of the house and retreat to our unfinished apartment, which—despite our best efforts since arriving in 2009—was still little more than a bedroom adjoining a dusty void of bricks and concrete. Being exiled to such a cave-like environment would have been problematic at the best of times, but we would be calling it "home" in the Croatian mid-winter, without any insulation, and with Dijana five months pregnant.

At one point we seriously considered packing our things and flying back to the UK, even if it meant leaving our in-laws (one of whom had serious heart problems) to fend for themselves without us. Though enraged by our decision to renounce their religion, they were rightly horrified at the thought of their pregnant daughter living in an exposed, inhospitable part of the building. Rather than countenance our leaving the country, they briefly entertained the idea of finding somewhere else to live locally and surrendering the

[15] Such was my elation that I was inspired to put together a special music video to mark the event for YouTube, titled *We Love You Jessica Liberty—A Message To My Newborn Daughter.*

house to our care, which would have also entailed shunning us completely as Dad was already doing.

Eventually, we were able to sit them down and thrash out an agreement whereby we could all live under the same roof and interact amicably so long as religion was kept off the agenda. They would turn a blind eye to my filming "apostate" YouTube videos and writing against the organization so long as I did it upstairs in our part of the house and we made no attempts at influencing them to join us. It was made clear that under no circumstances was I to do activism in their part of the property, or try to involve or mention them in my work in any way. They also stipulated that they would no longer eat with us at the same table, which was their way of applying 1 Corinthians 5:11 (in which Christians are urged to "not even eat" with an avowed sinner).

Despite successfully negotiating a peace accord, our predicament remained dire. We set up a wood-burning stove to give us a bit of heat, but our accommodation was far from palatial—and Jessica's due date in May loomed. Fortunately, since I had documented our exit on JWsurvey.org and on social media, many ex-Witnesses were alert to our situation. Four ex-JWs in particular—Julia Barrick, Annette Getzschman, Candace Conti and her mother Kathleen—decided to rally together and organize a baby shower. Our aim was to have at least our bathroom built and functional by the time Jessica was born. We ended up being about five months behind schedule in that regard—but, even so, the flow of gifts and money was overwhelming and made an otherwise bleak and stressful period far more bearable. By the time Jessica arrived, she had all the clothes and accessories she could possibly need thanks to the support and solidarity extended to us by our fellow "apostates" from all over the world. It certainly did not go unnoticed by my in-laws that our fellow unbelievers were not fitting the Watchtower stereotype of being cold, heartless and selfish.

By the summer of 2014, much of the pain of our exit was behind us and we could both look back on our decision without any regrets. If anything, the backlash and animosity from our former "brothers and sisters" had only served to underscore the urgency of disentangling ourselves from such a toxic group—a group in which recognizing the divine mandate of a bunch of men in New York means the difference between a warm embrace and being treated as something less than human.

Even so, we knew there was a missing ingredient. We were now on our own, adrift from any real sense of community. Our geographical isolation in a quiet rural village 20 minutes' drive from the nearest town did not help. Apart from my occasional games of football with some of my fellow villagers, we did not really interact with our neighbors—certainly not with the closeness that we were accustomed to in the Witness fold. So when an ex-JW Facebook friend, whom I had previously only met on Skype, asked whether I wanted to join him and his family for a holiday on the Croatian coast, our rather precarious financial predicament left us with a dilemma. Do we play it safe and stay at home for the next few days to conserve funds, or do we throw caution to the wind by spending what little money we have on a trip to the coast for a holiday with virtual strangers?

To this day I still cannot fully explain why, but something told me this was something the three of us needed to do—even if we could not justify it financially. Patrick Haeck was a charismatic Belgian with an infectious smile who was a fan of my work on JWsurvey. Based on our Skype conversations, he seemed the sort of person I could enjoy spending time with—and I felt we needed all the friends we could get. I thus spent the week just before our proposed rendezvous sending out emails to any translation clients who owed us money, pleading with them to pay. But when the day came for us to drive out to meet Patrick at his rented apartment in Pula, our bank account total was still depressingly close to zero. I sent out another flurry of emails, hoping that at least somebody would pay straight up. Finally, two or three payments trickled through on PayPal. We now had just enough money to buy some diapers for Jessica and put some fuel in the tank for the four-hour drive. We threw our things in the car, and off we went!

On our arrival in Pula, Patrick came to meet us at a pre-arranged roadside location (the place where he was staying was hard to find) before leading us on to his rented apartment. With him was his wife Belinda, his two daughters and one of their boyfriends, together with another Belgian family of ex-Witnesses including four school-age children. We were warmly greeted and immediately felt at ease in the relaxed vibe of our new friends, who immediately set about preparing a barbecue banquet. Especially noticeable was the hum of children running around carefree and having a good time—something we simply had not experienced since we were last in company with Witnesses. Over fine Belgian beer and grilled barbecue fare we chatted about our shared experience and I learned of how the other couple who were staying nearby, Bjorn and Priskilla, were close to Patrick because he had always looked out for Priskilla, an abuse victim, since his days as an elder.[16] Patrick also told us the bizarre story of his own exit from the Witnesses, which involved a PowerPoint presentation about 607 B.C.E. and an infestation of wild ducks.[17]

We were invited to stay with Patrick's family. His daughter and her boyfriend even gave up their room and slept on the couch so we could be comfortable. As the vacation went on, we felt more and more cocooned in an atmosphere of unconditional love and friendship. We both noticed how eerie it was that, in the five days we spent with Patrick and his expanded family, whom he jokingly referred to as his "cult," we never witnessed one dispute or acrimonious outburst—something we were both accustomed to from vacationing with Witness friends and family. Our time with Patrick was precisely what we were in need of: a reminder that

---

[16] Priskilla's abuse as a child was handled appallingly by Witness elders. Her husband, Bjorn, also carries scars from his Witness past. His disfellowshipped sister, Kaatje, committed suicide after repeated pleas to get reinstated fell on deaf ears.

[17] The back garden of Patrick's home in Belgian has a large pond. In 2006, when he was a well-known Witness elder, it was invaded by ducks. Patrick approached the local authorities and appealed for them to do something about the problem, but they refused to get involved. Eventually, he took matters into his own hands and decided to cull the ducks using a miniature crossbow, which was perfectly legal. Nevertheless, the media were alerted and the matter received publicity, much to the consternation of Patrick's fellow elders. As the backlash worsened, Patrick decided to tender his resignation. Four years later, his elders came to hear of a PowerPoint presentation he had prepared debunking the notion that 607 B.C.E. is significant as a date in Bible prophecy. They phoned Patrick to arrange a judicial committee hearing (apostasy trial), but hung up on him when he mentioned he would be bringing his lawyer. Finally, Patrick was disfellowshipped *in absentia*, but he has never looked back. To this day, he credits the ducks with his awakening.

***A group shot with our new Belgian friends toward the end of our time together in Pula (Patrick is in the center, with the white T-shirt)***

we could still enjoy that special sense of community despite no longer being in a cult. We just needed to put forth a little effort to find it.

It was not long after we returned home that our uplifting vacation experience received something of an encore. Patrick telephoned and asked if it would be agreeable for him and Belinda to come visit us before they headed back to Belgium. They had just dropped their youngest daughter off at Zagreb Airport (which is only an hour from where we live) because she needed to get home more urgently. They wanted to see where we lived, even if it was only for a brief visit. I told them that of course they could come, but I knew before I put the phone down that it would be complicated to entertain our guests. Firstly, despite some small progress, our apartment was still barely habitable. At that stage we were still without a working bathroom. We basically only had a bedroom and a large unfinished space, containing our desks and computers, framed by a bare brick wall and some windows. By now, we were accustomed to such basic conditions, but how would our guests react? Secondly, Dijana's parents were downstairs and would almost certainly shun our guests if they needed to go down and use the building's only bathroom.

As soon as Patrick and Belinda arrived, we ushered them upstairs and put on a small buffet for them. We showed them around and explained our modest progress since first arriving in 2009. At one point, Patrick went downstairs to use the bathroom. Thankfully, however, there was no awkwardness with Dijana's parents, who had secluded themselves in their room (I suppose, in their own way, this was their version of showing kindness—by not putting themselves in a position where they would have to be unkind).

As hard as Patrick and Belinda tried, it was difficult for them to conceal their shock at our circumstances. Normally very exuberant and talkative, Patrick stared at the walls and ceiling, apparently deep in thought.

"I can see you're shocked. This is pretty basic, but we're hoping to improve things," I said, trying to lighten the mood.

**Our "cave" during Patrick and Belinda's visit**

"I'm not shocked," he replied. "I'm just trying to think how I can help."

Shortly after saying this, Patrick excused himself and went outside to his car. He returned with a carry-case full of various tools, all neatly organized and strapped with velcro.

"These are yours. Don't worry, I can easily get a replacement box," he said.

I thanked him for the thoughtful gesture, which went above and beyond my expectations. After all, Dijana and I were happy simply to belong to such a fantastic group of friends after so recently being cut adrift from our Witness community. But I was to learn that Patrick had more help in mind while he had been carefully studying our walls and roof, as would become clear in future Skype and Facebook conversations. Patrick knew that Jessica did not yet have her own bedroom, and he noticed our roof was without insulation with winter approaching. His idea was to return two months later and remedy both those problems himself—which is exactly what he did.

To this day, Dijana and I pinch ourselves when we think about it, but I suppose when you have good friends with a willingness to help, this is the sort of magic that can result. Patrick, Belinda, their daughter Oriana and soon-to-be son-in-law Matthias drove across Europe in October 2014 and rolled up on our driveway to begin what they called their "humanitarian mission." They brought with them a huge trailer, every last square inch of which was crammed with tools and materials, including enough drywall and floor laminate for Jessica's room, and enough insulated ceiling panels to finish the ceiling for the whole apartment. Though one or two of their friends back in Belgium had kindly

**A group shot after work on Jessica's room was complete (From left: Matthias, me, Dijana and Jessica, Patrick, Belinda and Oriana)**

contributed toward the materials, the majority was paid for out of their own pockets.

After Mission HQ had been established downstairs in Dijana's parents' part of the house (they had vacated beforehand for a few days—again, to avoid any awkwardness) Patrick and Matthias set to work almost immediately by punching a hole through the wall of the "cave" that would be Jessica's bedroom window. Within three days of relentless high-intensity work, which continued to as late as 2 or 3 a.m. some nights, Jessica had a new bedroom complete with wallpaper, laminate floor and furnishings from IKEA. The half of the open space in our apartment where we spent most of our time also now had a ceiling with insulation. Not content with all that, Patrick left me enough ceiling panels for me to finish the other side of the apartment and a giddying amount of tools and equipment for future work—the total value of which I dare not estimate. We could never have dreamed of such kindness from our Witness friends or family who were shunning us, which made it even more special. And, perhaps sweetest of all, it was a source of wonder for Dijana's parents when they returned from self-enforced exile to behold what our "mentally diseased" and supposedly self-absorbed apostate friends had created for their granddaughter

Another two months passed, and Dijana, Jessica and I again found ourselves reunited with our "happiness cult"—the Haeck family and friends—this time in Belgium for what would be our first ever Christmas celebration. We were invited to stay for four weeks over Christmas and the New Year, during which time we enjoyed more gratuitous lashings of fun and laughter. The simple joy of going for a drink with friends and making a complete idiot of myself, something I had not been able to do for years, was revisited with Patrick, Matthias and Bjorn as my partners in crime on a night out in Ghent. (The evening climaxed with me being discovered, inebriated, in a compromising situation with a Christmas tree.) The pure thrill on children's faces as they opened their presents was something Dijana and I were able to behold for the very first time. And, of course, Jessica was the star of the show—constantly bombarded with doting admirers from all directions. She was the epitome of cuteness posing for the camera in front of the Christmas tree in her red and white outfit.

As the festivities started to wind down, Patrick and I had a long conversation at his kitchen table one evening over some extremely good single malt. He wanted to know more about my mother. He too had lost a parent—his father—at a relatively young age, so he could empathize.

I told Patrick of my final moments with Mum; the conversations we had in which she divulged things I could never otherwise have known, but which would

***Jessica poses for her first Christmas***

prove invaluable in helping me piece everything together once the time came for me to wake up. I told him about the letter I wrote to her that she never had chance to read because her mind deteriorated so rapidly toward the end.

Patrick stared at me with his piercing blue eyes.

"Lloyd, I want you to promise me something," he said.

"What?" I asked.

"This book you've told me you are writing—I want you to promise me you will include a new letter to your mother in it."

Slightly taken aback, and wondering whether it might be the whiskey talking (it probably was), I promised Patrick I would do this—even though inwardly I was baffled as to how I might satisfy this odd request. After all, I am now free from religion, so I no longer indulge in any fantasies of being reunited with Mum in some idyllic afterlife. But, nearly two years later as my story comes to an end, I cannot think of a more fitting way to conclude than with a tribute to a very special woman.

*Dear Mum*

*It's 2016, and I'm alive and happy.*

*I am married to a beautiful, intelligent Croatian woman, Dijana, who two years ago gave birth to your granddaughter, Jessica Liberty. Jessica is a gorgeous, happy, talkative little person with the same curly brown hair as you and I.*

*It's sad that you can't hold her and play with her, but we are determined that she will grow up knowing who her grandmother is and learning from your incredible kindness and strength.*

*At my baptism, you gave me a Bible in which you wrote that I should "stay awake, stand firm, grow mighty." Mum, I have done all those things. Especially have I stood firm against a harmful cult that is tearing our family apart, torturing Dad and Hannah with false hopes of seeing you again, and threatening future generations.*

*I know when you left us you believed strongly that Jehovah's Witnesses are God's one true organization on*

*earth. I don't blame you for reaching that conclusion—especially after what you told me about the difficult years before you met Dad. But the organization you joined has proved itself over many decades to be nothing more than a self-perpetuating system of deceit and hypocrisy. And you once told me that if there was one thing you hated more than anything else, it was hypocrisy. I know that, given some more time together, you would have at least given me chance to explain myself if I had tried showing you that, in fact, we were being lied to all along. And I still smile when I think of the time you questioned Dad, without any hesitation, over those crazy paragraphs I showed you in the "Daniel" book. You were braver than I was back then.*

*Just before you died, I wrote you a letter telling you of my fond memories from our walk in the Lake District when we passed by Loughrigg Tarn. You never managed to read the letter because your mind faded too quickly, but I wrote of how that magical day, when we strolled through the meadows in the splendor of the English countryside, was the closest to paradise I have ever been.*

*But the magic had nothing to do with any outbreak of Armageddon, real or fabricated. It didn't come as the result of billions of people being obliterated in a mass slaughter for the "crime" of not recognizing the authority of a group of men in New York. That wouldn't be any kind of "magic" worth remembering. The magic was a mother and her son taking a walk in beautiful surroundings—a place that you, me, Dijana and Jessica could still enjoy today if you were here with us. The magic was real. It was a memory we made together—and it was a memory I will always cherish.*

*If there is one thing I've learned from my efforts to "grow mighty," it is that reality itself is beautiful and diminishes in value only when diluted by false claims, failed expectations and unproven dogma. Rather than sink into a state of guilt and self-pity after leaving what we assumed was the "Truth," I feel I have grown as a human being and embraced reality. I have learned to accept my place in the cosmos and contribute in whatever infinitesimal way I can to the ongoing struggles of humanity. And it is your legacy of courage, kindness and honesty that I can credit for growing in that way.*

*Sometimes I find myself pondering the question: "If Mum could see me now, would she be proud?" I've come to realize that this question has two answers. Of course, if your mind belonged to Watchtower and you didn't know the real truth, you would be deeply ashamed of me and would join Dad in shunning me and Dijana—even if it meant never seeing your granddaughter. But the authentic, strong-minded, kind, loving, empathetic, free-spirited Lesley you always were would be proud of me—and would be by my side cheering me on in battling a monstrous bully.*

*Even if I know and accept that I can never see you again, in my mind and heart that's exactly who you are and what you are doing.*

*With all my love and fondest memories, always,*

*Your son,*

***Never forgotten. Always in my heart.***

# Postscript

AS I was putting the finishing touches to this book, I learned of a young man in Canada named Ryan who had recently awoken from his Witness indoctrination and who credited my activism work as having contributed in some way to this process. After speaking with him, I found his story compelling and noted many parallels with my own experience. Ryan kindly agreed to let me make his story a late addition to *The Reluctant Apostate.* I consider it a fascinating case study on how Witnesses are waking up in this internet age, and an example of how the needlessly draconian actions of elders (and their paranoia regarding any form of dissent) prove counterproductive in stemming this flow.

Ryan was born in Nova Scotia in 1991 to believing parents, both of whom were pioneers. Ryan's parents both assisted the legal department at the Canadian Bethel and ran a company employing other Witnesses. Ryan was five, and an only child, when his parents separated. By the time Ryan was eight, his mother was remarried and living in British Columbia. His father moved to live nearby and would spend time with Ryan on weekends, but sadly he committed suicide due to problems with depression when Ryan was only 13. Raised to be a model Witness, Ryan began commenting and giving talks at meetings at an early age and went on to get baptized at 17.

Fast forward to 2014, and 22-year-old Ryan found himself pioneering and starting a new job at a Witness-owned company that employed over 1,800 staff—

mostly Witnesses.[1] He was rewarded with a number of duties in the congregation, appeared on stage at assemblies before hundreds of people, and even declined an invitation to Bethel.[2] Despite his advancement and opportunities within the organization, Ryan reflects on this period in his life as a low point. "I was so busy I had little to no time for a social life," he says. "Looking back, I was incredibly depressed, but at the time I felt I was doing the right thing and that one day it would pay off."

Increasingly despondent about his predicament and desperate to spread his wings, Ryan decided a change was needed. Rather than living in the suburbs, he decided to move to the city (Vancouver) and join a congregation in need of young blood. He was initially overwhelmed by the reception he received from his new congregation, but it took only a couple of meetings for the initial fervor to subside. "Suddenly, no one really talked to me, and when I would approach others the conversations would be very brief," he recalls. "It was

---

[1] This phenomenon of companies comprised almost entirely of Witnesses is quite common. I myself worked for such an enterprise (a lawn treatment company) for a few years while pioneering in my early twenties and the experience was not entirely uplifting. I am also aware that other cult-like organizations such as the Exclusive Brethren are known to have similar arrangements (not necessarily church-sponsored) offering devout staff the benefit of reduced entanglements in matters where a religious stand may be necessary (in the case of JWs: no office Christmas parties or birthday celebrations to worry about), as well as an easier ride getting time off to attend religious events.

[2] At one assembly, Ryan was interviewed about his decision to pioneer. At another, he featured in a demonstration aimed at stressing how wrong it is to participate in paintball. A 1989 *Awake!* describes paintball as "morally obscene" and advises: "War is an abhorrent thing. That is why a Christian gets no thrill or exhilaration from simulating or perpetuating it, dramatizing it."

left to me to put the effort in to get to know my new congregation better."

Ryan tried to stay positive and busied himself alongside his new comrades in the recently-launched cart witnessing program. But the sense of anticlimax and loneliness on having reached his goal of independence and some standing within the congregation gradually intensified. Ryan's goal was to be appointed as a ministerial servant, but he had his reservations. "Being a ministerial servant felt like more work, and finding a wife felt tedious, as I was not interested in the majority of girls my age because I found it difficult to connect and engage in meaningful conversation," he explains. "My plan was to wait until I was older, when finding a marriage mate might be easier."

Ryan traveled to the 2014 regional convention as a fully-believing Jehovah's Witness who did not harbor any doubts. As he puts it: "The promise of a paradise and resurrection was something very close to my heart—especially after losing my father at 13. I was terrified of not making it into the paradise and everyone else, including my father, wondering where I was." There was simply no reason for Ryan to question a theology that promised him so much. Even so, he found the vibe at the convention unsettling. On arriving at the venue for the first morning he was disturbed by the large screens showing members of the Governing Body, along with the JW.org logo displayed prominently. "Immediately, it struck me as Orwellian," he recalls, "but I tried to quickly tame my thinking."

As the convention progressed, Ryan found himself increasingly troubled by what he was hearing. One particular moment of mental rebellion came when an emotional video was shown depicting a woman being resurrected in the future paradise and reunited with her sister, who had been at her bedside as she died. "The whole audience was in tears," says Ryan, "but to me, the video felt strangely manipulative. I was sitting beside a couple of friends and they whispered to me, 'Are you okay?' I nodded affirmatively, yet they continued to show their shock and concern. They said, 'Because your dad died, remember?' It didn't make sense to them that I wasn't sobbing like everyone else."

In the talk that followed, the speaker made comments to the effect that those in attendance had to do all they could for Jehovah if they wanted to see their dead loved ones again. "It felt like blackmail," says Ryan, "holding the relationship with my father hostage unless I did exactly as they stated."

The same convention saw the release of the book *God's Kingdom Rules!*—the slimmed-down replacement to the *Proclaimers* book referred to previously. On flicking through it, Ryan could not help but conclude that it presented a whitewashed version of Watchtower history. "It seemed I was finally seeing cracks in the organization," he confesses.

Rather than being an uplifting experience, Ryan's three days at the convention had left him feeling isolated and confused. The Governing Body were featured prominently on giant screens as the audience "clapped like seals at everything that was said." Ryan felt dejected and alone. He could feel himself disengaging from beliefs and convictions he had held dear only days earlier.

When he got home on the Sunday evening, Ryan decided to visit the Ex-Jehovah's Witness Sub-Reddit page.[3] A few clicks later, he found himself on the

---

[3] The Ex-JW Sub-Reddit can be found at: http://www.reddit.com/r/exjw/

JWfacts.com website reading an article that calmly and logically debunked Watchtower's claim (central to its 1914 doctrine) that Jerusalem was destroyed in 607 B.C.E. "It shattered my entire world," he says. "I began to think about a reality where Jehovah's Witnesses were wrong. The thought became overwhelming and I closed JWfacts and vowed to never return."

But no matter how hard he tried, Ryan could not calm the tsunami of doubt that was slowly engulfing his mind. He even began contemplating suicide and returned to the Ex-JW Reddit page in desperation to share his dark thoughts. Others began commenting to reassure him and offer support, but Ryan started to panic and deleted his account. He later returned and found that somebody had opened up a new post expressing concern and trying to reach out to him, but Ryan was struggling to process his rapidly changing reality. "It was a confusing time, so I decided not to return to Reddit. I felt like I was losing my mind. It was a very dark period." Ryan continued to flirt with ideas of suicide over the next few days and even began researching ways to do it.

Thankfully, Ryan found a moment of clarity and decided he needed to talk to someone. He messaged a friend on Facebook who had been raised a Witness but had never been baptized. "I heard from other friends that he no longer believed," Ryan explains. "I valued his opinion as I thought he was extremely intelligent." Knowing that his friend had also been at the convention, Ryan was anxious to know his thoughts on it. "He listened and empathized. He mentioned he saw my post on Reddit and understood. I was shocked. Kindly, he did not pressure or overwhelm me even though he wanted to tell me more."

After this conversation, Ryan began to feel guilty about the encounter. By the time he returned home, he had decided never to talk to his friend again. "I convinced myself I was weak in faith. I decided to study harder; pray more frequently."

A few days later, another friend of Ryan's, named Kalvin, asked him what he had done over the weekend. Ryan blurted out that he had met up for a coffee with the unbaptized friend, but stressed that this friend was struggling spiritually and he had tried to encourage him.

A month passed, and Ryan received a phone call from one of his elders requesting that he attend a meeting at the Kingdom Hall on a Friday night the following week. "When I asked him what the meeting would be about, as I had no idea, he said that it would be best if I just waited for the meeting," Ryan recounts. "I began to feel sick in anticipation. Not knowing really affected me. I was constantly nauseous and found it hard to sleep."

When the evening of the meeting finally arrived, Ryan was taken into a side room of the Kingdom Hall. He felt intimidated, having never experienced anything like it before. Ryan was asked if he knew why he was there. "When I said no, they asked me to try and guess. They were being very pushy. I didn't want to admit to something incriminating for no reason." Ryan was again asked if he had any idea why the meeting had been arranged, before being questioned as to whether he believed the faithful and discreet slave were God's organization. When he replied "yes," the elders sighed in relief.

The reason for the meeting was then revealed: Kalvin had reported Ryan's rendezvous with a "well-known apostate," his unbaptized friend. Ryan explained that he was not aware that his friend was an apostate and knew that he still attended meetings with his parents. It became clear that Ryan's elders knew very little about the individual themselves and were just going off what Kalvin had told them. Ryan asked why Kalvin had not approached him directly about the matter if he was so concerned, but the elders told him he felt "unequipped" to do so.[4]

As the meeting progressed, Ryan was asked if he had read any "bad books." Ryan answered honestly that he had not. Sensing the direction in which the interrogation was going, Ryan resolved that if asked about JWfacts.com he would admit to visiting it, but for some reason nothing was mentioned about apostate websites. "Afterward, I thought perhaps it was Jehovah looking out for me," he admits.

Kalvin had also informed the elders that Ryan was having "emotional issues," which Ryan was asked to explain. He admitted that he had been struggling with depression for a few years, but had been able to ease himself off medications through a strict diet, exercise and plenty of sleep. Ryan was then asked why he was depressed, and whether the elders in his last congregation had known of this. Finding this new line of questioning uncomfortable, Ryan said that his previous elders had known about his depression and that it was possibly in some way connected with his father's suicide due to depression. "I could sense their awkwardness, and they proceeded to change the subject and

---

[4] According to Matthew 18:15, Witnesses are supposed to approach a suspected wrongdoer privately to level an accusation before bringing the matter before the elders, but this requirement is frequently overlooked in cases where Witnesses are acting as informants.

show me a printout about putting on the spiritual suit of armor, including 'the shield of faith,'" he recalls. To this day, Ryan regrets divulging such personal information to his elders given their subsequent treatment of him.

As the meeting drew to a close, Ryan was told he could keep all of his privileges in the congregation. Ryan mentioned that he had been requesting a shepherding call since his arrival and yet no elders had visited. He was told that they would arrange a visit with him shortly. As Ryan departed the meeting, he sensed it had ended amicably. "I felt stupid for worrying so much and I tried to be as positive as I could in light of the circumstances."

A few days later, at work, Ryan received a phone call from his congregation coordinator, who also happened to be one of his many Witness coworkers. He was anxious to know if Ryan had "some kind of book." Ryan replied that he had no idea what he was talking about. The elder replied that he had it from a "reliable source" that he did indeed have this book, the title of which he refused to divulge. "Again, I said 'no,' and he finally said that, if I just told him the truth, it would be easier on me in the long run." Ryan insisted he had no book that he ought not to have as a Witness, which was actually true. Frustrated at this exchange, Ryan decided to confide in his mother about the elder's bizarre questioning. Little did he know, this would spark curiosity in her about the mysterious forbidden book (*Crisis of Conscience*, we can only assume) and lead her to embark on her own journey of waking up.

By November 2014, Ryan's two-week pioneer school was approaching. After the tumultuous events in the wake of the convention that summer, Ryan looked forward to the prospect of having his faith renewed by two weeks of intensive study. Eager to confirm his attendance, Ryan approached his congregation coordinator and asked whether everything was going to be okay. "He insisted everything was fine, but I just had to wait for the elders to follow up with me. He explained he was following proper procedure. He told me to wait until one of the elders returned from his vacation." With the school only two weeks away, Ryan sensed he would somehow be prevented from going. His intuition would prove correct.

Ryan was asked to attend another meeting with the elders—again on a Friday evening—but this time at an elder's home. He had to travel for an hour in the snow on foot to get there due to not having a car (no ride was offered). Curiously, the room in which the meeting took place adjoined the elder's property, but was accessible only from the outside. "In the room, there were two chairs facing my chair," said Ryan. "It reminded me of an interrogation room."

The elders told Ryan that because of his previous association with his unbaptized friend, whom they considered apostate, he no longer qualified to attend the school. Ryan pleaded with them, explaining that he had to attend if he was to continue as a pioneer. In response, the elders could only read scriptures and repeat their advice from the previous meeting about "putting on the spiritual suit of armor." When Ryan raised with them the strange phone call about the book, his elders shrugged: "Oh, that was a misunderstanding."

Ryan was told he could continue pioneering and they would review his qualifications for attending pioneer school next year. It was late by the time the meeting finished (about 10 p.m., as Ryan recalls). He made his way back home in the snow and "cried the entire time."

Resolving to get himself back in his elders' good books, Ryan threw himself into pioneering—but he was saddened to see the few friends he had moving out of the congregation, one by one. "We even had a local needs[5] that admitted the congregation had issues, but encouraged us to stay and to avoid saying bad things about it," he recalls.

Ryan confided in a handful of his friends about his despair at the situation and soon learned that he was not the only one who was frustrated. Some of his friends urged him to change congregations, as they feared he would "die spiritually" if he remained under the direction of such an unreasonable body of elders. One of his friends even emailed him information that would be considered by Witnesses as "apostate," but Ryan recoiled at what he saw as an affront to his faith—a faith he was desperately trying to nurture back to health.

Determined to give his beliefs a firm foundation, Ryan committed himself to more study and research. Could it be that, if his faith were strengthened, this would serve as a springboard to further progress in the organization in spite of his elders? "In reality, all it did was confuse me," he confesses.

Now that Ryan was viewing meetings and assemblies with a more critical eye, the information flowing from the platform started to grate. "I began to notice how guilt seemed to be the primary motivator, not love, as I had previously thought," he explains. One particular assembly, in March 2015, was especially irksome.

---

[5] A "local needs" is a special talk that elders can give tailored to the perceived needs of the congregation.

The audience was told of the importance of Witness males serving as ministerial servants from youth. This, in Ryan's mind, was just one more reason why he could be considered a failure and would never live up to Watchtower's expectations despite his best efforts.

By the time the Memorial rolled around on April 3, 2015, Ryan was reaching his wits' end. He was "extremely depressed and isolated" and had broken out in a skin condition across his chest that his doctor would later diagnose as hives likely caused by extreme stress.

A number of factors in Ryan's personal life were coming to a head: one of his closest friends had married, making him more distant than before; there was a bitter stand-off with his pioneer partner following a disagreement, and a Witness girl he had grown fond of had been deported back to Australia. A perfect storm was brewing and the collapse of Ryan's beleaguered faith was imminent. He could not have known it then, but the Memorial that Friday evening would be his last meeting at the Kingdom Hall.

Ryan needed a ride to the event, and it was his "friend" and whistleblower Kalvin who would oblige. Because the Memorial is the most important event on the Witness calendar, elders will often assign a number of baptized men in the congregation to act as ushers or attendants. Ryan and Kalvin had been assigned to the parking lot, so they had to be there early. When it finally came time for the talk, Ryan again felt irritated by the speaker's tone. It did not help that the speaker was his coordinator—the same guy who had badgered him at work over a mysterious book he was not supposed to have—who was now exuding warmth and loving concern from the platform. His talk seemed to focus on guilt-tripping inactive Witnesses (who might have ventured back to the Kingdom Hall for the Memorial observance) into returning to the fold permanently. The audience was urged to "think of the children," because "the end is very close." Compounding Ryan's frustration was the fact that he was among the first to arrive for the event and the last to leave. "I was exhausted from rushing home from work and heading straight to the Memorial. While I just wanted to get home to go to sleep, I was at the mercy of Kalvin," recalls Ryan. "I was the last to get dropped off at 11 p.m."

The following Saturday morning would normally have seen Ryan busily donning his suit and tie and departing for door-to-door work with the rest of the congregation. But this Saturday morning felt different. Ryan decided to skip the preaching work and just lie in bed for a bit. That weekend he was without internet due to changing his service provider, so he would have plenty of time on his hands to try to sort through the many conflicting thoughts whirring through his mind. As he lay in bed, he began to dissect his Memorial experience with the aim of trying to understand why it had bothered him so much. Soon, all his doubts from the previous year came flooding back. "I recall that I just stared at the ceiling and thought about what life would be like if I was not a Witness," he admits. "After a few hours of this contemplation, I became anxious and needed to get out of the house."

The more Ryan pondered his predicament, the more anxious he became. He decided to head straight for a local sensory deprivation chamber (or "float tank") he had used before to help calm his mind and manage his depression. He felt this would be the ideal opportunity to take some time out and process his thoughts in total solitude. In the darkness and silence of the chamber, Ryan had his epiphany: "This *cannot* be the truth."

A few weeks before, Ryan had watched a new movie titled *Going Clear: Scientology and the Prison of Belief* (a multi Emmy Award-winning film by Alex Gibney based on the book of the same title by Lawrence Wright). On reflection, he realized there were clear parallels between Scientology and Jehovah's Witnesses.[6] He was particularly moved by the interviews toward the end, in which ex-Scientologists had expressed shame at being duped by the cult, but sympathy for those still inside who could not bring themselves to go through the pain of accepting that their beliefs are untrue. Ryan could now feel this pain intensely as he began seriously contemplating how much he would lose if he left the Witnesses. Despite his eureka moment, Ryan left the float tank feeling despondent and stopped by the liquor store for something to soften this inner turmoil.

The next morning was a Sunday. Again, Ryan chose to stay in bed rather than put on his suit and tie. Still without internet, he revisited Reddit on his phone. The thought occurred to him that perhaps Armageddon was real, but Jehovah's Witnesses would not be the only survivors. Ryan resolved to broaden his research to encompass Christianity as a whole, without the teachings of Watchtower superimposed.

The following day at work, Ryan indulged in learning more about other branches of Christian belief during some downtime. He went for lunch with a coworker who was a non-JW believing Christian and

---

[6] *Going Clear* is one of many documentary films that can be used effectively to help indoctrinated Witnesses understand the control mechanisms common among cults. Other recommendations include *Meet the Mormons* (the Channel Four documentary, not the LDS-approved film of the same name) and the two Louis Theroux BBC documentaries on the Westboro Baptist Church, namely *The Most Hated Family in America*, and *The Most Hated Family in America in Crisis*.

sought his input. "He was very supportive and shared how he believed in God and Jesus but not organized religion." Ryan was finally starting to see alternatives to being a Witness.[7]

Later, as he looked around his office, he began drawing parallels between what he knew of Bethel service and the JW-owned company he was working for. It dawned on him that perhaps his employers might be taking advantage of him because he was a Witness and pioneer. "At the time of my interview, one and a half years prior, I had been promised I would receive sick days, vacation days and employee benefits," he explained. "This had not yet happened." His work life seemed to parallel his struggle for acceptance in the congregation. Here too, promises had been made that he would be appointed a ministerial servant if he just "kept doing what he was doing." A pattern of failed expectations was unfolding.

The next day, Ryan did not go into work. His internet was back, so he returned to Reddit and decided to start researching the story of Ray Franz, as well as other areas of controversy surrounding Watchtower and its teachings. His aim was not to affirm his doubts—rather, he aimed to uncover solid information that could refute the more damning arguments against his cherished beliefs. "I desperately wanted to be convinced the Jehovah's Witnesses had the truth," he admits. But the few Watchtower apologist websites he stumbled across were strewn with

---

7 Ryan relates how a number of non-JW workmates helped him, enabling him to experience for the first time the joy of unconditional friendships. One of these was an atheist who encouraged Ryan to look at the work of Christopher Hitchens for the other side of the argument on religion. When Ryan later told him of his epiphany that the Witnesses were not "the truth," his friend replied: "I knew this day would come!"

logical fallacies. "I recall finally turning off the computer and distracting myself for the rest of the day."

As Wednesday morning arrived, it was time for Ryan to once more immerse himself in life as a Witness. He was scheduled for a shift doing cart witnessing in downtown Vancouver and had to be there at 8:30 a.m. "I remember thinking how exhausting and abnormal it was to keep this pace," he reflects.

On arriving at his spot, Ryan found himself paired with a pretty, single girl his age whom some of his friends had been coaxing him to meet. Initially excited at the chance to get to know her, the disappointment slowly grew as it became obvious that there was no chemistry between the two. Ryan began to wonder whether he would ever find someone with whom he could gel intellectually while rooted to the treadmill of life as a Witness pioneer. He noticed that between them he was not the only one struggling to find happiness. "I recall how she kept bringing up how many times Satan tried to pressure her and how she couldn't wait for the New System to get here," he relates. "It just depressed me."

Making the situation more awkward was recent direction from the organization that those involved in cart witnessing were to hold tablets to their chests and play videos as pedestrians walked by, transforming Ryan and his partner into bizarre, evangelical versions of the Teletubbies. "To me, this felt stupid and ridiculous," says Ryan, who believes the practice was discontinued shortly thereafter. "Seeing how unhappy the pioneers were and how ineffective the work was, I realized I did not want to continue." Another piece of the jigsaw had fallen into place. "I was sacrificing so much to just stand there. I even had a man approach me and say 'It's a beautiful day, why are you wasting your time doing this?'" This honest observation resonated with Ryan. "I decided I couldn't do this anymore. It wasn't right."

Immediately on getting home, Ryan visited the Reddit page again. One of the threads featured a video by Peter Gregerson (who, you will recall, was the friend of Ray Franz). "I didn't turn it off, because it was not aggressive and seemed like an assembly talk," Ryan explains. By this stage he was desperately searching for the truth, so he decided to watch the full video. It was apparent that Gregerson was a sincere, knowledgeable person with no apparent anger or animosity toward the Witnesses. Following along with his Bible, Ryan could see the verses were correctly applied.

When the video ended, Ryan noticed a recommendation pop up for another video—this time from the John Cedars channel. The title was: "What If Jehovah's Witnesses Are Right?" This is a video I had made rather hurriedly only a few weeks earlier after noticing somebody on Facebook pose a similar hypothetical question. In the video, I made the argument (also made earlier in this book) that if the claims Jehovah's Witnesses make about Armageddon were followed to their logical conclusion, survivors would be forced to live in a world built over the corpses of billions of men, women and children all slaughtered for the sole 'crime' of not being Jehovah's Witnesses. Worse still, Armageddon survivors would need to spend the rest of eternity praising the perpetrator of the worst atrocity in recorded history. Ryan did not know this would be the nature of the video before clicking the play button and he was skeptical about videos filmed by former Witnesses in front of webcams, but he was intrigued by the premise of an apostate playing devil's advocate.

"I kept watching because I could sense you were sincere," he told me. "Once I had finished, I was disturbed and felt stupid because I had never really given that subject much thought. I believed that honest-hearted ones would survive Armageddon."

Ryan decided to fact-check my video on *Watchtower Library* and soon confirmed that what I said was true.[8] Though Watchtower is always reluctant to be open about whether only Witnesses will survive Armageddon, this has been a key tenet of the organization's doctrine for decades. After all, if Jehovah will spare anyone who is a good person despite them not being a Witness (a claim often made by less-informed Witness apologists), then what is the point of the preaching work? Why not wait for Armageddon to come and go, and then debrief all the bewildered survivors who were lucky enough to make it through?

"I realized I did not want to live on a paradise earth that was built on the graves of billions," recalls Ryan. "I could not believe that birds would eat the corpses of everyone except Jehovah's Witnesses. At that point, I lost faith in the hope of the paradise and the grieving process started."

Ryan lingered on my channel and decided to watch my very first vlog, recorded in November 2013 (during the countdown to my apostasy trial), in which I used two Bible verses to explain my reasons for leaving Watchtower. One was Philippians 4:8, in which Paul urges Christians to consider "whatever things are true." The other was Deuteronomy 18:20, in which Is-

---

[8] *Watchtower Library* is a piece of software allowing Witnesses to study Watchtower publications going back a number of decades using keywords. There is a limited online version of it (*Watchtower ONLINE LIBRARY*) on JW.org, but most of the featured publications only date as far back as 2000.

raelites were ordered not to fear any prophet who spoke in God's name but whose predictions did not come to pass. These points from my video further resonated with Ryan.

"It summed up how I felt. I felt like I was taking an honest stance with myself," Ryan relates. "I truly wished someone would prove me wrong and I wished there was empirical evidence that proved the Jehovah's Witnesses were the truth and I hadn't been misled my entire life. That video also helped me to not fear the Watch Tower Society. Watching the video, it was what really gave me the strength to say 'enough is enough.'"

Ryan was now finally awake and had granted himself full permission to see what information the internet had to offer. He felt moved to post a message on my Facebook page under his real name. Normally I struggle to keep up with checking emails and messages, let alone answering them, but I found myself relating to Ryan's words. His message read as follows:

> Hey I just wanted to thank you. I spent all day watching your videos from the start and reading your story. I could really relate to your upbringing and it just had the ring of truth. I'm only 23 but I was raised a witness, and I've been a regular pioneer for 3 years. I also did a college course similar to yours. Now I can begin to make the tough changes I need to begin to have a real life. Thank you.

After getting Ryan's permission, I decided to post his message on my Facebook timeline. Two days later, one of my Facebook friends made the following comment:

> Ummm.....so I read this post John Cedars and though I was happy for the young man I felt really downhearted because I have a son the same age who is a pioneer whom have been trying to "wake up."

> Then I got the call this morning. That WAS my son. John Cedars you just saved my boy's life. Ignore the crazy people. You are saving lives.

The part about saving her son's life was probably an exaggeration on Ryan's mother's part (although this could well turn out to be true if Ryan were to ever find himself in need of a blood transfusion). It should also be acknowledged that Ryan was well on the path to waking himself up before stumbling on my channel. Even so, I cannot help but be thrilled that a video I made on the spur of the moment exploring Witness beliefs about Armageddon ended up being "the straw that broke the camel's back" for someone.

I mentioned in the final chapter about the "bridge" of activism, and how hands reaching across that bridge from former Witnesses both dead and alive can serve to either encourage or repel doubting Witnesses from taking the final few steps. I will always derive great joy from knowing that, in the case of Ryan, the hands of myself, Peter Gregerson, Ryan's friends at work, and a number of sincere and supportive ex-Witnesses (including those on Reddit) were collectively able to pull him those last few feet toward mental freedom.[9] There is also considerable relief that this outcome was achieved relatively quickly, since any delay could have been catastrophic given his emotional state.

Transitioning to a new life outside the Witnesses came at a heavy price for Ryan. He was forced out

---

[9] Deborah Frances-White, who happens to be both an ex-Witness and a well-known comedian, has also contributed to Ryan's journey to mental freedom. She makes the story of her visit to Canada to help Ryan in the aftermath of his awakening, including an incredible stand-off with some elders who detained her against her will, the subject of an episode of her BBC Radio 4 series *Deborah Frances-White Rolls the Dice.* The episode in question is titled "Saving Brother Ryan."

of his job at the JW-owned company and made to start over from scratch.[10] It took over a year for him to find consistent work, with an inevitable impact on his finances. Though not disfellowshipped, virtually all his Witness friends have abandoned him preemptively. His former best friend and roommate told him: "If you want to speak to me, you can find me in a Kingdom Hall." He spotted another of his 'friends' taking his photograph while he was with his mother eating at a restaurant. One elder even cornered Ryan in a grocery store and told him to "pick a date" for his judicial hearing. All of this has caused considerable stress and exacerbated his depression, but Ryan now feels he is over the worst, and has no regrets. "I feel like despite having to rebuild my life and community, I've made massive personal growth. I'm a different person now," he told me. "Even though I'm not quite where I want to be in my life yet, I view those

***Ryan today***

[10] Ryan believes he was fired from his job for growing a beard and refusing to have any further meetings with elders. One day his boss asked to have a "chat" with him after work. Ryan thought it might finally be the promotion he had been promised. Instead, he was led into a room where another manager, who happened to be an elder, was waiting. After being told this was his last day and they were terminating his contract early, Ryan found himself being escorted from the building. "I did *not* expect that to happen at all," said Ryan. "It was probably the most shocking part."

challenging times as a positive and believe I'll be able to handle anything life throws at me now."

A number of factors in Ryan's story stand out for me. For example, I cannot help but note the irony of the obsessive behavior of his elders. Rather than coaxing him back to the fold, their paranoia and accusatory stance only served to help usher him out the door. It must be stressed that not all elders conduct themselves in such a heavy-handed, paranoid manner. I would say the majority of elders that I know personally are reasonable individuals who appear genuine in their desire to help and encourage Witnesses as best they can. But as my experience in Bramhall congregation highlighted, it only takes one overbearing, rule-oriented, fastidious character to spoil things for an entire congregation. And because Watchtower is built on a foundation of placing rules and procedures above the welfare of individuals, an environment is fostered in which narcissistic thugs such as Ryan's inquisitors can thrive.

Also noticeable in Ryan's story was the increasing role played by the internet in helping to wake up Witnesses. In Ryan's case, he gave himself permission to tentatively seek out information—first through Reddit and then on YouTube. In my case, Wikipedia was a neutral staging area for seeking objective analysis of Watchtower beliefs before spreading the parameters of my search to encompass ex-JW sources. But what few realize is that even Witnesses who do not consciously want to look at "apostate" information are finding themselves drawn to it by search engines.

I released a video in January 2015 explaining this phenomenon in more detail. Titled *Why Online Activism Really Is Working*, the video showed some of the web traffic results for JWsurvey over the previous few years. The figures demonstrated that there is a notable difference in readership between blog articles on stories that ordinary Witnesses would not have heard about (i.e. child abuse cases, leaked videos, controversial GB talks) and articles about developments Witnesses would almost certainly be familiar with, such as the death of a GB member or the release of a new Bible revision.

The highest number of visits one can hope for in one day when writing on a subject Witnesses do not know about is currently somewhere between 5,000 and 8,000.[11] By contrast, JWsurvey's coverage of the release of the 2013 revision of the *New World Translation* attracted a peak of 18,000 visits in a single day in October 2013. Such surges in visitor numbers (or "Google waves," as I like to call them) can only be accounted for by thousands of Witnesses simultaneously trying to locate information on new developments and being inadvertently directed to websites like JWsurvey by search engines. In short, it cannot be said that Witnesses will only visit an apostate website when they have resolved to do so. Google has changed everything. It is now possible for Witnesses to be confronted by videos or blog articles offering critical information about their religion whether they seek them out or not. If the information is presented in a calm, objective, reasonable spirit, there is every chance of a Witness going from total ignorance to serious doubts in just a few clicks.

This brings us to another feature of Ryan's story, namely the content of "apostate" sources and the manner in which information critical of Watchtower

---

[11] For example, on March 30, 2016, we received 8,000 visits for an article about a leaked *Circuit Overseer Guidelines* document—again, not something ordinary Witnesses would know about.

is shared. When telling me about his awakening, Ryan was keen to stress that efforts by some of his more deviant friends to push him toward apostate information did not prove helpful. In fact, they only made him raise the barriers; strengthening his resolve to steer clear of such material and delaying his exit. Thankfully, Ryan is able to use this experience in his own efforts to tactfully assist in easing Witnesses out of their indoctrination. He told me he is especially anxious to utilize the most productive approaches in reaching through to those heavily under Watchtower's spell: "I realize the importance of using honesty, logic, and extreme sensitivity when trying to pull a Jehovah's Witness off their treadmill. It is almost an art form."

I would echo those sentiments. An analogy I often use is that of a surgeon performing complex surgery. He or she could approach the operation with a steady hand and a scalpel, or a clumsy hand and a meat cleaver, but the latter is likely to only make the situation worse for the patient. Similarly, there is an "art" (as Ryan puts it) to helping people out of cult indoctrination and getting it right can be the difference between pulling people across the bridge or pushing them off it.

That is not to say there are only a few who are sufficiently qualified to help wake people from cults. Ryan's story showed that a number of supportive ex-JWs on Reddit were able to gently steer him in the right direction, thereby contributing to his awakening. But it is obvious to most people who have embarked on the road to recovery that the principle of *best practice* can be applied to such efforts. In short, there is a right way and a wrong way to go about attempting to extricate people from cult influence.

In *Combating Cult Mind Control*, Steven Hassan urges against "hysterical tirades" when reaching out to cult victims. "Getting emotionally aggressive with a cult member almost always backfires," he observes, while also pointing out that resentment directed at such ones is misplaced:

> Get angry with the cult. Get angry at all mind control cults. But don't get angry with the person who has been victimized. It isn't their fault.

And in his second book *In Search of Christian Freedom* (the follow-up to *Crisis of Conscience*) Ray Franz expressed his dismay at former Witnesses who approach believers in a belittling, sneering manner:

> Vindictive speech, ridicule, name-calling, magnifying minor faults far out of proportion, refusing to give persons the benefit of a doubt, to admit the possibility of their being sincerely, even if mistakenly, motivated, making no allowance for their wrong actions being the product of victimization through erroneous conceptions—none of this does anything for the cause of truth.

Franz, who clung to his faith in the Bible after leaving Watchtower, also pointed out that certain aggressive tactics such as picketing Witnesses outside their places of worship is counter-productive and, in his view, un-Christian.[12]

> Some who have terminated their affiliation with the Witness organization have engaged in picketing of Kingdom Halls or assemblies of Jehovah's Witnesses, have engaged in unusual tactics evi-

---

[12] I personally doubt that the majority of those who stand outside Witness conventions holding signs that say "Come to Jesus" or "Only those who are born again can be saved!" are actually "apostates," or former Witnesses. I would imagine most are simply members of evangelical denominations hoping for easy pickings.

> dently designed to gain the attention of the news media. This is nothing new. Persons opposed to the Watch Tower organization have been doing this from the time I was a child half a century ago. In the case of some involved, I know that their sole motive is to bring certain injustices and misrepresentations to light. I cannot answer as to the motive of others. In either case, I am not attempting to pass any judgment on them themselves in saying that I personally view such methods as not only counterproductive but also as reflecting unfavorably on the one we are committed to serve, Christ Jesus.

Unfortunately, even many ex-JWs who profess Christianity entirely ignore such advice and insist on besieging Witnesses in the street or at their place of worship—in some cases even infiltrating Kingdom Halls to yell at them or brazenly disrespect their rituals.[13] You would think it obvious that such behavior is "counterproductive" (as Franz put it) to the goal of freeing Witnesses from their indoctrination, but a worrying number of ex-Witnesses not only support such confrontational tactics—they will stop at nothing in their efforts to silence those who urge restraint.

I learned this the hard way in November 2014, when I decided to join Franz and others in taking a stand against what I call "aggressive activism" after a spike in videos on Facebook showing ex-JWs picketing Kingdom Halls and goading Witnesses in public. As a result of offering my honest opinion that people who indulge in such behavior are clearly more interested in

---

[13] A common practice is for some ex-Witnesses to post YouTube videos of themselves attending the Memorial for the sole purpose of standing and drinking the wine before telling the bewildered and distressed congregation members (who they have just insulted) how misled they are.

helping themselves feel better than helping Witnesses escape indoctrination, I found myself on the receiving end of a furious backlash of character assassination that continues to this day. At various times I have been accused of being a wife beater, a cyberbully, a traitor, a cult leader, a stalker, and even a sexual predator.[14] I have been told to expect violence against me if I travel to certain locations. My wife and I have received intimidating cards and letters at our home address, with one sender claiming they would be meeting us on holiday. The tide of hatred has been such that we no longer feel free to attend ex-Witness meet-ups with our daughter in case there is an ugly confrontation.

It is a sad irony that, over the years I have been engaged in my ex-JW activism work, by far the majority of opposition has come, not from Watchtower, but from fellow ex-JWs. As infuriating as this is, it is reassuring to know that regressive activism (as I call it) is not unique to the ex-JW movement.[15] My friends in the ex-Scientology and ex-Exclusive Brethren communities report similar abuse and infighting instigated by ex-cult members who simply cannot tolerate views and opinions being voiced that differ from theirs.

The reasons for these attitudes are not hard to find. When someone escapes a cult, they are left with con-

---

[14] Dijana could not help but laugh at a video in which, among many other things, I was accused of abusing her because, apparently, she bore the appearance of a battered wife. Her response: "Thanks very much!"

[15] I call it "regressive activism" because regressive activists tend to support or adopt aggressive methods that are unhelpful and (in the case of picketing) were only used in the past because there were few alternatives for raising awareness. They are also regressive in devoting considerable time and energy to campaigning against fellow ex-members who they disagree with, rather than focusing their energies on meaningful ex-cult advocacy and recovery work.

siderable anger. They can choose to channel this anger in productive ways, effectively turning a negative into a positive by devoting energy to exploring effective methods for raising awareness and helping others escape. Or, in the case of regressive activists, years or decades of pent-up resentment and bitterness is unleashed, not only on those still inside the cult (who need support and understanding, not shouting and vitriol), but on fellow ex-cult members who fail to conform to their expectations in some way (for example, by failing to support their religious views, or somehow betraying their idea of the "community"). The ex-member who has offended them becomes, in their eyes, just as worthy an opponent as the cult itself—and must be vanquished at all costs.

There have been times when I have found such animosity almost impossible to handle and have seriously contemplated walking away from my work altogether. As someone who struggles with depression, these attacks can take their toll emotionally in ways the "trolls" apparently choose not to contemplate. As much as I want to use my knowledge and experience to help people, I must keep in mind my duties as a father. If I am stricken by dark moods for days at a time due to the nature of the work I do, my daughter inevitably pays the price by being robbed of a parent who can give her the joy and happiness she deserves.

Thankfully, at least for the time being, the situation is manageable and I am learning to completely ignore these attacks when they come. I also have the benefit of an extremely supportive wife who understands the importance of my work and does whatever she can to keep me in fighting form.

I especially draw strength from reading stories such as Ryan's when they appear in my inbox or online. As I mentioned earlier, nothing gives me more joy than the thought of children being born who will never know what it means to be raised a Witness because their parents or grandparents watched one of my videos, or read one of my articles, and were prompted to do research.

There are few things more beautiful than helping people whom you will never meet, or who may be born years after you are dead, and may never even know that you have improved their lives in some way. That, in essence, is my new spirituality—and it is infinitely more satisfying than fantasies of palm trees, pandas and tables brimming with fruit. We do not need to cheat death if we can live on through the difference we make in the lives of those who will follow, even in the smallest, most imperceptible of ways.

Nobody can say for a certainty whether or not there is an afterlife. As Hitchens said: "I like surprises!" What we can say for sure is that the bridge will always be there and, whatever personal struggles we may face, we all have the opportunity to stand on it, arms outstretched.

Appendix A

# Helpful Books, Online Resources and Contact Information

**Books (Cited or recommended)**


Bergman, Jerry (1999). *Jehovah's Witnesses: A Comprehensive and Selectively Annotated Bibliography.* Greenwood Press.

Cole, Marley (1955). *Jehovah's Witnesses: The New World Society.* Vantage Press.

Crompton, Robert (1996). *Counting the Days to Armageddon: Jehovah's Witnesses and the Second Presence of Christ.*

Dawkins, Richard (2006). *The God Delusion.* Bantam Press.

Dickerson, Tami (2011). *Jehovah's Witnesses and the United Nations: How the Watchtower Society Fooled Millions.* Createspace.

Franz, Raymond (2004). *Crisis of Conscience.* Fourth edition. Commentary Press.

Franz, Raymond (2007). *In Search of Christian Freedom.* Second edition. Commentary Press.

Gruss, Edmond Charles (2001). *Jehovah's Witnesses: Their Claims, Doctrinal Changes, and Prophetic Speculation. What Does the Record Show?* Xulon Press.

Gruss, Edmond Charles (2003). *The Four Presidents of the Watch Tower Society (Jehovah's Witnesses).* Xulon Press.

Harris, Sam (2006). *The End of Faith: Religion, Terror, and the Future of Reason.* Simon & Schuster.

Harris, Sam (2007). *Letter To A Christian Nation.* Bantam Press.

Harrison, Barbara Grizutti (1978). *Visions of Glory: A History and a Memory of Jehovah's Witnesses.* Simon and Schuster.

Hassan, Steven (2012). *Freedom of Mind: Helping Loved Ones Leave Controlling People, Cults, and Beliefs.* Freedom of Mind Press.

Hassan, Steven (2015). *Combating Cult Mind Control: The #1 Best-selling Guide to Protection, Rescue, and Recovery from Destructive Cults.* Freedom of Mind Press.

Hitchens, Christopher (2007). *God is Not Great: How Religion Poisons Everything.* Atlantic Books.

Jonsson, Carl Olof (2008). *The Gentile Times Reconsidered—Chronology and Christ's Return.* Fourth edition. Commentary Press

Kelly, Richard (2008). *Growing Up In Mama's Club.* Parker Ridge Publishing.

Kelly, Richard (2012). *The Ghosts from Mama's Club.* Parker Ridge Publishing.

Kelly, Richard (2015). *Mariuca and Marilyn: Saying Goodbye to Mama's Club: Exploring the Effects of Undue Influence.* Parker Ridge Publishing.

Kostelniuk, James (2000). *Wolves Among Sheep: The True Story of Murder in a Jehovah's Witness Community.* Word Alive Press.

Lalich, Janja (2009). *Take Back Your Life: Recovering From Cults & Abusive Relationships: Recovering from Cults and Abusive Relationships.* Bay Tree Publishing.

McDaniel, Debbie (2015). *Out with Consequences: A Journey out of Jehovah's Witnesses.* CreateSpace.

McMillan, A. H. (1957). *Faith on the March.* Prentice-Hall.

Penton, M. James (1985). *Apocalypse Delayed: The Story of Jehovah's Witnesses.* University of Toronto Press.

Penton, M. James (2004). *Jehovah's Witnesses and the Third Reich.* University of Toronto Press.

Rient, Robert (2016). *Witness.* Outpost19.

Schnell, William J. (1956). *Thirty Years a Watch Tower Slave.* Baker Book House.

Talon, Brock (2013). *Journey to God's House: An Inside Story of Life at the World Headquarters of Jehovah's Witnesses in the 1980s.* Brock Talon Enterprises.

Terry, Scott (2012). *Cowboys, Armageddon, and the Truth: How a Gay Child Was Saved from Religion.* Lethe Press.

Zieman, Bonnie (2015). *EXiting the JW Cult: A Healing Handbook: For Current & Former Jehovah's Witnesses.* Createspace.

Zieman, Bonnie (2016). *The Challenge to Heal: A Recovery Guide to Help Reclaim Your Life After Leaving Any High-Control Group.* CreateSpace.

Zydek, Frederick (2009). *Charles Taze Russell: His Life and Times: The Man, the Millennium and the Message.* Createspace.

## Online Resources

AJWRB.org—A website that debunks Watchtower dogma regarding blood transfusions.

AvoidJW.org—An excellent resource for doubting Witnesses, including an online repository of out-of-print Watchtower literature stretching back to the 1800s.

Ex-JW.com—John Hoyle's excellent website contains a very useful archive of some of his Watchtower investigations.

FreedomofMind.com—Cult expert Steve Hassan's website offers a number of free resources for those seeking to better understand cult mind control and how it works.

FriendlyAtheist.com—Hemant Mehta's excellent blog serves up a steady stream of news about religion from an atheist/humanist perspective, and frequently comments on goings-on with Jehovah's Witnesses.

JWfacts.com—Unquestionably the best one-stop resource for an objective analysis of Witness teachings, including various scandals from Watchtower history.

JWsurvey.org—A website allowing current and former Jehovah's Witnesses to catch up on some of the latest JW-related news and developments, and express their views in an annual global survey.

OpenMindsFoundation.org—The Open Minds Foundation has been set up to help facilitate growing awareness of undue influence in society.

Quotes-Watchtower.co.uk—A rather dated, "retro" website, but nonetheless a fantastic resource for reading, at a glance, some of the more embarrassing quotes from Watchtower literature on a range of subjects.

Reddit.com/r/exjw/—An online community of ex-JWs dissecting the latest news and events involving Watchtower. The "exjw" sub-Reddit offers a wonderful resource for those in the process of leaving and in need of a hearing ear.

ReluctantApostate.co—The official website for this book, which will be kept up-to-date with helpful supplementary information and news on the author's latest videos and publications.

WatchtowerDocuments.org—Barbara Anderson's website has an impressive array of documents for those researching Watchtower history.

## Contact Information

**If you need support with leaving Jehovah's Witnesses** I would recommend reaching out anonymously online and benefiting from the many who either share your predicament or have been through it recently. The "exjw" sub-Reddit is a great resource for this purpose, allowing you to sign up and start posting safely and privately. Alternatively, you can set up an anonymous Facebook account (be very careful to make sure that you are in no way visible to any JW friends who can see your activity) and join one of the many Ex-JW Facebook groups. "Ex-Jehovah's Witness Recovery Group 3!" is one of the largest and best-moderated of these groups. Unfortunately, at present there are limited resources if you are looking for more personalized support. However, AAWA.co (Advocates for Awareness of Watchtower Abuses) has an email address that you are welcome to try: Support@AAWA.co

**If you need support with leaving religion** there is an excellent organization named "Faith to Faithless," based in the UK (website: faithtofaithless.com). Faith to Faithless is run by former Muslims, but aims to help those escaping all abusive religions—including Jehovah's Witnesses.

**If you need support with depression or suicidal feelings** please seek help urgently! If you are alone and need someone to talk to, here are some organizations you can call:

National Suicide Hotline (USA): 1 800 273 8255

National Suicide Hotline (Canada): 1 800 448 1833

Samaritans (UK): 08457 90 90 90

Samaritans (Ireland): 1850 60 90 90

Lifeline (Australia): 13 11 14

Lifeline (New Zealand): 0800 543 354.

I would also strongly recommend seeking out professional therapy or counseling. When selecting a therapist or counselor, it would be best to find one with some knowledge of cults and mind control. This is because, unfortunately, not all mental health professionals are experienced in this area.

If you are receiving therapy or counseling from a professional who wants to learn more about cult mind control/undue influence, feel free to share Bonnie Zieman's useful downloadable printouts at this URL: https://bonniezieman.com/downloads/

**If you are a victim of child sex abuse as a Jehovah's Witness** and would like legal advice on pursuing Watchtower for the abuse you have suffered, here are details of some law firms I would recommend:

(USA)

**The Zalkin Law Firm**
12555 High Bluff Drive
Suite 301
San Diego CA 92130
Telephone: (858) 259-3011
Website: www.zalkin.com/what-we-do/sexual-abuse-cases/jehovahs-witness-abuse/

(United Kingdom)

**AO Advocates**
The Pearce Building, 7th Floor
West Street
Maidenhead SL6 1RL
Telephone: 01628 567 549
Website: www.aoadvocates.com/jehovahs-witnesses-new/

**Bolt Burdon Kemp**
Providence House
Providence Place

Islington
London N1 0NT
Telephone: 0203 8135 144
Website: www.boltburdonkemp.co.uk/child-abuse/church/

(Australia)

**Artemis Legal**
Suite 307, 32 Delhi Rd
North Ryde
New South Wales
Telephone: 1300 887 390
Website: www.artemislegal.com.au

## APPENDIX B

# Internet Chart Data

The table below lists the countries with their corresponding internet availability percentage (IAP), as provided by internetworldstats.com, and the average number of publishers taken from the latest available issues of the *Yearbook*. Some territories for which data is not sufficiently available (including the "other lands" listed in Appendx C) were omitted.

| Country | IAP | Avg. Pub. in 2012 | Avg. Pub. in 2013 | Avg. Pub. in 2014 | Avg Pub. in 2015 |
|---|---|---|---|---|---|
| St. Maarten | 0.0% | 311 | 334 | 336 | 340 |
| Niger | 2.4% | 290 | 288 | 282 | 272 |
| Chad | 3.3% | 609 | 628 | 646 | 687 |
| St. Martin | 3.4% | 299 | 294 | 311 | 313 |
| Congo. Dem. Republic of | 3.8% | 163,349 | 174,687 | 180,343 | 176,585 |
| Central African Republic | 4.1% | 2,474 | 2,491 | 2,471 | 2,544 |
| Ethiopia | 4.4% | 9,300 | 9,515 | 9,768 | 10,013 |
| Burundi | 4.7% | 10,511 | 11,082 | 11,852 | 12,577 |
| Guinea-Bissau | 4.8% | 123 | 130 | 133 | 141 |
| Sierra Leone | 5.2% | 1,840 | 1,882 | 1,937 | 2,037 |
| Madagascar | 5.3% | 25,779 | 27,591 | 29,385 | 30,941 |
| Togo | 5.5% | 16,612 | 17,348 | 18,158 | 19,067 |
| Malawi | 6.3% | 78,225 | 80,175 | 82,671 | 80,776 |
| Mozambique | 7.1% | 47,906 | 49,765 | 51,637 | 53,027 |
| Guinea | 7.9% | 692 | 708 | 737 | 765 |
| Congo. Republic of | 8.2% | 5,526 | 5,835 | 6,193 | 6,080 |
| Liberia | 9.2% | 5,728 | 5,843 | 6,022 | 6,112 |
| Solomon Islands | 9.2% | 1,717 | 1,742 | 1,787 | 1,915 |
| Burkina Faso | 9.7% | 1,518 | 1,563 | 1,598 | 1,656 |
| Benin | 11.5% | 10,545 | 10,872 | 11,352 | 11,716 |
| Mali | 12.7% | 274 | 275 | 286 | 284 |
| Haiti | 12.8% | 17,403 | 18,236 | 18,899 | 19,552 |

| Country | IAP | Avg. Pub. in 2012 | Avg. Pub. in 2013 | Avg. Pub. in 2014 | Avg Pub. in 2015 |
|---|---|---|---|---|---|
| Papua New Guinea | 13.4% | 3,792 | 3,770 | 3,868 | 3,916 |
| Kiribati | 13.8% | 120 | 134 | 142 | 136 |
| Tanzania | 14.5% | 14,478 | 15,137 | 15,761 | 16,129 |
| South Sudan | 17.4% | 1,103 | 1,207 | 1,201 | 1,218 |
| Cameroon | 17.7% | 35,604 | 36,288 | 37,319 | 37,869 |
| Pakistan | 17.8% | 842 | 868 | 928 | 960 |
| Gambia | 18.6% | 197 | 204 | 208 | 230 |
| Myanmar | 19.3% | 3,705 | 3,803 | 3,941 | 4,099 |
| Nepal | 19.9% | 1,665 | 1,833 | 2,004 | 2,204 |
| **Total Publishers for 0-20%** | | **462,537** | **484,528** | **502,176** | **504,161** |
| **Growth for 0-20%** | | | **4.8%** | **3.6%** | **0.4%** |
| Zambia | 20.4% | 156,898 | 160,211 | 168,693 | 171,167 |
| St. Barthélemy | 21.4% | 23 | 24 | 24 | 26 |
| Côte d'Ivoire | 22.0% | 8,786 | 9,190 | 9,781 | 10,302 |
| Lesotho | 22.8% | 3,648 | 3,640 | 3,871 | 3,837 |
| Namibia | 23.4% | 1,891 | 2,012 | 2,208 | 2,247 |
| Equatorial Guinea | 23.9% | 1,359 | 1,442 | 1,574 | 1,653 |
| Rwanda | 24.8% | 20,604 | 22,152 | 23,507 | 25,061 |
| Wallis & Futuna Islands | 24.9% | 61 | 49 | 46 | 44 |
| São Tomé & Príncipe | 25.2% | 634 | 673 | 708 | 754 |
| Cambodia | 25.7% | 546 | 684 | 802 | 894 |
| Swaziland | 26.8% | 2,938 | 2,937 | 2,983 | 3,063 |
| Timor-Leste | 27.0% | 194 | 207 | 242 | 282 |
| Marshall Islands | 27.3% | 178 | 175 | 171 | 183 |
| Sri Lanka | 27.4% | 5,132 | 5,359 | 5,615 | 5,775 |
| Angola | 29.5% | 86,802 | 94,182 | 102,753 | 111,123 |
| Ghana | 29.6% | 109,085 | 113,392 | 119,199 | 124,004 |
| Sudan | 29.6% | 495 | 456 | 515 | 595 |
| Vanuatu | 29.8% | 492 | 520 | 525 | 557 |
| Honduras | 30.4% | 20,122 | 21,165 | 22,077 | 22,653 |
| Uganda | 31.1% | 5,691 | 6,093 | 6,468 | 6,832 |
| Botswana | 31.2% | 2,045 | 2,070 | 2,122 | 2,099 |
| Micronesia | 31.3% | 169 | 168 | 167 | 154 |
| Nicaragua | 31.8% | 23,453 | 24,984 | 26,169 | 27,054 |
| Cuba | 33.6% | 94,810 | 95,656 | 95,592 | 95,825 |
| Samoa | 34.2% | 450 | 496 | 522 | 519 |
| Guatemala | 34.9% | 33,017 | 35,598 | 37,192 | 38,140 |
| Palau | 36.1% | 80 | 75 | 78 | 80 |

| Country | IAP | Avg. Pub. in 2012 | Avg. Pub. in 2013 | Avg. Pub. in 2014 | Avg Pub. in 2015 |
|---|---|---|---|---|---|
| Kyrgystan | 36.2% | 4,804 | 4,882 | 4,936 | 5,071 |
| French Guiana | 36.3% | 2,138 | 2,211 | 2,288 | 2,373 |
| India | 36.5% | 34,995 | 36,869 | 39,355 | 41,866 |
| Gabon | 38.5% | 3,560 | 3,641 | 3,816 | 3,972 |
| Bhutan | 38.6% | 0 | 0 | 0 | 3 |
| Bangladesh | 38.9% | 161 | 181 | 211 | 243 |
| Tuvalu | 39.2% | 62 | 53 | 60 | 64 |
| **Total Publishers for 20-40%** | | **625,323** | **651,447** | **684,270** | **708,515** |
| **Growth for 20-40%** | | | **4.2%** | **5.0%** | **3.5%** |
| Cape Verde | 40.5% | 1,936 | 1,995 | 2,042 | 2,098 |
| American Samoa | 40.6% | 204 | 213 | 218 | 218 |
| Guyana | 41.4% | 2,680 | 2,758 | 2,846 | 2,941 |
| Bolivia | 41.9% | 21,957 | 23,014 | 23,976 | 24,836 |
| British Virgin Islands | 42.7% | 264 | 265 | 260 | 256 |
| Ukraine | 43.4% | 149,199 | 149,597 | 149,787 | 141,364 |
| Mayotte | 44.3% | 101 | 117 | 130 | 147 |
| Suriname | 44.4% | 2,536 | 2,644 | 2,765 | 2,849 |
| Réunion | 45.0% | 2,887 | 2,899 | 2,961 | 2,980 |
| Fiji | 45.9% | 2,734 | 2,807 | 2,938 | 2,958 |
| Paraguay | 45.9% | 8,781 | 8,947 | 9,309 | 9,719 |
| Zimbabwe | 46.5% | 38,637 | 39,999 | 41,688 | 43,361 |
| Belize | 46.6% | 2,198 | 2,352 | 2,425 | 2,515 |
| Guadeloupe | 46.7% | 8,089 | 7,993 | 8,025 | 8,058 |
| Tonga | 46.8% | 225 | 223 | 216 | 208 |
| Turks and Caicos | 48.6% | 302 | 315 | 323 | 332 |
| Georgia | 48.9% | 17,577 | 17,964 | 18,100 | 18,279 |
| Moldova | 49.2% | 20,020 | 19,856 | 19,846 | 19,776 |
| Mongolia | 49.5% | 317 | 366 | 405 | 435 |
| St. Helena | 50.1% | 117 | 116 | 115 | 118 |
| El Salvador | 50.4% | 37,721 | 38,643 | 39,346 | 39,643 |
| Grenada | 50.4% | 547 | 553 | 578 | 579 |
| Senegal | 50.7% | 1,116 | 1,136 | 1,150 | 1,168 |
| San Marino | 50.8% | 199 | 203 | 204 | 202 |
| Indonesia | 51.4% | 22,862 | 23,596 | 24,489 | 25,361 |
| Nigeria | 52.0% | 312,251 | 320,589 | 329,757 | 338,955 |
| Philippines | 52.6% | 178,467 | 185,387 | 190,930 | 199,551 |
| South Africa | 52.6% | 89,929 | 91,848 | 95,369 | 96,631 |
| Jamaica | 53.2% | 11,838 | 11,843 | 11,889 | 11,815 |

| Country | IAP | Avg. Pub. in 2012 | Avg. Pub. in 2013 | Avg. Pub. in 2014 | Avg Pub. in 2015 |
|---|---|---|---|---|---|
| Nauru | 53.7% | 15 | 16 | 15 | 11 |
| Northern Marianas | 54.2% | 224 | 209 | 213 | 209 |
| Kazakhstan | 54.3% | 17,175 | 17,321 | 17,475 | 17,545 |
| Monserrat | 55.1% | 16 | 21 | 18 | 19 |
| Virgin Islands. U.S. | 55.8% | 615 | 593 | 602 | 586 |
| Mexico | 56.0% | 749,585 | 777,429 | 802,903 | 818,481 |
| Norfolk Island | 56.0% | 7 | 9 | 8 | 5 |
| Romania | 56.3% | 39,803 | 40,154 | 40,371 | 40,370 |
| Bulgaria | 56.7% | 1,925 | 2,026 | 2,149 | 2,290 |
| Dominican Republic | 57.1% | 34,132 | 35,331 | 36,240 | 36,946 |
| Colombia | 58.6% | 152,280 | 157,395 | 161,876 | 165,089 |
| Peru | 58.6% | 110,651 | 114,153 | 117,211 | 120,260 |
| Belarus | 59.0% | 4,965 | 5,300 | 5,579 | 5,828 |
| Mauritius | 59.6% | 1,733 | 1,740 | 1,749 | 1,785 |
| Turkey | 59.6% | 2,171 | 2,291 | 2,408 | 2,514 |
| **Total Publishers for 40-60%** | | **2,050,988** | **2,112,226** | **2,170,904** | **2,209,291** |
| **Growth for 40-60%** | | | **3.0%** | **2.8%** | **1.8%** |
| Thailand | 60.1% | 3,508 | 3,737 | 4,022 | 4,258 |
| Seychelles | 60.3% | 327 | 331 | 331 | 333 |
| Azerbaijan | 61.0% | 1,064 | 1,149 | 1,120 | 1,303 |
| Montenegro | 61.0% | 233 | 248 | 265 | 270 |
| Venezuela | 61.5% | 124,670 | 129,284 | 134,913 | 138,860 |
| Italy | 62.0% | 245,326 | 247,259 | 248,871 | 250,277 |
| Albania | 62.7% | 4,635 | 4,923 | 5,190 | 5,381 |
| Greece | 63.2% | 29,003 | 28,804 | 28,677 | 28,592 |
| Palestinian Territory | 63.2% | 64 | 68 | 70 | 71 |
| St. Vincent & the Grenadines | 64.5% | 355 | 340 | 332 | 336 |
| Dominica | 65.4% | 422 | 427 | 423 | 437 |
| Cook Islands | 65.9% | 176 | 190 | 194 | 194 |
| Serbia | 66.2% | 3,816 | 3,851 | 3,857 | 3,861 |
| St. Lucia | 66.5% | 711 | 721 | 740 | 727 |
| Brazil | 67.5% | 737,951 | 748,940 | 767,449 | 787,470 |
| Poland | 67.5% | 124,292 | 123,278 | 122,381 | 121,018 |
| Portugal | 67.6% | 49,049 | 48,843 | 48,706 | 48,633 |
| Macedonia | 68.1% | 1,329 | 1,320 | 1,323 | 1,293 |
| Malaysia | 68.1% | 4,124 | 4,440 | 4,668 | 4,804 |
| Niue | 68.2% | 23 | 26 | 25 | 24 |
| Kenya | 68.4% | 24,223 | 24,965 | 25,820 | 26,578 |

| Country | IAP | Avg. Pub. in 2012 | Avg. Pub. in 2013 | Avg. Pub. in 2014 | Avg Pub. in 2015 |
|---|---|---|---|---|---|
| Bosnia and Herzegovina | 68.7% | 1,191 | 1,182 | 1,180 | 1,170 |
| Anguilla | 69.0% | 65 | 68 | 64 | 62 |
| Armenia | 69.7% | 11,019 | 10,965 | 10,978 | 11,019 |
| Russia | 70.5% | 162,748 | 164,187 | 165,322 | 172,977 |
| St. Kitts & Nevis | 71.1% | 255 | 261 | 256 | 259 |
| Uruguay | 71.6% | 11,386 | 11,464 | 11,471 | 11,614 |
| Macao | 72.6% | 239 | 283 | 298 | 294 |
| Israel | 72.7% | 1,348 | 1,391 | 1,450 | 1,511 |
| Slovenia | 72.8% | 1,983 | 1,948 | 1,930 | 1,911 |
| Malta | 73.2% | 570 | 578 | 623 | 665 |
| Croatia | 75.0% | 5,552 | 5,509 | 5,412 | 5,372 |
| Panama | 75.6% | 14,242 | 15,007 | 15,626 | 16,224 |
| Lebanon | 75.9% | 3,581 | 3,602 | 3,659 | 2,671 |
| Hungary | 76.1% | 22,593 | 22,526 | 22,444 | 22,400 |
| Martinique | 76.4% | 4,711 | 4,771 | 4,749 | 4,755 |
| Guam | 76.6% | 748 | 730 | 733 | 740 |
| Spain | 76.9% | 107,986 | 108,254 | 108,900 | 109,457 |
| Trinidad & Tobago | 77.2% | 9,216 | 9,347 | 9,503 | 9,543 |
| Barbados | 78.5% | 2,484 | 2,492 | 2,524 | 2,506 |
| Argentina | 79.4% | 142,435 | 143,620 | 145,277 | 147,379 |
| Czech Republic | 79.7% | 15,352 | 15,329 | 15,407 | 15,741 |
| Chile | 79.9% | 72,420 | 73,658 | 74,498 | 75,168 |
| **Total Publishers for 60-80%** | | **1,947,425** | **1,970,316** | **2,001,681** | **2,038,158** |
| **Growth for 60-80%** | | | **1.2%** | **1.6%** | **1.8%** |
| Hong Kong | 80.2% | 5,262 | 5,435 | 5,557 | 5,509 |
| St. Pierre and Miquelon | 80.4% | 14 | 15 | 15 | 14 |
| Aruba | 80.5% | 877 | 915 | 931 | 953 |
| Gibraltar | 82.0% | 113 | 114 | 124 | 127 |
| Latvia | 82.0% | 2,327 | 2,290 | 2,296 | 2,275 |
| Cayman Islands | 82.1% | 221 | 223 | 228 | 217 |
| Lithuania | 82.1% | 3,095 | 3,126 | 3,130 | 3,101 |
| Ireland | 82.5% | 5,930 | 6,078 | 6,210 | 6,281 |
| Austria | 83.1% | 20,795 | 20,873 | 20,990 | 21,216 |
| Slovakia | 83.1% | 11,094 | 11,056 | 11,105 | 11,276 |
| Ecuador | 83.8% | 76,587 | 79,586 | 82,547 | 85,468 |
| France | 83.8% | 121,331 | 122,456 | 124,298 | 125,519 |
| Taiwan | 83.8% | 8,366 | 8,853 | 9,256 | 9,582 |
| Estonia | 84.2% | 4,152 | 4,108 | 4,091 | 4,074 |

| Country | IAP | Avg. Pub. in 2012 | Avg. Pub. in 2013 | Avg. Pub. in 2014 | Avg Pub. in 2015 |
|---|---|---|---|---|---|
| Kosovo | 84.4% | 207 | 222 | 237 | 236 |
| Bahamas | 84.8% | 1,602 | 1,594 | 1,630 | 1,630 |
| Belgium | 85.0% | 24,131 | 24,243 | 24,531 | 24,661 |
| Puerto Rico | 85.2% | 25,827 | 25,752 | 25,709 | 25,585 |
| Costa Rica | 86.9% | 21,172 | 28,316 | 29,086 | 29,601 |
| Antigua | 87.1% | 475 | 481 | 478 | 462 |
| New Caledonia | 87.2% | 1,936 | 1,983 | 2,047 | 2,164 |
| Switzerland | 87.2% | 17,696 | 18,038 | 18,323 | 18,611 |
| Germany | 88.4% | 162,705 | 162,459 | 163,246 | 163,871 |
| United States of America | 88.6% | 1,156,150 | 1,167,723 | 1,186,598 | 1,195,081 |
| Greenland | 90.1% | 154 | 147 | 145 | 145 |
| Japan | 91.0% | 216,892 | 215,986 | 215,294 | 214,523 |
| New Zealand | 91.2% | 13,742 | 13,789 | 13,884 | 13,929 |
| Britain | 91.6% | 131,629 | 132,515 | 134,308 | 134,491 |
| Australia | 92.1% | 64,884 | 65,596 | 66,484 | 66,753 |
| Korea. Republic of | 92.1% | 99,970 | 100,276 | 100,289 | 99,950 |
| Curaçao | 93.1% | 1,811 | 1,883 | 1,931 | 1,987 |
| Canada | 93.3% | 112,710 | 113,111 | 113,617 | 114,123 |
| Finland | 93.5% | 18,710 | 18,643 | 18,588 | 18,496 |
| Bonaire | 94.0% | 103 | 110 | 116 | 118 |
| Sweden | 94.6% | 22,043 | 22,033 | 22,156 | 22,236 |
| Faroe Islands | 94.7% | 108 | 112 | 117 | 112 |
| Luxembourg | 94.7% | 2,013 | 1,988 | 2,028 | 2,042 |
| Cyprus | 95.0% | 2,439 | 2,468 | 2,467 | 2,536 |
| Liechtenstein | 95.2% | 85 | 89 | 88 | 85 |
| Netherlands | 95.5% | 29,292 | 29,356 | 29,495 | 29,508 |
| Andorra | 95.9% | 164 | 163 | 169 | 170 |
| Denmark | 96.0% | 14,281 | 14,380 | 14,462 | 14,564 |
| Falkland Islands | 96.2% | 12 | 11 | 10 | 11 |
| Bermuda | 96.3% | 462 | 457 | 463 | 448 |
| Norway | 96.3% | 10,959 | 11,133 | 11,359 | 11,472 |
| Iceland | 98.2% | 356 | 370 | 368 | 367 |
| **Total Publishers for 80-100%** | | **2,414,884** | **2,440,555** | **2,470,501** | **2,485,580** |
| **Growth for 80-100%** | | | **1.1%** | **1.2%** | **0.6%** |

APPENDIX C

# “Other Lands”

The chart below lists population figures (in thousands of inhabitants) for the “other lands” as of 2015:

| | | | |
|---|---|---|---|
| Afghanistan | 32,527 | North Korea | 25,155 |
| Algeria | 39,667 | Oman | 4,491 |
| Bahrain | 1,377 | Qatar | 2,235 |
| Brunei | 423 | Saudi Arabia | 31,540 |
| China | 1,376,049 | Singapore | 5,604 |
| Djibouti | 888 | Somalia | 10,787 |
| Egypt | 91,508 | Syria | 18,502 |
| Eritrea | 5,228 | Tajikistan | 8,482 |
| Iran | 79,109 | Tunisia | 11,254 |
| Iraq | 36,423 | Turkmenistan | 5,374 |
| Jordan | 7,595 | United Arab Emirates | 9,157 |
| Kuwait | 3,892 | Uzbekistan | 29,893 |
| Laos | 6,802 | Vietnam | 93,448 |
| Libya | 6,278 | Western Sahara | 573 |
| Mauritania | 4,068 | Yemen | 26,852 |
| Morocco | 34,378 | | |

(Source: UN)

The following page shows these “other lands” highlighted on a world map.

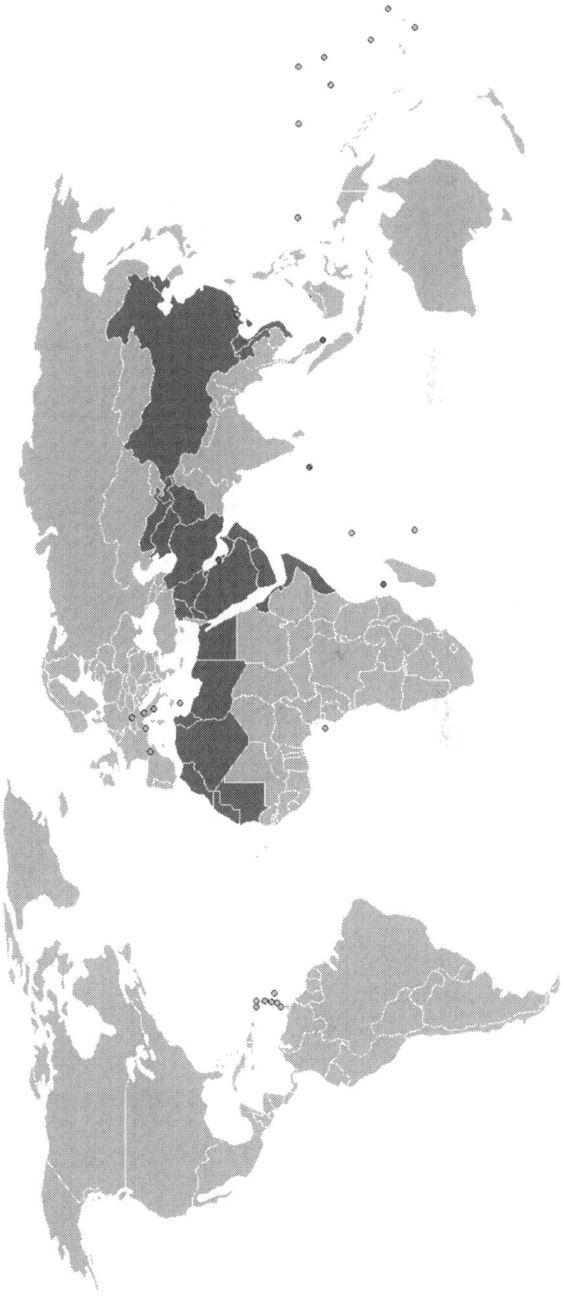

APPENDIX D

# Newspaper Articles on the Bonham Story

1

## Doubt tears at denomination

### World's continuation led to Jehovah's Witnesses exodus

By LISA ELLIS

Staff Writer

Ralph Deal shook his head and let out a bitter half-laugh. From the stack of papers, he pulled yet another document that he said demonstrates more than a century of false prophecies and contradictory teachings by Jehovah's Witnesses.

"I joke and kid about it, but it's really not funny," said Deal, a Bonham businessman baptized as a Witness in 1961 and thrown out last June. "It's cost 25 years of my life."

Deal and three fellow dissenters won a battle Friday in Fannin County Justice of the Peace Court to get control of the property of the Bonham congregation of Jehovah's Witnesses. But the denomination has appealed and countersued.

Although the East Texas case may be the first in the country involving who owns Witness property, it reflects more than six years of turmoil in this 650,000-member denomination, best known for its aggressive door-to-door evangelism.

Since 1979, three members of the national Governing Body have resigned or been ousted, critics say. Thousands of members have left, at least five ex-members have filed lawsuits and several, discarding a tradition of quiet departures, have written books about their dissatisfaction.

Critics said the defections began after the world failed to end in 1975 as leaders had predicted. Spokesmen for the denomination, known as the Watchtower Bible and Tract Society, refused to answer questions concerning the Bonham case, prophecies or any other issues.

Members of the Watchtower Society, founded in 1879 by Charles Taze Russell, believe that Jesus was not divine but the incarnation of the archangel Michael.

They teach that the world will end soon, that 144,000 select members will rule with Jesus in heaven and that millions of other believers will live in an earthly paradise.

But the rate of growth in believers dropped precipitously, despite intensive evangelism efforts, after the 1975 deadline passed. Between 1970 and 1975, U.S. membership increased 44.2 percent, but in the next five-year period the growth was only 0.8 percent.

Facing an exodus that some have estimated ran as high as 1 million people in a decade, the Governing Body in 1981 ordered members not to speak to anyone —

See SUIT on Page 32

2

# Suit reflects Witnesses' turmoil

SUIT — From Page 31

even a family member — who had been "disfellowshipped," on pain of suffering the same penalty.

"The Watchtower Society has drawn its wagons into a circle and treated the rest of us like Indians," said James Penton, a Canadian history professor, former Witness and author of two books on the church.

"By their paranoia they have suppressed a lot of people who are loyal Jehovah's Witnesses, and that has just increased the dissidence."

Deal, like many others, started searching through rare old Witness books and magazines for answers to his questions after the failure of the 1975 prophecy.

"For a number of years prior to 1975 . . . the circuit overseers were coming to (us) our kingdom hall and saying we had only (so many) months to evangelize before the end," said Deal, an elder of the Bonham congregation before he was disfellowshipped.

"In 1976, the Witnesses began to fall into shock and the attendance at meetings fell as people left," he added. "And I said to myself, if that is God's organization they certainly didn't have connection (on that prophecy)."

Through his research, Deal said he discovered that the Witnesses had incorrectly predicted the world's demise on at least two prior dates, 1918 and 1925. He said his study also convinced him that the denomination's claim to authority to interpret the Bible was faulty.

In late 1984, he confronted a district Witness official with his questions. "The man just sat there and looked at me for two minutes. Then I said, 'The reason you don't answer is that there is none.' "

Deal sent his questions to the New York headquarters. "They didn't want to answer the questions," said Tony Jones, who was the congregation's top official then. "We (the elders) sent a letter to New York, along with our own questions. They sent us a letter saying, 'It does not appear you brothers can handle the situation.' "

A committee from Houston was sent to investigate, and, after receiving their report, the national headquarters removed all elders last June and replaced them with four men moved in from elsewhere.

Shortly after, building locks were changed. When trustee Wesley Ruddell obtained a copy and made some for other dissenters, the locks were changed again, Jones said.

The Houston committee disfellowshipped Deal, and some other dissatisfied members drifted away. But, in December, the group decided to fight back.

Aided by Ron Reed, a California attorney who has handled numerous ex-Witness cases, Jones and two trustees filed a petition for possession, contending that the building was taken forcibly from the trustees.

The plaintiffs include two of the three trustees elected by the Bonham congregation. Legal documents list the trustees as holding title on behalf of the congregation.

But Ron Clark, the Sherman attorney representing the denomination's Brooklyn headquarters, said his side is arguing that it should control the Bonham congregation because it is a "structured" or "hierarchical" body. For example, the headquarters chooses elders who govern local congregations.

"Under the law, (in) that type of church, when there is a split the group that remains with the main body is the one that is entitled to keep possession of property," Clark said.

The congregation also has replaced the plaintiffs as trustees. In separate meetings last month, the trustees were voted out of office and disfellowshipped.

The Bonham case is important because it would set a legal precedent for ownership of property among the Witnesses, Reed said. "I am optimistic, but I also know that the Watchtower Society will have to fight this with everything they've got."

# Bonham church wins legal battle

by MILES WRIGHT
*Staff Writer*

BONHAM — Leaders and congregation members of the Jehovah's Witness church here declared a precedent-setting victory on Friday in their legal battle with the denomination's national organization, the Watchtower Society.

DEAL

A dispute had arisen over the legal ownership of the Kingdom Hall here, and local members predict the case will create a major impact on congregations across the nation.

After hearing almost six hours of testimony, Justice of the Peace Don Jones ruled that Richard Scovill, Luther Brodgen and other leaders of the Watchtower Society unlawfully changed locks and took possession of the church from the local congregation. Immediately after the decision, an appeal was filed to re-hear the case in County Court.

Plaintiff's attorney David Mercot of Henderson said the case illustrates how leaders of the Jehovah's Witnesses are "like the Russian government — saying one thing yet doing another."

The dispute arose last summer when "pioneer" Ralph Deal sent 14 letters to the Watchtower Bible and Tract Society in New York asking for answers to particular theological questions. He testified Friday that no response was heard from the Society until "local overseer" Tony Jones was told by letter to resolve the problem.

JONES

When the questions persisted, Deal testified, a committee representing the Watchtower Society came to Bonham on July 14 to select new officers for the church. After new officers were chosen two days later, the group changed the locks on the church and began meeting on Fridays instead of the traditional Sunday-Tuesday-Thursday meetings.

Deal, disillussioned with the handling of the situation, published a public apology on July 31 in the *Bonham Daily Favorite* for misleading local citizens in regards to the church.

Deal, along with Jones, Wesley Ruddell and Tommy Johnson, were contacted by letter that they

(Please see Bonham, Page A2)

# Bonham congregation 'stands up' to Society

(Continued from Page A1)

had been disfellowshipped — dismissed for disciplinary reasons — from the church. Jones, Ruddell and Johnson filed a lawsuit to retain possession of the Kingdom Hall.

During a recess Friday, Bercot said that "if we are successful here today this will strike like the Liberty Bell to get congregations to stand up for themselves.

"What is so ironic is the Jehovah's Witnesses have been so active in bringing civil right suits but they deny that to their own members.

"The impact I think will be that other individual witnesses and congregations that are dissatifsied with the unanswered questions of the Watchtower Society will be encouraged to stand up. For 40 years or more, the Watchtower Society acted like the local congregations were their pawns while in public denying any heirarchy.

"Right now there are hundreds of thousands of Jehovah's Witnesses that are asking questions. They are afraid to do anything," he added.

"The people in Bonham had the courage to stand up to the Watchtower Society, and I think you'll be seeing a lot more of this across the nation."

Deal stated that all he wanted was "answers to my questions." Under cross-examination, he said the essential difference between his arrival in Bonham in 1963 and the arrival of Scovill and Brogden was "the group was glad to see *me*."

The title to the property is filed with the county under "Trustees of the Bonham Congregation of Jehovah's Witnesses."

Ruddell said he filed the lawsuit because the local members were "rousted" from the church. "We were intimidated to do exactly as they said," he commented.

Deal, an ordained minister, was accused in the trial of starting his own sect, but he claimed he simply led non-religious historical research to either confirm or disprove events in the Bible.

The Jehovah's Witnesses were founded in 1884 by Charles T. Russell. During his lifetime, only leaders of the movement were considered "Faithful and Discreet Slaves," but following his death church leaders began considering every Jehovah's Witness a "Faithful and Discreet Slave."

The denomination is distinguished by its "doomsday theology" and belief that only 144,000 people will go to Heaven.

Rudell said, "The question is exactly who are the 'Faithful and Discreet Slaves.' When the question was given to the circuit overseer, he could not answer it."

Church member Richard Dobbs said, "What it boils down to is it is a man-made religion."

Another point of inquiry involved the changing dates for doomsday to occur. Dates cited by church leaders have included 1914, 1920, 1925 and 1938.

According to restricted-access communiques from the Watchtower Society to its circuit and district overseers, and obtained by the *Sherman Democrat*, it instructs elders to "discern between one who is a trouble-making apostate and a Christian who becomes weak in faith...The former one should be dealt with decisively..."

Apostate is defined by the organization as "persons stubbornly holding to and speaking about or deliberately spreading teachings contrary to Bible truth as taught by Jehovah's Witnesses."

Mercot said Jehovah's Witnesses are "losing a lot of members, and there is evidence they have the highest dropout rate of any large denomination in the United States."

He said the future will probably have two congregations at the church — "puppets" of the Watchtower Society and the "real local congregation." Several families moved to Bonham to become part of the Watchtower Society's congregation.

Scovill and Brogden were unavailable for comment about the outcome of the trial.

The Bonham Daily F
Serving All Of Fannin County Since 1892
… 190 SUNDAY, MARCH 2, 1986 BONHAM, TEXAS Copyright, …

LEGAL BATTLEGROUND- The Bonham Jehovah's Witnesses legal battle took another twist Friday in a district court hearing. Judge Ray Grisham ruled that clear legal title must be decided before any other legal questions can be answered. Pictured from left to right, Watchtower representitive William Mollenfont, Court stenographer Deana Bryn, Judge Ray Grisham, and Attorney Ronald Clark. (Daily Favorite exclusive photo by Charles McClure)

5

# Equal access granted in church case

BY CHARLES MCCLURE
Staff Writer

The controversial legal battle concerning the Jehovah's Witnesses Bonham Kingdom Hall took another suprising turn Friday in a Distict Court injunction held in Sherman.

Without hearing final arguements, District Judge Ray Grisham ruled in favor of the Luther Brogdon, Bennie Bolin, Ronald H. Williams, the plaintiffs in the injunction hearing to overrule Fannin County Justice of the Peace Don Jones' decision to grant a Forcible Entry and Detainer to defendants Tony Jones, Ralph Deal, Wesley Ruddell, and Tommy Johnson. However, both sides were claiming victory.

The reason that the defense was pleased by the decision was that they were given equal access to the building. The plaintiffs were happy because the judges' decision means that the case comes down to who actually has legal title to the Bonham Kingdom Hall.

6

In his decision, Grisham stated that "I have a tremedous amount of respect for Judge (Don) Jones, however, I think that since this court is going to have to hear the title case anyway, that title is the real issue here."

"I believe Judge Grisham made a decision based on the evidense he heard. It is a temporary solution. By nature, it is a brief hearing to make a temporary decision to provide a solution until a permanent ruling can be made," said plaintiffs attorney Ronald Clark of Sherman.

"We are pleased with the decision and we will exercise the courts decision in good faith." said David Bercot, the defense attorney from Henderson.

Now it is up to the court to decide who will get legal title to the Bonham Kingdom Hall. Whatever the decision, it will set legal precedent for the Jehovah's Witnesses in the United States.

7

(3-21 86)

# Doors chained in violation of order

BY CHARLES MCCLURE
Staff Writer

There has already been a great deal of legal litigation heard by various courts on the controversy surrounding the Jehovah's Witnesses Bonham Kingdom Hall. On Friday, February 28, Judge Ray Grisham of the 336 District Court ruled on an injunction brought before the court by Watchtower (the parent organization of the Jehovah's Witnesses) representatives.

The purpose of the injunction was to stop an appeal hearing in County Court on an earlier ruling by Fannin County Justice of the Peace Don Jones. The Jones decision involved a petition on forcible entry and detainer.

Grisham agreed that legal title was indeed the issue that needed to be answered before any other legal questions could be addressed. However, in his ruling, Grisham ordered that both parties would have to share the Kingdom Hall until the title case could be decided.

But the Watchtower representatives were not pleased with the decision. They hired Attorney Sam Boyd of Dallas to assist Ronald Clark of Sherman. Boyd filed a non-suit, effectively dismissing the injunction ruling. The action put the case back at step one.

Again chains, new locks, and no-trespassing signs adorned the Kingdom Hall, a direct violation of Grisham's ruling. But this time, they took it one step further and removed all identification designating the building as a Jehovah's Witnesses Kingdom Hall.

"Twice the local congregation has been given possession of the building by two different courts. Again they find themselves right back where they started, which is being unlawfully locked out of their own building," said Attorney David Bercot, the lawyer for the local faction forced out of the church.

The addition of Boyd has put a new twist into the case. Boyd maintains that the case should have been heard on a Federal level to begin with, "These are matters that the U.S. Supreme Court is going to have to deal with eventually anyway," says Boyd.

So, in effect, all questions concerning the case have been removed to federal court. "It's not that there is no forum for these issues, it's simply that this case would have been appealed to the Texas Supreme Court and then on to the U.S. Supreme Court."

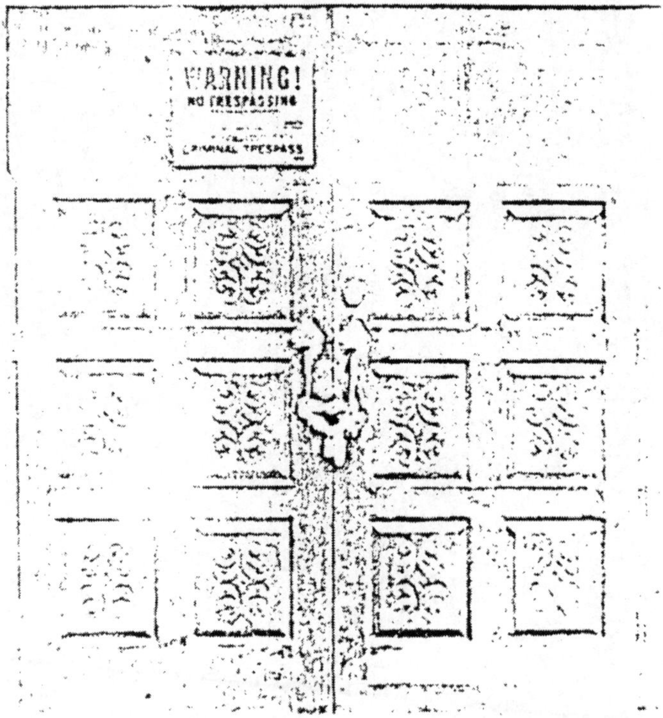


TAKE THESE CHAINS THAT BIND- Once again the Jehovah's Witnesses Bonham Kingdom Hall is the center of legal debate. And once again, new locks, chains, and no trosspassing signs adorn th doors of the building. (Dail Favorite photo by Charles Mc Clure)

# Jehovah's Witnesses case in federal court

by MILES WRIGHT
*Staff Writer*

A removal petition filed in the Eastern District Federal Court in Sherman late Wednesday afternoon will delay the contempt of court hearing over possession of the Bonham Jehovah's Witnesses Kingdom Hall.

The hearing was scheduled to begin in 336th District Judge Ray Grisham's court Thursday morning.

The petition automotically shifts the contempt of court proceeding to the federal court from state district court.

David Bercot of Henderson, attorney for ousted local members of the church, called the filing a "delay tactic" intended to extend the Watchtower Bible and Tract Society's control over the Bonham Kingdom Hall.

He added that the plaintiffs' motive was clear, considering they were the ones shifting the case from county court to district court.

But Ron Clark, attorney for the new congregation at the Bonham Kingdom Hall, said the action was meant to consolidate the different court filings so the case could be settled at one time in federal court.

He added that the hearing date in federal court would be determined by the motions filed in the next few weeks.

The federal court will either hear the contempt of court case or transfer it back to 336th District Court. Bercot said he feels "99 percent sure" the case will be returned to district court since plaintiffs in a district suit cannot request removal.

Clark countered by saying Bercot's clients were actually the plaintiffs due to earlier counter-filings.

Grisham ordered the two sides in the case to share the Kingdom Hall until the case could be settled in court. The local members claim the "transplanted" congregational leaders have failed to follow Grisham's order and placed new locks on the church building.

Bercot said he advised his clients "not to come down to their level and fight in the streets" by forcibly entering the building.

## House burglarized

McKINNEY — Dawna Anderson, of 1905 Inwood Street in McKinney, told the McKinney Police

# ..hurch on the firing line

**(Ed's note: This is the last in a three part series analyzing the history of the Jehovah's Witnesses, the ongoing rebellion within the church, and it's relationship to the Bonham Precedence setting legal battle.)**

BY CHARLES MCCLURE

Staff Writer

To understand just what the Governing Body of the Jehovah's Witnesses means to the body of the church, we must look at the Bible to Matthew 24:45, "Who then is the faithful and discreet slave whom his master put in charge of his household to give them their food at the proper time."

To Jehovah's Witnesses, this refers to the Governing Body. In other words, the Governing Body is God's organization to interpret Bible teachings.

This plays a very large part in the situation now going on in Bonham.

The controversy started in the spring of 1985 when an elder of the Bonham congregation, Ralph Deal, started to question some of the theology contained in many of the Watchtower publications. He posed these questions in a series of letters that he forwarded to the Society in New York.

Deal never received a reply to his letters, but instead, was excommunicated from the church. Although some members of the church were aware of Deal's questions, they did not perceive a threat to the Bonham congregation. But on June 18, 1985, the elders and "presiding overseer" of the church were removed in an surprising maneuver by the Watchtower Society.

On that night, as members of the church were arriving for a regular Bible study, they were surprised the find the church packed with Jehovah's Witnesses from other congregations. The out-numbered locals watched in amazement as Richard Scofield, one of the people moved in from another congregation, read the letter from the Watchtower Society removing the Bonham elders and replacing them with others. Scofield was named presiding overseer, with Luther Bragdon as elder. Also changed were locks on the Bonham Kingdom Hall — in effect, taking possession of the church.

A number of original members of Kingdom Hall filed a petition with the former presiding overseer, Tony Jones, and former elders and church trustees Tommy Johnson Jr. and Wesley Ruddell, asking them to file a Forcible Entry and Detainer lawsuit against Bragdon and Scofield.

The petition was filed with Fannin County Justice of the Peace Don Jones. The result was ex-communication for the petitioners.

Scofield and Bragdon filed a separate lawsuit in district court against trustees of the church to determine legal title of the Bonham Kingdom Hall.

Scofield's attorneys claim that the former trustees are trying to gain superior title to the church by circumventing state law. They maintain that the Jehovah's Witnesses are governed by a group of elected officials, not a local congregation.

The forcible entry and detainer case was heard by Fannin County Justice of the Peace on Friday, February 7. Judge Jones, who ruled in favor of the plaintiffs, Jones, Ruddell, and Johnson, said, "I don't feel the court has the sanctity to decide a religious issue. This court certainly does not have the right to decide the issue of legal title."

Jones stressed the fact that this was a case of forcible entry and detainer, pointing out that the locks were changed with no prior notification.

However, Jones' decision was overturned by the District Court on Friday of this week. According to Judge Ray Grisham, clear legal title has to be established in this case before any other rulings can be made.

In that court hearing, the Grisham stated in his ruling that the evidense led him to believe that the organization was congregational, not heirarchical, as the Watchtower Society claims it to be.

In the upcoming title case, the plaintiffs (Ronald Williams and Luther Bragdon) maintain that the church is heirarchical organization while the defense (Jones, Ruddell, Johnson, and Deal) alleges that the Watchtower has contradicted itself on policy.

Even some church athorities are unsure of policy. Ray Martin, a circuit overseer for the church, stated under oath that Jehovah's Witnesses were democratic in nature.

What makes the case important is the fact that the decision will set legal precedent for property title among the Jehovah's Witnesses. If the defense should win, the Watchtower Society fears the ruling may trigger a mass exodus within the church.

11

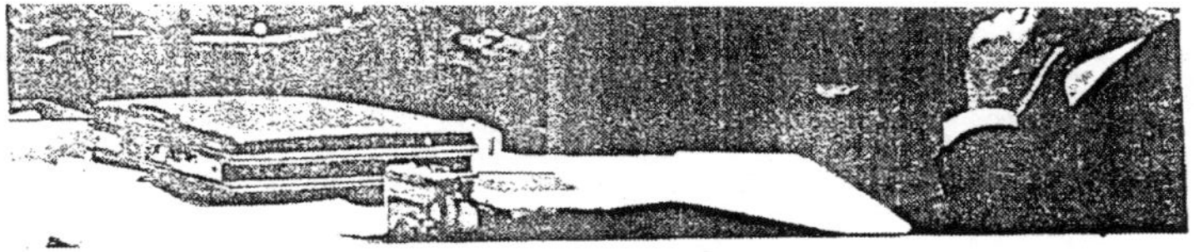

**WHO IS RIGHT? The Bonham Kingdom Hall was the subject in question at a court hearing to decide a forcible entry and detainer suit Friday at the Fannin County Courthouse. Fannin County Justice of the Peace Don Jones (pictured on far right) ruled in favor of plaintiffs Wesley Ruddell, Tommy Johnson, and Tony Jones. The plaintiffs maintain that defendants Richard Scofield and Luther Bradgon took possession of the church illegally. The decision is being appealed to the Fannin County Court at Law. The case drew press from all over the Texhoma area and the court was packed with interested members of the Jehovah's Witnesses. (pictured left) The defendants have filed a district court case that will decide the question of legal title of the Bonham Kingdom Hall. There are possible legal precedents involved. (Daily Favorite photos by Charles McClure)**

# Jehovah's Witnesses to appeal ruling

BY CHARLES MCCLURE
**Staff Writer**

On Friday, Fannin County Justice of the Peace Don Jones made a ruling in favor of the plaintiffs on a Forcible Entry and Detainer after hearing five hours of testimony concerning the Jehovah's Witnesses' Bonham Kingdom Hall.

The controversial suit was filed by plaintiffs' Wesley Ruddell, Tommy Johnson, Jr., and Tony M. Jones against Richard Scofield and Luther Brogdon.

The plantiffs argued that Scofield and Brogdon had illegally taken possession of the Bonham Kingdom Hall on the night of June 18, 1985. The plaintiffs alleged that the locks on the building were changed and that they were removed from their appointments as elders without prior notice.

The lawsuit led to the eventual excommunication of the plaintiffs by the Watchtower Bible and Tract Society of New York, the governing body of the Jehovah's Witnesses.

The plaintiffs maintained that the congregation of the church, and not the Watchtower Society, had legal ownership of the church. The defendants argued that the Watchtower Bible and Tract Society are a hierarchical organization while the plaintiffs alleged that the Watchtower Society was a theocratic organization.

The defense called Bill Mallenfont, a representitive of the Watchtower Society who testified that trustees were "just a figurehead, or a puppet." for the governing body.

The plaintiffs have maintained all along that outsiders from other congregations were sent in to intimidate the former elders and other members of the church. Ray Martin, a circut overseer for the Jehovah's Witnesses, testified that the church had to send in other people to stablize the Bonham Congregaton.

On cross examination by the plaintiffs' attorney, Martin first testified that the organization was hierarchical. Under furhter questioning by the plaintiffs attorneys he testified that the organization was actually democratic.

When defendant Richard Scofield was called to the stand to testify, he said that the church had held a meeting on January 15 of this year to appoint new trustees. He testified that 15 of the 25 voting members had been members of the church previous to June 18, 1985. Later, Eddie Johnson, a witness for the defense, testified that there were only eight original members of the church voting on the January 15 ballot.

It came out under cross-examination that defendant Scofield had at one time been excommunicated from the Jehovah's Witnesses but had been later reinstated. Although Judge Jones ruled that the reason for Scofields' disfellowship from the church was not pertinent to the question at hand, Scofield attempted to justify his charactar and the plaintiffs' attorney was allowed to pursue the question of why he was removed from the church.

But before he could question Scofield on the subject, the Watchtower attorney, Richard Long, objected to the line of questioning. The court errupted in chaos. The plaintiffs maintained that Long did not have legal right to practice law in the State of Texas. Jones agreed but refused the plaintiffs the right to pursue the line of questioning.

After all the testimony was heard, Jones ruled in favor of the plaintiffs. "I don't feel the court has the sanctity to decide a religious issue. This court certainly does not have the right to decide the issue of legal title."

But Jones brought out the fact that this was a case of forciable entry and detainer, and said that the locks on the building were changed and no notification of such action was given prior to the incident.

The defense plans to appeal the decision.

The numbered clippings reproduced in facsimile on the previous pages are taken from the following sources:

(1-2) *Dallas Times Herald*, February 9, 1986

(3-4) *Sherman Democrat*, February 9, 1986

(5-6) *The Bonham Daily Favorite*, March 2, 1986

(7-8) *The Bonham Daily Favorite*, March 21, 1986

(9) *Sherman Democrat*, March 22, 1986

(10-11) *The Bonham Daily Favorite*, unknown dates

Appendix E

# The 1975 Discrepancy

The Israelite jubilee, by definition, was held every 50th year following the Israelites' entry into the Promised Land. Thus, there were seven Sabbath cycles in a 50-year period. Since each Sabbath cycle ended in a Sabbath year, this meant that year 49 of the cycle was a Sabbath. According to the Bible, year 50 was also a Sabbath—a special Sabbath known as a "jubilee."

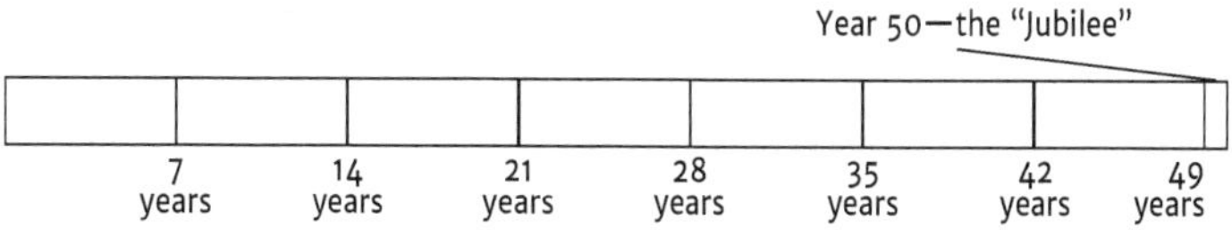


By applying the "thousand years as one day" principle (Psalm 90:4; 2 Peter 3:8), Watchtower long taught that the 7,000-year period from Adam's creation (in 4026 B.C.E., according to their literature) constituted the final creative day, or "God's rest." They argued that this day of rest brought to a conclusion a "creative week," which was explained in the February 1, 1973, *Watchtower* (p. 82) as being 49,000 years in duration:

> Since each of the creative "days" or periods was evidently seven thousand years long, the whole creative "week" takes in 49,000 years.

Though Freddie was eager to use this 49,000-year creative period to extrapolate a 1975 apocalypse, he was apparently less eager to assert the date at the opposite end of the timescale. If 1975 precisely marked the end of six thousand years from Adam's creation, then the first creative "week" (heralded with the immortal words "In the beginning . . .") would have had to, by necessity, start in 46,026 B.C.E.—but nowhere in Watchtower literature (at least to my knowledge) is this date to be found. (More than likely, Freddie did not want to double his chances of being caught out by giving a false date for both the apocalypse *and* the beginning of creation.)

Apart from grossly misrepresenting the length of Earth's various formative processes, Freddie's calculations posed another problem. They were inconsistent when it came to his 1975 teaching. Rather than heralding the "Jubilee" of God's 49,000 years of creation, 1975—by Freddie's logic—marked only 48,000 years from 'in the beginning.' According to his own reasoning, Witnesses would have had to wait until 2975 C.E.—7,000 years from Adam's creation—for the "creative week" of 49,000 years to end. In other words, despite all the fanfare about "stay alive 'til '75," 1975 was still a "day," or 1,000 years, too early for the jubilee celebration to commence.

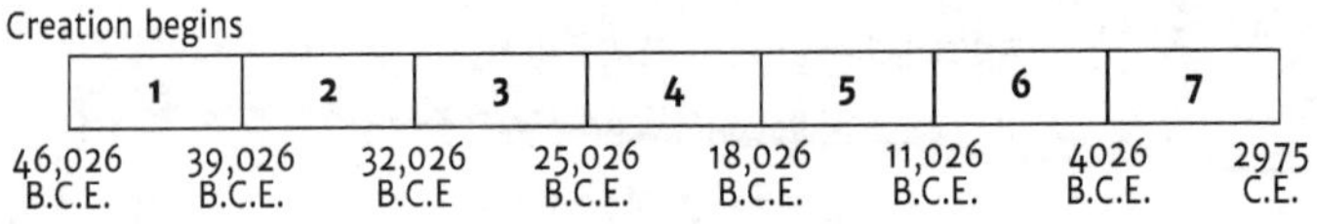


The following chart shows more clearly why, based on Freddie's math, Witnesses should have expected the grand jubilee to start in 2975 C.E.—even if doctrinal tinkering was to miraculously shift the Jubilee by 1,000 years to the year 1975.

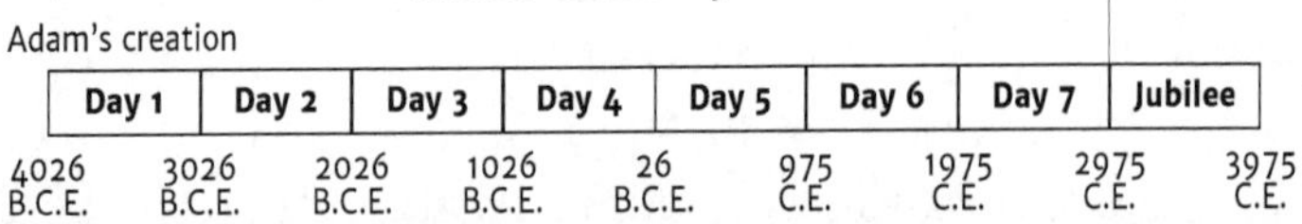

As you might expect, Fred Franz never satisfactorily addressed the mathematical discrepancy behind his 1975 teaching. Instead, he effectively combined the two consecutive millenniums ("Day 7" and the "Jubilee" on the chart above), claiming that it would be "appropriate" for these to be "a great jubilee sabbath."—*Life Everlasting*, p. 30.

This discrepancy would not be addressed for another 21 years, when the January 1, 1987, *Watchtower* (p. 30) published a "Questions From Readers" article admitting that "it might seem that the Jubilee would foreshadow the time following the end of a creative week of 49,000 years" (in other words, the time following 2975). But, rather than adhere to the numerical pattern that formed the basis for this belief in the first place, Watchtower did little more than describe its expectations as "fitting" (italics in the original):

> . . . the liberation and restoration that marked the Jubilee year in ancient Israel will find a fitting parallel *during* the coming Millennial Sabbath.

So the jubilee could encompass the "Millennial Sabbath" from the year 48,000 (1975) to the year 49,000 (2975) irrespective of this not technically being the jubilee.

In summary, it is one thing to claim that the seventh period of one thousand years from the creation of Adam is a "Sabbath." It is another thing entirely to invoke the jubilee system of celebrating every fiftieth year for this period. Once you insist on a method of calculation, you should use it consistently.*

---

* The July 15, 2004, *Watchtower* reaffirmed that the organization's expectations were "fitting," but with a unique twist: the symbolic jubilee for the "anointed" (heaven-bound Witnesses) now began in 33 C.E. following Jesus' resurrection, but for the "other sheep" (Witnesses who would inherit earthly

When 1975 passed by without incident, the January 1, 1976, *Watchtower* (p. 30) offered the following explanation:

> Although the time of Adam's creation can be determined, the beginning of God's "rest day" cannot. This is so because there was a time lapse of unspecified length between Adam's creation and the creation of Eve. Not until after the creation of Eve did God's "rest day" begin. The start of that day being unknown, its end is likewise unknown.

In other words, because nobody knew how long it took for Eve to join Adam in the Garden of Eden, it was anyone's guess when the "rest day" (or seventh creative "day") began, and hence it was impossible to know when Armageddon would arrive. Incredibly, this flimsy reasoning has yet to be officially contradicted. It comprises one of a number of "ghost teachings" (as I like to call them) from which Watchtower has long since moved on, but which were never formally disavowed. Rutherford's insistence that the Pyramid of Gizeh was built by Satan (see Chapter Six) as a revision of Russell's earlier assertion (that Jehovah built it) is another example of this intriguing phenomenon.

---

paradise) their jubilee would still occur during the 1000-year reign of Christ.

# Appendix F
# UN Letters

UNITED NATIONS NATIONS UNIES

POSTAL ADDRESS—ADRESSE POSTALE: UNITED NATIONS, N.Y. 10017
CABLE ADDRESS—ADRESSE TELEGRAPHIQUE: UNATIONS NEWYORK

REFERENCE:

11 October 2001

To Whom It May Concern:

Recently the NGO Section had been receiving numerous inquiries regarding the association of the **Watchtower Bible and Tract Society of New York** with the Department of Public Information (DPI). This organization applied for association with DPI in 1991 and was granted association in 1992. By accepting association with DPI, the organization agreed to meet criteria for association, including support and respect of the principles of the Charter of the United Nations and commitment and means to conduct effective information programmes with its constituents and to a broader audience about UN activities.

In October 2001, the **Watchtower Bible and Tract Society of New York** requested termination of its association with DPI. Following this request, the DPI has made a decision to disassociate the **Watchtower Bible and Tract Society of New York** as of 9 October 2001.

We appreciate your interest in the work of the United Nations.

Yours sincerely,

Paul Hoeffel
Chief
NGO Section
Department of Public Information

DPI NGO
NON-GOVERNMENTAL ORGANIZATIONS
SECTION

United Nations, DPI/NGO Resource Centre, Room L-1B-31
Tel: (212) 963-7233, 7234, 7078 • Fax: (212) 963-2819 • E-mail: dpingo@un.org

4 March 2004

To Whom It May Concern,

Recently the NGO Section has been receiving numerous inquiries regarding the association of the **Watchtower Bible and Tract Society of New York** with the Department of Public Information (DPI). This organization applied for association with DPI in 1991 and was granted association in 1992. By accepting association with DPI, the organization agreed to meet criteria for association, including support and respect of the principles of the Charter of the United Nations and commitment and means to conduct effective information programmes with its constituents and to a broader audience about UN activities.

In October 2001, the Main Representative of the **Watchtower Bible and Tract Society of New York** to the United Nations, Giro Aulicino, requested termination of its association with DPI. Following this request, the DPI made a decision to disassociate the **Watchtower Bible and Tract Society of New York** as of 9 October 2001.

Please be informed that it is the policy of the Department of Public Information of the United Nations to keep correspondence between the United Nations and NGOs associated with DPI confidential. However, please see below the paragraph included in all letters sent to NGOs approved for association in 1992:

"The principal purpose of association of non-governmental organizations with the United Nations Department of Public Information is the redissemination of information in order to increase public understanding of the principles, activities and achievements of the United Nations and its Agencies. Consequently, it is important that you should keep us informed about your organization's information programme as it relates to the United Nations, including sending us issues of your relevant publications. We are enclosing a brochure on the "The United Nations and Non-Governmental Organizations", which will give you some information regarding the NGO relationship."

In addition, the criteria for NGOs to become associated with DPI include the following:

- that the NGO share the principles of the UN Charter;
- operate solely on a not-for-profit basis;
- have a demonstrated interest in United Nations issues and a proven ability to reach large or specialized audiences, such as educators, media representatives, policy makers and the business community;
- have the commitment and means to conduct effective information programmes about UN activities by publishing newsletters, bulletins and pamphlets, organizing conferences, seminars and round tables; and enlisting the cooperation of the media.

We expect that you will share this information with your concerned colleagues, as we are unable to address the scores of duplicate requests regarding the Watchtower Bible and Tract Society that are being directed to our offices. Thank you for your interest in the work of the United Nations.

Sincerely,

Paul Hoeffel
Chief
NGO Section

APPENDIX G

# Magazine Printing Decrease Calculations

### December 2005

*The Watchtower*

| | |
|---|---|
| Circulation per issue: | 26,439,000 (Source: *w05* 12/15 p. 2) |
| Total monthly pages per copy: | 64 (two 32-page magazines) |
| Total monthly pages printed: | 1,692,096,000 |

*Awake!*

| | |
|---|---|
| Circulation per issue: | 22,842,000 (Source: *g05* 12/22 p. 2) |
| Total monthly pages per copy: | 64 (two 32-page magazines) |
| Total monthly pages printed: | 1,461,888,000 |

Total monthly pages printed for both magazines: **3,153,984,000**

### January 2006

*The Watchtower*

| | |
|---|---|
| Circulation per issue: | 26,439,000 (Source: *w06* 1/1 p. 2) |
| Total monthly pages per copy: | 64 (two 32-page magazines) |

| | |
|---|---|
| Total monthly pages printed: | 1,692,096,000 |

*Awake!*

| | |
|---|---|
| Circulation per issue: | 32,412,000 (Source: *g* 1/06 p. 2) |
| Total monthly pages per copy: | 32 (one 32-page magazine) |
| Total monthly pages printed: | 1,037,184,000 |

Total monthly pages printed for both magazines: **2,729,280,000**

**January 2008**

*The Watchtower* (Public edition)

| | |
|---|---|
| Circulation per issue: | 37,100,000 (Source: *w08* 1/1 p. 2) |
| Total monthly pages per copy: | 32 (one 32-page magazine) |
| Total monthly pages printed: | 1,187,200,000 |

*The Watchtower* (Study edition)

| | |
|---|---|
| Circulation per issue: | 9,500,000 (Source: *w08*-U 1/15 p. 2) |
| Total monthly pages per copy: | 32 (one 32-page magazine) |
| Total monthly pages printed: | 304,000,000 |

*Awake!*

| | |
|---|---|
| Circulation per issue: | 35,754,000 (Source: *g* 1/08 p. 2) |

| | |
|---|---|
| Total monthly pages per copy: | 32 (one 32-page magazine) |
| Total monthly pages printed: | 1,144,128,000 |

Total monthly pages printed for both magazines: **2,635,328,000**

## January 2013

*The Watchtower* (Public edition)

| | |
|---|---|
| Circulation per issue: | 44,978,000 (Source: *w13* 1/1 p. 2) |
| Total monthly pages per copy: | 16 (one 16-page magazine) |
| Total monthly pages printed: | 719,648,000 |

*The Watchtower* (Study edition)

| | |
|---|---|
| Circulation per issue: | 14,500,000 (Source: *w13*-U 1/15 p. 2) |
| Total monthly pages per copy: | 32 (one 32-page magazines) |
| Total monthly pages printed: | 464,000,000 |

*Awake!*

| | |
|---|---|
| Circulation per issue: | 43,524,000 (Source: *g* 1/13 p. 2) |
| Total monthly pages per copy: | 16 (one 16-page magazine) |
| Total monthly pages printed: | 696,384,000 |

Total monthly pages printed for both magazines: **1,880,032,000**

**January 2016**

*The Watchtower* (Public edition)

| | |
|---|---|
| Circulation per issue: | 58,987,000 (Source: *wp16.01* p. 2) |
| Total monthly pages per copy: | 8 (one 16-page magazine every two months) |
| Total monthly pages printed: | 471,896,000 |

*The Watchtower* (Study edition)

| | |
|---|---|
| Circulation per issue: | 15,252,000 (Source: *w16.01*-U p. 2) |
| Total monthly pages per copy: | 32 (one 32-page magazine) |
| Total monthly pages printed: | 488,064,000 |

*Awake!*

| | |
|---|---|
| Circulation per issue: | 57,761,000 (Source: *g16.01* p. 2) |
| Total monthly pages per copy: | 8 (one 16-page magazine every two months) |
| Total monthly pages printed: | 462,088,000 |

Total monthly pages printed for both magazines: **1,422,048,000**

Total drop in printing from December 2005 to January 2016: **54.91%**

**Please note:** I have included above the calculations for key stages in magazine printing reduction since 2005. The graph in Chapter Eight is based on more detailed data (including some extrapolations) derived from calculating the printing for each magazine issue since January 2005. Though not all the data has been shown in this Appendix, it can easily be calculated using the same method shown above by those who wish to delve deeper. It should also be pointed out that there are two unknown anomalies when it comes to magazine printing, namely (1) whether the "simplified edition" of *The Watchtower* is counted in the published circulation figures for the "study edition," and (2) to what extent the figures are influenced by large-print *Watchtowers* (which are printed as 64-page magazines). Ultimately, Watchtower is the gatekeeper of this information and will know precisely what its monthly magazine printing figures are, and the precise extent to which these have fallen. Nevertheless, the data shown above encompasses the overwhelming bulk of magazine printing for the organization, and is therefore useful in measuring the scaling down of operations in recent years.

APPENDIX H

# Extrapolation on the Number of Child Abuse Victims

What follows is an extrapolation of the numbers of victims and perpetrators for Britain, Canada and the United States based on the fact that (1) 1,006 alleged child molesters were recorded by Watchtower in Australia between 1950 and 2014, and (2) these 1,006 alleged perpetrators are said to have abused at least 1,800 victims. Publisher numbers for all four countries are based on *Yearbook* figures

| Year | Australia | | Britain | | Canada | | United States | |
|---|---|---|---|---|---|---|---|---|
| | Publishers | Victims | Publishers | Victims | Publishers | Victims | Publishers | Victims |
| 1950 | 4502 | 3.38 | 20842 | 15.67 | 16013 | 12.04 | 98468 | 74.02 |
| 1951 | 5098 | 3.83 | 23080 | 17.35 | 18669 | 14.03 | 118462 | 89.05 |
| 1952 | 5716 | 4.30 | 24847 | 18.68 | 20338 | 15.29 | 126626 | 95.18 |
| 1953 | 6302 | 4.74 | 26104 | 19.62 | 22350 | 16.80 | 139966 | 105.21 |
| 1954 | 6874 | 5.17 | 27145 | 20.40 | 23944 | 18.00 | 153969 | 115.74 |
| 1955 | 7603 | 5.72 | 28073 | 21.10 | 25306 | 19.02 | 163875 | 123.18 |
| 1956 | 8244 | 6.20 | 30342 | 22.81 | 25677 | 19.30 | 169835 | 127.66 |
| 1957 | 9359 | 7.04 | 34004 | 25.56 | 28541 | 21.45 | 187762 | 141.14 |
| 1958 | 10613 | 7.98 | 37416 | 28.13 | 30933 | 23.25 | 202141 | 151.95 |
| 1959 | 11834 | 8.90 | 40884 | 30.73 | 32861 | 24.70 | 221240 | 166.31 |
| 1960 | 12746 | 9.58 | 43650 | 32.81 | 34603 | 26.01 | 232632 | 174.87 |
| 1961 | 13650 | 10.26 | 44974 | 33.81 | 36459 | 27.41 | 248681 | 186.93 |
| 1962 | 14634 | 11.00 | 46842 | 35.21 | 37227 | 27.98 | 267436 | 201.03 |
| 1963 | 15045 | 11.31 | 47053 | 35.37 | 37418 | 28.13 | 280052 | 210.52 |
| 1964 | 15821 | 11.89 | 48849 | 36.72 | 38790 | 29.16 | 292052 | 219.54 |
| 1965 | 16156 | 12.14 | 48982 | 36.82 | 39293 | 29.54 | 302450 | 227.35 |

| Year | Australia | | Britain | | Canada | | United States | |
|---|---|---|---|---|---|---|---|---|
| | Publishers | Victims | Publishers | Victims | Publishers | Victims | Publishers | Victims |
| 1966 | 16588 | 12.47 | 49073 | 36.89 | 39554 | 29.73 | 305481 | 229.63 |
| 1967 | 17317 | 13.02 | 50154 | 37.70 | 40237 | 30.25 | 311378 | 234.06 |
| 1968 | 18305 | 13.76 | 52805 | 39.69 | 41458 | 31.16 | 323688 | 243.32 |
| 1969 | 19838 | 14.91 | 55876 | 42.00 | 43265 | 32.52 | 343673 | 258.34 |
| 1970 | 21474 | 16.14 | 59705 | 44.88 | 45734 | 34.38 | 371561 | 279.30 |
| 1971 | 22721 | 17.08 | 62813 | 47.22 | 48100 | 36.16 | 402893 | 302.85 |
| 1972 | 23309 | 17.52 | 64434 | 48.44 | 49233 | 37.01 | 418239 | 314.39 |
| 1973 | 23547 | 17.70 | 65348 | 49.12 | 50650 | 38.07 | 439489 | 330.36 |
| 1974 | 26012 | 19.55 | 71944 | 54.08 | 56108 | 42.18 | 506367 | 380.64 |
| 1975 | 27610 | 20.75 | 75168 | 56.50 | 58380 | 43.88 | 534765 | 401.98 |
| 1976 | 27936 | 21.00 | 76694 | 57.65 | 60573 | 45.53 | 544644 | 409.41 |
| 1977 | 28078 | 21.11 | 75136 | 56.48 | 60940 | 45.81 | 530374 | 398.68 |
| 1978 | 27864 | 20.95 | 73859 | 55.52 | 60540 | 45.51 | 513673 | 386.13 |
| 1979 | 28468 | 21.40 | 74862 | 56.27 | 61281 | 46.06 | 521370 | 391.91 |
| 1980 | 29995 | 22.55 | 78346 | 58.89 | 62938 | 47.31 | 543457 | 408.52 |
| 1981 | 31086 | 23.37 | 80824 | 60.76 | 65867 | 49.51 | 563452 | 423.55 |
| 1982 | 33153 | 24.92 | 83564 | 62.82 | 68410 | 51.42 | 581934 | 437.44 |
| 1983 | 35982 | 27.05 | 87732 | 65.95 | 73139 | 54.98 | 616058 | 463.09 |
| 1984 | 39052 | 29.36 | 92616 | 69.62 | 76866 | 57.78 | 648704 | 487.63 |
| 1985 | 41299 | 31.04 | 97370 | 73.19 | 80614 | 60.60 | 678510 | 510.04 |
| 1986 | 42998 | 32.32 | 101863 | 76.57 | 84343 | 63.40 | 710344 | 533.97 |
| 1987 | 44649 | 33.56 | 105082 | 78.99 | 87459 | 65.74 | 734378 | 552.03 |
| 1988 | 46733 | 35.13 | 108599 | 81.63 | 90846 | 68.29 | 762960 | 573.52 |
| 1989 | 49095 | 36.90 | 112742 | 84.75 | 94176 | 70.79 | 788709 | 592.87 |
| 1990 | 51541 | 38.74 | 115511 | 86.83 | 97752 | 73.48 | 816417 | 613.70 |
| 1991 | 53484 | 40.20 | 118100 | 88.78 | 100991 | 75.91 | 846028 | 635.96 |
| 1992 | 55039 | 41.37 | 120648 | 90.69 | 103412 | 77.73 | 866362 | 651.24 |
| 1993 | 56345 | 42.35 | 122245 | 91.89 | 105201 | 79.08 | 878841 | 660.62 |
| 1994 | 57780 | 43.43 | 123194 | 92.60 | 106664 | 80.18 | 889570 | 668.69 |
| 1995 | 59474 | 44.71 | 125138 | 94.07 | 109168 | 82.06 | 912002 | 685.55 |
| 1996 | 60216 | 45.26 | 124623 | 93.68 | 110235 | 82.86 | 921123 | 692.41 |
| 1997 | 59892 | 45.02 | 123318 | 92.70 | 109880 | 82.60 | 929471 | 698.68 |
| 1998 | 60226 | 45.27 | 123191 | 92.60 | 109664 | 82.43 | 944218 | 709.77 |
| 1999 | 59768 | 44.93 | 121723 | 91.50 | 108437 | 81.51 | 940650 | 707.09 |
| 2000 | 59392 | 44.64 | 120592 | 90.65 | 107742 | 80.99 | 945000 | 710.36 |

| Year | Australia | | Britain | | Canada | | United States | |
|---|---|---|---|---|---|---|---|---|
| | Publishers | Victims | Publishers | Victims | Publishers | Victims | Publishers | Victims |
| 2001 | 58993 | 44.35 | 119655 | 89.94 | 107218 | 80.60 | 945689 | 710.87 |
| 2002 | 59934 | 45.05 | 120801 | 90.81 | 108217 | 81.35 | 972754 | 731.22 |
| 2003 | 60510 | 45.49 | 120478 | 90.56 | 108409 | 81.49 | 988236 | 742.86 |
| 2004 | 60533 | 45.50 | 120514 | 90.59 | 108012 | 81.19 | 992809 | 746.29 |
| 2005 | 60399 | 45.40 | 121166 | 91.08 | 107534 | 80.83 | 995071 | 747.99 |
| 2006 | 60692 | 45.62 | 122412 | 92.02 | 107618 | 80.90 | 1008281 | 757.92 |
| 2007 | 62022 | 46.62 | 125808 | 94.57 | 108974 | 81.92 | 1042528 | 783.67 |
| 2008 | 62159 | 46.72 | 126580 | 95.15 | 109086 | 82.00 | 1059253 | 796.24 |
| 2009 | 63454 | 47.70 | 128435 | 96.54 | 110467 | 83.04 | 1096502 | 824.24 |
| 2010 | 63951 | 48.07 | 129230 | 97.14 | 111193 | 83.58 | 1115786 | 838.74 |
| 2011 | 64498 | 48.48 | 130808 | 98.33 | 111970 | 84.17 | 1145723 | 861.24 |
| 2012 | 64884 | 48.77 | 131629 | 98.95 | 112710 | 84.72 | 1156150 | 869.08 |
| 2013 | 65596 | 49.31 | 132515 | 99.61 | 113111 | 85.03 | 1167723 | 877.78 |
| 2014 | 66484 | 49.98 | 134308 | 100.96 | 113617 | 85.41 | 1186598 | 891.97 |
| **Total** | 2394572 | | | | | | | |
| **Victims** | | **1800** | | **4158.64** | | **3515.26** | | **30567.53** |
| **Perpetrators** | | **1006** | | **2324.22** | | **1964.64** | | **17083.85** |
| **Vict./Perp.** | | | | | **1.789264414** | | | |
| **Ratio** | | | | | **1330.317778** | | | |
| **Total Victims** | | | | | **40041** | | | |
| **Total Perpetrators** | | | | | **22379** | | | |

APPENDIX I

# Gerrit Lösch's Statement

FILED
Clerk of the Superior Court
FEB 05 2014

Megan S. Wynne, Esq., SBN 183707
Ashley A. Escudero, Esq., SBN250473
MORRIS POLICH & PURDY LLP
One America Plaza
600 West Broadway, Suite 500
San Diego, California 92101
Tel: (619) 557-0404
Fax: (619) 557-0460

Donald T. Ridley, Esq.
*Pro Hac Vice*
THE MANDEL LAW FIRM
370 Lexington Avenue, Suite 505
New York, NY 10017
Tel: (212) 697-7383
Fax: (212) 681-6157

Attorneys for Gerrit Lösch

FILED
Clerk of the Superior Court
'14 FEB 5 ... 4:34
FEB 05 2014
By:____________ Deputy

**SUPERIOR COURT OF THE STATE OF CALIFORNIA**

**COUNTY OF SAN DIEGO**

JOSE LOPEZ, an Individual,

Plaintiff,

v.

DOE 1, LINDA VISTA CHURCH; DOE 2, SUPERVISORY ORGANIZATION; DOE 3, PERPETRATOR; and DOES 4 through 100, inclusive,

Defendants.

CASE NO. 37-2012-00099849-CU-PO-CTL

**DECLARATION OF GERRIT LÖSCH IN SUPPORT OF MOTION TO QUASH ORDER GRANTING PLAINTIFF'S MOTION TO COMPEL DEPOSITION OF GERRIT LÖSCH**

| | |
|---|---|
| Hearing Date: | TBD |
| Time: | TBD |
| Dept: | C-65 |
| Judge: | Joan M. Lewis |
| Complaint Filed: | June 29, 2012 |
| Trial Date: | June 27, 2014 |

I, Gerrit Lösch, declare as follows:

1. I am over 18 years of age, of sound mind, and competent to make this Declaration. I have personal knowledge of the matters contained herein, and they are all true and correct.

2. I provide this Declaration to support the Motion to Quash Order Granting Plaintiff's "Motion to Compel the Deposition of Gerrit Lösch and the Underlying Notice of

Taking the Deposition of Gerrit Lösch, with Production of Documents Required – Videorecorded for Use at Trial."

3. If called upon to testify in this civil action, I would provide the information contained in this Declaration.

4. I was not served with the Notice of Deposition, but I learned that Plaintiff vacated the original deposition date after Watchtower objected to the Notice.

5. I recently learned that this Court entered an Order compelling Watchtower Bible and Tract Society of New York, Inc. (sued as Doe 1; hereinafter referred to as "Watchtower") to produce me for deposition, but I have not been served with a copy of the Court's Order.

6. I am a member of the ecclesiastical Governing Body of Jehovah's Witnesses, having been appointed to serve in that capacity on July 1, 1994. I was not on the Governing Body in 1986 when the Plaintiff alleges he was abused by Gonzalo Campos.

7. The Governing Body of Jehovah's Witnesses is the highest ecclesiastical authority for the faith of Jehovah's Witnesses, and it exercises spiritual oversight for Jehovah's Witnesses worldwide.

8. I am not, and never have been, a corporate officer, director, managing agent, member, or employee of Watchtower. I do not direct, and have never directed, the day-to-day operations of Watchtower. I do not answer to Watchtower. I do not have, and never have had, any authority as an individual to make or determine corporate policy for Watchtower or any department of Watchtower.

9. Watchtower does not have, and never has had, any authority over me.

10. I have no personal knowledge of any facts or circumstances concerning the subject matter of this case because, among other things:

(a) I do not supervise or work for, and I have never supervised or worked for, the Watchtower Legal Department or the U.S. Service Department.

(b) I did not move to live in the United States until July, 1990.

(c) Prior to July 1990, I resided in Austria.

(d) I do not know and have never met the Plaintiff, Jose Lopez.



(e) I do not know and have never met Leticia Lopez, the mother of Plaintiff Jose Lopez.

(f) I do not know and have never met the Defendant, Gonzalo Campos, who is sued as Doe 3.

11. I am a resident of the State of New York, as I live and work in Brooklyn where the world headquarters of Jehovah's Witnesses is located.

I declare under penalty of perjury under the laws of the State of California that the foregoing is true and correct, and that this Declaration is executed this 4th day of February 2014.

Gerrit Lösch

APPENDIX J

# 1947 *Awake!* Article on Excommunication

## Are You Also Excommunicated?

IF YOU are one of the 138,000,000 people in the world that were born and raised as "Protestants", then you are already excommunicated by the Roman Catholic Hierarchy. This means that you are looked upon with the blackest contempt by the Vatican, being cursed and damned with the Devil and his angels. Says the *Catholic Encyclopedia:*

With the foregoing exceptions [infidels, pagans, Mohammedans, and Jews], all who have been baptized are liable to excommunication, even those [protestants] who have never belonged to the true Church, since by their baptism they are really her subjects, though of course rebellious ones. Moreover, the Church excommunicates not only those who abandon the true faith to embrace [protestant] schism or heresy, but likewise the members of heretical and schismatic communities who have been born therein.

All those belonging to such lodges as the Masonic, Fenians, Independent Order of Good Templars, Odd Fellows, the Masonic, Fenians, Independent Order of Good Templars, Odd Fellows, Sons of Temperance, or the Knights of Pythias, are also excommunicated.

This is "canon law" which the Roman Catholic Hierarchy seeks to enforce on the pretext that it is God's law. The authority for excommunication, they claim, is based on the teachings of Christ and the apostles, as found in the following scriptures: Matthew 18:15-19; 1 Corinthians 5:3-5; 16:22; Galatians 1:8, 9; 1 Timothy 1:20; Titus 3:10. But the Hierarchy's excommunication, as a punishment and "medicinal" remedy (*Catholic Encyclopedia*), finds no support in these scriptures. In fact, it is altogether foreign to Bible teachings.—Hebrews 10:26-31.

Where, then, did this practice originate? The *Encyclopædia Britannica* says that papal excommunication is not without pagan influence, "and its variations cannot be adequately explained unless account be taken of several non-Christian analogues of excommunication." The superstitious Greeks believed that when an excommunicated person died the Devil entered the body, and therefore, "in order to prevent it, the relatives of the deceased cut his body in pieces and boil them in wine." Even the Druids had a method of expelling those who lost faith in their religious superstitions. It was therefore after Catholicism adopted its pagan practices, A.D. 325, that this new chapter in religious excommunication was written.

Thereafter, as the pretensions of the Hierarchy increased, the weapon of excommunication became the instrument by which the clergy attained a combination of ecclesiastical power and secular tyranny that finds no parallel in history. Princes and potentates that opposed the dictates of the Vatican were speedily impaled on the tines of excommunication and hung over persecution fires. Not only individuals, but whole countries, were so treated: France, in 998; Germany, in 1102; England, in 1208. Even Rome itself was excommunicated in 1155. Luther and his forty-one "errors" were similarly "cursed" in 1520. Likewise Napoleon in 1809 and Victor Emmanuel in 1860.

The excommunication of Frederick II furnishes a good example of the dire effects produced by these papal "curses" in the thirteenth century.

Five times king and emperor as he was, Frederick, placed under the bau of the church, led henceforth a doomed existence. The mendicant monks stirred up the populace to acts of fanatical enmity. To plot against him, to attempt his life by poison or the sword, was accounted virtuous. . . . Hunted to the ground and broken-hearted, Frederick expired at the end of 1250.—*Encyclopædia Britannica.*

*Excommunication as a papal force* was greatly reduced with the fall of the "Holy Roman Empire". So much so that this generation does not observe such ruthless consequences of the past befalling Tito and his associates who were recently excommunicated. (See *Awake!* November 22, 1946.)

*In recounting all of these facts one is* at a loss to find an explanation why the "crimes" of Tito and his associates are greater than (or as great as) those of Franco, Mussolini and Hitler, and their gang of cutthroats. Only when we turn to the *Catholic Encyclopedia* do we find the answer. There it is stated:

*The Church's right to excommunicate is* based on her status as a spiritual society, whose members, governed by legitimate authority, seek one and the same end through suitable means. Members who, by their obstinate disobedience, reject the means of attaining this common end deserve to be removed from such a society.

*Here, then, is the explanation why the* Axis dictators were not excommunicated. They were 'seeking the one and same end' with the Roman Catholic Church.

Appendix K

# "War of Words" Article in *The Independent* —September 27, 2011

**War of words breaks out among Jehovah's Witnesses**

*Attack on 'mentally diseased' worshippers who leave church provokes outcry*

by Jerome Taylor

The official magazine for Jehovah's Witnesses has described those who leave the church as "mentally diseased", prompting an outcry from former members and insiders concerned about the shunning of those who question official doctrine.

An article published in July's edition of *The Watchtower* warns followers to stay clear of "false teachers" who are condemned as being "mentally diseased" apostates who should be avoided at all costs. "Suppose that a doctor told you to avoid contact with someone who is infected with a contagious, deadly disease," the article reads. "You would know what the doctor means, and you would strictly heed his warning. Well, apostates are 'mentally diseased', and they seek to infect others with their disloyal teachings."

A copy of the magazine, distributed by Jehovah's Witnesses around the world, was given to *The Independent* by a current member of the church who has become unhappy with official teaching but is afraid to leave for fear of losing his family.

"Many like me remain associated with the Witnesses out of fear of being uncovered as an 'apostate' and ousted, not just from the organisation, but from their own friends and families," said the man, who would only give the name John. "I find I am now branded as 'mentally diseased' – giving any who discover my true beliefs free licence to treat me with disdain."

As a faith with a centralised leadership, many forms of discipline are used to counter criticism of doctrine, with punishments ranging from restriction of official duties to excommunication. Those who have been thrown out of the church often find themselves ostracised by fellow believers.

A growing number of former and current Witnesses have begun to argue that the church's use of the word "mentally diseased" to describe defectors could be in breach of Britain's religious hatred laws. A group of former Witnesses in Portsmouth have now made an official complaint to Hampshire Police about the article and police are currently investigating.

Angus Robertson, a former Witness "elder" from Hampshire, who was present at the meeting with police officers, said: "The way scripture is being used to bully people must be challenged. If a religion was preaching that blacks or gays were mentally diseased there would understandable outrage."

Critics are also considering whether to complain to the Charity Commission. The Watchtower Bible and Tract Society of Britain, which prints church doctrine in the UK, is a registered charity.

Rick Fenton, a spokesperson for the Watchtower Society, insisted last night that ostracisation was "a personal matter for each individual to decide for himself". "Any one of Jehovah's Witnesses is free to express their feelings and to ask questions," he said. "If a person changes their mind about Bible-based teachings they once held dear, we recognise their right to leave."

# War of words breaks out among Jehovah's Witnesses

## Attack on 'mentally diseased' worshippers who leave church provokes outcry

By Jerome Taylor
Religious Affairs Correspondent

THE OFFICIAL magazine for Jehovah's Witnesses has described those who leave the church as "mentally diseased", prompting an outcry from former members and insiders concerned about the shunning of those who question official doctrine.

An article published in July's edition of *The Watchtower* warns followers to stay clear of "false teachers" who are condemned as being "mentally diseased" apostates who should be avoided at all costs. "Suppose that a doctor told you to avoid contact with someone who is infected with a contagious, deadly disease," the article reads. "You would know what the doctor means, and you would strictly heed his warning. Well, apostates are 'mentally diseased', and they seek to infect others with their disloyal teachings."

A copy of the magazine, distributed by Jehovah's Witnesses around the world, was given to *The Independent* by a current member of the church who has become unhappy with official teaching but is afraid to leave for fear of losing his family.

"Many like me remain associated with the Witnesses out of fear of being uncovered as an 'apostate' and ousted, not just from the organisation, but from their own friends and families," said the man, who would only give the name John. "I find I am now branded as 'mentally diseased' – giving any who discover my true beliefs free licence to treat me with disdain."

**Those who have been thrown out of the church often find themselves excluded, even by their own families**

As a faith with a centralised leadership, many forms of discipline are used to counter criticism of doctrine, with punishments ranging from restriction of official duties to excommunication. Those who have been thrown out of the church often find themselves ostracised by fellow believers.

A growing number of former and current Witnesses have begun to argue that the church's use of the word "mentally diseased" to describe defectors could be in breach of Britain's religious hatred laws. A group of former Witnesses in Portsmouth have now made an official complaint to Hampshire Police about the article and police are currently investigating.

Angus Robertson, a former Witness "elder" from Hampshire, who was present at the meeting with police officers, said: "The way scripture is being used to bully people must be challenged. If a religion was preaching that blacks or gays were mentally diseased there would understandable outrage."

Critics are also considering whether to complain to the Charity Commission. The Watchtower Bible and Tract Society of Britain, which prints church doctrine in the UK, is a registered charity.

Rick Fenton, a spokesperson for the Watchtower Society, insisted last night that ostracisation was "a personal matter for each individual to decide for himself". "Any one of Jehovah's Witnesses is free to express their feelings and to ask questions," he said. "If a person changes their mind about Bible-based teachings they once held dear, we recognise their right to leave."

The magazine, which is distributed around the world
REX FEATURES

THE OFFENDING ARTICLE

Taken from 'Will you heed Jehovah's warnings?' *The Watchtower*, 15 July 2011

"Jehovah, the Great Physician, tells us to avoid contact with them. We know what he means, but are we determined to heed his warning in all respects? What is involved in avoiding false teachers? We do not receive them into our homes or greet them. We also refuse to read their literature, watch television programmes that feature them, examine their websites, or add our comments to their blogs. Why do we take such a firm stand?

"Because of love. We love 'the God of truth', so we are not interested in twisted teachings that contradict his Word of truth."

# Notes

The following list contains the sources for any quotes in the text that are not (1) already clearly stated, or (2) based on personal conversations or correspondence. Some Watchtower publications are abbreviated as follows:

- *w* = *Zion's Watch Tower, The Watch Tower* or *The Watchtower,*
- *g* = *The Golden Age, Consolation* or *Awake!;*
- *km* = *Kingdom Ministry, Our Kingdom Ministry* or *Our Christian Life and Ministry—Meeting Workbook;*
- *yb* = *Yearbook of Jehovah's Witnesses;*
- *jv* = *Jehovah's Witnesses—Proclaimers of God's Kingdom.*

Quotes from audio/video sources are numbered in brackets—e.g. "(01)"—to indicate where they can be located in the "Audio and Video Sources" section of this book's website (ReluctantApostate.co).

**Please note:** With a few rare exceptions, Watchtower publications are entirely accessible in digital form if you know where to look. If you have the *Watchtower Library* (a PC application running on Microsoft Windows, distributed among Jehovah's Witnesses) you can use it to find *Watchtower* magazines dating back to 1950 and *Awake!* magazines, books and many other publications dating back to 1970. If you do not have access to *Watchtower Library,* most recent publications (dating back to 2000) are available on the *Watchtower ONLINE LIBRARY* (URL: http://wol.jw.org/). For older publications (which I quote from extensively), I can recommend the literature archive on AvoidJW.org (URL: http://avoidjw.org/literature/). The magazine archive in particular is extensive and was extremely helpful to me when researching this book.

**INTRODUCTION**

1. "spiritually destitute condition": *w13* 9/15 p. 28, par. 4.
2. "untainted by the filth": *w10* 7/15 p. 9.

**CHAPTER ONE—HOW TO MAKE A JEHOVAH'S WITNESS**

1. "Imagine that you know that": *km* 3/14 p. 1.
2. "I'm not interested": *Reasoning From the Scriptures*, p. 16.
3. "could have produced the variety" (ftn.): *Insight on the Scriptures*, Vol. 1, p. 165.
4. "If the situation is really that serious": *Reasoning From the Scriptures*, p. 76.
5. "Jehovah's Witnesses take note": Ibid., p. 69.
6. "On the basis of the sacrifice of Jesus Christ": *Organized to Do Jehovah's Will* (2015), p. 209.
7. "The idea that people knowingly": *Freedom of Mind: Helping Loved Ones Leave Controlling People, Cults and Beliefs*, pp. 68-69.
8. "ungodly conduct": *w05* 12/15 p. 6.
9. "marked by debauched behavior": Ibid., p. 7.
10. "serves the purposes of Satan": *Life—How Did It Get Here? By Evolution, or by Creation?* p. 6.
11. "The theory of evolution is contrary to reality": Ibid., p. 4.
12. "nations of the UN beast": *w86* 10/1 p. 20.
13. "The global congregation of Jehovah's Witnesses": *Revelation—Its Grand Climax At Hand!*, p. 91.

**CHAPTER TWO—THE PAGE-FOLDING PIONEER**

14. "If you are not yet pioneering": *w13* 9/15 p. 27, par. 2.
15. "What secular job could possibly be as exciting": *Youths—What Will You Do With Your Life?*, p. 4.
16. "If you are a young person": *g69* 5/22 p. 15.
17. "A well-intentioned teacher": *w08* 9/1 p. 10.
18. "Young people, ask yourself": January 2015 JW Broadcasting episode (01).
19. "By the end of 1914, they were expecting" (ftn.): *Pay Attention to Daniel's Prophecy!*, p. 142.

## CHAPTER THREE—GOD'S PROMISE OF PARADISE

1. "just a little less than an acre": *Reasoning From the Scriptures*, p. 340.
2. "cause procreation to cease on earth": Ibid., p. 116.
3. "scrolls will be opened" (ftn): *w16.03* p. 21-22.
4. "than a superficial confession of faith": *w10* 8/1 p. 8.
5. "allowing for hundreds of thousands to be gathered": *w97* 1/1 p. 16, par. 12.
6. "The slain are gonna be from one end of the earth": Anthony Morris talk (02).
7. "I've seen what happens to humans when they're mangled": Anthony Morris talk (03).
8. "Jehovah is perhaps gonna use radiation": Gerrit Lösch talk (04).
9. "The carnage will be earth wide": *w14* 2/15 p. 7, par. 18.
10. "extensive preaching campaign": *w13* 9/15 p. 11, par. 19.
11. "Despite the opposition of Satan": *w12* 8/15 pp. 3-7.
12. "Human emotions today": *w87* 6/1 p. 31.
13. "In Jehovah's due time, all will be revealed": *w05* 5/1 p. 22, par. 20.
14. "Is there sound reason for hoping": *w14* 8/15 p. 29.

## CHAPTER FOUR—JEHOVAH'S WITNESSES AND SEX

1. "self-abuse": *w85* 4/15 p. 16, par. 6.
2. "steppingstone to homosexuality": *w76* 2/15 p. 123, par. 15.
3. "Feelings of guilt plagued me for many years": *Questions Young People Ask—Answers That Work, Volume 2*, p. 240.
4. "Some have contended": *w69* 12/15 p. 766.
5. "certain literature and photographs": *Crisis of Conscience* (4th Ed.), p. 47.
6. "gross unnatural conduct": *w72* 12/1 pp. 734-736.
7. "lewd practices on the part of a married person": *w74* 11/15 pp. 703-704.
8. "Women experienced painful embarrassment": *Crisis of Conscience* (4th Ed.), p. 48.
9. "half a man": Ibid., p. 52.
10. "Many, many problems have resulted": Ibid., p. 48.
11. "While both homosexuality and bestiality": *w72* 1/1 p. 32.
12. "emotional upset": *Crisis of Conscience* (4th Ed.), p. 55.
13. "genuinely disturbed": Ibid., p. 54.
14. "What, then, is the significance": *w72* 12/15 p. 768.

15. "if it becomes known": *w83* 3/15 p. 31.
16. "to highlight that it would be only": *Revelation—Its Grand Climax at Hand!*, p. 168 (footnote).
17. "can, and frequently does, lead into homosexuality": *w73* 9/15 p. 569.
18. "Is one who practices masturbation": *True Peace and Security—From What Source?*, p. 152, par. 19.
19. "With hearts full of gratitude": *w08* 8/15 p. 6, par. 15.
20. "public health hazard": *w01* 4/15 p. 32.

**CHAPTER FIVE—SHEPHERD THE FLOCK**

1. "To implement their decisions": *In Search of Christian Freedom*, p. 96.
2. "have freed themselves from the hierarchical": *w66* 4/1 p. 205, par. 20.
3. "In contrast with many religious groups": *w01* 1/15 p. 13.
4. "The female skull is lighter": *g67* 8/22 pp. 27-28.
5. "So now this shows that she's just not equipped": Samuel Herd talk (05).
6. "They are appointed after prayer": *w10* 9/15 p. 27, par. 10.
7. "Is there anything from your past": *"Shepherd the Flock of God"—1 Peter 5:2*, p.35; Letter to all bodies of elders dated July 13, 2014.
8. "1. Shepherd the Flock of God":*"Shepherd the Flock of God"—1 Peter 5:2*, pp. 4-5.
9. "safety lies in avoiding apostate": *w92* 7/15 pp. 12-13, par. 19.
10. "poorly documented Web entries": *yb11* p. 9.
11. "All of us must be ready to obey": *w13* 11/15 p. 20, par. 17.

**CHAPTER SIX—THE PASTOR**

1. "drawn into Mr. Miller's theory for a time": *Bible Examiner*, May 1849, p. 73.
2. "Brought up by a Presbyterian, indoctrinated from the Catechism": *w1916*, p.170-172.
3. "I should and do gratefully mention": *w1906* 7/15 p. 3821.
4. "it is quite obvious that Storrs contributed much": *Apocalypse Delayed* (2nd Ed.), pp. 16-17.
5. "We held together until the autumn": *Evidences for the Coming of the Lord in 1873, Or the Midnight Cry*, 1871 p. 26.

6. "I am still enforcing the 1873 arguments": *Advent Christian Times*, November 11, 1873, issue.
7. "When I opened I at once identified it with Adventism": *w1906* 7/15 p. 3822.
8. "I paid Mr. Barbour's expenses to come see me at Philadelphia": Ibid.
9. "money and instructions to prepare in concise book-form": Ibid.
10. "Let me urge you. A few months": *Three Worlds and the Harvest of This World*, p. 68.
11. "The Chronology is the best I have ever seen": *Bible Examiner*, July 1877, p. 317.
12. "I object to the time setting in any limited period": *Bible Examiner*, October 1877, p. 11.
13. "The doctrine of substitution, that is, punishing the innocent": *Herald of the Morning*, August 1878 p. 26.
14. "Unpleasant though it be, I feel it necessary": *Herald of the Morning*, September 1878 p. 39.
15. "If the 'Times of the Gentiles' began in October, 606 B. C." *What Pastor Russell Said*, pp. 75-76:
16. "Of course, if calculated from Nebuchadnezzar's own accession": *Horae Apocalypticae*, Vol. III (1844) p. 1429 (see also: *The Gentile Times Reconsidered*, by Carl Olof Jonsson, p. 40).
17. "practically the Bible topically arranged": *w1910* 9/15 p. 4685.
18. "Pleiades, in the north, has long been esteemed" (ftn.): *The New Creation*, p. 618.
19. "The constellation of the Pleiades is a small one" (ftn.): *Reconciliation*, p. 14.
20. "The testimony of God's Stone Witness and Prophet": *Thy Kingdom Come*, p. 313.
21. "The ancient structure thus being repeatedly": Ibid., p. 319.
22. "For some 35 years, Pastor Russell thought": *jv* p. 201.
23. "We now wonder why we ever believed": *w1928* 12/1 p. 361.
24. "colored people have less education than whites": *w1900* 4/15 p. 2618.
25. "if he could only be white like his employer": *w1900* 10/1 p. 2706.
26. "Can the Ethiopian Change His Skin?": *w1904* 2/15 pp. 52-53.
27. "We are not to forget that Africa is inhabited": *w1902* 7/15 pp. 215-216.

28. "We might have anticipated that many colored people": *w1914* 4/1 pp. 105-106.
29. "He proposed that on the ground of incompatibility": Transcript of record in *Russell v. Russell* (1907 on appeal) p. 130.
30. "Q. I want you to tell us what your husband did": "Girl Kissed Pastor and Sat On His Knee," *Brooklyn Daily Eagle*, October 29, 1911 (see also: *Some Facts and More Facts about the Self-Styled "Pastor" Charles T. Russell*, by Rev. J. J. Ross, pp. 26-29).
31. "remember the higher interpretation of adultery": *w1903* 10/1 p. 3254.
32. "who find themselves in any degree of sympathy": *w1904* 2/15 p. 3323.
33. "'Rose' was quite childish in appearance": *w1906* 7/15 p. 3815.
34. "But the most conclusive facts disclosed by the record": *A Great Battle in the Ecclesiastical Heavens*, p. 18.
35. "and, so far as reasonably possible": *w1908* 6/15 p. 4192.
36. "It is required that you leave the door of your room open": *Dwelling Together in Unity* (2004), p. 23.
37. "there surely is room for slight differences of opinion": *w1912* 12/1, p. 5142.
38. "We see no reason for changing the figures": *w1894* 7/15 p. 1677.
39. "We call attention to a few slight changes": *w1915* 3/1 p. 5649.
40. "Seven hours before his death": *w1916* 12/1 p. 6012.

**CHAPTER SEVEN—THE JUDGE**

1. "I took the books home": *w1894* 4/15 p. 1646.
2. "According to Hayden Covington" (ftn.): *The Four Presidents of the Watch Tower Society*, p. 207.
3. "I direct that the entire editorial charge": *w1916* 12/1 p. 5999.
4. "One of the by-laws, which was suggested": *Light After Darkness*, pp. 5-6.
5. "Opposition soon mounted": *jv* p. 66.
6. "Early in his presidency, four of the seven Directors": *Crisis of Conscience* (4th Ed.), p. 61.
7. "the management was in his hands": *Light After Darkness*, p. 13.
8. "At a meeting of the Board of Directors in June": Ibid., p. 6.

9. "It turned out that although the four opposing directors": *jv* p. 67.
10. "did everything that he could to help his opposers": *Faith on the March,* p. 77.
11. "On his homeward journey he visited Pittsburgh": *Light After Darkness,* p. 7.
12. "hard-fisted church politics": *Apocalypse Delayed* (2nd Ed.), p. 51.
13. "In this connection we might add": *Light After Darkness,* p. 7.
14. "merely confirmed Brother Rutherford's position": *Jehovah's Witnesses In the Divine Purpose,* p. 71.
15. "had Rutherford ever been taken to court": *Apocalypse Delayed* (2nd Ed.), p. 52.
16. "Brother Russell had been unable to produce": jv p. 67.
17. "posthumous work of Pastor Russell": *The Finished Mystery* (1917), p. 2.
18. "Indeed, it is obvious, even upon a fairly cursory reading": *Counting the Days to Armageddon,* p. 85.
19. "no other periodicals": *w1916* 12/1 p. 5999.
20. "It was as if a bombshell had exploded!": *jv* p. 67.
21. "the disgruntled ex-directors and their supporters": Ibid., p. 68.
22. "hastened to him and using physical force": *Light After Darkness,* p. 8.
23. "The amount of work that Pastor Russell performed": *The Finished Mystery* (1917), p. 57.
24. "an open and utter violation of Christianity": Ibid., p. 250.
25. "strengthened God's people" (ftn.): *w16.03* p. 32.
26. "The Committee on Public Information": *A Paranoid State: The American Public, Military Surveillance and the Espionage Act of 1917,* p. 81.
27. "butchery": *The Finished Mystery* (1917), p. 247.
28. "Church of the Messiah": Ibid., p. 251.
29. "an outspoken pacifist and opponent to the war": *A Paranoid State: The American Public, Military Surveillance and the Espionage Act of 1917,* p. 88.
30. "compromisingly cutting out pages": *w55* 5/1 p. 267.
31. "On May 5, Rutherford visited a Bible Students' meeting": *A Paranoid State: The American Public, Military Surveillance and the Espionage Act of 1917,* pp. 92–93.
32. "in 1918 Jehovah's servants came into a measure" (ftn.): *w92* 3/15 p. 11, par. 18.

33. "according to the Scriptures, the clergymen": *Faith on the March*, p. 85.
34. "To make matters worse": *A Paranoid State: The American Public, Military Surveillance and the Espionage Act of 1917*, pp. 96–97.
35. "Rutherford, like other witnesses before him": Ibid., p. 97.
36. "At the trial, the prosecution inquired": Ibid., p. 100.
37. "not the most unbiased judge": Ibid., p. 105.
38. "Even without the cards apparently stacked against him": Ibid., p. 112.
39. "religious propaganda": *Faith on the March*, p. 99.
40. "At first we were put in the tailor shop": Ibid., p. 101.
41. "no other periodicals": *w1916* 12/1 p. 5999.
42. "courageous journal": *jv* p. 77.
43. "Abraham, Isaac, Jacob, and the other faithful prophets": *The Harp of God* (1921), pp. 339–340.
44. "We should, therefore, expect shortly after 1925": *The Way to Paradise*, p. 224.
45. "God's provided means for communication": *Preparation*, p. 146.
46. "is not of man, but of God": *w1922* 7/15 p. 217.
47. "of divine origin": Ibid. p. 218.
48. "1925 is definitely settled by the Scriptures": *w1923* 4/1 p. 106.
49. "1925 is a date definitely and clearly marked in Scriptures": *w1924* 7/15 p. 211.
50. "Question: Have the ancient worthies returned?": *w1926* 7/1 p. 196.
51. "I know I made an ass of myself": *w84* 10/1 p. 24.
52. "the Lord himself is running his organization": *yb33* p. 11.
53. "The Theocracy is at present administered" (ftn): *g40* 9/4 p. 25.
54. "An amusing incident took place": *30 Years a Watchtower Slave* (2001 reprint), pp. 51–52.
55. "not the custom and are not considered acceptable": *w16.09* p. 21.
56. "the very ground will revolt against the presence": *Universal War Near*, p. 62.
57. "of the Devil": *g28* 12/12, p. 168.
58. "covenant breakers": *yb36*, p. 22.
59. "guilty of death": Ibid.
60. "often express much that is out of harmony with the truth": *w38* 5/1 p. 139.

61. "parasites": *w34* 3/15 p. 84.
62. "think more highly of themselves": *w38* 2/15 p. 54.
63. "This red-covered song book was received" (ftn.): *Jehovah's Witnesses in the Divine Purpose*, p. 215.
64. "desirability of sobering the southern negro": *g1919* 10/15 p. 44.
65. "the heartiest laughs": *g1928* 7/25 p. 684.
66. "Centuries before, anticipating the settlement of North America": *g1927* 11/30 pp. 140-143.
67. "It is generally believed that the curse which Noah pronounced": *g1929* 7/24 p. 702.
68. "God promised to restore Palestine to the Jews": *Life*, p. 54.
69. "Not every man who is a descendant of Abraham": *g1927* 2/23 p. 343.
70. "Before anyone can truly be a Jew": *Favored People*, p. 4.
71. "the New Testament has been made offensive": *Life*, p. 221.
72. "The Jews were evicted from Palestine": *Vindication*, Vol. 2, pp. 257-258.
73. "Among the powerful men who control the commerce": Ibid., p. 55.
74. "The people now on earth and which are called Jews": *Favored People*, p. 5.
75. "When the nation of the Jews repudiated their covenant" (ftn): Ibid., p. 8.
76. "a strong protest to Hitler and his government": *w55* 8/1 p. 462.
77. "Instead of being against the principles advocated": *yb34* p. 136.
78. "The greatest and the most oppressive empire": Ibid., p. 134.
79. "once the bulwark of democracy": *Face the Facts*, p. 16.
80. "When the totalitarian Catholic combine gains control": Ibid., p. 20.
81. "It has been the commercial Jews of the British-American empire": *yb34* p. 134.
82. "For instance, critics claim that the Witnesses decorated": *g98* 7/8 p. 12.
83. "This statement clearly did not refer to the Jewish people in general": Ibid., p. 14.
84. "from clerical, especially Catholic quarters": *Jehovah's Witnesses and the Third Reich*, p. 290.

85. "In a similar manner, the administration of our Society": Ibid., p. 291.
86. "Up to this hour there never has been the slightest bit of money": *yb34* p. 134.
87. "At the convention, it was stated that there are no opposing views": *Jehovah's Witnesses and the Third Reich*, p. 292.
88. "a strong protest to Hitler and his government": *w55* 8/1 p. 462.
89. "the Witnesses, along with millions of other Germans": *g98* 7/8 p. 11.
90. "By these principles we mean the statements in Section 24": *Jehovah's Witnesses and the Third Reich*, p. 294.
91. "This letter was probably written by": Ibid., p. 284.
92. "together with": *g98* 7/8 p. 12.
93. "As authorized by the Watch Tower": *Jehovah's Witnesses and the Third Reich*, p. 296.
94. "Early the following year": *jv* p. 693.
95. "have been warned that those who oppose God": *g34* 4/25 p. 453.
96. "Hitler Government, Berlin Germany": *g34* 10/24 p. 51.
97. "jumped to his feet and with clenched fists": *Jehovah's Witnesses in the Divine Purpose*, p. 142.
98. "It is true that the Witnesses would have suffered": *Jehovah's Witnesses and the Third Reich*, p. 163.
99. "the most cruel and sadistic treatment imaginable": *jv* p. 660.
100. "many ordinary German Witnesses lost their jobs": *Jehovah's Witnesses and the Third Reich*, p. 168.
101. "over a hundred Jehovah's witnesses" (ftn): *yb74* p. 170.
102. "obligated themselves, by written statement" (ftn): *Jehovah's Witnesses and the Third Reich*, p. 159 (ftn).
103. "did not compromise their faith" (ftn): *yb99* p. 67.
104. "Really, our colored brothers have a great cause for rejoicing": *w52* 2/1 p. 95.
105. "QUESTION: Will husband and wife live together": g1930 4/2 p. 446.
106. "It was in 1919 that the Federation of Churches": *Vindication*, Vol. 1, p. 155.
107. "In many of the church organizations": Ibid., p. 156.
108. "The father represents Jehovah": Ibid., p. 158.
109. "festival derived from the custom of mother worship": *Reasoning From the Scriptures*, p. 182.

110. "nowhere in the Bible do we find that parents are to be worshipped": *g56* 5/8 p. 25.
111. "teach and preach and prophesy in the churches": *Vindication*, Vol. 1, p. 160.
112. "The purpose of here mentioning women": Ibid., pp. 160–161.
113. "until lasting peace comes to the earth" (ftn): *Children*, p. 366.
114. "the blight, the delusions and illusions" (ftn): *g37* 1/27 p. 272.
115. "often said in his public talks": *The Four Presidents of the Watch Tower Society*, p. 30.
116. "Then the divine mandate shall be carried out": *w41* 9/15 p. 287.
117. "Fisher wanted to bring Rutherford, as an ex-officio elder": *Jehovah's Witnesses and the Third Reich*, p. 364 (ftn.).
118. "The charge in George H. Fisher's letter": *g1927* 5/4 p. 506.
119. "abandoned her non-Jehovah's Witness husband": *Jehovah's Witnesses and the Third Reich*, p. 102.
120. "If your wife was paralyzed, what would you do?": Article by Jerry Bergman, PhD (URL: http://ed5015.tripod.com/JwCovington99.htm).
121. "Then he pointed in the distance": Barbara Anderson testimony (06).
122. "I also talked to his wife during my visit" (ftn.): Article by Jerry Bergman Ph.D. (URL: http://ed5015.tripod.com/JwCovington99.htm).
123. "In some cases adultery is not proved" (ftn.): *"Shepherd the Flock of God"—1 Peter 5:2*, p. 129.
124. "above reproach": *w80* 9/1 p. 24, par. 12.
125. "Who is primarily to blame for the marital problems?" (ftn.): *"Shepherd the Flock of God"—1 Peter 5:2*, p. 33.
126. "side benefit" (ftn.): *God's Kingdom Rules!*, p. 167.
127. "Dear Brother Rutherford": *Jehovah's Witnesses and the Third Reich*, p. 369.
128. "filled with false, slanderous and libelous statements": *w39* 10/15 pp. 316–317.
129. "The Biblical injunctions against unclean, filthy speaking": *Jehovah's Witnesses and the Third Reich*, p. 371.
130. "shows disrespect for the Creator of speech": *g08* 3/08 p. 20.

131. "Under your tutelage": *Jehovah's Witnesses and the Third Reich*, p. 372.
132. "Alcoholic beverages may be brought into the home": *Dwelling Together in Unity* (2004), p. 23.
133. "the enemy of God": *Prohibition and the League of Nations: Born of God or the Devil—Which?*, p. 12.
134. "playing into the hands of Satan": Ibid., p. 14.
135. "I am of the opinion that the American people": Ibid., p. 30.
136. "Although Jehovah's Witnesses have done everything possible": *Apocalypse Delayed* (2nd Ed.), p. 72.
137. "It was with this thought in mind": *Jehovah's Witnesses and the Third Reich*, p. 365.
138. "one of the most disagreeable and revolting discoveries": "Discoveries of Barbara Anderson" on WatchtowerDocuments.org (URL: http://watchtowerdocuments.org/life-discoveries-barbara-anderson/).
139. "Shortly after coming to Bethel we were shocked": *Jehovah's Witnesses and the Third Reich*, p. 369.
140. "kind, approachable man": *w98* 5/1 p. 27.
141. "a kindly man": *w94* 8/1 p. 23.
142. "with the management of all his earthly belongings": *w07* 4/1 p. 22, par. 5.
143. "Rutherford had always manifested": *Faith on the March*, p. 73.
144. "To me, titles mean nothing": "Judge Rutherford, Leader of Jehovah Witnesses, Got His Start in St. Louis," *Globe Democrat*, August 10, 1941, issue.
145. "We publish to the world": *Jehovah's Witnesses and the Third Reich*, pp. 370-371.
146. "Judge Rutherford, president of the Watch Tower Society": *The Messenger* (1931), p. 6.
147. "In the 1920's, under a doctor's treatment": *jv* p. 76.
148. "no money has been drawn from the funds": *g30* 3/19 p. 406.
149. "some of the most beautiful residences": *Jehovah's Witnesses: Their Claims, Doctrinal Changes, and Prophetic Speculation*, p. 216.
150. "1. Not one but two 16-cylinder cars": *Jehovah's Witnesses and the Third Reich*, p. 366.
151. "To place the value of this automobile in perspective": *Witnesses of Jehovah*, p. 45.
152. "Before Judge Rutherford would accept and use the home": *The Messenger* (1931), pp. 6-8.

153. "The climate is the same as that of Palestine": Ibid., p. 8.
154. "On the part of Judge Rutherford": Ibid.
155. "The house has served as a testimony": *Salvation*, p. 311.
156. "facing the rising sun": *g42* 5/27 p. 6.
157. "followed the course of Satan": Ibid., p. 16.
158. "The owner and I began to talk about Rutherford": Barbara Anderson testimony (07).
159. "very disappointed in Knorr and Franz" (ftn.): *The Four Presidents of the Watch Tower Society*, p. 214.
160. "In late 1941, when Judge Rutherford lay on his deathbed": *Crisis of Conscience* (4th Ed.), p. 99.

## CHAPTER EIGHT—RISE OF THE SLAVE

1. "Seeing then that The Servant of Jehovah is The Christ": *w1927* 2/15 p. 53.
2. "a flair for organization": *Jehovah's Witnesses—The New World Society*, p. 211.
3. "On one occasion, Brother Knorr spoke to me": *w14* 4/15 p. 15.
4. "Nathan was very progressive": *w04* 7/1 p. 27.
5. "made-up English word": Bart Ehrman blog post (URL: http://ehrmanblog.org/is-jehovah-in-the-bible/).
6. "Knorr heard about the little enterprise": *Visions of Glory: A History and a Memory of Jehovah's Witnesses*, p. 159.
7. "When he started pulling away from the table": *The Ghosts from Mama's Club*, pp. 22-24.
8. "He kept calling N. H. Knorr, the president then": Article by Jerry Bergman, Ph.D. (URL: http://ed5015.tripod.com/JwCovington99.htm).
9. "the ushers acted strictly within their rights" (ftn.): *Religion*, p. 295.
10. "When he was not in his president's 'uniform' or role": *Crisis of Conscience* (4th Ed.), p. 90.
11. "Brothers, you can argue all you want": *Apocalypse Delayed* (2nd Ed.), p. 245.
12. "Q. In matters spiritual has each member": Pursuer's Proof in the case of *Walsh v. Clyde*, p. 100 (see also: *Crisis of Conscience* [4th Ed.], pp. 75-76).
13. "restlessness within the larger Witness community": *Apocalypse Delayed* (2nd Ed.), p. 214.

14. "Why me? What can I do?": *Crisis of Conscience* (4th Ed.), p. 76.
15. "strictly spiritual field": *w71* 12/15 p. 761.
16. "If we let the brothers do this": *Crisis of Conscience* (4th Ed.), p. 118.
17. "administrative authority and responsibility": Ibid., p. 57.
18. "down here and turn it over": Ibid., p. 82.
19. "caused him to bump into things": *jv* p. 108.
20. "Where is the proof that things aren't working well": *Crisis of Conscience* (4th Ed.), p. 89.
21. "I would be less than honest if I did not admit": Ibid., p. 98.
22. "All but two raised their hands in favor": Ibid., p. 105.
23. "his voice strained and shaking with emotion": Ibid., p. 106.
24. "I now began to realize": Ibid., p. 273.
25. "Up until 1980, aside from my wife": Ibid., p. 285.
26. "tactfully": Ibid., p. 300.
27. "The elder in the suit moved around the room": JW-survey.org article by Joanna Foreman, "Nestor Kuilan—Surviving the Fall from Watchtower's Trapdoor."
28. "They did everything but put your name": *Crisis of Conscience* (4th Ed.), p. 357.
29. "knew it was not right": Ibid., p. 368.
30. "So most of the college students go for that reason": Gerrit Lösch talk (08).
31. "I remember telling a friend of mine once": Anthony Morris talk (09).
32. "Now, I have to mention this, something I've observed": Anthony Morris talk (10).
33. "What will be the disastrous result": Anthony Morris talk (11).
34. "Now sometimes young ones feel": David Splane talk (12).
35. "You know, all five of us, we have something in common": Mark Sanderson talk (13).
36. "unscriptural practice": *w86* 3/15 p. 4.
37. "We cannot set a specific date": *w07* 5/1 p. 31.
38. "a number of factors—including past religious beliefs": *w11* 8/15 p. 22.
39. "Are all those anointed ones throughout the earth": *w09* 6/15 p. 24.
40. "Who, then, is the faithful and discreet slave?": *w13* 7/15 p. 22, par. 10.

41. "a small band of loyal Bible Students": Ibid., p. 23, par. 12.
42. "not a Bible teaching": *Reasoning From the Scriptures*, p. 37.
43. "No wonder that for many Catholics": *w14* 7/15 p. 19.
44. "willing to accept such an arrangement": *Crisis of Conscience* (4th Ed.), p. 153.
45. "The letter that you quoted of February 4": Ibid., p. 158.
46. "It is because Jehovah's Witnesses refuse to buy": *g76* 8/8 p. 5.
47. "where many died from malnutrition": *Apocalypse Delayed* (2nd Ed.), p. 145.
48. "At Lilongwe in central Malawi": *w68* 2/1 p. 71.
49. "For some of our dear sisters, the persecution was especially harrowing": *yb99* pp. 182, 189.
50. "don't any of you be specific in saying anything": *w66* 10/15 p. 631.
51. "The Jubilee year of God's ancient law": *Life Everlasting in Freedom of the Sons of God*, p. 30.
52. "Does God's rest day parallel the time man has been on earth": *g66* 10/8 pp. 19–20.
53. "Well now, as Jehovah's Witnesses, as runners": Charles Sunutko talk (14).
54. "Just think, brothers, there are only about ninety months left": *km* 3/68, p. 4.
55. "This is not the time to be toying": *w68* 8/15 p. 500, par. 35.
56. "Reports are heard of brothers selling their homes": *km* 5/74, p. 3.
57. "Sell your house, sell everything you own": Tape recording of "Divine Purpose" district assembly, Utrecht, the Netherlands, August 1974 (see also: *Expecting Armageddon: Essential Readings in Failed Prophecy*, by John R. Stone, p. 194).
58. "Thousands of Witness young people became pioneers": *Apocalypse Delayed* (2nd Ed.), p. 95.
59. "But it is not advisable for us to set our sights": *w76* 7/15 p. 441, par. 15.
60. "With the appearance of the book": *w80* 3/15 p. 17, par. 5.
61. "Today materialistic scientists": *Life Everlasting in Freedom of the Sons of God*, p. 16.
62. "disgusting thing that causes desolation": *w84* 4/1 p. 17, par. 10.

63. "In the larger fulfillment": *w13* 7/15 p. 5, par. 6.
64. "Ascribing to human organizations": *w89* 9/1 p. 7.
65. "Yes, the nations will use the scarlet-colored wild beast": *Revelation—Its Grand Climax At Hand!*, p. 258, par. 21.
66. "as they do other governmental bodies of the world": *w95* 10/1 p. 7.
67. "For 50 years the United Nations organization": Ibid., p. 3.
68. "nonneutral organization": *"Shepherd the Flock of God"—1 Peter 5:2*, p. 112.
69. "contemporary people of a certain historical period": *w95* 11/1 p. 17, par. 6.
70. "the peoples of earth who see the sign": Ibid., p. 19, par. 12.
71. "the modern-day John class": *w08* 2/15 p. 24, par. 15.
72. "until the last of the faithful anointed ones dies": Ibid., p. 24 (ftn.).
73. "easy way to keep the generation straight": David Splane video (15).
74. "certainly on Thursday and Friday": "Monster typhoon exposes an ill-prepared Philippines," November 13, 2013 (URL: http://www.reuters.com/article/us-philippines-typhoon-preparations-idUSBRE9AC0KZ20131113).
75. "Zion's Watch Tower has, we believe, JEHOVAH for its backer": *w1879* August p. 20.
76. "The Governing Body very much feels the urgency": Stephen Lett video (16).
77. "not yet certain of Jehovah's will regarding Warwick": *w12* 8/15 p. 17.
78. "Because of this merger": *w12* 8/15 p. 16.
79. "Every family head realizes that where the household income is limited": Samuel Herd announcement (17).
80. "In the belief that the end is near": JWsurvey.org article by Kyle Racki, "Betrayed and exploited: Dismissed 'special pioneer' lashes out against downsizing."

## CHAPTER NINE—BLOOD AND TEARS

1. "God's loyal love is more precious": Outline for talk no. 6 "Jehovah's 'Loyal Love Is Better Than Life'" (*CO-tk16*-E No. 6 12/15), p. 2.
2. "Many people would preserve their own life at all costs": Outline for talk no. 13 "Be Loyal, as Jesus Was

(Symposium)—When Facing Death" (*CO-tk16*-E No. 13 2/16), p. 1.

3. "How foolish it would be to gamble": *w70* 4/15 p. 249.
4. "Would a Christian break God's law": *What Does the Bible Really Teach?*, p. 130, par. 15.
5. "Well, this is quite touching": Anthony Morris talk (18).
6. "One night when Josh was in the hospital": *g95* 1/22, p. 13.
7. "The New Brunswick Court of Appeal's decision": Ibid., p. 12.
8. "a good example of faith": Anthony Morris talk (19).
9. "In former times thousands of youths died": *g94* 5/22 p. 2.
10. "Ernestine had no further transfusions": Ibid., p. 15.
11. "When doctors wanting court orders to give blood": Ibid., p. 12.
12. "Their ongoing support and care": "Court win allows for life-saving treatment," September 8, 2013 (URL: http://www.stuff.co.nz/national/health/9139314/Court-win-allows-for-life-saving-treatment).
13. "Occasionally, a doctor will urge a patient to deposit" (ftn.): *w00* 10/15 p. 30.
14. "it was advisable that the Gentile christians abstain": *w1909* 4/15 p. 4374.
15. "In New York city a housewife": *g40* 12/25 p. 19.
16. "it behooves all worshippers of Jehovah who seek eternal life": *w45* 7/1 p. 201.
17. "deliberately opposed to God's requirements": *w61* 1/15 p. 64.
18. "willfully and unrepentantly takes a blood transfusion": *Correspondence Guidelines* (2007), p. 15.
19. "have their start in the intestines": *g1928* 11/28 p. 133.
20. "one of the chief causes of diseased and enlarged tonsils": *g1919* 11/26 p. 153.
21. "bob up and down for a while": *g1926* 2/10 p. 310.
22. "they are destructive and sure to harm the grandchildren": *g36* 9/23 p. 828.
23. "a curse to humanity": *g32* 10/26 p. 35.
24. "applied to cuts": *g31* 12/1 p. 12.
25. "It's cheaper and less painful": *g1926* 4/7 p. 438.
26. "it has never been proven that a single disease is due to germs": *g1924* 1/16 p. 250.
27. "Sleep on the right side or flat on your back": *g1929* 11/13 p. 107.

28. "never prevented anything and never will": *g1921* 10/12 p. 17.
29. "for the individual that has to face it to decide": *w52* 12/15 p. 764.
30. "The recipient in some cases has seemed to adopt": *w75* 9/1 p. 519.
31. "Moral insanity, sexual perversions, repression" (ftn.): *w61* 9/15 p. 564, par. 16.
32. "Jehovah's Witnesses hold that accepting whole blood": *w00* 6/15 p. 29.
33. "To produce sufficient gamma globulin for one injection" (ftn.): *In Search of Christian Freedom*, p. 722.
34. "The blood, it is claimed, belongs to God": Ibid., pp. 288-289.
35. "Hemoglobin—33% of red cells": *km* 11/06 p. 5.
36. "In one trial involving 688 patients" (ftn.): "There will be blood" August 2, 2010 (URL: http://www.independent.co.uk/news/science/there-will-be-blood-2041051.html).
37. "With or without the peel an orange is still an orange": *In Search of Christian Freedom*, p. 290.
38. "Bloodwork and a bone marrow biopsy revealed": JWsurvey.org article by Karenne Saylor, "The Friday Column: The Blood Issue and Leukemia: One Man's Story."
39. "To support Jehovah's Witnesses" (ftn.): *jv* p. 185.
40. "Selma recalls a lesson she learned": *w12* 2/15 p. 29, par. 12.
41. "But to me, these are minor changes" (ftn.): "Behind the Scenes: 'Witness to Murder'" (URL: http://watchtowerwatch.com/blog/behind-the-scenes-witness-to-murder).

**CHAPTER TEN—SUFFER THE LITTLE CHILDREN**

1. "In recent weeks, the press in this country has focused attention": Letter to all congregations in the United Kingdom, dated July 14, 2002.
2. "Satan's system of things will soon come to its end": *w14* 5/15 p. 26, par. 1.
3. "It may not be too long, but we must endure": *w90* 1/1 p. 27, par. 21.
4. "Honestly, Mr. Zalkin, the efforts that we've made": "Jehovah's Witnesses use 1st Amendment to hide child sex abuse claims," February 14, 2015 (URL: https://

www.revealnews.org/article/jehovahs-witnesses-use-1st-amendment-to-hide-child-sex-abuse-claims/).

5. "Our goal is not to destroy the Jehovah's Witnesses": Irwin Zalkin interview (20).
6. "The process of being a Jehovah's Witness": Karen Morgan & John Viney interview (21).
7. "Following the original trial and judgment": "Jehovah's Witnesses face £1m legal bill after young girl was sexually abused by one of its members" July 8, 2016 (URL: http://www.leicestermercury.co.uk/jehovah-s-witnesses-face-1m-legal-bill-after-young-girl-was-sexually-abused-by-one-of-its-members/story-29491614-detail/story.html).
8. "once this has died down": "Submissions of Senior Counsel Assisting the Royal Commission," p. 36, par. 148.
9. "drag Jehovah's name through the mud": Ibid., p. 38, par. 155.
10. "The abuse definitely changed who I was": "Transcript (Day 147): 27 July," p. 40 of PDF.
11. "At trial, my father denied all charges against him": "Transcript (Day 148): 28 July," pp. 57–58 of PDF.
12. "Evidence will be put before the Royal Commission": "Opening Submissions by Senior Counsel Assisting," p. 14, par. 69.
13. "The Archdiocese of Baltimore has long been committed" (ftn.): "How the Church Responds to Sexual Abuse Allegations—Questions and Answers" (URL: http://www.archbalt.org/about-us/abuse-allegations-qanda.cfm).
14. "Another way we can contribute to the oneness": Stephen Lett video (22).
15. "Our policy as an organization": Anthony Morris video (23).
16. "In God's due time all who embrace his kingdom": *g82* 6/22 p. 12.
17. "I accept that child abuse is a problem": Geoffrey Jackson testimony (24).
18. "Stewart: Would you disagree, then, with anyone who said": Geoffrey Jackson testimony (25).
19. "Is it not the case that had Jesus been asked": Geoffrey Jackson testimony (26).
20. "It is important to note that the two contrasting situations": "Case Study 29—Statement of Geoffrey William Jackson," pp. 4–5.

21. "It is submitted that Mr. Jackson was evasive": "Submissions of Senior Counsel Assisting the Royal Commission," p. 76, par. 336.
22. "Stewart: Perhaps you can address that question specifically": Geoffrey Jackson testimony (27).
23. "If ever there was a group that needs the sun to shine on them": Rick Simons interview (28).
24. "all wrong": Roman Vargas video (29).
25. "dress and grooming is disturbing to the congregation": *Circuit Overseer Guidelines* (October 2015), Chapter 10, point 9.
26. "Stewart: And when a person is disfellowshipped": Kevin Bowditch testimony (30).

**CHAPTER ELEVEN—8 MILLION HOSTAGES**

1. "We should, I think, look upon modern despotisms": *The End of Faith*, p. 151.
2. "This is very hard. From where you are standing": "Dear Graham Norton: I've lost my beloved wife to religion," March 6, 2015 (URL: http://www.telegraph.co.uk/lifestyle/wellbeing/graham-norton/11452997/Dear-Graham-Norton-Ive-lost-my-beloved-wife-to-religion.html).
3. "Consider just one example of the good that can come": *w12* 4/15 p. 12, par. 17.
4. "persons residing in the United Kingdom and elsewhere": Summary Information Return 2013 for charity no. 1077961, dated May 14, 2014.
5. "If the religions of Christendom" (ftn.): *w96* 4/15 p. 15, par. 18.
6. "discussed and argued out": *w44* 5/15 p. 151.
7. "According to this Scripture the very most that the church could do": *w1919* 3/1 p. 6397.
8. "quietly laid before the representative members of the congregation": *w1944* 5/15 p. 152.
9. "What is the congregation going to do now": *w52* 3/1 p. 141, par. 13.
10. "Satan's influence through the disfellowshiped member": *w52* 11/15 p. 703.
11. "Say, for purposes of illustration": *w70* 7/1 p. 406, par. 19.
12. "Persons who make themselves 'not of our sort'": *w81* 9/15 p. 23, par. 16.
13. "Suppose that a doctor told you to avoid contact": *w11* 7/15 p. 16, par. 6.

## CHAPTER TWELVE—A PRISONER NO MORE

1. "have not invented a new religion": "Are Jehovah's Witnesses a Cult?" JW.org FAQ article (URL: https://www.jw.org/en/jehovahs-witnesses/faq/are-jehovahs-witnesses-a-cult/).
2. "One can view cults as a kind of lens": Sam Harris podcast (31).
3. "It is also important to recognize": *Combating Cult Mind Control* (25th Anniversary Ed.), pp. 48-49.
4. "Imagine if your neighbor claimed to believe": Sam Harris speech (32).
5. "Isn't it a remarkable coincidence that almost everyone": Richard Dawkins speech (33).
6. "She was informed, she signed documents" (ftn.): "Jehovah's Witness who died after giving birth understood risk of refusing blood, Quebec health minister says," October 20, 2016 (URL: http://www.cbc.ca/news/canada/montreal/jehovahs-witness-quebec-eloise-dupuis-1.3813974).
7. "Gay Byrne: Suppose it's all true": Stephen Fry interview (34).
8. "Any God who would allow children by the millions to suffer and die": Sam Harris speech (35).
9. "It can take people many years to recover": "Undue Influence" press conference (36).

## POSTSCRIPT

1. "hysterical tirades": *Combating Cult Mind Control* (25th Anniversary Ed.), p. 237.
2. "Vindictive speech, ridicule, name-calling": *In Search of Christian Freedom*, p. 652.
3. "Some who have terminated their affiliation": Ibid., p. 651.
4. "I like surprises": Hitchens debate panel video (37).

# Index